2003
600+ AGENTS WHO SELL WHAT YOU WRITE
GUIDE TO
LITERARY AGENTS

EDITED BY RACHEL VATER

WRITER'S DIGEST BOOKS
CINCINNATI, OH

Editorial Director, Annuals Department: Barbara Kuroff
Supervisory Editor: Alice Pope
Assistant Editor: Erin Nevius

Writer's Digest Books websites: www.writersdigest.com and www.writersmarket.com

2003 Guide to Literary Agents. Copyright © 2002 by Writer's Digest Books.

International Standard Serial Number 1078-6945
International Standard Book Number 1-58297-146-3
Cover image by Photonica/Toshi Sasaki

Cover illustration by Matthew DeRhodes and Wendy Dunning

Attention Booksellers: This is an annual directory of F&W Publications.
Return deadline for this edition is January 15, 2004.

contents at a glance

Contents

LITERARY AGENTS

SCRIPT AGENTS: NONFEE-CHARGING & FEE-CHARGING

Working with Script Agents

214 Listings

Both nonfee-charging and fee-charging agents interested in representing screenplays, plays, or television scripts are listed in this section.

◢ *insider* report

INDEPENDENT PRODUCTION COMPANIES

253 Listings

Markets for film and television scripts and stage plays are listed here.

◢ *insider* report

SCRIPT CONTESTS

260 Listings

Contests, fellowships and awards offer many opportunities for writers and can launch a successful script writing career.

INDEPENDENT PUBLICISTS

Working with Independent Publicists

269 Listings

The Independent Publicists listed in this section help spread the word about you and your book.

WRITERS' CONFERENCES

RESOURCES

INDEXES

From the Editor

Now that you've finished writing your masterpiece, it's time to send it out into the world. You could spend months waiting for a response, or worse, have your manuscript returned unopened because the publisher or producer won't consider unagented work. What's a writer to do? If only you could give yourself an edge, get your manuscript priority with the readers, make your work stand out in some way. If only you had an *agent!*

A good agent knows the marketplace, and by submitting her clients' work directly to the best potential buyers, she gets respect for her clients, getting their work out of the slush pile and into a publisher's or producer's hands. But her work doesn't end there. Once an agent has interest from a prospective buyer, she'll use her expertise to negotiate the contract to protect the author's interests, helping him keep his valuable rights and negotiating a fair price for his work. Writers who are serious about their careers know that having an agent represent them is essential to their success.

But how can you get an agent? In this book, you'll find listings for hundreds of **literary agents** and **script agents** who are looking for new clients to represent—and articles written by actual agents giving you the inside scoop on the best ways to impress them. You'll find examples of how to write a query letter that you can confidently submit to an agent as well as advice for networking at conferences. There are other guidebooks and websites that list agents, but many of these include agents who've made few legitimate sales or have a bad reputation with other industry pros. Not only are our listings carefully screened; you'll learn how to spot a scam artist before it's too late (page 56) and the easy way to check out an agent's credentials.

To meet with agents face-to-face and learn more about the industry, see our list of **conferences** with suggestions on the best ones to attend for the type of material you write (page 283). Whether you write scripts or books, you'll benefit from attending workshops, panels and seminars where you can ask questions and get the answers you need.

Especially for nonfiction writers and novelists, consult our listings for **publicists** (page 265), who arrange everything from radio and television interviews to visual displays.

New this year for screenwriters, we've included listings for the most respected **script contests** (page 260.) Placing in one of these high-profile contests can earn you prize money, land you a writing job or internship, or catch the attention of an industry pro who wants to buy your script! But don't stop there. Check out the listings of small- to medium-budget **independent production companies** on page 253. Smaller production companies are often more open to working with newer writers and can help you build the credentials you need to break into this tough but rewarding industry.

Take advantage of the articles and listings in this book, and give your writing career its best chance to succeed.

Rachel Vater

literaryagents@fwpubs.com
www.writersdigest.com

Quick Start Guide to Using Your *Guide to Literary Agents*

Starting a search for a literary agent can seem overwhelming, whether you've just finished your first book or you have several publishing credits on your resume. You are more than likely eager to start pursuing agents—anxious to see your name on the spine of a book. But before you go directly to the listings of agencies in this book, take a few minutes to familiarize yourself with the way agents work and how you should approach them. By doing so, you will be more prepared for your search, and ultimately save yourself time and unnecessary grief.

Read the articles

The book divides agents into two sections: nonfee-charging literary agents and script agents. Both sections begin with feature articles that give advice on the best strategies for contacting agents and provide perspectives on the author/agent relationship. The articles about literary agents are organized into four sections appropriate for each stage of the search process: **Before You Start, Finding the Right Agent, Contacting Agents** and **Before You Sign**. You may want to start by reading through each article, then refer back to relevant articles during each stage of your search for an agent.

Because there are many ways to make that initial contact with an agent, we've provided Insider Reports throughout the book. These personalized interviews with agents and published authors offer both information and inspiration for any writer hoping to find representation.

Decide what you're looking for

An independent publicist can promote your work—before or after an agent or publisher has taken an interest in it. Often publicists can drum up media time for their clients and help them get the exposure they need to make a sale or increase the number of copies sold.

A literary or script agent will actually present your work directly to editors or producers. It's his job to get his client's work published or sold and to negotiate a fair contract. In the literary agents and script agents sections, we list each agent's contact information and explain what type of work the agency represents and how to submit it for consideration.

For face-to-face contact, many writers prefer to meet agents at conferences. In this way, writers can assess an agent's personality, attend workshops, and usually have a chance to get more feedback on their work than they can by submitting their work through the mail and waiting for a response. The section for writers' conferences is divided into regions and lists only those conferences where agents will be in attendance. In many cases, private consultations can be arranged, and agents attend with the hope of finding new clients to represent.

For script writers, we have new contests and producers sections this year. Winning a contest can help you gain recognition in the film industry, land an internship, or impress an agent. Or use the producers section to market your work directly to independent production companies. Once you have some experience in the industry, you'll make important connections, find additional work, and have the credentials to impress an agent to help you with your long-term career goals.

Frequently asked questions about the Guide to Literary Agents

Why do you include agents who are not currently seeing clients?
We provide some information on well-known agents who have not answered our request for information. Because of these agents' reputations, we feel the book would be incomplete without an acknowledgement of their companies. Some agents even ask that their listings indicate they are currently closed to new clients.

Why do you exclude fee-charging agents?
There is a great debate in the publishing industry about whether literary agents should charge writers a reading or critiquing fee. There are fee-charging agents who make sales to prominent publishers. However, we have received a number of complaints in the past years regarding fees and therefore we've chosen to list only those agents who do not charge fees to writers.

Why are some agents not listed in the *Guide to Literary Agents*?
Some agents may not have returned our request for information. We have taken others out of the book because we received very serious complaints about that agency. Refer to the index to see why an agency in last year's book isn't in this edition.

Do I need more than one agent if I write in different genres?
More than likely not. If you have written in one genre and want to switch to a new style of writing, ask your agent if he is willing to represent you for your new endeavor. Most agents will continue to represent clients no matter what genre they use. Occasionally an agent may feel he has no knowledge of a certain genre and will make recommendations to his client. Regardless, you should always talk to your agent about any potential career move.

Why don't you list foreign agents?
Most U.S. agents have relationships with agents in other countries, called "foreign co-agents." It is more common for a U.S. agent to work with a co-agent to sell a client's book abroad, than for a writer to work directly with a foreign agent. We do, however, list agents in England and Canada who sell to both U.S and foreign publishers.

Do agents ever contact a writer who is self-published?
Occasionally. If a self-published author attracts the attention of the press or if her book sells extremely well, an agent might approach the author in hopes of representing her.

Why won't the agent I queried return my material?
An agent may not return your query or manuscript for several reasons. Perhaps you did not include a self-addressed, stamped envelope (SASE). Many agents will throw away a submission without a SASE. Or, the agent may have moved. To avoid using expired addresses, use the most current edition of the *Guide to Literary Agents*. Another possibility is that the agent is simply swamped with submissions. Agents can be overwhelmed with queries, especially if the agent has recently spoken at a conference or has been featured in an article or book.

Do I Need an Agent?

If you have a book ready to be published, you may be wondering if you need a literary agent. If you're not sure whether you want to work with an agent, consider the following factors.

WHAT CAN AN AGENT DO FOR YOU?

An agent will believe in your writing and know an audience interested in what you write exists somewhere. As the representative for your work, your agent will tell editors your manuscript is the best thing to land on her desk this year. But beyond being enthusiastic about your book, there are a lot of benefits to using an agent.

For starters, today's competitive marketplace can be difficult to break into, especially for previously unpublished writers. Many larger publishing houses will only look at manuscripts from agents. In fact, approximately 80 percent of books published by the major houses are sold to them by agents.

But an agent's job isn't just getting your book through a publisher's door. That's only a small part of what an agent can do for you. The following describes the various jobs agents do for their clients, many of which would be difficult for a writer to do without outside help.

Agents know editors' tastes and needs

An agent possesses information on a complex web of publishing houses and a multitude of editors to make sure her clients' manuscripts are placed in the hands of the right editors. This knowledge is gathered through relationships she cultivates with acquisition editors—the people who decide which books to present to their publisher for possible publication. Through her industry connections, an agent becomes aware of the specializations of publishing houses and their imprints, knowing that one publisher only wants contemporary romances while another is interested solely in nonfiction books about the military. By networking with editors over lunch, an agent also learns more specialized information—which editor is looking for a crafty Agatha Christie-style mystery for the fall catalog, for example.

Agents track changes in publishing

Being attentive to constant market changes and vacillating trends is also a major requirement of an agent's job. He understands what it may mean for clients when publisher A merges with publisher B and when an editor from house C moves to house D. Or what it means when readers—and therefore editors—are no longer interested in westerns, but instead can't get their hands on enough Stephen King-style suspense novels.

Agents get your manuscript read faster

Although it may seem like an extra step to send your manuscript to an agent instead of directly to a publishing house, the truth is an agent can prevent writers from wasting months sending manuscripts to the wrong places or being buried in someone's slush pile. Editors rely on agents to save them time as well. With little time to sift through the hundreds of unsolicited submissions arriving weekly in the mail, an editor is naturally going to prefer a work that has already been approved by a qualified reader. For this reason, many of the larger publishers accept agented submissions only.

Agents understand contracts

When publishers write contracts, they are primarily interested in their own bottom line rather than the best interests of the author. Writers unfamiliar with contractual language may find themselves bound to a publisher with whom they no longer want to work or prevented them from getting royalties on their first book until they have written several. An agent uses her experience to negotiate a contract that benefits the writer while still respecting some of the publisher's needs.

Agents negotiate—and exploit—subsidiary rights

Beyond publication, a savvy agent keeps in mind other opportunities for your manuscript. If your agent believes your book will also be successful as an audio book, a Book-of-the-Month club selection, or even a blockbuster movie, he will take these options into consideration when shopping your manuscript. These additional mediums for your writing are called "subsidiary rights." Part of an agent's job is to keep track of the strengths and weaknesses of different publishers's subsidiary rights offices to determine the deposition of these rights to your work. After the contract is negotiated, the agent will seek additional money-making opportunities for the rights he kept for his client.

Agents get escalators

An escalator is a bonus that an agent can negotiate as part of the book contract. It is commonly given when a book appears on a bestseller list or if a client appears on a popular television show. For example, a publisher might give a writer a $50,000 bonus if she is picked for a book club. Both the agent and the editor know such media attention will sell more books, and the agent negotiates an escalator to ensure the writer benefits from this increase in sales.

Agents track payments

Because an agent only receives payment when the publisher pays the writer, it is in her best interests to make sure the writer is paid on schedule. Some publishing houses are notorious for late payments. Having an agent distances you from any conflict over payment and allows you to spend your time writing instead of on the phone.

Agents are strong advocates

Besides standing up for your right to be paid on time, agents can ensure your book gets more attention from the publisher's marketing department, a better cover design, or other benefits you may not know to ask for during the publishing process. An agent can also provide advice during each step of this process as well as guidance about your long-term writing career.

WHEN MIGHT YOU NOT NEED AN AGENT?

Although there are many reasons to work with an agent, an author can benefit from submitting his own work. For example, if your writing focuses on a very specific area, you may want to work with a small or specialized publisher. These houses are usually open to receiving material directly from writers. Smaller houses can often give more attention to a writer than a large house, providing editorial help, marketing expertise, and other advice directly to the writer.

Some writers use a lawyer or entertainment attorney instead of an agent. If a lawyer specializes in intellectual property, he can help a writer with contract negotiations. Instead of giving the lawyer a commission, the lawyer is paid for his time only.

And, of course, some people prefer working independently instead of relying on others to do their work. If you are one of these people, it is probably better to shop your own work instead of constantly butting heads with an agent. And despite the benefits of working with an agent, it is possible to sell your work directly to a publisher—people do it all the time!

FAQs About Agents

BY JENNY BENT

Why do I need an agent?

You may not, in fact, need an agent. If you already have an offer for your book, or if your book will be published by a professional or educational publishing house that will not offer a significant advance against royalties, you may wish to use an attorney instead. Alternatively, if you regularly receive million dollar offers for your books, you may wish to use an attorney to avoid paying an agent a 15% commission of your millions. An attorney can negotiate your deal and vet your contract for you. One caveat: please, please, please, use an attorney who has experience negotiating book contracts. Using your tax attorney or divorce lawyer can just lead to disaster—it could even lead to the cancellation of your contract by your extremely frustrated publisher.

Jenny Bent

Okay, let's ask that again. Why do I need an agent?

You need an agent if you have written or plan to write a book that is directed to a large, general audience, and you want guidance in approaching the correct houses and editors to publish the book. You need an agent if you have no contacts of your own within publishing. Editors are more receptive to submissions from agents because they regard the agent as the first screening process, and have come to expect a submission of a certain quality from that agent. You also need an agent to negotiate your advance, to protect you from tricky contract language that takes away all of your rights in the book, to explain your mysterious royalty statement, to yell at publicity when they are studiously ignoring your book, to persuade you that "Yodeling for Dummies" will not be an instant bestseller and probably should not be the follow-up to your novel, and in general, to help guide your career in the often mysterious and even horrifying world of publishing. An agent also helps you sell the subsidiary rights to your book—foreign, audio, electronic, and film/TV—that can add up to significant income beyond your advance if you retain them rather than giving them to the publisher.

Fine, so I need an agent. What should I look for in an agent?

First, find someone who will actually take your calls. If your agent is too important to talk to you from the very beginning of the relationship, it may be a good idea to look elsewhere for representation. Keep in mind that your agent will be the only link to the above-mentioned terrifying world of publishing, and let that guide you to find an agent who you actually like and

---

JENNY BENT *is a literary agent with the firm of Harvey Klinger, Inc. in New York City. She holds a BA and MA in English literature from Cambridge University and has over ten years experience working in the publishing industry. She represents clients who write commercial and literary fiction as well as nonfiction on a variety of topics, including memoir, health, and women's issues. Please see her website, www.jennybent.com, for a complete project list and specific submission guidelines.*

feel you will work well with. Moving on to other, more practical items, look for an agent who has a respectable track record. Ask for a client or project list so you can see the titles he or she has sold and make sure your book seems like it will fit into that kind of list. As a general rule, it's best to avoid agents who charge reading fees, but there are exceptions to this. Agents have a kind of governing board called the Association of Authors Representatives (AAR) and one of the rules for membership is that an agent not charge reading fees. The AAR also has a very good list of questions to ask prospective agents at their website. Keep in mind that you should ask an agent these questions after they've indicated that they want to represent you, and never before.

Now that I know I need an agent, how do I convince an agent that he or she needs me? In other words, how do I get an agent?

Treat the publication of your book just like you would your career and really devote a great deal of time and effort to implementing a publication plan. The most important thing to know is that it is virtually impossible for an agent to sell a book by someone with no experience or credentials. If you are writing literary fiction, for example, you will have a far easier time catching an agent's eye if you graduated from a prestigious MFA program, know a few important writers who will blurb your book, have publication credits in major literary magazines, and have won some prizes and awards. I know that as a serious literary writer, the idea of doing all this yucky pandering stuff is probably disgusting to you. You're just going to have to get over that, I'm afraid, if you want to see your book published by a major New York house.

If you are writing nonfiction, credentials are even more important. For self-help or pop-psychology, it is, again, just about impossible to get a good publisher to buy your book unless you have some sort of national platform already in place. A local column or local radio show is a great start, but publishers (and hence agents) won't be interested unless you have a nationally syndicated radio show, or a nationally syndicated column, or a regular column in the New York Times, or you lecture regularly across the country to large groups, or you appear regularly on The Today Show or Dateline.

This may seem discouraging, but unfortunately it's the truth. To get the kind of credentials you need, simply start small (with the local radio show or column or by lecturing at your local community center) and keep building from there. If you want to write history or biography or other narrative nonfiction, you again need impressive credentials—affiliation with a major publication or prestigious learning institution—and published credits on your topic.

Once you have your credentials in place, and your book or proposal written, start researching agents. The best way to get to an agent is to be referred to him or her by another client. If you know anyone who is successfully published, ask for an introduction. The next best way is by meeting the agent at a conference or event—so network, network, network. The final way is to research the agents that are out there, and send out a targeted mailing to a select list of the agents you've identified as the best matches for you.

I have my (carefully researched) list of agents. Now, how do I write a query letter that will catch an agent's eye?

If you've built up your credentials as I've suggested above, and you list them clearly and concisely in your letter, I can almost guarantee you that you will hear from an interested agent. Beyond that, your letter should be well-written and impeccably neat (most agents have zero tolerance for typos), include biographical information (always), and a short, concise description of your project. Presentation can actually make a difference, so if you have very well designed letterhead or a glossy folder, by all means use it. Keep in mind that agents get hundreds of submissions every month or even every week; if you can make yours stand out in a positive way, you're already a step ahead. Having said that, I do recommend avoiding cutesy stuff like

little kittens or teddy bears (unless you're doing a book about little kittens or teddy bears)—
think professional, rather than adorable.

What is the one thing most important to know as I go on my quest to find an agent?

Never, ever, cold call an agent. Agents HATE that. If you are friendly with John Grisham, and
he has read your work and suggested you call his agent, well, that is an exception. Or, if you are
John Grisham, and you're looking for a new agent, then by all means, pick up the phone. But
otherwise, it's best to start with a letter including lots of information about you and your project.
Follow up with a phone call or e-mail if you don't hear back in about a month. E-mail is best,
because agents won't generally return long-distance phone calls from people they don't know.

I have an agent who wants to represent me, but he lives in Minnesota. Do I need a New York agent?

When I was an agent working out of Washington, DC, I got this question all the time. My answer
is always the same: there are talented, reputable agents working all over the country—in San
Francisco, New Orleans, Dallas and Washington. What's important is that the agent have a good
track record, not a New York address.

My prospective agent just sent me a ten-page author-agent agreement. I can't even understand it, but I don't want to lose the chance for representation. What do I do?

This one is easy. Never, ever, sign a legal document you don't understand without consulting a
lawyer first. Again, this should only be a lawyer who has knowledge of and experience with
publishing. I caution people to be careful about signing contracts that give the agent rights to
their book for an unlimited amount of time, or don't have a termination clause, or sign up
multiple projects all at once. If, for whatever reason, it doesn't work out with your agent, you
want to be able to part ways without engaging in a massive lawsuit. Also, don't be shy (but do
be polite!) about asking for modifications or additions to your agent's contract—most agents
are willing to be flexible about this. A reputable agent should not get defensive or touchy if you
have a lawyer look over the contract, or if you ask for (reasonable) changes. If your agent does
react badly, it may be a sign that he or she is not the best agent for you.

What should I expect from my agent?

Open lines of communication. Too often I hear from people who have worked with agents, but
don't even know where the agent submitted their manuscripts, or indeed, what the responses
were. Ask your agent if he or she will provide you with a submission list, will keep you informed
of all positive and negative responses to your submission, and provide you with copies of any
relevant correspondence upon request. Also make sure that your agent keeps your advance
money in a separate, non-interest bearing account, and that he or she will write you your advance
checks in a timely manner.

What to Expect from Your Agent

BY GAIL ROSS

Gail Ross

Authors have different ideas of what an agent should provide. Some want their agent to be strictly a business associate, others want their agent as a friend, encourager, and editor. Whatever your preference, an agent can be invaluable at all phases of your book's life, from the first idea to negotiating a termination with your publisher.

The book idea and proposal

Some authors prefer to come to their agents with fully developed book ideas; others want regular brainstorming sessions. In either case, your agent should be an excellent resource for what is currently selling in the industry. A good agent will know what publishers are looking for (and which editors are looking for what). This does not mean an agent should try to talk you out of writing the book in the way you had planned, but rather he or she should offer advice on what you can reasonably expect a publisher to accept for publication.

It's important that you and your agent discuss at the start what type of advance you will need to write the book. We often ask our clients, "Realistically, what do you need to complete the project?" and work from there. An agent should be able to predict how much money you might reasonably expect from a book. Naturally, if what you can accept is higher than what you can expect, you and your agent will have to do some re-thinking.

Most agents will help clients edit and redraft proposals. Proposals can be extremely difficult to write, and we often read and edit several versions before the best format is found.

Selling your book

Naturally, you can expect a lot from your agent during the selling phase of your book. Once the proposal is ready, agents will usually call editors to generate interest. Submissions occasionally work better if they are sent unannounced to editors, but in the vast majority of cases agents call editors to feel out their initial reaction and to be sure they are the best person at a particular house to see your proposal. A final list of interested editors will then be drawn up, and the proposal and a cover letter sent to each. Usually a deadline is set for responses, generally two to six weeks after the proposal is sent, depending on the urgency of the project and length of the proposal (naturally, you can expect a faster response time for five-page proposals than for

GAIL ROSS *is a lawyer, publishing consultant, and literary agent. She negotiates with major publishers and producers in the sales and distribution of literary properties and their video, audio, film and other rights through the Gail Ross Literary Agency. Ms. Ross writes and lectures frequently on publishing issues. She is the co-author of* The Writer's Lawyer *(Times Books), a definitive, practical guide to the law for writers and editors. Ms. Ross represents such best selling books as* You're Fifty—Now What?, *by Charles Schwab;* Raising Cain, *by Dan Kindlon and Michael Thompson; and* Uncovering Clinton, *by Michael Isikoff. Ms. Ross also is a partner in the law firm of Lichtman, Trister, Singer & Ross where she focuses on the legal aspects of publishing and media law. In addition, she advises clients on copyright, libel, trademark, electronic publishing and licensing issues.*

novels). August and late December are generally slow periods in publishing, and most agents will hold off sending proposals during these times. Your agent will follow up the proposal with phone calls to check on editors' interest, and will send supplementary material as requested.

Once some initial interest is expressed, your agent may decide a trip to New York to visit with editors makes sense. Generally, agents accompany authors on these trips. If you are an especially engaging author, and/or if your book will require frequent personal appearances, then face-to-face interviews are especially useful. This also gives you a time to interview the editors, though keep in mind that if editors are excited about your book, what they promise you in an initial interview may be more than they actually deliver.

You and your agent should discuss early what type of editor you want. Some editors are "hands on" from start to finish, offering detailed suggestions; others only edit the finished manuscript; different styles work better for different authors. Sometimes, several editors will make close bids on your book, and the decision will come down to which editor you and your agent feel would be the best match to work with you.

Auctions

In the best case scenario (but certainly not routinely), several publishers want to buy your book. Your agent will then set up an auction. There are two basic ways of handling an auction, with several variations on both depending on the circumstances. In one, the agent asks for "best bids," where each publisher is given the chance to submit their best price for the book, including size of advance, "pay out" (how the advance will be paid, e.g., half on signing the contract, half on delivery), subsidiary rights, and sometimes what publicity is planned (these variables are often called "deal points"). You are then free to choose the best package.

The other type of auction is one where publishers bid off each other's offers throughout the day. Each editor submits his/her first bid in the morning, and then the lowest bidder is called back with the price of the highest. Prices rise throughout the day (hopefully). If done properly, you are once again free to choose the best package, but as a practical matter, more often than not the highest advance offer wins. If there are enough players bidding for your book, an auction will take more than one day to complete. Your agent will be able to tell you which type of auction is the best for your book.

Watching your financial livelihood argued about all day can be both exciting and stressful. It's important that you are easily available during your auction so you and your agent can discuss the various options.

Contract negotiations

Once you have decided on a publisher, your agent will review the contract (though it can take three to six weeks after you sell your book before you actually see a contract). While many publishers will insist that their contract is "boilerplate" and unchangeable, we've never met any clause that couldn't occasionally be revised. (You shouldn't confuse the "deal points" listed above, however, with things that can be changed at the contract phase. With only the rarest of exceptions, all money questions are settled at the time of the auction or when the agent agrees to sell your book to a certain publisher.) Hopefully, your agent will have negotiated contracts with your publisher before, and so will know what changes they have agreed to in the past.

Payment

Your agent will receive all your money from your publisher. Generally, the check is deposited in the agent's account and a check is written to you from this account. The agent will subtract his or her percentage, and sometimes expenses (photocopying, etc.), from your check (you should be able to get details of your expenses if you ask). Your agent should also send you copies of all statements from your publisher.

Avoiding pitfalls

So except for handling money, is there any need for agents after they find a publisher and negotiate a deal? Absolutely. First-time authors very reasonably think that once they have a contract, both publisher and author have a vested interest in making the book the best it can be in order to sell as many copies as possible. While generally true, there are unfortunately many pitfalls along the way that may make you believe otherwise. A good agent can help you through them. For example:

Editors change jobs and houses all the time. Publishing salaries are low, and the best way to make more money is often to go to another house. We have clients who, over the course of one book, had to work with three different editors. There is no guarantee that the new editor will be as interested (or interested at all) in the books he or she inherits. Agents can try to make sure your book doesn't get lost in the shuffle and the publisher delivers on all that has been promised. Agents can also try to have your book assigned to another editor who is more interested in the project.

Agents can also help you handle the publicity department. As most veteran authors know, publicity departments are mysterious places in which the staff seems determined to keep your book in a warehouse. Agents can try to insure publicity has a plan, and push publishers to be sure your book gets attention. (Publishers know an agent may not bring future projects to the house if too many mistakes are made.) Agents do not, however, arrange publicity for your book. While they may set up the occasional book party or send copies to important people they know, they are generally there to give you advice on how you can handle the publicity for your book, not to handle it themselves.

Agents can monitor whether royalty statements arrive on time, and whether (more importantly) checks arrive on time. They also can and do spend considerable energy complaining when these don't arrive on time, or although prompt, are incomprehensible.

Subsidiary rights

You can expect your agent to try to sell any rights that you have retained (magazine excerpts, audio, foreign, television, motion picture, etc.) Often, these rights are sub-agented out to foreign representatives or movie agents. For both publishers and agents, subsidiary rights are often difficult to sell.

Managing your career

Agents can also be helpful in long term management of your career. Keep your agent updated on your changing goals and activities. Let him/her know if you're looking for a new project; magazine and book editors sometimes call agents looking for writers. Your agent can help you map out future plans and book ideas, and help you make the most of your career.

Finally, a brief look at what your agent expects from you

Monetary: Most agents take a percentage (e.g., 15% plus expenses such as photocopying, etc.) of all the monies you earn on your books, with a higher percentage taken for foreign rights (since foreign sub-agents also must be paid). You should be sure to sign an agreement with your agent at the start of your relationship, stating what the financial arrangements will be.

Information: The more you can tell the agent about your book, the better off you will be. What may not seem important to you before a contract is signed may be very important after the book is published. Any unusual expenses you might incur in writing the book, for example, should be brought up before the contract is negotiated. Say you want to use four lines from a popular song to open your first chapter. Buying permissions to use song lyrics can be expensive, and your publisher isn't likely to pay for them if you bring them up after the contract is signed (they may not pay for them even if you ask before signing, but at least there is a chance). Think about what publishing details will be the most important to you, and let your agent know. If consultation on the cover (not always possible, but worth asking for) is essential to you, tell your agent. Should your book come out at any special time? Are you concerned about a libel suit? Again, the more you can tell your agent before the contract is signed, the less hassles you will have later.

It is also important to tell your agent anything about you that might be helpful in selling your proposal or book. Have you just won an award for your writing? Did a well-known person compliment your book or book idea? Is your cousin the head of Cosmopolitan? A movie producer? Let your agent know.

It's often a good idea to send your agent, as well as your editor, portions of the manuscript as you go along. Some agents will make suggestions on your manuscript, and it also helps agents keep track of your book's progress.

Education: Learn as much as you can about the publishing industry. Ask your agent and other writers for books and magazines on the industry that they have found useful, and consider joining a writer's organization. The more you know, the better for your writing career. It's not always possible for your agent to know all the particulars of your situation, so be sure you know enough to ask the right questions and give the right information.

Four Editors Share Straight Talk about Agents

BY WILL ALLISON

Editors at big publishing houses generally agree that agents make their jobs easier. A good agent identifies promising books, sees that those books reach the appropriate editors, acts as a buffer between the publisher and writer during contract negotiations, and facilitates the editor/author relationship once a deal has been struck. However, for editors at smaller publishing houses (including university presses), agents can sometimes be more of a hindrance than a help—a reflection of the differences between academic and commercial publishing.

The editors in the following roundtable interview represent one university press and three imprints of big New York publishing houses.

Beverly Jarrett is the director and editor-in-chief of the University of Missouri Press, which publishes about sixty books a year, including short-story collections and nonfiction scholarly works in areas such as women's studies, black studies, intellectual history, and heartland studies (books about Middle America). Jarrett has worked with a wide range of authors including Cleanth Brooks, Kelly Cherry, James Dickey, George Garrett, Heather Ross Miller, Howard Nemerov, Elaine Palencia, Dabney Stuart, James Whitehead, and Steve Yarbrough.

Susan Allison is vice president and associate editorial director of Berkley Publishing Group, a division of Penguin Putnam. She is also editor-in-chief of Ace Science Fiction and Fantasy, the oldest continuously operating science fiction publisher in the United States, which produces about seventy-five titles a year. Her authors include William Gibson (*All Tomorrow's Parties*), Joe Haldeman (*Forever Peace*), Robin McKinley (*Spindle's End*), and Patricia McKillip (*Winter Rose*).

Sara Ann Freed is editor-in-chief of Mysterious Press, an imprint of Warner Books that publishes thirty-six crime, mystery, and suspense novels each year.

Brian Tart is vice president and editor-in-chief of Dutton, an imprint of Penguin Putnam that publishes fifty hardcover books each year, including both fiction and nonfiction for a general readership. Tart's fiction authors include Darin Strauss (*Chang and Eng*), Sharyn McCrumb (*The Songcatcher*), Michael McGarrity (*Under the Color of Law*), John Martel (*The Alternate and Billy Strobe*), and Douglas Kelley (*The Captain's Wife*). His nonfiction authors include Dave Pelzer (*A Man Named Dave*), Dan Savage (*The Kid*), Chris Kraft (*Flight: My Life in Mission Control*), James Dodson (*The Dewsweepers*), Randall Robinson (*The Debt and The Reckoning*), and Simon Worrall (*The Poet and the Murderer*).

In what ways do agents make your job easier or harder?

Beverly Jarrett, University of Missouri Press: I honestly can't think of a way that an agent has made my life easier. Some of the ways in which agents have made the process more difficult are by asking for unreasonable and unrealistic terms in a contract, and by being slow to respond to a legitimate offer from the press, but being fast or rushing to make demands for a decision

WILL ALLISON (willalliso@aol.com) is editor at large of Zoetrope: All-Story, former executive editor of STORY, and former editor of Novel & Short Story Writer's Market.

from a press whose imprint is reviewed and overseen by outside readers and a faculty press committee.

Susan Allison, Ace Books: To start with, many authors are unaccustomed to talking about money. They may also be unclear on what fair market price is for the kind of book they're selling, and they're very likely sure that publishing companies exist to cheat them, etc. An experienced agent can ease that fear, reassure the author that the offer is fair (assuming it is), and talk the author through details of contractual language. All of this would be my job, without an agent.

Later in the process, if the author and I are unhappy with each other for any reason, a good agent provides a sounding board for both sides. If I read a draft of a newly delivered manuscript and have serious problems with it, talking my responses through with the agent first is a tremendous help. And I assume that if an author is mad at me, it's a big help to be able to call the agent, vent a little, and get some help figuring out what to do.

Sara Ann Freed, Mysterious Press: Good agents always make life easier for an editor. The best agents are a continual advocate for the writer and help pave a career path. They make suggestions for strengthening manuscripts. They help make decisions about copy and jackets. They understand both the writer's needs and publishing realities, so they can mediate any differences of opinion. And they make certain that both the writer and the publisher keep their promises.

Brian Tart, Dutton: Agents generally make an editor's life easier, not harder. The agent is the author's advocate, but so is the editor. We are not working at cross-purposes, but toward the same end: we both want to make the book the best it can be and to make the publication the most successful it can be. Agents also spend a lot of their time looking for authors and books, and editors rely on them to bring in good projects. An editor thinks that if an agent has agreed to take the project on, he must believe that it is good and has potential. Editors know to take projects sent in from agents seriously. This frees up time for an editor to do what he or she is supposed to do: edit books.

Do you prefer to work with agented or unagented authors? And do agented and unagented book proposals receive the same treatment at your publishing house?

Beverly Jarrett, University of Missouri Press: I don't think I personally have a preference. I have no objection to working with an agented author, and I have on several occasions signed authors who were promising and good finds for the press through work with that author's agent. If and when we can establish a relationship with a particular agent, and that has happened a few times, then we begin to feel a bit like we have a real relationship—one is thinking of the needs of the other.

I would have to say that book proposals do receive the same treatment from us regardless of whether the proposal/author is agented or unagented, with one exception. Agents often set outrageous deadlines for decisions. If we are very interested in the manuscript to start with, we might try our best to meet one of these excessive deadlines. The only reason for that is the unspoken threat that the agent will take the project elsewhere if we don't make a decision fairly promptly.

Susan Allison, Ace Books: Many companies take the position that they don't even look at unagented submissions. One of my jobs for Berkley is to run Ace Books, the long-established science fiction and fantasy imprint, and Ace certainly looks at unagented manuscripts. I think most of the science fiction and fantasy publishers do. So you don't need an agent to sell a book to Ace, but it's almost always the case that after we've made a deal, the author does get an agent. If you have a deal in hand, it's easier to get a decent agent. Contracts are complicated and important, and authors reasonably enough want somebody to help them through the legal language. This is perfectly fine. (It doesn't make that first novel worth any more money, though.)

Of course a submission that comes in from an agent I respect gets top-tier attention. Respected agents don't just send piles of paper out; they know the editors they submit to, and they phone in advance to say, "I'm sending you a first novel I really liked, and I think you'll like it too." The fact that the book has had a knowledgeable first reading is a very important endorsement. An agent like this will also make sure the book doesn't sit on the editor's floor for months!

It should be said, however, that I could be an agent tomorrow if I had stationery printed up today, and so could anybody reading this article, so just having an unknown agent send in a manuscript is no help at all, especially if that agent is a "manuscript mill" from whom I get three books a week, not one of them suitable.

Sara Ann Freed, Mysterious Press: I work only with agented authors. If I meet writers at a conference or through an introduction, I encourage them to find an agent before submitting the work. One of the writers on our list called me and asked me to read his novel and said he thought of us because he was a huge fan of Donald E.Westlake, whom we publish. I loved his manuscript, but I told him to find an agent. His agent is wonderful and is passionate about the books he represents. He makes sure he not only finds the right editor, but that other book people hear about it, the movie agents know about it, and foreign publishers see the book.

Unagented writers often have lingering doubts about the contracts that are offered to them. Would the publisher have given betters terms? There are new areas to consider: electronic publishing, print on demand, web marketing. Agents know the market and can better judge the publisher's offer. And on the publisher's end, agents can help sort out any disputes that might arise throughout the editing and publishing process.

Brian Tart, Dutton: I prefer to work with agents because they usually have a knowledge of the industry so they can explain things to the author and put things into perspective. We give agented proposals and manuscripts from agents the priority because of the large number of proposals we get a day. We have to triage somehow, and agents are a good way to do that. We get back to everyone eventually who sends in a proposal. But proposals represented by agents get personal attention, while unsolicited manuscripts and proposals usually are sent back with a form letter if they are rejected.

How does the presence of an agent affect your working relationship with an author?

Beverly Jarrett, University of Missouri Press: I'd have to say in some cases there is no effect at all. We have good relationships with almost all of our authors. I have occasionally had an author contact me and say that his agent said the royalties hadn't been paid. Then I have no hesitation about reporting to my author friend that the royalties had not been paid because the agent failed to submit the proper forms. That's just an unusual little example. For the most part, especially if we do maintain some sort of independent working relationship with our authors, the existence of an agent is in no way troublesome.

Susan Allison, Ace Books: This of course depends entirely on my relationship with the agent, as well as with the author. In general these days, authors' relationships with their agents outlast relationships with their editors, who may move to another house, get fired, or not be able to pay as much money for the next book as somebody else. However, it's also true that my relationship with any agent I've known for twenty years is complex and outlasts my relationship with many of his/her clients.

The editor/author relationship is intense and difficult, involving very emotional issues of power, self-worth, and self-exposure. In my experience, it's wise to have a third party there to defuse the bad times and to help celebrate the good. I'm assuming the best here, though: I'm assuming a triad in which all three sides respect each other, talk reasonably honestly, and want the best for the book. (I'm also assuming an agent I enjoy talking to.)

Sara Ann Freed, Mysterious Press: It depends on the agent. Some agents adopt a hands-off approach. Others encourage a constant three-way dialogue. Occasionally an agent will take an "it's us against them approach" to publishers, and that isn't helpful. This can end an author's career quickly!

Very few books get big promotion and advertising budgets, so publishers, writers, and agents all need to work together creatively to help get books out to the reader.

Brian Tart, Dutton: It allows me to talk business with the agent and editorial issues with the author, which is a good thing. This is a business, and discussing financial issues and negotiating contracts can be sensitive, and it's better to handle that with an agent than with the author so no one takes it personally. I always have a relationship with the author, and most if not all agents try to facilitate that relationship. It is very rare for an agent not to try to forge a strong editor/author relationship.

How would you characterize your relationship with agents—collaborative, combative, or something in between?

Beverly Jarrett, University of Missouri Press: But for the foolishness of elaborate demands on the contract (which get dropped fairly promptly) and excessive scheduling rushes, I would say our relationship with agents is fairly pleasant. We don't have what you would call a collaborative relationship with any agent, but neither do we have what I would think of as a combative relationship with one either. For the most part, I think once we each understand that the other is speaking honestly and straightforwardly, then we have no difficulty at all in dealing with agents.

Susan Allison, Ace Books: I talk to a wide range of agents, but I expect 75% of my business is with half a dozen of them. The relationship at its best is collaborative. Sometimes even in dark times it's collaborative; an understanding agent can help an editor and author get out of a difficult relationship with as little damage to everyone as possible. (There are times of course when combative situations are unavoidable, and not all relationships can be salvaged.) The fact that the relationship between author and agent is transferable to another publisher, and the relationship between editor and agent is transferable to another author, gives the whole situation more emotional elasticity.

Sara Ann Freed, Mysterious Press: At Mysterious Press and Warner Books we deal with a great many agents. Like other editors, I get more manuscripts from agents I know well and from agents who specialize in crime fiction. One develops a certain trust about an agent's taste and instincts after a while, and those manuscripts are put aside for serious weekend reading! I prefer to work with agents who are thoughtful, forthright, and honest—and so do the writers. A good agent, by the way, can live anywhere: I get manuscripts not only from agents in New York and Los Angeles, but also from Boise and Boston.

Brian Tart, Dutton: All of the above. I deal with a wide range of agents. They are a necessary part of the business, and I cannot see working without them. Some agents are combative, others nurturing. Some are hands on and call every day, and others call once a year. An editor has to establish a unique relationship with each agent: one size does not fit all. I try to be as open as possible—there really isn't much to hide in our business—and I feel that if they are getting the information they seek in a timely manner, then they will be happier.

Revision and Editing

BY ALBERT ZUCKERMAN

You've diligently studied writing techniques, developed a number of outlines for your book, finished one outline that feels rock solid, and written a complete draft of your novel. What now? Put it aside for a week or two. Reread it with all the cool objectivity you can muster. Try to consider it as if someone else wrote it. Be ruthless in pinpointing its weaknesses. Then figure out how you're going to eliminate them. It's time for a second draft, and you may well have to repeat the process with a third or fourth. Although Dick Francis and Harold Robbins are reputed to write their books only one time through, most popular authors do at least two completed scripts followed by a final polish. Sidney Sheldon is said to do a dozen complete rewrites, and for Saul Bellow ten times is not unusual.

The point is that the likelihood of your novel being terrific in every respect the first time you set it down is from slight to nonexistent. Liken yourself to a sculptor fashioning a complex figure or set of figures from a great block of stone. On a first go-round, you chisel the stone down to roughly the shape you seek, but overall it lacks precise definition. On a second try, you manage to carve some portions finely, but others still resist the form you feel they should have. Finally, after what feels like an infinite amount of tedious and laborious chopping, shaping and smoothing, the sculpture emerges as you imagined it.

Difficult as this work may seem, it should be the most enjoyable part of the job. And for most writers, it is. Creating from nothing, with a blank piece of paper in front of you and the choices open to you seeming almost infinite, is generally considered the toughest part of writing a novel. Once your story and characters have begun to take shape, to achieve enough reality so you can at least start to believe in them and what they do, then you have real concrete stuff in front of you: words, lines, pages, the raw material of fiction on which you can bring to bear your innate artistic feel for character and storytelling as well as the craft you hopefully have acquired from this book.

Authors who, because they've had some success, think that whatever they set down needs no further work and should be published as is do so at their peril. For a few years in the mid-1980s, I represented a gifted novelist who had achieved enormous popularity in Britain but whose books had never caught on in the United States. I was hired to launch him here, and I made some modestly attractive deals for him for already completed works. Then he sent me a new manuscript that had patches of brilliance but also some important structural flaws. I carefully analyzed the novel and wrote him a ten- or twelve-page letter, pointing out how he might improve his book. By return mail, he fired me. His British publisher had loved the book. What did I know? He wanted enthusiasm from his agent, not advice. Since then, he has written eight or more novels, none of which have brought him recognition in the United States.

ALBERT ZUCKERMAN *has been a literary agent and book doctor to some two dozen blockbuster novels. At Writer's House, he presides over a firm which represents hundreds of leading writers in all categories. Author of two published novels, winner of the 1964 Stanley Drama Award, former writer for three television series, he also taught playwriting at the Yale School of Drama. He lives in New York with his wife. This article is an excerpt from his book,* Writing the Blockbuster Novel, *copyright © 1994 by Al Zuckerman. Used with permission of Writer's Digest Books, an imprint of F&W Publications, Inc. Visit your local bookseller or call 1-800-448-0915 to obtain your copy.*

Once you have gone through your manuscript a number of times, patiently and carefully restructuring, you think it's pretty damn good, marvelous even. So what do you do next? Send it to an agent or publisher? No. You look for confirmation or, more likely, for professional editorial assistance or guidance.

EDITING

Virtually all popular best-selling novelists need and get help from others in enriching their characters and maximizing the drama of their work. Established writers who are paid large advances, often before they commit even one word to paper, are provided by their publishers with editors who pore over their manuscripts and make detailed comments and suggestions on outlines and successive drafts of a manuscript. Authors sometimes also have editorially skilled agents who work with them or novelist colleagues with whom they exchange critiques. But the genre author, the midlist author, or the new author who lacks these personal connections and who is trying to break into this Top Writer rarified circle—who submits a manuscript that is meritorious but in some respect faulty, slow, obscure, in short, anything less than a mesmerizing knockout—is usually not accorded editorial succor from a publisher and most likely gets rejected.

Editors in publishing houses are overworked. They put in a full day in the office fielding phone calls from authors and agents, from publicity, marketing and production departments within their companies; attending meetings about covers, new acquisitions, production scheduling; interviewing, hiring and firing assistants; and negotiating with management for books they want to acquire, for promotion budgets for these books, and for pay increases and promotions for themselves. The result is that most of their editing and usually all of their reading gets relegated to nights and weekends, of which there are never enough, given the avalanche-like onslaught of manuscripts that keep piling in on them. The bulk of their time has to be devoted to contracted-for projects, books in which their company has already made an often sizeable investment, an investment that has to be nurtured and protected by the editors, who slave to help the author get the book into its optimal condition. All this leaves the editor precious little time or strength for a new author, unless what she presents is somehow marvelous.

FINDING AN EXPERT READER

So you've got this much sweated-over manuscript that you think is marvelous. Your spouse and your best friends are even more enthusiastic. What now? Don't trust yourself or the people who love you. Find a professional novelist, someone you don't know personally and who has no stake in your ego or making you feel good. Offer to pay this person to read your work, to provide you with an honest opinion as to its fine qualities and weaknesses and give you written suggestions as to how you might improve and strengthen it.

How do you find such a person? It's probably easier than you think. The owner of manager of your nearby bookstore or of one in the nearest big city will usually know the local authors. They generally come in for signing parties when their books are published or at the very least to autograph their copies in stock. Check out these authors' writing and choose one whose work has some affinity to yours. Then contact her. Be prepared to pay what it takes. If you've invested a year or several years in writing your novel, one you're hoping will bring you a worldwide readership and make you financially comfortable, you owe it to yourself to be able to get a read-through and general letter for $500 to $1,000, and a detailed critique with a marked-up manuscript for $2,000 to $5,000, depending on the length of your novel and the eminence of the author you're approaching.

If you're low on cash or simply cannot find an established novelist who will, even for a price, critique your manuscript, then I suggest that you join or form a novel workshop. Most universities have them, but they also can be purely private and meet in lodges, churches and writers' homes. In such a group, you would read your chapters aloud to other authors or would-be authors, and the group (which sometimes will have a novelist or an editor as a leader) would comment and make suggestions, letting you know which of your characters are engaging, repellent, or boring, which episodes in your story are riveting and which are dull, and whether the strands of your plot hang together from beginning to end.

In your roles as a self-critic, you must then sift through this criticism and advice, whether from a known novelist or from a group in a workshop, and make your own decisions about which suggestions to implement and how to implement them and which suggestions to ignore. Keep in mind, though, that none of us can be objective about our own work. So, if you get complaints, the likelihood is strong that there are problems, even though the suggestions you've been given on how to address these problems may or may not be exactly right.

PUBLISHING

After you've worked over your novel with the help of an individual or a group, you would be wise to get a reading from a second professional who has never seen it before. The first person who worked with you is likely to be all caught up in the improvements you've made and aware of how much better the book is. But that's not the same as being coolly objective. A person who is reading your work cold will be better equipped to advise you if your novel is or isn't ready to submit.

Okay, you have torn apart the manuscript and rewritten it from beginning to end. Your novelist-mentor or your workshop colleagues or, better yet, your second outside professional has now told you that you've done one hell of a job, your novel is as good as anything on *The New York Times* best-seller list, and you are as ready to shoot for the big time as you ever will be. Now what?

FINDING AN AGENT

You need an agent, and not just any agent. So who are these agents, you ask, and how do I get one? Again, it's not so hard. Pick an author you admire and whose writing you believe has a kinship with yours. To find out who represents that author, go to the bookstore (or library) and ask to see the current catalog of that author's publisher. Most publishers' catalogs contain "rights information," i.e., who (invariably the author's agent) controls motion picture and/or translation rights. This information is sometimes at the bottom of the page on which the author's new book is described or in a special section in the rear of the catalog. If the catalog contains no such disclosure, which is occasionally the case, then look up the name of the publisher's Subsidiary Rights Director in Literary Marketplace (LMP), call or write that person, and tell her you're interested in acquiring motion picture rights to your author's novel. You will then be directed to the agency or agent.

Now you know the name of the agent. What do you do about it? Top agents are as busy or busier than the orthopedist for whom you might have to wait three months for an appointment. Their first obligation is to the authors they already represent, the ones whose incomes provide the agents' livelihoods. These authors keep turning in outlines and manuscripts that have to be read, getting offers from publishers and movie companies that have to be negotiated, and experiencing an endless stream of problems with publishers about payments, jackets, deadlines, publication dates, publicity tours, titles, editorial content, personality conflicts, printing errors, all of which the agent must attend to and struggle to sort out before he can consider work from a potential new client. So don't be surprised if your attempt to communicate doesn't get a prompt reply.

The crux now is how you communicate. First, don't bother trying to telephone. Heavyweight agents just don't have the time to listen to a spiel from someone they don't know, unless the caller has "name recognition," either his own or that of someone (usually an author or an editor) known to the agent. It's almost always far better to write. Fiction is a written medium, and if you manage to write an enticing letter, the agent may feel there's a chance you've written a good book.

If you've published fiction before, either novels or short stories, the agent will be inclined to consider you more seriously than if you haven't. And if you enclose a letter of recommendation from a published novelist, from a teacher of writing, or best of all, from a client of the agent, that too will help stimulate a response. Experience in nonfiction, journalism or screenwriting has more value than no professional writing background, but writers whose prior work is in these areas often have a tough time making a go of the novel form. If you never have had anything published, it may be premature of you to be thinking about an agent. My advice would be first to try and place some short stories or excerpts from your novel in literary or mass-circulation magazines. Once you succeed in this, you'll have the beginnings of a literary track record that should encourage an agent to want to consider your novel.

Once an agent takes on your manuscript, there's not much you can do until either he lets you know he has struck out with it, or he calls you with an offer for publication. If your work is declined, don't give up. If a good agent liked your novel well enough to expend time, energy and money in making a bunch of submissions, there is a decent chance that, with a careful analysis of the publishers' rejection letters and further help from a freelance editor, you may be able to successfully revise it. On the other hand, if a call comes with an offer, and your agent advises acceptance, take it. One of the things you're paying him for, after all, is his expert advice.

Your first step in the publication process will be additional revision. I have placed novels by relatively unknown writers for sums in the neighborhood of $1,000,000, and even these manuscripts required a fair bit of rewriting. Once this work is completed, about a year goes by between the manuscript's "final acceptance" and its appearance in bookstores.

If you've managed to write an unforgettable novel on a subject with wide appeal, your agent and publisher (with some help from you) should be able to guide your book to the success it deserves.

How to Find the Right Agent

A writer's job is to write. A literary agent's job is to find publishers for her clients' books. Any writer who has endeavored to attract the attention of a publishing house knows this is no easy task. But beyond selling manuscripts, an agent must keep track of the ever-changing industry, writers' royalty statements, fluctuating reading habits, and the list continues.

Because publishing houses receive more unsolicited manuscripts each year, securing an agent is becoming more of a necessity. Nevertheless, finding an eager *and* reputable agent is a difficult task. Even the most patient of writers can become frustrated, even disillusioned. Therefore, as a writer seeking agent representation, you should prepare yourself before starting your search. By learning effective strategies for approaching agents, as well as what to expect from an author/agent relationship, you will save yourself time—and quite possibly, heartache. This article provides the basic information on literary agents and how to find one who will best benefit your writing career.

Make sure you are ready for an agent

With an agent's job in mind, you should ask yourself if you and your work are at a stage where you need an agent. Look at the "Ten Step Checklists for Fiction and Nonfiction Writers," and judge how prepared you are for contacting an agent. Have you spent enough time researching or polishing your manuscript? Sending an agent an incomplete project not only wastes your time but may turn him off in the process. Literary agents are not magicians. An agent cannot sell an unsalable property. He cannot solve your personal problems. He will not be your banker, CPA, social secretary, or therapist. Instead, he will endeavor to sell your book because that is how he earns his living.

Moreover, your material may not be appropriate for an agent. Most agents do not represent poetry, magazine articles, short stories, or material suitable for academic or small presses—the agents' commission earned does not justify spending time submitting these type of works. Those agents who do take on such material generally represent authors on larger projects first, and then represent these smaller items only as a favor for their clients.

If you strongly believe your work is ready to be placed with an agent, make sure you are personally ready to be represented. In other words, before you contact an agent, consider the direction in which your writing career is headed. Besides skillful writers, agencies want clients with the ability to produce more than one book. Most agents will say they represent careers, not books. So as you compose your query letter—your initial contact with an agent—briefly mention your potential. Let an agent know if you've already started drafting your second novel. Let him know that for you writing is more than a half-hearted hobby.

The importance of research

Nobody would buy a used car without at least checking the odometer, and the savvy shopper would consult the blue books, take a test drive, and even ask for a mechanic's opinion. Because you want to obtain the best possible agent for your writing, you should do some research on the business of agents before sending out query letters. Understanding how agents operate will help you find an agent appropriate for your work, as well as alert you about the types of agents to avoid.

Before You Contact an Agent: A Ten-step Checklist for Fiction Writers

9 **Finish your novel** or short story collection. An agent can do nothing for fiction without a finished product.

9 **Revise your novel.** Have other writers offer criticism to ensure your manuscript is as finished as you believe possible.

9 **Proofread.** Don't let your hard work go to waste by turning off an agent with typos or poor grammar.

9 **Publish** short stories or novel excerpts in literary journals, proving to potential agents that editors see quality in your writing.

9 **Research** to find the agents of writers you admire or whose work is similar to your own.

9 **Use the indexes** in this book to construct a list of agents open to new writers and looking for your type of fiction (i.e., literary, romance, mystery).

9 **Rank your list.** Use the listings in this book to determine the agents most suitable for you and your work, and to eliminate inappropriate agencies.

9 **Write your synopsis.** Completing this step early will help you write your query letter and save you time later when agents contact you.

9 **Compose your query letter.** As an agent's first impression of you, this brief letter should be polished and to the point.

9 **Read about the business** of agents so you are knowledgeable and prepared to act on any offer.

We often receive complaints from writers regarding agents *after* they have already lost money or their work is tied into a contract with an ineffective agent. If they'd put the same amount of effort into researching agents as they did writing their manuscript, they would have saved themselves unnecessary grief.

The best way to educate yourself is to read all you can about agents and other authors. The articles in this book will give you insight not only on how to contact an agent but also how the author/agent relationship works. Organizations such as the Association of Authors' Representatives (AAR), the National Writers Union (NWU), American Society of Journalists and Authors (ASJA), and Poets & Writers, Inc. all have informational material on agenting. (These, along with other helpful organizations, are listed in the back of this book.) *Publishers Weekly* covers publishing news affecting agents and others in the publishing industry in general; discusses specific events in the "Hot Deals" and "Behind the Bestsellers" columns; and occasionally lists individual author's agents in the "Forecasts" section. Their website, www.publishers-weekly.com, also offers a wealth of information about specific agents.

Even the Internet has a wide range of sites devoted to agents. Through the different forums provided on the Web, you can learn basic information about preparing for your initial contact or more specific material about individual agents. Keep in mind, however, that not everything printed on the Web is a solid fact; you may come across the site of a writer who is bitter because an agent rejected his manuscript. Your best bet is to use the Internet to supplement your other research. For particularly useful sites, refer to "Websites of Interest" in the back of this book.

Through your research, you will discover the need to be wary of some agents. Anybody can go to the neighborhood copy center and order business cards which say she is a literary agent. But that title does not mean she can sell your book. She may ask for a large sum of money, then disappear from society. Becoming knowledgeable about the different types of fees agents may charge is a *crucial* step to take before contacting any agent. Before paying any type of fee, read "Understanding Fees—What Writers Must Know" on page 31.

Before You Contact an Agent:
A Ten-step Checklist for Nonfiction Writers

9 **Formulate a concrete idea** for your book. Sketch a brief outline making sure you have enough material for an entire book-length manuscript.

9 **Research** works on similar topics to understand the competition and determine how yours is unique.

9 **Compose sample chapters.** This step should indicate how much time you will need to finish and if your writing needs editorial help.

9 **Publish** completed chapters in journals. This validates your work to agents and provides writing samples for later in the process.

9 **Polish your outline** to refer to while drafting a query letter and avoid wasting time when agents contact you.

9 **Brainstorm** three to four subject categories that best describe your material.

9 **Use the indexes in this book** to find agents interested in at least two of your subject areas and looking for new clients.

9 **Rank your list.** Narrow your list further by reading the listings of agencies you found in the indexes; organize the list according to your preferences.

9 **Write your query.** Describe your premise and your experience professionally and succinctly, to give an agent an excellent first impression of you.

9 **Read about the business** of agents so you are knowledgeable and prepared to act on any offer.

An agent also may not have any connections with others in the publishing industry. An agent's reputation with editors can be her major strength or weakness. While it's true that even top agents are not able to sell every book they represent, an inexperienced agent who submits too many inappropriate submissions will quickly lose her standing with any editor. It is acceptable to ask an agent for recent sales before he agrees to represent you, but keep in mind that some agents consider this information confidential. If an agent does give you a list of recent sales, you can call the publishers' contracts department to ensure the sale was actually made by that agent.

The pros and cons of location

For years, the major editors and agents were located in New York. If a writer wanted to be published with a big-name house, he had to contact a New York agency. But this has changed over time for many reasons. For starters, publishing companies are appearing all over the country—San Francisco, Seattle, Chicago, Minneapolis. And naturally, agents are locating closer to these smaller publishing hubs.

The recent advances in technology have also had an impact on the importance of location. Thanks to fax machines, the Internet, e-mail, express mail, and inexpensive long-distance telephone rates, an agent no longer needs to live in New York to work closely with a New York publisher. Besides, if a manuscript is truly excellent, a smart editor will not care where the agent lives.

Nevertheless, there are simply more opportunities for agents located in New York to network with editors. They are able to meet face-to-face over lunch. The editor can share his specific needs, and the agent can promote her newest talent. As long as New York remains the publishing capital of the world, the majority of agents will be found there, too.

Contacting agents

Once your manuscript is prepared and you have a solid understanding of how literary agents work, the time is right to contact an agent. Your initial contact is the first impression you make on an agent; therefore, you want to be professional and brief.

Because approaching agents is an important topic, we've included several articles on contacting agents in this book: "Basics of Contacting a Literary Agent" on page 36; "How to Write a Query Letter" on page 38; "Queries That Made It Happen" on page 43; "Outline and Synopsis Workshop" on page 48; and "How to Write a Nonfiction Proposal" on page 53.

Again, research plays an important role in getting an agent's attention. You'll want to show her you've done your homework. Read the listings in this book to learn her areas of interest, check out her website to learn more details about how she operates business, and find out the names of some of her clients. If there is an author whose book is similar to yours, call the author's publisher. Someone in the contracts department can tell you the name of the agent who sold the title, provided an agent was used. Contact that agent, and impress her with your knowledge of her agency.

Evaluate any offer

Once you've received an offer of representation, you must determine if the agent is right for you. As flattering as any offer may be, you need to be confident that you are going to work well with this person and that this person is going to work hard to sell your manuscript.

You need to know what you should expect once you enter into a business relationship. You should know how much editorial input to expect from your agent; how often he gives updates about where your manuscript has been and who has seen it; and what subsidiary rights the agent represents.

More importantly, you should know when you will be paid. The publisher will send your advance and any subsequent royalty checks directly to the agent. After deducting his commission—usually 10 to 15 percent—your agent will send you the remaining balance. Most agents charge a higher commission of 20 to 25 percent when using a co-agent for foreign, dramatic, or other specialized rights. As you enter into a relationship with an agent, have him explain his specific commission rates and payment policy.

As your potential partner, you have the right to ask an agent for information that convinces you she knows what she's doing. Be reasonable about what you ask, however. Asking for recent sales is okay; asking for the average size of clients' advances is not. Remember, agents are very busy. Often asking a general question like, "How do you work?" or requesting a sample contract, can quickly answer your concerns. If you are polite and he responds with anger or contempt, that tells you something you need to know about what working together would be like.

Evaluate the agent's level of experience. Agents who have been in the business awhile have a larger number of contacts, but new agents may be hungrier, as well as more open to previously unpublished writers. Talk to other writers about their interactions with specific agents. Writers' organizations such as the National Writers Association (NWA), the American Society of Journalists and Authors (ASJA), and the National Writers Union (NWU) maintain files on agents their members have dealt with, and can share this information by written request or through their membership newsletters.

Understand any contract before you sign

Some agents offer written contracts, some do not. If your prospective agent does not, at least ask for a "memorandum of understanding" that details the basic relationship of expenses and commissions. If your agent does offer a contract, be sure to read it carefully, and keep a copy for yourself. Because contracts can be confusing, you may want to have a lawyer or knowledgeable writer friend check it out before you sign anything.

The National Writers Union (NWU) has drafted a Preferred Literary Agent Agreement and a pamphlet, *Understand the Author-Agent Relationship*, which is available to members. (Membership is $74 and open to all writers actively pursuing a writing career. See "Professional Organizations" in the back of the book for their address.) The union suggests clauses that delineate such issues as:

- the scope of representation (One work? One work with the right of refusal on the next? All work completed in the coming year? All work completed until the agreement is terminated?)
- the extension of authority to the agent to negotiate on behalf of the author
- compensation for the agent, and any co-agent, if used
- manner and time frame for forwarding monies received by the agent on behalf of the client
- termination clause, allowing client to give about thirty days to terminate the agreement
- the effect of termination on concluded agreements as well as ongoing negotiations
- arbitration in the event of a dispute between agent and client

If things don't work out

Because this is a business relationship, a time may come when it is beneficial for you and your agent to part ways. Unlike a marriage, you don't need to go through counseling to keep the relationship together. Instead, you end it professionally on terms upon which you both agree.

First check to see if your written agreement spells out any specific procedures. If not, write a brief, businesslike letter, stating that you no longer think the relationship is advantageous and you wish to terminate it. Instruct the agent not to make any new submissions and give her a thirty- to sixty-day limit to continue as representative on submissions already under consideration. You can ask for a list of all publishers who have rejected your unsold work, as well as a list of those who are currently considering it. If your agent charges for office expenses, you will have to reimburse him upon terminating the contract. For this reason, you may want to ask for a cap on expenses when you originally enter into an agency agreement. If your agent has made sales for you, he will continue to receive those monies from the publisher, deduct his commission and remit the balance to you. A statement and your share of the money should be sent to you within thirty days. You can also ask that all manuscripts in his possession be returned to you.

FINAL THOUGHTS

Finding an agent is a challenge, but one may be necessary if you want a commercially successful book. Selecting an agent is a task which deserves a lot of time and careful consideration. Above all, it is important to find a person whom you trust and who believes in your work. And now that you know the steps to take to find a literary agent, get started on the right foot and select the right agent for you.

Matching an Agent's Talent to Yours

BY DONALD MAASS

Far worse than having no agent is having the wrong agent. Well over half my clients are ex-clients of some other agency. What went wrong? There are as many answers as there are clients, but some common themes are lack of communication, lack of editorial feedback, indifference, poor follow-through, lack of expertise with a given market and so on. Some of the ex-agents are part-timers, not in New York or, occasionally when I meet them, just not on the same planet.

Donald Maass

How did those authors wind up with those agents? One factor is haste. Getting an agent is a profound personal validation for a writer, and at a certain point—generally when success is close enough to taste, yet somehow elusive—the writer simply cannot stand to wait any longer. He signs up with the first agent who says "yes." A couple of years later, the mistake becomes evident. A divorce is needed, but of course divorce is a messy business and dating again is a scary prospect. Some writers put it off too long.

Do you need a new agent? If you do, you will probably know. Calls go unreturned. Marketing reports are scanty. In many ways, your agent does not seem involved with you. I am not talking about being taken for granted; that happens, and it usually can be cured with an honest phone call. No, I am talking about plain indifference, which can be just as hurtful as lack of experience.

To be fair, that indifference may be plain weariness. If you are impossibly demanding, sweating every detail, living or dying depending on the tone of your agent's voice in your last phone call, then your agent may have cause to be tired of you. Conversely, if you are indifferent to your career, writing weakly or all over the place, and frankly are not making money, then your agent may also be justified in his attitude.

True lack of experience is another matter. With your breakout novel in hand, you may be wondering if your agent is up to the job. Does he have the contacts, the savvy and the clout to get you a major deal and keep you on course throughout the publication process? One sign is how helpful your agent is before you are done writing: Is he giving you early feedback, is he cheering you on? Once the manuscript is done, is there quality evaluation and detailed planning for the sale?

You cannot measure those things if your attitude is, "Oh, I just let my agent handle that." You have to be involved. You will want to have some idea of what you need in terms of publisher, deal, format and so forth. If your agent is not on the same page, fine. Listen. If his ideas make

DONALD MAASS, *author of seventeen novels, has more than twenty years of experience as a literary agent, representing dozens of novelists in the science fiction, fantasy, crime, mystery, romance and thriller categories. He speaks at writers conferences throughout the country and lives in New York City. He is also the former president of the Association of Authors' Representatives. This article is an excerpt reprinted from his book* Writing the Breakout Novel, *copy © 2001 by Donald Maass. Used with permission of Writer's Digest Books, an imprint of F&W Publications, Inc. Visit your local bookseller or call 1-800-448-0915 to obtain your copy.*

sense, you might want to go with them. If they do not, talk about it. If your agent is excited, then at least he is on your side.

For one reason or another, you may find that the first publishing person with whom you connect is an editor. You may have interested one at a writers conference. If so, you probably have started a correspondence, and may even have received revision suggestions and more than one reading. If so, congratulations! There is nothing wrong with this route into publishing.

However, once it becomes clear that the editor would like to buy your book, it is time to get an agent. If an offer has been made, do not say yes or no; instead, ask if you may take the time to find an agent. Most editors will gladly consent. They are professionals. They know that a good agent can be an asset to everyone. As for timing, do not worry. Your agent search will not take long with an offer on the table.

How do you find an agent? Ask several sources for referrals. Check the guidebooks. Be sure that the agents to whom you are talking know your field. That is as easy as asking about their other clients and recent sales. Also be sure that what they have to say about your novel is specific, insightful and sensitive. The same goes for their outlook on the market and your upcoming deal.

With luck, you will have a choice of several good agents. Who will be right for you may come down to chemistry, but I recommend you consider agents who are members of the Association of Authors' Representatives, Inc.; AAR, for short. The membership requirements and Canon of Ethics of this national trade organization are the only standards for experience and fair dealing in the otherwise unregulated business of literary agency. I am a member. Many good agents are.

Whether or not you have an offer on the table, what is the best way to approach your prospects? Oh boy, do I have some advice for you!

The pitch

Query letter, fax, phone call, e-mail? The guidebooks will tell you what each agent prefers. Generally speaking, skip fax and e-mail. The first feels arrogant, I don't know why but it does, and the second is too casual. If you have an offer from a publisher in hand, a phone call is appropriate, if a little nerve-wracking.

With no offer in hand, a query letter with a SASE (that is, a self-addressed stamped envelope with sufficient postage to return to you the agent's reply and/or your material) is a businesslike way to make your first approach.

Do not be intimidated by the legendary volume of agents' query mail, the so-called "slush pile." (My office receives several hundred letters a week.) A well-written letter and a solid premise always stand out. When the good ones come in, my staff knows to get them on my desk right away. Hot prospects usually have written to my competition as well, and experience has taught me that the first agent to phone the prospective client is quite often the one who wins out.

Now, the pitch: Why are novelists so bad at selling their own stories? Never mind, I know why. This is the crucial moment, though, when it pays to practice the art of the pitch. A good query letter has four components: introduction, summary, credentials, closing. The first and last should be, and usually are, short. It is the middle two that give people problems.

First, the summary: How to sum up your long, layered break-out novel in 100-200 words? It is a challenge, but there are guidelines. First, remember the purpose of your query letter is not to tell the whole plot or convince me you are the hottest new writer since last week. Rather, the purpose of your query is simply to get me to read your manuscript. With that in mind, a summary gets easier.

There are only three things you need to get me, or anybody, hooked on a story: setting, protagonist, problem. Deliver those briefly and with punch, and you have a basic pitch. Conveying some of your story's layers is a tougher challenge. My advice is to be brief and to focus on the elements that lend your story plausibility (its real-world inspiration, briefly stated, can help), inherent conflict, originality and gut emotional appeal. No-no's to avoid are adjectives, superlatives and anything more than a word or two on your theme.

Also, skip all that junk about the size of the audience for your novel. Your ambition, years of effort, professional attitude, willingness to promote, etc., are also unnecessary. You are ahead of yourself. What matters at this stage is your story.

Publishing credentials, though, can be helpful to include. Prior novel publications always make me sit up and take notice, although self-publication has the opposite effect—unless it resulted in an Edgar Award nomination, or similar recognition. Short story sales to recognized magazines are also good. Journalistic experience, professional articles, ad writing and the like are nice but do not imply skill as a novelist.

What if you have never been published? What if this is your first piece of writing? No doubt about it, you may have a tough time persuading any top agent that your book is worth a look. The novel is a vastly complicated art form that takes years to master. For that reason, I am happier to hear that the offered manuscript is the author's third or fourth. That said, the right first novel pitched well can be a big winner.

There are other things that get my attention too. An M.F.A. in writing or study with a reputable teacher are pluses. So are referrals from published novelists. The best recommendation of all, needless to say, is a novel that sounds dynamite. Work on your pitch. Mention your models. If your premise is good, your approach professional and your skill evident, it is entirely possible to interest even a top New York agent.

Avoiding Bad Agents

BY LORI PERKINS

At writers' conferences I am often asked how to tell a good agent from a bad agent. This is usually followed by the question: What do you think of reading fees?

If an agent is a member of a writer's organization or has a good reputation within an organization's membership, it's a good indication that he is a good agent.

Literary agents do not have to pass a test or take an oath of office. However, many of us have joined the Association of Author's Representatives (AAR), which requires that we sign a very basic canon of ethics. It requires that we make our living exclusively from selling books, that we charge no more than a 15 percent commission and that we pay our authors within thirty days of receipt of their monies. I would say that any agent who is a member of AAR is a reputable agent. Lack of membership in AAR does not mean that an agent is disreputable, however—some of us are just much more independent than others, and many don't live in the New York City area and therefore can't take advantage of the full benefits of the organization.

Reading fees are a dicey subject among agents, so much so that they were one of the reasons why the two professional organizations of literary agents were unable to unite for years. In 1996, the Society of Author's Representatives (SAR) and the International Literary Agents Association (ILLA) joined to become AAR. The AAR finally decided to create a grandfather clause to include those agents who already charged reading fees before all members were required to sign the new canon of ethics, but not allow any new members to charge reading fees. Their feeling on this was that agents should make their living from selling books, not reading them, editing them, packaging them or illustrating them, which are different jobs than selling.

One AAR member who charges a reading fee defended this practice by reminding us that our time is worth money. I have solved that dilemma for myself by not reading material that fails to capture my imagination right away. This is what most agents do and is why agents often reject books based on the first page or even the query letter.

Many writers feel that agents don't give their work a chance because we make our decision on such a small amount of written material. If you feel your work picks up steam later on, you should rewrite the book. If you need editorial guidance to do so or you want a detailed review of your material, then you should consider paying a reader's fee. However, if you just want a simple yes or no from an agent because you feel your work is ready for submission, send it to the agents who don't charge a fee. If they see something redeeming in the book and it needs work, they will tell you so. You can then take a writer's workshop or hire a book doctor on your own.

The sleazy agent I once worked for charged reading fees. At one time I was one of the readers, which was a good thing for the writers who paid me to read their work—I did go on to become a successful agent, so my three pages of advice to them were very professional. But there's no guarantee that the person who reads your book will be the agent herself, or even someone with

LORI PERKINS *is the founder of L. Perkins Associates, a literary agency in Riverdale, NY. She is an adjunct professor at New York University where she teaches a class in Literary Agenting for N.Y.U.'s Center for Publishing. This article is excerpted from* The Insider's Guide to Getting an Agent *copyright © 1999 by Lori Perkins. Used with permission of Writer's Digest Books, an imprint of F&W Publications, Inc. Visit your local bookseller or call 1-800-448-0915 to obtain your copy.*

a more professional background than your own. Often, readers are fellow unpublished writers.

I did take on one of the novels I was paid to read, and sold it. Another writer who paid us to read his manuscript later won a Whiting Award and was published by Farrar Straus & Giroux. But neither one of those authors needed to pay us first. They were both exceptional writers to begin with and could easily have gotten an agent without paying a fee.

Many writers think that if they pay the reader's fee they will have a better chance of being taken on by the agency. I like to think of that as The Publisher's Clearing House Approach to publishing (buy a magazine subscription and maybe Ed McMahon will ring your bell with a million-dollar check). That's not the way publishing should work. Your writing should open doors, not your money.

Another question that comes up at these writers' conferences: "Is it essential that an agent be in New York?" Remember, the book publishing industry is in New York, so a New York agent is more likely to have up-to-the-minute industry information.

That does not mean that good, successful literary agents don't exist outside of New York. Most regions have at least one good agent who works with local authors. (It's nice to be able to meet with your agent face to face, although most New York agents travel so often that we do manage to meet most of our clients.) Whether you choose a New York agent goes back to the decisions you have to make about whether you want to be a big fish in a little pond or a guppy in a great lake.

Understanding Fees—What Writers Must Know

Before starting your search for an agent, it is extremely important to have an understanding of the various fees some agencies charge. Most agents make their living from the commissions they receive after selling their clients' books, and these are the agents we've listed. Charging writers for office expenses incurred on their behalf is standard, though there are agents who do not charge for this service. Agents also typically make 15% commission on sales. The editors at Writer's Digest discourage the payment of any other fees to agents.

Office expenses

Many agents—both those who do and do not charge additional fees—ask the author to pay for photocopying, postage, and long-distance phone calls. An agent should only ask for office expenses *after* agreeing to represent the writer. These expenses should be discussed upfront, and the writer should receive an accounting for them. This money is sometimes returned upon sale of the manuscript. Be wary if there is an upfront fee amounting to hundreds of dollars, which is excessive.

Reading fees

Agents who do not charge reading fees earn their money from commissions. Agencies that do charge reading fees often do so to cover the cost of additional readers or the time spent reading that could have been spent selling. This practice can save the agent time and open the agency to a larger number of submissions and may allow the agent time to consider each manuscript more extensively. Whether such promises are kept depends upon the honesty of the agency. You may pay a fee and never receive a response from the agent, or you may pay someone who will not submit your manuscript to publishers. In this book, we have not included those literary agents who charge reading fees.

Reading fees vary from $25 to $500 or more. The fee is usually nonrefundable, but sometimes agents agree to refund the money if they take a writer on as a client or if they sell the writer's manuscript. Keep in mind, however, that payment of a reading fee does not ensure representation. If you find that a literary agent listed in this book charges a reading fee, please contact the editor.

Officially, the AAR (Association of Authors' Representatives) in their Canon of Ethics prohibits members from directly or indirectly charging a reading fee, and the WGA (Writers Guild of America) does not allow WGA signatory agencies to charge a reading fee to WGA members, as stated in the WGA's Artists' Manager Basic Agreement. A signatory may charge you a fee if you are not a member, but most signatory agencies do not charge a reading fee as an across-the-board policy.

Critique fees

Sometimes a manuscript will interest an agent, but he will point out areas still needing development. Some agencies offer criticism services for an additional fee. Like reading fees, payment of a critique fee does not ensure representation. When deciding if you will benefit from having someone critique your manuscript, keep in mind that the quality and quantity of comments vary widely. The critique's usefulness will depend on the agent's knowledge of the market. Also be aware that an agent who spends a significant portion of his time commenting on manuscripts will have less time to actively market work he currently represents. We strongly advise writers not to use critiquing services offered through an agency. Instead, we recommend hiring a freelance editor or joining a writer's group until your work is ready to be submitted to agents who do not charge fees.

Other agents may refer a writer to a freelance editor or a "book doctor." Make sure you research any critiquing service before sending your work, and don't be charmed by fancy brochures and compliments about your writing. Also, beware of agents who hurriedly refer you to editorial services. While it is not illegal to make a referral, some agents may abuse this practice.

The WGA has issued a rule that its signatories cannot make referrals to book doctors, and the AAR frowns on them as well, particularly if an agent is receiving financial compensation for making the referral. The WGA believes that, while an agent may have good intentions, it would be too difficult to differentiate those agents trying to help writers from those who may have a financial or professional interest in an editing relationship that develops at their suggestion.

Finding reputable freelance editors and literary agents

How can you sift the reputable from the disreputable when you live far from the centers of publishing activity and feed on hope to keep your dreams alive? When you have been rejected by an entire flotilla of agents, and someone out there offers you (for a "small" fee) the opportunity to have your manuscript read by a self-styled "professional" or better yet, offers you publication if you will come up with an "advance" toward it, could this be the opportunity knocking at the door? Use the following guidelines to help you decide.

Read *Publishers Weekly* for several months before you will need the services of either a book doctor or a literary agent, focusing on new agents who come out of substantial publishing (not necessarily agenting) experience.

Attend writers' conferences, and ask around for names of freelance editors and agents with whom people have had positive experiences.

From freelance editors, request an advance breakdown of fees before signing any contract including the cost of a reading and editorial letter and the cost of a sebsequent in-depth editorial job. Beware of empty promises. A freelance editor cannot guarantee you publication.

Ask freelance editors if they will provide samples of previous editing jobs, and discuss the level of editing you will receive for the fees you pay.

Request a list of published writers who have worked with this editor, and try to check it out by looking at Acknowledgment pages, etc., unless you are fortunate enough to have access to one of these writers.

Ask your librarian or local bookseller if the name of the editor you are considering is at all familiar. Librarians and booksellers read *Publishers Weekly* and attend book conventions, where they sometimes meet editors. They can also make inquiries for you and steer you toward a reputable editor.

Familiarize yourself with what services a good agent can and should be able to provide.

Getting an Agent is a Contact Sport

BY LINDA MEAD

More individuals are writing and seeking agents to represent their work than ever before. It also seems that the agent population hasn't grown accordingly. At any given time, I have three boxes filled with queries that have to be read and 98% of these queries will be turned down. So how is a writer going to become part of the 2% that will hook an agent?

GET IN THE GAME

Let's talk about finding an agent first. There are numerous resources available to writers that list and/or describe agents and agencies. Some of these include magazines, directories, the Internet, and books like this one. Attend literary events, writers' conferences and visit writing groups. While sorting through these resources, compile an "A" list (agents you would love to represent you) and a "B" list

Linda Mead

(agents you would be happy to have represent you). Make the list as long as you wish, noting how each agency wants to be queried.

KNOW YOUR POSITION

Be clear about where your work fits by categorizing it. If you are unsure of the genre or sub-category of your work (other than fiction and non-fiction), go to the bookstore and find other similar books (besides, you should know your competition). If you are still unsure, make an effort to categorize the book by earmarking several possible slots into which it could fit. A writers' group or your local bookseller can sometimes be helpful. There is nothing more disheartening than submitting your "historical" fiction that you have mislabeled as "western" only to have it rejected on the basis that the agency doesn't handle "westerns." An opportunity missed?

PLAY BY THE RULES

Each agency specifies how it wishes to receive submissions. Don't deviate from these requests. It could work against you. I received a query letter recently that was written in the form of dialogue because the author was also a playwright. While amusing and certainly a unique approach, it didn't get to the point quickly enough to pique my interest.

Author: I have a wonderful story to tell that will change the world!
Agent: What is the book about?
I wondered as I plowed through the rest of the dialogue.

BEHAVE LIKE A PRO

Some agents will look at queries or proposals online, but that is not an invitation to chat or use their e-mail address as an educational tool. Several agents I know have received queries

LINDA MEAD *is a founding member of the LitWest Group, an agency handling nonfiction and fiction. As an agent, she seeks nonfiction projects that are life affirming and practical, even unusual. She is the co-author, with Suze Orman, of* You've Earned It, Don't Lose It *(Newmarket Press) and author of* Investing with Giants *(Wiley). Read more at www.litwest.com.*

from writers asking what a query letter is, how to pitch a project or even what a SASE is. It's perfectly okay not to know these things, but agents can't spend their time—their client's time—educating the public. That's what writers' conferences, writing groups, reference books, and other resources are for. Time is money for an agent, who needs to be spending that time finding new talent and selling projects. So, learn the game before you try to find a manager.

One last word about e-mail queries: Viruses are a constant threat and often are transmitted through attachments (even with anti-virus software, it's not worth the risk). If an agency accepts e-mail queries, it's best to incorporate your sample into the text of the e-mail or, if available, use their website query format.

THROW A SMOOTH, FAST PITCH

An important element of your query letter is the pitch. Whether your work is fiction or non-fiction, we need to know certain things about it. Your pitch is the distillation of your ideas in three to five sentences—or less.

For works of non-fiction, cover these issues: What is the concept of the book? Who is the audience and why do they need this book? Why are you the right person to write this book? How is your book different from similar books on the market? (See, the trip to the bookstore was worthwhile.)

For fiction and narrative nonfiction books, the following points should be covered: Who are the main characters? Where does the story take place? What events set up the story? What happens to change the circumstances of the story and create tension? How is the story resolved?

Here's the hard part. You'll have to be a great salesperson and writer and fit all of this information onto one page. So don't waste words. I had one author write an entire paragraph telling me that he was going to tell me about his book!

STRUT YOUR STUFF

Before queries are sent out, you should have your materials ready to submit the moment an agent requests them. This means having a completed proposal and sample chapters for a nonfiction project. For fiction, you'll need to have a final, edited manuscript ready to send. No first drafts. Follow the proper formats for proposals and manuscripts.

PLAN A STRATEGY

Don't feel that you have to query agents one at a time. Unless they ask for an exclusive on your full manuscript and tell you that they will have an answer for you within a week, query several agents at a time. Turn around times for proposals and manuscripts stretch from four to eight weeks (and beyond), so you may be old and gray before you find that perfect match if you don't send out simultaneous queries.

MAKE IT EASY TO GET RECRUITED

If you want to hear from the agent, make sure to include a self-addressed, stamped envelope (SASE) for the response or return of your work. Otherwise, it becomes scrap paper. If you wish to know that the work was received, include a self-addressed, stamped postcard. It costs less than "return receipt" postage and is just as effective.

WATCH YOUR BACK

Every agent manages their business a little differently, but, with a little information, you can avoid major pitfalls.

Reader's fees

It's just not necessary to pay anyone to read your work. An agent's job is to read and evaluate based on their needs. The person who charges to read your work is not an agent. There are plenty more to query who don't charge a fee.

Editorial fees

Some agencies also have editorial services. If your writing needs editorial work and the agent provides that service, ask for referrals outside of the company that you can interview. Don't be swayed to sign with an agent under the conditions that you must also pay for their editorial services. They should not go hand-in-hand. Get a second professional editorial opinion before having the scalpel wielded.

Agency fees

Many agents charge back such costs as photocopying and postage. Find out what the agency policies are: Do they require an up-front payment for office costs? What do charge-back fees include? What are the agency percentages on foreign and ancillary rights?

The agency agreement

Some agents have written agreements, some work on a handshake. Always look over any written agreement and ask questions. Either way, know what you're getting into.

THE LIFE OF A PRO

As a writer in today's market, you have the daunting task of being an all-encompassing talent: writer, salesperson, marketing genius, publicist, and so much more. It's not an enviable position. As Gustav Flaubert said, "Writing is a dog's life, but the only life worth living." Believe in yourself and your work, and keep writing.

Time Out: Query Quirk Alert!

- Don't pontificate. We know how much you treasure and want to sell your work.
- Don't complain about your woes as a writer. The last thing agents want to hear is that you are going to be evicted and need some money fast.
- Know to whom you are writing. I have received queries addressed to Ms. West (because our company's name is LitWest Group), Lieutenant Mead (because I sign my name LT Mead) and even received e-mails addressed to other agents (circular file!)
- Gifts don't help. Talent does.
- Don't call or e-mail and ask, "Did you receive . . .?" or "Have you read . . .?" Try to be patient. If the process is taking too long for you, move on.

Basics of Contacting a Literary Agent

Once you and your manuscript are thoroughly prepared, the time is right to contact an agent. Finding an agent can often be as difficult as finding a publisher. Nevertheless, there are three ways to maximize your chances of finding the right agent: Obtain a referral from someone who knows the agent; meet the agent in person at a writers' conference; submit a query letter or proposal; or attract the agent's attention with your own published writing.

Referrals

The best way to get your foot in an agent's door is to be referred by one of his clients, or by an editor or another agent he has worked with in the past. Because an agent trusts his clients, he will usually read referred work before over-the-transom submissions. If you are friends with anyone in the publishing business who has connections with agents, ask politely for a referral. However, don't be offended if another writer will not share the name of his agent.

If you don't have a wide network of publishing professionals, use the resources you do have to get an agent's attention.

Conferences

Going to a conference is your best bet for meeting an agent in person. Many conferences invite agents to either give a speech or simply be available for meetings with authors. And agents view conferences as a way to find writers. Often agents set aside time for one-to-one discussions with writers, and occasionally they may even look at material writers bring to the conference. If an agent is impressed with you and your work, she may ask for writing samples after the conference. When you send your query, be sure to mention the specific conference where you met and that she asked to see your work.

Because this is an effective way to connect with agents, we've asked agents to indicate in their listings which conferences they regularly attend. We've also included a section of conferences, starting on page 283, where you can find out more information about a particular conference.

Submissions

The most common way to contact an agent is by a query letter or a proposal package. Most agents will accept unsolicited queries. Some will also look at outlines and sample chapters. Almost none want unsolicited complete manuscripts. Check the **How to Contact** subhead in each listing to learn exactly how an agent prefers to be solicited. Never call—let the writing in your query letter speak for itself.

Because a query letter is your first impression on an agent, it should be professional and to the point. As a brief introduction to your manuscript, a query letter should only be one page in length, or at maximum, two pages.

- The first paragraph should quickly state your purpose—you want representation.
- In the second paragraph, mention why you have specifically chosen to query him. Perhaps he specializes in your areas of interest or represents authors you admire. Show him you have done your homework.
- In the next paragraph or two, describe the project, the proposed audience, why your book will sell, etc. Be sure to mention the approximate length and any special features.
- Then discuss why you are the perfect person to write this book, listing your professional

credentials or relative experience.

- Close your query with an offer to send either an outline, sample chapters, or the complete manuscript—depending on your type of book.

For examples of actual query letters that led authors straight to publication, see "Queries That Made It Happen" on page 43. For helpful hints on outlines and synopses, see "Outline and Synopsis Workshop" on page 48.

Agents agree to be listed in directories such as the *Guide to Literary Agents* to indicate to writers what they want to see and how they wish to receive submissions. As you start to query agents, make sure you follow their individual submission directions. This, too, shows an agent you've done your research. Like publishers, agencies have specialties. Some are only interested in novel-length works. Others are open to a wide variety of subjects and may actually have member agents within the agency who specialize in only a handful of the topics covered by the entire agency.

Before querying any agent, first consult the Agent Specialties Indexes in this book for your manuscript's subject, and identify those agents who handle what you write. Then, read the agents' listing to see if they are appropriate for you and for your work. For more information on targeting your submissions see "Matching an Agent's Talent to Yours" on page 26.

Publishing credits

Some agents read magazines or journals to find writers to represent. If you have had an outstanding piece published in a periodical, you may be contacted by an agent wishing to represent you. In such cases, make sure the agent has read your work. Some agents send form letters to writers, and such agents often make their living entirely from charging reading fees, not from commissions on sales.

However, many reputable and respected agents do contact potential clients in this way. For them, you already possess attributes of a good client: you have publishing credits and an editor has validated your work. To receive a letter from a reputable agent who has read your material and wants to represent you is an honor.

Occasionally, writers who have self-published or who have had their work published electronically may attract an agent's attention, especially if the self-published book has sold well or received a lot of positive reviews.

Recently, writers have been posting their work on the Internet in hope of attracting an agent's eye. With all the submissions most agents receive, they likely have little time to peruse writer's websites. Nevertheless, there are agents who do consider the Internet a resource for finding fresh voices. Only the future will show how often writers are discovered through this medium.

How to Write a Query Letter

BY JODIE RHODES

Every day thousands of writers blow their chance because they don't understand how to write a compelling query letter. An astounding number of writers fail to write one at all, just sending along pages from a manuscript with no explanation of what the material is. Those go straight into the rejection pile without even a glance.

Jodie Rhodes

Think of a query letter as a sincere, honest communication between you and the agent. The purpose is not to sell but to inform. But what dooms some query letters to rejection while others stir interest and lead to a request for the manuscript?

Following are all too typical letters in which writers apparently believed they had amazing ideas but clearly never had a "reality moment" about the absurdity of their plots. I think too much viewing of B movies that run at 3AM on obscure cable channels did them in.

These are actual queries I've received, with the writers' names charitably omitted.

> *This action/adventure novel is about a dark military program which takes a top navy seal and replaces the lower part of his brain with parts cloned from the DNA of a tiger!*

You will note the author doesn't even capitalize Navy Seal, which leads one to odd thoughts indeed.

> *A man angry at his company which has robbed him of his retirement funds makes neckties that constrict on their own. He seeks his revenge on the whole society by a series of murders where the ties do the choking for him. Such is the plot of* Haunted Neckties.

I had to read it twice in order to believe it actually said this.

> *This riveting and bittersweet story deals with loneliness, love, betrayal, sexual desire, child abuse, suicide, sexual identity, fear of insanity, eating disorders, sexual assault, molestation, delusional behavior, multiple personality and murder. The manuscript will frighten, amuse, disturb you but still leave you with a good feeling.*

Apparently the writer decided to cover all the bases.

> *This is at once a gay love story, a plea for handicapped liberation and a sanguine tale of greed, murder and revenge. My pen name is necessary because the narrative's explicit depictions of incontinence management and gay sex could arouse the interest of the culture police.*

Words totally fail me on this one.

JODIE RHODES *is a literary agent in La Jolla, California, a published novelist, former university level writing teacher, and editor. She gives seminars at The Learning Annex, writes columns for national and regional magazines and conducts clinics and workshops for local area writers. Of the 32 books she's sold in the past two years, 99% were by new writers.*

Where writers really shoot themselves in the foot is with the queries they write for mysteries, suspense novels and thrillers. Instead of coming up with a truly fresh, unique idea, they bury us in advertising words. I am sure they're really impressed by their copy, but the truth is it's so generic they all sound the same. Here are typical examples I hope you will never write—or if you've written them before you will instantly stop.

Corporate espionage. Now. A field alive with ex-agents, remnants of the Cold War who span the globe from San Francisco to the former U.S.S.R. A race against the clock by Emily who must discover the true inner self stripped from her by unknown forces.

A young Madison Avenue's aberrant lust for obscene personal wealth. A seasoned corporate entrepreneur who revels in a twisted code of ethics. A bizarre entourage of greedy Wall Street parasites. A caring, loving family swept along for the ride.

A fat and happy United States, unaware a conspiracy spawned in the aftermath of Watergate is about to achieve its goal as public servants subservient to a secret Council placed in powerful positions plot the assassination of the president-elect.

Former PI Jimmy Gates wants to sail off into the sunset but his ex-wife, drag queens, nanotechnology 20 years ahead of current science, a mad scientist and love conspires to keep him tied to the dock.

Then there's the desperate writer who tries for our sympathies. I must admit I did feel for these two, in between uncontrollable laughter.

I know there are rules for query letters like this and I apologize right here and now for not following them. My original plan was to write a full five chapters of perfect coherence but that plan went out the window about two hours ago when I threw up my hands after hours of editing and realized there's nothing more I can do. I'm at the end of some sort of rope here. There's a voice in the words I am enclosing and I hope you can find it.

Would you like to read a good novel? I hope so because I've written one. I'd like to send it to you, no strings attached, all of it or part of it or as much or as little of it as you like, with more than none of it, in any case, and I enclose a SASE so you can indicate your preference, though I'm afraid your preference will be for none of it but what the hell, I have to make the effort, don't I, and what do you have to lose except a little time and effort and really, reading it is no effort and you never really know, do you?

What stands out most of all from these queries is the bald fact they totally forgot to tell us what their book is about. A query letter filled with generalities is doomed from the start. It's specifics we need. Compare these, which give us vivid word pictures, to the first group, which are just a collection of adjectives and adverbs. Fiction by unknown writers is so difficult to sell that you must hook us immediately with the opening line of your query letter. Since novels by unknown writers are almost impossible to sell, you must create an intriguing scene in the first sentence of your query.

Street Kids *(by James River), a semi-autobiographical novel, is the story of two teenage runaways who meet on the streets of LA, join forces to survive, become close as blood brothers, then find themselves aligned with rival crime crews, the leaders of which order each to kill the other.*

Dark Horse *(by Shelby Weeks) is the story of an angry bitter boy, a proud but desperately lonely girl and a beautiful horse marked for death.*

Death in a Minor Key (by Paul Hall) opens with a young whore found dead in a hotel room. On the sidewalk under her window lies the shattered body of a Mexican construction worker. Several miles away an elegantly dressed woman walks out the door of a trendy restaurant and is struck down by a speeding car that appears abruptly out of the rain swept night. Linda Hartigan, founder of Global Electronics, comes home to find her cat and its newborn kittens lying dead on her bed. The following day Detective John Connally receives an anonymous note that says, "Guess what happens next?"

The easiest query letters to write are usually for nonfiction books, where you have either a true story to tell or factual information to give on which you're an authority. Below are some samples of these. But before we get to that, I believe it would be helpful for you to see a query letter for a novel where the author has no credentials of her own, yet presents a compelling letter that contains all the information an agent needs.

Julie Martinez is a rookie, fresh out of the Police Academy. She looks too young to be a cop, which is why they put her undercover at Jefferson High, an inner city school in Detroit where over half the kids are hooked on drugs. She's supposed to nail the drug supplier, not fall in love with him.

Double Sting is the first book in the Julie Martinez mystery series and runs 70,000 words. The character of Julie grows and matures with each new book in the series. I was fortunate enough to spend time with a very savvy and extremely compassionate young female detective who gave me a world of fascinating insider information about a cop's world.

I would be happy to send you either a partial or the complete manuscript. A SASE is enclosed for your convenience.

Take a close look at how three very short paragraphs sum up the entire essence of this writer's book. We not only know who the protagonist is but quite a bit about her, including the trouble she's in. We know what the plot of the story is, that it's the first in a mystery series, that it runs 70,000 words, that the author has completed it and, of key importance, the author has done her homework and interviewed a real female detective so the material in the book is authentic. Also note, with the exception of describing the real detective, there's not a single adjective or adverb in the entire letter. Keep a copy of this at your side when you write your query letter.

Nonfiction queries do not need dramatic openings like fiction queries, but they do need compelling subject matter written by authors with proven expertise on their subject. If you have no name recognition and no outstanding credentials in the area you are writing about, your only chance is to find a recognized authority who will endorse your book and/or do a foreword.

The exception is the memoir, where your life experiences are your credentials. However, your life experiences better be compelling. Authors from different cultures and different racial and ethnic backgrounds have built-in credentials, but their writing must be powerful and luminous to have a chance in this crowded market. Below are some nonfiction queries that catch the eye.

Mexico's Isthmus is known for its women. Handsome, bold and exquisitely dressed, they are so unlike most Mexican women that they are renowned throughout the region as Amazons. For decades anthropologists and filmmakers alike have been fascinated with these women who comprise the only living matriarchal society in the world. Strangely, however, no one until now has written a book about them. I'm a widely published travel writer who's fluent in Spanish and spent seven years researching this culture with the help of Julin Contreras, Director of Tehuantepec's Casa de Cultura. The book gives information on white healers and black magicians, The Day of the Dead, Boxcar Women, Shutting

Down the Pan American Highway and the Midwives of Juchitan. (Into the Heart of Amazons, written by Tom DeMott.)

A Woman's Voyage With The Merchant Marines is the true story of my shipping out to sea as the lone woman on a rust bucket oil tanker. It's a world that few people know: a world of men that almost no woman has ever experienced. The arc of the memoir is a terrifying storm at sea where death seems a certainty. At that moment I realized it wasn't death that scared me but life. The scariest part of being in that storm was the involuntary opening of my heart. When that happens, as frightening as it feels, anything is possible. I mean anything. (Changing Course, written by Jeanne Lutz.)

I was born to a white mother and a black father, went to an all white Catholic school and every important person they taught me about was white. All the TV Stars my classmates talked about were white. The only blacks I saw were on the six o'clock news: murderers, rapists, drug addicts. So I decided to be white. When kids called me zebra and oreo, I told myself being called a cookie was not too bad and zebras were pretty cool animals. I worked hard in school but I worked hardest at being white. Then the world told me if you are half black, you are black. And if you are one eighth black, you are black. And if we find out there's a speck of blackness in you, you are black. (Living in a Black and White World, written by Ann Pearlman.)

The most important thing to keep in mind when you're writing a query letter is the need to give us a sense of your book, something that makes it your book and no one else's. A well-known author once said the book you write should be the book only you can write. Don't write for the market, which means your sole purpose is to sell it. These are invariably the most poorly written books.

Sincerity, honesty, genuine passion for your book, these are things we respond to. And please do your homework first. Research everything. If you're writing a mystery, thriller or suspense novel that involves cops, go talk to cops. If it's about doctors or scientists, find real ones and interview them. You should know 20 times more about your book than ever appears on the printed page. That's how you produce a book with that invaluable stamp of authenticity.

Finally, if you feel no emotion when you're writing it, neither will the reader. If you know your book inside out, know the characters and care about them, this will come through in your query letter. Never try to sell us or impress us. Just tell it like it is.

Query Tips

- Create your own letterhead so you appear professional. Nothing could be easier. Simply type your name, address, phone number and e-mail on a piece of paper and center it at the top of the page, then make photocopies of it on quality paper.
- Use a basic business letter format in writing the query. The text is single spaced with double spaces between paragraphs.
- Write very short paragraphs. This makes the page visually attractive and reader friendly. Four short paragraphs that take up almost a full page look shorter and very much easier to read than one long paragraph that fills three-quarters of a page.
- Keep the query letter to a single page. You would need to have very important information about the book and your background to warrant a two page query.
- Proofread your query letter. Typos, misspellings and clumsy, incoherent sentences in a simple one-page letter inspire no confidence at all in your manuscript.
- Be very careful you send the right letter to the right agent. If you're printing out a large number of letters, it's easy to leave in the name from a previous letter. Few things make a more negative impression than receiving a query letter addressed to another agent.
- Follow the agent's submission guidelines. If they only ask for a query, don't send sample chapters. If they do ask for sample pages of your manuscript, be sure and include them.
- Always enclose a SASE if you want a response.

Query Mistakes to Avoid

- Don't use "cute" stationary or odd type fonts. Use plain paper, standard type faces, 12-point type.
- Don't waste time telling us you're writing in hopes our agency will represent your book. Trust me, we already figured that out without your telling us. Get immediately into the heart of the matter.
- Don't try to sell us by telling us how great the book is or comparing it to those written by bestselling authors.
- Don't mention that your family, friends or "readers" loved it.
- Don't tell if it's been professionally edited. We'll almost certainly see flaws in it and wonder what in the world it looked like before it was "professionally edited."
- Don't say this is your third or sixth or twentieth book or how many other books you've written. Keep your rejections to yourself.
- Don't boast that you've been published by iUniverse or Xlibris. They're vanity presses and only emphasize your lack of success to date. Of course, if you've actually been published by a reputable royalty paying house, do mention that.
- Don't send sample chapters that are not the opening chapters. When you send us chapters 13, 15 and 25 for example, you're saying that chapters 1 through 12 were so boring, superficial and weakly written that you didn't dare send them.

Queries That Made It Happen

BY TERRI SEE

If your mother is a literary agent, congratulations! If not, you will likely face the same challenge as every other would-be writer in getting results from your query. To introduce yourself and your book with a letter that dazzles and impresses (without resorting to peculiar fonts and stationery) can be a daunting task. But what literary agents want is quite straightforward: a letter that explains who you are, what your book is about, and what qualifies you to write it. Depending on your subject matter, it may be helpful to do some research and include information on your competition in the marketplace. Perhaps your book really is the first of its kind and, if so, you have a powerful selling point.

Tempt with an irresistible opening sentence. Create curiosity with interesting, tight lines and cut any fat. You have one or two minutes to catch the reader's attention, so make them count. A well-composed letter will hint of your writing ability, but remember that in this brief introduction clarity is paramount. Be sure that the description of your book is not only intriguing but also complete in concept, so that it does not leave the reader hanging, wondering "is that it?"

Stick to your strengths and be careful not to be "all sizzle and no steak." One very common mistake writers make is pretending to be something they are not. Most agents can sense this and will discard the submission. Be confident, but be honest. Avoid commenting that your book will "make millions" or "change the world" but if you have been published before, mention it. It can work to your advantage.

Choose good quality paper, but showy colors and flashy designs are unnecessary. Your words are what should capture and hold the agent's attention, so concentrate your efforts there. Also, check and double check your spelling and punctuation and mind the spelling of the agent's name (Aaron or Erin? Terry or Terri?). Spell-check and grammar-check programs are helpful, but they can be wrong. They will not catch the improper use of a word and often confuse "your" with "you're," "it's" with "its" and a host of other problems.

It always helps to have a second pair of eyes, so ask someone qualified to proofread your letter in order to avoid mistakes. Overall, think of your letter as your messenger. Its details and presentation will go a long way to illustrate your professionalism. Consider how long it took you to write your book. Certainly your query letter is worth polishing until it fairly represents all that work.

Following are the query letters of two authors, Grace Tiffany and Jim Brown, along with their stories of finding an agent and getting a first novel published. Their agents, in turn, explain their first impressions and how these queries sold them on representing the writers. While the authors have distinctly different styles, both query letters landed them representation with an agent whose enthusiasm matched their own. To sell her literary novel, Tiffany focused on historical fact, which played up her research skills and sparked the interest of agent Carolyn French. Brown plugged the high concept of his commercial novel to capture the imagination of agent Mark David Ryan.

Let their stories inspire you to find the perfect slant for your query letter.

TERRI SEE *is a freelance writer living near Philadelphia. She is a former editor for Writer's Digest Books.*

Grace Tiffany

How Grace Tiffany found her agent is an interesting tale of chance encounters and second chances. It began when her sister met a writer in a Brooklyn laundromat. When her sister raved about Tiffany's book, the writer recommended the Fifi Oscard Agency. Tiffany followed the writer's recommendation and contacted Ms. Oscard, who set her up with Carolyn French. Having taught Shakespeare at four major universities, Tiffany had the ideal background for writing the book in question—a work of literary fiction based on the life of William Shakespeare. As luck would have it, French, too, had intensively studied Shakespeare and found personal interest in Tiffany's subject matter. It seemed the perfect connection.

© Nick Lucking

After examining the manuscript, however, French felt it would not sell well and chose not to represent it. "It was beautiful, but too long and weighty with extraneous material," she says. But she believed that Tiffany had strong writing talent and gave her advice about changing the book, encouraging her to keep at it. "This was the kind of writer I like, a literary writer," French says, "and even though I was turning her down, I wanted her to know she was a good writer." She believes that good writers know what to accept and what not to accept when being given advice, and what works for them. "I will say 'this doesn't work for me' and why, and hope that it helps."

Although Tiffany had been published numerous times before, this was her first novel, so she took French's advice, followed her own instincts, and made careful revisions. "Basically I wrote a better book," she says, adding that what greatly helped her writing was learning to listen to criticism and make changes accordingly, instead of feeling angry or insulted. "I would not change things just because someone said I should, but—if enough readers say the same thing they are probably right. Everyone said that my first manuscript was too long and slow in getting started. Finally I decided I didn't want to be the only person in the world other than my mother who didn't think it was too long. So I turned it into a shorter book."

More than a year after their initial discussion, Tiffany sent French a query letter for *My Father Had a Daughter*, or *Judith Shakespeare's Tale*. Because their first contact was by phone, the job of writing the query letter was somewhat less precarious. "Mine was a personal letter to an agent I knew something about." She knew from previous conversation that French had a "special interest in Shakespeare," and appealed to that. She also mentioned that she revised the manuscript along the lines of French's suggestions. "I actually quoted her exact words back to her," Tiffany recalls. By referring to previous contact and showing the agent that she had followed her advice, Tiffany hoped to persuade her to read the second manuscript. Prepared by the first submission, French says she knew Tiffany was a good writer and eagerly read the letter and manuscript. She was more than pleased at what she found. "This one was delightful and lush. The story was *right there*. I was right there in Stratford, immersed in the climate of the times. I couldn't put it down!" French remembers.

When asked what she found most gratifying or beneficial about having French as her agent, Tiffany says, "Her enthusiasm about my book and knowledge of the historical period on which it is based was very helpful. Also, because she genuinely liked the book, she put great energy into it and it sold quickly." French sent the manuscript to four publishers and says that they all wanted it. *My Father Had a Daughter* was purchased by Penguin Putnam for a May 2003 Berkley Signature Edition.

There was one more happy twist in this simpatico writer-agent connection. French had, to this point, only represented plays. "I had not sold a novel before, but I truly loved the book and believed in it. So this experience changed us both," she adds.

December 1, 2001

Ms. Carolyn French
Fifi Oscard Agency
24 W. 40th Street
New York, NY 10078

Dear Ms. French:

A year and a half ago we spoke on the phone about Shakespeare, and you were good enough to review a rather lengthy historical novel I had written about him (entitled Bottom's Dream). You made some helpful comments about it, which I have taken into account in structuring a new novel out of one strand of the old one. I would be happy to hear your thoughts on this shorter work, and for your agency to represent it if you find it entertaining and marketable.

The book is entitled *Judith*, and is a first-person narrative and a fictional account of the life of Judith Shakespeare, youngest daughter of the playwright, between the ages of 3 and 31. Little is known of Judith Shakespeare, but here are the raw historical facts on which I base my story. She was born in Stratford, England in 1585 the twin of a brother (Hamnet), who died when they both were 11. She remained in Stratford throughout her life, as did her sister, Susanna, who was married to a local doctor famed for his bizarre cures. When Judith was 31 she married Tom Quiney, the son of a good friend of her father's (and a local vintner), then gave birth to a son, whom she named "Shakespeare."

Parallel historical facts which figure in my story have to do with the building of the Globe Theater in 1599 and the career of Nathan Field, a boy actor who grew up to be a romantic rake and one of the leading players in Shakespeare's company.

So much for the facts. An outline of the novel accompanies this letter, as does a stamped and self-addressed envelope for your reply.

Thank you for you renewed consideration.

Sincerely,

Grace Tiffany

Jim Brown

"What if, as an initiation, you were buried alive for one hour, with an air tank and a radio? Then you learned that the people who put you there had just been killed in a car wreck? What if you saw a woman being slashed to death by an impossible storm of glass? Or a man being choked by a severed hand? And what if you had less than 72 hours to explain it all—with science?" Are you riveted? Would you continue reading? Literary agent Mark David Ryan did, then immediately called the author, Jim Brown, to ask for an exclusive 24-hour look at the complete manuscript for *The Hill*. He then stayed up all night reading it. Asked what grabbed his attention, Ryan, president of New Brand Agency Group says, "He opened by describing a 'high concept' premise—an irresistible 'what if . . .'—and illustrated his story-telling ability in the style of his letter."

Jim Brown attributes the action-packed style of his query letter to his years of work in television news. As an anchorman he has written thousands of "teases"—pre-program blurbs that reveal just enough about an upcoming story to keep viewers tuned in. "I took that concept and increased it by a factor of ten. Sort of a tease on steroids," Brown says. Also from television tease writing is his "you-oriented" phrasing (as in "What if . . . *you* were buried alive") which piques interest and personalizes the story for the reader.

Brown went through dozens of drafts and contends that in some respects it is easier to write a book than a good query letter. "Instead of five hundred pages, you have one. Every line is crucial—designed to make someone want to read the next," he explains, adding that his approach was initially wrong. "Originally I thought, 'I wrote a book and I need an agent.' Then it occurred to me that since I was trying to sell myself as a creative person, I needed to show some of that creativity in the letter." When he finally had a letter he liked, he submitted it to numerous agencies. Within a few weeks he had several responses, but chose Ryan for his enthusiasm and similar vision. "I didn't just want to sell a book. I wanted to start a career," Brown says.

Although his first love was writing, Jim Brown paid his dues in some less gratifying vocations. Before entering a career in broadcasting at the tender age of 16, he worked every job from milking cows and pumping gas to cutting lawns and tarring roofs. "These jobs had one thing in common," he says. "I was equally inept at them all."

A teacher noticed his natural abilities and steered him toward broadcasting. "I've always been curious, always asking questions and talking. My teacher decided that my big mouth and natural ability to make things up under pressure, along with my deep voice, made me a natural in broadcasting." So Brown's teacher set up an interview with the local radio station and his media career began. But all the while he was quietly writing and focusing on the craft.

Continuing to write until he felt ready for publication, Brown was then positioned to take advantage of his broadcasting background to promote his writing. And it carried weight with his agent. Ryan was impressed with his strong writing background, but also happy that Brown would be exceptionally media savvy due to his work in broadcasting. Another plus was the subject matter of *The Hill*. "It is easier to get publicity for stories relevant to our times," Ryan says.

Jim Brown always wanted to be a writer and maintains that if he never sold another word, he would continue to write: "Growing up I found it hard to believe that something so personal could also be profitable. Getting paid to write? That would be like getting paid to eat or sleep." As happens to many writers, his familiars instructed him to get a "real job." "Nine to five. Punch that time clock. I worked enough real jobs to know they weren't for me. I don't mind working, but I hate being bored," Brown says. The opening of his query letter attests to that.

The Hill was sold to Ballantine Books, and has gone on to auction for feature film. Success! The power of a query well written.

June 17, 2000

Mark Ryan
New Brand Agency Group
3389 Sheridan Street, #317
Hollywood, FL 33021

Dear Mr. Ryan:

What if, as an initiation, you were buried alive for one hour, with an air tank and a radio? Then you learned that the people who put you there had just been killed in a car wreck? What if you saw a woman being slashed to death by an impossible storm of glass? Or a man being choked by a severed hand? And what if you had less than 72 hours to explain it all—with science?

To give you a little background on myself: I'm an award-winning journalist, a television anchorman, and have written a weekly column for three years. My storytelling and writing has received national recognition. I've also been instrumental getting Northwest writers such as John Saul and Chuck Palunuck on-air interviews and publicity for their latest work.

Additionally, I am an avid writer and reader, and I've tracked the progress and development of many best-selling authors.

I appreciate you taking the time to read the sample chapters of *The Hill*. The full manuscript is ready for your request. I look forward to your response.

Thanks again for your time.

Sincerely,

Jim Brown

Outline and Synopsis Workshop

BY IAN BESSLER

You've written your Great American Novel or your Nonfiction Tome. After mailing out a punchy, carefully composed query letter, you receive word back that an agent is interested in finding out more about your project. Your task now is to put together a full proposal package. This usually includes a cover letter, three sample chapters (or the first 100 pages of a fiction manuscript) and an outline or synopsis. Outline or synopsis? What's the difference?

Agents often use the terms interchangeably, but there is indeed a difference. In general, "outline" refers to nonfiction, while "synopsis" refers to fiction.

Nonfiction is defined by logical and meaningful structure. Your goal when selling a nonfiction project is to detail the logical presentation of facts, ideas and arguments; a nonfiction outline is therefore primarily a structural skeleton showing how each part relates to the whole and in what order the reader encounters each element.

On the other hand, fiction is defined by conflict. Your goal when selling a novel manuscript is to show the characters, the flow of events and how these events are propelled forward by the conflict. A novel synopsis, therefore, is a condensed narrative version of your story from beginning to end that, ideally, reads like your novel, conveys a similar style of writing and sells your novel by grabbing the reader's attention much like the full-scale manuscript.

The nonfiction outline and the novel synopsis are useful means for both the writer and the agent to "step back" from the manuscript and look at the larger outlines of structure and plot.

THE NONFICTION OUTLINE

The nonfiction outline serves as an annotated table of contents and describes the structure of a book that you either have written or intend to write. It is also a tool used to sell that book to an editor or agent, as well as a valuable labor-saving device for you as a writer. It can indicate what you're getting into and guide how you develop the book idea. Creating an outline for your idea can help impose form and point out further avenues of research and development.

If you intend to pitch an idea for a nonfiction book that has not yet been completed, the outline must convince an agent or editor that the proposed idea has been developed in a way that is both wide-ranging and detailed enough to produce a book-length manuscript's worth of material. They need to know your idea will support a book and not just an article. Your outline must also demonstrate you have a clear grasp of the level of research needed to complete the project and deliver the manuscript on time. If you have not thoroughly investigated what is involved in researching the book, you may begin writing only to lose focus when you come across books, people to interview and other areas of research you had not realized were essential to a thorough treatment of your idea.

The following list covers several pointers for generating an outline:

- **DESCRIBE:** Describe what each section of the book does—how it arranges and presents the material you have gathered on the topic—and not the topic itself. For instance, if the topic of the chapter is the Marine Corps boot camp training process, your outline of the chapters should begin with something like this: "The chapter assesses the boot camp process where recruits are stripped of their individual identities, broken down and then

---

IAN BESSLER *is the editor of* Songwriter's Market, *a fiction writer and musician.*

SAMPLE NONFICTION OUTLINE

Psychedelic Rawk: 1965 to Present

Chapter 1
Designed to Blow Your Mind:
the Psychedelic Sound, the Studio and the Road   23 pages, 10 photos.

The first chapter launches a discussion of the term "psychedelic"; the corresponding aesthetic and musical features generally considered psychedelic; the associated sound studio technologies; and elements of the live psychedelic music experience. It is divided into three sections.

The first section scrutinizes the aesthetics and musical characteristics of psychedelic rock. It argues that psychedelic music is based on an aesthetic of sound fetishizing radically new, sensual or shocking sound textures, including the perception of familiar sounds as "strange" or "weird" when placed into new contexts. It argues for a wider interpretation of the term "psychedelic" to include any sort of music that allows listeners to defamiliarize themselves with common musical and everyday sounds. As an expansion of this argument, it discusses the inherently slippery and imprecise nature of music terminology and notes the numerous crossover points between psychedelic rock and other genres and schools of musical thought, including "art rock" artists such as Frank Zappa, Captain Beefheart, the Velvet Underground and Brian Eno. It expands on these points with a discussion of other common features of psychedelic music, including nonstandard song structures, avant-garde influences, collage, "found" sounds, studio chatter and soundscapes.

The second section chronicles the development of specific studio techniques/technologies and the part they have historically played in allowing the expression of the psychedelic aesthetic. It discusses the early multi-track and effects experiments of Les Paul; the innovations of tape loops, phasing, automatic double-tracking and sophisticated mixing techniques refined during mid- to late-Sixties Beatles, Pink Floyd and Jimi Hendrix recording sessions; and modern refinements in sampling, digital effects and computer manipulation of sound.

The third section sketches out a brief overview of the rise of new instrumental and sound-system technology that has made it possible to bring the psychedelic music aesthetic into a live performance context, including new synthesizer technology, the widespread use of small portable effects processors and innovations in PA technology made possible by touring psychedelic bands such as the Grateful Dead and Pink Floyd. This section ends the chapter by scrutinizing other elements of the live psychedelic experience, including the crowd experience, audience participation and musical improvisation, as well visual projections and light shows ranging from the early blobs and phantasms of Haight-Ashbury to modern computerized lighting systems.

Photos: Syd Barrett w/early Pink Floyd, Jefferson Airplane, Brian Eno, Frank Zappa, a photo of the inside of Abbey Road studios in the mid-1960s, Jimi Hendrix in the studio w/engineer Eddie Kramer, Roger Waters onstage w/Pink Floyd, the early-1970s Grateful Dead onstage w/the Wall of Sound, a crowd of Deadheads, a blob projection from the mid-1960s Fillmore West.

rebuilt as Marines. It is divided into three sections. The first part discusses . . ." Once again, the focus is on what the chapter does (it "assesses"), how it is constructed ("divided into three sections") and what information goes in what sections ("The first part discusses . . ."), rather than on a detailed explication of the topic itself.

- **STAY PRESENT:** Write the outline in the present tense for clarity.
- **STAY ACTIVE:** Avoid using the passive voice whenever possible. Avoid a sentence form like this: "The issue of combat unit cohesion is explored." Instead, use a form more like this: "The chapter explores combat unit cohesion." Consistent use of the active voice maintains clarity and punch in the outline.
- **HOOK:** Give each chapter a hook title with impact and clarity. For example, if the book on Marine training is titled *Parris Island Blues*, a chapter encapsulating Marine Corp history could be titled "The Leatherneck Chronicles."
- **BE VIVID:** Use vivid and active verbs to tell what the chapter does. The chapter doesn't just "talk about" the topic, it *unearths* information, *confronts* the possibilities, *expands* a viewpoint or *blasts* a commonly held misconception. Action verbs can liven up your outline and serve as an additional tool for maintaining the active interest of the agent or editor, but be sure not to repeat the same verb too many times.
- **PHOTOS AND ILLUSTRATIONS:** In the upper right-hand corner of the first page of each chapter outline, give a page count for the chapter and a tally of the number of photos and illustrations you intend to use. At the end of each chapter outline, include a short paragraph detailing any photographs or illustrations incorporated into the chapter.

The example outline on page 49 models the principles listed above.

THE NOVEL SYNOPSIS

A well-written synopsis is an important tool when marketing your novel, and many agents and editors will use it to judge your ability to tell a story. The synopsis is a condensed narrative version of the novel. It should hook the editor or agent by showcasing the central conflict of the book and the interlocking chain of events set off by that conflict. It should incorporate every chapter of your book, and distill every main event, character and plot twist. A synopsis should highlight the element of human drama and emotion that explains *why* the characters in a novel took their particular path. When crafting your synopsis, these pointers form a set of guidelines to lead you through the process of condensing your manuscript:

- **FORMAT:** Type a heading in the upper left-hand corner of the first page, featuring the title of your novel, the genre, an estimated word count for the full manuscript and your name. At the end of the synopsis, type out "THE END" to signify the conclusion of the story.
- **STAY PRESENT:** Write the synopsis in the present tense and third-person point of view. Even if your novel is written in first person, use third person for the synopsis. This allows for consistency and ease in summarizing. Such a summary will also help when an agent pitches the work to an editor.
- **DON'T HOLD BACK:** Tell the entire story, including the ending. Do not tease—tell who lives, who dies, who did it and so on. At this stage of the query process, the agent or editor has already been hooked by your brilliant query letter with the clever teaser, and now they want an overview of the entire project, so don't leave anything out.
- **HOOK:** Start with a hook detailing your primary character and the main conflict of the novel. Give any pertinent information about the lead character, such as age, career, marital status, etc., and describe how that character manifests or is drawn into the primary conflict.
- **SPOTLIGHT:** The first time you introduce a character, spotlight that character by capitalizing his name. If possible, weave the character's initial description into the flow of the text, but don't stray from the narrative with a lengthy or overly-detailed character sketch.
- **CONDENSE:** Don't defeat the purpose of the synopsis by letting it run too long. A

SAMPLE NOVEL SYNOPSIS

Obelisk
  Science Fiction
  75,000 words
  by Maxwell Parker
  ARCAS KANE, newly minted agent for the Imperial Galactic Security Apparatus, is eager for promotion within the ranks. Security Apparatus Director DELSIN HISTER, leader of an Imperial faction hostile to the current ruler, sees Kane's ambitions and picks the young man for a mission on the fringe of the galaxy, where archaeologists make a startling discovery.
  Buried in the sands of a sparsely populated desert world they find artifacts from times beyond the reckoning of even the oldest histories of the Imperium. The artifacts include obsidian obelisks, perfectly preserved and carved with glyphs and signs. Using bits of lore preserved by the desert planet's nonhuman natives, the scientists decipher part of the message and send news of their discovery.
  Kane arrives with the crew of a supply ship and finds the archaeologists murdered, the artifacts destroyed. He searches through bits of surviving scientific data. The obelisks describe a planet, the mythical home system of the human race. The obelisks tell of the abandonment of the home world and the wandering of the human race. They also refer to an ancient doomsday weapon, the source of the destruction.
  Kane questions the wary natives. He learns that two of the archaeologists escaped in a ship to retrace the ancient wanderers' steps back to the home planet. He reports in to Hister, who orders Kane to follow.
  He departs with the reluctant crew of the supply ship. They spend weeks hopping from world to world, following the trail. Beautiful AVA, the supply ship's executive officer, seduces Kane, and jealous hostility flares between Kane and the ship's captain. Crew members die in mysterious accidents. Suspicion falls on Kane. He suspects a mole among the crew and wonders if he is himself a pawn.
  He catches the archaeologists. They find the hulking ruins of a colony generation ship floating lifelessly in orbit around an obscure star system. A search of the colony ship's archives reveals detailed descriptions of the home planet's location and the doomsday device. Hister is shadowing the pursuit. He overtakes them in an Imperial warship. Hister congratulates them on their discovery and urges them all on to the home planet.
  Nothing is left of the planet but a charred, sterilized cinder. They detect a beacon in the ruins of a city on the surface. In a bunker beneath the city, they find an artificial intelligence unit waiting for the return of its masters. In between senile harangues by the AI, they coax out the complete history of the war and the formula for the doomsday device.
  After returning to orbit, Hister announces that Kane and the others have reached the end of their usefulness and must be liquidated. Hister intends to take the doomsday device information for his own use. Hister's minions lead Kane, Ava and the others away to be ejected from the airlocks. The supply ship's engines explode where it sits docked with the warship. Kane, Ava and one of the archaeologists narrowly escape in a life pod as the ship comes apart at the seams. Hister is sucked into the vacuum of space as the bridge ruptures. Ava reveals her identity as the mole, a spy for the Imperial loyalists. They seal themselves into hibernation pods to wait for rescue by loyalist forces.
  THE END

workable rule of thumb for calculating the length of the synopsis is to condense every 25 pages of your novel synopsis down to 1 page. If you follow this formula for a 200-page novel manuscript, you should wind up with 8 pages of synopsis. This formula is not set in stone, however, since some agents like to see even more compression and will frequently ask for a two-page synopsis to represent an entire novel. If in doubt, ask the agent what length he prefers, and tailor your synopsis to his requirement, no more, no less.

- **CUT OUT THE FAT:** Be concise. Include only details of the action essential to the story, and excise excessive adjectives and adverbs. Dialogue is rarely used, but at the same time don't be afraid to feature pivotal quotes, descriptive gems or a crucial scene when you know it will enhance the impact of your synopsis at critical points.
- **RETELL:** Work from your manuscript chapter by chapter, and briefly retell the events of each chapter. You should tell one complete account of your book, although you may use paragraphs to represent chapters or sections. Whenever possible, use a style reflecting the tone of the actual novel—if the novel is dark and moody in tone, then a dark and moody tone is called for in the synopsis.
- **BE SEAMLESS:** Do not intrude in the narrative flow with authorial commentary, and do not let the underlying story framework show in your synopsis. Don't use headings such as "Setting" or phrases like "At the climax of the conflict . . ." or "The next chapter begins with . . ." In short, do not let it read like a nonfiction outline. Your goal is to entrance the agent or editor with the story itself and not to break the spell by allowing the supporting scaffolding to show. These elements should already be self-evident and woven into the narrative. You should also avoid reviewing your own story; the agent or the editor will make his own judgment. Your work should hopefully speak for itself.

The example synopsis on page 51 condenses an entire novel in one page. This is an extreme example of compression as noted above but a demonstration of the principles involved.

A FEW LAST BITS

A few final tips to consider:

9   Include two SASEs with your submission, a #10 business-size SASE for reply and a larger SASE big enough to hold your manuscript, along with enough postage for its return.

9   Be sure your proposal package is either laser-printed or neatly typed (no dot matrix) on clean paper sufficiently strong to stand up to handling (do not use erasable bond or onionskin). Also, put a blank piece of paper at the end of the manuscript to protect the last page.

9   Be sure to use proper manuscript format (one-inch margins on all four sides of the page, double-spaced, one-sided and left-justified only).

9   Resist the urge to cover your manuscript with copyright symbols. Under current copyright law, your work is protected as soon as you put it into tangible form. To many agents and editors, a manuscript sporting copyright symbols is the mark of an amateur.

Not all agents or editors have boiled down an explicit set of nuts-and-bolts guidelines, but the methods outlined in this article will provide you with a repeatable set of steps for framing your ideas with clarity and precision. For further treatments of nonfiction outline issues, refer to *How to Write a Book Proposal*, by Michael Larsen (Writer's Digest Books). For further advice on constructing a synopsis, refer to *Your Novel Proposal: From Creation to Contract*, by Blythe Camenson and Marshall J. Cook (Writer's Digest Books) or *The Marshall Plan for Novel Writing*, by Evan Marshall (Writer's Digest Books).

How to Write a Nonfiction Proposal

BY JEFF KLEINMAN

When selling nonfiction, you don't have to write the entire book: in fact, it's often preferable not to. That way the editor and publisher can put their own "spin" on it, providing their own input to make it as marketable as possible to the audience that they (and you) intend to target.

Instead of an entire book, you write a "proposal"—it's just like a business plan, and tells the publisher how you propose to write the book. It's not a long document—anywhere from 10 to 80 pages—but it's a crucial one.

That said, you should keep the following issues in mind when you're actually sitting down to write:

Jeff Kleinman

Sales tool

A proposal is a sales tool, and you need to think of it as such. The agent uses it to sell the book to the editor; the editor uses it to sell the book to the publisher and other editors, to the marketing people, possibly to booksellers and other publishers (for foreign sales), and so forth. The first thing to keep in mind is that you can't be subtle, and can't be modest: if you are, no doubt at least half the people reading your proposal just won't get it.

Complete & concrete

Although the proposal is not supposed to be complete, you should still try to connect as many dots as you possibly can, to make the proposal as complete—and concrete—as possible. Even if your vision of the book changes over time, you still want the editor to feel comfortable and confident that you know what you're doing: that you can write the book, and you know how you're going to do it. The more ways you're able to satisfy the concerns, the better. For example, in your Chapter Outline (see below), you could estimate the number of pages per chapter—even if you really don't have a clue how long the chapter will be, since you haven't written it yet.

OK, now you hopefully have some general idea on what the proposal will do; here are the issues that every proposal should cover. You can use the sections as I've outlined them here, or modify them as you see fit: the importance is not to cram everything under a specific heading, but instead to give the editor (and/or agent) the most solid, concrete understanding of your book as you possibly can.

Overview: *1-3 Pages. This is exactly like the "Executive Summary" of a business plan, if you've ever written one. Here, as clearly and briefly as possible, you set out the highlights of the book: what it's about, why it's an important subject, who will be reading it, who the author is, why we should care what the author says, what will set it apart on the bookshelf. Editors,*

JEFF KLEINMAN *is an agent with Graybill & English, LLC, where he specializes in representing narrative nonfiction and prescriptive (how to) books on a wide variety of topics, including historical, health, parenting, self-help, memoir, art, and equestrian books. He holds a B.A. with High Distinction from the University of Virginia (English), an M.A. from the University of Chicago (Italian Language & Literature), and a J.D. from the Case Western Reserve University School of Law.*

when they're interested in a book, fill out a so-called "Tip Sheet" that they pass around in Editorial Meetings. The Tip Sheet will include the following information:
- Title and subtitle;
- "Sales handle" or "log line"—a single-sentence description describing the proposal in a clever nutshell;
- Production specs, including estimated word count, approximate delivery date, and the need/availability for photographs, graphics, or illustrations;
- A paragraph-length positioning "memo", describing where the book will fit in the publishing world;
- The most relevant comparative titles;
- Other relevant marketing information;
- A brief description of the author and the author's credentials, including the author's previous publishing history.

I like the editor to be able to find all the information that will be in the Tip Sheet right in the Overview. You'll be covering all of these issues in far more detail in the rest of the proposal.

Author: *1-5 Pages.* Who are you, and why are you the best person in the whole world to write this book? That's the biggest question that a publisher will ask—these credentials can quite easily make or break a book sale. This is no time to be modest: include exactly why you are the best person for the job—so if you've written other books on the subject; have advanced degrees; get interviewed in the media; lecture regionally, nationally, and/or internationally; have great personal contacts for marketing the book; whatever—include them here. Your credentials may be nothing more than a passionate interest in the subject, which is also fine—but tell us.

Annotated Chapter Outline: *Varies on the proposal, but plan on spending 1 page per chapter, assuming that an "average" chapter is 20 pages long.* As clearly and concisely as you can, set out what each chapter will do, and how the book will be organized. Try to write it as interestingly as possible (so try to avoid "this chapter will discuss . . .," which just adds extra verbiage), but at the same time, make it very clear to the editor that you're providing only a summary—that there's a lot more material you haven't been able to cover.

Sample Chapter: *15-30 pages; may include several sample chapters, but it may not be necessary.* Other than the Author's Credentials, this section is the most important part of the proposal. Here you show that you can write well, communicate effectively, organize your material efficiently, and keep the reader's interest. Obviously what chapter you choose to use will depend on what material you already have available, but you want this chapter to be a representative (i.e., "sample") chapter of the book—not an introduction, or summary. I always try to tell authors to use the easiest, sexiest material for the sample chapters: the stuff that the author has the most material on already, the stuff that people have already demonstrated an interest in, and so forth.

For narrative nonfiction (by way of example), you should try to show the editor how you address the following types of issues:
- How you introduce and develop your characters, and how they will interact;
- How you will deal with facts and technical jargon;
- How you set a scene;
- The kind of momentum/pacing the book will have;
- How you will handle (if at all) dialogue and other "novelistic" elements.

You've now dealt with the "personal," most important aspects of the proposal; now you need to concentrate on the supplemental information to really sell it. In order to do this effectively, the basic premise to keep in mind is that you need to fit your book in with the rest of the publishing world. My break-down into three sections here is fairly arbitrary, but all the issues need to be addressed somehow.

Positioning: *1-2 pages, maybe less.* The positioning section fits your book into the greater world of publishing. Go out and find several wildly successful books on whatever subject—it doesn't have to be at all similar to yours—with authors who have credentials that are similar to yours, with marketing contacts that are similar to yours, and explain how your book "will be the next" wildly successful book because it has a lot of "package" similarities. The big thing here is to be reasonable and realistic: find books by authors whose credentials really are similar to yours, with a writing style or world view or angle that is somehow similar to yours. "This is the Longitude for dog lovers," and so forth.

Market: *2-8 pages; may include letters of support from celebrities, sponsoring organizations, etc.* Who are your readers, and how will you reach them? Do you give lectures and seminars? Have a great website? Any great publicity tools already in your pocket? (e.g., Dateline wants to do a special on you.) This tends to be a hard section to write, but it really helps if you've gone out and gotten information to give the publisher on how many, and what kind, of people will be interested in purchasing your book—it shows you're a "go-getter" and will be effective at selling your book even without the publisher's support. FYI—never rely on a publisher's plans for publicity—authors always complain that publishers don't do enough to get the book into the public eye, so you need to be your own best advocate. Show it here.

Competing Works: *1-4 pages.* Go to your local bookstore and determine where (literally—the physical location) your book will fit on the shelf. Then find the titles that are your book's closest competitors. It's important to show that the book has a niche—that a bookseller will know where to put it, so it doesn't get lost and remain unsold. On the other hand, your book can't get lost among dozens of other similar titles—so explain what sets your book apart from the others. Perhaps you can fill in the following sentence: "My book is the first book that _____." How you set your book apart may depend on your subject matter, but you should never disparage another book. (After all, it may have the same publisher/editor who will be looking at your proposal.) You should just explain why yours is different (meaning "better"). It also helps if you can reasonably compare your book to another that has done exceptionally well—but be sure that the writing style, content, and subject matter are similar enough that you won't sound silly or overly grandiose.

So that's it. I know it seems like a lot, but when everything's said and done, you're writing one chapter, putting together an outline, and then putting on a lot of ribbons and bows to make this into an effective sales tool. Good luck!

Scam Alert!

BY RACHEL VATER

If you were going into business with another person, you'd make sure you knew him, felt comfortable with him, had the same vision as he did—and that he'd never had trouble with the law or a history of bankruptcy, wouldn't you? As obvious as this sounds, many writers take for granted that any agent who expresses interest in their work is trustworthy. They'll sign a contract before asking any questions, cross their fingers for luck, and simply hope everything will turn out okay.

But don't fall into this trap. Doing a little research ahead of time can save you a lot of frustrations later. So how do you check up on an agent? How do you spot a scam before you're already taken in by it?

BEFORE YOU SUBMIT

First, research the agency itself. What kind of reputation does it have? If it's a well-established literary agency, and all the agents are AAR members, you should be safe from scams.

All AAR members are required to abide by a certain code of ethics, and they are not permitted to charge any fees to writers. Even if an agent is not a member of AAR, he should not be charging fees to his clients. His salary should be earned exclusively with commissions. If you feel he may be violating the code of ethics, you can contact the AAR at www.aar-online.org or by writing to: The Association of Authors' Representatives, Inc. P.O. Box 237201, Ansonia Station, New York, NY 10003.

A writer should never pay any fees to an agent, including reading fees, retainers, marketing fees, or submission fees. And rather than paying an agent for a critique service, join a writers group. Invest your time instead of your money. Give feedback to others in exchange for their feedback to you. Then, when you feel your book is in the best possible shape it can be in, ask an English teacher or editor friend to read it over for you.

BEFORE YOU SIGN

If you have any concerns about the agency's practices, ask the agent about them before you sign. Once an agent is interested in representing you, he should be willing to answer any questions or concerns that you have. If he is rude or unresponsive, or tries to tell you that the information is confidential or classified, the agent is uncommunicative at best and at worst, is already trying to hide something from you.

An agent should be willing to discuss his recent sales with you: how many, what type of books, and to what publishers. If it's a new agent without a track record, be aware that you're taking more of a risk signing with him than with a more established agent. However, even a new agent should not be new to publishing. Many agents were editors before they were agents, or they worked at an agency as an assistant. This experience in publishing is crucial for making contacts in the publishing industry and learning about rights and contracts. So ask him how long he's been an agent and what he did before becoming an agent. Ask him to name a few editors off the top of his head who he thinks may be interested in your work and why they sprang to mind. Has he sold to them before? Do they publish books in your genre?

If an agent has no contacts in the business, he has no more clout than you do yourself. Without publishing prowess, he's just an expensive mailing service. Anyone can make photocopies, slide them into an envelope and address them to "Editor," but without a contact name and a familiar return address on the envelope—or a phone call from a trusted colleague letting an editor know it's on the way and why it's a perfect fit for her publisher—it will land in the slush pile with all the other submissions that don't have representation. And you can do your own mailings with higher priority than such an agent could.

Occasionally, an agent will charge for the cost of photocopies, postage, and long-distance phone calls made on your behalf, and this is acceptable, so long as he keeps an itemized account of the expenses and you've agreed on a ceiling cost. Be sure to talk over any expenses you don't understand until you have a clear grasp of what you're paying for.

Other times, an agent will recognize the value of the content of your work, but will recommend hiring an editor to revise it before he is comfortable submitting it to publishers. In this case, you may find an editor (someone with references you'll check) who understands your subject matter or genre and has some experience getting manuscripts into shape. Occasionally, if your story is exceptional or your ideas and credentials are marketable, but your writing needs help, you will work with a ghostwriter or co-author who will share a percentage of your commission or work with you at an agreed upon cost per hour.

An agent may refer you to editors he knows, but you may instead choose to find an editor in your area you've selected for yourself. Many editors do freelance work and would be happy to help you with your writing project. Of course, before entering into an agreement, make sure you know what you'll be getting for your money. Ask the editor for writing samples, references, or critiques he's done in the past. Make sure you feel comfortable working with him before you give him your business.

An honest agent will not make any money for referring you to an editor.

Some agents claim that charging a reading fee cuts down on the number of submissions they receive, and while that is a very real possibility, I recommend writers work with non fee-charging agents if at all possible. Non fee-charging agents have a stronger incentive to sell your work. After all, until they make a sale, they don't make a dime.

Agencies who charge fees don't have the same urgency to sell your work. If you do the math, you can see how much money they're bringing in without selling anything: If an agency has 300 clients, each sending in quarterly marketing fees of $100, the agent is making $400 a year from each client. That's $120,000 a year—and that doesn't include the reading fees or any other fees they collect.

AFTER YOU'VE SIGNED

Periodically, you should ask your agent for a full report of where your manuscript has been sent including the publishing house and the editor he sent it to. Then, contact a few of the editors/ publishers on the list and see if they know your agent and have a strong working relationship with him.

If the agent has ever successfully sold anything to her before (or at least sent her some promising work before), an editor should remember his name. It's a small world in publishing, and news of an agent's reputation spreads very fast.

But this industry is all about contacts, and if you can't find a worthy agent to do this for you, it's entirely possible to do it yourself. Think about it: the agent was once an unknown too. He or she made first contact by knocking on doors or schmoozing it up at conferences. You can do this too. The doors aren't locked to outsiders—they're just harder to find.

It might seem like making toast before baking the bread, but if you can find an interested editor, publisher or producer at a conference or by referral, she can probably recommend an agent to you, or you can choose one yourself based on reputation. If you mention a credible person interested in your work, any agent would be delighted to take over the contract negotiations for you. And letting a legitimate agent haggle over your contract for you instead of going at it yourself will help you keep your rights and negotiate the best advance.

If you've been scammed . . .

. . . or if you're trying to prevent a scam, the following resources should be of help:

Contact The Federal Trade Commission, Bureau of Consumer Protection (CRC-240, Washington DC 20580, 1-877-FTC-HELP(382-4357)). While they won't resolve individual consumer problems, the FTC depends on your complaints to help them investigate fraud, and your speaking up may even lead to law enforcement action. Contact them by mail or phone, or visit their website at www.ftc.gov.

Volunteer Lawyers for the Arts (1 E. 53rd St., New York NY 10022) is a group of volunteers from the legal profession who assist with questions of law pertaining to the arts, all fields. You can phone their hotline at (212)319-ARTS (2787), ext. 9 and have your questions answered for the price of the phone call. For further information you can also visit their website at www.vlany.org.

Better Business Bureau (check local listings or visit www.bbb.org)—the folks to contact if you have a complaint or if you want to investigate a publisher, literary agent or other business related to writing and writers.

It's also recommended that you contact your state's attorney general with information about scamming activity. Don't know your attorney general's name? Go to www.attorneygeneral.gov/ags. Here you'll find a wealth of contact information, including a complete list of links to the attorney general's website for each state.

Not everyone has this gift for making contacts, so many writers must rely on agents for the agents' pre-existing contacts. The trouble is, unless you know an agent's track record, you're taking his word for it that he indeed has these contacts. If he doesn't, even if he lives right there in California, he's no more able to sell your work for you than you are, even if you're living in Massachusetts. So check out his references and make sure he's made recent sales with legitimate publishers or production companies.

As a side note, agents should return their clients' phone calls or e-mails quickly and keep them informed about prospects. An agent should also consult his clients about any offers before accepting or rejecting them.

IF YOU'VE BEEN SCAMMED

If you have trouble with your agent, and you've already tried to resolve it yourself to no avail, it may be time to call for help. Please alert the writing community to protect others. If you find agents online, in directories, or in this book who aren't living up to their promises or are charging you money when they're listed as non fee-charging agents, please let the webmaster or editor of the publication know. Sometimes they can intervene for an author, and if no solution can be found, they can at the very least remove a listing from their directory so that no other authors will be scammed in the future. All efforts are made to keep scam artists out, but in a world where agencies are bought and sold, a reputation can change overnight.

If you have complaints about any business you can call the Better Business Bureau to report them. The BBB will at least file it, and that way, if anyone contacts the BBB before dealing with the business, the BBB will inform them that there are unresolved complaints against the business. Their website is www.bbb.org, or you may send a written complaint to: The Council of Better Business Bureaus, 4200 Wilson Blvd., Suite 800, Arlington, VA 22203-1838. Or call (703)276-0100 or fax them at (703)525-8277.

Finally, legal action may seem like a drastic step, but people do it sometimes. You can file a suit with the Attorney General and try to find some other people who want to sue for fraud with you. The Science Fiction Writers of America Website, www.sfwa.org, offers sound advice on recourse you can take in these situations. (See this page for further details: www.sfwa.org/beware/overview.html.)

If you live in the same state as your agent, it may be possible to settle the score in small claims court, a viable option for collecting smaller damages and a way to avoid lawyer fees. The jurisdiction of the small claims court includes cases in which the claim is $5,000 or less (this varies from state to state, but should still cover the amount you're suing for.) Keep in mind suing takes a lot of effort and time. You'll have to research all the necessary legal steps. If you have lawyers in your family, that could be a huge benefit if they'll agree to help you organize your case, but legal assistance is not necessary.

And authors occasionally do fight back and win. For instance, in a case against an agent named Dorothy Deering, many scammed authors came together to testify against her literary agency. After bilking writers out of millions of dollars, she was found guilty of fraud, and she's now in prison.

Some authors have been taken for more money than you can imagine. Promises of publication made them write checks for thousands of dollars. This can be one of the most frustrating road blocks on the path to publication, leaving authors feeling betrayed and angry.

MOVING ON AND STARTING AGAIN

Above all, if you've been scammed, don't waste time blaming yourself. It's not your fault if someone lies to you. In cases like this, it's good to believe in karma. People who do good, who

---

Warning Signs! Beware of:

- Excessive typos or poor grammar in an agent's correspondence.
- A form letter accepting you as a client, praising generic things about your book that could apply to any book. An agent should call or send a personalized letter. A good agent doesn't take on a new client very often, so when she does, it's a special occasion that warrants a personal note or phone call.
- Unprofessional contracts that ask you for money up front, contain clauses you haven't discussed, or are covered with amateur clip-art or silly borders.
- Rudeness when you inquire about any points you're unsure of. Don't employ any business partner who doesn't treat you with respect, as an equal.
- Pressure, by way of threats, bullying, or bribes. A good agent is not desperate to represent more clients. He invites worthy authors, but leaves the final decision up to them.
- Promises of publication. No agent can guarantee you a sale. Not even the top agents sell everything they choose to represent. They can only send your work to the most appropriate places, have it read with priority, and negotiate you a better contract if a sale does happen.
- A print-on-demand book contract or any contract offering you no advance. You can sell your own book to an e-publisher any time you wish without an agent's help. An agent should pursue traditional publishing routes with respectable advances. (There are a few exceptions: Some larger publishing houses are developing new lines of e-books, but they also offer fair advances.)

These websites may be of further interest to you:

"Sharks in the Water: Old Publishing Scams for the New Millenium" at http://www.sff.net/people/alicia/artscam.htm

"Before You Write That Check" at http://www.writer.org/scamkit.htm

"Hunting for a Literary Agent: Which to Keep and Which to Shoot" at http://www.sfwa.org/writing/agents.htm

are kind, who help you—they'll be rewarded. People who scam, cheat, lie and steal—they'll get what's coming to them. It might take a while for their actions to catch up to them, and you might wonder how they can even look at themselves in the mirror without feeling overwhelming guilt, but they'll get theirs. Respect in the literary world is built on reputation, and word about bad agents gets around. Editors ignore their submissions. Writers begin to avoid them. Without clients or buyers, a swindling agent will find his business collapsing.

Meanwhile, you'll keep writing and believing in yourself. You'll be able to face yourself in the mirror. One day, you'll see your work in print and you'll tell everyone what a rough road it was to get there, but how you wouldn't trade it for anything in the world.

Because writing is a part of us. It's what we do, what we love. And sometimes, it's how we make sense of the world and come to understand events in our lives and heal from them. And without our consent, no one can break our spirit or take that away from us.

What to Ask—and Not Ask—an Agent

If an agent is interested in representing your work, congratulations! Nevertheless, you may have some concerns about whether this agent is the best person for you. The following is a list of appropriate questions to ask an agent who offers you a contract. Because an agent is busy, you'll want to pick only five or six of the questions most important to you to ask.

These are questions you ask only *after* the agent agrees to take you on as a client. In other words, don't take up the agent's time with these questions if you are only considering sending the agent a query letter. Also listed below are questions that you'll want to avoid asking—doing so may cause an agent to doubt your professionalism.

Do ask:

1) What about my work interests you?
2) What can I do to be a good client?
3) Who are some other authors you represent and what are examples of recent sales you've made for those authors?
4) How much career guidance do you give clients?
5) Are you interested in representing me for this one title or throughout my writing career?
6) What is your commission? Does your commission change if you use a foreign or film co-agent?
7) Do you charge clients for office expenses? If so, what is your policy? Do you have a ceiling amount for such expenses?
8) Do you charge any other fees (i.e., reading fee, critiquing fee)?
9) What are your agency's strengths?
10) How often should I expect to be in contact with you?
11) Will you show me rejections from publishers if I request them?
12) Will you consult with me before accepting any offer?
13) Do you work with independent publicists?
14) What are your policies if, for whatever reason, we decided to part company?
15) Do you offer a written contract? If not, what legal provisions can be made to avoid any misunderstandings between us?

For a list of further questions recommended by the Association of Author's Representatives, go to www.aar-online.org.

Don't ask:

1) What are some recent advances you've negotiated for your clients?
2) Can I have the phone numbers for some of your clients to use as references?
3) Can you call me at this specific time?
4) How much money are you going to get for my book?
5) Who do I need to talk to in order to get my book made into a movie?

Entertainment Attorneys: Contract Specialists

BY JOSHUA EASTON

Let's say you decided not to use an agent. Maybe you had enough confidence in your own salesmanship to try selling the book yourself. Maybe you met an editor at a conference who made you an offer of publication you were afraid to refuse. So you agreed. But now that you're holding that contract in your hand, you feel your confidence beginning to ebb. What are all these clauses? Will you look like an amateur if you ask the editor what some of this legal mumbo-jumbo means in plain English? Will the publisher withdraw his offer if he feels you're making unreasonable requests to retain some of your rights? What if you're concerned that you've already signed away some of your rights and you'd like to renegotiate? What started out as a friendly agreement begins to get messy, and you're starting to wonder whom you can turn to for advice.

Robert Mendelsohn

"Have you been injured in an accident? We can help!" Conspicuously placed on the backs of phone books and on the sides of buses, advertisements for personal injury attorneys pledge to get compensation for the harm you may have suffered. Though writers *may* confer with one of these injury lawyers in the unfortunate event of an accident, writers *should* consult with an entertainment attorney when they need help negotiating or revising their contracts with a publisher or protecting their intellectual property. Attorneys who represent writers prefer to avoid "accidents," and much of their practice is preventing disputes from arising through negotiation of publishing agreements.

Robert Mendelsohn, an attorney in Cincinnati, represents various individuals and organizations in the entertainment industry, specifically writers, musicians, and record labels. Practicing for almost nineteen years, he has become an active participant in the Cincinnati writers' community. He is a member of the Cincinnati Writer's Project and the Entertainment Law Committee of the Cincinnati Bar Association. He also speaks on book publishing topics to various local writers' groups and clubs.

Mendelsohn says part of his practice is to represent writers on a number of fronts. "Recently, I have been retained to review a literary agent agreement on behalf of a novice author. I also draft query letters for some of my clients, although I'm not a literary agent. Another area I handle is setting up the writer's or publisher's business entity (corporation, Limited Liability Company) and representing them in their various business/legal endeavors. Attorneys like myself also represent writers and publishers in litigation-related matters." Here Mendelsohn shares some of his expertise on a number of legal issues writers may face when seeking to publish their work.

JOSHUA EASTON, *a Kentucky native, received his J.D. from Tulane Law School in New Orleans last spring and currently lives in Washington D.C. where he practices writing and dabbles in law.*

How did you become interested in representing writers?

Several years ago I was contacted by a friend of mine who has written several articles and books on various insurance-related subjects. Actually, he is quite a prolific and experienced author on the topic. In this particular instance, my friend had been contacted to write an insurance article for a local Cincinnati publication. He had submitted the article and it had been published in a later edition. My friend called me to complain that he never received payment per the requirement of the contract and asked if I would handle the matter. After reviewing the contract, I noted how one-sided it was and how it became a little more than a simple breach of contract/collection case. From that point on, I began my involvement in representing writers and became active in the writing community as part of my overall entertainment law practice. By the way, after reviewing the agreement and drafting a demand letter, my friend soon received his money!

What are some of the books or writers you have represented? What specifically has that work entailed?

Among the writers I represent are authors of both fiction and nonfiction work. These individuals have written books on such diverse subjects as romance, military history and weaponry, politics, and insurance industry topics. One writer I represented asked me to review his book contract. This particular agreement with the publisher was even more one-sided than usual, and I was able to point out and rework some of the more unconscionable clauses, which my client had brought to the attention of the publisher. The publisher agreed to many of the suggestions, and, as a result, the playing field was more level regarding the author's rights.

What are the legal issues a writer should keep in mind early on the road to getting published?

One of the obvious early issues regarding sending out a manuscript is to copyright the document. This will ensure the writer some protection from possible infringement on his or her product by another party. After the author receives a book -publishing contract, early on he or she should review the section regarding the manuscript and note its language. The language should include the right for the writer to revise the manuscript within a set time frame before the publisher rejects it and any rejection must be for a good faith reason. Also, the author's work should be sufficiently described in the manuscript in order to prevent any disagreement over the book's contents as sent in manuscript form.

Are there particular rights a writer should be careful to protect in a contract?

There are some areas in any publishing agreement that an author should review closely and negotiate if necessary. Work for hire provisions and non-compete clauses should be avoided. The right to revise or rewrite the manuscript should be included. An accounting of copies sold should be reported, and publicity should be addressed.

Could you elaborate?

Work for hire provisions create an employer/employee relationship with the publisher under which any work that you perform under the employ of the publisher could belong to them. Avoid work for hire agreements. The right to revise/rewrite the manuscript protects your ability to make your changes to the work but does not give the publisher a second chance to reject your book. A non-compete clause could allow a publisher to block you from working for another publisher or freelancing. Such provisions can also be applied to speaking at conferences. Keep these out of your contract or limit their length to a year or less if possible. An "accounting" clause gives the writer access to know how many books are being sold, given away, or offered as promotional copies. Finally, you probably want some language about publicity in a contract if possible, creating a duty in the publisher to publicize your work.

Do you have any general suggestions for writers working on collaborative efforts?

The writers involved should decide at the outset how they will allocate the rights, royalties and advances among themselves and should make a contractual agreement. A second agreement should be made between the collaborators and the publisher. One particular problem that may arise is when one of the collaborators has original artwork as part of the manuscript. Any drawings or designs have additional copyright protection and royalties that should be recognized in the collaborative agreement.

Are there any legal issues a writer should keep in mind if some of their work is reprinted on the Internet?

This is an area I am just getting involved in. One issue that comes to mind concerns permission for a writer's work to be reprinted. The writer should provide written (or receive as the case may be) permission in this instance. This will prevent infringement issues and ensure legal compliance with copyright rules. Also, the writer should look at his agreement with the publisher to determine the extent of these rights—any additional royalties received, publicity matters, etc. Also, concerning any reprint on the Internet, common law contract rules apply regarding consideration, term, breach, default, etc.

What rights are available to writers using vanity presses to get "published?"

While I have not been involved with the so-called vanity press, I am familiar with their process. I understand that various consumer and government organizations (e.g. FTC) have investigated and in some cases sanctioned some of them. The contracts put out by these presses are very one-sided and need to be reviewed carefully. Also, they usually require an upfront investment from the writer. Finally, check out these companies before you leap—see which one offers the best deal. Negotiate as many favorable terms as you can to protect your rights.

How can a writer find an attorney with the right experience? Is there an effective way to locate and make contact with such an attorney?

Believe it or not, local Yellow Pages may list attorneys who represent writers, usually under the "Lawyers" section designated "Entertainment Law." I am listed in that manner. Another way is to speak with other writers or publishers and obtain a reference. Some lawyers, such as myself, belong to writers' groups and speak to like organizations. The local bar association referral service will also maintain a list of attorneys who represent writers.

Generally, do you find writers or do they find you?

It actually works both ways. Sometimes when I am discussing an unrelated matter with a client (real estate, incorporation, etc.) I discover that the individual has written a book, short story or the like. I then tell them that I represent writers and they may contact me later to draft or review a book contract. I also meet writers at meetings or when I give presentations to writers' groups. I once met several authors at a presentation I made on how to review a book contract.

What should a writer know about the costs for an attorney to write or review a contract or for performing other legal services related to publishing a book or protecting the author's interests after it is published?

The writer should inquire as to the lawyer's fee schedule. Most lawyers bill on an hourly basis for their legal services and the rate will vary depending upon the lawyer. I bill at $125 per hour and also perform some work on a fixed fee basis. I understand that some attorneys charge a percentage fee much like a literary agent.

When is it to a writer's advantage to use an attorney as an alternative to an agent? Would an author ever want to use both?

Many times I am asked if I do act as a literary agent. My answer is usually no. I do not shop a book or manuscript unless I know someone in the publishing business who I can contact on behalf of the writer, as my work concerns protecting an author's rights. An author should really utilize the services of both an attorney and a literary agent. The literary agent shops the manuscript, helps with the query letter, usually has the contacts in the publishing industry and acts as a "salesperson" for the author. The attorney reviews the agreements (even the literary agent agreement!), gets involved in the contract negotiation and handles the intellectual property aspects if necessary.

How might their services differ in what they can offer a writer and where might an attorney or agent's job overlap?

There are advantages to using an attorney versus an agent if the attorney has the connections in the publishing world and can effectively market your manuscript. The attorney already possesses the technical skills to review and negotiate the publishing agreement. The one area where the roles overlap is in the negotiation and contract area where some agents do have the skills necessary to effectively market the manuscript on the front end and review and negotiate the final agreement.

Any final suggestions as to what a writer should be looking for in an entertainment attorney?

As in any other business relationship, the attorney should be one that the writer is comfortable with, both on a professional and personal level. The entertainment attorney should be experienced in that field (publishing, e.g.). The attorney also should be approachable and responsive to the writer's needs and concerns, just as within any other legal field, and should always return the writer's calls. The attorney should also be able to provide guidance and be proactive in the writer's endeavors, especially in the case of a new writer who is on the verge of being published for the first time. New and experienced writers alike are depending upon the attorney to guide them through the complex maze of publishing and book contracts.

Know Your Rights

BY DONYA DICKERSON

Most writers who want to be published envision their book in store fronts and on their friends' coffee tables. They imagine book signings and maybe even an interview on *Oprah*. Usually the dream ends there—having a book published seems exciting enough. In actuality, a whole world of opportunities exists for published writers beyond seeing their books in print. These opportunities are called "subsidiary rights."

Subsidiary rights, or sub-rights, are the additional ways that a book—that you're writing—can be presented. Any time a book is made into a movie or excerpted in a magazine, a subsidiary right has been sold. If these additional rights to your book are properly "exploited," you'll not only see your book in a variety of forms, but you'll also make a lot more money than you would have on book sales alone.

Unfortunately, the terminology of subsidiary rights can be confusing. Phrases like "secondary rights," "traditional splits," or "advance against royalty" could perplex any writer. And the thought of negotiating the terms of these rights with a publisher is daunting.

Although there are many advantages to working with agents, the ability to negotiate sub-rights is one of their most beneficial attributes. Through her experience, an agent knows which publishing houses have great sub-rights departments. If she knows a house can make money with a right, she will grant that right to the publisher when the contract is negotiated. Otherwise, she'll keep, or "retain," certain rights for her clients, which she will try to exploit by selling them to her own connections. In an interview in the *2000 Guide to Literary Agents*, writer Octavia Butler said that working with an agent, "is certainly a good thing if you don't know the business. It's a good way to hang onto your foreign and subsidiary rights, and have somebody actively peddling those rights because there were years when I lived off subsidiary rights."

If you want to work with an agent, you should have a basic understanding of sub-rights for two reasons. First, you'll want to be able to discuss these rights with your agent intelligently (although you should feel comfortable asking your agent any question you have about sub-rights). Secondly, different agents have more expertise in some sub-right areas than others. If you think your book would make a great movie, you should research the agents who have strong film connections. A knowledge of sub-rights can help you find the agent best suited to help you achieve your dreams.

An agent negotiates sub-rights with the publishing house at the same time a book is sold. In fact, the sale of certain sub-rights can even determine how much money the publisher offers for the book. But the author doesn't get paid immediately for these rights. Instead, the author is paid an "advance against royalties." An advance is a loan to the author that is paid back when the book starts earning money. Once the advance is paid, the author starts earning royalties, which is a pre-determined percentage of the book's profit.

The agent always keeps certain rights, the publisher always buys certain rights, and the others are negotiated. When an agent keeps a right, she is then free to sell it at will. If she does sell it, the money she receives from the purchasing company goes immediately to the author, minus the agent's commission. Usually the companies who purchase rights pay royalties instead of a one-time payment.

If the publisher keeps the right, any money that is made from it goes toward paying off the advance more quickly. Because the publisher kept the right, they will keep part of the money it makes. For most rights, half the money goes to the publisher and half goes to the writer, although for some rights the percentages are different. This separation of payment is called a "traditional split" because it has become standard over the years. And, of course, the agent takes her commission from the author's half.

Most agents have dealt with certain publishers so many times that they have pre-set, or "boilerplate," contracts, which means they've already agreed to the terms of certain rights, leaving only a few rights to negotiate. The following describes the main sub-rights and discusses what factors an agent takes into account when deciding whether or not to keep a right. As you read through this piece, carefully consider the many opportunities for your book, and encourage your agent and publisher to exploit these rights every chance they get.

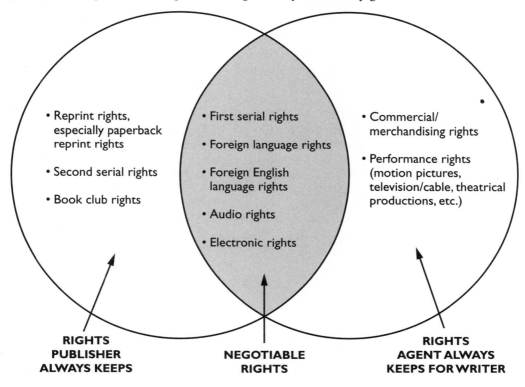

- Reprint rights, especially paperback reprint rights
- Second serial rights
- Book club rights

- First serial rights
- Foreign language rights
- Foreign English language rights
- Audio rights
- Electronic rights

- Commercial/ merchandising rights
- Performance rights (motion pictures, television/cable, theatrical productions, etc.)

RIGHTS PUBLISHER ALWAYS KEEPS

NEGOTIABLE RIGHTS

RIGHTS AGENT ALWAYS KEEPS FOR WRITER

RIGHTS THE PUBLISHER ALWAYS KEEPS

The following sub-rights are always kept by the publisher and are often called "non-negotiable rights." Money earned from these rights is split between the publisher and the author, and the author's share goes toward paying back the advance. Selling these rights helps the advance earn out faster which hopefully means the writer will receive royalty checks sooner.

Reprint rights

In publishing, a "reprint right" refers to the paperback edition of the book. When a hardcover book is reprinted in paperback, the reprint right has been used. According to Donald Maass, of the Donald Maass Literary Agency, "In deals with major trade publishers, it's a long-standing practice to grant them control of reprint rights. However, in some cases, a small press deal for instance, we withhold these rights." Traditionally, if a hardcover book sold really well, paperback houses bought the rights to reprint the book in a more affordable version. Any money earned from the paperback was then split fifty/fifty between the publisher and writer. Paperback houses often paid substantial amounts of money for these reprint rights.

But the recent consolidation of publishing houses has changed the value of reprint rights. "In the old days," explains Maass, "most books were hardcover, and paperbacks were cheap versions of the book. Today, so many paperback publishers have either merged with a hardcover publisher or begun their own hardcover publisher, that the business of selling reprint rights has diminished." Now, many publishers make what is called a "hard/soft deal" meaning the house will first print the book in hardcover, and, if the book sells well, they reprint the book in paperback. This type of deal can still benefit writers because they no longer have to split the money earned from reprint with the publisher. Instead, they earn royalties from both the hardcover and paperback versions.

Book club rights

These days it seems that a book club exists for every possible interest. There are the traditional book clubs, like Book-of-the-Month and its paperback counterpart, the Quality Paperback Book Club. But there are also mystery book clubs, New Age book clubs, book clubs for writers and artists, and even online book clubs. And many major publishers, like Scholastic or Doubleday, have their own book clubs. Most book clubs are very selective, and you should be flattered if your book is chosen for a book club. Like reprint rights, any money made from book club rights is split fifty/fifty between the publisher and the writer. If an agent believes a book will appeal to a certain book club's audience, she will target the manuscript to publishers who have good relationships with—or who own—that book club.

Serial rights

A serial is an excerpt of the book that appears in a magazine or in another book. To have your book serialized is wonderful because excerpts not only make additional money for you, but they also provide wonderful publicity for your book. There are actually two types of serial rights: first serial and second serial. First serial means the excerpt of the book is available before the book is printed. A second serial is an excerpt that appears after the book is already in bookstores. First serial rights are actually negotiable—sometimes the right to use them is kept by the agent. Usually an agent's decision is based upon her knowledge of the publications available in the book's subject. If she doesn't know the various magazines, she will let the publisher have this right. Second serial rights, however, are almost always granted to the publisher.

Nonfiction books are more commonly excerpted than fiction. Nonfiction usually stands alone well, and magazines are always eager to use these excerpts because they usually cost less than hiring a freelancer to write original material. Recently, though, serialized fiction has regained popularity. In the past year, John Grisham's *A Painted House* made a giant splash by appearing, in six installments, in *The Oxford American*. According to Marc Smirnoff, editor of *The Oxford American*, response to Grisham's story has been "overwhelming. I've heard from several people who think it is the best writing John has done. John wanted to challenge himself and we're always looking for exciting work to publish." Grisham's success will certainly create opportunities for other writers who want to have their novels serialized.

RIGHTS NEGOTIATED BETWEEN THE AGENT AND PUBLISHER

The owner of these sub-rights is always determined when the book is sold. Often an agent and editor must compromise for these rights. In other words, an agent may agree to sell foreign rights if she can keep electronic rights. Or an editor will offer more money if he can obtain the audio rights to a book.

Foreign language rights

If your book might appeal to audiences in a non-English-speaking country, then you'll want an agent who has good connections with foreign co-agents. According to James Vines of The Vines Agency, Inc., a "foreign co-agent is someone who specializes in the sales of foreign publishing rights and who has good relationships with the heads of publishing houses throughout the world. These agents work on behalf of a New York City agency and approach the foreign publishers with manuscripts and proposals. They will typically have appointments booked at big trade shows like Frankfurt, London Book, BEA. That's where a lot of the big foreign deals happen." Usually an agent charges a 20 percent commission when a foreign co-agent is used, and the two split the earnings.

"All of my clients have benefited from the sale of foreign rights," continues Vines. For example, "*Kokology*, by Tadahiko Nagao and Isamu Saito started as a big phenomenon in Japan, selling over four million copies there. A game you play about psychology, it's one of those ideas that crosses all languages and cultural boundaries because it's uniquely human—we all want to know more about ourselves." Vines sold the book to Simon & Schuster, then worked with a co-agent to sell it all over the world.

When agents are considering how a book will do abroad, they must be aware of trends in other countries. "Most agents try to stay on top of the foreign markets as much as possible and listen to what foreign co-agents have to say," says Vines. "Trends vary from territory to territory, and I try to keep those trends in mind. For example, in the United Kingdom the *Bridget Jones* phenomena is still in full swing. In Germany, historical novels are popular." Vines also points out that writers can benefit from different sub-rights over a period of time depending on how well a sub-right is selling. "Three or four years ago we were selling more film rights than we are now—studios are not as hungry as they were. Interestingly, as their interest tapered off, the foreign interest increased."

Many publishing houses have foreign counterparts, and often an agent will grant the publisher these rights if she knows the book can be printed by one of these foreign houses. If the publisher has foreign language rights, the author receives an average of 75 percent of any money made when the book is sold to a foreign publisher.

British rights

Like foreign language rights, the owner of a book's British rights can sell the book to publishers in England. Australia was once included in these rights, but Australian publishers are becoming more independent. If an agent keeps these rights, she will use a co-agent in England and the two will likely split a 20 percent commission. If a publisher has these rights, the traditional split is eighty/twenty with the author receiving the larger share.

Electronic rights

Stephen King caused a big commotion in the publishing world first by using an electronic publisher for his book, *Riding the Bullet*, and then by self-publishing his serialized novel, *The Plant*. Many publishing professionals worried that King would start a trend drawing writers away from publishers, while others claimed only high-profile writers like King could ever compete successfully against the vast amounts of information on the Web. Regardless, King's achievement showed that readers are paying attention to the Internet.

Basically, electronic rights refer to the hand-held electronic, Internet, and print-on-demand versions of a book. This right is currently one of the hottest points of contention between agents and publishers because the potential for these rights is unknown—it is quite possible that electronic versions of a book will make a lot of money one day.

This area of publishing is changing so rapidly that both agents and editors struggle with how to handle electronic rights. Many publishers believe any version of a book is the same material as the printed book, and, therefore, they should own the rights. Agents worry, however, that if the publisher lets the book go out of print, the rights to the book will never be returned to the author.

Audio rights

Before people feared that the Internet would cause the end of traditional book publishing, people worried that audio versions of books would erase the need to have printed books. In actuality, audio books have complimented their printed counterparts and have proved to be a fantastic source of additional income for the person who owns the rights to produce the book in audio form—whether through cassette tape or compact disc.

Many publishers own audio imprints and even audio book clubs, and if they are successful with these ventures, an agent will likely grant the audio rights to the publisher. The traditional split is fifty/fifty. Otherwise, the agent will try to save this right and sell it to a company that can turn it into a profit.

RIGHTS THE WRITER ALWAYS KEEPS

When a book is sold, an agent always reserves two rights for his authors: performance and merchandising. Some books are naturally more conducive to being made into films or products. And when they do, there is usually a lot of money to be made. And a smart agent can quickly identify when a book will be successful in these areas.

Performance rights

Many writers fantasize about seeing their book on the big screen. And a lot of times, agents share this dream—especially for best-selling titles. If your agent feels your book will work well as a movie, or even as a television show or video game, she will sell these rights to someone in the entertainment industry. This industry works fairly differently than the publishing industry. Usually a producer "options" the right to make your book into a movie. An option means the producer can only make the movie during a specific amount of time, like a year. If the movie isn't made during that time period, the rights revert back to you. You can actually option these rights over and over—making money for every option—without the book ever being made into a movie.

As with foreign rights, agents usually work with another agent to sell performance rights. Usually these agents live in Los Angeles and have the connections to producers that agents outside California just don't have. A 20 percent commission is the norm for what agents take from any money made from performance rights and split between the two agents who partnered to sell these rights.

Merchandising rights

Merchandising rights create products—like calendars, cards, action figures, stickers, dolls, and so on—that are based on characters or other elements of your book. Few books transfer well into such products, but they can be successful when they do. Keep in mind that if a producer options the performance rights to your book, the merchandising rights are usually included in the deal.

Agent Steven Malk, of Writers House, made wonderful use of these two rights for his client, Elise Primavera, and her book, *Auntie Claus* (Silver Whistle/Harcourt). According to Malk, "When I first read the manuscript of *Auntie Claus* and saw a couple of Primavera's sample illustrations, I immediately knew the book had a lot of possibilities in the sub-rights realm. First of all, the character of Auntie Claus is extremely memorable and unique, and, from a visual standpoint, she's stunning. Also, the basic concept of the book is completely fresh and original, which is very hard to accomplish with a Christmas book.

"The first thing I did was to approach Saks Fifth Avenue with the idea of featuring *Auntie Claus* in their Christmas windows. In addition to using the book as the theme for their window displays, they created some merchandise that was sold through Saks. It's a perfect project for them; the character of Auntie Claus is so sophisticated and refined, and it seemed ideal for their windows."

"Shortly after that, the movie rights were optioned by Nickelodeon with Wendy Finerman attached as a producer—she produced *Forrest Gump* and *Stepmom*. Nickelodeon is currently developing the project, and, when it's released, more merchandise will likely follow."

Like Malk did for Primavera, many agents successfully exploit subsidiary rights every day. If you want the most for your book, look for an agent who has the know-how and connections to take your publishing dream to its fullest potential. And use the information in this article to help your agent make the most of your subsidiary rights.

Listing Policy and Complaint Procedure

Listings in *Guide to Literary Agents* are compiled from detailed questionnaires, phone interviews, and information provided by agents. The industry is volatile, and agencies change frequently. We rely on our readers for information on their dealings with agents and changes in policies or fees that differ from what has been reported to the editor of this book. Write to us if you have new information, questions, or problems dealing with the agencies listed.

Listings are published free of charge and are not advertisements. Although the information is as accurate as possible, the listings are *not* endorsed or guaranteed by the editor or publisher of *Guide to Literary Agents*. If you feel you have not been treated fairly by an agent or representative listed in *Guide to Literary Agents*, we advise you to take the following steps:

9 First try to contact the agency. Sometimes one phone call or a letter can clear up the matter.

9 Document all your correspondence with the agency. When you write to us with a complaint, provide the name of your manuscript, the date of your first contact with the agency and the nature of your subsequent correspondence.

9 We will enter your letter into our files and attempt to contact the agency.

9 The number, frequency, and severity of complaints will be considered in our decision whether or not to delete the listing from the next edition.

Guide to Literary Agents reserves the right to exclude any agency for any reason.

Markets

Literary Agents

Agents listed in this section generate 98 to 100 percent of their income from commission on sales. They do not charge for reading, critiquing, or editing. Sending a query to a nonfee-charging agent means you pay only the cost of postage to have your work considered by an agent with an imperative to find salable manuscripts: Her income depends on finding the best publisher for your manuscript.

Because her time is more profitably spent meeting with editors, she will have little or no time to critique your writing. Agents who don't charge fees must be selective and often prefer to work with established authors, celebrities, or those with professional credentials in a particular field.

Some agents in this section may charge clients for office expenses such as photocopying, foreign postage, long distance phone calls, or express mail services. Make sure you have a clear understanding of what these expenses are before signing any agency agreement. While most agents deduct expenses from the advance or royalties before passing them on to the author, a few agents included in this section charge their clients a one-time "marketing" or "handling" fee up front. These agents have a ($) preceding their listing.

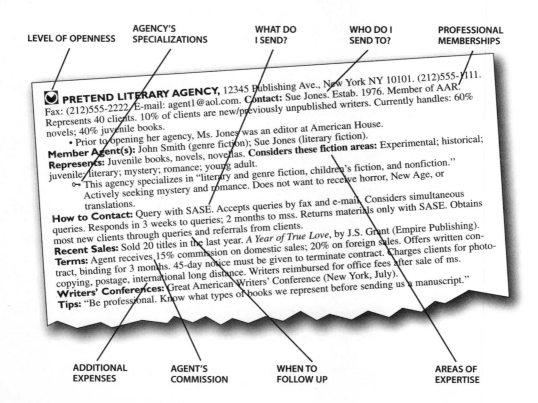

LEVEL OF OPENNESS   AGENCY'S SPECIALIZATIONS   WHAT DO I SEND?   WHO DO I SEND TO?   PROFESSIONAL MEMBERSHIPS

PRETEND LITERARY AGENCY, 12345 Publishing Ave., New York NY 10101. (212)555-1111. Fax: (212)555-2222. E-mail: agent1@aol.com. **Contact:** Sue Jones. Estab. 1976. Member of AAR. Represents 40 clients. 10% of clients are new/previously unpublished writers. Currently handles: 60% novels; 40% juvenile books.

- Prior to opening her agency, Ms. Jones was an editor at American House.

Member Agent(s): John Smith (genre fiction); Sue Jones (literary fiction).
Represents: Juvenile books, novels, novellas. **Considers these fiction areas:** Experimental; historical; juvenile; literary; mystery; romance; young adult.

   This agency specializes in "literary and genre fiction, children's fiction, and nonfiction." Actively seeking mystery and romance. Does not want to receive horror, New Age, or translations.

How to Contact: Query with SASE. Accepts queries by fax and e-mail. Considers simultaneous queries. Responds in 3 weeks to queries; 2 months to mss. Returns materials only with SASE. Obtains most new clients through queries and referrals from clients.
Recent Sales: Sold 20 titles in the last year. *A Year of True Love*, by J.S. Grant (Empire Publishing).
Terms: Agent receives 15% commission on domestic sales; 20% on foreign sales. Offers written contract, binding for 3 months. 45-day notice must be given to terminate contract. Charges clients for photocopying, postage, international long distance. Writers reimbursed for office fees after sale of ms.
Writers' Conferences: Great American Writers' Conference (New York, July).
Tips: "Be professional. Know what types of books we represent before sending us a manuscript."

ADDITIONAL EXPENSES   AGENT'S COMMISSION   WHEN TO FOLLOW UP   AREAS OF EXPERTISE

Quick Reference Icons

At the beginning of each listing, you will find one or more of the following symbols to help you quickly identify features particular to that listing.

N Agency new to this edition.

✓ Change in address, contact information or phone number from last year's edition.

$ Agents who charge fees to previously unpublished writers only.

▣ Agents who make sales to electronic publishers.

✦ Canadian agency.

🌐 International agency.

Level of Openness

Each agency has an icon indicating its openness to submissions. Before contacting any agency, check the listing to make sure it is open to new clients.

○ Newer agency actively seeking clients.

◑ Agency seeking both new and established writers.

◐ Agency prefers to work with established writers, mostly obtains new clients through referrals.

◎ Agency handling only certain types of work or work by writers under certain circumstances.

⊘ Agency not currently seeking new clients. We include these agencies to let you know they are currently not open to new clients. *Unless you have a strong recommendation from someone well respected in the field, our advice is to avoid approaching these agents.*

For quick reference, a chart of these icons and their meanings is printed on the inside covers of this book.

Canadian and International agents are included in this section. Canadian agents have a (✦) preceding their listing while International agents have a (🌐) preceding their listing. Remember to include an International Reply Coupon (IRC) with your self-addressed envelope when contacting Canadian and International agents.

SUBHEADS

Each listing is broken down into subheads to make locating specific information easier. In the first section, you'll find contact information for each agency. You'll also learn if they belong to any professional organizations which can tell you a lot about an agency. For example, members of the Association of Authors' Representatives (AAR) are prohibited from charging reading or evaluating fees. (An explanation of all organizations' acronyms is available on page 320.) Further information is provided which indicates an agency's size, its willingness to work with a new or previously unpublished writer, and its general areas of interest.

Member Agents: Agencies comprised of more than one agent list member agents and their individual specialties to help you determine the most appropriate person for your query letter.

Represents: Here agencies specify what nonfiction and fiction subjects they consider. Make sure you query only agents who represent the type of material you write. To help narrow your search, check the **Agents Specialties Index** in the back of the book.

⚷ Look for the key icon to quickly learn an agent's areas of specialization or specific strengths (i.e., editorial or marketing experience, sub-rights expertise, etc.). Agents mention here what specific areas they are currently seeking as well as subjects they do *not* wish to receive.

How to Contact: Most agents open to submissions prefer initially to receive a query letter briefly describing your work. (See "Queries That Made It Happen" on page 43.) Some agents ask for an outline and a number of sample chapters, but you should send these only if requested to do so. Here agents also mention if they accept queries by fax or e-mail, if they consider simultaneous submissions, and their preferred way of meeting new clients.

Recent Sales: To give a sense of the types of material they represent, agents provide specific titles they've sold as well as a sampling of clients' names. Some agents consider their client list confidential and may only share names once they agree to represent you.

Terms: Provided here are details of an agent's commission, whether a contract is offered and for how long, and what additional office expenses you might have to pay if the agent agrees to represent you. Standard commissions range from 10 to 15 percent for domestic sales, and 15 to 20 percent for foreign or dramatic sales with the difference going to the co-agent who places the work.

Writers' Conferences: A great way to meet an agent is at a writers' conference. Here agents list the ones they attend. For more information about a specific conference, check the **Writers' Conferences** section starting on page 283.

Tips: Agents offer advice and additional instructions for writers looking for representation.

> ### For More Information
> For a detailed explanation of the agency listings and for more information on approaching agents, read "Basics of Contacting a Literary Agent" and "How to Write a Query Letter." Be sure to read the informative articles at the beginning of this book to fully understand the process a writer should go through when finding a literary agent.

SPECIAL INDEXES TO HELP YOUR SEARCH

Additional Nonfee-charging Agents: Many literary agents are also interested in scripts; many script agents will also consider book manuscripts. Nonfee-charging script agents who primarily sell scripts but also handle at least 10 to 15 percent book manuscripts appear among the listings in this section, with the contact information, breakdown of work currently handled, and a note to check the full listing in the script section. Those nonfee-charging script agencies that sell scripts and less than 10 to 15 percent book manuscripts may not appear in this section. Complete listings for these agents appear in the Script Agents section.

Agents Specialties Index: In the back of the book on page 325 is an index which organizes agencies according to the subjects they are interested in receiving. This index should help you compose a list of agents specializing in your areas. Cross-referencing categories and concentrating on agents interested in two or more aspects of your manuscript might increase your chances of success.

Agencies Indexed by Openness to Submissions: This index lists agencies according to their receptivity to new clients.

Geographic Index: For writers looking for an agent close to home, this index lists agents state-by-state.

Agents Index: Often you will read about an agent who is an employee of a larger agency and you may not be able to locate her business phone or address. Starting on page 380 is a list of agents' names in alphabetical order along with the name of the agency they work for. Find the name of the person you would like to contact, then check the agency listing.

Listing Index: This index lists all agencies, independent publicists, and writers' conferences listed in the book.

NONFEE-CHARGING AGENTS

DOMINICK ABEL LITERARY AGENCY, INC., 146 W. 82nd St., #1B, New York NY 10024. Estab. 1975. Member of AAR. Represents 100 clients.
Represents: Nonfiction books, novels. **Considers these fiction areas:** Detective/police/crime; mystery/suspense.
Terms: Agent receives 10% commission on domestic sales; 20% commission on foreign sales. No written contract.

CAROLE ABEL LITERARY AGENT, 160 W. 87th St., New York NY 10024. Member of AAR.
   ● This agency did not respond to our request for information. Query before submitting.

ABS LITERARY AGENCY, INC., P.O. Box 397, Ashland OR 97520-0014. (541)488-6934. Fax: (541)488-6937. E-mail: agent@abs-book.com. **Contact:** Ms. W. Gail Manchur. Estab. 1998. Adheres to AAR Code of Ethics; registered with AuthorLink and other selective agency lists that have standards that must be met prior to listing; was invited in 2000 to be a signatory to the WGA, but declined because we do not represent scripts. Represents 10 clients. 20% of clients are new/unpublished writers. Currently handles: 10 nonfiction books; 90 novels.
   ● I have over 25 years of experience as a freelance editor of scholarly works, technical works, textbooks, nonfiction, and fiction works, having worked on books published by Greenwood Press, Prentice-Hall, and Collectors Press, Inc., among others. I also have experience in book design and production.
Member Agents: Although relatively new, we are highly selective and offer representation to approximately one out of every 200 queries; or one out of every 75 to 100 full, requested submissions. In the first 18 months after establishing our agency, we focused on selecting very special, highly-talented writers, whether previously published or not, and working with them to polish and refine their manuscripts. We slowly worked on establishing important connections with publishers and editors and other agents, including attending the 1999 BEA in Los Angeles, where we had a table in the Rights Section. We were very pleased and proud that our first two sales were to well-established royalty publishers.
Represents: Nonfiction books, novels. **Considers these nonfiction areas:** Child guidance/parenting; cooking/foods/nutrition; how-to; self-help/personal improvement; true crime/investigative. **Considers these fiction areas:** Action/adventure; detective/police/crime; historical; literary; mainstream/contemporary; mystery/suspense; psychic/supernatural; science fiction (hard science fiction only); thriller.
   ⟳ Fresh, innovative fiction and nonfiction. Do your marketing research and know your market for your work. Do not want "formula" fiction, horror, swords and dragons fantasy, pornography, children's or juvenile or young adult stories, poetry, memoirs, autobiographies, romance, westerns. Query first for all other genre.
How to Contact: Query with SASE, will accept e-mail queries that follow our guidelines for content. Guidelines are published at our website http://www.abs-book.com/guidelines.htm. I prefer to be the only reader of REQUESTED full manuscript submissions. Accepts e-mail queries. No fax queries. Responds in 2 months to queries; four to mss. Returns materials only with SASE. Obtains most new clients through my Internet listings (AuthorLink, Literary Agents, etc.) and word of mouth, but some come through recommendations and referrals from publishers.
Recent Sales: Sold 2 titles in the last year. Other clients include Miguel O. Conner, J.J. Johnson Jr., Ron Nance, F. Gordon Robinson, Anthony Ramphos, Alice Schriber, Osvaldo Salas.
Terms: Agent receives 15 commission on domestic sales; 20 commission on foreign sales. Offers written contract. Contract is open-ended, allowing for cancellation by either party, without explanation, upon 30-day notice sent by Certified Mail, return receipt requested. Some rights remain with Agency for limited period after cancellation of contract. As stated earlier, 30-day notice must be given to terminate contract.
Tips: Check our guidelines first and then follow them faithfully. Browse our website, as we offer many pages of valuable information for new writers, especially information on how to write a PROPER synopsis (most writer's just don't know how), and how to get your manuscript noticed among the hundreds sitting on the editor's desk. Articles we have written that have been published elsewhere by Internet organizations also appear on our Web site.

ACACIA HOUSE PUBLISHING SERVICES LTD., 51 Acacia Rd., Toronto, Ontario M4S 2K6, Canada. (416)484-8356. Fax: (416)484-8356. E-mail: fhanna.acacia@rogers.com. **Contact:** (Ms.) Frances Hanna. Estab. 1985. Represents 50 clients. Works with a small number of new/unpublished writers. Currently handles: 30% nonfiction books; 70% novels.
   ● Ms. Hanna has been in the publishing business for 30 years, first in London (UK) as a fiction editor with Barrie & Jenkins and Pan Books, and as a senior editor with a packager of mainly illustrated books. She was condensed books editor for 6 years for *Reader's Digest* in Montreal, senior editor and foreign rights manager for (the then) W.M. Collins & Sons (now HarperCollins) in Toronto. Her husband, Vice President Bill Hanna, has over 40 years experience in the publishing business.

Member Agents: Bill Hanna, vice president (business, self-help, modern history).
Represents: Nonfiction books, novels. **Considers these nonfiction areas:** Animals; biography/autobiography; language/literature/criticism; memoirs; military/war; music/dance; nature/environment; theater/film; travel. **Considers these fiction areas:** Action/adventure; detective/police/crime; literary; mainstream/contemporary; mystery/suspense; thriller.
   O- This agency specializes in contemporary fiction: literary or commercial. Actively seeking "outstanding first novels with literary merit." Does not want to receive horror, occult, science fiction.
How to Contact: Query with outline and SASE. *No unsolicited mss.* No e-mail or fax queries. Responds in 6 weeks to queries. Returns materials only with SASE.
Recent Sales: Sold over 50 titles in the last year. Also made numerous international rights sales. This agency prefers not to share information on specific sales or clients.
Terms: Agent receives 15% commission on English language sales, 20% on dramatic sales, 25% commission on foreign sales. Charges clients for photocopying, postage and courier, as necessary.
Tips: "I prefer that writers be previously published, with at least a few articles to their credit. Strongest consideration will be given to those with, say, three or more published books. However, I *would* take on an unpublished writer of outstanding talent."

☑ AGENTS INC. FOR MEDICAL AND MENTAL HEALTH PROFESSIONALS, P.O. Box 4956, Fresno CA 93744. (559)438-8289. **Contact:** Sydney H. Harriet, Ph.D., Psy. D., director. Estab. 1987. Member of APA. Represents 49 clients. 70% of clients are new/unpublished writers. Currently handles: 80% nonfiction books; 20% novels; multimedia.
   • Prior to opening his agency, Dr. Harriet was a professor of English, psychologist, and radio and television reporter.
Member Agents: Sydney Harriet, Ph.D., director.
Represents: Nonfiction books, novels. **Considers these nonfiction areas:** Cooking/foods/nutrition; health/medicine (mind-body healing); psychology; science/technology; self-help/personal improvement; sociology; sports (medicine, psychology); law. **Considers these fiction areas:** *Currently representing previously published novelists only.*
   O- This agency specializes in writers who have education and experience in the business, legal and health professions. It is helpful if the writer is licensed but not necessary. Prior nonfiction book publication not necessary. For fiction, previously published fiction is prerequisite for representation. Does not want memoirs, autobiographies, stories about overcoming an illness, science fiction, fantasy, religious materials and children's books.
How to Contact: Query with SASE. Considers simultaneous queries and submissions. Responds in 1 month to queries; 1 month to mss.
Recent Sales: Sold 4 titles in the last year. *Infantry Soldier*, by George Neil (University of Oklahoma Press); *SAMe, The European Arthritis and Depression Breakthrough*, by Sol Grazi, M.D. and Maria Costa (Prima); *What to Eat if You Have Diabetes*, by Danielle Chase M.S. (Contemporary); *How to Turn Your Fat Husband Into a Lean Lover*, by Maureen Keane (Random House).
Terms: Agent receives 15% commission on domestic sales; 20% commission on foreign sales. Offers written contract, binding for 6-12 months (negotiable). Writers reimbursed for office fees after the sale of ms.
Writers' Conferences: "Scheduled as a speaker at a number of conferences across the country in 2001-2002. Contact agency to book authors and agents for conferences."
Tips: "Remember, query first. Do not call to pitch an idea. The only way we can judge the quality of your idea is to see how you write. Please, unsolicited manuscripts will not be read if they arrive without a SASE. Currently we are receiving more than 200 query letters and proposals each month. Send complete proposal/manuscript only if requested. Please, please ask yourself why someone would be compelled to buy your book. If you think the idea is unique, spend the time to create a query and then a proposal where every word counts. Fiction writers need to understand that the craft is just as important as the idea. 99% of the fiction is rejected because of sloppy overwritten dialogue, wooden characters, predictable plotting and lifeless narrative. Once you finish your novel, put it away and let it percolate, then take it out and work on fine-tuning it some more. A novel is never finished until you stop working on it. Would love to represent more fiction writers and probably will when we read a manuscript that has gone through a dozen or more drafts. Because of rising costs, we no longer can respond to queries, proposals, and/or complete manuscripts without receiving a return envelope and sufficient postage."

THE PUBLISHING FIELD is constantly changing! Agents often change addresses, phone numbers, or even companies. If you're still using this book and it is 2004 or later, buy the newest edition of *Guide to Literary Agents* at your favorite bookstore or order directly from Writer's Digest Books at (800)448-0915.

THE AHEARN AGENCY, INC., 2021 Pine St., New Orleans LA 70118-5456. (504)861-8395. Fax: (504)866-6434. E-mail: pahearn@aol.com. **Contact:** Pamela G. Ahearn. Estab. 1992. Member of RWA. Represents 25 clients. 20% of clients are new/unpublished writers. Currently handles: 10% nonfiction books; 90% novels.

• Prior to opening her agency, Ms. Ahearn was an agent for eight years and an editor with Bantam Books.

Represents: Nonfiction books, novels, short story collections (if stories previously published). **Considers these nonfiction areas:** Animals; biography/autobiography; child guidance/parenting; current affairs; ethnic/cultural interests; gay/lesbian issues; health/medicine; history; music/dance; popular culture; self-help/personal improvement; theater/film; true crime/investigative; women's issues/studies. **Considers these fiction areas:** Action/adventure; contemporary issues; detective/police/crime; ethnic; family saga; feminist; gay/lesbian; glitz; historical; humor/satire; literary; mainstream/contemporary; mystery/suspense; psychic/supernatural; regional; romance; thriller.

> ☞ This agency specializes in historical romance; also very interested in mysteries and suspense fiction. Does not want to receive category romance.

How to Contact: Query with SASE. Accepts e-mail queries, no attachments. Considers simultaneous queries. Responds in 6 weeks to queries; 10 weeks to mss. Obtains most new clients through recommendations from others, solicitations, conferences.

Recent Sales: *Moonlight Becomes Her*, by Meagan McKinney (Kensington); *After the Abduction*, by Sabrina Jeffries (Avon); *The Pillow Book of Lady Wisteria*, by Laura Joh Rowland (St. Martin's Press).

Terms: Agent receives 15% commission on domestic sales; 20% commission on foreign sales. Offers written contract, binding for 1 year; renewable by mutual consent.

Writers' Conferences: Midwest Writers Workshop; Moonlight & Magnolias; RWA National Conference (Orlando); Virginia Romance Writers (Williamsburg VA); Florida Romance Writers (Ft. Lauderdale FL); Golden Triangle Writers Conference; Bouchercon (Monterey, November); Malice Domestic (DC, May).

Tips: "Be professional! Always send in exactly what an agent/editor asks for, no more, no less. Keep query letters brief and to the point, giving your writing credentials and a very brief summary of your book. If one agent rejects you, keep trying—there are a lot of us out there!"

N M © JOSEPH AJLOUNY LITERARY AGENCY, (Specialized: humor, popular culture and reference), Federal Bureau of Entertainment 29205 Greening Blvd., Farmington Hills MI 48334-2945. (248)932-0090. Fax: (248)932-8763. E-mail: jsapub@aol.com. Website: www.the-feds.com. **Contact:** Joseph Ajlouny, director. Estab. 1988. Signatory of WGA; member of Mid-America Publishers Association, Michigan Publishers Association. Represents 80 clients. 20% of clients are new/previously unpublished writers. Currently handles: 60% nonfiction books; 20% stage plays; 5% syndicated material; 15% licensing.

• Prior to becoming an agent, Mr Ajlouny was an editor of art books and Ms. Foss was a journalist.

Member Agents: Gwen Foss (humor, popular reference, science); Joseph S. Ajlouny (theatricals, licensing, history).

Represents: Nonfiction books, scholarly books, musical theater, science and technical books. **Considers these nonfiction areas:** Art/architecture/design; biography/autobiography; crafts/hobbies; current affairs; history; how-to; humor; language/literature/criticism; music/dance/theater/film; popular culture; science/technology; sports.

> ☞ This agency specializes in humorists and satirists; popular reference and cultural titles on film, TV, sports, art and music. Does not want to receive relationship or employment humor; self-improvement; memoirs by recovering addicts; religious narratives or novels.

Also Handles: Playscripts only. **Considers these script subject areas:** Comedy; erotica; experimental; musical theater; interactive theater. Actively seeking interactive (participatory theatrical scripts).

How to Contact: Query with SASE. Accepts queries by e-mail. Considers simultaneous queries. Responds in 1 month to queries; 2 months to mss. Returns material only with SASE. Obtains most new clients through queries/solicitations.

Recent Sales: Sold 16 titles and 6 script projects in the last year. *Techno Rebels*, by Dan Sicko (Billboard Books); *How to Live Forever*, by Joey West (Gramercy); *The Avant Garde Prima Donna*, by A. Booten (Random House); *Pass the Pepper*, by Annette Wong (Bantam).

Terms: Agent receives 15% commission on domestic sales; 20% on foreign sales. Offers written contract. 60-day notice must be given to terminate contract. Charges clients for annual administration fee of $50/title payable from earned royalties only.

Writers' Conference: Oakland Writers Conference (Rochester Hills, MI, October).

M ALIVE COMMUNICATIONS, INC., 7680 Goddard St., Suite 200, Colorado Springs CO 80920. (719) 260-7080. Fax: (719)260-8223. Website: www.alivecom.com. Estab. 1989. Member of CBA. Represents 200+ clients. 5% of clients are new/unpublished writers. Currently handles: 50% nonfiction books; 30% novels; 4% story collections; 5% novellas; 10% juvenile books; 1% syndicated material.

Member Agents: Rick Christian, president (blockbusters, bestsellers); Greg Johnson (popular/commercial nonfiction and fiction, Christian organizations); Kathryn Helmers (popular/literary nonfiction and fiction, spirituality, memoir); Jerry "Chip" MacGregor (popular/commercial nonfiction and fiction, new authors with breakout potential); Linda Glasford (gift, women's fiction/nonfiction, Christian living); Lee Hough (popular/commercial nonfiction and fiction, thoughtful spirituality, children's).

Represents: Nonfiction books, novels, short story collections, novellas, juvenile books. **Considers these nonfiction areas:** Biography/autobiography; business/economics; child guidance/parenting; how-to; religious/inspirational; self-help/personal improvement; sports; women's issues/studies. **Considers these fiction areas:** Action/ adventure; contemporary issues; detective/police/crime; family saga; historical; humor/satire; juvenile; literary; mainstream/contemporary; mystery/suspense; religious/inspirational; thriller; westerns/frontier; young adult.

    ○━ This agency specializes in fiction, Christian living, how-to, children's and commercial nonfiction. Actively seeking inspirational/literary/mainstream fiction and work from authors with established track records and platforms. Does not want poetry, young adult paperback, scripts, dark themes.

How to Contact: Works primarily with well-established, best-selling and career authors.

Recent Sales: Sold 300 titles in the last year. *Left Behind series*, by Tim LaHaye and Jerry B. Jenkins (Tyndale); *Let's Roll*, by Lisa Beamer (Tyndale); *The Message*, by Eugene Peterson (NavPress); *Hometown Legend*, by Jerry B. Jenkins (Warner); *Racing to Win*, by Joe Gibbs (Multnomah).

Terms: Agent receives 15% commission on domestic sales; 25% commission on foreign sales. Offers written contract; 60-day written notice notice must be given to terminate contract.

Reading List: Reads literary, religious, and mainstream journals to find new clients. "Our goal is always the same—to find writers whose use of language is riveting and powerful."

Tips: "Rewrite and polish until the words on the page shine. Endorsements and great connections may help, provided you can write with power and passion. Network with publishing professionals by making contacts, joining critique groups, and attending writers' conferences in order to make personal connections in publishing and to get feedback. Alive Communications, Inc. has established itself as a premiere literary agency. Based in Colorado Springs, we serve an elite group of authors who are critically acclaimed and commercially successful in both Christian and general markets."

◪ **LINDA ALLEN LITERARY AGENCY**, 1949 Green St., Suite 5, San Francisco CA 94123-4829. (415)921-6437. **Contact:** Darlene Dozier, Esq., agent. Estab. 1982. Member of AAR. Represents 35-40 clients.

Represents: Nonfiction books (adult), novels (adult). **Considers these nonfiction areas:** Current affairs; health/ medicine; history; multicultural; food/wine, narrative. **Considers these fiction areas:** Historical; multicultural; narrative, current affairs, food/wine, health.

How to Contact: Query with SASE. Considers simultaneous queries. Responds in 3 weeks to queries. Returns materials only with SASE. Obtains most new clients through recommendations from others.

Recent Sales: This agency prefers not to share information on specific sales.

Terms: Agent receives 15% commission on domestic sales. Charges for photocopying.

◪ **ALLRED AND ALLRED LITERARY AGENTS**, 7834 Alabama Ave., Canoga Park CA 91304-4905. (818)346-4313. **Contact:** Robert Allred. Estab. 1991. Represents 5 clients. 100% of clients are new/unpublished writers. Currently handles: nonfiction books; novels; movie scripts; TV scripts.

    ● Prior to opening his agency, Mr. Allred was a writer, assistant producer, associate director and editorial assistant.

Member Agents: Robert Allred (all); Kim Allred (all).

Represents: Nonfiction books, novels, short story collections, juvenile books, scholarly books, textbooks. **Considers these nonfiction areas:** Anthropology/archaeology; art/architecture/design; biography/autobiography; cooking/foods/nutrition; crafts/hobbies; current affairs; education; ethnic/cultural interests; health/medicine; history; how-to; humor/satire; interior design/decorating; juvenile nonfiction; language/literature/criticism; military/ war; music/dance; New Age/metaphysics; photography; popular culture; psychology; religious/inspirational; science/technology; self-help/personal improvement; sociology; sports; theater/film; true crime/investigative; women's issues/studies. **Considers these fiction areas:** Action/adventure; confession; detective/police/crime; ethnic; family saga; fantasy; feminist; gay/lesbian; glitz; historical; horror; humor/satire; juvenile; literary; mainstream/ contemporary; mystery/suspense; psychic/supernatural; regional; religious/inspirational; romance (contemporary, gothic, historical, regency); science fiction; sports; thriller; westerns/frontier; young adult.

Represents: Feature Film; TV Movie of the Week; Episodic Drama; Sitcom; Animation; Documentary; Soap Opera; Syndicated Material; Variety Show.

Considers these script subject areas: action/adventure; biography/autobiography; cartoon/animation; comedy; contemporary issues; detective/police/crime; erotica; ethnic; experimental; family saga; fantasy; feminist; gay/ lesbian; glitz; historical; horror; juvenile; mainstream; multicultural; multimedia; mystery/suspense; psychic/ supernatural; regional; religious/inspirational; romantic comedy; romantic drama; science fiction; sports; teen; thriller; western/frontier.

How to Contact: Query with SASE. Submit first 25 pages for book submissions. For scripts, send entire ms. Include 1-2 page synopsis and SASE. No e-mail or fax queries. Considers simultaneous queries. Responds in 3 weeks to queries; 2 months to mss. Returns materials only with SASE. Obtains most new clients through recommendations from others, solicitations.

Recent Sales: Sold 5 titles in the last year. *Diamond in the Rough*, by Richard Blacke (Wide Western); *Red Rose, White Rose*, by Betty Stuart (Sunset Publications).

Terms: Agent receives 10% commission on domestic sales; 10% commission on foreign sales. Offers written contract, binding for 1 year; 100% of business is derived from commissions on ms sales.

Tips: "The synopsis must cover the entire length of the project from beginning to end. A professional appearance in script format, dark and large type, and simple binding go a long way to create good first impressions in this business, as does a professional business manner. We must be able to at least estimate the potential of the whole project before we can expend the time reading it in its entirety. Writers who try to sell us with overblown hyperbole or titillate our curiosity by vaguely hinting at a possible outcome do themselves a disservice; agents don't have time for reading sales copy—just tell us what it's about, and let us make the decision about whether we want to see the entire project."

ALTAIR LITERARY AGENCY, 141 Fifth Ave., Suite 8N, New York NY 10010. (212)505-3320. **Contact:** Nicholas Smith, partner. Estab. 1996. Member of AAR. Represents 75 clients. Currently handles: 90% nonfiction books; 5% novels; 5% juvenile activity books.
Member Agents: Andrea Pedolsky, partner (art/architecture/design, personal finance, contemporary issues, sports, spirituality, women's issues, illustrated books, self help, literary fiction); Nicholas Smith, partner (archaeology, art, design, history, music, natural history, photography, popular culture, popular reference, science, illustrated books.)
Represents: Nonfiction books. **Considers these nonfiction areas:** Biography/autobiography (no person currently alive); history (natural history and science, esp. museum-related); money/finance (personal finance, published journalists only); popular culture (esp. pre-1970s music); science/technology. **Considers these fiction areas:** Historical (pre-20th century).
  O— This agency specializes in nonfiction with an emphasis on authors who have a direct connection to their topic, and a high level of public exposure. Actively seeking solid, well-informed authors who have or are developing a public platform for the subject specialty. Interested in book to museum exhibition.
How to Contact: Query with SASE. See website for more specific query information. Considers simultaneous queries. Responds in 1 month to queries; 1 month to mss. Obtains most new clients through recommendations from others, solicitations, author queries.
Recent Sales: *Love Dharma*, by Geri Larkin (Tuttle); *Solar-System: A Pull-Out Book*, by Christine Malloy with the American Museum of Natural History (Chronicle Books).
Terms: Agent receives 15% commission on domestic sales; 20% commission on foreign sales. Offers written contract, binding for 1 year; 60-day notice must be given to terminate contract. Charges clients for postage, copying, messengers and Fedex and UPS.
Tips: "Beyond being able to write a compelling book, have an understanding of the market issues that are driving publishing today."

MIRIAM ALTSHULER LITERARY AGENCY, 53 Old Post Rd. N., Red Hook NY 12571. (845)758-9408. Fax: (845)758-3118. **Contact:** Miriam Altshuler. Estab. 1994. Member of AAR. Represents 40 clients. Currently handles: 45% nonfiction books; 45% novels; 5% story collections; 5% juvenile books.
  • Ms. Altshuler has been an agent since 1982.
Represents: Nonfiction books, novels, short story collections, juvenile books. **Considers these nonfiction areas:** Biography/autobiography; ethnic/cultural interests; history; language/literature/criticism; memoirs; multicultural; music/dance; nature/environment; popular culture; psychology; sociology; theater/film; women's issues/studies. **Considers these fiction areas:** Literary; mainstream/contemporary; multicultural; thriller.
How to Contact: Query with SASE. Prefers to read materials exclusively. No e-mail or fax queries. Considers simultaneous queries. Responds in 2 weeks to queries; 3 weeks to mss. Returns materials only with SASE. Obtains most new clients through recommendations from others.
Terms: Agent receives 15% commission on domestic sales; 20% commission on foreign sales. No written contract. Charges clients for overseas mailing, photocopies, overnight mail when requested by author.
Writers' Conferences: Bread Loaf Writers' Conference (Middlebury VT, August).

BETSY AMSTER LITERARY ENTERPRISES, P.O. Box 27788, Los Angeles CA 90027-0788. **Contact:** Betsy Amster. Estab. 1992. Member of AAR. Represents over 65 clients. 35% of clients are new/unpublished writers. Currently handles: 65% nonfiction books; 35% novels.
  • Prior to opening her agency, Ms. Amster was an editor at Pantheon and Vintage for 10 years and served as editorial director for the Globe Pequot Press for 2 years. "This experience gives me a wider perspective on the business and the ability to give focused editorial feedback to my clients."
Represents: Nonfiction books, novels. **Considers these nonfiction areas:** Biography/autobiography; business/economics; child guidance/parenting; ethnic/cultural interests; gardening; health/medicine; history; money/finance; psychology; sociology; women's issues/studies. **Considers these fiction areas:** Ethnic; literary.
  O— Actively seeking "strong narrative nonfiction, particularly by journalists; outstanding literary fiction (the next Michael Chabon or Jhumpa Lahiri); and high profile self-help and psychology, preferably research-based." Does not want to receive poetry, children's books, romances, westerns, science fiction.
How to Contact: For fiction send query, first 3 pages and SASE. For nonfiction send query or proposal with SASE. No e-mail or fax queries. Considers simultaneous queries. Responds in 1 month to queries; 2 months to mss. Obtains most new clients through recommendations from others, solicitations, conferences.

Recent Sales: *Nature Lessons*, by Lynette Brasfield (St. Martin's); *I Know I'm in There Somewhere*, by Helene Brenner, Ph.D. (Penguin Putnam); *The Highly Sensitive Child*, by Elaine Aron, Ph.D. (Broadway). Other clients include Robin Chotzinoff, Mariá Amparo Escandón, Joy Nicholson, Jan DeBlieu, Katie Singer, Frank Clifford, Mary Rakow, Louise Steinman, Diana Wells, Dwight Allen.

Terms: Agent receives 15% commission on domestic sales; 20% commission on foreign sales. Offers written contract, binding for 1-2 years; 60-day notice must be given to terminate contract. Charges for photocopying, postage, long distance phone calls, messengers and galleys and books used in submissions to foreign and film agents and to magazines for first serial rights.

Writers' Conferences: Squaw Valley; Pacific Northwest Conference; San Diego Writers Conference; UCLA Writers Conference

MARCIA AMSTERDAM AGENCY, 41 W. 82nd St., New York NY 10024-5613. (212)873-4945. **Contact:** Marcia Amsterdam. Estab. 1970. Signatory of WGA. Currently handles: 15% nonfiction books; 70% novels; 5% movie scripts; 10% TV scripts.

● Prior to opening her agency, Ms. Amsterdam was an editor.

Represents: Nonfiction books, novels, feature film, TV movie of the week, sitcom. **Considers these nonfiction areas:** Child guidance/parenting; popular culture; self-help/personal improvement. **Considers these fiction areas:** Action/adventure; detective/police/crime; horror; mainstream/contemporary; mystery/suspense; romance (contemporary, historical); science fiction; thriller; westerns/frontier; young adult. **Considers these script subject areas:** Comedy; mainstream; mystery/suspense; romantic comedy; romantic drama.

How to Contact: Submit outline, 3 sample chapter(s), SASE. Responds in 1 month to queries.

Recent Sales: *Rosey in the Present Tense*, by Louise Hawes (Walker); *Flash Factor*, by William H. Lovejoy (Kensington). *Movie/TV MOW script(s) optioned/sold: Mad About You*, by Jenna Bruce (Columbia Tristar TV).

Terms: Agent receives 15% commission on domestic sales; 20% commission on foreign sales; 10% commission on dramatic rights sales. Offers written contract, binding for 1 year. Charges clients for extra office expenses, foreign postage, copying, legal fees (when agreed upon).

Tips: "We are always looking for interesting literary voices."

BART ANDREWS & ASSOCIATES, 7510 Sunset Blvd., Suite 100, Los Angeles CA 90046. Phone/fax: (310)271-9916. **Contact:** Bart Andrews. Estab. 1982. Represents 25 clients. 25% of clients are new/unpublished writers. Currently handles: 100% nonfiction books.

Represents: Nonfiction books. **Considers these nonfiction areas:** Biography/autobiography; music/dance; theater/film; TV.

○➠ This agency specializes in nonfiction only, and in the general category of entertainment (movies, TV, biographies, autobiographies).

How to Contact: Query with SASE. Considers simultaneous queries. Responds in 1 week to queries; 1 month to mss.

Recent Sales: Sold 25 titles in the last year. *Roseanne*, by J. Randy Taraborrelli (G.P. Putnam's Sons); *Out of the Madness*, by Rose Books packaging firm (HarperCollins).

Terms: Agent receives 15% commission on domestic sales; 15% (after subagent takes his 10%) commission on foreign sales. Offers written contract. Charges clients for all photocopying, mailing, phone calls, postage, etc; Writers reimbursed for office fees after the sale of ms.

Writers' Conferences: Frequently lectures at UCLA in Los Angeles.

Tips: "Recommendations from existing clients or professionals are best, although I find a lot of new clients by seeking them out myself. I rarely find a new client through the mail. Spend time writing a query letter. Sell yourself like a product. The bottom line is writing ability, and then the idea itself. It takes a lot to convince me. I've seen it all! I hear from too many first-time authors who don't do their homework. They're trying to get a book published and they haven't the faintest idea what is required of them. There are plenty of good books on the subject and, in my opinion, it's their responsibility—not mine—to educate themselves before they try to find an agent to represent their work. When I ask an author to see a manuscript or even a partial manuscript, I really must be convinced I want to read it—based on a strong query letter—because of wasting my time reading just for the fun of it."

ANUBIS LITERARY AGENCY, 79 Charles Gardner Rd., Leamington Spa, Warwickshire CV313BG, Great Britain. 01926 832644. Fax: 01926 311607. **Contact:** Steve Calcutt. Estab. 1994. Represents 25 clients. 50% of clients are new/unpublished writers. Currently handles: 100% novels.

● Prior to becoming an agent, Mr. Calcutt taught creative writing for Warwick University plus American history—US Civil War.

Member Agents: Maggie Heavey (crime); Steve Calcutt (horror/science fiction).

Represents: Novels. **Considers these fiction areas:** Detective/police/crime; fantasy; historical; horror; science fiction.

○➠ "We are very keen on developing talented new writers. We give support, encouragement and editorial guidance." Actively seeking horror fiction. Does not want to receive children's, nonfiction, journalism or TV/film scripts.

How to Contact: Query with SASE, submit proposal package, outline, IRCs. Returns materials only with SASE or IRCs. No e-mail or fax queries. Accepts simultaneous queries and submissions. Responds in 6 weeks to queries; 3 months to mss. Obtains most new clients through solicitations.
Recent Sales: *When There Were Heroes*, by Elon Salmon (Dewi Lewis). Other clients include Richard Irvine, Steve Savile, Lesley Asquith, E.K. Salmon, Zoe Sharp, Anthea Ingham.
Terms: Agent receives 15% commission on domestic sales; 20% commission on foreign sales. No written contract.

⬤ APPLESEEDS MANAGEMENT, 200 E. 30th St., Suite 302, San Bernardino CA 92404. (909)882-1667.
Contact: S. James Foiles. Estab. 1988. 40% of clients are new/unpublished writers. Currently handles: 15% nonfiction books; 85% novels.
Represents: Nonfiction books, novels. **Considers these nonfiction areas:** True crime/investigative. **Considers these fiction areas:** Detective/police/crime; mystery/suspense.
How to Contact: Query with SASE. Responds in 2 weeks to queries; 2 months to mss.
Recent Sales: This agency prefers not to share information on specific sales.
Terms: Agent receives 10-15% commission on domestic sales; 20% commission on foreign sales. Offers written contract, binding for 1-7 years.
Tips: "Appleseeds specializes in mysteries with a detective who could be in a continuing series because readership of mysteries is expanding."

⬤ ARCADIA, 31 Lake Place North, Danbury CT 06810. **Contact:** Victoria Gould Pryor. Member of AAR.
  ● This agency did not respond to our request for information. Query before submitting.

⬤ AUTHENTIC CREATIONS LITERARY AGENCY, 875 Lawrenceville-Suwanee Rd., Suite 310-306, Lawrenceville GA 30043. (770)339-3774. Fax: (770)339-7126. E-mail: marylee@authenticcreations.com. Website: www.authenticcreations.com. **Contact:** Mary Lee Laitsch. Estab. 1993. Represents 70 clients. 30% of clients are new/unpublished writers. Currently handles: 60% nonfiction books; 40% novels.
  ● Prior to becoming agents, Ms. Laitsch was a librarian and elementary school teacher; Mr. Laitsch was an attorney and a writer.
Member Agents: Mary Lee Laitsch; Ronald Laitsch; Jason Laitsch.
Represents: Nonfiction books, novels, scholarly books. **Considers these nonfiction areas:** Anthropology/archaeology; biography/autobiography; child guidance/parenting; crafts/hobbies; current affairs; history; how-to; science/technology; self-help/personal improvement; sports; true crime/investigative; women's issues/studies.
Considers these fiction areas: Action/adventure; contemporary issues; detective/police/crime; family saga; literary; mainstream/contemporary; mystery/suspense; romance; sports; thriller.
How to Contact: Query with SASE. No e-mail or fax queries. Considers simultaneous queries. Responds in 2 weeks to queries; 2 months to mss.
Recent Sales: Sold 15 titles in the last year. *Frankenstein—The Legacy* , by Christopher Schildt (Simon & Schuster); *Night of Dracula*, by Christopher Schildt (Simon & Schuster).
Terms: Agent receives 15% commission on domestic sales; 15% commission on foreign sales. Charges clients for photocopying.
Tips: "The tragic events of September 11 followed by the anthrax scare have changed the nature of the marketplace. Agents need to be aware of these changes and guide their authors into new directions that tap into this new market."

⬤ THE AXELROD AGENCY, 49 Main St., P.O. Box 357, Chatham NY 12037. (518)392-2100. Fax: (518)392-2944. E-mail: steve@axelrodagency.com. **Contact:** Steven Axelrod. Estab. 1983. Member of AAR. Represents 20-30 clients. 1% of clients are new/unpublished writers. Currently handles: 5% nonfiction books; 95% novels.
  ● Prior to becoming an agent, Mr. Axelrod was a book club editor.
Represents: Nonfiction books, novels. **Considers these fiction areas:** Mystery/suspense; romance; women's.
How to Contact: Query with SASE. Considers simultaneous queries. Responds in 3 weeks to queries; 6 weeks to mss. Returns materials only with SASE. Obtains most new clients through recommendations from others.
Recent Sales: This agency prefers not to share information on specific sales.
Terms: Agent receives 15% commission on domestic sales; 20% commission on foreign sales. No written contract.
Writers' Conferences: Romance Writers of America (July).

⬤ JULIAN BACH LITERARY AGENCY, 22 E. 71st St., New York NY 10021. Member of AAR.
  ● This agency did not respond to our request for information. Query before submitting.

☑ ⬤ MALAGA BALDI LITERARY AGENCY, 204 W. 84th St., Suite 3C, New York NY 10024. (212)579-5075. Fax: (212)579-5078. E-mail: mbaldi@aol.com. **Contact:** Malaga Baldi. Estab. 1985. Represents 40-50 clients. 80% of clients are new/unpublished writers. Currently handles: 60% nonfiction books; 40% novels.
  ● Prior to becoming an agent, Malaga Baldi worked in a bookstore.

Represents: Nonfiction books, novels. **Considers these nonfiction areas:** Agriculture/horticulture; animals; anthropology/archaeology; art/architecture/design; biography/autobiography; business/economics; current affairs; ethnic/cultural interests; gay/lesbian issues; government/politics/law; health/medicine; history; interior design/decorating; language/literature/criticism; memoirs; money/finance; music/dance; nature/environment; photography; psychology; science/technology; sociology; theater/film; travel; true crime/investigative; women's issues/studies. **Considers these fiction areas:** Action/adventure; contemporary issues; detective/police/crime; erotica; ethnic; experimental; feminist; gay/lesbian; historical; literary; mainstream/contemporary; mystery/suspense; regional; thriller/espionage.

> ◻━ This agency specializes in quality literary fiction and nonfiction. Actively seeking well-written fiction and nonfiction. Does not want to receive child guidance, crafts, juvenile nonfiction, New Age/metaphysics, sports, family saga, fantasy, glitz, juvenile fiction, picture book, psychic/supernatural, religious/inspirational, romance, science fiction, western or young adult.

How to Contact: Query with SASE. No e-mail or fax queries. Considers simultaneous queries. Responds after a minimum of 10 weeks.

Recent Sales: Sold 15 titles in the last year. *The Ravens Cliff* series, by Geoffrey Huntington (Judith Regan/HarperCollins).

Terms: Agent receives 15% commission on domestic sales; 20% commission on foreign sales. Offers written contract. Charges clients "an initial fee of $50 to cover photocopying expenses. If the manuscript is lengthy, I prefer the author to cover expenses of photocopying."

⬤ **BALKIN AGENCY, INC.**, P.O. Box 222, Amherst MA 01004. (413)548-9835. Fax: (413)548-9836. **Contact:** Rick Balkin, president. Estab. 1972. Member of AAR. Represents 50 clients. 10% of clients are new/unpublished writers. Currently handles: 85% nonfiction books; 5% scholarly books; 5% textbooks; 5% reference books.

● Prior to opening his agency, Mr. Balkin served as executive editor with Bobbs-Merrill Company.

Represents: Nonfiction books, scholarly books, textbooks. **Considers these nonfiction areas:** Animals; anthropology/archaeology; biography/autobiography; current affairs; health/medicine; history; how-to; language/literature/criticism; music/dance; nature/environment; popular culture; science/technology; sociology; translation; travel; true crime/investigative.

> ◻━ This agency specializes in adult nonfiction. Does not want to receive fiction, poetry, screenplays, computer books.

How to Contact: Query with SASE, proposal package, outline. No e-mail or fax queries. Responds in 1 week to queries; 2 weeks to mss. Returns materials only with SASE. Obtains most new clients through recommendations from others.

Recent Sales: Sold 30 titles in the last year. *The Liar's Tale*, (W.W. Norton Co.); *Adolescent Depression*, (Henry Holt); *Eliz. Van Lew: A Union Spy in the Heart of the Confederacy*, (biography, Oxford U.P.).

Terms: Agent receives 15% commission on domestic sales; 20% commission on foreign sales. Offers written contract, binding for 1 year. Charges clients for photocopying and express or foreign mail.

Tips: "I do not take on books described as bestsellers or potential bestsellers. Any nonfiction work that is either unique, paradigmatic, a contribution, truly witty or a labor of love is grist for my mill."

⬤ **LORETTA BARRETT BOOKS INC.**, 101 Fifth Ave., New York NY 10003. (212)242-3420. Fax: (212)807-9579. **Contact:** Loretta A. Barrett or Nick Mullendore. Estab. 1990. Member of AAR. Represents 90 clients. Currently handles: 60% nonfiction books; 40% novels.

● Prior to opening her agency, Ms. Barrett was vice president and executive editor at Doubleday for 25 years.

Represents: Nonfiction books, novels. **Considers these nonfiction areas:** Americana; animals; anthropology/archaeology; biography/autobiography; business/economics; child guidance/parenting; computers/electronic; cooking/foods/nutrition; creative nonfiction; current affairs; education; ethnic/cultural interests; gay/lesbian issues; government/politics/law; health/medicine; history; how-to; humor/satire; interior design/decorating; memoirs; military/war; money/finance; multicultural; nature/environment; New Age/metaphysics; philosophy; popular culture; psychology; science/technology; self-help/personal improvement; sex; sociology; spirituality; sports; theater/film; travel; true crime/investigative; women's issues/studies. **Considers these fiction areas:** Action/adventure; confession; contemporary issues; detective/police/crime; ethnic; family saga; feminist; gay/lesbian; glitz; historical; humor/satire; literary; mainstream/contemporary; mystery/suspense; religious/inspirational; spiritual; sports; thriller.

> ◻━ This agency specializes in general interest books. No children's or juvenile.

How to Contact: Query with SASE. No e-mail or fax queries. Considers simultaneous queries. Responds in 1 month to queries. Returns materials only with SASE.

CHECK THE AGENT SPECIALTIES INDEX to find agents who are interested in your specific nonfiction or fiction subject area.

Recent Sales: *A Lady First*, by Letitia Baldrige (Viking); *The Singularity is Near*, by Ray Kurzweil (Viking); *Flesh Tones*, by MJ Rose (Ballantine Books); *The Lake of Dead Languages*, by Carol Goodman (Ballantine Books); *The Bad Witness*, by Laura Van Wormer (Mira Books).

Terms: Agent receives 15% commission on domestic sales; 20% commission on foreign sales. Offers written contract. Charges clients for shipping and photocopying.

Writers' Conferences: San Diego State University Writer's Conference; Maui Writer's Conference.

possible **☑ ⊘ JENNY BENT, HARVEY KLINGER, INC.**, 301 W. 53rd St., New York NY 10019. (212)581-7068. Fax: (212)315-3823. E-mail: JenLBent@aol.com. Website: www.jennybent.com. **Contact:** Jenny Bent. Member of AAR. Represents 60 clients. 40% of clients are new/unpublished writers. Currently handles: 70% nonfiction books; 30% novels.

• Prior to joining her agency, Ms. Bent worked as an editor in book publishing and magazines.

Represents: Nonfiction books, novels. **Considers these nonfiction areas:** Animals; biography/autobiography; ethnic/cultural interests; health/medicine; history; popular culture; psychology; self-help/personal improvement; women's issues/studies. **Considers these fiction areas:** Ethnic; literary; mainstream/contemporary; romance.

O➔ Actively seeking quality fiction and nonfiction from well-credentialed authors. Does not want to receive science fiction, New Age fiction, mysteries, thrillers, children's, self-help from non-credentialed writers.

How to Contact: Query with SASE, submit proposal package, outline, résumé, publishing history, author bio. Please always include a bio or résumé with submissions or queries. Accepts e-mail queries, but no attachments. Considers simultaneous queries and submissions. Responds in 1 month to queries; 2 months to mss. Returns materials only with SASE. Obtains most new clients through recommendations from others, solicitations, conferences.

Recent Sales: Sold 20 titles in the last year. *Red Ant House*, by Ann Cummins (Houghton Mifflin); *Makeover Moms Meal Club*, by Liz Weiss and Janice N. Bissey (Broadway).

Terms: Agent receives 15% commission on domestic sales; 25% commission on foreign sales. Offers written contract; 30-day notice must be given to terminate contract. Charges for overnight mail, out-of-office photocopies (deducted from advance).

⊘ PAM BERNSTEIN & ASSOCIATES, INC., 790 Madison Ave., Suite 310, New York NY 10021. (212)288-1700. Fax: (212)288-3054. Estab. 1992. Member of AAR.

• Prior to becoming an agent, Ms. Bernstein served as vice president with the William Morris Agency. Currently not accepting submissions.

trial Carmen *possible* **⊘ MEREDITH BERNSTEIN LITERARY AGENCY**, 2112 Broadway, Suite 503A, New York NY 10023. (212)799-1007. Fax: (212)799-1145. Estab. 1981. Member of AAR. Represents 100 clients. 20% of clients are new/unpublished writers. Currently handles: 50% nonfiction books; 50% novels.

• Prior to opening her agency, Ms. Bernstein served in another agency for 5 years.

Member Agents: Meredith Bernstein; Elizabeth Cavanaugh.

Represents: Nonfiction books, novels. **Considers these nonfiction areas:** Animals (pets); business/economics (and e-commerce); child guidance/parenting; creative nonfiction; government/politics/law; health/medicine; psychology; science/technology; spirituality. **Considers these fiction areas:** Literary; mystery/suspense; romance; women's fiction.

O➔ This agency does not specialize, "very eclectic."

How to Contact: Query with SASE. No e-mail or fax queries. Considers simultaneous queries. Obtains most new clients through recommendations from others, conferences, also develops and packages own ideas.

Recent Sales: *The Botox Book*, by Dr. Michael Kane (St. Martin's); *No More Knee Pain*, by Dr. George Kessler (Berkley).

Terms: Agent receives 15% commission on domestic sales; 20% commission on foreign sales. Charges clients $75 disbursement fee/year.

Writers' Conferences: Southwest Writers Conference (Albuquereque, August); Rocky Mountain Writers' Conference (Denver, September); Golden Triangle (Beaumont TX, October); Pacific Northwest Writers Conference; Austin League Writers Conference; Willamette Writers Conference (Portland, OR); Lafayette Writers Conference (Lafayette, LA); Surrey Writers Conference (Surrey, BC.); San Diego State University Writers Conference (San Diego, CA).

Tips: "Don't give up."

⊘ DANIEL BIAL AGENCY, 41 W. 83rd St., Suite 5-C, New York NY 10024-5246. (212)721-1786. Fax: (309)213-0230. E-mail: dbialagency@juno.com. **Contact:** Daniel Bial. Estab. 1992. Represents under 50 clients. 15% of clients are new/unpublished writers. Currently handles: 95% nonfiction books; 5% novels.

• Prior to opening his agency, Mr. Bial was an editor for 15 years.

Represents: Nonfiction books, novels. **Considers these nonfiction areas:** Animals; anthropology/archaeology; biography/autobiography; business/economics; child guidance/parenting; cooking/foods/nutrition; current affairs; ethnic/cultural interests; gay/lesbian issues; government/politics/law; history; how-to; humor/satire; language/literature/criticism; memoirs; military/war; money/finance; music/dance; nature/environment; New Age/metaphysics; popular culture; psychology; religious/inspirational; science/technology; self-help/personal improvement; sociology; spirituality; sports; theater/film; travel; true crime/investigative; women's issues/studies. **Considers these fiction areas:** Action/adventure; comic books/cartoon; confession; contemporary issues; detective/police/crime; erotica; ethnic; feminist; gay/lesbian; humor/satire; literary.

How to Contact: Submit proposal package, outline. Responds in 2 weeks to queries. Returns materials only with SASE. Obtains most new clients through recommendations from others, solicitations, "good rolodex"

Recent Sales: This agency recently had a number one New York Times bestseller with *Osama Bin Ladin: The Man Who Declared War on America*, by Yossef Bodansky.

Terms: Agent receives 15% commission on domestic sales; 25% commission on foreign sales. Offers written contract, binding for 1 year with cancellation clause. Charges clients for overseas calls, overnight mailing, photocopying, messenger expenses.

Tips: "Good marketing is a key to success at all stages of publishing—successful authors know how to market themselves as well as their writing."

BIGSCORE PRODUCTIONS INC., P.O. Box 4575, Lancaster PA 17604. (717)293-0247. Fax: (717)293-1945. E-mail: bigscore@bigscoreproductions.com. Website: www.bigscoreproductions.com. **Contact:** David A. Robie. Estab. 1995. Represents 15-25 clients. 25% of clients are new/unpublished writers.

● Mr. Robie is also the president of Starburst Publishers, an inspirational publisher that publishes books for both the general and Christian markets.

Represents: Nonfiction books, novels.

○➤ This agency specializes in inspirational and self-help nonfiction and fiction.

How to Contact: See website for guidelines. Query by e-mail or mail. No email attachments unless requested. No fax queries. Considers simultaneous queries. Responds in 1 month to proposals.

Terms: Agent receives 15% commission on domestic sales. Offers written contract, binding for 6 months. Charges clients for shipping, ms photocopying, ms photocopying and preparation, and books for subsidiary rights submissions.

Tips: "Very open to taking on new clients. Submit a well-prepared proposal that will take minimal fine-tuning for presentation to publishers. Nonfiction writers must be highly marketable and media savvy—the more established in speaking or in your profession, the better. Bigscore Productions works with all major general and Christian publishers."

VICKY BIJUR, 333 West End Ave., Apt. 513, New York NY 10023. Member and past president of AAR.

● This agency did not respond to our request for information. Query before submitting.

DAVID BLACK LITERARY AGENCY, 156 Fifth Ave., New York NY 10010. (212)242-5080. Fax: (212)924-6609. **Contact:** David Black, owner. Estab. 1990. Member of AAR. Represents 150 clients. Currently handles: 90% nonfiction books; 10% novels.

Member Agents: Susan Raihofer (general nonfiction to literary fiction); Gary Morris (commercial fiction to psychology); Joy E. Tutela (general nonfiction to literary fiction); Laureen Rowland (business, health).

Represents: Nonfiction books, novels. **Considers these nonfiction areas:** Biography/autobiography; business/economics; government/politics/law; history; memoirs; military/war; money/finance; multicultural; sports. **Considers these fiction areas:** Literary; mainstream/contemporary; commercial.

○➤ This agency specializes in business, sports, politics, and novels.

How to Contact: Query with SASE, outline. No e-mail or fax queries. Considers simultaneous queries. Responds in 2 months to queries. Returns materials only with SASE.

Recent Sales: *Body for Life*, by Bill Phillips with Mike D'Orso (HarperCollins); *Walking with the Wind*, by John Lewis with Micke D'Orso (Simon & Schuster).

Terms: Agent receives 15% commission on domestic sales. Charges clients for photocopying and books purchased for sale of foreign rights.

BLEECKER STREET ASSOCIATES, INC., 532 LaGuardia Place, #617, New York NY 10012. (212)677-4492. Fax: (212)388-0001. **Contact:** Agnes Birnbaum. Estab. 1984. Member of AAR, RWA, MWA. Represents 60 clients. 20% of clients are new/unpublished writers. Currently handles: 75% nonfiction books; 25% novels.

● Prior to becoming an agent, Ms. Birnbaum was a senior editor at Simon & Schuster, Dutton/Signet and other publishing houses.

Represents: Nonfiction books, novels. **Considers these nonfiction areas:** Animals; biography/autobiography; business/economics; child guidance/parenting; computers/electronic; cooking/foods/nutrition; current affairs; ethnic/cultural interests; government/politics/law; health/medicine; history; how-to; memoirs; military/war; money/finance; nature/environment; New Age/metaphysics; popular culture; psychology; religious/inspirational; science/technology; self-help/personal improvement; sociology; sports; true crime/investigative; women's issues/studies. **Considers these fiction areas:** Ethnic; historical; literary; mystery/suspense; romance; thriller; women's (interest).

○➤ "We're very hands-on and accessible. We try to be truly creative in our submission approaches. We've had especially good luck with first-time authors." Does not want to receive science fiction, westerns, poetry, children's books, academic/scholarly/professional books, plays, scripts, short stories.

How to Contact: Query with SASE. No email, phone or fax queries. Considers simultaneous queries. Responds in 2 weeks to queries; 1 month to mss. Returns materials only with SASE. Obtains most new clients through recommendations from others, solicitations, conferences, "plus, I will approach someone with a letter if his/her work impresses me."

Recent Sales: Sold 34 titles in the last year. *The Art of War*, by Bevin Alexander (Crown); *Mars on a Budget*, by Andrew Mishkin (Berkley Books); *Ghosts*, by Brad Steiger (Visible Ink Press).

Terms: Agent receives 15% commission on domestic sales; 25% commission on foreign sales. Offers written contract; 30-day notice must be given to terminate contract. Charges for postage, long distance, fax, messengers, photocopies, not to exceed $200.

Tips: "Keep query letters short and to the point; include only information pertaining to book or background as writer. Try to avoid superlatives in description. Work needs to stand on its own, so how much editing it may have received has no place in a query letter."

REID BOATES LITERARY AGENCY, 69 Cooks Crossroad, Pittstown NJ 08867. (908)730-8523. Fax: (908)730-8931. E-mail: boatesliterary@att.net. **Contact:** Reid Boates. Estab. 1985. Represents 45 clients. 5% of clients are new/unpublished writers. Currently handles: 85% nonfiction books; 15% novels; very rarely story collections.

How to Contact: No unsolicited queries of any kind. New clients by personal referral only.

Recent Sales: Sold 20 titles in the last year. This agency prefers not to share information on specific sales.

Terms: Agent receives 15% commission on domestic sales; 20% commission on foreign sales. Charges clients for photocopying costs above $50.

BOOK DEALS, INC., 244 Fifth Ave., Suite 216, New York NY 10001-7604. (212)252-2701. Fax: (212)591-6211. E-mail: bookdeals@aol.com. Website: www.bookdealsinc.com. **Contact:** Caroline Francis Carney. Estab. 1996. Member of AAR. Represents 40 clients. 15% of clients are new/unpublished writers. Currently handles: 85% nonfiction books; 15% novels.

- Prior to opening her agency, Ms. Carney was editorial director for a consumer book imprint within Times Mirror and held senior editorial positions in McGraw-Hill and NYIF/Simon & Schuster.

Represents: Nonfiction books, novels (commercial and literary). **Considers these nonfiction areas:** Business/economics; child guidance/parenting; ethnic/cultural interests; health/medicine (nutrition); history; how-to; money/finance; multicultural; popular culture; psychology (popular); religious/inspirational; science/technology; self-help/personal improvement; spirituality. **Considers these fiction areas:** Ethnic; literary; mainstream/contemporary; women's (contemporary); urban literature.

- This agency specializes in highly commercial nonfiction and "authors with large circles of influence." Actively seeking well-crafted fiction and nonfiction from authors with engaging voices and impeccable credentials.

How to Contact: Query with SASE. Accept e-mail queries.

Recent Sales: Sold 25 titles in the last year. *Eat Right for Your Personality Type*, by Dr. Robert Kushner & Nancy Kushner (St. Martin's Press); *Self-Proclaimed*, by Rochelle Shapiro (Simon & Schuster); *Par for the Course*, by Alice Dye and Mark Shaw (HarperCollins).

Terms: Agent receives 15% commission on domestic sales; 20% commission on foreign sales. Offers written contract. Charges clients for photocopying and postage.

Tips: "If you have Internet access, please visit our website before submitting a query letter. It has a lot of insider tips to assist you in your search."

THE BOOK PEDDLERS, 15245 Minnetonka Blvd., Minnetonka MN 55345-1510. **Contact:** Vicki Lansky. Member of AAR.

- This agency did not respond to our request for information. Query before submitting.

BOOKENDS, LLC, 136 Long Hill Rd., Gillette NJ 07933. (908)604-2652. E-mail: editor@bookends-inc.com. Website: www.bookends-inc.com. **Contact:** Jessica Faust or Jacky Sach. Estab. 1999. Represents 50 clients. 60% of clients are new/unpublished writers. Currently handles: 50% nonfiction books; 50% novels.

- Prior to opening their agency, Ms. Faust and Ms. Sach worked at such publishing houses as Berkley, Penguin Putnam, Macmillan and IDG.

Member Agents: Jessica Faust (mysteries, romance, relationships, business, finance, pets, general self-help); Jacky Sach (suspense thrillers, mysteries, literary fiction, spirituality, pets, general self-help).

Represents: Nonfiction books, novels. **Considers these nonfiction areas:** Animals; biography/autobiography; business/economics; child guidance/parenting; cooking/foods/nutrition; crafts/hobbies; current affairs; ethnic/cultural interests; gay/lesbian issues; health/medicine; how-to; humor/satire; memoirs; money/finance; New Age/metaphysics; psychology; religious/inspirational; self-help/personal improvement; women's issues/studies. **Considers these fiction areas:** Contemporary issues; detective/police/crime; ethnic; family saga; feminist; glitz; historical; literary; mainstream/contemporary; mystery/suspense; romance; thriller.

- BookEnds specializes in genre fiction and personality driven nonfiction. Actively seeking romance, mystery, women's fiction, literary fiction and suspense thrillers. For nonfiction, relationships, business, general self-help, women's interest, parenting, pets, spirituality, health and psychology. Does not want to receive children's books, screenplays, science fiction, poetry, technical/military thrillers.

How to Contact: Submit outline, 3 sample chapter(s). Considers simultaneous queries. Responds in 6 weeks to queries; 8-10 weeks to mss. Returns materials only with SASE. Obtains most new clients through recommendations from others, solicitations, conferences.

Recent Sales: Sold 40 titles in the last year. *Women at Ground Zero*, by Mary Carouba and Susan Hagen (Alpha); *Soapmaking: A Magickal Guide*, by Alicia Grosso (Career Press); *Streetwise Guide to Publicity*, by Sandra Beckwith (Adams Media); *Managing your Parents' Money*, by Sharon Burns, Ph.D., and Dr. Ray Laforge (McGraw-Hill); *And a Hard Rain Fell*, by John Ketwig (Sourcebooks); *Pills for Pets*, by Debra Eldredge (Kensington Books); *Drawing for Dummies*, by Brenda Hodinnott (Hungry Minds).

Terms: Agent receives 15% commission on domestic sales; 20% commission on foreign sales. Offers written contract. Charges clients for photocopying, messenger, cables, overseas postage, long-distance phone calls, copies of the published book when purchases for subsidiary rights submissions. Expenses will not exceed $150.

Writers' Conferences: Central Florida Romance Writers Conference (Orlando FL, September); Emerald Coast Writers Conference (Seattle WA, October); Southwest Writers (Albuquerque NM, September); Harriet Austin (Athens GA, July).

Tips: "When submitting material be sure to include any information that might be helpful to the agent. In your query letter you should include the title of the book, your name, your publishing history and a brief 1 or 2 sentence description of the book. Also be sure to let the agent know if you see this book as part of a series and if you've already begun work on other books. Once an agent has expressed interest in representing you it is crucial to let her know who has seen your book and even supply copies of any correspondence you've had with prospective editors."

BOOKS & SUCH, (Specialized: Christian market), 4788 Carissa Ave., Santa Rosa CA 94505. (707)538-4184. Fax: (707)538-3937. E-mail: jkgbooks@aol.com. Website: janetgrant.com. **Contact:** Janet Kobobel Grant. Estab. 1996. Member of CBA (associate). Represents 40 clients. 20% of clients are new/unpublished writers. Currently handles: 42% nonfiction books; 46% novels; 2% juvenile books; 10% children's picture books.

• Before becoming an agent, Ms. Grant was an editor for Zondervan and managing editor for Focus on the Family.

Represents: Nonfiction books, novels, juvenile books. **Considers these nonfiction areas:** Child guidance/parenting; humor/satire; juvenile nonfiction; religious/inspirational; self-help/personal improvement; women's issues/studies. **Considers these fiction areas:** Contemporary issues; family saga; historical; juvenile; mainstream/contemporary; picture books; religious/inspirational; romance; young adult.

Oㅠ This agency specializes in "general and inspirational fiction, romance, and in the Christian booksellers market." Actively seeking "material appropriate to the Christian market."

How to Contact: Query with SASE. Considers simultaneous queries. Responds in 1 month to queries; 2 months to mss. Returns materials only with SASE. Obtains most new clients through recommendations from others, conferences.

Recent Sales: Sold 31 titles in the last year. *Gentle Passages*, by Robin Jones Gunn (Multnomah Publishers); *Fair Haven*, by BJ Hoff (W Publishing). Other clients include Janet McHenry, Jane Orcutt, Gayle Roper, Stephanie Grace Whitson.

Terms: Agent receives 15% commission on domestic sales; 15% commission on foreign sales. Offers written contract; 2-month notice must be given to terminate contract. Charges clients for postage, photocopying, telephone calls, fax and express mail.

Writers' Conferences: Romance Writers of America; Mt. Hermon Writers Conference (Mt. Hermon CA, March 22-26); Glorieta Writers Conference (Santa Fe NM, October).

Tips: "The heart of my motivation is to develop relationships with the authors I serve, to do what I can to shine the light of success on them, and to help be a caretaker of their gifts and time."

GEORGES BORCHARDT INC., 136 E. 57th St., New York NY 10022. (212)753-5785. Fax: (212)838-6518. Estab. 1967. Member of AAR. Represents 200 clients. 10% of clients are new/unpublished writers. Currently handles: 60% nonfiction books; 37% novels; 1% novellas; 1% juvenile books; 1% poetry.

Member Agents: Anne Borchardt; Georges Borchardt; DeAnna Heindel; Valerie Borchardt.

Represents: Nonfiction books, novels. **Considers these nonfiction areas:** Anthropology/archaeology; biography/autobiography; current affairs; history; memoirs; travel; women's issues/studies. **Considers these fiction areas:** Literary.

Oㅠ This agency specializes in literary fiction and outstanding nonfiction.

How to Contact: Responds in 1 week to queries; 1 month to mss. Obtains most new clients through recommendations from others.

Recent Sales: Sold 100 titles in the last year. *An Atonement*, by Ian McEwan (Nan Talese-Doubleday); *Brown*, by Richard Rodriguez (Viking Penguin).

Terms: Agent receives 15% commission on domestic sales; 20% commission on foreign sales. Offers written contract. "We charge clients cost of outside photocopying and shipping manuscripts or books overseas."

insider report

The Night-Shift Novelist: Squeezing in time to write and research

William Casey Moreton knows a thing or two about hard work: In the nine years between starting his political thriller, *The Greater Good*, and its sale to Atria Books (a division of Pocket), Moreton spent his nights and weekends working in warehouses, doing back-breaking manual labor. And through this near-decade, Moreton held onto the hope that, one day, he'd be able to make a living as an author. And then, one morning after getting home from work, he answered the phone and found that it was happening.

"It was surreal. If you've been rejected for nine years, and then that first person calls and says they think you've written something great and they want to represent you . . . man, it was absolutely surreal, it was unbelievable." The phone call was from Frank Weimann of the Literary Group, the man who wasted no time in selling Moreton's book to Emily Bestler at Pocket Books. "He thought I had something that was going to really work. Then he sold it so fast, and that was unbelievable—he sold it within four weeks of signing me up."

Moreton hadn't always had literary aspirations, though. Growing up in Rogers, Arkansas, Moreton enjoyed reading as a child and even dabbled at writing short stories, but he never gave any thought to making a career out of it. After graduating from Southwest Baptist University, a tiny university in Missouri, with a bachelor of arts in religious studies, Moreton didn't know what he wanted to do, so he went to work in a warehouse to pay the bills. "We lived in Missouri at the time, and it's a pretty rural community, there's not a lot of industry. So I started working in a warehouse, filling orders. It's rough, hot, sweaty work, the pay's not too great, and it breaks you down after a while."

But it was during this time that Moreton came up with the idea of writing a book. "I guess I was reading a thriller of some sort, and I thought, 'I can do that.' So I started piddling with it and, before I knew it, I was pretty serious." The process of writing the book and pulling 12-hour warehouse shifts proved a challenge, but Moreton came up with a way to do both at the same time. "I would keep 3×5 index cards and a pencil in my back pocket, and as I was working through the night, I would stop periodically and jot down my story. That's how the bulk of the story was written—it was just a minute here and a minute there, and when I'd get home in the morning, I'd try to find the time to type it up on the computer."

Piece by piece he put together the thriller that his agency details on their website, www.theliterarygroup.com, with this gripping premise: "Hours before a renowned assassin's bullet rips through his bedroom window, Vice President James Ettinger makes a confession on a videotape that could bring the current White House administration to its knees. Suddenly, the race is on to find the video tape, and those responsible for his death will stop at nothing to make sure Ettinger's final words are never heard." But coming up with a high-concept premise and learning to write a commercially successful book required research. "I knew what I liked to read,"

Moreton says, "but it took a long time to figure out what to write about and how to come up with a sellable story. I'd read a lot, not necessarily because I like to, but to figure out what sells and doesn't sell. There's so much stuff that's published, but I'd look at what's successful, the books that make it onto the bestseller list and the ones that don't, and I'd compare what I do with those." Moreton describes this process as "painful," as it forced him to evaluate the work that he was producing. "As a novelist, at least with me, you live in doubt of whether it's good enough. I think the best sellers in the world would tell you the same thing, regardless of the level of their success. You never, I think, reach a point where you're absolutely confident with what you do. I think the most important thing is you have to be honest with yourself and decide whether you have the ability to do what it is you want to do."

Moreton discovered that there was a lot he needed to know in order to get the attention of agents. "When I started working on the manuscript, the process of getting it published never occurred to me, so I just plowed ahead and tried to get it done. Then when I got to a point where I thought I was ready to submit, I found you have to put nearly as much effort into your query letter and into approaching an agent as you do to writing your book. I learned that [agents] receive hundreds and hundreds of these letters every month, and that's all they do is read, and they want something as brief as possible. My letters started out being 300 or 400 words—something about me, something about the book—and I learned that you've got to be as short as possible, because that's how you get their attention." He also turned to print resources (including *Guide to Literary Agents*) for tips. "I always used to buy them because they had the little articles in there, and I would just read and reread them, looking for some little morsel of information that would help me. And I was always buying *Writer's Digest* magazine, hoping for something that would help me out. And they did. You glean a little bit of information from a lot of different sources."

Another thing Moreton discovered was that seeking an agent involves learning how to cope with rejection. "It took me a long, long time and probably 200 rejections before anyone even asked to see the manuscript. It was a terribly long and arduous process. It's all about rejection, learning how to cope with rejection, and figuring out what you're doing wrong, figuring out what succeeds in the literary world." He began to gain some perspective that helped him deal with the frustration of constant rejection. "There's really two different levels of rejection—there's the letter getting rejected, and then there's the manuscript being rejected, and you've got to separate the two. I got 300 or more rejections on my letters, but I think only a couple of agents rejected the actual manuscript. When you look at it like that it doesn't feel nearly as bad, but you have to wade through so many of those letters before somebody will ask for even a partial manuscript."

And then Weimann called, and Moreton realized exactly why he had persevered all those years and not given up. "I was waiting for somebody within the industry to give me [validation]. It's one thing when friends and family say it's good, and it's another thing when somebody within the industry says it's good." Weimann was able to secure a two-book contract for Moreton, a deal that the author sees as justification for the nine years of seeking publication. "It's just unbelievable—as I sat down to start the second book, I knew that it would be published and that all I had to do was worry about writing it. When I get done with it, I won't have to worry about sending out letters and hoping I can find somebody who will be interested in it. It's very empowering. It gives me a tremendous amount of freedom. And to know that some-body believes in my work—it's really hard to describe how that feels."

Moreton's quick to point out that his success was as much a matter of perseverance as it was the quality of his work and encourages aspiring writers to hang in there in the face of rejection. "If you've really got the goods, it's just about not giving up. I've had conversations with Brad Meltzer and he told me, 'You only need one person to say yes.' That's really what it comes down to."

"Mainly it's deciding that you've got whatever talent is required, and it's about telling stories. It's not a matter of how good a 'writer' you are—a good 'writer' is about good grammar and punctuation and being accurate—but storytelling is just about sitting around the fire and telling stories and keeping people on the edge of their seats. If you come to a point where you realize you've got a way with words to tell a story, and you believe what you're doing is worthwhile, then it's all about perseverance. As any agent will tell you, they reject thousands of letters and hundreds of manuscripts a year, but their job is to find a couple of manuscripts a year that are publishable. They've got to have new novelists every year to publish, so I figured, if I hang in there long enough, I'll get my shot at some point."

Moreton's currently writing his second novel, and he's still employed at a warehouse, working the weekend night shift in the computer department of a Wal-Mart distribution center—though the sale of *The Greater Good* will soon allow him to be a full-time writer.

—*Rodney Wilson*

THE BOSTON LITERARY GROUP, 156 Mount Auburn St., Cambridge MA 02138-4875. (617)547-0800. Fax: (617)876-8474. E-mail: agent@bostonliterary.com. **Contact:** Elizabeth Mack. Estab. 1994. Member of PEN New England. Represents 30 clients. 25% of clients are new/unpublished writers. Currently handles: 100% nonfiction books.
Member Agents: Kirsten Wainwright (psychology, biography, health, current events, memoir, business); Heather Moehn (science, history, fiction).
Represents: Nonfiction books. **Considers these nonfiction areas:** Animals; anthropology/archaeology; art/architecture/design; biography/autobiography; business/economics; child guidance/parenting; current affairs; ethnic/cultural interests; government/politics/law; health/medicine; history; military/war; money/finance; nature/environment; photography; psychology; science/technology; sociology; true crime/investigative; women's issues/studies.
  ☛ Actively seeking "nonfiction manuscripts that have something new and fascinating to say. Good writing skills are essential." Does not want to receive poetry, cookbooks, children's literature or fiction.
How to Contact: Query with SASE. Prefers to read materials exclusively. Accepts e-mail and fax queries. Responds in 6 weeks to queries. Returns materials only with SASE. Obtains most new clients through recommendations from others, journal articles.
Recent Sales: Sold 10 titles in the last year. *Zero: The Biography of a Dangerous Idea*, by Charles Seife (Viking Penguin); *The Skin We're In: Teaching Our Children to be Emotionally Strong*, by Janie Ward (Free Press); *The Change Monster*, by Jeannie Daniel Dock (Crown Business).
Terms: Agent receives 15% commission on domestic sales; 10% commission on foreign sales. Offers written contract, binding for 1 year; 60-day notice must be given to terminate contract. Charges clients for expenses associated with manuscript submissions (postage, photocopy); makes referrals to editing service. "We matchmake with development editors on promising projects."

BRADY LITERARY MANAGEMENT, P.O. Box 164, Hartland Four Corners VT 05049. **Contact:** Upton Brady. Estab. 1988. Represents 100 clients.
Represents: Nonfiction books, novels, short story collections, novellas. **Considers these fiction areas:** Literary; mainstream/contemporary.
How to Contact: Query with SASE, submit outline, 2 sample chapters for nonfiction; first 50 pages for fiction. Responds in 2 months to queries.
Recent Sales: This agency prefers not to share information on specific sales.
Terms: Agent receives 15% commission on domestic sales; 20% commission on foreign sales. Charges clients for extensive international postage and photocopying.

BRANDT & HOCHMAN LITERARY AGENTS INC., 1501 Broadway, New York NY 10036. (212)840-5760. Fax: (212)840-5776. **Contact:** Carl Brandt; Gail Hochman (current president of AAR); Marianne Merola; Charles Schlessiger; Meg Giles. Estab. 1913. Member of AAR. Represents 200 clients.
Represents: Nonfiction books, novels, short story collections, novellas, juvenile books, journalism. **Considers these nonfiction areas:** Biography/autobiography; current affairs; ethnic/cultural interests; government/politics/law; health/medicine; history; nature/environment; psychology; science/technology; theater/film; true crime/investigative; women's issues/studies. **Considers these fiction areas:** Action/adventure; contemporary issues; ethnic; family saga; historical; literary; mainstream/contemporary; mystery/suspense; romance; thriller; young adult.
How to Contact: Query with SASE. No fax queries. Considers simultaneous queries. Responds in 1 month to queries. Returns materials only with SASE. Obtains most new clients through recommendations from others.
Recent Sales: Sold 50 titles in the last year. This agency prefers not to share information on specific sales. Other clients include Scott Turow, Carlos Fuentes, Ursula Hegi, Michael Cunningham, Mary Pope Osborne.
Terms: Agent receives 15% commission on domestic sales; 20% commission on foreign sales. Charges clients for "manuscript duplication or other special expenses agreed to in advance."
Tips: "Write a letter which will give the agent a sense of you as a professional writer, your long-term interests as well as a short description of the work at hand."

THE JOAN BRANDT AGENCY, 788 Wesley Dr., Atlanta GA 30305-3933. (404)351-8877. **Contact:** Joan Brandt. Estab. 1980. Represents 30 clients. 50% of clients are new/unpublished writers. Currently handles: 45% nonfiction books; 45% novels; 10% juvenile books.
Represents: Nonfiction books, novels, short story collections. **Considers these fiction areas:** Contemporary issues; detective/police/crime; family saga; literary; mainstream/contemporary; mystery/suspense; thriller.
How to Contact: Query with SASE. No e-mail or fax queries. Considers simultaneous queries. Returns materials only with SASE. Obtains most new clients through solicitations.
Recent Sales: This agency prefers not to share information on specific sales.
Terms: Agent receives 15% commission on domestic sales; 20% commission on foreign sales. No written contract.

THE HELEN BRANN AGENCY, INC., 94 Curtis Rd., Bridgewater CT 06752. Member of AAR.
● This agency did not respond to our request for information. Query before submitting.

N BARBARA BRAUN ASSOCIATES, INC., 115 W. 18th St., 5th floor, New York NY 10011. **Contact:** Barbara Braun. Member of AAR.
● This agency did not respond to our request for information. Query before submitting.

M. COURTNEY BRIGGS, 100 N. Broadway Ave., 20th Floor, Oklahoma City OK 73102-8806. **Contact:** M. Courtney Briggs. Estab. 1994. 25% of clients are new/unpublished writers. Currently handles: 5% nonfiction books; 10% novels; 80% juvenile books; 5% multimedia.
● Prior to becoming an agent, Ms. Briggs was in subsidiary rights at Random House for 3 years; an associate agent and film rights associate with Curtis Brown, Ltd.; also an attorney for 10 years.
Represents: Nonfiction books, novels, juvenile books. **Considers these nonfiction areas:** Animals; biography/autobiography; health/medicine; juvenile nonfiction; self-help/personal improvement; young adult. **Considers these fiction areas:** Juvenile; mainstream/contemporary; picture books; young adult.
☞ M. Courtney Briggs is an agent and an attorney. "I work primarily, but not exclusively, with children's book authors and illustrators. I will also consult or review a contract on an hourly basis." Actively seeking children's fiction, children's picture books (illustrations and text), young adult novels, fiction, nonfiction.
How to Contact: Query with SASE. No e-mail or fax queries. Responds in 2 weeks to queries; 6 weeks to mss. Returns materials only with SASE. Obtains most new clients through recommendations from others.
Recent Sales: This agency prefers not to share information on specific sales.
Terms: Agent receives 15% commission on domestic sales; 25% commission on foreign sales. Offers written contract; 60-day notice must be given to terminate contract.
Writers' Conferences: National Conference on Writing & Illustrating for Children (August).

MARIE BROWN ASSOCIATES INC., 412 W. 154th St., New York NY 10032. (212)939-9725. Fax: (212)939-9728. E-mail: mbrownlit@aol.com. **Contact:** Marie Brown. Estab. 1984. Represents 60 clients. Currently handles: 75% nonfiction books; 10% juvenile books; 15% other.
Member Agents: Janell Walden Agyeman.
Represents: Nonfiction books, juvenile books. **Considers these nonfiction areas:** Art/architecture/design; biography/autobiography; business/economics; ethnic/cultural interests; history; juvenile nonfiction; music/dance; religious/inspirational; self-help/personal improvement; theater/film; women's issues/studies. **Considers these fiction areas:** Contemporary issues; ethnic; juvenile; literary; mainstream/contemporary.
☞ This agency specializes in multicultural and African-American writers.
How to Contact: Query with SASE. Prefers to read materials exclusively. Responds in 6 weeks to queries. Obtains most new clients through recommendations from others.

Recent Sales: *Satisfy My Soul*, by Colin Channer (Ballantine/One World); *The Reckoning and Exile*, by Randall Robinson (Dutton); *33 Things Every Girl Should Know About Women's History*, by Tonya Bolden (Crown).
Terms: Agent receives 15% commission on domestic sales; 20% commission on foreign sales. Offers written contract.

■ ◪ ◎ **ANDREA BROWN LITERARY AGENCY, INC., (Specialized: juvenile)**, P.O. Box 371027, Montara CA 94037-1027. (650)728-1783. Fax: (650)728-1732. E-mail: ablitag@pacbell.net. **Contact:** Andrea Brown, president. Estab. 1981. Member of WNBA, SCBWI. 10% of clients are new/unpublished writers. Currently handles: 95% juvenile nonfiction; 5% adult nonfiction books.
   • Prior to opening her agency, Ms. Brown served as an editorial assistant at Random House and Dell Publishing and as an editor with Alfred A. Knopf.
Member Agents: Andrea Brown (middle-grade, YA fiction, pop culture); Laura Rennert (adult fiction, picture books, photo books, historical); Laurel Newby (juvenile, biography, nonfiction).
Represents: Nonfiction books (juvenile). **Considers these nonfiction areas:** Animals; anthropology/archaeology; art/architecture/design; biography/autobiography; current affairs; ethnic/cultural interests; history; how-to; juvenile nonfiction; nature/environment; photography; popular culture; science/technology; sociology; sports; all nonfiction subjects for juveniles. **Considers these fiction areas:** Juvenile; young adult; all fiction genres for juveniles.
   ☛ This agency specializes in "all kinds of children's books—illustrators and authors." Considers all juvenile fiction areas; all genres of nonfiction.
How to Contact: Query with SASE. Accepts e-mail queries. No fax queries. Considers simultaneous queries. Responds in 3 to 4 months to queries. Obtains most new clients through recommendations from others, referrals from editors, clients and agents.
Recent Sales: *Not So Scary Monster Handbook*, by Dave Ross (Harper Collins); *Mercedes and the Candy Bomber*, by Margot Raven (Sleeping Bear Press).
Terms: Agent receives 15% commission on domestic sales; 20% commission on foreign sales. Offers written contract. Charges clients for shipping costs.
Writers' Conferences: Austin Writers League; SCBWI, Orange County Conferences; Mills College Childrens Literature Conference (Oakland CA); Asilomar (Pacific Grove CA); Maui Writers Conference; Southwest Writers Conference; San Diego State University Writer's Conference; Big Sur Children's Writing Workshop (Director); William Saroyan Conference; Columbus Writers Conference; Willamette Writers Conference.
Tips: "Query first—so many submissions come in it takes three to four months to get a response. Taking on very few picture books. Must be unique—no rhyme, no anthropomorphism. Handling some adult historical fiction."

◪ **CURTIS BROWN LTD.**, 10 Astor Place, New York NY 10003-6935. (212)473-5400. Also: 1750 Montgomery St., San Francisco CA 94111. (415)954-8566. **Contact:** Perry Knowlton, chairman; Timothy Knowlton, CEO; Peter L. Ginsberg, president. Member of AAR; signatory of WGA.
Member Agents: Laura Blake Peterson; Ellen Geiger; Emilie Jacobson, vice president; Maureen Walters, vice president; Virginia Knowlton (literary, adult, children's); Timothy Knowlton (film, screenplays, plays); Marilyn Marlow, executive vice president; Ed Wintle (film, screenplays, plays); Mitchell Waters; Elizabeth Harding; Douglas Stewart; Kristen Manges; Dave Barber (translation rights).
Represents: Nonfiction books, novels, short story collections, novellas, juvenile books, poetry books, movie scripts, feature film, TV scripts, TV movie of the week, stage plays. **Considers these nonfiction areas:** Agriculture/horticulture; Americana; animals; anthropology/archaeology; art/architecture/design; biography/autobiography; business/economics; child guidance/parenting; computers/electronic; cooking/foods/nutrition; crafts/hobbies; creative nonfiction; current affairs; education; ethnic/cultural interests; gardening; gay/lesbian issues; government/politics/law; health/medicine; history; how-to; humor/satire; interior design/decorating; juvenile nonfiction; language/literature/criticism; memoirs; military/war; money/finance; multicultural; music/dance; nature/environment; New Age/metaphysics; philosophy; photography; popular culture; psychology; recreation; regional; religious/inspirational; science/technology; self-help/personal improvement; sex; sociology; software; spirituality; sports; theater/film; translation; travel; true crime/investigative; women's issues/studies; young adult. **Considers these fiction areas:** Action/adventure; comic books/cartoon; confession; contemporary issues; detective/police/crime; erotica; ethnic; experimental; family saga; fantasy; feminist; gay/lesbian; glitz; gothic; hi-lo; historical; horror; humor/satire; juvenile; literary; mainstream/contemporary; military/war; multicultural; multimedia; mystery/suspense; New Age; occult; picture books; plays; poetry; poetry in translation; psychic/supernatural; regional; religious/inspirational; romance; science fiction; short story collections; spiritual; sports; thriller; transla-

---

IF YOU'RE LOOKING for a particular agent, check the Agents Index to find the specific agency where the agent works. Then check the listing for that agency in the appropriate section.

tion; westerns/frontier; young adult; women's. **Considers these script subject areas:** Action/adventure; comedy; detective/police/crime; ethnic; feminist; gay/lesbian; historical; horror; mainstream; mystery/suspense; psychic/supernatural; romantic comedy; romantic drama; thriller; western/frontier.

How to Contact: Query with SASE. Prefers to read materials exclusively. No unsolicited mss. No e-mail or fax queries. Responds in 3 weeks to queries; 5 weeks to mss. Obtains most new clients through recommendations from others, solicitations, conferences.

Recent Sales: This agency prefers not to share information on specific sales.

Terms: Offers written contract. Charges for photocopying, some postage. "There are no office fees until we sell a manuscript."

☑ ◯ **PEMA BROWNE LTD.**, P.O. Box 4063, North Hollywood CA 91617. Website: www.geocities.com/pemabrowneltd. **Contact:** Perry Browne or Pema Browne. Estab. 1966. Signatory of WGA. Represents 30 clients. Currently handles: 40% nonfiction books; 30% novels & romance novels; 25% juvenile books; 5% movie scripts. *maybe*

- Prior to opening their agency, Mr. Browne was a radio and TV performer; Ms. Browne was a fine artist and art buyer.

Member Agents: Pema Browne (children's fiction and nonfiction, adult nonfiction); Perry Browne (adult fiction, nonfiction).

Represents: Nonfiction books, novels, juvenile books, reference books. **Considers these nonfiction areas:** Business/economics; child guidance/parenting; cooking/foods/nutrition; ethnic/cultural interests; gay/lesbian issues; health/medicine; how-to; juvenile nonfiction; military/war; money/finance; nature/environment; New Age/metaphysics; popular culture; psychology; religious/inspirational; self-help/personal improvement; spirituality; sports; true crime/investigative; women's issues/studies; reference. **Considers these fiction areas:** Action/adventure; contemporary issues; detective/police/crime; erotica; ethnic; feminist; gay/lesbian; glitz; historical; humor/satire; juvenile; literary; mainstream/contemporary (commercial); mystery/suspense; picture books; psychic/supernatural; religious/inspirational; romance (contemporary, gothic, historical, regency); young adult.

- ☛ Actively seeking adult nonfiction, romance, juvenile, middle grade, some young adult, picture books, novelty books.

How to Contact: Query with SASE. No e-mail or fax queries. Responds in 6 weeks to queries; 2 months to mss. Returns materials only with SASE. Obtains most new clients through "editors, authors, *LMP*, *Guide to Literary Agents* and as a result of longevity!"

Recent Sales: *Soul Echoes*, by Dr. Thelma Freedman (Citadel Press); *Sweet Potato Pie*, by Kathleen Lindsey (Lee & Low).

Terms: Agent receives 15% commission on domestic sales; 20% commission on foreign sales.

Tips: "We do not review manuscripts that have been sent out to publishers. If writing romance, be sure to receive guidelines from various romance publishers. In nonfiction, one must have credentials to lend credence to a proposal. Make sure of margins, double-space and use clean, dark type."

N ◯ HOWARD BUCK AGENCY, 80 Eigth Ave., Suite 1107, New York NY 10011. (212)807-7855. **Contact:** Howard Buck or Mark Frisk. Estab. 1981. Represents 75 clients. Currently handles: 75% nonfiction books; 25% novels. *no*

Represents: Nonfiction books, novels. **Considers these nonfiction areas:** Americana; anthropology/archaeology; art/architecture/design; biography/autobiography; business/economics; computers/electronic; cooking/foods/nutrition; creative nonfiction; current affairs; education; ethnic/cultural interests; gay/lesbian issues; government/politics/law; health/medicine; history; humor/satire; language/literature/criticism; memoirs; military/war; money/finance; multicultural; music/dance; nature/environment; philosophy; photography; popular culture; psychology; recreation; regional; religious/inspirational; science/technology; sex; sociology; software; spirituality; sports; theater/film; translation; travel; true crime/investigative; women's issues/studies. **Considers these fiction areas:** Action/adventure; confession; contemporary issues; detective/police/crime; ethnic; experimental; family saga; feminist; gay/lesbian; glitz; historical; humor/satire; literary; mainstream/contemporary; military/war; multicultural; multimedia; mystery/suspense; psychic/supernatural; regional; romance; short story collections; thriller; translation; women's.

- ☛ "We do not read original screenplays."

How to Contact: Query with SASE. Responds in 6 weeks to queries. Obtains most new clients through recommendations from others.

Recent Sales: This agency prefers not to share information on specific sales.

Terms: Agent receives 15% commission on domestic sales. Offers written contract. Charges client for office expenses, postage and photocopying.

◯ **KNOX BURGER ASSOCIATES, LTD.**, 39 ½ Washington Square South, New York NY 10012. Member of AAR.

- This agency did not respond to our request for information. Query before submitting.

⬛ SHEREE BYKOFSKY ASSOCIATES, INC., 16 W. 36th St., 13th Floor, New York NY 10018. Fax: (212)244-0129. E-mail: shereebee@aol.com. Website: www.shereebee.com. **Contact:** Sheree Bykofsky. Estab. 1984, incorporated 1991. Member of AAR, ASJA, WNBA. Currently handles: 80% nonfiction books; 20% novels.

● Prior to opening her agency, Ms. Bykofsky served as executive editor of The Stonesong Press and managing editor of Chiron Press. She is also the author or co-author of more than 17 books. Ms. Bykofsky teaches publishing at NYU and The Learning Anex.

Member Agents: Janet Rosen, associate; Megan Buckley, associate.

Represents: Nonfiction books, novels. **Considers these nonfiction areas:** Americana; animals; anthropology/archaeology; art/architecture/design; biography/autobiography; business/economics; child guidance/parenting; computers/electronic; cooking/foods/nutrition; crafts/hobbies; creative nonfiction; current affairs; education; ethnic/cultural interests; gardening; gay/lesbian issues; government/politics/law; health/medicine; history; how-to; humor/satire; interior design/decorating; language/literature/criticism; memoirs; military/war; money/finance; multicultural; music/dance; nature/environment; New Age/metaphysics; philosophy; photography; popular culture; psychology; recreation; regional; religious/inspirational; science/technology; self-help/personal improvement; sex; sociology; software; spirituality; sports; theater/film; translation; travel; true crime/investigative; women's issues/studies. **Considers these fiction areas:** Literary; mainstream/contemporary.

O➡ This agency specializes in popular reference nonfiction. "I have wide-ranging interests, but it really depends on quality of writing, originality, and how a particular project appeals to me (or not). I take on very little fiction unless I completely love it—it doesn't matter what area or genre." Does not want to receive poetry, material for children, screenplays.

How to Contact: Query with SASE. No unsolicited mss or phone calls. Considers simultaneous queries. Responds in 1 week to queries; 1 month to mss. Returns materials only with SASE. Obtains most new clients through recommendations from others.

Recent Sales: Sold 100 titles in the last year. *10 Sure Signs a Movie Character Is Doomed and Other Movie Lists*, by Richard Roerer (Hyperion); *A Witness Above*, by Andy Straka (Signet); *Open Your Mind, Open Your Life*, by Taroa Gold (Andrews & McMeel).

Terms: Agent receives 15% commission on domestic sales; 15% commission on foreign sales. Offers written contract, binding for 1 year. Charges for postage, photocopying and fax.

Writers' Conferences: ASJA (New York City); Asilomar (Pacific Grove CA); Kent State; Southwestern Writers; Willamette (Portland); Dorothy Canfield Fisher (San Diego); Writers Union (Maui); Pacific NW; IWWG; and many others.

Tips: "Read the agent listing carefully, and comply with guidelines."

CARLISLE & COMPANY, 24 E. 64th St., New York NY 10021. (212)813-1881. Fax: (212)813-9567. E-mail: mtessler@carlisleco.com. Website: www.carlisleco.com. **Contact:** Michelle Tessler. Estab. 1998. Member of AAR. Represents 100 clients. Currently handles: 60% nonfiction books; 35% novels; 5% story collections.

● Prior to opening his agency, Mr. Carlisle was the Vice President of William Morris for 18 years.

Member Agents: Michael Carlisle; Christy Fletcher; Emma Parry; Michelle Tessler; Affiliates: Donald S. Lamm, Robert Bernstein, Paul Bresnick.

Represents: Nonfiction books, novels. **Considers these nonfiction areas:** Biography/autobiography; business/economics; cooking/foods/nutrition; health/medicine; history; memoirs; popular culture; psychology; science/technology; lifestyle. **Considers these fiction areas:** Literary; mainstream/contemporary.

O➡ This agency has "expertise in nonfiction. We have a strong focus on editorial input on fiction before submission." Does not want to receive science fiction, fantasy, or romance.

How to Contact: Query with SASE. Responds in 10 days to queries; 3 weeks to mss. Obtains most new clients through recommendations from others.

Recent Sales: Sold 80 titles in the last year. *The Founding*, by Jay Winik (HarperCollins); *The Piano Turner*, by Daniel Philippe Mason (Knopf); *The Americans*, by David M. Kennedy (Viking).

Terms: Agent receives 15% commission on domestic sales; 20% commission on foreign sales. Offers written contract, binding for 1 book only.

Writers' Conferences: Squaw Valley Community Conference (California).

Tips: "Be sure to write as original a story as possible. Remember, you're asking the public to pay $25 for your book."

⬛ MARIA CARVAINIS AGENCY, INC., 1350 Avenue of the Americas, Suite 2905, New York NY 10019. (212)245-6365. Fax: (212)245-7196. E-mail: mca@mariacarvainisagency.com. **Contact:** Maria Carvainis, president; Frances Kuffel, executive vice president. Estab. 1977. Member of AAR, Authors Guild, ABA, MWA, Novelists Inc., RWA; signatory of WGA. Represents 70 clients. 10% of clients are new/unpublished writers. Currently handles: 34% nonfiction books; 65% novels; 1% poetry.

● Prior to opening her agency, Ms. Carvainis spent more than 10 years in the publishing industry as a senior editor with Macmillan Publishing, Basic Books, Avon Books (where she worked closely with Peter Mayer), and Crown Publishers. Ms. Carvainis has served as a member of the AAR Board of Directors and AAR Treasurer, as well as serving as chair of the AAR Contracts Committee. She presently serves on the AAR Royalty Committee.

Member Agents: Frances Kuffel (Executive Vice President); Anna Del Vecchio (Contracts Associate); Moira Sullivan (Editorial Associate); Elise Shin (Editorial Assistant).
Represents: Nonfiction books, novels. **Considers these nonfiction areas:** Biography/autobiography; history; business/economics; health/medicine; memoirs; science/technology (pop science); women's issues/studies. **Considers these fiction areas:** Literary; mainstream/contemporary; mystery/suspense; historical; romance; thriller; young adult; middle grade.

O⊶ Does not want to receive science fiction or children's.

How to Contact: Query with SASE. Responds in 1 week to queries; 3 months to mss. Obtains most new clients through recommendations from others, conferences, 60% from conferences/referrals; 40% from query letters.
Recent Sales: *The Crush*, by Sandra Brown (Warner Books); *The Guru Guide to Money Management*, by Joseph H. Boyett and Jimmie T. Boyett (John Wiley and Sons); *Trophy Widow*, by Michael Kahn (TOR/Forge); *Paint it Black*, by P.J. Parrish (Kensington); *A Summer to Remember*, by Mary Balogh (Delacorte); *The Truest Heart; the Hidden Heart*, by Candace Camp (Mira Books); *The Floating World*, by Cynthia Gralla (Ballantine Books); *His Wicked Promise*, by Samantha James (Morrow/Avon); *The Airedale Heiress*, by Lee Charles Kelley (Morrow/Avon). Other clients include Sue Erikson Boland, Pam Conrad, Phillip DePoy, Carlos Dews, FDNY Emerald Society Pipes & Drums, Cindy Gerard, Fred Haefle, Hugo Mager, Kristine Rolofson, Janet Mansfield Soares, Charlie Smith, Peter Stark, Ernest Suarez.
Terms: Agent receives 15% commission on domestic sales; 20% commission on foreign sales. Offers written contract, binding for 2 years on a book-by-book basis. Charges clients for foreign postage, bulk copying.
Writers' Conferences: BEA; Frankfurt Book Fair.

◐ ◎ **MARTHA CASSELMAN LITERARY AGENCY, (Specialized: cookbooks)**, P.O. Box 342, Calistoga CA 94515-0342. (707)942-4341. Fax: (707)942-4358. **Contact:** Martha Casselman. Estab. 1978. Member of IACP. Represents 30 clients. Currently handles: 100% nonfiction books.
Represents: Nonfiction books (food-related proposals and cookbooks). **Considers these nonfiction areas:** Agriculture/horticulture; anthropology/archaeology; biography/autobiography; cooking/foods/nutrition; health/ medicine; women's issues/studies.

O⊶ This agency specializes in "nonfiction, especially food books." Does not want to receive children's book material.

How to Contact: Query with SASE, proposal package, outline, 3 sample chapter(s). Do not send any submission without querying first. Does not accept fax or e-mail queries. Considers simultaneous queries. Responds in 3 weeks to queries. Obtains most new clients through recommendations from others.
Recent Sales: Sold 10 titles in the last year.
Terms: Agent receives 15% commission on domestic sales; 20% commission on foreign sales. Charges clients for photocopying, overnight and overseas mailings.
Writers' Conferences: IACP; other food-writers' conferences.
Tips: "No tricky letters; no gimmicks; always include SASE or mailer, or we can't contact you."

◐ **CASTIGLIA LITERARY AGENCY**, 1155 Camino Del Mar, Suite 510, Del Mar CA 92014. (858)755-8761. Fax: (858)755-7063. **Contact:** Julie Castiglia. Estab. 1993. Member of AAR, PEN. Represents 50 clients. Currently handles: 55% nonfiction books; 45% novels.
Member Agents: Winifred Golden; Julie Castiglia.
Represents: Nonfiction books, novels. **Considers these nonfiction areas:** Animals; anthropology/archaeology; biography/autobiography; business/economics; child guidance/parenting; cooking/foods/nutrition; current affairs; ethnic/cultural interests; health/medicine; history; language/literature/criticism; money/finance; nature/environment; New Age/metaphysics; psychology; religious/inspirational; science; self-help/personal improvement; sociology; women's issues/studies. **Considers these fiction areas:** Contemporary issues; ethnic; literary; mainstream/ contemporary; mystery/suspense; women's (especially).

O⊶ Does not want to receive horror, screenplays or academic nonfiction.

How to Contact: Query with SASE. No fax queries. Responds in 2 months to mss. Returns materials only with SASE. Obtains most new clients through recommendations from others, solicitations, conferences.
Recent Sales: Sold 25 titles in the last year. *Ready to Roll*, by Doug Keister (Viking Penguin); *Red Tile Style*, by Arrel Gellner (Penguin); *West of Kabul, East of New York*, by Tamim Ansary (Farrar, Straus & Giroux).
Terms: Agent receives 15% commission on domestic sales; 25% commission on foreign sales. Offers written contract; 6-week notice must be given to terminate contract. Charges clients for Fed Ex or Messenger.
Writers' Conferences: Southwestern Writers Conference (Albuquerque NM, August); National Writers Conference; Willamette Writers Conference (OR); San Diego State University (CA); Writers at Work (Utah); Austin Conference (TX).
Tips: "Be professional with submissions. Attend workshops and conferences before you approach an agent."

◐ **JAMES CHARLTON ASSOCIATES**, 680 Washington St., #2A, New York NY 10014. (212)691-4951. Fax: (212)691-4952. **Contact:** Lisa Friedman. Estab. 1983. Currently handles: 100% nonfiction books.
Represents: Nonfiction books. **Considers these nonfiction areas:** Child guidance/parenting; cooking/foods/ nutrition; health/medicine; how-to; humor/satire; military/war; popular culture; sports.

O⊸ This agency specializes in military history, sports.

How to Contact: Query with SASE. Responds in 2 weeks to queries. Obtains most new clients through recommendations from others.

Recent Sales: Sold 15 titles in the last year. *The Violence Handbook*, by Dr. George Gellert (West View); *Wisdom of the Popes*, by Tom Craughwell (St. Martin's Press).

Terms: Agent receives 15% commission on domestic sales. Offers written contract; 60-day cancellation notice must be given to terminate contract.

Writers' Conferences: Oregon Writer's Conference (Portland); Oklahoma Writer's Conference.

JANE CHELIUS LITERARY AGENCY, 548 Second St., Brooklyn NY 11215. Member of AAR.
● This agency did not respond to our request for information. Query before submitting.

LINDA CHESTER AND ASSOCIATES, 630 Fifth Ave., New York NY 10111. E-mail: submissions @lindachester.com. Website: www.lindachester.com. Member of AAR.
● This agent specializes in nonfiction, spirituality, memoir/biography, pop culture/art, business, health/ psychology, self-help and gift books. Query by e-mail only before submitting.

CINE/LIT REPRESENTATION, P.O. Box 802918, Santa Clarita CA 91380-2918. E-mail: cinelit@ao l.com. Website: www.cinelit.com. **Contact:** Mary Alice Kier. Member of AAR.
● This agency did not respond to our request for information. Query before submitting. Cine/Lit is an entertainment, management and producing partnership formed by Anna Cottle and Mary Alice Kier.

WM CLARK ASSOCIATES, 355 W. 22nd St., New York NY 10011. (212)675-2784. Fax: (646)349- 1658. E-mail: query@wmclark.com. Website: www.wmclark.com. **Contact:** William Clark. Estab. 1999. Member of AAR. 4.25% of clients are new/unpublished writers. Currently handles: 50% nonfiction books; 50% novels.
● Prior to opening WCA, Mr. Clark was an agent at the Virginia Barber Literary Agency and William Morris Agency.

Represents: Nonfiction books, novels, short story collections. **Considers these nonfiction areas:** Art/architec- ture/design; biography/autobiography; current affairs; ethnic/cultural interests; history; memoirs; music/dance; popular culture; religious/inspirational (Eastern religion philosophy only); science/technology; sociology; theater/ film; translation. **Considers these fiction areas:** Contemporary issues; ethnic; historical; literary; mainstream/ contemporary; Southern fiction.
O⊸ "As one of the new breed of media agents recognizing their expanded roles in today's ever-changing media landscape, William Clark represents a diverse range of commercial and literary fiction and quality nonfiction to the book publishing, motion picture, television, and new media fields."

How to Contact: Prefers to read materials exclusively. E-mail queries only. Responds in 1 month to queries. Obtains most new clients through recommendations from others.

Recent Sales: Sold 25 titles in the last year. *Bjork*, by Bjork (Bloomsbury); *Dante's Path*, by Bonney and Richard Schaub (Penguin/Bill Shinker); *Boogie Woogie*, by Danny Moynihan (St. Martin's Press); *Housebroken*, by David Eddie (Riverhead); *Savvy in the City Guides*, (St. Martin's Press); *Stardust Melodies*, by Will Friedwald (Alfred A. Knopf); *Mark Hampton: The Art of Friendship*, by Duane Hampton (HarperCollins). Other clients include Molly Jong-Fast, William Monahan, Cornelia Bailey, James St. James, Jonathan Stone, Dr. Doreen Virtue, Mian Mian.

Terms: Agent receives 15% commission on domestic sales; 20% commission on foreign sales. Offers written contract.

Tips: "E-mail queries should include a general description of the work, a synopsis/outline if available, biographi- cal information, and publishing history, if any."

CLAUSEN, MAYS & TAHAN, LLC, 249 W. 34th St., Suite 605, New York NY 10001-2815. (212)239- 4343. Fax: (212)239-5248. E-mail: cmtassist@aol.com. **Contact:** Stedman Mays, Mary M. Tahan. Estab. 1976. 10% of clients are new/unpublished writers. Currently handles: nonfiction books; novels.

Member Agents: Stedman Mays; Mary M. Tahan; Rachelle Leon.

Represents: Nonfiction books, novels. **Considers these nonfiction areas:** Biography/autobiography; cooking/ foods/nutrition; health/medicine; history; how-to; humor/satire; memoirs; money/finance; psychology; religious/ inspirational; spirituality; women's issues/studies; fashion/beauty/style; relationships; also rights for books op- tioned for TV movies and feature films.

How to Contact: Query with SASE, proposal package, outline. No e-mail or fax queries. Considers simultane- ous queries. Responds in 3 weeks to queries; 1 month to mss. Returns materials only with SASE.

Recent Sales: *The Okinawa Program*, by Bradley J. Willcox, M.D., D. Craig Willcox, Ph.D and Makoto Suzuki, M.D.; *The Power of Apology*, by Beverly Engel (Wiley & Sons); *The Rules for Online Dating*, by Ellen Fein and Sherrie Schneider (Pocket Books); *The Anti-Inflammation Diet*, by Richard Fleming, M.D. with Tom Monte (Putnam).

Terms: Agent receives 15% commission on domestic sales; 20% commission on foreign sales. Charges clients for postage, shipping, and photocopying.

Tips: "Research proposal writing and the publishing process. Always study your book's competition. Send a proposal and outline instead of complete manuscript for faster response. Always pitch books in writing, not over the phone."

◐ **CLIENT FIRST—A/K/A LEO P. HAFFEY AGENCY**, P.O. Box 128049, Nashville TN 37212-8049. (615)463-2388. E-mail: c1st@nashville.net. Website: www.c-1st.com. **Contact:** Robin Swensen. Estab. 1990. Signatory of WGA. Represents 21 clients. 25% of clients are new/unpublished writers. Currently handles: 40% novels; 60% movie scripts.
   • See the expanded listing for this agency in Script Agents.

◐ **RUTH COHEN, INC. LITERARY AGENCY**, P.O. Box 2244, La Jolla CA 92038-2244. (858)456-5805. **Contact:** Ruth Cohen. Estab. 1982. Member of AAR, Authors Guild, Sisters in Crime, RWA, SCBWI. Represents 45 clients. 15% of clients are new/unpublished writers. Currently handles: 60% novels; 40% juvenile books.
   • Prior to becoming an agent, Ms. Cohen served as directing editor at Scott Foresman & Company (now HarperCollins).
Represents: Novels (adult), juvenile books. **Considers these fiction areas:** Ethnic; historical; juvenile; literary; mainstream/contemporary; mystery/suspense; picture books; young adult.
   O– This agency specializes in "quality writing in contemporary fiction, women's fiction, mysteries, thrillers and juvenile fiction." Does not want to receive poetry, westerns, film scripts or how-to books.
How to Contact: Submit outline, 1 sample chapter(s). Does not accept fax or e-mail queries. Accepts simultaneous queries. Responds in 3 weeks to queries. Returns materials only with SASE. Obtains most new clients through recommendations from others, solicitations.
Recent Sales: This agency prefers not to share information on specific sales.
Terms: Agent receives 15% commission on domestic sales; 20% commission on foreign sales. Offers written contract, binding for 1 year. Charges for foreign postage, phone calls, photocopying submissions and overnight delivery of mss when appropriate.
Tips: "As the publishing world merges and changes, there seem to be fewer opportunities for new writers to succeed in the work that they love. We urge you to develop the patience, persistence and preserverance that have made this agency so successful. Prepare a well-written and well-crafted manuscript, and our combined best efforts can help advance both our careers."

◉ **JOANNA LEWIS COLE, LITERARY AGENT**, 404 Riverside Dr., New York NY 10025. Member of AAR.
   • This agency did not respond to our request for information. Query before submitting.

◖ **FRANCES COLLIN LITERARY AGENT**, P.O. Box 33, Wayne PA 19087-0033. **Contact:** Frances Collin. Estab. 1948. Member of AAR. Represents 90 clients. 1% of clients are new/unpublished writers. Currently handles: 50% nonfiction books; 48% novels; 1% textbooks; 1% poetry.
Represents: Nonfiction books, novels. **Considers these nonfiction areas:** Anthropology/archaeology; biography/autobiography; health/medicine; history; nature/environment; true crime/investigative. **Considers these fiction areas:** Detective/police/crime; ethnic; family saga; fantasy; historical; literary; mainstream/contemporary; mystery/suspense; psychic/supernatural; regional; romance (historical); science fiction.
How to Contact: Query with SASE. Considers simultaneous queries. Responds in 1 week to queries; 2 months to mss. Obtains most new clients through recommendations from others.
Recent Sales: This agency prefers not to share information on specific sales.
Terms: Agent receives 15% commission on domestic sales; 20% commission on foreign sales. Offers written contract. Charges clients for overseas postage for books mailed to foreign agents; photocopying of mss, books, proposals; copyright registration fees; registered mail fees; passes along cost of any books purchased.

◖ **COMMUNICATIONS AND ENTERTAINMENT, INC.**, 2851 S. Ocean Blvd., #5K, Boca Raton FL 33432-8407. (561)391-9575. Fax: (561)391-7922. E-mail: jlbearde@bellsouth.net. **Contact:** James L. Bearden. Estab. 1989. Represents 10 clients. 50% of clients are new/unpublished writers. Currently handles: 10% novels; 5% juvenile books; 40% movie scripts; 40% TV scripts.
   • See the expanded listing for this agency in Script Agents.

◖ **DON CONGDON ASSOCIATES INC.**, 156 Fifth Ave., Suite 625, New York NY 10010. (212)645-1229. Fax: (212)727-2688. E-mail: dca@doncongdon.com. **Contact:** Don Congdon, Michael Congdon, Susan Ramer, Cristina Concepcion. Estab. 1983. Member of AAR. Represents 100 clients. Currently handles: 60% nonfiction books; 40% novels.
Represents: Nonfiction books, novels. **Considers these nonfiction areas:** Anthropology/archaeology; biography/autobiography; child guidance/parenting; cooking/foods/nutrition; creative nonfiction; current affairs; ethnic/cultural interests; government/politics/law; health/medicine; history; humor/satire; language/literature/criticism; memoirs; military/war; multicultural; music/dance; nature/environment; popular culture; psychology; science/

technology; sociology; theater/film; travel; true crime/investigative; women's issues/studies. **Considers these fiction areas:** Action/adventure; detective/police/crime; horror; humor/satire; literary (especially); mainstream/ contemporary; multicultural; mystery/suspense; short story collections; thriller; women's.

How to Contact: Query with SASE. Responds in 1 week to queries; 1 month to mss. Obtains most new clients through recommendations from others.

Recent Sales: *Eisenhower*, by Carlo D'Este (Holt); *Bachelor Girl*, by Betsy Israel (Morrow); *The Ice Maiden*, by Edna Buchanan (HarperCollins); *I, Rhoda Madding, Go Hunting with my Daddy*, by Ellen Gilchrist (Little, Brown).

Terms: Agent receives 15% commission on domestic sales. Charges client for extra shipping costs, photocopying, copyright fees and book purchases.

Tips: "Writing a query letter with a self-addressed stamped envelope is a must. No phone calls."

CONNOR LITERARY AGENCY, 2911 W. 71st St., Minneapolis MN 55423. (612)866-1426. Fax: (612)869-4074. E-mail: coolmkc@aol.com. **Contact:** Marlene Connor Lynch. Estab. 1985. Represents 50 clients. 30% of clients are new/unpublished writers. Currently handles: 50% nonfiction books; 50% novels.
- Prior to opening her agency, Ms. Connor served at the Literary Guild of America, Simon and Schuster and Random House. She is the author of *What is Cool: Understanding Black Manhood in America* (Crown).

Member Agents: Deborah Coker (children's books).

Represents: Nonfiction books, novels, especially with a minority slant. **Considers these nonfiction areas:** Child guidance/parenting; cooking/foods/nutrition; crafts/hobbies; current affairs; ethnic/cultural interests; government/ politics/law; health/medicine; how-to; humor/satire; interior design/decorating; language/literature/criticism; money/finance; photography; popular culture; self-help/personal improvement; sports; true crime/investigative; women's issues/studies; relationships. **Considers these fiction areas:** Historical; horror; literary; mainstream/ contemporary; multicultural; thriller; women's; suspense.

How to Contact: No unsolicited queries, thank you. Obtains most new clients through recommendations from others, conferences, grapevine.

Recent Sales: *Outrageous Commitments*, by Dr. Ronn Elmore (HarperCollins); *Seductions*, by Snow Starborn (Sourcebooks); *Simplicity's Simply the Best Sewing Book, Revised Edition*.

Terms: Agent receives 15% commission on domestic sales; 25% commission on foreign sales. Offers written contract, binding for 1 year.

Writers' Conferences: National Writers Union, Midwest Chapter; Agents, Agents, Agents; Texas Writer's Conference; Detroit Writer's Conference.

Tips: "Seeking previously published writers with good sales records and new writers with real talent."

THE DOE COOVER AGENCY, P.O. Box 668, Winchester MA 01890. (781)721-6000. Fax: (781)721-6727. **Contact:** Doe Coover, president. Estab. 1985. Represents over 100 clients. Currently handles: 80% nonfiction books; 20% novels.
- Prior to becoming agents, Ms. Coover and Ms. Mohyde were editors for over a decade.

Member Agents: Doe Coover (cooking, general nonfiction); Colleen Mohyde (literary and commercial fiction, general nonfiction and journalism); Rebecca Staffel (literary and commercial fiction, general nonfiction and journalism); Frances Kennedy (assistant).

Represents: Nonfiction books, novels. **Considers these nonfiction areas:** Anthropology/archaeology; biography/autobiography; business/economics; child guidance/parenting; cooking/foods/nutrition; ethnic/cultural interests; health/medicine; history; language/literature/criticism; memoirs; money/finance; nature/environment; psychology; sociology; travel; true crime/investigative; women's issues/studies. **Considers these fiction areas:** Literary; mainstream/contemporary (commercial).
- This agency specializes in cookbooks, serious nonfiction—particularly books on social issues—as well as fiction (literary and commercial), journalism and general nonfiction. Does not want children's books.

How to Contact: Query with SASE, outline. No e-mail or fax queries. Considers simultaneous queries. Returns materials only with SASE. Obtains most new clients through recommendations from others, solicitations.

Recent Sales: Sold 25-30 titles in the last year. *The Gourmet Cookbook*, by Gourmet Magazine (W.W. Norton); *I Hear America Eating*, by Jane and Michael Stern (Houghton Mifflin Company); *Best 100 Books Every Child and Adult Should Read*, by Anita Silvey (Houghton Mifflin Company). *Movie/TV MOW script(s) optioned/sold: Stella Landry*, by Robin McCorquodale; *A Crime in the Neighborhood*, by Suzanne Berne. Other clients include Peter Lynch, Deborah Madison, Sandra Shea, Rick Bayless, Marion Cunningham, Robert Clark and Adrea Bernardi.

Terms: Agent receives 15% commission on domestic sales; 15% commission on foreign sales.

Writers' Conferences: BEA.

CORE CREATIONS, LLC, 9024 S. Sanderling Way, Littleton CO 80126. (303)683-6792. E-mail: agent@e oncity.com. Website: www.eoncity.com/agent. **Contact:** Calvin Rex. Estab. 1994. Represents 10 clients. 70% of clients are new/unpublished writers. Currently handles: 30% nonfiction books; 60% novels; 5% novellas; 5% games.
- Prior to becoming an agent, Mr. Rex managed a small publishing house.

Member Agents: Calvin Rex.

Represents: Nonfiction books, novels, novellas. **Considers these nonfiction areas:** Gay/lesbian issues; how-to; humor/satire; psychology; true crime/investigative. **Considers these fiction areas:** Detective/police/crime; horror; science fiction.

> O⌐ This agency specializes in "bold, daring literature." Agency has strong "experience with royalty contracts and licensing agreements."

How to Contact: Query with SASE, outline/proposal. Responds in 3 weeks to queries; 3 months to mss. Obtains most new clients through recommendations from others, solicitations, through the Internet.

Terms: Agent receives 15% commission on domestic sales; 20% commission on foreign sales. Offers written contract. Charges clients for postage (applicable mailing costs).

Writers' Conferences: Steamboat Springs Writers Group (Colorado, July); Rocky Mountain Fiction Writers Colorado Gold Conference.

Tips: "Have all material proofread. Visit our webpage before sending anything. We want books that dare to be different. Give us a unique angle, a new style of writing, something that stands out from the crowd!"

CORNERSTONE LITERARY, INC., 4500 Wilshire Blvd., 3rd floor, Los Angeles CA 90010. (323)930-6039. Fax: (323)930-0407. Website: www.cornerstoneliterary.com. **Contact:** Helen Breitwieser. Estab. 1998. Member of AAR; Author's Guild. Represents 40 clients. 75% of clients are new/unpublished writers.

> • Prior to founding her own boutique agency, Ms. Breitwieser was a literary agent at The William Morris Agency.

Represents: Nonfiction books, novels, short story collections. **Considers these nonfiction areas:** Multicultural; women's issues/studies; narrative nonfiction. **Considers these fiction areas:** Detective/police/crime; erotica; ethnic; family saga; glitz; historical; humor/satire; literary; mainstream/contemporary; multicultural; mystery/suspense; New Age; romance; thriller.

> O⌐ Actively seeking first fiction, literary. Does not want to receive science fiction, westerns, children's books, poetry, screenplays, fantasy, gay/lesbian, horror.

How to Contact: Query with SASE. Responds in 2 weeks to queries; 2 months to mss. Returns materials only with SASE. Obtains most new clients through recommendations from others.

Recent Sales: Sold 42 titles in the last year. *Last Breath*, by Rachel Lee (Warner); *Cold Silence*, by Danielle Girard (NAL). Other clients include Stan Diehl, Elaine Coffman, Carole Matthews, Kayla Perrin, Candice Proctor.

Terms: Agent receives 15% commission on domestic sales; 20% commission on foreign sales. Offers written contract, binding for 1 year; 60-day notice must be given to terminate contract.

Tips: "Don't query about more than one manuscript."

CRAWFORD LITERARY AGENCY, 94 Evans Rd., Barnstead NH 03218. (603)269-5851. Fax: (603)269-2533. E-mail: CrawfordLit@att.net. **Contact:** Susan Crawford. Estab. 1988. Represents 40 clients. 10% of clients are new/unpublished writers. Currently handles: 50% nonfiction books; 50% novels.

Member Agents: Susan Crawford; Lorne Crawford (commercial fiction); Scott Neister (scientific/techno thrillers); Kristen Hales (parenting, psychology, New Age, self help).

Represents: Nonfiction books, novels (commercial fiction). **Considers these nonfiction areas:** Religious/inspirational; self-help/personal improvement; women's issues/studies; celebrity/media. **Considers these fiction areas:** Action/adventure; mystery/suspense; thriller (medical).

> O⌐ This agency specializes in celebrity and/or media-based books and authors. Actively seeking action/adventure stories, medical thrillers, suspense thrillers, celebrity projects, self-help, inspirational, how-to and women's issues. Does not want to receive short stories, poetry.

How to Contact: Query with SASE. Considers simultaneous queries. Responds in 3 weeks to queries. Returns materials only with SASE. Obtains most new clients through recommendations from others, solicitations, conferences.

Recent Sales: Sold 42 titles in the last year. *Handy at Home*, by Richard Karn and George Mair (St. Martin's Press); *Float Like a Butterfly and Sting Like a Bee*, by Maryum Ali (Beyond Words). Other clients include John Travolta, Kat Carney, Cal Morris, MD, Mimi Donaldson, Linda Seger.

Terms: Agent receives 15% commission on domestic sales; 20% commission on foreign sales. Offers written contract, binding for 90 days; 100% of business is derived from commissions on ms sales.

Writers' Conferences: International Film & Television Workshops (Rockport ME); Maui Writers Conference.

Tips: "Keep learning to improve your craft. Attend conferences and network."

N ⊘ THE CREATIVE CULTURE, INC., 2853 Broadway, Suite 1715, New York NY 10003. **Contact:** Debra Goldstein. Member of AAR.

> • This agency did not respond to our request for information. Query before submitting. Handles nonfiction.

RICHARD CURTIS ASSOCIATES, INC., 171 E. 74th St., Suite 2, New York NY 10021. (212)772-7363. Fax: (212)772-7393. Website: www.curtisagency.com. Estab. 1969. Member of RWA, MWA, WWA, SFWA; signatory of WGA. Represents 100 clients. 1% of clients are new/unpublished writers. Currently handles: 80% nonfiction books; 20% novels.

• Prior to opening his agency, Mr. Curtis was an agent with the Scott Meredith Literary Agency for 7 years and has authored over 50 published books.

Member Agents: Richard Curtis; Jennifer Hackworth; Amy Victoria Meo.

Represents: Nonfiction books, novels, scholarly books. **Considers these nonfiction areas:** Agriculture/horticulture; Americana; animals; anthropology/archaeology; art/architecture/design; biography/autobiography; business/economics; child guidance/parenting; computers/electronic; cooking/foods/nutrition; crafts/hobbies; creative nonfiction; current affairs; education; ethnic/cultural interests; gardening; gay/lesbian issues; government/politics/law; health/medicine; history; how-to; humor/satire; interior design/decorating; juvenile nonfiction; language/literature/criticism; memoirs; military/war; money/finance; multicultural; music/dance; nature/environment; New Age/metaphysics; philosophy; photography; popular culture; psychology; recreation; regional; religious/inspirational; science/technology; self-help/personal improvement; sex; sociology; software; spirituality; sports; theater/film; translation; travel; true crime/investigative; women's issues/studies.

O━ This agency specializes in general and literary fiction and nonfiction, as well as genre fiction such as science fiction, romance, horror, fantasy, action-adventure.

How to Contact: Query with SASE, outline, 3 sample chapter(s). No e-mail or fax queries. Responds in 1 month to queries; 1 month to mss. Obtains most new clients through recommendations from others, solicitations, conferences.

Recent Sales: Sold 100 titles in the last year. *Vitals*, by Greg Bear (Random House); *Hard Case*, by Dan Simmons (St. Martin's Press); *A Capital Holiday*, by Janet Dailey (Kensington). Other clients include Jennifer Blake, Leonard Maltin, Earl Mindell and Barbara Parker.

Terms: Agent receives 15% commission on domestic sales; 20% commission on foreign sales. Offers written contract, binding for book-by-book basis. Charges for photocopying, express, fax, international postage, book orders.

Writers' Conferences: Romance Writers of America; World Fantasy Conference.

⬤ **JAMES R. CYPHER, THE CYPHER AGENCY**, 816 Wolcott Ave., Beacon NY 12508-4261. (845)831-5677. Fax: (845)831-5677. E-mail: jimcypher@prodigy.net. Website: pages.prodigy.net/jimcypher/. **Contact:** James R. Cypher. Estab. 1993. Member of Authors Guild. Represents 27 clients. 19% of clients are new/unpublished writers. Currently handles: 100% nonfiction books.

• Prior to opening his agency, Mr. Cypher worked as a corporate public relations manager for a Fortune 500 multi-national computer company for 28 years.

Represents: Nonfiction books. **Considers these nonfiction areas:** Biography/autobiography; current affairs; ethnic/cultural interests; gay/lesbian issues; government/politics/law; health/medicine; history; how-to; language/literature/criticism; memoirs (travel); money/finance; music/dance; nature/environment; popular culture; psychology; science/technology; self-help/personal improvement; sociology; sports; theater/film; travel (memoirs); true crime/investigative; women's issues/studies.

O━ Actively seeking a wide variety of topical nonfiction. Does not want to receive humor; pets; gardening; cooking books; crafts; spiritual; religious or New Age topics.

How to Contact: Query with SASE, proposal package, outline, 2 sample chapter(s). Accepts e-mail and fax queries. Considers simultaneous queries. Responds in 2 weeks to queries; 6 weeks to mss. Obtains most new clients through recommendations from others, conferences, networking on online computer service.

Recent Sales: Sold 7 titles in the last year. *Perfect Poison: How a Trusted VA Hospital Nurse Became a Cold-Blooded Serial Killer*, by M. William Phelps (Kensington); *Fishing the Web: The Best 500 Fishing Web Sites*, by Craig Buddo (Stoeger Publications); *Prophets Without Honor: A Requiem for Moral Patriotism*, by William M. Strabala and Michael J. Palecek (Algora Publishing); *The Masters: A Hole-by-Hole History*, by David Sowell (Brassey's, Innc.); *Gay Perspective: What our Homosexuality Tells Us About the Nature of Life, the Universe and God*, by Toby Johnson (Alyson Publications); *Postcards from Pit Road: An Irreverent Account of the 2002 NASCAR Season*, by Monte Dutton (Brassey's, Inc.).

Terms: Agent receives 15% commission on domestic sales; 20% commission on foreign sales. Offers written contract; 30-day cancellation notice must be given to terminate contract. 100% of business is derived from commissions on ms sales. Charges clients for postage, photocopying, overseas phone calls and faxes.

N ⬤ **LAURA DAIL LITERARY AGENCY, INC.**, 250 West 57th Street, Suite 1314, New York NY, 10107. Website: www.ldlainc.com/news.html. **Contact:** Laura Dail. Member of AAR.

• This agency did not respond to our request for information. Query before submitting.

⬤ **DARHANSOFF & VERRILL LITERARY AGENTS**, 236 W. 26th St., Suite 802, New York NY 10001. (917)305-1300. Fax: (917)305-1400. Estab. 1975. Member of AAR. Represents 120 clients. 10% of clients are new/unpublished writers. Currently handles: 25% nonfiction books; 60% novels; 15% story collections.

Member Agents: Liz Darhansoff; Charles Verrill; Leigh Feldman.

Represents: Novels, short story collections. **Considers these fiction areas:** Literary.

O━ Specializes in literary fiction.

How to Contact: Obtains most new clients through recommendations from others.

Recent Sales: *At Home in Mitford*, by Jan Karon (Viking); *Cold Mountain*, by Charles Frazier (Atlantic Monthly Press). Other clients include Arthur Golden.

JOAN DAVES AGENCY, 21 W. 26th St., New York NY 10010. (212)685-2663. Fax: (212)685-1781. **Contact:** Jennifer Lyons, director. Estab. 1960. Member of AAR. Represents 100 clients. 10% of clients are new/unpublished writers.

poss.

Represents: Nonfiction books, novels. **Considers these nonfiction areas:** Biography/autobiography; gay/lesbian issues; popular culture; translation; women's issues/studies. **Considers these fiction areas:** Ethnic; family saga; gay/lesbian; literary; mainstream/contemporary.

☞ This agency specializes in literary fiction and nonfiction, also commercial fiction.

How to Contact: Query with SASE. No e-mail or fax queries. Considers simultaneous queries. Responds in 3 weeks to queries; 6 weeks to mss. Returns materials only with SASE. Obtains most new clients through recommendations from others, solicitations.

Recent Sales: Sold 70 titles in the last year. *Confessions of a Dangerous Mind*, by Chuck Barris (Miramax); *Complete Works of Isaac Babel*, ed. by Nathalie Babel (W.W. Norton); *Red Ribbons and the Broken Memory Tree*, by April Reynolds (Henry Holt).

Terms: Agent receives 15% commission on domestic sales; 20% commission on foreign sales. Offers written contract, binding for per-book basis; 100% of business is derived from commissions on ms sales. Charges for office expenses.

Tips: "A few queries translate into representation."

LIZA DAWSON ASSOCIATES, 240 W. 35th St., Suite 500, New York NY 10001. (212)465-9071 or (212)629-9212. **Contact:** Liza Dawson, Rebecca Kurson, Caitlin Blasdell. Member of AAR, MWA, Women's Media Group. Represents 50 clients. 10% of clients are new/unpublished writers. Currently handles: 60% nonfiction books; 40% novels.

11/21/03 - no ✱ sounds right

● Prior to becoming an agent, Ms. Dawson was an editor for 20 years, spending 11 years at William Morrow as vice president and 2 at Putnam as executive editor. Ms. Kurson was an associate editor at Farrar Straus; Ms. Blasdell was a senior editor at HarperCollins and Avon.

Member Agents: Liza Dawson; Rebecca Kurson (science, women's issues, narrative nonfiction, literary fiction); Caitlin Blasdell (science fiction, business books, commercial fiction).

Represents: Nonfiction books, novels, scholarly books. **Considers these nonfiction areas:** Biography/autobiography; business/economics; child guidance/parenting; health/medicine; history; memoirs; psychology; sociology; women's issues/studies. **Considers these fiction areas:** Ethnic; family saga; historical; literary; mystery/suspense; regional; thriller.

☞ This agency specializes in readable literary fiction, thrillers, mainstream historicals and women's fiction, academics, historians, business, journalists and psychology. "My specialty is shaping books and ideas so that a publisher will respond quickly." Actively seeking talented professionals. Does not want to receive westerns, sports, computers, juvenile.

How to Contact: Query with SASE. Responds in 3 weeks to queries; 6 weeks to mss. Obtains most new clients through recommendations from others, conferences.

Recent Sales: Sold 40 titles in the last year. *Darjeeling*, by Bharti Kirchner (St. Martin's); *Wild Mothers*, (Algonquin); *My Mother's Island*, by Marnie Mueller (Curbstone); *Life or Debt*, by Stacy Johnson (Ballantine); *The Summer of My Greek Taverna*, by Tom Stone (Simon & Schuster); *Poker Nation*, by Andy Bellin (HarperCollins).

Terms: Agent receives 15% commission on domestic sales; 20% commission on foreign sales. Offers written contract. Charges clients for photocopying and overseas postage.

Writers' Conferences: Pacific Northwest Book Conference (Seattle, July).

Reading List: Reads *The Sun*, *New York Review of Books*, *The New York Observer*, *Utne Reader*, and *The Wall Street Journal* to find new clients.

Tips: "Please include a detailed bio with any query letter, let me know somehow that you've done a little research, that you're not just interested in any agent but someone who is right for you."

DeFIORE AND COMPANY, 72 Spring St., Suite 304, New York NY 10012. (212)925-7744. Fax: (212)925-9803. E-mail: info@defioreandco.com. Website: www.defioreandco.com. **Contact:** Brian DeFiore. Estab. 1999. Represents 35 clients. 50% of clients are new/unpublished writers. Currently handles: 70% nonfiction books; 30% novels.

poss.

● Prior to becoming an agent, Mr. DeFiore was Publisher of Villard Books 1997-1998; Editor-in-Chief of Hyperion 1992-1997; Editorial Director of Delacorte Press 1988-1992.

Member Agents: Brian DeFiore (popular nonfiction, business, pop culture, parenting, commercial fiction); Mark S. Roy (literary fiction, spirituality, health and fitness, lifestyle, gay & lesbian).

Represents: Nonfiction books, novels. **Considers these nonfiction areas:** Biography/autobiography; business/economics; child guidance/parenting; cooking/foods/nutrition; gay/lesbian issues; health/medicine; money/finance; multicultural; popular culture; psychology; religious/inspirational; self-help/personal improvement; sports. **Considers these fiction areas:** Ethnic; gay/lesbian; literary; mainstream/contemporary; mystery/suspense; thriller.

How to Contact: Query with SASE. Considers simultaneous queries. Responds in 2 weeks to queries; 6 weeks to mss. Returns materials only with SASE. Obtains most new clients through recommendations from others.

Recent Sales: Sold 15 titles in the last year. *Other Fish In The Sea*, by Lisa Kusel (Hyperion); *You Got Nothing Coming*, by Jimmy A. Lerner (Broadway Books); *Mr. Fix-It Introduces You to Your Home*, by Lou Manfredini (Ballantine). Other clients include David Rensin, Loretta LaRoche, Jason Starr, Joel Engel, Christopher Keane, Robin McMillan, Jessica Teich, Ronna Lichtenberg, Fran Sorin, Christine Dimmick.
Terms: Agent receives 15% commission on domestic sales; 20% commission on foreign sales. Offers written contract; 10-day notice must be given to terminate contract. Charges clients for photocopying, overnight delivery (deducted only after a sale is made).
Writers' Conferences: Maui Writers Conference (Maui HI, September); Pacific Northwest Writers Association Conference.

 DH LITERARY, INC., P.O. Box 990, Nyack NY 10960-0990. (212)753-7942. E-mail: dhendin@aol.com. **Contact:** David Hendin. Estab. 1993. Member of AAR. Represents 30 clients. Currently handles: 80% nonfiction books; 10% novels; 10% scholarly books.
• Prior to opening his agency, Mr. Hendin served as president and publisher for Pharos Books/World Almanac as well as senior VP and COO at sister company United Feature Syndicate.
Represents: Nonfiction books, novels. **Considers these nonfiction areas:** High-concept. **Considers these fiction areas:** Considers fiction by referral only.
How to Contact: Query by e-mail only. Send printed material only if requested.
Recent Sales: *Star Spangled Manners*, by Judith Martin (Norton); *Dead End Jobs* (mystery series), by Elaine Viets (Penguin/Putnam); *Coined by God*, by Jeffrey McQuain and Stanley Malless (Norton).
Terms: Agent receives 15% commission on domestic sales; 20% commission on foreign sales. Offers written contract, binding for 1 year. Charges for out of pocket expenses for overseas postage specifically related to sale. No other fees.

 DHS LITERARY, INC., 2528 Elm St., Suite 350, Dallas TX 75226. (214)363-4422. Fax: (214)363-4423. E-mail: submissions@dhsliterary.com. Website: www.dhsliterary.com. **Contact:** David Hale Smith, president. Estab. 1994. Represents 35 clients. 15% of clients are new/unpublished writers. Currently handles: 60% nonfiction books; 40% novels.
• Prior to opening his agency, Mr. Smith was an editor at a newswire service.
Represents: Nonfiction books, novels. **Considers these nonfiction areas:** Biography/autobiography; business/economics; child guidance/parenting; cooking/foods/nutrition; current affairs; ethnic/cultural interests; popular culture; sports; true crime/investigative. **Considers these fiction areas:** Detective/police/crime; ethnic; literary; mainstream/contemporary; mystery/suspense; thriller.
⊶ This agency specializes in commercial fiction and nonfiction for adult trade market. Actively seeking thrillers, mysteries, suspense, etc., and narrative nonfiction. Does not want to receive poetry, short fiction, children's books.
How to Contact: One-page queries via e-mail only. No paper queries accepted unless requested by agency. Will request more material if appropriate. Considers simultaneous queries. Responds in 1 month to queries. Obtains most new clients through recommendations from others, editors and agents.
Recent Sales: Sold 35 titles in the last year. *The Curve of the World*, by Marcus Stevens (Algonquin); *City on Fire*, by Bill Minutaglio (Morrow).
Terms: Agent receives 15% commission on domestic sales; 25% commission on foreign sales. Offers written contract; 10-day notice must be given to terminate contract. Charges for client expenses, i.e., postage, photocopying. 100% of business is derived from commissions on sales.
Tips: "Remember to be courteous and professional, and to treat marketing your work and approaching an agent as you would any formal business matter. When in doubt, always query first via e-mail. Visit our website for more information."

 SANDRA DIJKSTRA LITERARY AGENCY, 1155 Camino del Mar, PMB 515, Del Mar CA 92014-2605. (858)755-3115. Fax: (858) 794-2822. E-mail: sdla@dijkstraagency.com. **Contact:** Jill Marr. Estab. 1981. Member of AAR, Authors Guild, PEN West, Poets and Editors, MWA. Represents 200 clients. 30% of clients are new/unpublished writers. Currently handles: 50% nonfiction books; 45% novels; 5% juvenile books.
• We specialize in a number of fields.
Member Agents: Sandra Dijkstra.

FOR EXPLANATIONS OF THESE SYMBOLS, SEE THE INSIDE FRONT AND BACK COVERS OF THIS BOOK

Represents: Nonfiction books, novels. **Considers these nonfiction areas:** Anthropology/archaeology; business/ economics; child guidance/parenting; cooking/foods/nutrition; ethnic/cultural interests; government/politics/law; health/medicine; history; language/literature/criticism; military/war; money/finance; nature/environment; psychology; science/technology; sociology; women's issues/studies. **Considers these fiction areas:** Ethnic; literary; mainstream/contemporary; mystery/suspense; thriller.

How to Contact: Submit proposal package, outline, sample chapter(s), author bio, SASE. No e-mail or fax queries. Responds in 6 weeks to queries; 6 weeks to mss. Obtains most new clients through recommendations from others, solicitations, conferences.

Recent Sales: Sold over 40 titles in the last year. *The Hottentot Venus*, by Barbara Chase-Riboud (Doubleday); *The Lady, The Chef and The Whore*, by Marisol Konczal (Harper Collins); *End of Adolescence*, by Robert Epstein (Harcourt).

Terms: Agent receives 15% commission on domestic sales; 20% commission on foreign sales. Offers written contract. Charges clients for expenses "to cover domestic costs so that we can spend time selling books instead of accounting expenses. We also charge for the photocopying of the full ms or nonfiction proposal and for foreign postage."

Writers' Conferences: "Have attended Squaw Valley, Santa Barbara, Asilomar, Southern California Writers Conference, Rocky Mountain Fiction Writers, to name a few. We also speak regularly for writers groups such as PEN West and the Independent Writers Association."

Tips: "Be professional and learn the standard procedures for submitting your work. Give full biographical information on yourself, especially for a nonfiction project. Send no more than 50 pages of your manuscript, a very brief synopsis, detailed author bio (awards, publications, accomplishments) and a SASE. We will not respond to submissions without a SASE. Nine page letters telling us your life story, or your book's, are unprofessional and usually not read. Tell us about your book and write your query well. It's our first introduction to who you are and what you can do! Call if you don't hear within six weeks. Be a regular patron of bookstores and study what kind of books are being published. READ. Check out your local library and bookstores—you'll find lots of books on writing and the publishing industry that will help you! At conferences, ask published writers about their agents. Don't believe the myth that an agent has to be in New York to be successful—we've already disproved it!"

⊘ THE JONATHAN DOLGER AGENCY, 49 E. 96th St., Suite 9B, New York NY 10128. (212)427-1853. **Contact:** Herbert Erinmore; President: Jonathan Dolger. Estab. 1980. Member of AAR. Represents 70 clients. 25% of clients are new/unpublished writers.

Represents: Nonfiction books, novels, illustrated books.

   Oⁿ This agency specializes in adult trade fiction and nonfiction, and illustrated books.

How to Contact: Query with SASE.

Recent Sales: Sold 15-20 titles in the last year. This agency prefers not to share information on specific sales.

Terms: Agent receives 15% commission on domestic sales; 25% commission on foreign sales. Charges clients for "standard expenses."

Tips: "Writer must have been previously published if submitting fiction. Prefers to work with published/established authors; works with a small number of new/previously unpublished writers."

◐ JANIS A. DONNAUD & ASSOCIATES, INC., 525 Broadway, 2nd Floor, New York NY 10012. (212)431-2664. Fax: (212)431-2667. E-mail: jdonnaud@aol.com. **Contact:** Janis A. Donnaud. Member of AAR; signatory of WGA. Represents 40 clients. 5% of clients are new/unpublished writers. Currently handles: 100% nonfiction books.

   ● Prior to opening her agency, Ms. Donnaud was Vice President, Associate Publisher, Random House Adult Trade group.

Represents: Nonfiction books. **Considers these nonfiction areas:** Biography/autobiography; child guidance/ parenting; cooking/foods/nutrition; narrative nonfiction; current affairs; health/medicine; humor/satire; psychology (pop).

   Oⁿ This agency specializes in health, medical, cooking, humor, pop psychology, narrative nonfiction, photography, biography, parenting, current affairs. "We give a lot of service and attention to clients." Actively seeking serious narrative nonfiction; cookbooks; health and medical by experts with an established platform in their area of specialty. Does not want to receive fiction, poetry, mysteries, juvenile books, romances, science fiction, young adult, religious fantasy.

How to Contact: Query with SASE, description of book and 2-3 pages of sample material. Prefers to read materials exclusively. Accepts e-mail and fax queries. No e-mail attachments. Responds in 1 month to queries; 1 month to mss. Obtains most new clients through recommendations from others.

Recent Sales: Sold 25 titles in the last year. *The Flamboya Tree: Memoirs of a Mother's Wartime Courage*, by Clara Kelly (Random House); *Nancy Silverton's Sandwiches*, by Nancy Silverton (Knopf).

Terms: Agent receives 15% commission on domestic sales; 20% commission on foreign sales; 20% commission on dramatic rights sales. Offers written contract; 30-day notice must be given to terminate contract. Charges clients for messengers, photocopying, purchase of books.

JIM DONOVAN LITERARY, 4515 Prentice St., Suite 109, Dallas TX 75206. Fax: (214)696-9412. **Contact:** Jim Donovan, president; Kathryn Lindsey. Estab. 1993. Represents 25 clients. 25% of clients are new/unpublished writers. Currently handles: 75% nonfiction books; 25% novels.

Member Agents: Jim Donovan (president); Kathryn Lindsey.

Represents: Nonfiction books, novels. **Considers these nonfiction areas:** Biography/autobiography; business/economics; child guidance/parenting; current affairs; health/medicine; history; military/war; money/finance; music/dance; nature/environment; popular culture; sports; true crime/investigative. **Considers these fiction areas:** Action/adventure; detective/police/crime; historical; horror; literary; mainstream/contemporary; mystery/suspense; sports; thriller; westerns/frontier.

　　O— This agency specializes in commercial fiction and nonfiction. Does not want to receive poetry, humor, short stories, juvenile, romance or religious work.

How to Contact: Query with SASE. For nonfiction, send query letter. For fiction, send 2- to 5-page outline and 3 sample chapters. No e-mail or fax queries. Considers simultaneous queries and submissions. Responds in 1 month to queries; 1 month to mss. Obtains most new clients through recommendations from others, solicitations.

Recent Sales: Sold 24 titles in the last year. *Unitas*, by Dan McGraw (Doubleday); *Monsters*, by Jim Dent (St. Martin's Press).

Terms: Agent receives 15% commission on domestic sales; 20% commission on foreign sales. Offers written contract, binding for 1 year; written notice must be given to terminate contract. Charges clients for some postage and photocopying—"author is notified first." Writers reimbursed for office fees after the sale of ms.

Tips: "The vast majority of material I receive, particularly fiction, is not ready for publication. Do everything you can to get your fiction work in top shape before you try to find an agent. I've been in the book business since 1981, in retail (as a chain buyer), as an editor, and as a published author. I'm open to working with new writers if they're serious about their writing and are prepared to put in the work necessary—the rewriting—to become publishable."

DORIAN LITERARY AGENCY, Upper Thornehill, 27 Church Rd., St. Mary Church, Torquay Devon TQ1 4Q4, England. 44 (0) 1803 312095. Fax: 44 (0) 1803 312095. **Contact:** Dorothy Lumley. Estab. 1986. Member of Association of Authors & Agents, UK. Represents 50 clients. 10% of clients are new/unpublished writers. Currently handles: 100% novels.

　　● Prior to becoming an agent, Ms. Lumley was a paperback editor.

Member Agents: Dorothy Lumley (popular adult fiction).

Represents: Novels. **Considers these fiction areas:** Detective/police/crime; family saga; fantasy; historical; horror; literary; mainstream/contemporary; mystery/suspense; romance; science fiction; thriller; young adult.

　　O— This agency is a small specialist agency that offers personal service and editorial input. Does not want to receive poetry, nonfiction of specialist type, autobiographies, plays, children's books.

How to Contact: Query with SASE, submit proposal package, outline, 1-3 sample chapter(s), IRCs. No e-mail or fax queries. Considers simultaneous queries. Responds in 2 weeks to queries; 6 weeks to mss. Returns materials only with SASE. Obtains most new clients through recommendations from others.

Recent Sales: Sold 25 titles in the last year. They include popular historical fiction, thrillers, contemporary crime and horror.

Terms: Agent receives 12½% commission on domestic sales; 15% (to USA) commission on foreign sales. Charges clients for photocopying of mss, extra copies of book for rights sales.

Writers' Conferences: Romantic Novelists Association; Crime Writers Association; World Fantasy.

Tips: "I am forced to be very selective, as this is a small one-person agency. I prefer traditional storytelling with warm, sympathetic characters."

DOYEN LITERARY SERVICES, INC., 1931 660th St., Newell IA 50568-7613. (712)272-3300. Website: www.barbaradoyen.com. **Contact:** (Ms.) B.J. Doyen, president. Estab. 1988. Represents 20 clients. 20% of clients are new/unpublished writers. Currently handles: 90% nonfiction books; 10% novels.

　　● Prior to opening her agency, Ms. Doyen worked as a published author, teacher, guest speaker and wrote and appeared in her own weekly TV show airing in 7 states.

Represents: Nonfiction books, novels. **Considers these nonfiction areas:** Agriculture/horticulture; Americana; animals; anthropology/archaeology; art/architecture/design; biography/autobiography; business/economics; child guidance/parenting; computers/electronic; cooking/foods/nutrition; crafts/hobbies; creative nonfiction; current affairs; education; ethnic/cultural interests; gardening; gay/lesbian issues; government/politics/law; health/medicine; history; how-to; humor/satire; interior design/decorating; juvenile nonfiction; language/literature/criticism; memoirs; military/war; money/finance; multicultural; music/dance; nature/environment; New Age/metaphysics; philosophy; photography; popular culture; psychology; recreation; regional; religious/inspirational; science/technology; self-help/personal improvement; sex; sociology; software; spirituality; sports; theater/film; translation; travel; true crime/investigative; women's issues/studies; young adult. **Considers these fiction areas:** Contemporary issues; family saga; historical; literary; mainstream/contemporary; occult; psychic/supernatural.

　　O— This agency specializes in nonfiction and occasionally handles genre and mainstream fiction for adults. Actively seeking business, health, how-to, psychology; all kinds of adult nonfiction suitable for the major trade publishers. Prefers fiction from published novelists only. Does not want to receive pornography, children's, poetry.

How to Contact: Query with SASE. No e-mail or fax queries. Considers simultaneous queries and submissions. Responds in 2 weeks to mss. Responds immediately to queries. Returns materials only with SASE.

Terms: Agent receives 15% commission on domestic sales; 20% commission on foreign sales. Offers written contract, binding for 1 year.

Tips: "Our authors receive personalized attention. We market aggressively, undeterred by rejection. We get the best possible publishing contracts. We are very interested in nonfiction book ideas at this time; will consider most topics. Many writers come to us from referrals, but we also get quite a few who initially approach us with query letters. Do not use phone queries unless you are successfully published or a celebrity. It is best if you do not collect editorial rejections prior to seeking an agent, but if you do, be up-front and honest about it. Do not submit your manuscript to more than one agent at a time—querying first can save you (and us) much time. We're open to established or beginning writers—just send us a terrific letter with SASE!"

ROBERT DUCAS, The Barn House, 244 Westside Rd., Norfolk CT 06058. (860)542-5733. Fax: (860)542-5469. E-mail: robertducas@aol.com. **Contact:** Robert Ducas. Estab. 1981. 15% of clients are new/unpublished writers. Currently handles: 70% nonfiction books; 28% novels; 2% scholarly books.
- Prior to opening his agency, Mr. Ducas ran the *London Times* and the *Sunday Times* in the U.S. from 1966 to 1981.

Represents: Nonfiction books, novels, novellas. **Considers these nonfiction areas:** Animals; biography/autobiography; business/economics; current affairs; gay/lesbian issues; government/politics/law; health/medicine; history; memoirs; military/war; money/finance; nature/environment; science/technology; sports; travel; true crime/investigative. **Considers these fiction areas:** Action/adventure; contemporary issues; detective/police/crime; family saga; literary; mainstream/contemporary; mystery/suspense; sports; thriller.
- This agency specializes in nonfiction, journalistic exposé, biography, history. Does not want to receive women's fiction.

How to Contact: Query with SASE. Responds in 2 weeks to queries; 2 months to mss. Obtains most new clients through recommendations from others.

Recent Sales: Sold 10 titles in the last year. This agency prefers not to share information on specific sales.

Terms: Agent receives 15% commission on domestic sales; 20% commission on foreign sales. Charges clients for photocopying, postage, messengers, overseas couriers to subagents.

DUNHAM LITERARY, 156 Fifth Avenue, Suite 625, New York NY 10010-7002. (212)929-0994. Website: www.dunhamlit.com. **Contact:** Jennie Dunham. Estab. 2000. Member of AAR. Represents 50 clients. 15% of clients are new/unpublished writers. Currently handles: 25% nonfiction books; 25% novels; 50% juvenile books.
- Prior to opening her agency, Ms. Dunham worked as a literary agent for Russell & Volkening.

Member Agents: Donna Lieberman (mainstream fiction and nonfiction, mysteries, suspense, thrillers).

Represents: Nonfiction books, novels, short story collections, juvenile books. **Considers these nonfiction areas:** Anthropology/archaeology; art/architecture/design; biography/autobiography; business/economics; current affairs; education; ethnic/cultural interests; gay/lesbian issues; government/politics/law; health/medicine; history; juvenile nonfiction; language/literature/criticism; music/dance; nature/environment; photography; popular culture; psychology; science/technology; sociology; sports; women's issues/studies. **Considers these fiction areas:** Ethnic; juvenile; literary; mainstream/contemporary; mystery/suspense; picture books; thriller (especially); young adult.

How to Contact: Query with SASE. No e-mail or fax queries. Responds in 1 week to queries; 2 months to mss. Obtains most new clients through recommendations from others, solicitations.

Recent Sales: Sold 45 titles in the last year. *Living Dead Girl*, by Tod Goldberg; *Native New Yorkers*, by Evan Pritchard; *Molly*, by Nancy Jones; *Hidden Witness*, by Jackie Napolean Wilson; *Letters of Intent*, by Anna Bondoc and Meg Daly; *And Baby Makes Four*, by Hilory Wanger; *A Positive Life*, by River Huston and photographed by Mary Berridge; *Everything Motorcycles* and *WICCA for Couples*, by A.J. Drew; *Ezmereld Chronicles: Initiation At Beltane*, by Tamarin Laurel; *Reflexology Sox*, by Michelle Kluck; *Devoted to Deity*, by Judy Harrow; *Magick Made Easy* and *Goddess In My Pocket*, by Trish Telesco; *Clever Beatrice*, illustrated by Heather Solomon; *Lincoln*, illustrated by David A. Johnson; *Who Will Tell My Brother?*, by Marlene Carvell; *Pirates*, by C. Drew Lamm; *Young Naturalist's Handbook of Butterflies/Beetles*, by Robert Sabuda and Matthew Reinhart; *Animal Popposites*, by Matthew Reinhart; *The Tale of Tricky Fox*, illustrated by Barbara McClintock; *Molly and the Magic Wishbone*, by Barbara McClintock; *Dancing Mathilda*, by Sarah Hager.

Terms: Agent receives 15% commission on domestic sales; 20% commission on foreign sales. Writers reimbursed for office fees after the sale of ms.

HENRY DUNOW LITERARY AGENCY, 27 W. 20th St., Suite 1003, New York NY 10011. E-mail: henry@dunowcarlson.com. Website: www.dunowcarlson.com. Member of AAR.
- This agency did not respond to our request for information. Query before submitting.

Member Agents: Jennifer Carlson; Kyung Cho (literary fiction and commercial love stories, serious narrative nonfiction, history and science).

DUPREE/MILLER AND ASSOCIATES INC. LITERARY, 100 Highland Park Village, Suite 350, Dallas TX 75205. (214)559-BOOK. Fax: (214)559-PAGE. E-mail: dmabook@aol.com. **Contact:** Submissions Department. President: Jan Miller. Estab. 1984. Member of ABA. Represents 200 clients. 20% of clients are new/unpublished writers. Currently handles: 75% nonfiction books; 25% novels.

Member Agents: Jan Miller; Michael Broussard; Shannon Miser-Marven (business affairs); Kym Elizondo.

Represents: Nonfiction books, novels, scholarly books, syndicated material. **Considers these nonfiction areas:** Agriculture/horticulture; Americana; animals; anthropology/archaeology; art/architecture/design; biography/autobiography; business/economics; child guidance/parenting; computers/electronic; cooking/foods/nutrition; crafts/hobbies; creative nonfiction; current affairs; education; ethnic/cultural interests; gardening; gay/lesbian issues; government/politics/law; health/medicine; history; how-to; humor/satire; interior design/decorating; juvenile nonfiction; language/literature/criticism; memoirs; military/war; money/finance; multicultural; music/dance; nature/environment; New Age/metaphysics; philosophy; photography; popular culture; psychology; recreation; regional; religious/inspirational; science/technology; self-help/personal improvement; sex; sociology; software; spirituality; sports; theater/film; translation; travel; true crime/investigative; women's issues/studies; young adult. **Considers these fiction areas:** Action/adventure; contemporary issues; detective/police/crime; ethnic; experimental; family saga; feminist; gay/lesbian; glitz; historical; humor/satire; literary; mainstream/contemporary; mystery/suspense; picture books; psychic/supernatural; religious/inspirational; sports; thriller.

　　○┓ This agency specializes in commercial fiction, nonfiction.

How to Contact: Query with SASE, outline. Considers simultaneous queries. Responds in 2 months to mss. Obtains most new clients through recommendations from others, conferences, lectures and "very frequently through publisher's referrals."

Recent Sales: Sold 25 titles in the last year. *Self Matters*, by Dr. Phil McGraw (Simon & Schuster); *Life Strategies for Teens*, by Jay McGraw (Simon & Schuster); *Bringing the Family Back to the Table*, by Art Smith (Hyperion).

Terms: Agent receives 15% commission on domestic sales. Offers written contract. Charges clients $20 processing fee and express mail charges.

Writers' Conferences: Southwest Writers (Albuquerque NM); Brazos Writers (College Station TX).

Tips: If interested in agency representation, "it is vital to have the material in the proper working format. As agents' policies differ, it is important to follow their guidelines. The best advice I can give is to work on establishing a strong proposal that provides sample chapters, an overall synopsis (fairly detailed) and some bio information on yourself. Do not send your proposal in pieces; it should be complete upon submission. Remember you are trying to sell your work and it should be in its best condition."

DWYER & O'GRADY, INC., (Specialized: children's books), P.O. Box 239, Lempster NH 03605-0239. (603)863-9347. Fax: (603)863-9346. **Contact:** Elizabeth O'Grady. Estab. 1990. Member of SCBWI. Represents 20 clients. Currently handles: 100% juvenile books.

　　● Prior to opening their agency, Mr. Dwyer and Ms. Grady were booksellers and publishers.

Member Agents: Elizabeth O'Grady (children's books); Jeff Dwyer (children's books).

Represents: Juvenile books. **Considers these nonfiction areas:** Juvenile nonfiction. **Considers these fiction areas:** Juvenile; picture books; young adult.

　　○┓ This agency represents only writers and illustrators of children's books. Does not want to receive submissions that are not for juvenile audiences.

How to Contact: Not accepting new clients. No unsolicited mss. Obtains most new clients through recommendations from others, direct approach by agent to writer whose work they've read.

Recent Sales: Sold 22 titles in the last year. Clients include Kim Ablon, Mary Azarian, Tom Bedett, Odds Bodkin, Donna Clair, Leonard Jenkins, E.B. Lewis, Rebecca Rule, Steve Schuch, Virginia Stroud, Natasha Tarpley, Zong-Zhou Wang, Rashida Watson.

Terms: Agent receives 15% commission on domestic sales; 20% commission on foreign sales. Offers written contract; 30-day notice must be given to terminate contract. Charges clients for "photocopying of longer manuscripts or mutually agreed upon marketing expenses."

Writers' Conferences: Book Expo; American Library Association; Society of Children's Book Writers & Illustrators.

JANE DYSTEL LITERARY MANAGEMENT, INC., One Union Square West, Suite 904, New York NY 10003. (212)627-9100. Fax: (212)627-9313. E-mail: miriam@dystel.com. Website: www.dystel.com. **Contact:** Miriam Goderich. Estab. 1994. Member of AAR. Represents 300 clients. 50% of clients are new/unpublished writers. Currently handles: 65% nonfiction books; 25% novels; 10% cookbooks.

　　● Jane Dystel Literary Management recently acquired the client list of Bedford Book Works.

Member Agents: Stacey Glick; Jane Dystel; Miriam Goderich; Michael Bourret.

Represents: Nonfiction books, novels, cookbooks. **Considers these nonfiction areas:** Animals; anthropology/archaeology; biography/autobiography; business/economics; child guidance/parenting; cooking/foods/nutrition; current affairs; education; ethnic/cultural interests; gay/lesbian issues; government/politics/law; health/medicine; history; humor/satire; military/war; money/finance; New Age/metaphysics; popular culture; psychology; religious/inspirational; science/technology; true crime/investigative; women's issues/studies. **Considers these fiction areas:** Action/adventure; contemporary issues; detective/police/crime; ethnic; family saga; gay/lesbian; literary; mainstream/contemporary; mystery/suspense; thriller (especially).

O━ This agency specializes in commercial and literary fiction and nonfiction plus cookbooks.

How to Contact: Query with SASE. Accepts e-mail queries. Considers simultaneous queries. Responds in 1 month to queries; 6 weeks to mss. Obtains most new clients through recommendations from others, solicitations, conferences.

Recent Sales: *Redbone*, by Ron Stodghill (Farrar Straus & Giroux); *The Courier*, by Jay MacLarby (Pocket Books); *The Sparrow* and *Children of God*, by Mary Russell; *Water Carry Me*, by Thomas Moran; *Today, I Am a Ma'am*, by Valerie Harper; *Lidia's Italian-American Kitchen*, by Lidia Bastianich.

Terms: Agent receives 15% commission on domestic sales; 19% commission on foreign sales. Offers written contract, binding for book to book basis. Charges for photocopying. Galley charges and book charges from the publisher are passed on to the author.

Writers' Conferences: West Coast Writers Conference (Whidbey Island WA, Columbus Day weekend); University of Iowa Writer's Conference; Pacific Northwest Writer's Conference; Pike's Peak Writer's Conference; Santa Barbara Writer's Conference; Harriette Austin's Writer's Conference; Sandhills Writers Conference.

Tips: "Work on sending professional, well written queries that are concise and addressed to the specific agent the author is contacting. No dear Sirs/Madam."

N: THE E.S. AGENCY, 7220 Brattle Court, Sacramento CA 95842. (916)332-3959. Fax: (916)332-3960. E-mail: edley07@cs.com. **Contact:** Ed Silver. Estab. 1994. Signatory of WGA. Represents 50 clients. 50% of clients are new/unpublished writers. Currently handles: 30% movie scripts; 10% TV scripts; 60% novels/nonfiction.

Member Agents: Ed Silver.

Represents: Action/adventure; comedy; detective/police/crime; mainstream; mystery/suspense; romantic comedy; romantic drama; thriller/espionage.

O━ Does not want to receive TV series or episodic.

How to Contact: Query with SASE. Accepts queries by e-mail. Considers simultaneous queries. Responds in 1 month to queries. Discards unwanted queries. Obtains most new clients through recommendations from others, queries/solicitations.

Recent Sales: Optioned 3 titles in the last year.

Terms: Agent receives 10% commission on screen; 15% on mss. Offers written contract. Immediate notice must be given to terminate contract. Charges clients for postage and photocopies.

Ø ANNE EDELSTEIN LITERARY AGENCY, 404 Riverside Dr., New York NY 10025. Member of AAR.

● This agency did not respond to our request for information. Query before submitting.

Ø Ⓞ EDUCATIONAL DESIGN SERVICES, INC., (Specialized: education), P.O. Box 253, Wantagh NY 11793-0253. (718)539-4107 or (516)221-0995. **Contact:** Bertram L. Linder, president; Edwin Selzer, vice president. Estab. 1979. Represents 17 clients. 70% of clients are new/unpublished writers. Currently handles: 100% textbooks.

Represents: Scholarly books, textbooks. **Considers these nonfiction areas:** Anthropology/archaeology; business/economics; child guidance/parenting; current affairs; education; ethnic/cultural interests; government/politics/law; history; language/literature/criticism; military/war; money/finance; science/technology; sociology; women's issues/studies; all K-12 market.

O━ This agency specializes in textual material for the educational market.

How to Contact: Query with SASE, proposal package, outline, 1-2 sample chapter(s). Considers simultaneous queries. Responds in 1 month to queries; 6 weeks to mss. Returns materials only with SASE. Obtains most new clients through recommendations from others, solicitations, conferences.

Recent Sales: Sold 4 titles in the last year. *How to Solve the Word Problems in Arithmetic Grades 6-8*, by P. Pullman (McGraw-Hill/Schaum); *How to Solve Math Word Problems on Standardized Tests*, by D. Wayne (McGraw-Hill/Schaum); *First Principles of Cosmology*, by E.V. Linder (Addison-Wesley Longman).

Terms: Agent receives 15% commission on domestic sales; 25% commission on foreign sales. Offers written contract. Charges clients for photocopying, actual postage/shipping costs.

Ø PETER ELEK ASSOCIATES, The Content Company, Inc., 5111 JFK Blvd. E., West New York NJ 07093. (201)558-0323. Fax: (201)558-0307. E-mail: info@theliteraryagency.com. **Contact:** Juliet Gentile. Estab. 1979. Represents 15 clients. Currently handles: 70% nonfiction books; 30% juvenile books.

Member Agents: Gerardo Greco (director of project development/multimedia).

Represents: Nonfiction books, juvenile books (nonfiction, picture books). **Considers these nonfiction areas:** Anthropology/archaeology; child guidance/parenting; juvenile nonfiction; nature/environment; popular culture; science/technology; true crime/investigative.

O━ This agency specializes in children's picture books, adult nonfiction.

How to Contact: Query with SASE, proposal package, outline. Prefers to read material exclusively. Accepts e-mail queries. No fax queries. Responds in 6 weeks to queries; 6 weeks to mss. Obtains most new clients through recommendations from others, studying bylines in consumer and trade magazines and in regional and local newspapers.

Recent Sales: Sold 8 titles in the last year. *Ghost of the Aby*, by James Camero (Da Capo); *D-Day*, by Dan van der Vat (Bloomsbury).

Terms: Agent receives 15% commission on domestic sales; 20% commission on foreign sales. If required, charges clients for wholesale photocopying, typing, courier charges.

Writers' Conferences: Frankfurt Book Fair (Frankfurt Germany, October); LIBF (England); Bologna Children's Book Fair (Italy); APBA, Sydney, Australia

Tips: "Do your research thoroughly before submitting proposal. Only fresh and original material considered."

ETHAN ELLENBERG LITERARY AGENCY, 548 Broadway, #5-E, New York NY 10012. (212)431-4554. Fax: (212)941-4652. E-mail: agent@ethanellenberg.com. Website: www.ethanellenberg.com. **Contact:** Ethan Ellenberg, Michael Psaltis. Estab. 1983. Represents 80 clients. 10% of clients are new/unpublished writers. Currently handles: 25% nonfiction books; 75% novels.

● Prior to opening his agency, Mr. Ellenberg was contracts manager of Berkley/Jove and associate contracts manager for Bantam.

Member Agents: Michael Psaltis (serious and commercial nonfiction, including science, health, popular culture, cooking, current events, politics, business, memoir and other unique projects; and commercial and literary fiction); Ethan Ellenberg.

Represents: Nonfiction books, novels. **Considers these nonfiction areas:** Biography/autobiography; health/medicine; history; military/war; New Age/metaphysics; religious/inspirational; science/technology. **Considers these fiction areas:** Fantasy; romance; science fiction; thriller; women's.

○► This agency specializes in commercial fiction, especially thrillers, romance/women's fiction and specialized nonfiction. "We also do a lot of children's books." For children's books: Send introductory letter (with credits, if any), up to 3 picture book mss, outline and first 3 chapters for longer projects, SASE. Actively seeking commercial and literary fiction, children's books, break-through nonfiction. Does not want to receive poetry, short stories, westerns, autobiographies.

How to Contact: For fiction: Send introductory letter (with credits, if any), outline, first 3 chapters and SASE. For nonfiction: Send query letter and/or proposal, 1 sample chapter if written. No fax queries. Accepts e-mail queries, no attachments. Considers simultaneous queries. Responds in 10 days to queries; 1 month to mss. Returns materials only with SASE.

Recent Sales: Has sold over 100 titles in the last 3 years. *On Punk's Wing*, by Ward Carroll (Dutton); *Shadow of the Warrior*, by Marcus Wynne (Tor Books); *The Tentmaker*, by Clay Reynolds (Berkley); *The Rover*, by Mel Odom (Tor Books); *Angelica*, by Sharon Shinn (Ace Books); *Reckless Embrace*, by Madeline Baker (Leisure Books); *Bliss River*, by Thea Devine (Kensington); *Just Beyond Tomorrow*, by Beatrice Small (Kensington); *My Friend Rabbit*, by Eric Rohmann (Millbrook Press); *A Taste of the Season*, by Diane Worthington (Chronicle Books); *Yoga Mini-Book* series, by Elaine Gavalas (Fireside/Simon & Schuster).

Terms: Agent receives 15% commission on domestic sales; 10% commission on foreign sales. Offers written contract. Charges clients for "direct expenses only limited to photocopying, postage, by writer's consent only."

Writers' Conferences: RWA National; Novelists, Inc.; and other regional conferences.

Tips: "We do consider new material from unsolicited authors. Write a good clear letter with a succinct description of your book. We prefer the first three chapters when we consider fiction. For all submissions you must include SASE for return or the material is discarded. It's always hard to break in, but talent will find a home. Check our website for complete submission guidelines. We continue to see natural storytellers and nonfiction writers with important books."

NICHOLAS ELLISON, INC., affiliated with Sanford J. Greenburger Associates, 55 Fifth Ave., 15th Floor, New York NY 10003. (212)206-6050. Fax: (212)436-8718. **Contact:** Alicka Pistek. Estab. 1983. Represents 70 clients. Currently handles: 50% nonfiction books; 50% novels.

● Prior to becoming an agent, Mr. Ellison was an editor at Minerva Editions, Harper & Row and editor-in-chief at Delacorte.

Member Agents: Alicka Pistek.

Represents: Nonfiction books, novels. **Considers these nonfiction areas:** Considers most nonfiction areas. **Considers these fiction areas:** Literary; mainstream/contemporary.

○► Does not want to receive self-help.

How to Contact: Query with SASE. Responds in 6 weeks to queries.

ALWAYS INCLUDE a self-addressed, stamped envelope (SASE) for reply or return of your query or manuscript.

Recent Sales: *Up Country*, by Nelson DeMille (Warner); *Equivocal Death*, by Amy Gutman (Little, Brown). Other clients include Olivia Goldsmith, P.T. Deutermann, Nancy Geary.
Terms: Agent receives 15% commission on domestic sales; 20% commission on foreign sales.

◑ **ANN ELMO AGENCY INC.**, 60 E. 42nd St., New York NY 10165. (212)661-2880, 2881. Fax: (212)661-2883. **Contact:** Lettie Lee. Estab. 1959. Member of AAR, MWA, Authors Guild.
Member Agents: Lettie Lee; Mari Cronin (plays); A.L. Abecassis (nonfiction).
Represents: Nonfiction books, novels. **Considers these nonfiction areas:** Biography/autobiography; business/economics; cooking/foods/nutrition; current affairs; health/medicine; history; how-to; money/finance; music/dance; popular culture; psychology; science/technology; self-help/personal improvement; theater/film. **Considers these fiction areas:** Contemporary issues; detective/police/crime; ethnic; family saga; historical; literary; mainstream/contemporary; mystery/suspense; regional; romance (contemporary, gothic, historical, regency); thriller.
How to Contact: Letter queries *only* with SASE. No fax queries. Responds in 3 months to queries. Obtains most new clients through recommendations from others.
Recent Sales: This agency prefers not to share information on specific sales.
Terms: Agent receives 15% commission on domestic sales; 20% commission on foreign sales. Offers written contract. Charges clients for "special mailings or shipping considerations or multiple international calls. No charge for usual cost of doing business."
Tips: "Query first, and when asked only please send properly prepared manuscript. A double-spaced, readable manuscript is the best recommendation. Include SASE, of course."

☑ ◻ **ELAINE P. ENGLISH**, Graybill & English, LLC, 1875 Connecticut Ave. NW, Suite 712, Washington DC 20009. (202)588-9798, ext. 143. Fax: (202)457-0662. E-mail: ElaineEngl@aol.com. Website: www.graybilla ndenglish.com. **Contact:** Elaine English. Member of AAR. Represents 7 clients. 75% of clients are new/unpublished writers. Currently handles: 100% novels.
● Ms. English is also an attorney specializing in media and publishing law.
Member Agents: Elaine English (women's fiction, including romance).
Represents: Novels. **Considers these fiction areas:** Historical; mainstream/contemporary; multicultural; romance (including single titles); women's.
　O� "While not as an agent, per se, I have been working in publishing for over fifteen years. Also, I'm affiliated with other agents who represent a broad spectrum of projects." Actively seeking women's fiction, including single title romances. Does not want to receive anything other than above.
How to Contact: Submit outline, 3 sample chapter(s), SASE. Responds in 3 weeks to queries; 2 months to mss. Returns materials only with SASE. Obtains most new clients through solicitations.
Terms: Agent receives 15% commission on domestic sales; 20% commission on foreign sales. Offers written contract; 30-day notice must be given to terminate contract. Charges only for expenses directly related to sales of manuscript (long distance, postage, copying).
Writers' Conferences: Washington Romance Writers (Harpers Ferry VA, April); Novelists, Inc. (New York NY, September); RWA Nationals (Denver CO, July); Georgia Romance Writers (Atlanta GA, November).

◪ **FELICIA ETH LITERARY REPRESENTATION**, 555 Bryant St., Suite 350, Palo Alto CA 94301-1700. (650)375-1276. Fax: (650)375-1277. E-mail: feliciaeth@aol.com. **Contact:** Felicia Eth. Estab. 1988. Member of AAR. Represents 25-35 clients. Works with established and new writers. Currently handles: 85% nonfiction books; 15% adult novels.
Represents: Nonfiction books, novels. **Considers these nonfiction areas:** Animals; anthropology/archaeology; biography/autobiography; business/economics; child guidance/parenting; current affairs; ethnic/cultural interests; gay/lesbian issues; government/politics/law; health/medicine; history; nature/environment; popular culture; psychology; science/technology; sociology; true crime/investigative; women's issues/studies. **Considers these fiction areas:** Ethnic; feminist; gay/lesbian; literary; mainstream/contemporary; thriller.
　Oᴀrt This agency specializes in "provocative, intelligent, thoughtful nonfiction on a wide array of subjects which are commercial and high-quality fiction; preferably mainstream and contemporary."
How to Contact: Query with SASE, outline. Considers simultaneous queries. Responds in 3 weeks to queries; 1 month to mss.
Recent Sales: Sold 7-10 titles in the last year. *Recovering the Power of the Ancestral Mind*, by Dr. Gregg Jacobs (Viking); *The Ulster Path*, by Will Ferguson (Grove/Atlantic); *Socrates Cafe*, by Chris Phillips (W.W. Norton); *Imperfect Harmony*, by Joshua Coleman (St. Martin's); *Baby Catcher: Chronicles of a Modern Midwife*, by Peggy Vincent (Charles Scribner's); *The Devil's Cup*, by Stewart Allen (Soho Press).
Terms: Agent receives 15% commission on domestic sales; 20% commission on foreign sales; 20% commission on dramatic rights sales. Charges clients for photocopying, express mail service—extraordinary expenses.
Writers' Conferences: Independent Writers of LA (Los Angeles); Conference of National Coalition of Independent Scholars (Berkley CA); Writers Guild.
Tips: "For nonfiction, established expertise is certainly a plus, as is magazine publication—though not a prerequisite. I am highly dedicated to those projects I represent."

FALLON LITERARY AGENCY, 15 E. 26th St., Suite 1609, New York NY 10010. Member of AAR.
● This agency did not respond to our request for information. Query before submitting. Agent: Eileen Fallon.

FARBER LITERARY AGENCY INC., 14 E. 75th St., #2E, New York NY 10021. (212)861-7075. Fax: (212)861-7076. E-mail: farberlit@aol.com. Website: www.donaldfarber.com. **Contact:** Ann Farber; Dr. Seth Farber. Estab. 1989. Represents 40 clients. 50% of clients are new/unpublished writers. Currently handles: 40% nonfiction books; 15% scholarly books; 45% stage plays.
Member Agents: Ann Farber (books); Seth Farber (theater); Donald C. Farber (attorney, all entertainment media).
Represents: Nonfiction books, novels, juvenile books, textbooks, stage plays. **Considers these nonfiction areas:** Child guidance/parenting; cooking/foods/nutrition; music/dance; psychology; theater/film. **Considers these fiction areas:** Action/adventure; contemporary issues; humor/satire; juvenile; literary; mainstream/contemporary; mystery/suspense; thriller; young adult.
How to Contact: Submit outline, 3 sample chapter(s), SASE. Considers simultaneous queries and submissions. Responds in 1 month to queries; 2 month to mss. Obtains most new clients through recommendations from others.
Recent Sales: Sold 5 titles in the last year. *The Eden Express*, by Mark Vonnegut (Seven Stories); *The Gardens of Frau Hess*, by Milton Marcus; *Hot Feat*, by Ed Bullins; *Bright Freedom Song*, by Gloria Houston (Harcourt Brace & Co.).
Terms: Agent receives 15% commission on domestic sales; 20% commission on foreign sales. Offers written contract, binding for 1 year. Client must furnish copies of ms, treatments and any other items for submission.
Tips: "Our attorney, Donald C. Farber, is the author of many books. His services are available to the agency's clients as part of the agency service at no additional charge."

FEIGEN/PARRENT LITERARY MANAGEMENT, 10158 Hollow Glen Circle, Bel Air CA 90077-2112. (310)271-4722. Fax: (310)274-0503. E-mail: feigenparrentlit@aol.com. **Contact:** Brenda Feigen, Joanne Parrent. Estab. 1995. Member of PEN USA West, Authors Guild, LA County Bar Association. Represents 35-40 clients. 20-30% of clients are new/unpublished writers. Currently handles: 40% nonfiction books; 30% novels; 25% movie scripts; 5% TV scripts.
● Ms. Feigen is also an attorney and producer; Ms. Parrent is also a screenwriter and author.
Member Agents: Brenda Feigen (books, books-to-film); Joanne Parrent (screenplays).
Represents: Nonfiction books, novels, feature film, TV movie of the week. **Considers these nonfiction areas:** Biography/autobiography; business/economics; current affairs; gay/lesbian issues; government/politics/law; health/medicine; how-to; memoirs; money/finance; psychology; self-help/personal improvement; theater/film; women's issues/studies. **Considers these fiction areas:** Family saga; feminist; gay/lesbian; literary. Must be professionally formatted and under 130 pages. **Considers these script subject areas:** Action/adventure; comedy; contemporary issues; family saga; feminist; gay/lesbian; thriller.
　This agency is actively seeking "material about women, including strong, positive individuals. The material can be fiction, memoir or biographical. Does not want to receive horror, science fiction, religion, pornography. "No poetry or short stories unless author has been published by a major house."
How to Contact: Prefers to read materials exclusively. Query only with 2-page synopsis, author bio. Accepts e-mail queries. No fax queries. Considers simultaneous queries. Responds in 3 weeks to queries; 6 weeks to mss. Returns materials only with SASE. Obtains most new clients through recommendations from other clients and publishers, through the Internet, and listings in *Literary Market Place*.
Recent Sales: Sold 6 titles and sold 1 script in the last year. *Defy the Darkness*, by Joe Rosenblum with David Kohn (Praeger); *The Courage to Care*, by Joanne Parrent (Macmillan). ***Movie/TV MOW script(s) optioned/sold:*** *Read Easy*, by Jay Milner (Tomorrow Entertainment).
Terms: Agent receives 15% commission on domestic sales; 20% commission on foreign sales. Offers written contract, binding for 1 year. Charges clients for postage, long distance calls, photocopying.
Tips: "If we like a book or screenplay we will either, at the writer's choice, represent it as agents or offer to produce it ourselves if the material is of real interst to us personally."

FEIGENBAUM PUBLISHING CONSULTANTS, INC., 61 Bounty Lane, Jericho NY 11753. (516)937-1909. Fax: (516)681-9121. E-mail: readrover5@aol.com. **Contact:** Laurie Feigenbaum. Represents 3 clients. 0% of clients are new/unpublished writers. Currently handles: 100% romance novels.
● In addition to being an agent, Ms. Feigenbaum was a contracts director.
Represents: Novels. **Considers these fiction areas:** Romance.
　This agency specializes in contract negotiation and permissions clearance. "I handle copyright and trademark registrations and research." Actively seeking romance. Does not want anything else.
How to Contact: Send outline/proposal, indicating any prior publishing experience. Accepts e-mail and fax queries. Considers simultaneous queries. Responds in 2 weeks to queries. Returns materials only with SASE. Obtains most new clients through recommendations from others.
Recent Sales: Sold 10 titles in the last year.
Terms: Agent receives 10% commission on domestic sales. No written contract.

Writers' Conferences: RWA.

▣ ▣ ◎ JUSTIN E. FERNANDEZ, AGENT/ATTORNEY, Cincinnati OH. E-mail: lit4@aol.com. **Contact:** Justin E. Fernandez. Estab. 1996. Represents 6-10 clients. 50% of clients are new/unpublished writers. Currently handles: 25% nonfiction books; 65% novels; 5% multimedia; 5% other.

• Prior to opening his agency, Mr. Fernandez, a 1992 graduate of the University of Cincinnati College of Law, served as a law clerk with the Ohio Court of Appeals, Second Appellate District (1992-94), and as a literary agent for Paraview, Inc., New York NY (1995-96).

Represents: Nonfiction books, novels, screenplays, digital art including e-books, video games and multimedia/ Internet works. **Considers these nonfiction areas:** Agriculture/horticulture; Americana; animals; anthropology/ archaeology; art/architecture/design; biography/autobiography; business/economics; child guidance/parenting; computers/electronic; cooking/foods/nutrition; crafts/hobbies; creative nonfiction; current affairs; education; ethnic/cultural interests; gardening; gay/lesbian issues; government/politics/law; health/medicine; history; how-to; humor/satire; interior design/decorating; juvenile nonfiction; language/literature/criticism; memoirs; military/war; money/finance; multicultural; music/dance; nature/environment; New Age/metaphysics; philosophy; photography; popular culture; psychology; recreation; regional; religious/inspirational; science/technology; self-help/personal improvement; sex; sociology; software; spirituality; sports; theater/film; translation; travel; true crime/ investigative; women's issues/studies; young adult. **Considers these fiction areas:** All well-written novella- to novel-length fiction.

How to Contact: Query first via e-mail only. Considers simultaneous queries. Obtains most new clients through referrals.

Terms: Agent receives 10% commission on domestic print sales, 15-25% on other sales depending upon project and particulars. Offers written contract.

Tips: "Query letters are business letters. Include facts such as book length (word count), genre, intended audience, favorable comparisons to other successful books of its type, and information about the book's niche (how much competition is there and what is it?) Keep personal data to a minimum unless it relates to publication credit or notoriety. Queries and manuscripts should be very carefully edited."

◎ FLAMING STAR LITERARY ENTERPRISES, 320 Riverside Dr., New York NY 10025. **Contact:** Joseph B. Vallely or Janis C. Vallely. Estab. 1985. Represents 100 clients. 25% of clients are new/unpublished writers. Currently handles: 100% nonfiction books.

• Prior to opening the agency, Joseph Vallely served as national sales manager for Dell; Janis Vallely was vice president at Doubleday.

Represents: Nonfiction books. **Considers these nonfiction areas:** Current affairs; government/politics/law; health/medicine; nature/environment; New Age/metaphysics; science/technology; self-help/personal improvement; spirituality; sports.

O➤ This agency specializes in upscale commercial nonfiction.

How to Contact: Query with SASE. Obtains most new clients through recommendations from others, solicitations.

Terms: Agent receives 15% commission on domestic sales; 20% commission on foreign sales. Offers written contract. Charges clients for photocopying, postage only. Writers reimbused for office fees after the sale of mss.

▣ ◎ FLANNERY LITERARY, (Specialized: juvenile books), 1140 Wickfield Court, Naperville IL 60563-3300. (630)428-2682. Fax: (630)428-2683. **Contact:** Jennifer Flannery. Estab. 1992. Represents 33 clients. 90% of clients are new/unpublished writers. Currently handles: 100% juvenile books.

• Prior to opening her agency, Ms. Flannery was an editorial assistant.

Represents: Juvenile books. **Considers these nonfiction areas:** Juvenile nonfiction; young adult. **Considers these fiction areas:** Juvenile; picture books; young adult.

O➤ This agency specializes in children's and young adult, juvenile fiction and nonfiction.

How to Contact: Query with SASE. Responds in 3 weeks to queries; 1 month to mss. Obtains most new clients through recommendations from others, solicitations.

Recent Sales: Sold 20 titles in the last year. This agency prefers not to share information on specific sales.

Terms: Agent receives 15% commission on domestic sales; 20% commission on foreign sales. Offers written contract, binding for life of book in print; 30-day notice must be given to terminate contract. 100% of business is derived from commissions on ms sales.

Writers' Conferences: SCBWI Fall Conference.

Tips: "Write an engrossing, succinct query describing your work."

◎ PETER FLEMING AGENCY, P.O. Box 458, Pacific Palisades CA 90272. (310)454-1373. **Contact:** Peter Fleming. Estab. 1962. Currently handles: 100% nonfiction books.

Represents: Nonfiction books.

O➤ This agency specializes in "nonfiction books: innovative, helpful, contrarian, individualistic, free market... with bestseller potential." Books should promote "abandoning special interests, corruption and patronage."

How to Contact: Query with SASE. Obtains most new clients through "through a different, one-of-a-kind idea for a book usually backed by the writer's experience in that area of expertise."

Recent Sales: *Rulers of Evil*, by F. Tupper Saussy (HarperCollins); *Why is it Always About You—Saving Yourself from the Narcissists in Your Life*, by Sandy Hotchkiss (Free Press).

Terms: Agent receives 15% commission on domestic sales; 25% commission on foreign sales. Offers written contract, binding for 1 year. Charges clients "only those fees agreed to in writing, i.e., NY-ABA expenses shared. We may ask for a TV contract, too."

Tips: "You can begin by self-publishing, test marketing with direct sales, starting your own website."

B.R. FLEURY AGENCY, P.O. Box 149352, Orlando FL 32814-9352. (407)895-8494. Fax: (407)898-3923 or (888)310-8142. E-mail: brfleuryagency@yahoo.com. **Contact:** Blanche or Margaret. Estab. 1994. Signatory of WGA. Currently handles: 30% nonfiction books; 60% novels; 10% movie scripts.

Represents: Nonfiction books, novels, feature film, TV movie of the week. **Considers these nonfiction areas:** Health/medicine; how-to; humor/satire; money/finance; New Age/metaphysics; self-help/personal improvement; spirituality; true crime/investigative. **Considers these fiction areas:** Fantasy; horror; humor/satire; literary; psychic/supernatural; thriller. **Considers these script subject areas:** Detective/police/crime; fantasy; horror; mystery/suspense; psychic/supernatural; thriller.

How to Contact: Prefers to read materials exclusively. Query with one-page letter, SASE; or call for information. Accepts 1-page e-mail queries, no attachments. Responds in 3 months to mss. Responds immediately to queries. Obtains most new clients through recommendations from others, listings.

Recent Sales: Sold 5 manuscripts and 1 screenplay in the last year. This agency prefers not to share information on specific sales.

Terms: Agent receives 15% commission on domestic sales. Offers written contract, binding for as per contract. Receives screenplay commission according to WGA guidelines. Charges clients for business expenses directly related to work represented.

Tips: "Read your work aloud with someone who is not in love with you before you send it to us." E-mail queries should be 1 page maximum, no attachments. Queries with attachments or additional information will be returned unread.

THE FOGELMAN LITERARY AGENCY, 7515 Greenville, Suite 712, Dallas TX 75231. (214)361-9956. Fax: (214)361-9553. E-mail: foglit@aol.com. Website: www.fogelman.com. Also: 599 Lexington Ave., Suite 2300, New York NY 10022. (212)836-4803. **Contact:** Evan Fogelman. Estab. 1990. Member of AAR. Represents 100 clients. 2% of clients are new/unpublished writers. Currently handles: 40% nonfiction books; 40% novels; 10% scholarly books; 10% TV scripts.

● Prior to opening his agency, Mr. Fogelman was an entertainment lawyer. He is still active in the field and serves as chairman of the Texas Entertainment and Sports Lawyers Association.

Member Agents: Evan Fogelman (nonfiction, women's fiction); Linda Kruger (women's fiction, nonfiction).

Represents: Nonfiction books, novels. **Considers these nonfiction areas:** Biography/autobiography; business/economics; child guidance/parenting; current affairs; education; ethnic/cultural interests; government/politics/law; health/medicine; popular culture; psychology; sports; true crime/investigative; women's issues/studies. **Considers these fiction areas:** Historical; literary; mainstream/contemporary; romance (all sub-genres).

O➔ This agency specializes in women's fiction and nonfiction. "Zealous advocacy" makes this agency stand apart from others. Actively seeking "nonfiction of all types; romance fiction." Does not want to receive children's/juvenile.

How to Contact: Query with SASE. Considers simultaneous queries. Responds in 3 months to mss. Responds 'next business day' to queries. Returns materials only with SASE. Obtains most new clients through recommendations from others.

Recent Sales: Sold 60 titles in the last year. Other clients include Caroline Hunt, Katherine Sutcliffe, Crystal Stovall.

Terms: Agent receives 15% commission on domestic sales; 10% commission on foreign sales. Offers written contract, binding for project-to-project.

Writers' Conferences: Romance Writers of America; Novelists, Inc.

Tips: "Finish your manuscript, and see our website."

THE FOLEY LITERARY AGENCY, 34 E. 38th St., New York NY 10016-2508. (212)686-6930. **Contact:** Joan Foley or Joseph Foley. Estab. 1961. Represents 10 clients. Rarely takes on new clients. Currently handles: 75% nonfiction books; 25% novels.

Represents: Nonfiction books, novels.

How to Contact: Query with letter, brief outline, SASE. Responds promptly to queries. Obtains most new clients through recommendations from others, taking on new clients rarely.

Recent Sales: This agency prefers not to share information on specific sales.

Terms: Agent receives 10% commission on domestic sales; 15% commission on foreign sales. 100% of business is derived from commissions on ms sales.

Tips: Desires brevity in querying.

FORT ROSS INC. RUSSIAN-AMERICAN PUBLISHING PROJECTS, 26 Arthur Place, Yonkers NY 10701-1703. (914)375-6448. Fax: (914)375-6439. E-mail: ftross@ix.netcom.com. Website: www.fortross.net. **Contact:** Dr. Vladimir P. Karsev. Estab. 1992. Represents about 100 clients. 2% of clients are new/unpublished writers. Currently handles: 50% nonfiction books; 40% novels; 10% juvenile books.
Member Agents: Ms. Olga Borodyanskaya, St. Petersburg, Russia, phone: 7-812-1738607 (fiction, nonfiction); Mr. Konstantin Paltchikov, Moscow, Russia, phone: 7-095-2035280 (romance, science fiction, fantasy, thriller); Kristin Olson, Prague, Czech Republic, phone: 420-2 2251-9639.
Represents: Nonfiction books, novels, juvenile books. **Considers these nonfiction areas:** Biography/autobiography; history; memoirs; psychology; self-help/personal improvement; true crime/investigative. **Considers these fiction areas:** Action/adventure; detective/police/crime; fantasy; horror; juvenile; mystery/suspense; romance (contemporary, gothic, historical, regency); science fiction; thriller; young adult.

　　○➔ This agency specializes in selling rights for Russian books and illustrations (covers) to American publishers and American books and illustrations for Europe; also Russian-English and English-Russian translations. Actively seeking adventure, fiction, mystery, romance, science fiction, thriller from established authors and illustrators for Russian and European markets.
How to Contact: Send published book or galleys. Accepts e-mail and fax queries. Considers simultaneous queries. Returns materials only with SASE.
Recent Sales: Sold 12 titles in the last year. *Mastering Judo with Vladimir Putin*, by Vladimir Putin et al (North Atlantic Books [USA]); *Max*, by Howard Fast (Baronet [Czech Republic]); *Kiss of Midas*, by George Vainer (Neri [Italy]); *Redemption*, by Howard Fast (Oram [Israel]); *Billion Dollars Cash*, by Anatoly Romov (Amber [Poland]).
Terms: Agent receives 10% commission on domestic sales; 20% commission on foreign sales. Offers written contract, binding for 2 years; 2-month notice must be given to terminate contract.
Tips: "Established authors and book illustrators (especially cover art) are welcome for the following genres: romance, fantasy, science fiction, mystery and adventure."

FORTHWRITE LITERARY AGENCY, 23852 W. Pacific Coast Hwy., Suite 701, Malibu CA 90265. (310)456-5698. Fax: (310)456-6589. E-mail: agent@kellermedia.com. Website: www.Kellermedia.com. **Contact:** Wendy Keller. Estab. 1989. Member of National Association for Female Executives, American Society for Training and Development, National Speakers Association. Represents 40 clients. 10% of clients are new/ unpublished writers. Currently handles: 90% nonfiction books; 10% foreign and other secondary rights.

　　● Prior to opening her agency, Ms. Keller was the associate publisher of Los Angeles' second largest Spanish-language newpaper. **Considers these nonfiction areas:** Art/architecture/design; biography/autobiography; business/economics; child guidance/parenting; cooking/foods/nutrition; crafts/hobbies; current affairs; health/medicine (and alternative health); history; how-to; interior design/decorating; nature/environment (ecology); psychology (pop); religious/inspirational; self-help/personal improvement; spirituality (inspirational); theater/film; women's issues/studies; home maintenance and management; writing; consumer reference.
Member Agents: Suzanne Boyd Smith and Melissa Lee (speakers and booking agents).

　　○➔ This agency specializes in "serving authors who are or plan to also be speakers. Our sister company is a speaker's bureau. We handle business books (sales, finance, marketing and management especially); self-help and how-to books on many subjects." Also handles foreign, ancillary, upselling (selling a previously published book to a larger publisher) and other secondary and subsidiary rights. Actively seeking "professional manuscripts by highly qualified authors." Does not want to read "fiction, get-rich-quick or first person narrative on health topics."
How to Contact: No unsolicited mss. Prefers e-mail queries, no attachments. Considers simultaneous queries. Responds in 2 weeks to queries; 6 weeks to mss. Returns materials only with SASE. Obtains most new clients through referrals, recommendations by editors, queries, satisfied authors, conferences.
Recent Sales: Sold 17 titles in the last year. *The Power Path*, by José and Lena Stevens (New World Library); *Connected for Life: Emotional Availability Between Parents and Children*, by Zeynep Biringen, Ph.D (Putnam/ Perigree).
Writers' Conferences: BEA; Frankfurt Booksellers' Convention; Maui Writer's Conference. Attends regional conferences and regularly talks on finding an agent, how to write nonfiction proposals, book marketing, query writing, creativity enhancement, persevering for creatives.

MARKET UPDATE FROM *WRITER'S MARKET* Looking for advice for getting published, pubishing trends, and information about the shifting writing marketplace? All are available free by subscribing to *Market Update From Writer's Market*. Our e-mail newsletter will deliver this invaluable information straight to your e-mailbox every two weeks absolutely free. Sign up at www.WritersMarket.com.

Tips: "Write only on a subject you know well, and be prepared to show a need in the market for your book. We prefer to represent authors who are already presenting their material publicly through seminars or other media."

⊘ FOX CHASE AGENCY, INC., Public Ledget Bldg. 930, Philadelphia PA 19106. Member of AAR.
• This agency did not respond to our request for information. Query before submitting.
Member Agents: A. L. Hart; Jo C. Hart.

⊘ LYNN C. FRANKLIN ASSOCIATES, LTD., 1350 Broadway, Suite 2015, New York NY 10018. (212)868-6311. Fax: (212)868-6312. **Contact:** Lynn Franklin and Claudia Nys. Estab. 1987. Member of PEN America. Represents 30-35 clients. 50% of clients are new/unpublished writers. Currently handles: 90% nonfiction books; 10% novels.
Represents: Nonfiction books, novels. **Considers these nonfiction areas:** Biography/autobiography; current affairs; health/medicine; history; memoirs; New Age/metaphysics; psychology; religious/inspirational (inspirational); self-help/personal improvement; spirituality. **Considers these fiction areas:** Literary; mainstream/contemporary (commercial).
  O─┐ This agency specializes in general nonfiction with a special interest in health, biography, international affairs, and spirituality.
How to Contact: Query with SASE. No unsolicited mss. Considers simultaneous queries. Responds in 2 weeks to queries; 6 weeks to mss. Obtains most new clients through recommendations from others, solicitations.
Recent Sales: *The Rich Part of Life*, by Jim Kokoris (St. Martin's Press/film rights secured by Columbia Pictures); *Health on Your Own Terms*, by Frank Lipman, M.D. (Tarcher/Putnam); *After Breast Cancer Treatment: A Survivor's Guide to Renewed Health and Happiness*, by Hester Hill Schnipper (Bantam/Dell); *Meeting Faith: the Forest Journals of a Black Buddhist Nun in Thailand*, by Faith Adiele (WW Norton).
Terms: Agent receives 15% commission on domestic sales; 20% commission on foreign sales. Offers written contract; 60-day notice must be given to terminate contract. 100% of business is derived from commissions on ms sales. Charges clients for postage, photocopying, long distance telephone if significant.

JEANNE FREDERICKS LITERARY AGENCY, INC., 221 Benedict Hill Rd., New Canaan CT 06840. (203)972-3011. Fax: (203)972-3011. E-mail: jfredrks@optonline.net. **Contact:** Jeanne Fredericks. Estab. 1997. Member of AAR, Authors Guild. Represents 90 clients. 10% of clients are new/unpublished writers. Currently handles: 98% nonfiction books; 2% novels.
  • Prior to opening her agency, Ms. Fredericks was an agent and acting director with the Susan P. Urstadt Inc. Agency. In an earlier career she held editorial positions in trade publishing, most recently as editorial director of Ziff-Davis Books.
Represents: Nonfiction books. **Considers these nonfiction areas:** Animals; biography/autobiography; child guidance/parenting; cooking/foods/nutrition; gardening; health/medicine (and alternative health); history; how-to; interior design/decorating; money/finance; nature/environment; photography; psychology; self-help/personal improvement; sports; women's issues/studies.
  O─┐ This agency specializes in quality adult nonfiction by authorities in their fields. Does not want to receive children's fiction.
How to Contact: Query first with SASE. Then send outline/proposal, 1-2 sample chapters and SASE. No fax queries. Accepts e-mail queries if short; no attachments. Considers simultaneous queries. Responds in 3 weeks to queries; 2 months to mss. Returns materials only with SASE. Obtains most new clients through recommendations from others, solicitations, conferences.
Recent Sales: Sold 20 titles in the last year. *From Storebought to Homemade*, by Emyl Jenkins; *Cowboys and Dragons: Achieving Successful American-Chinese Business Relations*, by Charles Lee (Dearborn); *Handbook to Life in the Medieval World*, by Madeleine Cosman (Facts on File).
Terms: Agent receives 15% commission on domestic sales; 25% commission on foreign sales with co-agent; without co-agent receives 20% commission on foreign sales. Offers written contract, binding for 9 months; 2-month notice must be given to terminate contract. Charges client for photocopying of whole proposals and mss, overseas postage, priority mail and express mail services.
Writers' Conferences: PEN Women Conference (Williamsburg VA, February); Connecticut Press Club Biennial Writer's Conference (Stamford CT, April); ASJA Annual Writers' Conference East (New York NY, May); BEA (New York, May).
Tips: "Be sure to research the competition for your work and be able to justify why there's a need for it. I enjoy building an author's career, particularly if s(he) is professional, hardworking, and courteous. Aside from ten years of agenting experience, I've had ten years of editorial experience in adult trade book publishing that enables me to help an author polish a proposal so that it's more appealing to prospective editors. My MBA in marketing also distinguishes me from other agents."

◐ SARAH JANE FREYMANN LITERARY AGENCY, 59 W. 71st St., Suite 9B, New York NY 10023. (212)362-9277. Fax: (212)501-8240. **Contact:** Sarah Jane Freymann. Represents 100 clients. 20% of clients are new/unpublished writers. Currently handles: 75% nonfiction books; 23% novels; 2% juvenile books.
Represents: Nonfiction books, novels, illustrated books. **Considers these nonfiction areas:** Animals; anthropology/archaeology; art/architecture/design; biography/autobiography; business/economics; child guidance/par-

enting; cooking/foods/nutrition; current affairs; ethnic/cultural interests; health/medicine; history; interior design/decorating; memoirs (narrative, non-fiction); nature/environment; psychology; religious/inspirational; self-help/personal improvement; women's issues/studies; lifestyle. **Considers these fiction areas:** Contemporary issues; ethnic; literary; mainstream/contemporary; mystery/suspense; thriller.

How to Contact: Query with SASE. Responds in 2 weeks to queries; 6 weeks to mss. Obtains most new clients through recommendations from others.

Recent Sales: *Serenity in Motion*, by Nancy O'Hara (Harmony 2003); *Seeing Red: Tales from the Communist Bloc*, by Stephanie Elizondo Griest (Random House 2003); *Asian Grilling*, by Su-Mei Yu (William Morrow 2002).

Terms: Agent receives 15% commission on domestic sales; 20% commission on foreign sales. Offers written contract. Charges clients for long distance, overseas postage, photocopying. 100% of business is derived from commissions on ms sales.

Tips: "I love fresh new passionate works by authors who love what they are doing and have both natural talent and carefully honed skill."

CANDICE FUHRMAN LITERARY AGENCY, 2440C Bush St., San Francisco CA 94115. **Contact:** Candice Fuhrman. Member of AAR. Not accepting new clients.

MAX GARTENBERG, LITERARY AGENT, 521 Fifth Ave., Suite 1700, New York NY 10175-0038. (212)292-4354. Fax: (973)535-5033. E-mail: gartenbook@att.net. **Contact:** Max Gartenberg. Estab. 1954. Represents 30 clients. 5% of clients are new/unpublished writers. Currently handles: 90% nonfiction books; 10% novels.

Represents: Nonfiction books, novels. **Considers these nonfiction areas:** Agriculture/horticulture; animals; art/architecture/design; biography/autobiography; child guidance/parenting; current affairs; health/medicine; history; military/war; money/finance; music/dance; nature/environment; psychology; science/technology; self-help/personal improvement; sports; theater/film; true crime/investigative; women's issues/studies.

How to Contact: Query with SASE. No e-mail or fax queries. Considers simultaneous queries. Responds in 2 weeks to queries; 6 weeks to mss. Obtains most new clients through recommendations from others, occasionally by "following up on good query letters."

Recent Sales: *Stealing Secrets, Telling Lies*, by James Gannon (Brassey's); *Encyclopedia of North American Sports History*, by Ralph Hickok (Facts-On-File).

Terms: Agent receives 15% commission on first domestic sales; 10% subsequent commission on domestic sales; 15-20% commission on foreign sales.

Tips: "This is a small agency serving established writers; new writers whose work it is able to handle are few and far between. Nonfiction is more likely to be of interest here than fiction, and category fiction not at all."

GELFMAN SCHNEIDER LITERARY AGENTS, INC., 250 W. 57th St., New York NY 10107. (212)245-1993. Fax: (212)245-8678. **Contact:** Jane Gelfman, Deborah Schneider. Estab. 1981. Member of AAR. Represents 150 clients. 10% of clients are new/unpublished writers.

Represents: Nonfiction books, novels. "We represent adult, general, hardcover fiction and nonfiction, literary and commercial, and some mysteries." **Considers these fiction areas:** Literary; mainstream/contemporary; mystery/suspense.

Does not want to receive romances, science fiction, westerns or children's books.

How to Contact: Query with SASE. No e-mail queries. Accepts simultaneous queries. Responds in 1 month to queries; 2 months to mss. Obtains most new clients through recommendations from others.

Terms: Agent receives 15% commission on domestic sales; 20% commission on foreign sales. Offers written contract. Charges clients for photocopying, messengers and couriers.

GHOSTS & COLLABORATORS INTERNATIONAL, (Specialized: ghostwriting), division of James Peter Associates, Inc., P.O. Box 358, New Canaan CT 06840. (203)972-1070. E-mail: gene_brissie@msn.com. **Contact:** Gene Brissie. Estab. 1971. Represents 75 clients. Currently handles: 100% nonfiction books.

Represents: Nonfiction collaborations and ghost writing assignments.

This agency specializes in representing only published ghostwriters and collaborators, nonfiction only.

How to Contact: Prefers to read materials exclusively.

Recent Sales: Sold 40 titles in the last year. Clients include Alan Axelrod, Carol Turkington, George Mair, Brandon Toropov, Richard Marek, Susan Shelly.

Terms: Agent receives 15% commission on domestic sales; 20% commission on foreign sales. Offers written contract.

Tips: "We would like to hear from professional writers who are looking for ghosting and collaboration projects. We invite inquiries from book publishers who are seeking writers to develop house-generated ideas and to work with their authors who need professional assistance."

THE GISLASON AGENCY, 219 Main St. SE, Suite 506, Minneapolis MN 55414-2160. (612)331-8033. Fax: (612)332-8115. E-mail: gislasonbj@aol.com. Website: www.thegislasonagency.com. **Contact:** Barbara J. Gislason, literary agent. Estab. 1992. Member of Minnesota State Bar Association, Art & Entertainment Law

Section (former chair), Internet Committee, Minnesota Intellectual Property Law Association Copyright Committee (former chair). Also a member of SFWA, MWA, RWA, Sisters in Crime, University Film Society (board member), Neighborhood Justice (board member) and American Academy of Acupuncture and Oriental Medicine (advisory board member). 80% of clients are new/unpublished writers. Currently handles: 25% nonfiction books; 75% novels.

• Ms. Gislason became an attorney in 1980, and continues to practice Art & Entertainment Law. She has been nationally recognized as a Leading American Attorney and a SuperLawyer.

Member Agents: Adam Kintopf (senior editor); Deborah Sweeney (fantasy, science fiction); Kellie Hultgren (fantasy, science fiction); Lisa Higgs (romance); Ally Ohlson (nonfiction); Kris Olson (mystery).

Represents: Nonfiction books, novels. **Considers these nonfiction areas:** Animals (behavior/communications); health/medicine (alternative); New Age/metaphysics; psychology (popular); science/technology; self-help/personal improvement; sociology; spirituality. **Considers these fiction areas:** Fantasy; mainstream/contemporary; mystery/suspense; romance; science fiction; thriller (legal).

O⊓ Do not send personal memoirs, poetry, screenplays or children's books.

How to Contact: Fiction: Query with synopsis, first 3 chapters and SASE. Nonfiction: Query with proposal and sample chapters; published authors may submit complete ms. Responds in 2 months to queries; 3 months to mss. Obtains most new clients through recommendations from others, conferences, *Guide to Literary Agents, Literary Market Place* and other reference books.

Recent Sales: *Historical Romance # 4*, by Linda Cook (Kensington); *Dancing Dead*, by Deborah Woodworth (HarperCollins); *Autumn World*, by Joan Verba, et al (Dragon Stone Press).

Terms: Agent receives 15% commission on domestic sales; 20% commission on foreign sales. Offers written contract, binding for 1 year with option to renew. Charges clients for photocopying and postage.

Writers' Conferences: Romance Writers of America; Midwest Fiction Writers; University of Wisconsin Writer's Institute. Also attend state and regional writers conferences.

Tips: "Cover letter should be well-written and include a detailed synopsis (if fiction) or proposal (if nonfiction), the first three chapters and author bio. Appropriate SASE required. We are looking for a great writer with a poetic, lyrical or quirky writing style who can create intriguing ambiguities. We expect a well-researched, imaginative and fresh plot that reflects a familiarity with the applicable genre. If submitting nonfiction work, explain how the submission differs from and adds to previously published works in the field. Scenes with sex and violence must be intrinsic to the plot. Remember to proofread, proofread, proofread. If the work was written with a specific publisher in mind, this should be communicated. In addition to owning an agency, Ms. Gislason practices law in the area of Art and Entertainment and has a broad spectrum of entertainment industry contacts."

◑ GOLDFARB & ASSOCIATES, 1501 M St. NW, Washington DC 20005-2902. (202)466-3030. Fax: (202)293-3187. E-mail: rglawlit@aol.com. **Contact:** Ronald Goldfarb. Estab. 1966. Currently handles: 75% nonfiction books; 25% novels; increasing TV and movie deals.

• Ron Goldfarb's book (his ninth), *Perfect Villains, Imperfect Heroes*, was published by Random House. His tenth, *TV or not TV: Courts, Television, and Justice* (NYU Press), 1998. His *RFK* book is coming out in paper this year and is about to be optioned for dramatic development.

Member Agents: Ronald Goldfarb, Esq. (nonfiction); Robbie Anna Hare; Kristin Auclair; Kimberlee Damen, Esq.; Louise Wheatley.

Represents: Nonfiction books, novels. **Considers these nonfiction areas:** Art/architecture/design; biography/autobiography; business/economics; cooking/foods/nutrition; creative nonfiction; current affairs; education; ethnic/cultural interests; government/politics/law; health/medicine; history; humor/satire; language/literature/criticism; memoirs; military/war; money/finance; multicultural; nature/environment; popular culture; sociology; sports; theater/film; travel; true crime/investigative; women's issues/studies. **Considers these fiction areas:** Action/adventure; contemporary issues; detective/police/crime; ethnic; literary; mainstream/contemporary; mystery/suspense; thriller.

O⊓ This agency specializes primarily in nonfiction but has a growing interest in well-written fiction. "Given our D.C. location, we represent many journalists, politicians and former federal officials. We arrange collaborations. We also represent a broad range of nonfiction writers and novelists." Actively seeking "fiction with literary overtones; strong nonfiction ideas." Does very little children's fiction or poetry.

How to Contact: No fax queries. Responds in 1 month to queries; 2 months to mss. Obtains most new clients through recommendations from others.

Recent Sales: Sold 35 titles in the last year. *Imperfect Justice*, by Stuart Eizenstat. Other clients include former Congressman John Kasich, Diane Rehm, Susan Eisenhower, Dan Moldea, Roy Gutman, Leonard Garment, Sargent Shriver, Harlem Jazz Museum.

Terms: Charges clients for photocopying, long distance phone calls, postage.

Writers' Conferences: Washington Independent Writers Conference; Medical Writers Conference; VCCA; participates in many ad hoc writers' and publishers' groups and events each year.

Tips: "We are a law firm which can help writers with related legal problems, Freedom of Information Act requests, libel, copyright, contracts, etc. As published authors ourselves, we understand the creative process."

◿ FRANCES GOLDIN, 57 E. 11th St., Suite 5B, New York NY 10003. Member of AAR.

• This agency did not respond to our request for information. Query with SASE before submitting.

Member Agents: Sam Stoloff (literary fiction, history, accessible sociology and philosophy, cultural studies, serious journalism and topical nonfiction with a progressive orientation).

GOODMAN ASSOCIATES, 500 West End Ave., New York NY 10024-4317. (212)873-4806. **Contact:** Elise Simon Goodman. Estab. 1976. Member of AAR. Represents 50 clients.
 • Arnold Goodman is current chair of the AAR Ethics Committee.
Member Agents: Elise Simon Goodman; Arnold P. Goodman.
Represents: Nonfiction books, novels. **Considers these nonfiction areas:** Americana; animals; anthropology/ archaeology; biography/autobiography; business/economics; child guidance/parenting; cooking/foods/nutrition; creative nonfiction; current affairs; education; ethnic/cultural interests; government/politics/law; health/medicine; history; language/literature/criticism; memoirs; military/war; money/finance; multicultural; music/dance; nature/ environment; philosophy; popular culture; psychology; recreation; regional; science/technology; sex; sociology; sports; theater/film; translation; travel; true crime/investigative; women's issues/studies. **Considers these fiction areas:** Action/adventure; contemporary issues; detective/police/crime; erotica; ethnic; family saga; historical; literary; mainstream/contemporary; military/war; multicultural; multimedia; mystery/suspense; occult; regional; romance; sports; thriller; translation.
 ⊶ Accepting new clients on a highly selective and limited basis. Does not want to receive poetry, articles, individual stories, children's or YA material.
How to Contact: Query with SASE. Responds in 10 days to queries; 1 month to mss.
Terms: Agent receives 15% commission on domestic sales; 20% commission on foreign sales. Charges clients for certain expenses: faxes, toll calls, overseas postage, photocopying, book purchases.

CARROLL GRACE LITERARY AGENCY, P.O. Box 10938, St. Petersburg FL 33733. (727)865-2099. **Contact:** Pat Jozwiakowski, Sunny Mays. Estab. 1999. Represents 50 clients. 95% of clients are new/unpublished writers. Currently handles: 10% nonfiction books; 90% novels.
Member Agents: Ms. Sunny Mays (acquisitions director/agent); Ms. Pat Jozwiakowski (agent).
Represents: Nonfiction books, novels. **Considers these nonfiction areas:** History; true crime/investigative; women's issues/studies. **Considers these fiction areas:** Action/adventure; detective/police/crime; family saga; fantasy; historical; horror; literary; mainstream/contemporary; mystery/suspense (amateur sleuth, cozy); psychic/ supernatural; romance (contemporary, gothic, historical, regency); thriller; westerns/frontier.
 ⊶ This agency specializes in romance, fantasy, mystery/suspense, psychic supernatural, timeswept (romance with time travel). They are not accepting new clients at this time.
How to Contact: Query with SASE, synopsis, 1st sample chapter(s), SASE. No postage strips on SASE. No e-mail or fax queries. Considers simultaneous queries. Responds in 6 weeks to queries; 2 months to mss.
Recent Sales: Sold 1 title in the last year. *Tunnel Vision*, by Rob Marshall (Algora).
Terms: Agent receives 15% commission on domestic sales; 20% commission on foreign sales. Offers written contract, binding for length of time determined on a book-by-book basis; 90-day notice must be given to terminate contract. No return of mss without SASE. Charges clients for photocopying, international and express postage, faxes.
Tips: "Make sure your manuscript is as near to finished as possible—be neat and orderly. Study manuscript formatting, check your manuscript for spelling, grammar and punctuation errors."

[N] THE THOMAS GRADY AGENCY, 209 Bassett St., Petaluma CA 94952-2668. E-mail: tom@tgrady. com. Website: www.tgrady.com. **Contact:** Thomas Grady. Estab. 1997. Member of AAR.
 • Prior to opening his agency, Mr. Grady worked in trade book publishing for over 20 years as an editor, editorial director and publisher at Harper San Francisco.
 ⊶ This agency specializes in religion, spirituality, psychology and personal growth, biography and memoir. Does not want to receive children's books, plays, screenplays, or illustrated books, fiction or poetry.
How to Contact: Prefers e-mail query, may attach one document (Microsoft Word preferred), including a 1- or 2-page description, focusing on what is distinctive, fresh, original and marketable about it, 1-sentence statement of book's purpose and promise, analysis of competition and how yours differs, table of contents, page count estimate, sample (10-15 pages in a row), brief bio (qualifications for writing, marketing, publishing history), how much is complete or expected completion date. Responds in 6 weeks to queries.
Recent Sales: *Gerard Manley Hopkins: A Life*, by Paul Mariani (Viking); *Epiphanies: A Psychotherapist's Tales of Surprise and Healing*, by Ann Jauregui (Prima Publishing); *It's Not the Same Without You: Hope and Help for Alienated Catholics Coming Home*, by Mitch Finley (Doubleday).
Tips: Please mention whether the project has been seen by publishers or if it is currently with other agents.

[✓] [Ø] GRAYBILL & ENGLISH, 1875 Connecticut Ave. NW, Suite 712, Washington DC 20009. **Contact:** Nina Graybill. Member of AAR. See individual agent listings for Elaine P. English, Jeffrey M. Kleinman, Esq. and Lynn Whittaker.

[✓] ASHLEY GRAYSON LITERARY AGENCY, 1342 18th St., San Pedro CA 90732. Fax: (310)514-1148. Member of AAR.

Member Agents: Ashley Grayson (science fiction, fantasy, young adult); Carolyn Grayson (women's fiction, romance, children's, nonfiction); Dan Hooker (contemporary fiction, science fiction, horror, sports).
How to Contact: No e-mail or fax queries. Considers simultaneous queries.
Recent Sales: Sold 80 titles in the last year. *Tokyo Suckerpunch*, by Isaac Adamson (HarperCollins); *The Return*, by Buzz Aldrin and John Barnes (TOR/Forge).
Terms: Charges for "extraordinary expenses such as express mail service costs for overseas submissions."

◨ SANFORD J. GREENBURGER ASSOCIATES, INC., 55 Fifth Ave., New York NY 10003. (212)206-5600. Fax: (212)463-8718. Website: www.greenburger.com. **Contact:** Heide Lange. Estab. 1945. Member of AAR. Represents 500 clients.
Member Agents: Heide Lange; Faith Hamlin; Beth Vesel; Theresa Park; Elyse Cheney; Dan Mandel; Julie Barer.
Represents: Nonfiction books, novels. **Considers these nonfiction areas:** Agriculture/horticulture; Americana; animals; anthropology/archaeology; art/architecture/design; biography/autobiography; business/economics; child guidance/parenting; computers/electronic; cooking/foods/nutrition; crafts/hobbies; creative nonfiction; current affairs; education; ethnic/cultural interests; gardening; gay/lesbian issues; government/politics/law; health/medicine; history; how-to; humor/satire; interior design/decorating; juvenile nonfiction; language/literature/criticism; memoirs; military/war; money/finance; multicultural; music/dance; nature/environment; New Age/metaphysics; philosophy; photography; popular culture; psychology; recreation; regional; religious/inspirational; science/technology; self-help/personal improvement; sex; sociology; software; spirituality; sports; theater/film; translation; travel; true crime/investigative; women's issues/studies; young adult. **Considers these fiction areas:** Action/adventure; contemporary issues; detective/police/crime; ethnic; family saga; feminist; gay/lesbian; glitz; historical; humor/satire; literary; mainstream/contemporary; mystery/suspense; psychic/supernatural; regional; sports; thriller.
  ⊶ Does not want to receive romances or westerns.
How to Contact: Query with SASE. Considers simultaneous queries. Responds in 3 weeks to queries; 2 months to mss.
Recent Sales: Sold 200 titles in the last year. This agency prefers not to share information on specific sales. Clients include Andrew Ross, Margaret Cuthbert, Nicholas Sparks, Mary Kurcinka, Linda Nichols, Edy Clarke, Peggy Claude Pierre, Brad Thor, Dan Brown, Sallie Bissell.
Terms: Agent receives 15% commission on domestic sales; 20% commission on foreign sales. Charges for photocopying, books for foreign and subsidiary rights submissions.

☑ ⊕ ◨ GREGORY AND COMPANY AUTHORS' AGENTS, (formerly Gregory and Radice Authors' Agents), 3 Barb Mews, London W6 7PA, England. 020-7610-4676. Fax: 020-7610-4686. E-mail: info@gregoryandcompany.co.uk. Website: www.gregoryandcompany.co.uk. **Contact:** Jane Gregory, sales; Broo Doherty, editorial; Jane Barlow/Claire Morris, rights. Estab. 1987. Member of Association of Authors' Agents. Represents 60 clients. Currently handles: 10% nonfiction books; 90% novels.
  ● Prior to becoming an agent, Ms. Gregory was Rights Director for Chatto & Windus.
Member Agents: Jane Gregory (sales); Broo Doherty (editorial); Jane Barlow/Claire Morris (rights).
Represents: Nonfiction books, novels. **Considers these nonfiction areas:** Biography/autobiography; history. **Considers these fiction areas:** Action/adventure; detective/police/crime; historical; humor/satire; literary; mainstream/contemporary; multicultural; romance; thriller.
  ⊶ "Jane Gregory is successful at selling rights all over the world, including film and television rights. As a British agency we do not generally take on American authors." Actively seeking well-written, accessible modern novels. Does not want to receive horror, science fiction, fantasy, children's books, scripts, poetry.
How to Contact: Query with SASE, or submit outline, 3 sample chapters, SASE. Considers simultaneous queries. Returns materials only with SASE. Obtains most new clients through recommendations from others, conferences.
Recent Sales: Sold 100 titles in the last year. *Tokyo*, by Mo Hayder (Bantam UK/Doubleday USA); *Distant Echo*, by Val McDermid (HarperCollins UK/St. Martin's Press NY); *Fox Evil*, by Minette Walters (McMillan UK/Putnam USA); *Hello Bunny*, by Laura Wilson (Orion UK/Bantam USA); *Out of the Dark* by Natasha Cooper (Simon & Schuster UK/St. Martin's Press USA).
Terms: Agent receives 15% commission on domestic sales; 20% commission on foreign sales. Offers written contract; 3-month notice must be given to terminate contract. Charges clients for photocopying of whole typescripts and copies of book for submissions.
Writers' Conferences: CWA Conference (United Kingdom, Spring); Dead on Deansgate (Manchester, Autumn); Bouchercon (location varies, Autumn).

CONTACT THE EDITOR of *Guide to Literary Agents* by e-mail at literaryagents @fwpubs.com with your questions and comments.

BLANCHE C. GREGORY, INC., 2 Tudor City Place, New York NY 10017. (212)697-0828. Fax: (212)697-0828. Website: www.bcgliteraryagency.com. **Contact:** Gertrude Bregman. Member of AAR.
Member Agents: Lynda Gregory; Merry Gregory Pantano.
Represents: Nonfiction books, novels, juvenile books (some).
  • This agency is especially strong in international subrights sales.
How to Contact: Query with SASE. No e-mail or fax queries.
Recent Sales: This agency prefers not to share information on specific sales. Clients include Lilian Jackson Braun, Peter Miller, Thomas Savage, Martin Blumenson, Steven Ossad and Don Marsh.
Terms: Agent receives 15% commission on domestic sales; 20% commission on foreign sales. Charges clients for copying manuscript.

MAXINE GROFFSKY LITERARY AGENCY, 853 Broadway, Suite 708, New York NY 10003. Member of AAR.
  • This agency did not respond to our request for information. Query before submitting.

JILL GROSJEAN LITERARY AGENCY, 1390 Millstone Rd., Sag Harbor NY 11963-2214. (631)725-7419. Fax: (631)725-8632. E-mail: JILL6981@aol.com. Website: www.hometown.aol.com/JILL6981/myhomep age/index.html. **Contact:** Jill Grosjean. Estab. 1999. Represents 19 clients. 100% of clients are new/unpublished writers. Currently handles: 1% nonfiction books; 99% novels.
  • Prior to becoming an agent, Ms. Grosjean was manager of an independent bookstore. She also worked in publishing and advertising.
Represents: Nonfiction books (some), novels (mostly). **Considers these nonfiction areas:** Art/architecture/design; gardening; humor/satire; interior design/decorating; nature/environment; travel; women's issues/studies. **Considers these fiction areas:** Contemporary issues; historical; humor/satire; literary; mainstream/contemporary; mystery/suspense; regional; romance; thriller.
  • This agency offers some editorial assistance (i.e., line-by-line edits). Actively seeking literary novels and mysteries. Does not want to receive any nonfiction subjects not indicated above.
How to Contact: Query with SASE. Considers simultaneous queries. Responds in 1 week to queries; 1 month to mss. Returns materials only with SASE. Obtains most new clients through recommendations from others, solicitations.
Recent Sales: *I Love You Like a Tomato*, by Marie Giordano (Forge Books); *Nectar*, by David C. Fickett (Forge Books); *Spectres in the Smoke*, by Tony Broadbent (Thomas Dunne); *Free Bird*, by Greg Garrett (Kensington); *The Smoke*, by Tony Broadbent (Thomas Dunne).
Terms: Agent receives 15% commission on domestic sales; 20% commission on foreign sales. No written contract. Charges clients for photocopying, mailing expenses; writers reimbursed for office fees after the sale of ms.
Writers' Conferences: Book Passages Mystery Writer's Conference (Corte Madera CA, July).

THE GROSVENOR LITERARY AGENCY, 5510 Grosvenor Lane, Bethesda MD 20814. (301)564-6231. Fax: (301)581-9401. E-mail: dcgrosveno@aol.com. **Contact:** Deborah C. Grosvenor. Estab. 1995. Member of National Press Club. Represents 30 clients. 10% of clients are new/unpublished writers. Currently handles: 80% nonfiction books; 20% novels.
  • Prior to opening her agency, Ms. Grosvenor was a book editor for 18 years.
Represents: Nonfiction books, novels. **Considers these nonfiction areas:** Animals; anthropology/archaeology; art/architecture/design; biography/autobiography; business/economics; child guidance/parenting; current affairs; government/politics/law; health/medicine; history; how-to; language/literature/criticism; military/war; money/finance; music/dance; nature/environment; New Age/metaphysics; photography; popular culture; psychology; religious/inspirational; science/technology; self-help/personal improvement; sociology; spirituality; theater/film; translation; true crime/investigative; women's issues/studies. **Considers these fiction areas:** Contemporary issues; detective/police/crime; family saga; historical; literary; mainstream/contemporary; mystery/suspense; romance (contemporary, gothic, historical); thriller.
How to Contact: Send outline/proposal for nonfiction; send outline and 3 sample chapters for fiction. No e-mail or fax queries. Responds in 1 month to queries; 2 months to mss. Returns materials only with SASE. Obtains most new clients through recommendations from others.
Recent Sales: *Susan McDougal Unchained*, by Susan McDougal with Pat Harris (Carroll and Graf); *The Vatican Cover-up: The Papacy and the Church's Sexual Crisis*, by Jason Berry and Gerald Renner (The Free Press).
Terms: Agent receives 15% commission on domestic sales; 20% commission on foreign sales. Offers written contract; 10-day notice must be given to terminate contract.

H.W.A. TALENT REPRESENTATIVES, 3500 W. Olive Ave., Suite 1400, Burbank CA 91505. (818)972-4310. Fax: (818)972-4313. **Contact:** Kimber Wheeler. Estab. 1985. Signatory of WGA. 90% of clients are new/unpublished writers. Currently handles: 10% novels; 90% movie scripts.
  • See the expanded listing for this agency in Script Agents.

Represents: Novels, movie scripts, TV scripts. **Considers these script subject areas:** Action/adventure; comedy; contemporary issues; ethnic; family saga; fantasy; feminist; mystery/suspense; psychic/supernatural; romantic comedy; romantic drama; sports; thriller.
How to Contact: Query with SASE, outline/proposal.

REECE HALSEY AGENCY, 8733 Sunset Blvd., Suite 101, Los Angeles CA 90069. Fax: (310)652-7595. **Contact:** Kimberley Cameron (all queries) at Reece Halsey North. Estab. 1957. Member of AAR. Represents 40 clients. 30% of clients are new/unpublished writers. Currently handles: 30% nonfiction books; 60% novels; 10% movie scripts.

● The Reece Halsey Agency has an illustrious client list largely of established writers, including the estate of Aldous Huxley and has represented Upton Sinclair, William Faulkner and Henry Miller. Ms. Cameron has recently opened a Northern California office and all queries should be addressed to her at the Reece Halsey North office.
Member Agents: Dorris Halsey (by referral only); Kimberley Cameron.
Represents: Nonfiction books, novels. **Considers these nonfiction areas:** Biography/autobiography; current affairs; history; language/literature/criticism; popular culture; true crime/investigative; women's issues/studies. **Considers these fiction areas:** Action/adventure; contemporary issues; detective/police/crime; ethnic; family saga; historical; literary; mainstream/contemporary; mystery/suspense; science fiction; thriller; women's.

○━ This agency specializes mostly in books/excellent writing.
How to Contact: Query with SASE. Prefers to read materials exclusively. No e-mail or fax queries. Responds in 3 weeks to queries; 3 months to mss. Obtains most new clients through recommendations from others, solicitations.
Terms: Agent receives 15% commission on domestic sales; 10% commission on dramatic rights sales. Offers written contract, binding for 1 year. Requests 6 copies of ms if representing an author.
Writers' Conferences: Maui Writers Conference; ABA.
Tips: "Always send a well-written query and include a SASE with it!"

REECE HALSEY NORTH, 98 Main St., #704, Tiburon CA 94920. (415)789-9191. E-mail: info@reecehal seynorth.com. Website: www.reecehalseynorth.com or www.kimberleycameron.com. **Contact:** Kimberley Cameron. Estab. 1995. Member of AAR. Represents 40 clients. 30% of clients are new/unpublished writers. Currently handles: 30% nonfiction books; 70% novels.
Member Agents: Kimberley Cameron (Reece Halsey North); Dorris Halsey (by referral only, LA office).
Represents: Nonfiction books, novels. **Considers these nonfiction areas:** Biography; health; history; science; spirituality. **Considers these fiction areas:** Action/adventure; contemporary issues; detective/police/crime; ethnic; family saga; historical; horror; literary; mainstream/contemporary; mystery/suspense; science fiction; thriller; women's.

○━ This agency specializes in mystery, literary and mainstream fiction, excellent writing. The Reece Halsey Agency has an illustrious client list largely of established writers, including the estate of Aldous Huxley and has represented Upton Sinclair, William Faulkner and Henry Miller. Ms. Cameron has a Northern California office and all queries should be addressed to her at the Tiburon address.
How to Contact: Query with SASE. No e-mail or fax queries. Considers simultaneous queries. Responds in 1 month to queries; 3 months to mss. Obtains most new clients through recommendations from others, solicitations.
Recent Sales: *Jinn*, by Matthew Delaney (St. Martin's Press); *Final Epidemic*, by Earl Merkel (Dutton-NAL); *Sea Room*, by Norman Gautreau; *The Modern Gentleman*, by Phineas Mollod and Jason Tesauro.
Terms: Agent receives 15% commission on domestic sales. Offers written contract, binding for 1 year. Requests 8 copies of ms if representing an author.
Writers' Conferences: BEA; Maui Writers Conference; San Diego State University; Pacific Northwest; Cape Cod.
Reading List: Reads *Glimmer Train*, *The Sun*, *Zyzzyva* and *The New Yorker* to find new clients. Looks for "writing that touches the heart."
Tips: "Please send a polite, well-written query and include a SASE with it! You may also include the first ten pages of the manuscript."

THE MITCHELL J. HAMILBURG AGENCY, 11718 Barrington Ct., #732, Los Angeles CA 90049-2930. (310)471-4024. Fax: (310)471-9588. **Contact:** Michael Hamilburg. Estab. 1937. Signatory of WGA. Represents 70 clients. Currently handles: 70% nonfiction books; 30% novels.
Represents: Nonfiction books, novels, Considers all nonfiction and most fiction areas. **Considers these nonfiction areas:** Agriculture/horticulture; Americana; animals; anthropology/archaeology; art/architecture/design; biography/autobiography; business/economics; child guidance/parenting; computers/electronic; cooking/foods/nutrition; crafts/hobbies; creative nonfiction; current affairs; education; ethnic/cultural interests; gardening; gay/lesbian issues; government/politics/law; health/medicine; history; how-to; humor/satire; interior design/decorating; juvenile nonfiction; language/literature/criticism; memoirs; military/war; money/finance; multicultural; music/dance; nature/environment; New Age/metaphysics; philosophy; photography; popular culture; psychology; recreation; regional; religious/inspirational; science/technology; self-help/personal improvement; sex; sociology; software; spirituality; sports; theater/film; translation; travel; true crime/investigative; women's issues/studies;

young adult. **Considers these fiction areas:** Action/adventure; comic books/cartoon; confession; contemporary issues; detective/police/crime; erotica; ethnic; experimental; family saga; fantasy; feminist; gay/lesbian; glitz; gothic; hi-lo; historical; horror; humor/satire; juvenile; literary; mainstream/contemporary; military/war; multicultural; multimedia; mystery/suspense; New Age; occult; picture books; plays; poetry; poetry in translation; psychic/supernatural; regional; religious/inspirational; science fiction; short story collections; spiritual; sports; thriller; translation; westerns/frontier; young adult.

○➔ Does not want to receive romance.

How to Contact: Query with SASE, submit outline, 2 sample chapter(s). Responds in 1 month to mss. Obtains most new clients through recommendations from others, conferences, personal search.

Recent Sales: *Fatal North*, by Bruce Henderson (Dutton); *Wildlife Wars*, by Richard Leakey and Virginia Morell (St. Martin's Press); *The Siege of Shangri-La*, by Michael Macrae (Broadway Books).

Terms: Agent receives 10-15% commission on domestic sales.

Tips: "Good luck! Keep writing!"

◎ **JEANNE K. HANSON LITERARY AGENCY**, 5441 Woodcrest Dr., Edina MN 55424-1649. Member of AAR.

● This agency did not respond to our request for information. Query before submitting.

◎ **HARDEN CURTIS ASSOCIATES**, 850 Seventh Ave., Suite 405, New York NY 10019. **Contact:** Mary Harden. Member of AAR.

● This agency did not respond to our request for information. Query with SASE before submitting.

◎ **THE JOY HARRIS LITERARY AGENCY, INC.**, 156 Fifth Ave., Suite 617, New York NY 10010. (212)924-6269. Fax: (212)924-6609. E-mail: gen.office@jhlitagent.com. **Contact:** Joy Harris. Member of AAR. Represents 100 clients. Currently handles: 50% nonfiction books; 50% novels.

Member Agents: Leslie Daniels; Stéphanie Abou; Alexia Paul (associate member).

Represents: Nonfiction books, novels. **Considers these fiction areas:** Action/adventure; comic books/cartoon; confession; contemporary issues; detective/police/crime; ethnic; experimental; family saga; feminist; gay/lesbian; glitz; hi-lo; historical; humor/satire; literary; mainstream/contemporary; military/war; multicultural; multimedia; mystery/suspense; New Age; picture books; poetry; poetry in translation; regional; religious/inspirational; short story collections; spiritual; sports; thriller; translation; women's.

○➔ Does not want to receive screenplays.

How to Contact: Query with outline/proposal, SASE. Considers simultaneous queries. Responds in 2 months to queries. Obtains most new clients through recommendations from clients and editors.

Recent Sales: Sold 15 titles in the last year. This agency prefers not to share information on specific sales.

Terms: Agent receives 15% commission on domestic sales; 20% commission on foreign sales. Charges clients for some office expenses.

◐ **HARTLINE LITERARY AGENCY**, 123 Queenston Dr., Pittsburgh PA 15235-5429. (412)829-2495 or 2483. Fax: (412)829-2450. E-mail: joyce@hartlineliterary.com. Website: www.hartlineliterary.com. **Contact:** Joyce A. Hart. Estab. 1990. Represents 45 clients. 30% of clients are new/unpublished writers. Currently handles: 40% nonfiction books; 60% novels.

Member Agents: Joyce A. Hart, principal agent; Janet Benrey; Tamela Hancock Murray; Andrea Boeshaar.

Represents: Nonfiction books, novels. **Considers these nonfiction areas:** Business/economics; child guidance/parenting; cooking/foods/nutrition; money/finance; religious/inspirational; self-help/personal improvement; women's issues/studies. **Considers these fiction areas:** Action/adventure; contemporary issues; family saga; historical; literary; mystery/suspense (amateur sleuth, cozy); regional; religious/inspirational; romance (contemporary, gothic, historical, regency); thriller.

○➔ This agency specializes in the Christian bookseller market. Actively seeking adult fiction, self-help, nutritional books, devotional, business. Does not want to receive science fiction, erotica, gay/lesbian, fantasy, horror, etc.

How to Contact: Submit outline, 3 sample chapter(s). Accepts e-mail and fax queries. Considers simultaneous queries. Responds in 1 month to queries; 2 months to mss. Returns materials only with SASE. Obtains most new clients through recommendations from others.

Recent Sales: Sold 7 titles in the last year. *Betrayed* and *Traitor*, by Rosey Dow and Andrew Snaden (Promise Press); *I Don't Love You Anymore*, by Dr. David E. Clarke (Thomas Nelson Publishers); *A Name of Her Own*, by Jane Kirkpatrick (WaterBrook Press); *Footprints of God*, by Nancy Hoag (Fleming H. Revell); *The Fisherman*, by Larry Huntsperger (Fleming H. Revell).

Terms: Agent receives 15% commission on domestic sales. Offers written contract.

◐ **JOHN HAWKINS & ASSOCIATES, INC.**, 71 W. 23rd St., Suite 1600, New York NY 10010. (212)807-7040. Fax: (212)807-9555. E-mail: jha@jhaliterary.com. Website: jhaliterary.com. **Contact:** John Hawkins, William Reiss. Estab. 1893. Member of AAR. Represents over 100 clients. 5-10% of clients are new/unpublished writers. Currently handles: 40% nonfiction books; 40% novels; 20% juvenile books.

Member Agents: Moses Cardona; Warren Frazier; Anne Hawkins; John Hawkins; William Reiss; Elly Sidel.

Represents: Nonfiction books, novels, juvenile books. **Considers these nonfiction areas:** Agriculture/horticulture; Americana; animals; anthropology/archaeology; art/architecture/design; biography/autobiography; business/economics; child guidance/parenting; cooking/foods/nutrition; crafts/hobbies; creative nonfiction; current affairs; education; ethnic/cultural interests; gardening; gay/lesbian issues; government/politics/law; health/medicine; history; how-to; humor/satire; interior design/decorating; juvenile nonfiction; language/literature/criticism; memoirs; military/war; money/finance; multicultural; music/dance; nature/environment; New Age/metaphysics; philosophy; photography; popular culture; psychology; recreation; regional; science/technology; self-help/personal improvement; sex; sociology; software; spirituality; sports; theater/film; travel; true crime/investigative; women's issues/studies; young adult. **Considers these fiction areas:** Action/adventure; comic books/cartoon; contemporary issues; detective/police/crime; ethnic; experimental; family saga; fantasy; feminist; gay/lesbian; glitz; gothic; hi-lo; historical; horror; humor/satire; juvenile; literary; mainstream/contemporary; military/war; multicultural; multimedia; mystery/suspense; New Age; occult; picture books; plays; poetry; poetry in translation; psychic/supernatural; regional; religious/inspirational; science fiction; short story collections; spiritual; sports; thriller; translation; westerns/frontier; young adult; women's.
How to Contact: Query with SASE, submit proposal package, outline. Considers simultaneous queries. Responds in 1 month to queries. Returns materials only with SASE. Obtains most new clients through recommendations from others.
Recent Sales: *Dead Halt on the Lunatic Line*, by Sarah Rose (Random House); *Empire of Light*, by David Czuchlewski (Putnam).
Terms: Agent receives 15% commission on domestic sales; 20% commission on foreign sales. Charges clients for photocopying.

RICHARD HENSHAW GROUP, 127 W. 24th St., 4th Floor, New York NY 10011. (212)414-1172. Fax: (435)417-5208. E-mail: submissions@henshaw.com. Website: www.rich.henshaw.com. **Contact:** Rich Henshaw. Estab. 1995. Member of AAR, SinC, MWA, HWA, SFWA. Represents 35 clients. 20% of clients are new/unpublished writers. Currently handles: 30% nonfiction books; 70% novels.
• Prior to opening his agency, Mr. Henshaw served as an agent with Richard Curtis Associates, Inc.
Represents: Nonfiction books, novels. **Considers these nonfiction areas:** Animals; biography/autobiography; business/economics; child guidance/parenting; computers/electronic; cooking/foods/nutrition; current affairs; gay/lesbian issues; government/politics/law; health/medicine; how-to; humor/satire; military/war; money/finance; music/dance; nature/environment; New Age/metaphysics; popular culture; psychology; science/technology; self-help/personal improvement; sociology; sports; true crime/investigative; women's issues/studies. **Considers these fiction areas:** Action/adventure; detective/police/crime; ethnic; family saga; fantasy; glitz; historical; horror; humor/satire; literary; mainstream/contemporary; mystery/suspense; psychic/supernatural; romance; science fiction; sports; thriller.
○➝ This agency specializes in thrillers, mysteries, science fiction, fantasy and horror.
How to Contact: Query with SASE. Responds in 3 weeks to queries; 6 weeks to mss. Obtains most new clients through recommendations from others, solicitations, conferences.
Recent Sales: Sold 17 titles in the last year. *A Fine and Bitter Snow*, by Dana Stabenow (St. Martin's Press); *Training Our Own Minds*, by Susan Wise Bauer (W.W. Norton); *The Shadow Dancer*, by Margaret Coel (Berkley); *Little Girl Blue*, by David Cray (Carroll & Graf). Other clients include Penny Wagner, Stan Jones.
Terms: Agent receives 15% commission on domestic sales; 20% commission on foreign sales. No written contract. 100% of business is derived from commissions on ms sales. Charges clients for photocopying mss and book orders.
Tips: "While we do not have any reason to believe that our submission guidelines will change in the near future, writers can find up-to-date submission policy information on our website. Always include SASE with correct return postage."

THE JEFF HERMAN AGENCY LLC, 332 Bleecker St., #631, New York NY 10014. (212)941-0540. Fax: (212)941-0614. E-mail: jeff@jeffherman.com. Website: www.jeffherman.com. **Contact:** Jeffrey H. Herman. Estab. 1985. Represents 100 clients. 10% of clients are new/unpublished writers. Currently handles: 85% nonfiction books; 5% novels; 5% scholarly books; 5% textbooks.
• Prior to opening his agency, Mr. Herman served as a public relations executive.
Member Agents: Deborah Levine (vice president, nonfiction book doctor); Jeff Herman; Amanda White.
Represents: Nonfiction books. **Considers these nonfiction areas:** Business/economics; computers/electronic; government/politics/law; health/medicine (and recovery issues); history; how-to; psychology (pop); self-help/personal improvement; spirituality; popular reference.
○➝ This agency specializes in adult nonfiction.
How to Contact: Query with SASE. Accepts e-mail and fax queries. Considers simultaneous queries.
Recent Sales: Sold 35 titles in the last year. This agency prefers not to share information on specific sales.
Terms: Agent receives 15% commission on domestic sales. Offers written contract. Charges clients for copying, postage.

◑ **HILL & BARLOW AGENCY**, One International Place, Boston MA 02110. (617)428-3514. Fax: (617)428-3500. E-mail: doconnell@hillbarlow.com. Website: www.hillbarlow.com. **Contact:** Alexis Rizzuto. Estab. 1990. Represents 100 clients. 5% of clients are new/unpublished writers. Currently handles: 80% nonfiction books; 20% novels.
Member Agents: John Taylor (Ike) Williams, director (books, film, TV); Jill Kneerim, director (books); Rob McQuilkin, agent (books); Elaine Rogers, director of subsidiary rights (dramatic rights, foreign, audio).
Represents: Nonfiction books, novels. **Considers these nonfiction areas:** Anthropology/archaeology; biography/autobiography; business/economics; child guidance/parenting; current affairs; education; ethnic/cultural interests; gay/lesbian issues; government/politics/law; health/medicine; history; language/literature/criticism; money/finance; music/dance; nature/environment; New Age/metaphysics; popular culture; psychology; religious/inspirational; science/technology; self-help/personal improvement; sociology; spirituality; women's issues/studies. **Considers these fiction areas:** Ethnic; feminist; gay/lesbian; literary; mainstream/contemporary, general/popular.
O— This agency specializes in trade nonfiction and quality fiction for adults. Dramatic rights for books and life story rights only. Does not want to receive genre fiction.
How to Contact: Query with SASE, submit outline/proposal. No unsolicited material. Responds in 1 month to queries; 3 months to mss. Obtains most new clients through recommendations from others.
Recent Sales: *Will in the World*, by Stephen Greenblatt; *Nightingales*, by Gillian Gill; *The Millionaires*, by Brad Meltzer (Warner).
Terms: Agent receives 15% commission on domestic sales; 20% commission on foreign sales. Offers written contract; 4-month notice must be given to terminate contract. 100% of business is derived from commissions on ms sales. Charges clients for direct expenses (postage, phone, photocopying, messenger service).
Tips: "We are taking very few new clients for representation."

◐ **FREDERICK HILL BONNIE NADELL, INC.**, 1842 Union St., San Francisco CA 94123. (415)921-2910. Fax: (415)921-2802. **Contact:** Irene Moore. Estab. 1979. Represents 100 clients.
Member Agents: Fred Hill (president); Bonnie Nadell (vice president); Irene Moore (associate).
Represents: Nonfiction books, novels. **Considers these nonfiction areas:** Biography/autobiography; cooking/foods/nutrition (cookbooks); current affairs; government/politics/law; language/literature/criticism; women's issues/studies. **Considers these fiction areas:** Literary; mainstream/contemporary.
How to Contact: Query with SASE. No e-mail or fax queries. Considers simultaneous queries. Returns materials only with SASE.
Recent Sales: *The Race: The First Non-Stop, Round-the-World, No-Holds-Barred Sailing Competition*, by Tim Zimmermann; *Balance of Power*, by Richard North Patterson (Ballantine); *Native State*, by Tony Cohan (Broadway).
Terms: Agent receives 15% commission on domestic sales; 20% commission on foreign sales; 15% commission on dramatic rights sales. Charges clients for photocopying.

◑ **JOHN L. HOCHMANN BOOKS**, 320 E. 58th St., New York NY 10022-2220. (212)319-0505. **Contact:** Theodora Eagle. Director: John L. Hochman. Estab. 1976. Member of PEN. Represents 23 clients. Prefers to work with previously published/established authors. Currently handles: 100% nonfiction books.
Member Agents: Theodora Eagle (popular medical and nutrition books).
Represents: Nonfiction books, textbooks (college). **Considers these nonfiction areas:** Anthropology/archaeology; art/architecture/design; biography/autobiography; cooking/foods/nutrition; current affairs; gay/lesbian issues; government/politics/law; health/medicine; history; military/war; music/dance; sociology; theater/film.
O— This agency specializes in nonfiction books. "Writers must have demonstrable eminence in field or previous publications."
How to Contact: Query first with detailed chapter outline, titles and sample reviews of previously published books. Responds in 1 week to queries. Responds in one month to solicited manuscripts. Obtains most new clients through recommendations from authors and editors.
Recent Sales: Sold 6 titles in the last year. *Granite and Rainbow: The Life of Virginia Woolf*, by Mitchell Leaska (Farrar, Straus & Giroux); *Manuel Puig and the Spider Woman*, by Suzanne Jill Levine (Farrar, Straus & Giroux); *Part-Time Vegetarian*, by Louise Lambert-Lagasse (Stoddart).
Terms: Agent receives 15% commission on domestic sales; 25% commission on foreign sales.
Tips: "Detailed outlines are read carefully; letters and proposals written like flap copy get chucked. We make multiple submissions to editors, but we do not accept multiple submissions from authors. Why? Editors are on salary, but we work for commission, and do not have time to read manuscripts on spec."

◐ **BARBARA HOGENSON AGENCY**, 165 West End Ave., Suite 19-C, New York NY 10023. (212)874-8084. Fax: (212)362-3011. **Contact:** Barbara Hogenson, Sarah Feider. Estab. 1994. Member of AAR; signatory of WGA. Represents 60 clients. 5% of clients are new/unpublished writers. Currently handles: 35% nonfiction books; 15% novels; 50% stage plays.
• See expanded listing for this agency in Script Agents.

☑ ◐ ◎ **HOPKINS LITERARY ASSOCIATES, (Specialized: romance/women's fiction)**, 2117 Buffalo Rd., Suite 327, Rochester NY 14624-1507. (585)352-6268. **Contact:** Pam Hopkins. Estab. 1996. Member of AAR, RWA. Represents 30 clients. 5% of clients are new/unpublished writers. Currently handles: 100% novels.
Represents: Novels. **Considers these fiction areas:** Historical; mainstream/contemporary; romance; women's.
  ○┅ This agency specializes in women's fiction, particularly historical, contemporary and category romance as well as mainstream work.
How to Contact: Submit outline, 3 sample chapter(s). No e-mail or fax queries. Considers simultaneous queries. Responds in 2 weeks to queries; 1 month to mss. Returns materials only with SASE. Obtains most new clients through recommendations from others, solicitations, conferences.
Recent Sales: Sold 50 titles in the last year. *The Oklahomans*, by Merline Lovelace (MIRA); *The Charmer*, by Madeline Hunter (Bantam); *Nobody But You*, by Julie Kenner (Pocket); *Knock Me Off My Feet*, by Susan Donovan (St. Martin's Press).
Terms: Agent receives 15% commission on domestic sales; 20% commission on foreign sales. No written contract.
Writers' Conferences: Romance Writers of America.

◑ **HORNFISCHER LITERARY MANAGEMENT, INC.**, P.O. Box 50067, Austin TX 78763-0067. E-mail: jim@hornfischerliterarymanagement.com. Website: www.hornfischerliterarymanagement.com. **Contact:** Jim Hornfischer, president. Estab. 2001. Represents 45 clients. 20% of clients are new/unpublished writers. Currently handles: 90% nonfiction books; 10% novels.
  • Prior to opening his agency, Mr. Hornfischer was an agent with Literary Group International and held editorial positions at HarperCollins and McGraw-Hill. "I work hard to make an author's first trip to market a successful one. That means closely working with my clients prior to submission to produce the strongest possible book proposal or manuscript. My New York editorial background, at HarperCollins and McGraw-Hill, where I worked on books by a variety of bestselling authors such as Erma Bombeck, Jared Diamond and Erica Jong among others, is useful in this regard. In eight years as an agent I've handled two number 1 *New York Times* nonfiction bestsellers, and in 2001 one of my clients was a finalist for the Pulitzer Prize."
Represents: Nonfiction books, novels, feature film, TV movie of the week. **Considers these nonfiction areas:** Anthropology/archaeology; biography/autobiography; business/economics; child guidance/parenting; current affairs; government/politics/law; health/medicine; history; how-to; humor/satire; memoirs; military/war; money/finance; multicultural; nature/environment; popular culture; psychology; religious/inspirational; science/technology; self-help/personal improvement; sociology; sports; true crime/investigative. **Considers these fiction areas:** Literary; mainstream/contemporary; psychic/supernatural; religious/inspirational; thriller.
  ○┅ Actively seeking the best work of terrific writers. Does not want poetry, genre mysteries, romance or science fiction.
How to Contact: Submit proposal package, outline, 2 sample chapter(s). Considers simultaneous queries. Responds in 1 month to queries. Returns materials only with SASE. Obtains most new clients through recommendations from active clients; reading books and magazines; pursuing ideas with New York editors.
Recent Sales: *Flags of Our Fathers*, by James Bradley with Ron Powers (Bantam); *The Age of Gold: The California Gold Rush and the New American Dream*, by H.W. Brands (Doubleday); *My Life Has Stood a Loaded Gun*, by Theo Padnos (Talk Miramax Books); *Born Burning*, by Thomas Sullivan (New American Library); *Tom and Huck Don't Live Here Anymore*, by Ron Powers (St. Martin's Press). Other clients include Cathy and Joseph Garcia-Prats; Richard Goldstein; Don Graham; Sharon Simmons Hornfischer; John Mosier; Jan Reid; Clint Richmond; Mary Beth Rogers; Jan Jarboe Russell.
Terms: Agent receives 15% commission on domestic sales; 20% commission on foreign sales. Offers written contract; 30-day notice must be given to terminate contract. Reasonable expenses deducted from proceeds after book is sold.
Tips: "When you query agents and send out proposals, present yourself as someone who's in command of his material and comfortable in his own skin. Too many writers have a palpable sense of anxiety and insecurity. Take a deep breath and realize that—if you're good—someone in the publishing world will want you."

◉ **IMG LITERARY**, 825 Seventh Ave., New York NY 10019. **Contact:** Carolyn Krupp. Member of AAR. This agency did not respond to our request for information. Query before submitting.

◉ **INTERNATIONAL CREATIVE MANAGEMENT**, 40 W. 57th St., New York NY 10019. (212)556-5600. Fax: (212)556-5665. **Contact:** Literary Department. Member of AAR; signatory of WGA.

ALWAYS INCLUDE an International Reply Coupon (IRC) for reply or return of your material when sending query letters to non-U.S. countries.

Member Agents: Esther Newberg and Amanda Urban, department heads; Richard Abate; Lisa Bankoff; Sam Cohn; Kristine Dahl; Mitch Douglas; Liz Farrell; Sloan Harris; Heather Schroeder; Denise Shannon; Amy Williams.

How to Contact: Not currently accepting submissions. Obtains most new clients through recommendations from others.

Terms: Agent receives 10% commission on domestic sales; 15% commission on foreign sales.

J DE S ASSOCIATES INC., 9 Shagbark Rd., Wilson Point, South Norwalk CT 06854. (203)838-7571. **Contact:** Jacques de Spoelberch. Estab. 1975. Represents 50 clients. Currently handles: 50% nonfiction books; 50% novels.

• Prior to opening his agency, Mr. de Spoelberch was an editor with Houghton Mifflin.

Represents: Nonfiction books, novels. **Considers these nonfiction areas:** Biography/autobiography; business/economics; current affairs; ethnic/cultural interests; government/politics/law; health/medicine; history; military/war; New Age/metaphysics; self-help/personal improvement; sociology; sports; translation. **Considers these fiction areas:** Detective/police/crime; historical; juvenile; literary; mainstream/contemporary; mystery/suspense; New Age; westerns/frontier; young adult.

How to Contact: Query with SASE. Responds in 2 months to queries. Obtains most new clients through recommendations from authors and other clients.

Terms: Agent receives 15% commission on domestic sales; 20% commission on foreign sales. Charges clients for foreign postage and photocopying.

JABBERWOCKY LITERARY AGENCY, P.O. Box 4558, Sunnyside NY 11104-0558. (718)392-5985. Fax: (718)392-5985. **Contact:** Joshua Bilmes. Estab. 1994. Member of SFWA. Represents 40 clients. 25% of clients are new/unpublished writers. Currently handles: 15% nonfiction books; 75% novels; 5% scholarly books; 5% other.

Represents: Nonfiction books, novels, scholarly books. **Considers these nonfiction areas:** Biography/autobiography; business/economics; cooking/foods/nutrition; current affairs; gay/lesbian issues; government/politics/law; health/medicine; history; humor/satire; language/literature/criticism; military/war; money/finance; music/dance; nature/environment; popular culture; science/technology; sociology; sports; theater/film; true crime/investigative; women's issues/studies. **Considers these fiction areas:** Action/adventure; comic books/cartoon; contemporary issues; detective/police/crime; ethnic; family saga; fantasy; gay/lesbian; glitz; historical; horror; humor/satire; literary; mainstream/contemporary; psychic/supernatural; regional; science fiction; sports; thriller.

• This agency represents quite a lot of genre fiction and is actively seeking to increase amount of nonfiction projects. It does not handle juvenile or young adult. Book-length material only; no poetry, articles or short fiction.

How to Contact: Query with SASE. No mss unless requested. No e-mail or fax queries and submissions. Considers simultaneous queries and submissions. Responds in 2 weeks to queries. Returns materials only with SASE. Obtains most new clients through solicitations, recommendation by current clients.

Recent Sales: Sold 25 titles in the last year. *Living Dead in Dallas*, by Charlaine Harris (ACE); *The Speed of Dark*, by Elizabeth Moon (Ballantine); *Deathstalker Legacy*, by Simon Green (ROC); *Follow Me and Die*, by Ceil Currey (Cooper Square). Other clients include Tanya Huff, Kristine Smith, Edo Van Belkom.

Terms: Agent receives 12.5% commission on domestic sales; 20% commission on foreign sales. Offers written contract, binding for 1 year. Charges clients for book purchases, photocopying, international book/ms mailing, international long distance.

Writers' Conferences: Malice Domestic (Washington DC, May); World SF Convention (Toronto, August); Icon (Stony Brook NY, April).

Reading List: *New Republic*, *Analog* and various newspapers to find clients.

Tips: "In approaching with a query, the most important things to me are your credits and your biographical background to the extent it's relevant to your work. I (and most agents) will ignore the adjectives you may choose to describe your own work."

MELANIE JACKSON AGENCY, 250 W. 57th St., Suite 1119, New York NY 10107. Member of AAR.

• This agency did not respond to our request for information. Query before submitting.

JAMES PETER ASSOCIATES, INC., P.O. Box 358, New Canaan CT 06840. (203)972-1070. E-mail: gene_brissie@msn.com. **Contact:** Gene Brissie. Estab. 1971. Represents 75 individual and 6 corporate clients. 15% of clients are new/unpublished writers. Currently handles: 100% nonfiction books.

Member Agents: Gene Brissie.

Represents: Nonfiction books. **Considers these nonfiction areas:** Anthropology/archaeology; art/architecture/design; biography/autobiography; business/economics; child guidance/parenting; current affairs; ethnic/cultural interests; gay/lesbian issues; government/politics/law; health/medicine; history; language/literature/criticism; memoirs (political or business); military/war; money/finance; music/dance; popular culture; psychology; self-help/personal improvement; theater/film; travel; women's issues/studies.

O━ This agency specializes in nonfiction, all categories. "We are especially interested in general, trade and reference." Actively seeking "good ideas in all areas of adult nonfiction." Does not want to receive "children's and young adult books, poetry, fiction."

How to Contact: Submit proposal package, outline, SASE. Prefers to read materials exclusively. No e-mail or fax queries. Responds in 1 month to queries. Returns materials only with SASE. Obtains most new clients through recommendations from others, solicitations, contact "with people who are doing interesting things."

Recent Sales: Sold 50 titles in the last year. *Nothing to Fear*, by Dr. Alan Axelrod (Prentice-Hall); *Out of the Ordinary: A Biographical Dictionary of Women Explorers*, by Sarah Purcell and Edward Purcell (Routledge); *The Hellfighters of Harlem*, by William Harris (Carroll & Graf).

Terms: Agent receives 15% commission on domestic sales; 20% commission on foreign sales. Offers written contract.

JANKLOW & NESBITT ASSOCIATES, 598 Madison Ave., New York NY 10022. Member of AAR.
● This agency did not respond to our request for information. Query before submitting.

JCA LITERARY AGENCY, 27 W. 20th St., Suite 1103, New York NY 10011. (212)807-0888. Fax: (212)807-0461. **Contact:** Jeff Gerecke, Tony Outhwaite. Estab. 1978. Member of AAR. Represents 100 clients. 10% of clients are new/unpublished writers. Currently handles: 20% nonfiction books; 75% novels; 5% scholarly books.

Member Agents: Jeff Gerecke; Tony Outhwaite; Peter Steinberg.

Represents: Nonfiction books, novels. **Considers these nonfiction areas:** Anthropology/archaeology; biography/autobiography; business/economics; current affairs; government/politics/law; health/medicine; history; language/literature/criticism; memoirs; military/war; money/finance; music/dance; nature/environment; popular culture; science/technology; sociology; sports; theater/film; translation; true crime/investigative; women's issues/studies. **Considers these fiction areas:** Action/adventure; contemporary issues; detective/police/crime; family saga; historical; literary; mainstream/contemporary; mystery/suspense; sports; thriller.

O━ Does not want to receive screenplays, poetry, children's books, science fiction/fantasy, genre romance.

How to Contact: Query with SASE. No e-mail or fax queries. Considers simultaneous queries. Responds in 2 weeks to queries; 10 weeks to mss. Returns materials only with SASE. Obtains most new clients through recommendations from others, solicitations, conferences.

Recent Sales: *Alison's Automotive Repair Manuel*, by Brad Barkley (St. Martin's); *Line of Vision*, by David Ellis (Putnam); *The Heaven of Mercury*, by Brad Watson (Norton); *The Bone Orchard*, by Dan Judson (Bantam). Other clients include Ernest J. Gaines, W.E.B. Griffin, Polly Whitney, David J. Garrow.

Terms: Agent receives 15% commission on domestic sales; 20% commission on foreign sales. No written contract. "We work with our clients on a handshake basis." Charges for postage on overseas submissions, photocopying, mss for submission, books purchased for subrights submission, and bank charges, where applicable. "We deduct the cost from payments received from publishers."

Tips: "We do not ourselves provide legal, accounting, or public relations services for our clients, although some of the advice we give falls somewhat into these realms. In cases where it seems necessary we will recommend obtaining outside advice or assistance in these areas from professionals who are not in any way connected to the agency."

THE JENKS AGENCY, 24 Concord Ave., Suite 412, Cambridge MA 02138. (617)354-5099. E-mail: cbjenks@att.net. **Contact:** Carolyn Jenks. Estab. 1990. Signatory of WGA. 80% of clients are new/unpublished writers. Currently handles: 15% nonfiction books; 75% novels; 5% movie scripts; 5% stage plays; co-agents for TV in Los Angeles.
● Prior to opening her agency, Ms. Jenks was a managing editor, actor and producer.

Represents: Nonfiction books, novels, feature film, TV movie of the week. **Considers these nonfiction areas:** Animals; biography/autobiography; ethnic/cultural interests; history; language/literature/criticism; nature/environment; film; translation; women's issues/studies. **Considers these fiction areas:** Contemporary issues; ethnic; historical; literary; mainstream/contemporary; mystery/suspense; romance (contemporary); thriller. **Considers these script subject areas:** Contemporary issues; historical; mainstream; mystery/suspense; romantic comedy; romantic drama; thriller.

O━ This agency specializes in "development of promising authors." Actively seeking "exceptionally talented writers committed to work that makes a contribution." Does not want to receive gratuitous violence; drug scenes that are a cliche; war stories unless they transcend; sagas; or cliched coming of age stories.

How to Contact: Query with SASE, author bio. No fax queries. Accepts e-mail queries, no attachments. Responds in 2 weeks to queries; 6 weeks to mss. "Materials are not returned. Send copy that can be recycled."

Recent Sales: Sold 2 scripts in the last year. **Film/TV rights optioned/sold:** *The Red Tent*, by Anita Diamant (now a bestseller) (St. Martin's Press); *White Wings*, by Dan Montague (Japanese); *Hunger*, by Jane Ward (Forge).

Terms: Agent receives 15% commission on domestic sales; 15% commission on dramatic rights sales. Offers written contract.

Tips: "Query first in writing with SASE or to cbjenks@att.net. Do not send samples of writing by e-mail. Manuscripts will not be returned to the author. Send copy that can be recycled."

LAWRENCE JORDAN LITERARY AGENCY, a Morning Star Communications, LLC company, 345 W. 121st St., New York NY 10027. (212)662-7871. Fax: (212)662-8138. E-mail: ljlagency@aol.com. **Contact:** Lawrence Jordan, president. Estab. 1978. Represents 50 clients. 25% of clients are new/unpublished writers. Works with a small number of new/previously unpublished authors. Currently handles: 70% nonfiction books; 30% novels.

- Prior to opening his agency, Mr. Jordan served as an editor with Doubleday & Co.

Member Agents: Lawrence Jordan (mystery novels, sports, autobiographies, biographies, religion); Toni Banks (religion, women's studies, inspirational, autobiography, memoirs); Melanie Okadigwe (African American, Caribbean and African literature, speculative fiction, coming of age memoirs, women's studies, arts, travel, cookbooks, alternative health).

Represents: Nonfiction books, novels. **Considers these nonfiction areas:** Biography/autobiography; business/economics; cooking/foods/nutrition (cookbooks); health/medicine; memoirs; religious/inspirational; science/technology; self-help/personal improvement; sports; travel.

　　O→ This agency specializes in general adult fiction and nonfiction. Actively seeking spiritual and religious books, mystery novels, action suspense, thrillers, biographies, autobiographies, celebrity books. Does not want to receive poetry, movie scripts, stage plays, juvenile books, fantasy novels, science fiction.

How to Contact: Query with SASE, outline. Accepts e-mail queries. Responds in 3 weeks to queries; 6 weeks to mss.

Recent Sales: *Walk in the Light, While There is Light* and *The Godson*, by Leo Tolstoy, compiled by Lawrence Jordan (Revell); *Broken Silence: Opening Your Heart and Mind to Therapy—A Black Woman's Recovery Guide*, by D. Kim Singleton, Ph.D. (Ballantine); *The Undiscovered Paul Robeson, Volume II*, by Paul Robeson, Jr. (John Wiley).

Terms: Agent receives 15% commission on domestic sales; 20% commission on foreign sales; 20% commission on dramatic rights sales. 99% of business is derived from commissions on ms sales. Charges long-distance calls, photocopying, foreign submission costs, postage, cables and messengers.

NATASHA KERN LITERARY AGENCY, P.O. Box 2908, Portland OR 97208-2908. (503)297-6190. Website: www.natashakern.com. **Contact:** Natasha Kern. Estab. 1986. Member of RWA, MWA, SinC.

- Prior to opening her agency, Ms. Kern worked as an editor and publicist for New York publishers (Simon & Schuster, Bantam, Ballantine). "This agency has sold over 500 books."

Member Agents: Natasha Kern; Ruth Widener.

Represents: Adult commercial nonfiction and fiction. **Considers these nonfiction areas:** Animals; anthropology/archaeology; business/economics; child guidance/parenting; current affairs; ethnic/cultural interests; gardening; health/medicine; money/finance (personal finance); nature/environment; New Age/metaphysics; popular culture; psychology; religious/inspirational; science/technology; self-help/personal improvement; spirituality; women's issues/studies; investigative journalism. **Considers these fiction areas:** Ethnic; feminist; historical; mainstream/contemporary; mystery/suspense; religious/inspirational; romance (contemporary, historical); thriller (medical, scientific, historical).

　　O→ This agency specializes in commercial fiction and nonfiction for adults. "A full service agency." Does not represent sports, true crime, scholarly works, coffee table books, war memoirs, software, scripts, literary fiction, photography, poetry, short stories, children's, horror, fantasy, genre science fiction, stage plays or traditional Westerns.

How to Contact: Query with SASE, include submission history, writing credits, how long ms is. For fiction: send 2-3 page synopsis and 3-5 first pages. For nonfiction: overview, describe market and how ms is different/better than similar works, author bio and ms length. See website before querying. No e-mail or fax queries. Considers simultaneous queries. Responds in 3 weeks to queries.

Recent Sales: Sold 53 titles in the last year. *Firstborn*, by Robin Lee Hatcher (Tyndale); *Bone Mountain*, by Eliot Pattison (St. Martin's Press); *The Diamond Conspiracy*, by Nick Kublicki (Sourcebooks).

Terms: Agent receives 15% commission on domestic sales; 20% commission on foreign sales; 15% commission on dramatic rights sales.

Writers' Conferences: RWA National Conference, MWA National Conference and many regional conferences.

Tips: "Our idea of a Dream Client is someone who participates in a mutually respectful business relationship, is clear about needs and goals, and communicates about career planning. If we know what you need and want, we can help you achieve it. A dream client has a storytelling gift, a commitment to a writing career, a desire to learn and grow, and a passion for excellence. We want clients who are expressing their own unique voice and truly have something of their own to communicate. This client understands that many people have to work together for a book to succeed and that everything in publishing takes far longer than one imagines. Trust and communication are truly essential."

LOUISE B. KETZ AGENCY, 1485 First Ave., Suite 4B, New York NY 10021-1363. (212)535-9259. Fax: (212)249-3103. E-mail: ketzagency@aol.com. **Contact:** Louise B. Ketz. Estab. 1983. Represents 25 clients. 15% of clients are new/unpublished writers. Currently handles: 100% nonfiction books.

Represents: Nonfiction books. **Considers these nonfiction areas:** Business/economics; current affairs; history; military/war; science/technology; sports.

　　O→ This agency specializes in science, business, sports, history and reference.

How to Contact: Submit outline, 2 sample chapter(s), author bio, with qualifications for authorship of work. Responds in 6 weeks to mss. Obtains most new clients through recommendations from others, idea development. **Terms:** Agent receives 15% commission on domestic sales.

VIRGINIA KIDD AGENCY, INC., (Specialized: science fiction/fantasy), 538 E. Harford St., P.O. Box 278, Milford PA 18337-0728. (570)296-6205. Fax: (570)296-7266. E-mail: www.vkagency@ptd.net. **Contact:** Linn Prentis, Nanci McCloskey. Estab. 1965. Member of SFWA, SFRA. Represents 80 clients. **Member Agents:** Nanci McCloskey (science fiction, speculative fiction, fantasy, women's fiction); Linn Prentis (science fiction, speculative fiction, fantasy); Christine Cohen (historical fantasy). **Represents:** Novels. **Considers these fiction areas:** Fantasy (special interest in non-traditional fantasy); glitz; historical; literary; mainstream/contemporary; mystery/suspense; science fiction; young adult; speculative fiction.
   O— This agency specializes in "science fiction but we do not limit ourselves to it."
How to Contact: Submit synopsis, cover letter, SASE. Prefers to read materials exclusively. Considers simultaneous queries. Responds in 2 weeks to queries; 2 months to mss. Obtains most new clients through recommendations.
Recent Sales: Sold 75 titles in the last year. *Changing Planes*, by Ursula K. Le Guin (Harcourt Brace); *Stories of Your Life and Others*, Ted Chiang (Tor Books). Other clients include Gene Wolfe, Alan Dean Foster, Kage Baker, Wen Spencer, Eleanor Arnason, Katie Waitman, Margaret Ball.
Terms: Agent receives 15% commission on domestic sales; 30% commission on foreign sales; 20% commission on dramatic rights sales. Offers written contract; 60-day notice must be given to terminate contract. Charges clients occasionally for extraordinary expenses.
Tips: "If you have a novel of speculative fiction, romance, or mainstream that is really extraordinary, please query me, including a synopsis, a cv and a SASE."

KIRCHOFF/WOHLBERG, INC., AUTHORS' REPRESENTATION DIVISION, (Specialized: children's books), 866 United Nations Plaza, #525, New York NY 10017. (212)644-2020. Fax: (212)223-4387. **Contact:** Liza Pulitzer-Voges. Director of Operations: John R. Whitman. Estab. 1930s. Member of AAR, AAP, Society of Illustrators, SPAR, Bookbuilders of Boston, New York Bookbinders' Guild, AIGA. Represents 50 clients. 10% of clients are new/unpublished writers. Currently handles: 5% nonfiction books; 25% novels; 5% young adult; 65% picture books.
   • Kirchoff/Wohlberg has been in business for over 60 years.
Member Agents: Liza Pulitzer-Voges (juvenile and young adult authors).
   O— This agency specializes in only juvenile through young adult trade books.
How to Contact: Query with SASE, outline, a few sample chapter(s), for novels. For picture book submissions, please send entire ms. SASE required. No e-mail or fax queries. Considers simultaneous queries. Responds in 1 month to queries; 2 months to mss. Returns materials only with SASE. Obtains most new clients through recommendations from authors, illustrators and editors.
Recent Sales: Sold over 50 titles in the last year. *Loretta, Pinky Scout*, by Keith Graves (Scholastic); *Wallace's Lists*, by Barbara Bottner (HarperCollins).
Terms: Offers written contract, binding for not less than 1 year. Agent receives standard commission, "depending upon whether it is an author only, illustrator only, or an author/illustrator book."

JEFFREY M. KLEINMAN, ESQ., Graybill & English L.L.C, 1875 Connecticut Ave. NW, Suite 712, Washington DC 20009. (202)588-9798. Fax: (202)457-0662. E-mail: jmkagent@aol.com. Website: www.graybill andenglish.com/jmk. **Contact:** Jeff Kleinman. Estab. 1998. 50% of clients are new/unpublished writers.
   • Mr. Kleinman is an attorney.
Represents: Nonfiction books (particularly narrative nonfiction), novels. **Considers these nonfiction areas:** Agriculture/horticulture; animals; anthropology/archaeology; art/architecture/design; biography/autobiography; business/economics; child guidance/parenting; computers/electronic; cooking/foods/nutrition; crafts/hobbies; creative nonfiction; current affairs; education; ethnic/cultural interests; gay/lesbian issues; government/politics/law; health/medicine; history; how-to; humor/satire; interior design/decorating; language/literature/criticism; money/finance; music/dance; nature/environment; photography; popular culture; psychology; science/technology; self-help/personal improvement; sociology; theater/film; translation; true crime/investigative; women's issues/studies. **Considers these fiction areas:** Action/adventure; contemporary issues; ethnic; family saga; fantasy; feminist; gay/lesbian; glitz; historical; horror; humor/satire; literary; mainstream/contemporary; multimedia (tie-ins with literary projects); psychic/supernatural; regional; science fiction; thriller.
   O— This agency specializes in narrative nonfiction, nonfiction, fiction. Does not want to receive children's literature, romances, westerns or poetry.
How to Contact: Query with SASE, or send outline, 3 sample chapters. Accepts e-mail queries, no attachments. Considers simultaneous queries. Responds in 2 weeks to queries; 1 month to mss. Returns materials only with SASE. Obtains most new clients through recommendations from others, solicitations.
Recent Sales: Sold 12 titles in the last year. *Almost an Army*, by Philip Gerard (Dutton); *A Telling of Stars*, by Caitlin Sweet (Penguin/Putnam); *Bombproof Your Horse*, by Rick Pelicano (Trafalgar Square); *Learning to Speak Alzheimer's* (Houghton Mifflin); *Soaring Stones* (National Geographic); *The Color Solution* (St. Martin's).

Terms: Agent receives 15% commission on domestic sales; 20% commission on foreign sales. Offers written contract; 30-day notice must be given to terminate contract. Charges clients for postage, long distance, photocopying.

Writers' Conferences: Chesterfield Writer's Workshop (Chesterfield VA, March); Pacific Northwest Writers Association (Seattle WA, July); Henriette Austin Writers Conference (Atlanta GA, July); Mid-Atlantic Creative Nonfiction Summer Writer's Conference (Baltimore MD, August); Baltimore Writers (Baltimore MD, September).

Reading List: Reads *Smithsonian Magazine*, *Zoetrope* and Salon.com to find new clients. Looks for "great ideas and solid writing."

HARVEY KLINGER, INC., 301 W. 53rd St., Suite 21-A, New York NY 10019. (212)581-7068. Fax: (212)315-3823. E-mail: klingerinc@aol.com. **Contact:** Harvey Klinger. Estab. 1977. Member of AAR. Represents 100 clients. 25% of clients are new/unpublished writers. Currently handles: 50% nonfiction books; 50% novels.

Member Agents: Jenny Bent (literary fiction; commercial women's fiction; memoir; narrative nonfiction; self help/pop psychology); David Dunton (popular culture, with a speciality in music-related books; literary fiction; crime novels; thrillers); Wendy Silbert (narrative nonfiction; historical narrative nonfiction; politics; history; biographies; memoir; literary ficiton; business books; culinary narratives); Lisa Dicker, associate agent (literary fiction; sports; narrative nonfiction).

Represents: Nonfiction books, novels. **Considers these nonfiction areas:** Biography/autobiography; cooking/foods/nutrition; health/medicine; psychology; science/technology; self-help/personal improvement; spirituality; sports; true crime/investigative; women's issues/studies. **Considers these fiction areas:** Action/adventure; detective/police/crime; family saga; glitz; literary; mainstream/contemporary; mystery/suspense; thriller.

O→ This agency specializes in "big, mainstream contemporary fiction and nonfiction."

How to Contact: Query with SASE. No phone queries. Accepts e-mail queries. No fax queries. Responds in 2 months to queries; 2 months to mss. Obtains most new clients through recommendations from others.

Recent Sales: Sold 30 titles in the last year. *Swan Place*, by Augusta Trobaugh (Dutton); *Fund Your Future*, by Julie Stav (Berkley); *Auriel Rising*, by Elizabeth Redfern (Putnam); *A Love Supreme*, by Ashley Kahn (Viking); *Idiot Girls' Action Adventure Guide*, by Laurie Notaro; *Inside Medicine*, by Kevin Soden and Christine Dumas; *Where I Work and Other Stories*, by Ann Cummins (Houghton Mifflin); *Thirty Years of Shame*, by Mark Kemp (Free Press). Other clients include Barbara Wood, Terry Kay, Barbara De Angelis, Jill Conner Browne, Michael Farquhar, Greg Bottoms, Jeremy Jackson, Pamela Berkman, Jonetta Rose Barras, Paul Russell.

Terms: Agent receives 15% commission on domestic sales; 25% commission on foreign sales. Offers written contract. Charges for photocopying mss, overseas postage for mss.

THE KNIGHT AGENCY, P.O. Box 550648, Atlanta GA 30355. (404)816-9620. E-mail: knightagency@msn.com. Website: www.knightagency.net. **Contact:** Lisa Payne, manuscript coordinator. Estab. 1996. Member of AAR, RWA, Authors Guild. Represents 65 clients. 40% of clients are new/unpublished writers. Currently handles: 50% nonfiction books; 50% novels.

Member Agents: Deidre Knight (president, agent); Pamela Harty (agent); Lisa Wessling Payne (agency associate).

Represents: Nonfiction books, novels. **Considers these nonfiction areas:** Business/economics; child guidance/parenting; current affairs; ethnic/cultural interests; health/medicine; history; how-to; money/finance; music/dance; popular culture; psychology; religious/inspirational; self-help/personal improvement; theater/film. **Considers these fiction areas:** Literary; mainstream/contemporary (commercial); romance (contemporary, paranormal, romantic suspense, historical, inspirational); women's.

O→ "We are looking for a wide variety of fiction and nonfiction. In the nonfiction area, we're particularly eager to find personal finance, business investment, pop culture, self-help/motivational and popular reference books. In fiction, we're always looking for romance, women's fiction, commercial fiction."

How to Contact: Query with SASE. Accepts e-mail queries; no attachments. Considers simultaneous queries. Responds in 3 weeks to queries; 3 months to mss.

Recent Sales: Sold approximately 65 titles in the last year. *Dark Highlander*, by Karen Marie Moning (Bantam Dell); *The Healing Quilt*, by Lauraine Snelling (WaterBrook Press).

Terms: Agent receives 15% commission on domestic sales; 20-25% commission on foreign sales. Offers written contract, binding for 1 year; 30-day notice must be given to terminate contract. Charges clients for photocopying, postage, overnight courier expenses. "These are deducted from the sale of the work, not billed upfront."

Tips: "At the Knight Agency, a client usually ends up becoming a friend."

TO LEARN MORE ABOUT THE PUBLISHING INDUSTRY, look for the helpful resources in **Professional Organizations** and **Websites of Interest** listed in the back of this book.

LINDA KONNER LITERARY AGENCY, 10 W. 15th St., Suite 1918, New York NY 10011-6829. (212)691-3419. E-mail: ldkonner@cs.com. **Contact:** Linda Konner. Estab. 1996. Member of AAR, ASJA; signatory of WGA. Represents 65 clients. 5-10% of clients are new/unpublished writers. Currently handles: 100% nonfiction books.

Represents: Nonfiction books (adult only). **Considers these nonfiction areas:** Business/economics; child guidance/parenting; gay/lesbian issues; health/medicine (diet/nutrition/fitness); how-to; money/finance (personal finance); popular culture; psychology; self-help/personal improvement; women's issues/studies; relationships. ○➔ This agency specializes in health, self-help and how-to books.

How to Contact: Query with SASE, outline, sufficient return postage. Prefers to read materials exclusively for 2 weeks. Considers simultaneous queries. Obtains most new clients through recommendations from others, occasional solicitation among established authors/journalists.

Recent Sales: Sold 26 titles in the last year. *Lizzy's Ten Perfect Workouts*, by Liz Neporent (Ballantine); *Strength for Their Journey: The Five Disciplines Every African-American Parent Must Teach Her Child*, by Robert Johnson, MD, and Paula Stanford, MD (Doubleday).

Terms: Agent receives 15% commission on domestic sales; 25% commission on foreign sales. Offers written contract. Charges $85 one-time fee for domestic expenses; additional expenses may be incurred for foreign sales.

Writers' Conferences: American Society of Journalists and Authors (New York City, May).

Reading List: *New York Times Magazine* and women's magazines to find new clients.

ELAINE KOSTER LITERARY AGENCY, LLC, 55 Central Park West, Suite 6, New York NY 10023. (212)362-9488. Fax: (212)712-0164. **Contact:** Elaine Koster. Member of AAR, MWA. Represents 40 clients. 10% of clients are new/unpublished writers. Currently handles: 30% nonfiction books; 70% novels.
● Prior to opening her agency, Ms. Koster was president and publisher of Dutton NAL.

Represents: Nonfiction books, novels. **Considers these nonfiction areas:** Biography/autobiography; business/economics; child guidance/parenting; cooking/foods/nutrition; current affairs; ethnic/cultural interests; health/medicine; history; how-to; money/finance; nature/environment; New Age/metaphysics; popular culture; psychology; self-help/personal improvement; spirituality; women's issues/studies. **Considers these fiction areas:** Action/adventure; contemporary issues; detective/police/crime; ethnic; family saga; feminist; historical; literary; mainstream/contemporary; mystery/suspense (amateur sleuth, cozy, culinary, malice domestic); regional; thriller. ○➔ This agency specializes in quality fiction and nonfiction. Does not want to receive juvenile, screenplays, or science fiction.

How to Contact: Query with SASE, outline, 3 sample chapter(s). Prefers to read materials exclusively. No e-mail or fax queries. Responds in 3 weeks to queries; 1 month to mss. Returns materials only with SASE. Obtains most new clients through recommendations from others.

Recent Sales: Sold over 25 titles in the last year. *It's a Man's World*, by Travis Hunter (Strivers Row); *As the Crow Flies*, by M.G. Craig (Pocket Books); *Me Book of Salt*, by Monique Truong (Houghton Mifflin).

Terms: Agent receives 15% commission on domestic sales; 20% commission on foreign sales. Offers written contract. Charges clients for photocopying, messengers, express mail, books and book galleys, ordered from publisher to exploit other rights, overseas shipment of mss and books. 100% of business derived from commissions.

Tips: "We prefer exclusive submissions. Don't e-mail or fax submissions."

BARBARA S. KOUTS, LITERARY AGENT, P.O. Box 560, Bellport NY 11713. (631)286-1278. Fax: (361) 286-1278. E-mail: bkouts@aol.com. **Contact:** Barbara Kouts. Estab. 1980. Member of AAR. Represents 50 clients. 10% of clients are new/unpublished writers. Currently handles: 20% nonfiction books; 20% novels; 60% juvenile books.

Represents: Nonfiction books, novels, juvenile books. **Considers these nonfiction areas:** Biography/autobiography; child guidance/parenting; current affairs; ethnic/cultural interests; health/medicine; history; juvenile nonfiction; music/dance; nature/environment; psychology; self-help/personal improvement; theater/film; women's issues/studies. **Considers these fiction areas:** Contemporary issues; family saga; feminist; historical; juvenile; literary; mainstream/contemporary; mystery/suspense; picture books; young adult. ○➔ This agency specializes in adult fiction and nonfiction and children's books.

How to Contact: Query with SASE. Considers simultaneous queries. Responds in 1 week to queries; 2 months to mss. Obtains most new clients through recommendations from others, solicitations, conferences.

Recent Sales: *A Troubled Guest*, by Nancy Mairs (Beacon); *Sacajawea*, by Joseph Bruchac (Harcourt).

Terms: Agent receives 15% commission on domestic sales; 20% commission on foreign sales. Charges clients for photocopying.

Tips: "Write, do not call. Be professional in your writing."

IRENE KRAAS AGENCY, 256 Rancho Alegre Rd., Santa Fe NM 87508. (505)438-7715. Fax: (505)438-7783. Estab. 1990. Represents 30 clients. 75% of clients are new/unpublished writers. Currently handles: 100% novels.

Represents: Novels (adult). **Considers these fiction areas:** Action/adventure; detective/police/crime; mystery/suspense; science fiction; thriller (psychological).

O₋₇ This agency specializes in adult fiction. Actively seeking "books that are well-written with commercial potential." Does not want to receive romance, short stories, plays or poetry.

How to Contact: Submit cover letter, first 50 pages, SASE; must include return postage and/or SASE. No e-mail or fax queries. Considers simultaneous queries. Returns materials only with SASE.

Recent Sales: *Night Blooming*, by Chelsea Quinn Yarbro (Warner); *Goblin Wood*, by Hilari Bell (Harper/Avon); *Farsala Trilogy*, by Hilari Bell (Simon & Schuster); *Edge of the Sword Trilogy*, by Rebecca Tingle (Putnam); *Patriots in Petticoats*, by Shirley Raye Redmond (Random); *No Place Like the Chevy*, by Janet Lee Cary (Atheneum). Other clients include Denise Vitola, Duncan Long, Shirley-Raye Redmond, Torry England.

Terms: Agent receives 15% commission on domestic sales. Offers written contract, binding for 1 year. Charges clients for photocopying and postage.

Writers' Conferences: Southwest Writers Conference (Albuquerque); Pacific Northwest Conference (Seattle); Vancouver Writers Conference (Vancouver BC); Austin Writers Workshop; Wilamette Writers' Group.

[N] ⊘ **BERT P. KRAGES, ATTORNEY AT LAW**, 6665 S.W. Hampton St., Suite 200, Portland OR 97223-8354. (503)597-2525. E-mail: krages@onemain.com. Website: www.krages.com. **Contact:** Bert Krages. Estab. 2001. Represents 6 clients. 50% of clients are new/unpublished writers. Currently handles 95% nonfiction books; 5% scholarly books.

Member Agents: Bert Krages.

Represents: Nonfiction books, scholarly books. **Considers these nonfiction areas:** agriculture/horticulture; animals; anthropology/archaeology; art/architecture/design; biography/autobiography; business; child guidance/parenting; computers/electronics; cooking/food/nutrition; crafts/hobbies; current affairs; education; government/politics/law; health/medicine; history; how-to; military/war; money/finance/economics; nature/environment; photography; psychology; science/technology; self-help/personal improvement; sociology.

O₋₇ Agent has technical background and welcomes queries on such topics. Is also available to represent authors on an hourly basis who have secured a publisher and want assistance in contract matters. Actively seeking popular science, health and psychology.

How to Contact: Query with SASE. Accepts queries by e-mail. Considers simultaneous queries. Responds in 2 weeks to queries. Obtains most new clients through queries/solicitations.

Terms: Agent receives 15% commission on domestic sales; 20% on foreign sales. Offers written contract, binding for 1 year. 30-day notice must be given to terminate contract. Charges clients for direct expenses (e.g., postage, copying) deducted from royalty payments.

Tips: "The best way to get my attention is with a straightforward query that describes the work, market and writers credentials."

⊘ **STUART KRICHEVSKY LITERARY AGENCY, INC.**, 381 Park Ave., Suite 914, New York NY 10016. Member of AAR.

● Prior to opening his agency, Mr. Krichevsky was an agent at Sterling Lord Agency (now Sterling Lord Literistic) where he worked 15 years.

Represents: Nonfiction books; novels. Considers these fiction areas: mystery, suspense.

Recent Sales: *The Perfect Storm*, by Sebastian Junger; *In the Heart of the Sea*, by Nathaniel Philbrick; *Die Broke*, by Stephen M. Pollan and Mark Levine.

⊘ **EDDIE KRITZER PRODUCTIONS**, 8484 Wilshire Blvd., Suite 205, Beverly Hills CA 90211. (323)655-5696. Fax: (323)655-5173. E-mail: producedby@aol.com. Website: www.eddiekritzer.com. **Contact:** Larisa Wain, executive story editor. Estab. 1995. Represents 20 clients. 50% of clients are new/unpublished writers. Currently handles: 100% nonfiction books.

Member Agents: Eddie Kritzer (nonfiction).

Represents: Nonfiction books. **Considers these nonfiction areas:** Animals; biography/autobiography; business/economics; computers/electronic; cooking/foods/nutrition; current affairs; health/medicine; how-to; humor/satire; self-help/personal improvement; true crime/investigative.

O₋₇ "Looking for compelling stories for books, TV and features."

How to Contact: Query with SASE. Prefers to read materials exclusively. Discards unwanted queries and mss. Accepts e-mail and fax queries. Responds in 3 days to queries; 3 weeks to mss. Obtains most new clients through recommendations from others, solicitations.

Recent Sales: Sold 2 titles and sold 2 scripts in the last year. *Kids Say the Darndest Things*, by Art Linkletter (Workman). ***Movie/TV MOW script(s) optioned/sold:*** *Chat*, by Russ Thartwig (Renee Valente). Other clients include Dr. Alfred Jones, Dr. Bob Murphy, Arthur Satterfield

Terms: Agent receives 15% commission on domestic sales; 20% commission on foreign sales. Offers written contract.

Writers' Conferences: Michale Levine (Santa Monica, May).

Tips: "Be succinct."

EDITE KROLL LITERARY AGENCY INC., 12 Grayhurst Park, Portland ME 04102. (207)773-4922. Fax: (207)773-3936. **Contact:** Edite Kroll. Estab. 1981. Represents 40 clients. Currently handles: 40% juvenile books; 60% adult books.

• Prior to opening the agency, Edite Kroll served as a book editor and translator.

Represents: Adult and juvenile books. **Considers these adult book areas:** Government/politics/law (political issues/feminist); sociology (social issues/feminist); women's issues/studies; humor/satire (by author/artists). Juvenile: picture books (by author/artists), fiction.

O→ Does not want to receive fantasy or genre.

How to Contact: Query with SASE. For nonfiction, send outline and proposal. For juvenile fiction send outline and 1 sample chapter; for picture books and humor send text dummy. No e-mail or fax queries. Considers simultaneous queries. Responds in 1 month to queries; 2 months to mss.

Terms: Agent receives 15% commission on domestic sales; 20% commission on foreign sales. Charges clients for photocopying and legal fees with prior approval from writer.

 THE CANDACE LAKE AGENCY, 9200 Sunset Blvd., Suite 820, Los Angeles CA 90069. (310)247-2115. Fax: (310)247-2116. E-mail: clagency@bwkliterary.com. **Contact:** Candace Lake. Estab. 1977. Member of DGA signatory; signatory of WGA. 50% of clients are new/unpublished writers. Currently handles: 20% novels; 40% movie scripts; 40% TV scripts.

• See the expanded listing for this agency in Script Agents.

PETER LAMPACK AGENCY, INC., 551 Fifth Ave., Suite 1613, New York NY 10176-0187. (212)687-9106. Fax: (212)687-9109. E-mail: renbopla@aol.com. **Contact:** Loren G. Soeiro. Estab. 1977. Represents 50 clients. 10% of clients are new/unpublished writers. Currently handles: 20% nonfiction books; 80% novels.

Member Agents: Peter Lampack (psychological suspense, action/adventure, literary fiction, nonfiction, contemporary relationships); Sandra Blanton (foreign rights); Loren G. Soeiro (literary and commercial fiction, mystery, suspense, nonfiction, narrative nonfiction).

Represents: Nonfiction books, novels. **Considers these fiction areas:** Action/adventure; detective/police/crime; family saga; historical; literary; mainstream/contemporary; mystery/suspense; thriller; contemporary relationships.

O→ This agency specializes in commercial fiction, nonfiction by recognized experts. Actively seeking literary and commercial fiction, thrillers, mysteries, suspense, psychological thrillers. Does not want to receive horror, romance, science fiction, western, academic material.

How to Contact: Query with SASE. No unsolicited mss. Accepts e-mail queries. No fax queries. Considers simultaneous queries. Responds in 3 weeks to queries; 2 months to mss. Obtains most new clients through referrals made by clients.

Recent Sales: *Summer of Storms*, by Judith Kelman (Berkley); *Law of Gravity*, by Stephen Horn (HarperCollins); *Valhalla Rising*, by Clive Cussler (Putnam).

Terms: Agent receives 15% commission on domestic sales; 20% commission on foreign sales.

Writers' Conferences: BEA (Chicago, June).

Tips: "Submit only your best work for consideration. Have a very specific agenda of goals you wish your prospective agent to accomplish for you. Provide the agent with a comprehensive statement of your credentials: educational and professional."

MICHAEL LARSEN/ELIZABETH POMADA LITERARY AGENTS, 1029 Jones St., San Francisco CA 94109-5023. (415)673-0939. E-mail: larsenpoma@aol.com. Website: www.Larsen-Pomada.com. **Contact:** Mike Larsen or Elizabeth Pomada. Estab. 1972. Member of AAR, Authors Guild, ASJA, PEN, WNBA, California Writers Club. Represents 100 clients. 40-45% of clients are new/unpublished writers. Currently handles: 70% nonfiction books; 30% novels.

• Prior to opening their agency, Mr. Larsen and Ms. Pomada were promotion executives for major publishing houses. Mr. Larsen worked for Morrow, Bantam and Pyramid (now part of Berkley), Ms. Pomada worked at Holt, David McKay, and The Dial Press.

Member Agents: Michael Larsen (nonfiction); Elizabeth Pomada (narrative nonfiction, books of interest to women).

Represents: Nonfiction books (adult), novels. **Considers these nonfiction areas:** Anthropology/archaeology; art/architecture/design; biography/autobiography; business/economics; cooking/foods/nutrition; current affairs; ethnic/cultural interests; gay/lesbian issues; government/politics/law; health/medicine; history; how-to; humor/satire; interior design/decorating; memoirs; money/finance; music/dance; nature/environment; New Age/metaphysics; photography; popular culture; psychology; religious/inspirational; science/technology; self-help/personal improvement; sociology; sports; theater/film; travel; true crime/investigative; women's issues/studies; futurism. **Considers these fiction areas:** Action/adventure; contemporary issues; detective/police/crime; ethnic; experimental; family saga; fantasy; feminist; gay/lesbian; glitz; historical; humor/satire; literary; mainstream/contemporary; mystery/suspense; religious/inspirational; romance (contemporary, gothic, historical).

O→ "We have very diverse tastes. We look for fresh voices and new ideas. We handle literary, commercial and genre fiction, and the full range of nonfiction books." Actively seeking commercial and literary fiction. Does not want to receive children's books, plays, short stories, screenplays, pornography, poetry or stories of abuse.

How to Contact: Query with SASE, first 10 pages of completed novel and two page synopsis. For nonfiction, send title, promotion plan and proposal done according to our plan (see brochure and website). No e-mail or fax queries. Responds in 2 months to queries.

Recent Sales: Sold 15 titles in the last year. *Night Whispers*, by Pam Chun (Sourcebooks); *Marketing for Free*, by Jay C. Levinson (Houghton Mifflin); *Snoopy's Guide to the Writing Life*, introduction by Barnaby Conrad and foreward by Monte Schulz (Writer's Digest); *Fox on the Rhine*, by Michael Dobson and Doug Niles (Tor).

Terms: Agent receives 15% commission on domestic sales; 20% (30% for Asia) commission on foreign sales. May charge for printing, postage for multiple submissions, foreign mail, foreign phone calls, galleys, books, and legal fees.

Writers' Conferences: Book Expo America; Santa Barbara Writers Conference (Santa Barbara); Maui Writers Conference (Maui); ASJA.

Tips: "If you can write books that meet the needs of the marketplace, and you can promote your books, now is the best time ever to be a writer. We must find new writers to make a living so we are very eager to hear from new writers whose work will interest large houses and nonfiction writers who can promote their books. Please send a SASE for a free 16-page brochure and a list of recent sales."

☑ ◖ **THE MAUREEN LASHER AGENCY**, P.O. Box 46370, Los Angeles CA 90046. Fax: (323)654-5388. E-mail: mllaliterary@aol.com. **Contact:** Ann Cashman. Estab. 1980.

• Prior to becoming an agent, Ms. Lasher worked in publishing in New York.

Represents: Nonfiction books, novels. **Considers these nonfiction areas:** Animals; anthropology/archaeology; art/architecture/design; biography/autobiography; business/economics; child guidance/parenting; cooking/foods/ nutrition; current affairs; ethnic/cultural interests; government/politics/law; health/medicine; history; how-to; nature/environment; popular culture; psychology; science/technology; self-help/personal improvement; sociology; sports; true crime/investigative; women's issues/studies. **Considers these fiction areas:** Action/adventure; detective/police/crime; family saga; feminist; historical; literary; mainstream/contemporary; sports; thriller.

How to Contact: Query with SASE, submit outline, 1 sample chapter(s). No e-mail or fax queries.

Recent Sales: *United We Stand*, by Peter Kritter (Chronicle); *Walls Came Tumbling Down*, by H. Caldwell (Scribner); *Untitled companion book to PBS series*, by Regina Campbell (Morrow); *Relax, This Won't Hurt*, by Judith Reichman (Morrow); *Now This*, by Judy Muller (Putnam).

Terms: This agency charges clients for copying and postage for FedEx.

◖ **LAWYER'S LITERARY AGENCY, INC.**, 501 W. Broadway, Lobby C, San Diego CA 92101. (619)696-3300. Fax: (619)696-3808. E-mail: allenetling@legallanding.com or kr@legallanding.com. **Contact:** H. Allen Etling or Kevin Lee Randall. Estab. 1994. Represents 10 clients. 90% of clients are new/unpublished writers. Currently handles: 70% nonfiction books; 30% novels.

Represents: Nonfiction books, novels. **Considers these nonfiction areas:** Biography/autobiography (of lawyers); government/politics/law; true crime/investigative. **Considers these fiction areas:** Thriller (political).

☞ This agency specializes in true crime, including trial aspect written by attorneys, and lawyer biographies and autobiographies.

How to Contact: Query with SASE, outline, 3 sample chapter(s). Responds in 1 month to queries. Obtains most new clients through recommendations from others.

Recent Sales: Movie options for *Undying Love: A Key West Love Story*, by Ben Harrison (New Horizon Press).

Terms: Agent receives 15% commission on domestic sales. Offers written contract, binding for 1 year; 30-day notice must be given to terminate contract.

Tips: "Many of the best real stories are true crime stories—including depiction of the crime, background of the participants, official investigation by authorities, defense/prosecution preparation and the trial. There are hundreds of intriguing cases that occur annually in the US and not all of them are handled by attorneys who are household names. We are looking for the most compelling of these stories where there is also a good chance of selling TV movie/feature movie rights. Manuscripts can entail one case or multiple cases. Those involving multiple cases would probably resemble an attorney's biography. The story or stories can be told by defense and prosecution attorneys alike."

◖ **LAZEAR AGENCY INCORPORATED**, 800 Washington Ave. N., Suite 660, Minneapolis MN 55401. (612)332-8640. Fax: (612)332-4648. Website: www.lazear.com. **Contact:** Editorial Board. Estab. 1984. Represents 250 clients. Currently handles: 60% nonfiction books; 30% novels; 10% juvenile books.

• The Lazear Agency opened a New York Office in September 1997.

Member Agents: Jonathon Lazear; Wendy Lazear; Christi Cardenas; Anne Blackstone; Julie Mayo.

Represents: Nonfiction books, novels, juvenile books, feature film, TV scripts, syndicated material, licensing; new media with connection to book project. **Considers these nonfiction areas:** Agriculture/horticulture; Americana; animals; anthropology/archaeology; art/architecture/design; biography/autobiography; business/economics; child guidance/parenting; computers/electronic; cooking/foods/nutrition; crafts/hobbies; creative nonfiction; current affairs; education; ethnic/cultural interests; gardening; gay/lesbian issues; government/politics/law; health/medicine; history; how-to; humor/satire; interior design/decorating; juvenile nonfiction; language/literature/criticism; memoirs; military/war; money/finance; multicultural; music/dance; nature/environment; New Age/metaphysics; philosophy; photography; popular culture; psychology; recreation; regional; religious/inspirational; science/technology; self-help/personal improvement; sex; sociology; software; spirituality; sports; theater/film; translation; travel; true crime/investigative; women's issues/studies; young adult. **Considers these fiction areas:** Action/adventure; comic books/cartoon; confession; contemporary issues; detective/police/crime; erotica; ethnic; experimental; family saga; fantasy; feminist; gay/lesbian; glitz; gothic; hi-lo; historical; horror; humor/satire; juvenile; literary; mainstream/contemporary; military/war; multicultural; multimedia; mystery/suspense; New Age; occult; picture books; plays; poetry; poetry in translation; psychic/supernatural; regional; religious/inspirational; romance; science fiction; short story collections; spiritual; sports; thriller; translation; westerns/frontier; young adult; women's.

How to Contact: Query with SASE, outline/proposal. Highly selective. No phone calls. No e-mail or fax queries. Responds in 3 weeks to queries; 1 month to mss. Returns materials only with SASE. Obtains most new clients through recommendations from others, "through the bestseller lists, word-of-mouth."

Recent Sales: Sold over 50 titles in the last year. *Oh, The Things I Know*, by Al Franken (Dutton); *You Ain't Got no Easter Clothes*, by Laura Love (Hyperion).

Terms: Agent receives 15% commission on domestic sales; 20% commission on foreign sales. Offers written contract. Charges clients for photocopying, international express mail, bound galleys and finished books used for subsidiary rights sales. "No fees charged if book is not sold."

Reading List: Reads *The New Yorker*, *Harper's* and various newspapers and other magazines to find new clients. Looks for "originality, broad interest."

Tips: "The writer should first view himself as a salesperson in order to obtain an agent. Sell yourself, your idea, your concept. Do your homework. Notice what is in the marketplace. Be sophisticated about the arena in which you are writing."

⊘ SARAH LAZIN BOOKS, 126 Fifth Ave., Suite 300, New York NY 10011. Member of AAR.
   ● This agency did not respond to our request for information. Query before submitting.

⊘ THE NED LEAVITT AGENCY, 70 Wooster St., New York NY 10012. Member of AAR.
   ● This agency did not respond to our request for information. Query before submitting.

⊘ LESCHER & LESCHER LTD., 47 E. 19th St., New York NY 10003. (212)529-1790. Fax: (212)529-2716. E-mail: rl@lescherltd.com. **Contact:** Robert Lescher, Susan Lescher, Michael Choate. Estab. 1966. Member of AAR. Represents 150 clients. Currently handles: 80% nonfiction books; 20% novels.
Represents: Nonfiction books, novels. **Considers these nonfiction areas:** Cooking/foods/nutrition (cookbooks); wines. **Considers these fiction areas:** Mystery/suspense.
   0→ Does not want to receive screenplays or science fiction.
How to Contact: Query with SASE. Accepts queries by e-mail. Obtains most new clients through recommendations from others.
Recent Sales: Sold 25 titles in the last year. *Dead Aim*, by Thomas Perry (Random House); *Great Wine Estates*, by Robert M. Parker, Jr. (Simon & Schuster). Other clients include Neil Sheehan, Madeleine L'Engle, Calvin Trillin, Judith Viorst, Thomas Perry, Anne Fadiman, Frances FitzGerald, Paula Fox, J.F. Freedman and Robert M. Parker, Jr.
Terms: Agent receives 15% commission on domestic sales; 20-25% commission on foreign sales.

◉ JAMES LEVINE COMMUNICATIONS, INC., 307 Seventh Ave., Suite 1906, New York NY 10001. (212)337-0934. Fax: (212)337-0948. Website: www.jameslevine.com. Estab. 1989. Member of AAR. Represents 250 clients. 33% of clients are new/unpublished writers. Currently handles: 70% nonfiction books; 30% novels.
   ● Prior to opening his agency, Mr. Levine served as vice president of the Bank Street College of Education.
Member Agents: James Levine; Arielle Eckstut; Daniel Greenberg; Stephanie Kip Roston; Miek Coccia.
Represents: Nonfiction books, novels. **Considers these nonfiction areas:** Animals; art/architecture/design; biography/autobiography; business/economics; child guidance/parenting; computers/electronic; cooking/foods/ nutrition; gardening; gay/lesbian issues; health/medicine; money/finance; nature/environment; New Age/metaphysics; psychology; religious/inspirational; science/technology; self-help/personal improvement; sociology; spirituality; sports; women's issues/studies. **Considers these fiction areas:** Contemporary issues; literary; mainstream/contemporary; mystery/suspense; thriller (psychological); women's.
   0→ This agency specializes in business, psychology, parenting, health/medicine, narrative nonfiction, psychology, spirituality, religion, women's issues and commercial fiction.
How to Contact: See www.jameslevine.com for full submission procedure. Prefers e-mail queries. Obtains most new clients through recommendations from others.
Recent Sales: *Queen Bees and Wannabes: Helping Your Daughter Survive Cliques, Gossip, Boyfriends, and Other Realities of Adolescence*, by Rosalind Wiseman (Crown); *Chicken: A Self-Portrait*, by David Sterry (Regan Books/Harper Collins); *Raising Fences: A Black Man's Love Story*, by Michael Datcher (Riverhead/ Penguin Putnam); *21 Dog Years: Doing Time*, by Mike Daisey (Free Press/Simon and Schuster).
Terms: Agent receives 15% commission on domestic sales; 20% commission on foreign sales. Offers written contract, binding for variable length of time. Charges clients for out-of-pocket expenses—telephone, fax, postage and photocopying—directly connected to the project.
Writers' Conferences: ASJA Annual Conference (New York City, May).

Tips: "We work closely with clients on editorial development and promotion. We work to place our clients as magazine columnists and have created columnists for *McCall's* (renamed *Rosie's*) and *Child*. We work with clients to develop their projects across various media—video, software, and audio."

 **ELLEN LEVINE LITERARY AGENCY, INC.**, 15 E. 26th St., Suite 1801, New York NY 10010. (212)889-0620. Fax: (212)725-4501. **Contact:** Ellen Levine, Diana Finch, Louise Quayle. Estab. 1980. Member of AAR. Represents 200 clients. 20% of clients are new/unpublished writers. Currently handles: 50% nonfiction books; 5% juvenile books; 45% fiction.
Member Agents: Ellen Levine; Diana Finch; Louise Quayle.
Represents: Nonfiction books, novels, short story collections, juvenile books. **Considers these nonfiction areas:** Anthropology/archaeology; biography/autobiography; creative nonfiction; current affairs; health/medicine; history; memoirs; popular culture; psychology; religious/inspirational; science/technology; women's issues/studies; adventure; books by journalists in all areas. **Considers these fiction areas:** Literary; mystery/suspense; thriller; women's.
How to Contact: Query with SASE. Responds in 6 weeks to mss. Responds in 2 weeks to queries if SASE provided. Obtains most new clients through recommendations from others.
Recent Sales: *Diana's Boys*, by Christopher Andersen (William Morrow); *Lake Wobegon Summer 1956*, by Garrison Keillor; *Anil's Ghost* , by Michael Ondaatje; *The Frailty Myth*, by Colette Dowling (Random House). Other clients include Russell Banks, Cristina Garcia, Jane Heller, Michael Gross, Todd Gitlin.
Terms: Agent receives 15% commission on domestic sales; 20% commission on foreign sales. Charges clients for overseas postage, photocopying, messenger fees, overseas telephone and fax, books ordered for use in rights submissions.
Tips: "My younger colleagues at the agency (Quayle and Finch) are seeking both new and established writers. I prefer to work with established writers, mostly through referrals."

PAUL S. LEVINE LITERARY AGENCY, 1054 Superba Ave., Venice CA 90291-3940. (310)450-6711. Fax: (310)450-0181. E-mail: pslevine@ix.netcom.com. Website: www.netcom.com/~pslevine/lawliterary.html. **Contact:** Paul S. Levine. Estab. 1996. Member of the State Bar of California. Represents over 100 clients. 75% of clients are new/unpublished writers. Currently handles: 30% nonfiction books; 30% novels; 10% movie scripts; 30% TV scripts.
Represents: Nonfiction books, novels, movie scripts, feature film, TV scripts, TV movie of the week, episodic drama, sitcom, animation, documentary, miniseries, syndicated material. **Considers these nonfiction areas:** Art/architecture/design; biography/autobiography; business/economics; child guidance/parenting; computers/electronic; cooking/foods/nutrition; crafts/hobbies; creative nonfiction; current affairs; education; ethnic/cultural interests; gay/lesbian issues; government/politics/law; health/medicine; history; how-to; humor/satire; interior design/decorating; language/literature/criticism; memoirs; military/war; money/finance; music/dance; nature/environment; New Age/metaphysics; photography; popular culture; psychology; religious/inspirational; science/technology; self-help/personal improvement; sociology; sports; theater/film; true crime/investigative; women's issues/studies. **Considers these fiction areas:** Action/adventure; comic books/cartoon; confession; contemporary issues; detective/police/crime; erotica; ethnic; experimental; family saga; feminist; gay/lesbian; glitz; historical; humor/satire; literary; mainstream/contemporary; mystery/suspense; psychic/supernatural; regional; religious/inspirational; romance; sports; thriller; westerns/frontier. **Considers these script subject areas:** Action/adventure; biography/autobiography; cartoon/animation; comedy; contemporary issues; detective/police/crime; erotica; ethnic; experimental; family saga; fantasy; feminist; gay/lesbian; glitz; historical; horror; juvenile; mainstream; multimedia; mystery/suspense; psychic/supernatural; religious/inspirational; romantic comedy; romantic drama; science fiction; sports; teen; thriller; western/frontier.
  ☛ Actively seeking commercial fiction and nonfiction. Does not want to receive science fiction or children's material.
How to Contact: Query with SASE. Accepts e-mail and fax queries. Considers simultaneous queries. Responds in 1 day to queries; 2 months to mss. Returns materials only with SASE. Obtains most new clients through conferences, referrals, listings on various websites and through listings in directories.
Recent Sales: Sold 25 titles in the last year. This agency prefers not to share information on specific sales.
Terms: Agent receives 15% commission on domestic sales; 20% commission on foreign sales. Offers written contract. Charges clients for messengers, long distance, postage. "Only when incurred. No advance payment necessary."

FOR EXPLANATIONS OF THESE SYMBOLS,
SEE THE INSIDE FRONT AND BACK COVERS OF THIS BOOK

Writers' Conferences: California Lawyers for the Arts (Los Angeles CA); National Writers Club (Los Angeles CA); "Selling to Hollywood" Writer's Connection (Glendale CA); "Spotlight on Craft" Willamette Writers Conference (Portland OR); Women in Animation (Los Angeles CA); and many others.

ROBERT LIEBERMAN ASSOCIATES, 400 Nelson Rd., Ithaca NY 14850-9440. (607)273-8801. Fax: (801)749-9682. E-mail: RHL10@cornell.edu. Website: www.people.cornell.edu/pages/RHL10/. **Contact:** Robert Lieberman. Estab. 1993. Represents 30 clients. 50% of clients are new/unpublished writers. Currently handles: 20% nonfiction books; 80% textbooks.
Represents: Nonfiction books (trade), scholarly books, textbooks (college, high school and middle school level). **Considers these nonfiction areas:** Agriculture/horticulture; anthropology/archaeology; art/architecture/design; business/economics; computers/electronic; education; health/medicine; memoirs (by authors with high public recognition); money/finance; music/dance; nature/environment; psychology; science/technology; sociology; theater/film.
> **O—** This agency specializes in university/college level textbooks, CD-ROM/software and popular tradebooks in science, math, engineering, economics and other subjects. Does not want to receive fiction, self-help or screenplays.

How to Contact: Query with SASE or by e-mail. Prefers to read materials exclusively. Prefers e-mail queries. Considers simultaneous queries. Responds in 2 weeks to queries; 1 month to mss. Returns materials only with SASE. Obtains most new clients through referrals.
Recent Sales: Sold 15 titles in the last year. *Conflict Resolution*, by Baltos and Weir (Cambridge University Press).
Terms: Agent receives 15% commission on domestic sales; 20% commission on foreign sales. Offers written contract, binding for open-ended length of time; 30-day notice must be given to terminate contract. 100% of business is derived from commissions on ms sales. "Fees are sometimes charged to clients for shipping and when special reviewers are required."
Tips: "The trade books we handle are by authors who are highly recognized in their fields of expertise. Client list includes Nobel Prize winners and others with high name recognition, either by the public or within a given area of expertise."

LIMELIGHT MANAGEMENT, 33 Newman St., London W1T 1PY, England. (00)44 207 637 2529. Fax: (00)44 207 637 2538. E-mail: limelightmanagement@virgin.net. Website: www.limelightmanagement.com. **Contact:** Fiona Lindsay. Estab. 1990. Member of Association of Authors' Agents. Represents 70 clients. Currently handles: 100% nonfiction books; multimedia.
> • Prior to becoming an agent, Ms. Lindsay was a public relations manager of the Dorchester and was working on her law degree.

Represents: Nonfiction books, lifestyle TV. **Considers these nonfiction areas:** Agriculture/horticulture; art/architecture/design; cooking/foods/nutrition; crafts/hobbies; gardening; health/medicine; interior design/decorating; nature/environment; New Age/metaphysics; photography; self-help/personal improvement; sports; travel.
> **O—** This agency specializes in lifestyle subject areas, especially celebrity chefs, gardeners and wine experts. Actively seeking health, cooking, gardening. Does not want to receive any subject not listed above.

How to Contact: Query with SASE, or send outline/proposal; IRCs. Prefers to read materials exclusively. Accepts e-mail and fax queries. Responds in 1 week to queries. Returns materials only with SASE. Obtains most new clients through recommendations from others.
Recent Sales: Sold 45 titles in the last year. This agency prefers not to share information on specific sales. Clients include Oz Clarke, Antony Worrall Thompson, David Stevens, David Joyce, John Bly.
Terms: Agent receives 15% commission on domestic sales; 20% commission on foreign sales. Offers written contract; 2-month notice must be given to terminate contract.

RAY LINCOLN LITERARY AGENCY, Elkins Park House, Suite 107-B, 7900 Old York Rd., Elkins Park PA 19027. (215)782-8882. Fax: (215)782-8882. **Contact:** Mrs. Ray Lincoln. Estab. 1974. Represents 30 clients. 35% of clients are new/unpublished writers. Currently handles: 30% nonfiction books; 50% novels; 20% juvenile books.
Member Agents: Jerome A. Lincoln; Mrs. Ray Lincoln.
Represents: Nonfiction books, novels, juvenile books, scholarly books. **Considers these nonfiction areas:** Animals; anthropology/archaeology; art/architecture/design; biography/autobiography; business/economics; child guidance/parenting; cooking/foods/nutrition; crafts/hobbies; creative nonfiction; current affairs; ethnic/cultural interests; gardening; gay/lesbian issues; government/politics/law; health/medicine; history; interior design/decorating; juvenile nonfiction; language/literature/criticism; money/finance; music/dance; nature/environment; psychology; science/technology; self-help/personal improvement; sociology; sports; theater/film; women's issues/studies. **Considers these fiction areas:** Action/adventure; contemporary issues; detective/police/crime; ethnic; family saga; fantasy; feminist; gay/lesbian; historical; humor/satire; juvenile; literary; mainstream/contemporary; mystery/suspense; psychic/supernatural; regional; romance (contemporary, gothic, historical); sports; thriller; young adult.
> **O—** This agency specializes in biography, nature, the sciences, fiction in both adult and children's categories.

How to Contact: Query with SASE. Prefers to read materials exclusively. If requested, send an outline, 2 sample chapters, SASE. No e-mail or fax queries. Responds in 2 weeks to queries. Obtains most new clients through recommendations from others.
Recent Sales: *Alexander Hamilton: A Life*, by Willard Sterne Randall (HarperCollins); *Laser*, by Jerry Spinelli (HarperCollins); *Planet Walk*, by John Francis (Chelsea Green).
Terms: Agent receives 15% commission on domestic sales; 20% commission on foreign sales. Offers written contract. Charges clients for overseas telephone calls; upfront postage fee for unpublished authors only. "I request authors to do manuscript photocopying themselves."
Tips: "I always look for polished writing style, fresh points of view and professional attitudes. I send for balance of manuscript if it is a likely project."

WENDY LIPKIND AGENCY, 165 E. 66th St., New York NY 10021. (212)628-9653. Fax: (212)628-2693. **Contact:** Wendy Lipkind. Estab. 1977. Member of AAR. Represents 60 clients. Currently handles: 80% nonfiction books; 20% novels.
Represents: Nonfiction books, novels. **Considers these nonfiction areas:** Biography/autobiography; current affairs; health/medicine; history; science/technology; women's issues/studies; social history. **Considers these fiction areas:** Mainstream/contemporary; mystery/suspense (psychological suspense).
○┰ This agency specializes in adult nonfiction. Does not want to receive mass market originals.
How to Contact: Prefers to read materials exclusively. For nonfiction, query with outline/proposal. For fiction, query with SASE only. Responds in 1 month to queries. Returns materials only with SASE. Obtains most new clients through recommendations from others.
Recent Sales: Sold 10 titles in the last year. *One Small Step*, by Robert Mauner (Workman); *In the Land of Lyme*, by Pamela Weintraub (Scribner).
Terms: Agent receives 15% commission on domestic sales; 20% commission on foreign sales. Sometimes offers written contract. Charges clients for foreign postage, messenger service, photocopying, transatlantic calls, faxes.
Tips: "Send intelligent query letter first. Let me know if you sent to other agents."

LITERARY AND CREATIVE ARTISTS, INC., 3543 Albemarle St. NW, Washington DC 20008-4213. (202)362-4688. Fax: (202)362-8875. E-mail: LCADC@earthlink.net. Website: www.leadc.com. **Contact:** Muriel Nellis, Jane Roberts. Estab. 1981. Member of AAR, Authors Guild, associate member of American Bar Association. Represents 75 clients. Currently handles: 70% nonfiction books; 15% novels; 15% audio/video/film/TV.
Member Agents: Muriel Nellis; Jane Roberts; Stephen Ruwe.
Represents: Nonfiction books, novels, audio, film/TV rights. **Considers these nonfiction areas:** Biography/autobiography; business/economics; cooking/foods/nutrition; government/politics/law; health/medicine; how-to; memoirs; philosophy; human drama; lifestyle.
How to Contact: Query with SASE, outline, author bio. No unsolicited mss. Responds in 3 weeks to queries.
Recent Sales: *Katurran Odyssey*, by Terryl Whitlatch and David Wieger (Simon & Schuster); *Grow Younger, Live Longer*, by Deepak Chopra, M.D. and David Simon, M.D.; *The Way*, by Michael Berg (John Wiley and Sons); *Discover Your Genius*, by Michael Gelb (HarperCollins); *The 10 Lenses*, by Mark Williams (Capital Books); *Secondhand Smoke*, by Patty Friedmann (Counterpoint); *The Essential Zohar*, by Rav Philip Berg (Bell Tower Books); *American Roulette*, by Richard Marcus (Thomas Dunne Books).
Terms: Agent receives 15% commission on domestic sales; 25% commission on foreign sales; 25% commission on dramatic rights sales. Charges clients for long-distance phone and fax, photocopying, shipping.
Tips: "While we prefer published writers, it is not required if the proposed work has great merit."

THE LITERARY GROUP, 270 Lafayette St., 1505, New York NY 10012. (212)274-1616. Fax: (212)274-9876. E-mail: fweimann@theliterarygroup.com. Website: www.theliterarygroup.com. **Contact:** Frank Weimann. Estab. 1985. Represents 200 clients. 65% of clients are new/unpublished writers. Currently handles: 50% nonfiction books; 50% fiction.
Member Agents: Frank Weimann (fiction, nonfiction); Andrew Stuart (nonfiction); Priya Ratneshwar (fiction).
Represents: Nonfiction books, novels. **Considers these nonfiction areas:** Animals; anthropology/archaeology; biography/autobiography; business/economics; child guidance/parenting; cooking/foods/nutrition; crafts/hobbies; creative nonfiction; current affairs; education; ethnic/cultural interests; government/politics/law; health/medicine; history; how-to; humor/satire; juvenile nonfiction; language/literature/criticism; memoirs; military/war; money/finance; multicultural; music/dance; nature/environment; popular culture; psychology; religious/inspirational; science/technology; self-help/personal improvement; sociology; sports; theater/film; true crime/investigative; women's issues/studies. **Considers these fiction areas:** Action/adventure; contemporary issues; detective/police/crime; ethnic; family saga; fantasy; feminist; horror; humor/satire; mystery/suspense; psychic/supernatural; romance (contemporary, gothic, historical, regency); sports; thriller; westerns/frontier.
○┰ This agency specializes in nonfiction (true crime, military, history, biography, sports, how-to).
How to Contact: Query with SASE, outline, 3 sample chapter(s). Prefers to read materials exclusively. Responds in 1 week to queries; 1 month to mss. Returns materials only with SASE. Obtains most new clients through referrals, writers' conferences, query letters.

insider report

The agent's law: perseverence is key

Robert Preskill

Robert Preskill never expected his many literary aspirations would make perfect stepping stones to his career as an agent, but they built his path, one by one. As an undergraduate college student studying architecture at the University of Illinois, he found Ayn Rand's *The Fountainhead* enthralling. His enthusiasm for Rand's fiction energized him to study creative writing, and one of his first published articles appeared in, of all places, an architecture magazine.

Thus the first stepping stone was laid.

Teachers at Illinois such as Jean Thompson, Mark Costello, and Laurence Lieberman, who are also accomplished writers, encouraged Preskill's writing. "It was a nurturing program," he says, adding that it allowed him to work as an editor for the undergrad literary magazine, *Little America*. The editor in Preskill did not know it at the time, but reading manuscripts gave him a sense of the diversity of writers' works that ten years later would influence his decisions as a fledgling literary agent.

Although he emphasizes that "nothing is a smooth transition to anyplace else," his decision to study law became another stepping stone to his future. "It taught me the nuts and bolts about how to get what's fair, especially for the writer," he says. All along he continued to sharpen his writing skills as a reporter for a trade legal newspaper.

A year and a half after he graduated with a law degree, Preskill joined McGraw Hill where, for over four years, he inched closer to his agenting career, working in editing, production and sales. By the time he left both McGraw Hill and *Another Chicago Magazine*—the venerable literary publication he simultaneously worked for—he had inside knowledge of writing, editing, and the publishing industry.

Since June 1999, Preskill has operated his literary agency in San Francisco as part of a group of four agents called Lit West, LLC. This collaborative represents a recent kind of development among numerous agents these days on both coasts. In Lit West, Preskill and the agents are free to partner with agents outside the group, yet this core group of four shares ideas, strategies, and other administrative duties that provide Lit West with more clout. Their reliance on each other both sustains their collaboration and empowers them to expand, with the goal of always discovering new projects according to their different tastes.

Law school did impress upon Preskill the many ways contracts must be studied. He considers every possible route in which his client "might exploit his own work," he says, and then he highlights those points when he negotiates with the publisher. As an example, Preskill cites a negotiation he might have with a publisher over a project's electronic rights: if the author has *no* plan as to how electronic rights might increase book sales, while the publisher *can* demonstrate that they have a real plan to use them and have included a fair division of rights, then Preskill will recommend that the author accept the publisher's proposal for electronic rights in exchange for improving another facet of the book deal. But if the publisher has no such plan for electronic use, Preskill negotiates for the author to keep those rights.

Since logic and common sense are crucial in "the deal," law school taught Preskill what every competent agent should know: negotiating has more to do with personalities and relationships and the ability to say no. The course of a negotiation changes all the time, he says. For instance, there are editors who essentially know they are the only ones bidding; they might have true respect for what Preskill is offering, and their bid is generous. These are editors Preskill will come back to every time. "This has less to do with law and more with human nature," he says.

Preskill relates one classic story where an editor in a negotiation said, "We never do that." Preskill's experience in law school immediately told him this was a bluff. "It meant the editor did not understand the contract, was busy, confused, or did not care," he says. "If you, as an agent, know in your heart what your client reasonably needs, 'never' is never an effective answer."

As a writer, editor, attorney, and agent, Preskill knows how to become deeply involved in a project. He helps edit a manuscript, strategizes its marketability, pursues the best possible route for a deal, and works as closely with publishers as he does with his writers. And he prefers to work with writers who put great thought into what they are writing.

"This doesn't mean that a writer has to have been previously published," he says, "but prior publication is solid proof that the larger work evolved from something developed and tested. It also shows that someone else—an editor—thought the writing was worthy of publication. This really stands out."

Much of Preskill's vision of a manuscript harks back to what he learned in the best creative writing classes: how to be uncompromising in one's first drafts, and how a writer needs to step back and be self-effacing in the editing. "To rethink everything," he says. Changing a project to improve it is paramount if the work is to reach its highest quality.

Preskill recommends that writers be patient and thoughtful with their work, because he certainly will. While Preskill considers *all* parts of a book's selling potential, he considers most heavily whether a writer has "boiled down the essence of the project, so that the manuscript or proposal almost assumes an agent or publisher will say 'yes.' "

Preskill advises writers to be concise, including only those details that make it obvious to the agent why the project is interesting. "Any additional information, as in a lot of superfluous details not related to the book or things overcompensating the book, might push the agent against the project—quickly," he says. "Less is digestible."

How can a writer do this? "What I look at depends on the writing," he says. "What's the writing doing to interest me? At what quality level is this writing? How much has it been worked on so far?"

When Preskill takes on a manuscript it's also because the book is something he would like to read himself and can safely assume others would want to read. In that sense, writers should be self-critical about their writing and also read extensively for inspiration. "I'm a writer," Preskill says, "and often when I *read* good writing, *I* want to write something."

Whatever personal strategy a writer has in seeking an agent, Preskill urges writers to be vigilant and query, say, fifteen agents at once, maintaining a response deadline of three months. Within that span of time, it's favorable to place consistent yet polite follow-ups. "No need to hound the agent with demands, though. That's not a good move," he says.

Agents work now within such a vast range of sub-genres that if the writing is high-caliber and accessible, it will get noticed at some point. Preskill's advice to writers is identical to the advice he got when he wavered over pursuing agenting: The keys, he says, are perseverance, belief in one's work, and a never-say-quit attitude toward writing, knowing that a strong work ethic always outweighs pure luck.

—*Jeffrey Hillard*

Recent Sales: Sold 80 titles in the last year. *Inside Delta Force*, by Eric Haney; *The Greater Good*, by William Casey Moreton; *The Dead Room*, by Robert Ellis; *It's Only a Game*, by Terry Bradshaw. Other clients include James Bradley, Victoria Gotti, Judith Lansdowne.

Terms: Agent receives 15% commission on domestic sales; 15% commission on foreign sales. Offers written contract; 30-day notice must be given to terminate contract.

Writers' Conferences: Detroit Women's Writers (MI); Kent State University (OH); San Diego Writers Conference (CA); Maui Writers Conference (HI); Austin Writers' Conference (TX).

LITWEST GROUP, LLC, 379 Burning Tree Court, Half Moon Bay CA 94019. (650)726-3969. Fax: (650)726-4925. E-mail: linda@litwest.com. Website: www.litwest.com. **Contact:** Linda Mead. Represents 160 clients. 45% of clients are new/unpublished writers. Currently handles: 75% nonfiction books; 25% novels; TV, movie, Internet projects revolving around the book.

• Prior to opening the agency, Ms. Ellis was in academia, Mr. Preskill was in law and Ms. Mead and Ms. Boyle were in publishing. See individual listings for Robert Preskill and Linda Mead.

Member Agents: Linda Mead (business, personal improvement, memoir); Nancy Ellis (mystery/suspense/thriller, religion/spiritual, parenting, psychology, science); Rob Preskill (men's, thrillers, sports, literary); Katie Boyle (literary, women's issues, pop-culture, religion/spirituality).

Represents: Nonfiction books, novels, scholarly books. **Considers these nonfiction areas:** Biography/autobiography; business/economics; child guidance/parenting; current affairs; ethnic/cultural interests; health/medicine; history; how-to; humor/satire; memoirs; military/war; money/finance; multicultural; popular culture; psychology; religious/inspirational; self-help/personal improvement; sociology; sports; true crime/investigative; women's issues/studies. **Considers these fiction areas:** Contemporary issues; detective/police/crime; ethnic; family saga; feminist; historical; humor/satire; literary; mainstream/contemporary; multicultural; mystery/suspense; religious/inspirational; sports; thriller.

○┓ "We are multi-faceted." Actively seeking all subjects. Does not want to receive science fiction, horror, western, cookbooks.

How to Contact: Query with SASE, outline, 3 sample chapter(s). Accepts e-mail queries. Considers simultaneous queries and submissions. Responds in 1 month to queries; 2 months to mss. Returns materials only with SASE. Obtains most new clients through recommendations from others, solicitations, conferences.

Recent Sales: *Stone Soup for the World*, by Marianne Larned (Crown); *The Acne Cure*, by Stephen Dubrow, Ph.D. and Brenda Adderly (Rodale); *The Nature of Music*, by Maureen McCarthy Draper (Riverhead/Penguin/Putnam); *Esther Stories*, by Peter Orner (Houghton Mifflin). Other clients include Woodleigh Marx Hubbard, Jennifer Openshaw, Jed Diamond, Dr. Jay Gordon, Dr. Arthur White, Eric Harr, Brad Herzog, Martin Yan, Lyn Webster-Wilde, Larraine Segil, Bobby Unser.

Terms: Agent receives 15% commission on domestic sales; 20% commission on foreign sales. Offers written contract; 60-day notice must be given to terminate contract. Charges for postage and photocopying.

Writers' Conferences: Maui Writers Conference (Maui HI, Labor Day); San Diego State University Writers' Conference (San Diego CA, January); William Saroyan Writers Conference (Fresno CA, March); Santa Barbara (June) and many others.

Tips: "Clarity and precision about your work also helps the agent process."

LIVINGSTON COOKE, 457A Danforth Ave., Suite 201, Toronto Ontario M4K 1P1, Canada. (416)406-3390. Fax: (416)406-3389. E-mail: livcooke@idirect.ca. **Contact:** Elizabeth Griffen. Estab. 1992. Represents 200 clients. 30% of clients are new/unpublished writers. Currently handles: 50% nonfiction books; 30% novels; 10% movie scripts; 10% TV scripts.

• Prior to becoming an agent, Mr. Cooke was the publisher of Seal Books Canada.

Member Agents: David Johnston (film rights, literary fiction/nonfiction); Dean Cooke (literary fiction, nonfiction).

Represents: Nonfiction books, novels, juvenile books. **Considers these nonfiction areas:** Biography/autobiography; business/economics; child guidance/parenting; current affairs; gay/lesbian issues; health/medicine; popular culture; science/technology; young adult. **Considers these fiction areas:** Juvenile; literary.

○┅ Livingston Cooke represents some of the best Canadian writers in the world. "Through our contacts and sub-agents, we are building an international reputation for quality. Curtis Brown Canada is jointly owned by Dean Cooke and Curtis Brown New York. It represents Curtis Brown New York authors in Canada." Does not want to receive genre fiction (science fiction, fantasy, mystery, thriller, horror).

How to Contact: Query with SASE. Accepts e-mail and fax queries. Considers simultaneous queries. Responds in 1 month to queries; 6 weeks to mss. Returns materials only with SASE. Obtains most new clients through recommendations from others.

Recent Sales: Sold 40 titles and sold 4 scripts in the last year. *Clara Callan*, by Richard B. Wright (Harperflamingo Canada); *Stanley Park*, by Timothy Taylor (Knopf Canada); *Your Mouth is Lovely*, by Nancy Richler (Harper Collins); *Spirit Cabinet*, by Paul Quarrinton (Grove/Atlantic); *Lazarus and the Hurricane*, by S. Charton/ T. Swinton (St. Martin's Press); *Latitudes of Melt*, by Joan Clark (Knopf Canada); *Possesing Genius: The Bizarre Odyssey of Einstein's Brain*, by Caroline Abraham (Penguin Canada, St. Martin's Press); *Englishman's Boy*, by Guy Vanderhaeghe (Minds Eye); *Lazarus and the Hurricane*, by T. Swinton and S. Chaiton (Universal/Beacon). Other clients include Margaret Gibson, Richard Scrimger, Tony Hillerman, Robertson Davies, Brian Moore.

Terms: Agent receives 15% commission on domestic sales; 20% commission on foreign sales. Offers written contract. Charges clients for postage, photocopying, courier.

◪ **NANCY LOVE LITERARY AGENCY**, 250 E. 65th St., New York NY 10021-6614. (212)980-3499. Fax: (212)308-6405. **Contact:** Nancy Love. Estab. 1984. Member of AAR. Represents 60-80 clients. Currently handles: 90% nonfiction books; 10% novels.

Member Agents: Nancy Love.

Represents: Nonfiction books, novels (mysteries and thrillers only). **Considers these nonfiction areas:** Biography/autobiography; child guidance/parenting; cooking/foods/nutrition; current affairs; ethnic/cultural interests; government/politics/law; health/medicine; history; how-to; memoirs; nature/environment; New Age/metaphysics; popular culture; psychology; religious/inspirational; science/technology; self-help/personal improvement; sociology; spirituality; travel (armchair only, no how-to travel); true crime/investigative; women's issues/studies. **Considers these fiction areas:** Mystery/suspense; thriller.

○┅ This agency specializes in adult nonfiction and mysteries. Actively seeking health and medicine (including alternative medicine), parenting, spiritual and inspirational. Does not want to receive novels other than mysteries and thrillers.

How to Contact: Prefers to read materials exclusively. For nonfiction, send a proposal, chapter summary and sample chapter. For fiction, query first. Fiction is only read on an exclusive basis. No e-mail or fax queries. Considers simultaneous queries. Responds in 3 weeks to queries; 6 weeks to mss. Returns materials only with SASE. Obtains most new clients through recommendations from others, solicitations.

Recent Sales: Sold 20 titles in the last year. *The Tools People Use to Quit Addictions*, by Stauton Peele, Ph.D.(Crown); *The CIA and the Shah of Iran*, by Steven Kinzer (John Wiley).

Terms: Agent receives 15% commission on domestic sales; 20% commission on foreign sales. Offers written contract. Charges clients for photocopying "if it runs over $20."

Tips: "Nonfiction author and/or collaborator must be an authority in subject area and have a platform. Send a SASE if you want a response."

LOWENSTEIN ASSOCIATES, 121 W. 27th St., Suite 601, New York NY 10001. (212)206-1630. Fax: (212)727-0280. **Contact:** President: Barbara Lowenstein. Estab. 1976. Member of AAR. Represents 150 clients. 20% of clients are new/unpublished writers. Currently handles: 60% nonfiction books; 40% novels.

Member Agents: Barbara Lowenstein (president); Nancy Yost (agent); Eileen Cope (agent); Norman Kurz (business affairs); Dorian Karchmar (associate member).

Represents: Nonfiction books, novels. **Considers these nonfiction areas:** Animals; anthropology/archaeology; biography/autobiography; business/economics; child guidance/parenting; crafts/hobbies; creative nonfiction; current affairs; education; ethnic/cultural interests; gay/lesbian issues; government/politics/law; health/medicine; history; how-to; humor/satire; language/literature/criticism; memoirs; money/finance; music/dance; nature/environment; New Age/metaphysics; popular culture; psychology; religious/inspirational; science/technology; self-help/personal improvement; sociology; spirituality; sports; theater/film; travel; women's issues/studies. **Considers these fiction areas:** Contemporary issues; detective/police/crime; erotica; ethnic; feminist; gay/lesbian; historical; literary; mainstream/contemporary; mystery/suspense; romance (contemporary, historical, regency); thriller (medical).

○┅ This agency specializes in health, business, spirituality, creative nonfiction, literary fiction, commercial fiction, especially suspense, crime and women's issues. "We are a full-service agency, handling domestic and foreign rights, film rights, and audio rights to all of our books."

How to Contact: Query with SASE. Prefers to read materials exclusively. For fiction, send outline and first chapter. No unsolicited mss. Responds in 6 weeks to queries. Returns materials only with SASE. Obtains most new clients through recommendations from others, solicitations, conferences.

Recent Sales: Sold 75 titles in the last year. *Secrets of the Baby Whisperer*, by Tracy Hogg and Melinda Blau (Ballantine); *Insect Dreams*, by Marc Estrin (Putnam/Blue Hen); *Murad Magic!*, by Dr. Howard Murad (St. Martin's). Other clients include Ishmael Reed, Deborah Crombie, Leslie Glass, Stephanie Laurens, Dr. Grace Cornish, Stephen Raleigh Byler, Harriet Scott Chessman, Camron Wright, Tim Cahill, Gina Nahai, Kevin Young.

Terms: Agent receives 15% commission on domestic sales; 20% commission on foreign sales. Offers written contract, binding for book-by-book basis. Charges for large photocopy batches and international postage.
Writers' Conferences: Malice Domestic; Bouchercon.
Tips: "Know the genre you are working in and READ!"

🌐 ◐ **ANDREW LOWNIE LITERARY AGENCY LTD.**, 17 Sutherland St., London SW1V4JU, England. (0207)828 1274. Fax: (0207)828 7608. E-mail: lownie@globalnet.co.uk. Website: www.andrewlownie.co.uk. **Contact:** Andrew Lownie. Estab. 1988. Member of Association of Author's Agents. Represents 130 clients. 50% of clients are new/unpublished writers. Currently handles: 90% nonfiction books; 10% novels.
  ● Prior to becoming an agent, Mr. Lownie was a journalist, bookseller, publisher, author of 12 books, and previously a director of the Curtis Brown Agency.
Represents: Nonfiction books. **Considers these nonfiction areas:** Anthropology/archaeology; biography/auto-biography; current affairs; government/politics/law; history; memoirs; military/war; music/dance; popular culture; theater/film; true crime/investigative.
  ⊶ This agent has wide publishing experience, extensive journalistic contacts, and a specialty in showbiz memoir and celebrities. Actively seeking showbiz memoirs, narrative histories and biographies. Does not want to receive poetry, short stories, children's fiction, scripts, academic.
How to Contact: Query with SASE and/or IRCs. Submit outline, 1 sample chapter(s). Accepts e-mail and fax queries. Considers simultaneous queries. Responds in 1 week to queries; 1 month to mss. Returns materials only with SASE. Obtains most new clients through recommendations from others.
Recent Sales: Sold 50 titles in the last year. *Neil Kinnock: The Authorized Biography*, by Martin Westlake (Little Brown); *The Disappearing Duke*, by Andrew Crofts (Carroll & Graf); *Jihad*, by Tom Carew (Mainstream); *Warrior Race* (St. Martin's). Other clients include Norma Major, Guy Bellamy, Joyce Cary Eslate, Lawrence James, Juliet Barker, Patrick McNee, Sir John Mills, Peter Evans, Desmond Seward, Laurence Gardner, Richard Rudgley.
Terms: Agent receives 15% commission on domestic sales; 15% commission on foreign sales. Offers written contract, binding until author chooses to break it but valid while book is in print; 30-day notice must be given to terminate contract. Charges clients for some copying, postage, copies of books for submission.
Tips: "I prefer submissions in writing by letter."

◐ **DONALD MAASS LITERARY AGENCY**, 160 W. 95th St., Suite 1B, New York NY 10025. (212)866-8200. **Contact:** Donald Maass, Jennifer Jackson or Michelle Brummer. Estab. 1980. Member of AAR, SFWA, MWA, RWA. Represents over 100 clients. 5% of clients are new/unpublished writers. Currently handles: 100% novels.
  ● Prior to opening his agency, Mr. Maass served as an editor at Dell Publishing (NY) and as a reader at Gollancz (London). He is a former president of AAR.
Member Agents: Donald Maass (mainstream, literary, mystery/suspense, science fiction); Jennifer Jackson (commercial fiction, especially romance, science fiction, fantasy, mystery/suspense); Michelle Brummer (fiction: literary, contemporary, feminist, science fiction, fantasy, romance).
Represents: Novels. **Considers these fiction areas:** Detective/police/crime; fantasy; historical; horror; literary; mainstream/contemporary; mystery/suspense; psychic/supernatural; romance (historical, paranormal, time travel); science fiction; thriller; women's.
  ⊶ This agency specializes in commercial fiction, especially science fiction, fantasy, mystery, romance, suspense. Actively seeking "to expand the literary portion of our list and expand in romance and women's fiction." Does not want to receive nonfiction, children's or poetry.
How to Contact: Query with SASE. Returns material only with SASE. Considers simultaneous queries and submissions. Responds in 2 weeks to queries; 3 months to mss.
Recent Sales: Sold over 100 titles in the last year. *No Graves as Yet*, by Anne Perry (Ballantine); *Griffone*, by Nalo Hopkinson (Warner Aspect).
Terms: Agent receives 15% commission on domestic sales; 20% commission on foreign sales.
Writers' Conferences: *Donald Maass*: World Science Fiction Convention; Frankfurt Book Fair; Pacific Northwest Writers Conference; Bouchercon and others; *Jennifer Jackson*: World Science Fiction and Fantasy Convention; RWA National and others; *Michelle Brummer*: ReaderCon; Luna Con; Frankfurt.
Tips: "We are fiction specialists, also noted for our innovative approach to career planning. Few new clients are accepted, but interested authors should query with SASE. Subagents in all principle foreign countries and Hollywood. No nonfiction or juvenile works considered."

THE PUBLISHING FIELD is constantly changing! Agents often change addresses, phone numbers, or even companies. If you're still using this book and it is 2004 or later, buy the newest edition of *Guide to Literary Agents* at your favorite bookstore or order directly from Writer's Digest Books at (800)448-0915.

GINA MACCOBY AGENCY, P.O. Box 60, Chappaqua NY 10514. (914)238-5630. **Contact:** Gina Maccoby. Estab. 1986. Represents 35 clients. Currently handles: 33% nonfiction books; 33% novels; 33% juvenile books. Represents illustrators of children's books.
Represents: Nonfiction books, novels, juvenile books. **Considers these nonfiction areas:** Biography/autobiography; current affairs; ethnic/cultural interests; history; juvenile nonfiction; popular culture; women's issues/studies. **Considers these fiction areas:** Juvenile; literary; mainstream/contemporary; mystery/suspense; thriller; young adult.
How to Contact: Query with SASE. Considers simultaneous queries. Responds in 2 months to queries. Returns materials only with SASE. Obtains most new clients through recommendations from own clients.
Recent Sales: Sold 18 titles in the last year. *8th Air Force in WWII*, by Donald L. Miller; *The Crying Rocks*, by Janet Taylor Lisle; *You Read to Me, I'll Read to You*, by Mary Ann Hoberman.
Terms: Agent receives 15% commission on domestic sales; 25% commission on foreign sales. Charges clients for photocopying. May recover certain costs such as airmail postage to Europe or Japan or legal fees.

CAROL MANN AGENCY, 55 Fifth Ave., New York NY 10003. (212)206-5635. Fax: (212)675-4809. E-mail: kim@carolmannagency.com. **Contact:** Kim Goldstein. Estab. 1977. Member of AAR. Represents 100 clients. 25% of clients are new/unpublished writers. Currently handles: 70% nonfiction books; 30% novels.
Member Agents: Jim Fitzgerald (fiction, popular culture, biography); Carol Mann (literary fiction, nonfiction); Leylha Ahuile (Spanish and Latin American fiction and nonfiction).
Represents: Nonfiction books, novels. **Considers these nonfiction areas:** Anthropology/archaeology; art/architecture/design; biography/autobiography; business/economics; child guidance/parenting; current affairs; ethnic/cultural interests; government/politics/law; health/medicine; history; money/finance; psychology; self-help/personal improvement; sociology; women's issues/studies. **Considers these fiction areas:** Literary.
- ☛ This agency specializes in current affairs; self-help; popular culture; psychology; parenting; history. Does not want to receive "genre fiction (romance, mystery, etc.)."
How to Contact: Query with outline/proposal and SASE. Responds in 3 weeks to queries.
Recent Sales: *What About the Kids*, by Judith Wallerstein (Hyperion); *The Book of Illusions*, Paul Auster (Henry Holt); *E=mc2*, by David Bodanis (Walker). Other clients include novelist Marita Golden; journalists Tim Egan, Elizabeth Mehren, Pulitzer Prize winner Fox Butterfield and National Book Critic Award winner James Tobin; essayist Shelby Steele; sociologist Dr. William Julius Wilson; economist Thomas Sowell; and Tufts University's Elliot Pearson School of Education.
Terms: Agent receives 15% commission on domestic sales; 20% commission on foreign sales. Offers written contract.

MANUS & ASSOCIATES LITERARY AGENCY, INC., 375 Forest Ave., Palo Alto CA 94301. (650)470-5151. Fax: (650)470-5159. E-mail: manuslit@manuslit.com. Website: www.manuslit.com. **Contact:** Jillian Manus. Also: 445 Park Ave., New York NY 10022. (212)644-8020. Fax (212)644-3374. **Contact:** Janet Manus. Estab. 1985. Member of AAR. Represents 75 clients. 30% of clients are new/unpublished writers. Currently handles: 55% nonfiction books; 40% novels; 5% juvenile books.
- • Prior to becoming agents, Jillian Manus was associate publisher of two national magazines and director of development at Warner Bros. and Universal Studios; Janet Manus has been a literary agent for 20 years.
Member Agents: Jandy Nelson (self-help, health, memoirs, narrative nonfiction, literary fiction, multicultural fiction, thrillers); Stephanie Lee (self-help, memoirs, dramatic nonfiction, commercial literary fiction, multicultural fiction, quirky/edgy fiction).
Represents: Nonfiction books, novels. **Considers these nonfiction areas:** Biography/autobiography; business/economics; child guidance/parenting; creative nonfiction; current affairs; ethnic/cultural interests; health/medicine; how-to; memoirs; money/finance; nature/environment; popular culture; psychology; science/technology; self-help/personal improvement; women's issues/studies; Gen X and Gen Y issues. **Considers these fiction areas:** Literary; mainstream/contemporary; multicultural; mystery/suspense; romance; thriller; women's; Southern fiction; quirky/edgy fiction.
- ☛ This agency specializes in commercial literary fiction, narrative nonfiction, thrillers, health, pop psychology, women's empowerment. "Our agency is unique in the way that we not only sell the material, but we edit, develop concepts and participate in the marketing effort. We specialize in large, conceptual fiction and nonfiction, and always value a project that can be sold in the TV/feature film market." Actively seeking high-concept thrillers, commercial literary fiction, women's fiction, celebrity biographies, memoirs, multicultural fiction, popular health, women's empowerment, mysteries. Does not want to receive horror, romance, science fiction/fantasy, westerns, young adult, children's, poetry, cookbooks, magazine articles. Usually obtains new clients through recommendations from editors, clients and others; conferences; and unsolicited materials.
How to Contact: Query with SASE. If requested, submit outline, 2-3 sample chapter(s). Accepts e-mail and fax queries. Considers simultaneous queries. Responds in 2 months to queries; 6 weeks to mss. Returns materials only with SASE. Obtains most new clients through recommendations from others, solicitations, conferences.

A new agent explains the game

Stephanie Lee is a literary agent with Manus & Associates Literary Agency, Inc., a national firm representing independent authors for over 15 years from offices in both New York and the San Francisco Bay Area. Lee holds a degree in literature and fiction writing from Stanford University, has studied at Oxford University, and has worked closely with the last living editor of Hemingway. An award-winning writer herself, she is considered to be an editorial agent, actively involved in the development and marketing of her clients' work.

Stephanie Lee

Please tell me a little bit about your background. How did you get started in agenting?
I was one of those people who would ask, "A literary agent? What's that?" I had no idea writers needed agents, and I had no idea what agents did. I come from a writing background, and I studied short fiction at Stanford. I knew it would be difficult to make money as a writer (especially of short fiction!), but I really wanted to work with writing and writers nonetheless. A search for local internships led me to Manus & Associates, and as I learned more about the business of agenting, I was hooked! I kept expecting the agency to give me the boot after being an intern for over a year, but instead, I got a job.

What do you like most about agenting?
I really love talking to authors, working with them on their manuscripts, and developing ideas. I like getting my hands dirty. I like guiding writers through a process that can sometimes seem mysterious and frustrating. When you fall in love with a manuscript from the slush pile and then eventually hold the published book in your hand, you know that something magical has taken place.

What made you decide to work at an established agency rather than work independently? How might this alliance benefit the authors you represent?
As I mentioned, I knew nothing about agenting when I first came here, so I learned a lot from Manus & Associates. There is a certain loyalty and camaraderie here that makes us a very strong team. We all come from different backgrounds and possess different strengths, so we can call upon each other for support. I believe this is a great asset to our authors as well. Though a writer certainly works closely with one of us, that writer in effect can reap the benefits of the agency as a whole.

Where do you find most of your clients?
From the "slush pile," writers' conferences, references from other clients, or other publications

that I read such as magazines, literary journals, or newspapers.

How important is it for aspiring writers to attend conferences?

Conferences are wonderful. Writing can be such a solitary pursuit, and then when you're finished with a book, you have no idea what to do with it. Conferences are Information Central as well as Networking Central. Of course, many published writers have never been to a conference, but if you are considering attending one, I would strongly encourage it. You not only learn about the business, but you also have the opportunity to chat with a lot of writers just like yourself.

Have you found any clients through this channel?

Our agency has found several bestselling clients from conferences.

How can writers best create a favorable impression at a conference?

Don't be shy about signing up, but do practice pitching your book out loud to maximize any time you may have with an editor or agent.

What do you look for in a query letter?

Something unique! A good pitch. Not too much plot re-hash and explanation, but a killer, concise, persuasive pitch. I find it especially appealing if a writer has been previously published in journals or magazines, but it is not necessary. I also like to see that writers have done their homework, that they found me in a writer's guide to research what projects I like, or that they've read some of our clients' work. I like letters that are professional but that also allow the writer's personality and style to show though.

How rare is it to find a manuscript that shows promise?

You might say that I am a relatively "hungry" agent, but I still look for books for the same marketplace as everyone else, and today's marketplace is incredibly competitive. There is a lot of excellent writing out there, but unfortunately we cannot sell all of it. So I do find myself passing on a lot of work that I like. Sometimes I read manuscripts that I feel have a great deal of promise but that might not be ready to go yet. I tend to like books that are a little more off the beaten path, so I may be open to different kinds of projects, but ultimately, I not only want to take on projects that I love, but also ones I can sell.

Once you have a client, how involved are you in helping them edit their work?

My involvement varies depending on what each client needs. I do a lot of editing myself and work closely with my writers to polish up a manuscript. I usually only sign clients if I feel their manuscripts or proposals are pretty much ready to go, though on occasion, I will take somebody under sort of a developmental wing, with an eye toward representation. We also help our clients find ghostwriters or co-writers if necessary.

When there are multiple agents under one roof and a great manuscript is discovered, which agent considers offering representation?

We arm wrestle for it! Actually, though all of us share a love for great writing and great ideas, we can usually decide easily who would be the best agent for a specific writer. We also consult with each other a lot. If you've met us, you know that we are quite different and have different tastes, so if all of us agree that a certain project is intriguing, you can basically put your money on it.

When you train interns, what surprises them most about agenting? Once they learn what's involved, do most go on to become agents? What personal qualities do you think are most crucial for a newer agent to have?

This is an interesting question! I think what might be most surprising is the sheer volume of submissions, or how involved we really get with the editing and marketing aspects of a book. Many of our interns go on to work at other literary agencies, even TV/Film agencies in Hollywood, and also in editorial departments in publishing houses. As for personal qualities . . . well, of course a love of reading is a must, but there are as many different kinds of agents as there are people. Mostly, I think a newer agent needs to be tenacious, intrepid, supportive of her clients, and keenly attentive to a very dynamic marketplace.

Please share a recent publishing success story.

I recently sold a book to Crown called *Avoiding Prison and Other Noble Vacation Goals: The Adventures of a Nice Girl in Latin America*, by Wendy Dale. When Wendy's material first came to me through the slush pile, I was floored. She was young, hysterical and smart, a really personable mix of good girl/bad girl, but the pages also needed a lot of work. We edited the manuscript for almost a year. And then we sent it out to publisher after publisher without any offers. It took a long time for us to find just the right editor for her book, but we never gave up, and ultimately I feel very good about where Wendy is now.

The book will not be out until Summer 2003, so this is just the beginning of our story, but Wendy's book was an example of how success can be attained through sheer will and patience and team work. Wendy and I are also great friends, and having a book published by a large house is a dream come true in itself. Experiences like this make it difficult to choose just one success story, because there are so many kinds of success. Some clients might have bestselling, high-grossing books, while others might see smaller sales but garner a load of prestigious literary awards. In the end, putting pen to paper (fingers to keyboard) is a triumph in itself. I see these completed manuscripts come into the office and feel such admiration for people who committed themselves to their skill and their art.

What are the most exciting or fulfilling moments of your job?

When a client calls me or emails me and says, "Thank you, you really get me!" It's amazing to make a connection like that, where your business relationship isn't contentious or difficult, but more of a shared effort toward a common goal. I get paid to do what I love. What's more fulfilling than that?

—*Rachel Vater*

Recent Sales: *Lily Dale: The Town that Talks to the Dead*, by Christine Wicker (Harper Collins); *Avoiding Prison and Other Noble Vacation Goals*, by Wendy Dale (Crown); *Within These Walls: Memoirs of a Death House Chaplain*, by Carol Pickett with Carlton Stowers (St. Martin's); *Beyond Choice*, by Alexander Sanger (Public Affairs); *Geisha: A Life*, by Mineko Iwasaki with Rande Brown (Pocket Books). Other clients include Dr. Loraine Zappert, Marcus Allen, Carlton Stowers, Ann Brandt, Dr. Richard Marrs, Mary Loverde, Lisa Huang Fleishman, Judy Carter, Daryl Ott Underhill, Glen Kleier, Andrew X. Pham, Lalita Tademy, Frank Baldwin, Katy Robinson, K.M. Soehnlein, Joelle Fraser, Fred Luskin, Jim Schutze.
Terms: Agent receives 15% commission on domestic sales; 20-25% commission on foreign sales. Offers written contract, binding for 2 years; 60-day notice must be given to terminate contract. Charges for photocopying and postage.
Writers' Conferences: Maui Writers Conference (Maui HI, Labor Day); San Diego Writer's Conference (San Diego CA, January); Willamette Writers Conference (Willamette OR, July).
Tips: "Research agents using a variety of sources, including *LMP*, guides, *Publishers Weekly*, conferences and even acknowledgements in books similar in tone to yours."

MARCH TENTH, INC., 4 Myrtle St., Haworth NJ 07641-1740. (201)387-6551. Fax: (201)387-6552. E-mail: hchoron@aol.com. **Contact:** Harry Choron, vice president. Estab. 1982. Represents 40 clients. 30% of clients are new/unpublished writers. Currently handles: 75% nonfiction books; 25% novels.
Represents: Nonfiction books, novels. **Considers these nonfiction areas:** Biography/autobiography; current affairs; health/medicine; history; humor/satire; language/literature/criticism; music/dance; popular culture; theater/film. **Considers these fiction areas:** Confession; ethnic; family saga; historical; humor/satire; literary; mainstream/contemporary.
  O→ "Writers must have professional expertise in their field. Prefers to work with published/established writers."
How to Contact: Query with SASE. Accepts e-mail queries. Considers simultaneous queries. Responds in 1 month to queries. Returns materials only with SASE.
Recent Sales: Sold 8 titles in the last year. *Here and Now*, by Elena Dorfman and Heidi Adams (Avalon); *The Breathing Field*, by Wyatt Townley and Eric Dinyer (Bulfinch); *The 100 Simple Secrets of Successful People*, by David Niven (Harper SF); *Dilemmas*, by James Saywell and Ann-Marie Rotti (Villard); *Everything You Need to Know About Mercury Retrograde*, by Chrissie Blaze (Warner).
Terms: Agent receives 15% commission on domestic sales; 20% commission on foreign sales; 20% commission on dramatic rights sales. Charges clients for postage, photocopying, overseas phone expenses. "Does not require expense money upfront." Writers reimbursed for office fees after the sale of ms.

BARBARA MARKOWITZ LITERARY AGENCY, P.O. Box 41709, Los Angeles CA 90041-3032. (323)221-5722. **Contact:** Barbara Markowitz, president. Estab. 1980. Represents 14 clients. Currently handles: 25% nonfiction books; 25% novels; 50% juvenile books.
  ● Prior to opening her agency, Ms. Markowitz owned the well-known independent bookseller, Barbara's Bookstores, in Chicago.
Member Agents: Judith Rosenthal (psychology, current affairs, women's issues, biography); Barbara Markowitz.
Represents: Nonfiction books, novels, juvenile books. **Considers these nonfiction areas:** Biography/autobiography; current affairs; juvenile nonfiction; music/dance; nature/environment; popular culture; sports; theater/film; women's issues/studies. **Considers these fiction areas:** Contemporary issues; detective/police/crime; ethnic; historical; humor/satire; juvenile; mainstream/contemporary; mystery/suspense; sports; thriller; young adult.
  O→ This agency specializes in mid-level and YA; contemporary fiction; adult trade fiction and nonfiction. Actively seeking mid-level historical and contemporary fiction for 8- to 11-year-olds, 125-150 pages in length; adult mysteries/thrillers/suspense. Does not want to receive illustrated books, science fiction/futuristic, poetry.
How to Contact: Query with SASE, 2-3 sample chapter(s). No e-mail or fax queries. Considers simultaneous queries. Responds in 3 weeks to queries.
Recent Sales: Sold 6 titles in the last year. *Just Jane*, by William Lavender (HBJ); *Emako Blue*, by Brenda Woods (Putnam). Other clients include Mary Batten, Henry Garfield, Brenda Woods.
Terms: Agent receives 15% commission on domestic sales; 20% commission on foreign sales. Charges clients for mailing, postage.
Tips: "We do not agent pre-school or early reader books. Only mid-level and YA contemporary fiction and historical fiction. We receive an abundance of pre-school and early reader mss, which our agency returns if accompanied by SASE. No illustrated books. No sci-fi/fable/fantasy or fairy tales."

ELAINE MARKSON LITERARY AGENCY, 44 Greenwich Ave., New York NY 10011. (212)243-8480. Fax: (212)691-9014. Estab. 1972. Member of AAR; signatory of WGA. Represents 200 clients. 10% of clients are new/unpublished writers. Currently handles: 35% nonfiction books; 55% novels; 10% juvenile books.
Member Agents: Geri Thoma; Elizabeth Sheinkman; Elaine Markson.
Represents: Nonfiction books (quality), novels (quality).
  O→ This agency specializes in literary fiction, commercial fiction, trade nonfiction.

How to Contact: Obtains most new clients through recommendations from others.

Terms: Agent receives 15% commission on domestic sales; 20% commission on foreign sales. Charges for postage, photocopying, foreign mailing, faxing, and other special expenses.

N ☻ MILDRED MARMUR ASSOCIATES, LTD., 2005 Palmer Ave., Suite 127, Larchmont NY 10538. **Contact:** Mildred Marmur. Estab. 1987. Member of AAR.

Represents: Nonfiction books, novels. **Considers these nonfiction areas:** Biography/autobiography; business/economics; cooking/foods/nutrition; current affairs; ethnic/cultural interests; government/politics/law; health/medicine; history; money/finance; music/dance; nature/environment; religious/inspirational; science/technology; sports; theater/film; true crime/investigative; women's issues/studies. **Considers these fiction areas:** Detective/police/crime; family saga; feminist; juvenile; literary; mainstream/contemporary; mystery/suspense; thriller; young adult.

　O✦ This agency specializes in serious nonfiction.

How to Contact: Query with SASE. Responds in 1 month to queries. Obtains most new clients through recommendations from others.

Terms: Agent receives 15% commission on domestic sales; 20% commission on foreign sales. 100% of business is derived from commissions on ms sales.

Tips: "Browse in a bookstore or library and look at the acknowledgments in books similar to yours. If an author of a nonfiction book in your general area thanks his or her agent, send your manuscript to that person and point out the link. If you can't figure out who the agent is, try phoning the publisher. At least you'll have a more targeted person. Also, agents are more receptive to written submissions than to pitches over the phone."

☻ THE EVAN MARSHALL AGENCY, 6 Tristam Place, Pine Brook NJ 07058-9445. (973)882-1122. Fax: (973)882-3099. E-mail: evanmarshall@thenovelist.com. Website: www.thenovelist.com. **Contact:** Evan Marshall. Estab. 1987. Member of AAR, MWA. Currently handles: 100% novels.

　● Prior to opening his agency, Mr. Marshall served as an editor with New American Library, Everest House, and Dodd, Mead & Co., and then worked as a literary agent at The Sterling Lord Agency.

Represents: Novels. **Considers these fiction areas:** Action/adventure; erotica; ethnic; historical; horror; humor/satire; literary; mainstream/contemporary; mystery/suspense; religious/inspirational; romance (contemporary, gothic, historical, regency); science fiction; westerns/frontier.

How to Contact: Responds in 1 week to queries; 2 months to mss. Obtains most new clients through recommendations from others.

Recent Sales: *Something Real*, by J.J. Murray (Kensington); *The Ghost of Carnal Cove*, by Evelyn Rogers (Dorchester); *Lone Warrior*, by Bobbi Smith (Dorchester); *Mumbo Gumbo*, by Jerrilyn Farmer (Avon); *A Husband in Her Eyes*, by Karen Rose Smith (Silhouette).

Terms: Agent receives 15% commission on domestic sales; 20% commission on foreign sales. Offers written contract.

☻ HAROLD MATSON CO. INC., 276 Fifth Ave., New York NY 10001. **Contact:** Jonathan Matson. Member of AAR.

　● This agency did not respond to our request for information. Query before submitting.

Member Agents: Jonathan Matson (literary, adult); Ben Camardi (literary, adult, dramatic).

☻ JED MATTES, INC., 2095 Broadway, Suite 302, New York NY 10023-2895. Member of AAR.

　● This agency did not respond to our request for information. Query before submitting.

MARGRET McBRIDE LITERARY AGENCY, 7744 Fay Ave., Suite 201, La Jolla CA 92037. (858)454-1550. Fax: (858)454-2156. Estab. 1980. Member of AAR, Authors Guild. Represents 50 clients. 15% of clients are new/unpublished writers.

　● Prior to opening her agency, Ms. McBride worked at Random House, Ballantine Books and Warner Books.

Represents: Nonfiction books, novels, audio, video film rights. **Considers these nonfiction areas:** Biography/autobiography; business/economics; cooking/foods/nutrition; current affairs; ethnic/cultural interests; government/politics/law; health/medicine; history; how-to; money/finance; music/dance; popular culture; psychology; religious/inspirational; science/technology; self-help/personal improvement; sociology; women's issues/studies; style. **Considers these fiction areas:** Action/adventure; detective/police/crime; ethnic; historical; humor/satire; literary; mainstream/contemporary; mystery/suspense; thriller; westerns/frontier.

　O✦ This agency specializes in mainstream fiction and nonfiction. Does not want to receive screenplays.

How to Contact: Query with synopsis or outline and SASE. Considers simultaneous queries. Responds in 6 weeks to queries. Returns materials only with SASE.

Recent Sales: Sold 22 titles in the last year. *Incriminating Evidence*, by Sheldon Siegel (Bantam); *Fierce Conversations*, by Susan Scott (Viking); *Born on a Bad Day*, by Hazel Dixon-Cooper (Simon & Schuster); *The Art of Shen Ku*, by Zeek (Perigee).

Terms: Agent receives 15% commission on domestic sales; 25% commission on foreign sales. Charges for overnight delivery and photocopying.

[N] THE McCARTHY AGENCY, LLC, 7 Allen St., Rumson NJ 07760. **Contact:** Shawna McCarthy. Member of AAR. Estab. 1999.
- Prior to opening her agency, Ms. McCarthy was editor of *Asimov's Science Fiction Magazine*, senior editor at Bantam Spectra, senior editor at Workman Publishing and a literary agent with another agency. She is the founding editor of the world's bestselling fantasy magazine, *Realms of Fantasy*.

[O] GERARD McCAULEY, P.O. Box 844, Katonah NY 10536. (914)232-5700. Fax: (914)232-1506. Estab. 1970. Member of AAR. Represents 60 clients. 5% of clients are new/unpublished writers. Currently not accepting new clients. Currently handles: 65% nonfiction books; 15% scholarly books; 20% textbooks.
- This agency specializes in history, biography and general nonfiction.
How to Contact: Obtains most new clients through recommendations from others.
Recent Sales: Sold 30 titles in the last year. *Jack Johnson*, by Ken Burns (Knopf); *At War at Sea*, by Ronald Spector (Viking).
Terms: Agent receives 15% commission on domestic sales; 20% commission on foreign sales.

[O] ANITA D. McCLELLAN ASSOCIATES, 50 Stearns St., Cambridge MA 02138. Member of AAR.
- This agency did not respond to our request for information. Query before submitting.

[M] HELEN McGRATH, 1406 Idaho Ct., Concord CA 94521. (925)672-6211. Fax: (925)672-6383. E-mail: hmcgrath_lit@yahoo.com. **Contact:** Helen McGrath. Estab. 1977. Currently handles: 50% nonfiction books; 50% novels.
Represents: Nonfiction books, novels. **Considers these nonfiction areas:** Biography/autobiography; business/economics; current affairs; health/medicine; history; how-to; military/war; psychology; self-help/personal improvement; sports; women's issues/studies. **Considers these fiction areas:** Contemporary issues; detective/police/crime; literary; mainstream/contemporary; mystery/suspense; psychic/supernatural; romance; science fiction; thriller.
How to Contact: Submit proposal with SASE. *No unsolicited mss.* Responds in 2 months to queries. Obtains most new clients through recommendations from others.
Terms: Agent receives 15% commission on domestic sales. Offers written contract. Charges clients for photocopying.

[O] McHUGH LITERARY AGENCY, 1033 Lyon Rd., Moscow ID 83843-9167. (208)882-0107. Fax: (847)628-0146. E-mail: elisabetmch@turbonet.com. **Contact:** Elisabet McHugh. Estab. 1994. Represents (in the US and nine foreign countries) 71 clients. 35% of clients are new/unpublished writers. Currently handles: 50% nonfiction books; 50% fiction novels.
Represents: Nonfiction books, novels. **Considers these nonfiction areas:** Animals; anthropology/archaeology; biography/autobiography; child guidance/parenting; cooking/foods/nutrition; current affairs; education; gardening; health/medicine; history; how-to; memoirs; military/war; money/finance; multicultural; nature/environment; popular culture; recreation; religious/inspirational; science/technology; self-help/personal improvement; travel; true crime/investigative; women's issues/studies; young adult; alternative medicine. **Considers these fiction areas:** Historical; mainstream/contemporary; mystery/suspense; romance; thriller; westerns/frontier.
- Does not want to receive children's books, poetry, science fiction, fantasy, horror.
How to Contact: Query by e-mail. Considers simultaneous queries. Returns materials only with SASE.
Recent Sales: *Clark Gable* (McFarland & Co.); *Hassle-Free Business Travel* (Ten Speed Press); *Deadly Intent* (Bantam); *Never Again* (Harlequin).
Terms: Agent receives 15% commission on domestic sales; 20% commission on foreign sales. Does not charge any upfront fees. Offers written contract. "Client must provide all copies of manuscripts needed for submissions."
Tips: "Be professional."

[N] McINTOSH & OTIS, 353 Lexington Ave., 15th Floor, New York NY 10016. Member of AAR.
- This agency did not respond to our request for updated information. Query before submitting.
Member Agents: Tracey Adams (literary, children); Samuel L. Pinkus; Elizabeth A. Winick; Eugene Winick.

[O] CLAUDIA MENZA LITERARY AGENCY, 1170 Broadway, Suite 807, New York NY 10001. (212)889-6850. **Contact:** Claudia Menza. Estab. 1983. Member of AAR. Represents 111 clients. 50% of clients are new/unpublished writers.
- Prior to becoming an agent, Ms. Menza was an editor/managing editor at a publishing company.
Represents: Nonfiction books, novels. **Considers these nonfiction areas:** Current affairs; education; ethnic/cultural interests (especially African-American); health/medicine; history; multicultural; music/dance; photography; psychology; self-help/personal improvement; theater/film.
- This agency specializes in African-American fiction and nonfiction, and editorial assistance.
How to Contact: Submit outline, 1 sample chapter(s). Prefers to read materials exclusively. Responds in 2 weeks to queries; 4 months to mss. Returns materials only with SASE. Obtains most new clients through recommendations from others.
Recent Sales: This agency prefers not to share information on specific sales.

Terms: Agent receives 15% commission on domestic sales; 20% (if co-agent is used) commission on foreign sales; 20% commission on dramatic rights sales. Offers written contract.

HELEN MERRILL, LTD., 295 Lafayette St., Suite 915, New York NY 10012-2700. Member of AAR.
• This agency did not respond to our request for information. Query before submitting.
Member Agents: Beth Blickers

DORIS S. MICHAELS LITERARY AGENCY, INC., 1841 Broadway, Suite #903, New York NY 10023. Website: www.dsmagency.com. **Contact:** Doris S. Michaels, president. Estab. 1994. Member of AAR, WNBA.
Member Agents: Faye Bender.
Represents: Nonfiction books, novels. **Considers these nonfiction areas:** Art, biography, business, computers, current affairs, health, history, memoirs, classical music, pop culture, self-help, sports, women's issues. **Considers these fiction areas:** Literary (with commercial appeal and strong screen potential); women's. Considers these nonfiction areas: business, current affairs, biography and memoirs, self-help, history, health, classical music, art, sports, women't issues, computers and pop culture.

How to Contact: All unsolicited mss returned unopened. Query by e-mail; see submission guidelines on website before you send a query. Obtains most new clients through recommendations from others, conferences.
Recent Sales: Sold over 30 titles in the last year. *Cycles: How We'll Live, Work and Buy*, by Maddy Dychtwald (The Free Press); *In the River Sweet*, by Patricia Henley (Knopf); *Healing Conversations: What to Say When You Don't Know What to Say*, by Nance Guilmartin (Josey-Bass); *The Mushroom Man*, by Sophie Powell (Peguim Putnam).
Terms: Agent receives 15% commission on domestic sales; 20% commission on foreign sales. Offers written contract, binding for 1 year; 30-day notice must be given to terminate contract. 100% of business is derived from commissions on ms sales. Charges clients for office expenses, not to exceed $150 without written permission.
Writers' Conferences: BEA (New York, May); Frankfurt Book Fair (Germany, October); London Book Fair; Maui Writers Conference.

MARTHA MILLARD LITERARY AGENCY, 293 Greenwood Ave., Florham Park NJ 07932. (973)593-9233. Fax: (973)593-9235. E-mail: marmillink@aol.com. **Contact:** Martha Millard. Estab. 1980. Member of AAR, SFWA. Represents 50 clients. Currently handles: 25% nonfiction books; 65% novels; 10% story collections.
• Prior to becoming an agent, Ms. Millard worked in editorial departments of several publishers and was vice president at another agency for four and a half years.
Represents: Nonfiction books, novels. **Considers these nonfiction areas:** Art/architecture/design; biography/autobiography; business/economics; child guidance/parenting; cooking/foods/nutrition; current affairs; education; ethnic/cultural interests; health/medicine; history; how-to; juvenile nonfiction; memoirs; money/finance; music/dance; New Age/metaphysics; photography; popular culture; psychology; self-help/personal improvement; theater/film; true crime/investigative; women's issues/studies. **Considers these fiction areas:** Considers fiction depending on writer's credits and skills.
How to Contact: No unsolicited queries. No e-mail or fax queries. Obtains most new clients through recommendations from others.
Recent Sales: Sold 45 titles in the last year. *The Ill-Made Mute*, by Cecilia Dart-Thornton (Warner); *The Bear Daughter*, by Judith Berman (Putnam); *Restore Yourself*, by Victoria Houston (Simon & Schuster).
Terms: Agent receives 15% commission on domestic sales; 20% commission on foreign sales. Offers written contract.

THE MILLER AGENCY, 1 Sheridan Square, 7B, #32, New York NY 10014. (212)206-0913. Fax: (212)206-1473. E-mail: angela@milleragency.net. Website: www.milleragency.net. **Contact:** Angela Miller. Estab. 1990. Represents 100 clients. 5% of clients are new/unpublished writers. Currently handles: 75% nonfiction books.
Represents: Nonfiction. **Considers these nonfiction areas:** Anthropology/archaeology; art/architecture/design; biography/autobiography; business/economics; child guidance/parenting; cooking/foods/nutrition; current affairs; ethnic/cultural interests; gay/lesbian issues; health/medicine; language/literature/criticism; New Age/metaphysics; psychology; self-help/personal improvement; sports; women's issues/studies.
⌐ This agency specializes in nonfiction, multicultural arts, psychology, self-help, cookbooks, biography, travel, memoir, sports.
How to Contact: Query with SASE, submit outline, a few sample chapter(s). Accepts e-mail queries. Considers simultaneous queries. Responds in 1 week to queries. Obtains most new clients through referrals.
Recent Sales: Sold 25 titles in the last year.

FOR INFORMATION ON THE CONFERENCES agents attend, refer to the
Writers' Conferences section in this book.

Terms: Agent receives 15% commission on domestic sales; 20-25% commission on foreign sales. Offers written contract, binding for 2-3 years; 60-day notice must be given to terminate contract. 100% of business is derived from commissions on ms sales. Charges clients for postage (express mail or messenger services) and photocopying.

MOORE LITERARY AGENCY, 83 High St., Newburyport MA 01950-3047. (978)465-9015. Fax: (978)465-8817. E-mail: cmoore@moorelit.com; mmeehan@moorelit.com; dmckenna@moorelit.com. **Contact:** Claudette Moore, Mike Meehan, Deborah McKenna. Estab. 1989. 10% of clients are new/unpublished writers. Currently handles: 100% nonfiction books.
Represents: Nonfiction books. **Considers these nonfiction areas:** Business/economics; computers/electronic; technology.
  O→ This agency specializes in trade computer books (90% of titles); also handles business/hi-tech/general trade nonfiction.
How to Contact: Submit outline. Obtains most new clients through recommendations from others, conferences.
Recent Sales: *Programming Windows With C#*, by Charles Petzold (Microsoft Press); *Microsoft Word Inside and Out*, by Mary Milhollan and Katherine Murray (Microsoft Press); *C# for Dummies*, by Stephen R. Davis (Hungry Minds); *Lessons Learned in Software Testing,* by Cem Kaner, et al (John Wiley & Sons).
Terms: Agent receives 15% commission on domestic sales; 15% commission on foreign sales; 15% commission on dramatic rights sales. Offers written contract.

MAUREEN MORAN AGENCY, P.O. Box 20191, Park West Station, New York NY 10025-1518. (212)222-3838. Fax: (212)531-3464. E-mail: maureenm@erols.com. **Contact:** Maureen Moran. Represents 30 clients. Currently handles: 100% novels.
Represents: Novels. **Considers these fiction areas:** Women's.
  O→ This agency specializes in women's fiction, principally romance and mystery. Does not want to receive science fiction, fantasy or juvenile books.
How to Contact: Query with SASE, will accept email query without attachments. Does not read unsolicited mss. Considers simultaneous queries. Responds in 1 week to queries. Returns materials only with SASE.
Recent Sales: *Silver Scream*, by Mary Daheim; *The Older Woman*, by Cheryl Reavis.
Terms: Agent receives 10% commission on domestic sales; 15-20% commission on foreign sales. Charges clients for extraordinary expenses such as courier, messenger and bank wire fees by prior arrangement.
Tips: "This agency does not handle unpublished writers."

HOWARD MORHAIM LITERARY AGENCY, 841 Broadway, Suite 604, New York NY 10003. Member of AAR.
  ● This agency did not respond to our request for information. Query before submitting.

WILLIAM MORRIS AGENCY, INC., 1325 Ave. of the Americas, New York NY 10019. (212)586-5100. Fax: (212)903-1418. Website: www.wma.com. 151 El Camino Dr., Beverly Hills CA 90212. Member of AAR.
Member Agents: Owen Laster; Jennifer Rudolph Walsh; Suzanne Gluck; Joni Evans; Tracy Fisher; Mel Berger; Virginia Barber; Jay Mandel; Manie Barron.
Represents: Nonfiction books, novels.
How to Contact: Query with SASE. Considers simultaneous queries.
Recent Sales: This agency prefers not to share information on specific sales.
Terms: Agent receives 15% commission on domestic sales; 20% commission on foreign sales.

HENRY MORRISON, INC., 105 S. Bedford Rd., Suite 306A, Mt. Kisco NY 10549. (914)666-3500. Fax: (914)241-7846. **Contact:** Henry Morrison. Estab. 1965. Signatory of WGA. Represents 49 clients. 5% of clients are new/unpublished writers. Currently handles: 5% nonfiction books; 90% novels; 5% juvenile books.
Represents: Nonfiction books, novels. **Considers these nonfiction areas:** Anthropology/archaeology; biography/autobiography; government/politics/law; history; juvenile nonfiction. **Considers these fiction areas:** Action/adventure; detective/police/crime; family saga; historical.
How to Contact: Query with SASE. Responds in 2 weeks to queries; 3 months to mss. Obtains most new clients through recommendations from others.
Recent Sales: Sold 17 titles in the last year. *Long Lost*, by David Morrell (Warner Books); *Janson Deception*, by Robert Ludlum (St. Martin's Press); *Cons, Scams & Grifts*, (Warner/Mysterious Press); *Dhalgren*, by Samuel R. Delany (Vintage); *Shadowbrook*, by Beverly Swerling (Simon & Schuster); *The Ring of Five Dragons*, by Eric Van Lustbader (TOR Books). Other clients include Steve Samuel, Joe Gores, Samuel R. Delany, Beverly Byrnne, Patricia Keneally-Morrison, Molly Katz.
Terms: Agent receives 15% commission on domestic sales; 25% commission on foreign sales. Charges clients for ms copies, bound galleys and finished books for submissions to publishers, movie producers, foreign publishers.

⚙ **MULTIMEDIA PRODUCT DEVELOPMENT, INC.**, 410 S. Michigan Ave., Suite 724, Chicago IL 60605-1465. (312)922-3063. **Contact:** Jane Jordan Browne, president; Scott Mendel, vice president. Estab. 1971. Member of AAR, RWA, MWA, SCBWI. Represents 150 clients. 2% of clients are new/unpublished writers. Currently handles: 60% nonfiction books; 39% novels; 1% movie scripts.

• Prior to opening her agency Ms. Browne served as the managing editor, then as head of the juvenile department for Hawthorne Books, senior editor for Thomas Y. Crowell, adult trade department and general editorial and production manager for Macmillan Educational Services, Inc. Scott Mendel joined the agency in 1998 with a background in academia and the publishing industry, where he was the managing editor of *Positively Aware*, and did considerable freelance and technical writing.

Member Agents: Jane Jordan Browne, president; Scott Mendel, vice-president; Nik Vargas (generalist).

Represents: Nonfiction books, novels. **Considers these nonfiction areas:** Agriculture/horticulture; animals; anthropology/archaeology; biography/autobiography; business/economics; child guidance/parenting; cooking/foods/nutrition; crafts/hobbies; creative nonfiction; current affairs; ethnic/cultural interests; health/medicine; how-to; humor/satire; juvenile nonfiction; memoirs; money/finance; nature/environment; popular culture; psychology; religious/inspirational; science/technology; self-help/personal improvement; sociology; sports; travel; true crime/investigative; women's issues/studies. **Considers these fiction areas:** Contemporary issues; detective/police/crime; ethnic; family saga; glitz; historical; juvenile; literary; mainstream/contemporary; mystery/suspense; picture books; religious/inspirational; romance (contemporary, gothic, historical, regency, western); sports; thriller.

⚷ "We are generalists looking for professional writers with finely honed skill in writing. We are partial to authors with promotion savvy. We work closely with our authors through the entire publishing process, from proposal to after publication." Actively seeking highly commercial mainstream fiction and nonfiction. Does not want to receive poetry, short stories, plays, screenplays, articles.

How to Contact: Query by mail, SASE required. No unsolicited mss accepted. Prefers to read material exclusively. No e-mail or fax queries. Considers simultaneous queries. Responds in 1 week to queries; 6 weeks to mss. Returns materials only with SASE. Obtains most new clients through "referrals, queries by professional, marketable authors."

Recent Sales: Sold 50 titles in the last year. *The Chili Queen*, by Sandra Dallas (St. Martin's Press); *The Procrastinating Child: A Handbook for Adults to Help Children Stop Putting Things Off*, by Rita Emmett (Walker); *In the Castle of the Flynns*, by Michael Raleigh (Sourcebooks); *Remembered Prisoners of a Forgotten War*, by Lewis H. Carlson (St. Martin's Press).

Terms: Agent receives 15% commission on domestic sales; 20% commission on foreign sales. Offers written contract, binding for 2 years. Charges clients for photocopying, overseas postage, faxes.

Writers' Conferences: BEA (June); Frankfurt Book Fair (October); RWA (July); CBA (July); London International Book Fair (March); Boucheron (October); Guadalajara Book Fair (November).

Tips: "If interested in agency representation, be well informed."

⚙ **DEE MURA LITERARY**, (formerly Dee Mura Enterprises Inc.), 269 West Shore Dr., Massapequa NY 11758-8225. (516)795-1616. Fax: (516)795-8797. E-mail: samurai5@ix.netcom.com. **Contact:** Dee Mura, Karen Roberts, Frank Nakamura. Estab. 1987. Signatory of WGA. 50% of clients are new/unpublished writers.

• Prior to opening her agency, Ms. Mura was a public relations executive with a roster of film and entertainment clients, and worked in editorial for major weekly news magazines.

Represents: Nonfiction books, juvenile books, scholarly books, feature film, TV scripts, episodic drama, sitcom, animation, documentary, miniseries, variety show. **Considers these nonfiction areas:** Agriculture/horticulture; animals; anthropology/archaeology; biography/autobiography; business/economics; child guidance/parenting; computers/electronic; current affairs; education; ethnic/cultural interests; gay/lesbian issues; government/politics/law; health/medicine; history; how-to; humor/satire; juvenile nonfiction; memoirs; military/war; money/finance; nature/environment; science/technology; self-help/personal improvement; sociology; sports; travel; true crime/investigative; women's issues/studies. **Considers these fiction areas:** Action/adventure; contemporary issues; detective/police/crime; ethnic; experimental; family saga; fantasy; feminist; gay/lesbian; glitz; historical; humor/satire; juvenile; literary; mainstream/contemporary; mystery/suspense; psychic/supernatural; regional; romance (contemporary, gothic, historical, regency); science fiction; sports; thriller; westerns/frontier; young adult. **Considers these script subject areas:** Action/adventure; cartoon/animation; comedy; contemporary issues; detective/police/crime; family saga; fantasy; feminist; gay/lesbian; glitz; historical; horror; juvenile; mainstream; mystery/suspense; psychic/supernatural; religious/inspirational; romantic comedy; romantic drama; science fiction; sports; teen; thriller; western/frontier.

⚷ "We work on everything, but are especially interested in literary fiction, commercial fiction and nonfiction, thrillers and espionage, self-help, inspirational, medical, scholarly, true life stories, true crime, women's stories and issues." Actively seeking "unique nonfiction manuscripts and proposals; novelists who are great storytellers; contemporary writers with distinct voices and passion." Does not want to receive "ideas for sitcoms, novels, film, etc. or queries without SASEs."

How to Contact: Query with SASE. No fax queries. Accepts queries by e-mail without attachments. Considers simultaneous queries. Responds in 2 weeks to queries. Returns materials only with SASE. Obtains most new clients through recommendations from others, queries.

Recent Sales: Sold over 40 titles and sold 35 scripts in the last year.

Terms: Agent receives 15% commission on domestic sales; 20% commission on foreign sales. Offers written contract. Charges clients for photocopying, mailing expenses, overseas and long distance phone calls and faxes.
Tips: "Please include a paragraph on writer's background even if writer has no literary background and a brief synopsis of the project. We enjoy well-written query letters that tell us about the project and the author."

JEAN V. NAGGAR LITERARY AGENCY, 216 E. 75th St., Suite 1E, New York NY 10021. (212)794-1082. **Contact:** Jean Naggar. Estab. 1978. Member of AAR, Women's Media Group and Women's Forum. Represents 100 clients. 20% of clients are new/unpublished writers. Currently handles: 35% nonfiction books; 45% novels; 15% juvenile books; 5% scholarly books.
● Ms. Naggar served as president of AAR.
Member Agents: Alice Tasman (Senior Agent, narrative nonfiction, commercial/literary fiction, thrillers); Anne Engel (academic-based nonfiction for general readership); Jennifer Weltz (Director, Subsidiary Rights).
Represents: Nonfiction books, novels. **Considers these nonfiction areas:** Biography/autobiography; child guidance/parenting; current affairs; government/politics/law; health/medicine; history; juvenile nonfiction; memoirs; New Age/metaphysics; psychology; religious/inspirational; self-help/personal improvement; sociology; travel; women's issues/studies. **Considers these fiction areas:** Action/adventure; contemporary issues; detective/police/crime; ethnic; family saga; feminist; historical; literary; mainstream/contemporary; mystery/suspense; psychic/supernatural; thriller.
  ○→ This agency specializes in mainstream fiction and nonfiction, literary fiction with commercial potential.
How to Contact: Query with SASE. Prefers to read materials exclusively. No e-mail or fax queries. Responds in 1 day to queries; 2 months to mss. Returns materials only with SASE. Obtains most new clients through recommendations from others, solicitations, conferences.
Recent Sales: *Leaving Ireland*, by Ann Moore (NAL); *The Associate*, by Phillip Margolin (HarperCollins); *Quantico Rules*, by Gene Riehl (St. Martin's Press). Other clients include Jean M. Auel, Robert Pollack, Mary McGarry Morris, Elizabeth Gane, Susan Fromberg Schaeffer.
Terms: Agent receives 15% commission on domestic sales; 20% commission on foreign sales. Offers written contract. Charges for overseas mailing, messenger services, book purchases, long-distance telephone, photocopying. "These are deductible from royalties received."
Writers' Conferences: Willamette Writers Conference; Pacific Northwest Writers Conference; Breadloaf Writers Conference; Virginia Women's Press Conference (Richmond VA); Marymount Manhattan Writers Conference.
Tips: "Use a professional presentation. Because of the avalanche of unsolicited queries that flood the agency every week, we have had to modify our policy. We will now only guarantee to read and respond to queries from writers who come recommended by someone we know. Our areas are general fiction and nonfiction, no children's books by unpublished writers, no multimedia, no screenplays, no formula fiction, no mysteries by unpublished writers. We recommend patience and fortitude: the courage to be true to your own vision, the fortitude to finish a novel and polish and polish again before sending it out, and the patience to accept rejection gracefully and wait for the stars to align themselves appropriately for success."

NATIONAL WRITERS LITERARY AGENCY, division of GTR, Inc., 3140 S. Peoria #295, Aurora CO 80014. (720)851-1959. Fax: (720)851-1960. E-mail: aajwiii@aol.com or nationalwriters@aol.com. **Contact:** Andrew J. Whelchel III. Estab. 1987. Represents 52 clients. 20% of clients are new/unpublished writers. Currently handles: 40% nonfiction books; 34% novels; 20% juvenile books; 6% scripts.
Member Agents: Andrew J. Whelchel III (screenplays, nonfiction, mystery, thriller); Jason S. Cangialosi (nonfiction); Shayne Sharpe (novels, screenplays, fantasy).
Represents: Nonfiction books, textbooks. **Considers these nonfiction areas:** Animals; biography/autobiography; child guidance/parenting; education; government/politics/law; how-to; popular culture; science/technology; sports; travel. **Considers these fiction areas:** Action/adventure; juvenile; mainstream/contemporary; mystery/suspense; science fiction; sports; young adult.
  ○→ Actively seeking "music, business, cutting edge novels; pop culture, compelling true stories, science and technology." Does not want to receive "concept books, westerns, over-published self-help topics."
How to Contact: Query with outline and SASE. Accepts e-mail queries. No fax queries. Considers simultaneous queries. Responds in 6 weeks to queries; 2 months to mss. Returns materials only with SASE. Obtains most new clients through solicitations, conferences, or over the transom.
Recent Sales: Sold 22 titles in the last year. *Final Cut: Business Plans for Independent Films*, by Reed Martin (Faber & Faber); *Open Season* (Warner Brothers Pictures); *The Deadline*, by Ron Franscell (Repeat Offender Films).
Terms: Agent receives 15% commission on domestic sales; 20% commission on foreign sales; 10% commission on dramatic rights sales. Offers written contract; 30-day notice must be given to terminate contract.
Reading List: Reads *Popular Mechanics, The Futurist, Industry Standard, Money, Rolling Stone, Maxim, Details, Spin* and *Buzz* to find new clients.
Tips: "Query letters should include a great hook just as if you only had a few seconds to impress us. A professional package gets professional attention. Always include return postage!"

✔️ 🔲 🖊️ **KAREN NAZOR LITERARY AGENCY**, 100 Powdermill Road, PMB 182, Acton MA 01720. (978) 266-3792. Fax: (978) 263-6230. E-mail: query@nazor.org. **Contact:** Karen Nazor. Estab. 1991. Represents 35 clients. 15% of clients are new/unpublished writers. Currently handles: 75% nonfiction books; 10% novels; 10% electronic multimedia.

• Prior to opening her agency, Ms. Nazor served a brief apprenticeship with Raines & Raines and was assistant to Peter Ginsberg, president of Curtis Brown Ltd.

Member Agents: Kris Ashley (literary and commercial fiction).

Represents: Nonfiction books, novels, novellas. **Considers these nonfiction areas:** Biography/autobiography; business/economics; child guidance/parenting; computers/electronic; current affairs; ethnic/cultural interests; government/politics/law; history; how-to; music/dance; nature/environment; photography; popular culture; science/technology; sociology; sports; travel; women's issues/studies. **Considers these fiction areas:** Comic books/cartoon; ethnic; feminist; literary; regional; women's.

O→ This agency specializes in "good writers! Mostly nonfiction—arts, culture, politics, technology, civil rights, etc."

How to Contact: Query by e-mail without attachments. No unsolicited mss. Responds in 2 weeks to queries. Returns materials only with SASE.

Recent Sales: Sold 12 titles in the last year. *The Secret Life of Dust*, by Hannah Holmes (John Wiley & Sons); *Childhood and Adolescent Obsessive Compulsive Disorder*, by Mitzi Waltz (O'Reilly).

Terms: Agent receives 15% commission on domestic sales; 20% commission on foreign sales. Offers written contract. Charges clients for express mail services, photocopying costs.

Tips: "I'm interested in good writers who want a long term, long haul relationship. Not a one-book writer, but a writer who has many ideas, is productive, professional, passionate and meets deadlines!"

🖊️ **NEW BRAND AGENCY GROUP, LLC**, Website: www.literaryagent.net. **Contact:** Mark Ryan, Ingrid Elfver-Ryan. Estab. 1994. Represents 30 clients. 40% of clients are new/unpublished writers. Currently handles: 50% nonfiction books; 30% novels; 20% juvenile books.

Member Agents: Mark Ryan and Ingrid Elfver-Ryan (fiction and nonfiction with bestseller or high commercial potential....projects with national and/or international appeal likely to sell at least 100,000 copies.)

Represents: Nonfiction books, novels, juvenile books (books for younger readers). **Considers these nonfiction areas:** Biography/autobiography; business/economics; health; humor; juvenile nonfiction; memoirs; New Age/metaphysics; popular culture; psychology; religious/inspirational; self-help/personal improvement; sex; spirituality; women's issues/studies; body and soul, celebrity, family, finance, fitness, gift/novelty, leadership, men's issues, parenting, personal growth, relationships, success. **Considers these fiction areas:** Erotica (mainstream); fantasy; historical; horror; juvenile; literary; mainstream/contemporary; mystery; romance (mainstream); science fiction; thriller; westerns/frontier (mainstream); cross-genre, magical realism, supernatural, suspense.

O→ "We only work with authors we are passionate about on three levels: The financial promise of the work and its ability to entertain, educate, and inspire; the personality and character of the author; and the potential career of the author (future books and willingness and ability to promote). Actively seeking stories and voices that dare to be different."

How to Contact: Accepts e-mail queries only; submit electronic query at www.literaryagent.net. Responds in 1 day to queries; 1 week to mss. Obtains most new clients through queries and conferences.

Recent Sales: Sold 10 titles in the last year. *24/7*, by Jim Brown (Ballantine); *The Marriage Plan*, by Aggie Jordan, Ph.D. (Broadway/Bantam); *Father to Daughter*, by Harry Harrison (Workman).

Terms: Agent receives 15% commission on domestic sales. Offers written contract, binding for 6 months; 30-day notice must be given to terminate contract. 20% commission for subsidiary rights; charges for postage and phone costs.

Writers' Conferences: Sleuthfest (Ft. Lauderdale, March 15-17); Moving the Borders (Lexington, April 3); Author's Venue (Mesa, May 9-12); First Coast Festival (Jacksonville, May 16-18); Writing the Region (Gainesville, July 25-29); Rocky Mountain Fiction Writers' Conference (Denver, September 12-15); Missouri Writers' Conference (Kansas City, October 3-5), and many more.

🖊️ **NEW ENGLAND PUBLISHING ASSOCIATES, INC.**, P.O. Box 5, Chester CT 06412-0645. (860)345-READ and (860)345-4976. Fax: (860)344-3660. E-mail: nepa@nepa.com. Website: www.nepa.com. **Contact:** Elizabeth Frost-Knappman, Edward W. Knappman, Kristine Schiavi, Ron Formica, or Victoria Harlow. Estab. 1983. Member of AAR, ASJA, Authors Guild, Connecticut Press Club. Represents 125-150 clients. 15% of clients are new/unpublished writers.

Member Agents: Elizabeth Frost-Knappman (president); Edward W. Knappman (vice president); Kristine Schiavi (subsidiary rights agent); Ron Formica (managing editor); Victoria Harlow (research editor).

Represents: Nonfiction books. **Considers these nonfiction areas:** Biography/autobiography; business/economics; child guidance/parenting; government/politics/law; health/medicine; history; language/literature/criticism; military/war; money/finance; nature/environment; psychology; science/technology; self-help/personal improvement; sociology; true crime/investigative; women's issues/studies; reference.

O→ This agency specializes in adult nonfiction of serious purpose.

How to Contact: Send outline/proposal, SASE. Accepts e-mail and fax queries. Considers simultaneous queries. Responds in 1 month to queries; 5 weeks to mss. Returns materials only with SASE.

Recent Sales: Sold over 70 titles in the last year. *Swimming with Sharks*, by Peter Klimley (Simon and Schuster); *Turnaround: How Carlos Ghosn Rescued Nissan*, by David Magee (Harper Collins); *The Princeton Murder Project*, by Ann Waldron (Berkeley); *Elementary, My Dear: Thinking Logically*, by Deborah Bennett (Norton).
Terms: Agent receives 15% commission on domestic sales; 20% commission on foreign sales. Offers written contract, binding for 6 months. Charges clients for copying.
Writers' Conferences: BEA (Chicago, June); ALA (San Antonio, January); ALA (New York, July); ASJA (May); Frankfurt (October).
Tips: "Send us a well-written proposal that clearly identifies your audience—who will buy this book and why. Check our website for tips on proposals and advice on how to market your books. Never give up."

NINE MUSES AND APOLLO INC., 525 Broadway, Suite 201, New York NY 10012. (212)431-2665. **Contact:** Ling Lucas. Estab. 1991. Represents 50 clients. 10% of clients are new/unpublished writers. Currently handles: 90% nonfiction books; 10% novels.
• Ms. Lucas formerly served as vice president, sales & marketing director and associate publisher of Warner Books.
Represents: Nonfiction books. **Considers these nonfiction areas:** Animals; biography/autobiography; business/economics; current affairs; ethnic/cultural interests; health/medicine; language/literature/criticism; psychology; spirituality; women's issues/studies. **Considers these fiction areas:** Ethnic; literary; mainstream/contemporary (commercial).
↝ This agency specializes in nonfiction. Does not want to receive children's and young adult material.
How to Contact: Submit outline, 2 sample chapter(s), SASE. Prefers to read materials exclusively. Responds in 1 month to mss.
Recent Sales: Sold 20 titles in the last year. *Baron Baptiste Yoga*, by Baron Baptiste (Simon & Schuster/Fireside); *The Twelve Gifts of Birth*, by Charlene Costanzo (HarperCollins).
Terms: Agent receives 15% commission on domestic sales; 20-25% commission on foreign sales. Offers written contract. Charges clients for photocopying, postage.
Tips: "Your outline should already be well-developed, cogent, and reveal clarity of thought about the general structure and direction of your project."

THE BETSY NOLAN LITERARY AGENCY, 224 W. 29th St., 15th Floor, New York NY 10001. (212)967-8200. Fax: (212)967-7292. **Contact:** Donald Lehr, president. Estab. 1980. Member of AAR. Represents 200 clients. 10% of clients are new/unpublished writers. Currently handles: 90% nonfiction books.
Member Agents: Carla Glasser.
Represents: Nonfiction books. **Considers these nonfiction areas:** Cooking/foods/nutrition (cookbooks).
How to Contact: Query with outline. No e-mail or fax queries. Considers simultaneous queries. Responds in 6 weeks to queries. Returns materials only with SASE.
Recent Sales: Sold 15 titles in the last year. *Mangia*, by Sasha Muniak/Ricardo Diaz (HarperCollins); *The Buttercup Bake Shop Cookbook*, by Jennifer Appel (Simon & Schuster); *Desperation Dinners*, by Beverly Mills & Alicia Ross (Workman); *Bridgehampton Weekends*, by Ellen Wright (William Morrow).
Terms: Agent receives 15% commission on domestic sales; 20% commission on foreign sales.

THE NORMA-LEWIS AGENCY, 311 W. 43rd St., Suite 602, New York NY 10036. (212)664-0807. **Contact:** Norma Liebert. Estab. 1980. 50% of clients are new/unpublished writers. Currently handles: 60% juvenile books; 40% adult books.
Represents: Movie scripts, TV scripts, documentary, miniseries, stage plays, juvenile and adult nonfiction and fiction. **Considers these nonfiction areas:** Art/architecture/design; biography/autobiography; child guidance/parenting; cooking/foods/nutrition; crafts/hobbies; current affairs; ethnic/cultural interests; government/politics/law; health/medicine; history; juvenile nonfiction; music/dance; nature/environment; photography; popular culture; self-help/personal improvement; theater/film; true crime/investigative; women's issues/studies. **Considers these fiction areas:** Action/adventure; detective/police/crime; family saga; historical; horror; humor/satire; juvenile; mainstream/contemporary; mystery/suspense; picture books; romance (contemporary, gothic, historical, regency); thriller; westerns/frontier; young adult.
↝ This agency specializes in juvenile books (pre-school to high school).
How to Contact: Query with SASE. Prefers to read materials exclusively. Considers simultaneous queries. Responds in 6 weeks to queries. Returns materials only with SASE.

THE PUBLISHING FIELD is constantly changing! Agents often change addresses, phone numbers, or even companies. If you're still using this book and it is 2004 or later, buy the newest edition of *Guide to Literary Agents* at your favorite bookstore or order directly from Writer's Digest Books at (800)448-0915.

Recent Sales: *Viper Quarry*, by Dean Feldmeyer (Pocket Books); *Pitchfork Hollow*, by Dean Feldmeyer (Pocket Books).
Terms: Agent receives 15% commission on domestic sales; 20% commission on foreign sales.

HAROLD OBER ASSOCIATES, 425 Madison Ave., New York NY 10017. (212)759-8600. Fax: (212)759-9428. Estab. 1929. Member of AAR. Represents 250 clients. 10% of clients are new/unpublished writers. Currently handles: 35% nonfiction books; 50% novels; 15% juvenile books.
Member Agents: Phyllis Westberg; Pamela Malpas; Emma Sweeney; Knox Burger; Alexander C. Smithline; Craig Tenney (not accepting new clients).
Represents: Nonfiction books, novels, juvenile books. **Considers these nonfiction areas:** Considers all nonfiction areas. **Considers these fiction areas:** Considers all fiction subjects.
How to Contact: Query letter only with SASE. No fax queries. Responds in 1 week to queries; 6 weeks to mss. Obtains most new clients through recommendations from others.
Terms: Agent receives 15% commission on domestic sales; 20% commission on foreign sales. Charges clients for photocopying and express mail or package services.

FIFI OSCARD AGENCY INC., 110 W. 40th St., New York NY 10018. (212)764-1100. **Contact:** Literary Department. Estab. 1956. Member of AAR; signatory of WGA. Represents 108 clients. 5% of clients are new/unpublished writers. Currently handles: 60% nonfiction books; 10% novels; 30% stage plays.
Member Agents: Fifi Oscard; Peter Sawyer; Carmen Lavia; Kevin McShane; Ivy Fischer Stone; Carolyn French; Lindley Kirksey; Jerry Rudes.
Represents: Nonfiction books, novels (by referral only), stage plays.
   O➛ This agency specializes in history, celebrity biography and autobiography, pop culture, travel/adventure, performing arts, fine arts/design.
How to Contact: Query with outline. No unsolicited mss. Returns materials only with SASE.
Recent Sales: *Dances With Demons* (biography of Jerome Robbins), by Greg Lawrence (Putnam); *All Elevations Unknown*, by Sam Lightner, Jr. (Broadway); *Indiscretion*, by Elizabeth Nunez (One World Books); *King of Rock*, by Darryl McDaniels (St. Martin's Press); *Three Roosevelts*, by James Macgregor Burns and Susan Dunn (Atlantic Monthly Press); *Wit* (Faber & Faber); *True Hope*, by Frank Manley.
Terms: Agent receives 15% commission on domestic sales; 20% commission on foreign sales; 10% commission on dramatic rights sales. Charges clients for photocopying expenses.
Tips: "Writer must have published articles or books in major markets or have screen credits if movie scripts, etc."

PARAVIEW, INC., (Specialized: spiritual/New Age, self help), 12 Aldershot Rd., Walderslade, Chatham Kent ME5 OHX, England. E-mail: lhagan@paraview.com. Website: www.paraview.com. **Contact:** Lisa Hagan. Estab. 1988. Represents 75 clients. 50% of clients are new/unpublished writers. Currently handles: 80% nonfiction books; 10% novels; 10% scholarly books.
   • Ms. Hagan has agented since 1995.
Member Agents: Lisa Hagan (fiction and nonfiction self-help).
Represents: Nonfiction books, novels. **Considers these nonfiction areas:** Agriculture/horticulture; Americana; animals; anthropology/archaeology; art/architecture/design; biography/autobiography; business/economics; child guidance/parenting; computers/electronic; cooking/foods/nutrition; crafts/hobbies; creative nonfiction; current affairs; education; ethnic/cultural interests; gardening; gay/lesbian issues; government/politics/law; health/medicine; history; how-to; humor/satire; interior design/decorating; juvenile nonfiction; language/literature/criticism; memoirs; military/war; money/finance; multicultural; music/dance; nature/environment; New Age/metaphysics; philosophy; photography; popular culture; psychology; recreation; regional; religious/inspirational; science/technology; self-help/personal improvement; sex; sociology; software; spirituality; sports; theater/film; translation; travel; true crime/investigative; women's issues/studies; young adult. **Considers these fiction areas:** Action/adventure; contemporary issues; ethnic; feminist; literary; mainstream/contemporary; regional; romance; women's.
   O➛ This agency specializes in spiritual, New Age and self-help.
How to Contact: Query including, synopsis, author, bio via email. Responds in 1 month to queries; 3 months to mss. Obtains most new clients through recommendations from editors.
Recent Sales: Sold 40 titles in the last year. *Love Signs*, by Stacey Wolf (Warner); *Love Letters*, by Paula Roberts (New Page Books); *Tending Roses*, by Lisa Wingate (NAL); *The Last Vampire*, by Whitley Streiber (Pocket Books).
Terms: Agent receives 15% commission on domestic sales; 20% commission on foreign sales.
Writers' Conferences: BEA (Chicago, June); London Book Fair; E3—Electronic Entertainment Exposition.
Tips: "New writers should have their work edited, critiqued, and carefully reworked prior to submission. First contact should be via e-mail to lhagan@paraview.com."

THE RICHARD PARKS AGENCY, 138 E. 16th St., 5th Floor, New York NY 10003. (212)254-9067. Website: www.richardparksagency.com. **Contact:** Richard Parks. Estab. 1988. Member of AAR. Currently handles: 55% nonfiction books; 40% novels; 5% story collections.

• Prior to opening his agency, Mr. Parks served as an agent with Curtis Brown, Ltd.

Represents: Nonfiction books, novels. **Considers these nonfiction areas:** Animals; anthropology/archaeology; art/architecture/design; biography/autobiography; business/economics; child guidance/parenting; cooking/foods/nutrition; crafts/hobbies; current affairs; ethnic/cultural interests; gardening; gay/lesbian issues; government/politics/law; health/medicine; history; how-to; humor/satire; language/literature/criticism; memoirs; military/war; money/finance; music/dance; nature/environment; popular culture; psychology; science/technology; self-help/personal improvement; sociology; theater/film; travel; women's issues/studies. **Considers these fiction areas:** Considers fiction by referral only.

○→ Actively seeking nonfiction. Does not want to receive unsolicited material.

How to Contact: Query by mail only with SASE. No e-mail or fax queries. Considers simultaneous queries. Responds in 2 weeks to queries. Returns materials only with SASE. Obtains most new clients through recommendations and referrals.

Terms: Agent receives 15% commission on domestic sales; 20% commission on foreign sales. Charges clients for photocopying or any unusual expense incurred at the writer's request.

KATHI J. PATON LITERARY AGENCY, 19 W. 55th St., New York NY 10019-4907. (908)647-2117. E-mail: KJPLitBiz@aol.com. **Contact:** Kathi Paton. Estab. 1987. Currently handles: 65% nonfiction books; 35% novels.

Represents: Nonfiction books, novels, short story collections, book-based film rights. **Considers these nonfiction areas:** Business/economics; child guidance/parenting; money/finance (personal investing); nature/environment; psychology; religious/inspirational; women's issues/studies. **Considers these fiction areas:** Literary; mainstream/contemporary; short story collections.

○→ This agency specializes in adult nonfiction.

How to Contact: For nonfiction, send proposal, sample chapter and SASE. For fiction, send first 40 pages, plot summary or 3 short stories and SASE. Considers simultaneous queries. Obtains most new clients through recommendations from other clients.

Recent Sales: *Future Wealth*, by McInerney and White (St. Martin's Press); *Unraveling the Mystery of Autism*, by Karyn Seroussi (Simon & Schuster).

Terms: Agent receives 15% commission on domestic sales; 20% commission on foreign sales. Offers written contract. Charges clients for photocopying.

Writers' Conferences: Attends major regional panels, seminars and conferences.

Tips: "Write well."

L. PERKINS ASSOCIATES, 5800 Arlington Ave., Riverdale NY 10471. (718)543-5344. Fax: (718)543-5354. E-mail: lperkinsagency@yahoo.com. **Contact:** Lori Perkins. Estab. 1990. Member of AAR. Represents 50 clients. 10% of clients are new/unpublished writers.

• Ms. Perkins has been an agent for 18 years. Her agency has an affiliate agency, Southern Literary Group. She is also the author of *The Insider's Guide to Getting an Agent* (Writer's Digest Books).

Represents: Nonfiction books, novels. **Considers these nonfiction areas:** Popular culture. **Considers these fiction areas:** Fantasy; horror; literary (dark); science fiction.

○→ All of Ms. Perkins's clients write both fiction and nonfiction. "This combination keeps my clients publishing for years. I am also a published author so I know what it takes to write a book." Actively seeking a Latino *Gone With the Wind* and *Waiting to Exhale*, and urban ethnic horror. Does not want to receive "anything outside of the above categories, i.e., westerns, romance."

How to Contact: Query with SASE. Considers simultaneous queries. Responds in 6 weeks to queries; 3 months to mss. Returns materials only with SASE. Obtains most new clients through recommendations from others, solicitations, conferences.

Recent Sales: Sold 100 titles in the last year. *The Illustrated Ray Bradbury*, by Jerry Weist (Avon); *The Poet in Exile*, by Ray Manzarek (Avalon); *Behind Sad Eyes: The Life of George Harrison* (St. Martin's Press).

Terms: Agent receives 15% commission on domestic sales; 20% commission on foreign sales. No written contract. Charges clients for photocopying.

Writers' Conferences: San Diego Writer's Conference; NECON; BEA; World Fantasy.

Tips: "Research your field and contact professional writers' organizations to see who is looking for what. Finish your novel before querying agents. Read my book, *An Insider's Guide to Getting an Agent* to get a sense of how agents operate."

STEPHEN PEVNER, INC., 382 Lafayette Street, #8, New York NY 10003. (212)674-8403. Fax: (212)529-3692. E-mail: spevner@aol.com. **Contact:** Stephen Pevner. Estab. 1991.

Represents: Nonfiction books, novels, feature film, TV scripts, TV movie of the week, episodic drama, animation, documentary, miniseries. **Considers these nonfiction areas:** Biography/autobiography; ethnic/cultural interests; gay/lesbian issues; history; humor/satire; language/literature/criticism; memoirs; music/dance; New Age/metaphysics; photography; popular culture; religious/inspirational; sociology; travel. **Considers these fiction areas:** Comic books/cartoon; contemporary issues; erotica; ethnic; experimental; gay/lesbian; glitz; horror; humor/satire; literary; mainstream/contemporary; psychic/supernatural; thriller; urban. **Considers these script subject areas:** Comedy; contemporary issues; detective/police/crime; gay/lesbian; glitz; horror; romantic comedy; romantic drama; thriller.

O— This agency specializes in motion pictures, novels, humor, pop culture, urban fiction, independent filmmakers. Actively seeking urban fiction, popular culture, screenplays and film proposals.

How to Contact: Query with SASE, outline/proposal. Prefers to read materials exclusively. No e-mail or fax queries. Responds in 2 weeks to queries; 1 month to mss. Obtains most new clients through recommendations from others.

Recent Sales: *In the Company of Men* and *Bash*, by Neil LaBute; *The Vagina Monologues*, by Eve Ensler; *Guide to Life*, by The Five Lesbian Brothers; *Noise From Underground*, by Michael Levine. Other clients include Richard Linklater, Gregg Araki, Tom DiCillo, Genvieve Turner/Rose Troche, Todd Solondz.

Terms: Agent receives 15% commission on domestic sales; 20% commission on foreign sales. Offers written contract, binding for 1 year; 6-week notice must be given to terminate contract. 100% of business is derived from commissions on ms sales.

Tips: "Be persistent but civilized."

ALISON J. PICARD, LITERARY AGENT, P.O. Box 2000, Cotuit MA 02635. (508)477-7192. Fax: (508)477-7192 (Please contact before faxing.) E-mail: ajpicard@aol.com. **Contact:** Alison Picard. Estab. 1985. Represents 48 clients. 30% of clients are new/unpublished writers. Currently handles: 40% nonfiction books; 40% novels; 20% juvenile books.

• Prior to becoming an agent, Ms. Picard was an assistant at an NYC literary agency.

Member Agents: Alison Picard (mysteries/suspense/thriller, romance, literary fiction, adult nonfiction, juvenile books).

Represents: Nonfiction books, novels, short story collections, novellas, juvenile books. **Considers these nonfiction areas:** Animals; anthropology/archaeology; art/architecture/design; biography/autobiography; business/economics; child guidance/parenting; cooking/foods/nutrition; current affairs; education; ethnic/cultural interests; gay/lesbian issues; government/politics/law; health/medicine; history; how-to; humor/satire; juvenile nonfiction; memoirs; military/war; money/finance; multicultural; music/dance; nature/environment; New Age/metaphysics; popular culture; psychology; religious/inspirational; science/technology; self-help/personal improvement; translation; travel; true crime/investigative; women's issues/studies; young adult. **Considers these fiction areas:** Action/adventure; contemporary issues; detective/police/crime; erotica; ethnic; experimental; family saga; feminist; gay/lesbian; glitz; historical; horror; humor/satire; juvenile; literary; mainstream/contemporary; multicultural; mystery/suspense; New Age; picture books; psychic/supernatural; regional; religious/inspirational; romance; sports; thriller; young adult.

O— "Many of my clients have come to me from big agencies, where they felt overlooked or ignored. I communicate freely with my clients, and offer a lot of career advice, suggestions for revising manuscripts, etc. If I believe in a project, I will submit it to a dozen or more publishers, unlike some agents who give up after 4 or 5 rejections." Actively seeking commercial adult fiction and nonfiction, middle grade juvenile fiction. Does not want to receive sci-fi/fantasy, westerns, poetry, plays, articles.

How to Contact: Query with SASE. Considers simultaneous queries. Responds in 1 week to queries; 6 weeks to mss. Returns materials only with SASE. Obtains most new clients through recommendations from others, solicitations.

Recent Sales: Sold 27 titles in the last year. *The Shade of My Own Tree*, by Sheila Williams (Ballantine); *The Boldness of Boys*, by Susan Strong (Andrews McMeel); *The Complete Bridal Shower Planner*, by Sharon Naylor (Prima); *Nicole Kidman*, by James Dickerson (Kensington/Citadel); *Pierce Brosnan*, by Peter Carrick (Kensington/Citadel). Other clients include Caryl Rivers, Osha Gray Davidson, Amy Dean, David Housewright, Nancy Means Wright.

Terms: Agent receives 15% commission on domestic sales; 20% commission on foreign sales. Offers written contract, binding for 1 year; 1 week notice must be given to terminate contract.

Tips: "Please don't send material without sending a query first via mail or e-mail. For e-mail, use plain text only, no attachments. I don't accept phone or fax queries. Always enclose a SASE with a query."

PINDER LANE & GARON-BROOKE ASSOCIATES, LTD., 159 W. 53rd St., Suite 14E, New York NY 10019-6005. (212)489-0880. E-mail: pinderl@interport.com. **Contact:** Robert Thixton. Member of AAR; signatory of WGA. Represents 30 clients. 20% of clients are new/unpublished writers. Currently handles: 25% nonfiction books; 75% novels.

Member Agents: Nancy Coffey (contributing agent); Dick Duane; Robert Thixton.

Represents: Nonfiction books, novels. **Considers these fiction areas:** Contemporary issues; detective/police/crime; family saga; fantasy; gay/lesbian; literary; mainstream/contemporary; mystery/suspense; romance; science fiction.

O— This agency specializes in mainstream fiction and nonfiction. Does not want to receive screenplays, TV series teleplays or dramatic plays.

How to Contact: Query with SASE. No unsolicited mss. Responds in 3 weeks to queries; 2 months to requested mss. Obtains most new clients through referrals, queries.

Recent Sales: Sold 20 titles in the last year. *Diana & Jackie - Maidens, Mothers & Myths*, by Jay Mulvaney (St. Martin's Press); *The Sixth Fleet* (series), by David Meadows (Berkley); *Dark Fires*, by Rosemary Rogers (Mira Books).

Terms: Agent receives 15% commission on domestic sales; 30% commission on foreign sales. Offers written contract, binding for 3-5 years.

Tips: "With our literary and media experience, our agency is uniquely positioned for the current and future direction publishing is taking. Send query letter first giving the essence of the ms and a personal or career bio with SASE."

ARTHUR PINE ASSOCIATES, INC., 250 W. 57th St., Suite 417, New York NY 10019. (215)265-7330. Fax: (212)265-4650. Estab. 1966. Represents 100 clients. 25% of clients are new/unpublished writers. Currently handles: 60% nonfiction books; 40% novels.

Member Agents: Richard Pine (fiction, nonfiction); Catherine Drayton (fiction, nonfiction, children's); Lori Andiman (subsidiary rights); Sarah Piel (fiction, nonfiction); Matthew Guma (fiction, nonfiction).

Represents: Nonfiction books, novels. **Considers these nonfiction areas:** Business/economics; current affairs; health/medicine; money/finance; psychology; self-help/personal improvement. **Considers these fiction areas:** Detective/police/crime; family saga; literary; mainstream/contemporary; romance; thriller.

How to Contact: Query with SASE, outline/proposal. Prefers to read materials exclusively. No e-mail or fax queries. Responds in 3 weeks to queries. Obtains most new clients through recommendations from others.

Recent Sales: Sold 60 titles in the last year. *Have a Good Life*, by Campbell Armstrong (Crown); *The Bullfighter Checks Her Make-up*, by Susan Orlean (Random House); *Philistines at the Hedgerow: Passion and Property in the Hamptons*, by Steven Gaines (Little, Brown/Back Bay).

Terms: Agent receives 15% commission on domestic sales; 15% commission on foreign sales. Offers written contract.

Tips: "Our agency will consider exclusive submissions only. All submissions must be accompanied by postage or SASE. Will not read manuscripts before receiving a letter of inquiry."

JULIE POPKIN, 15340 Albright St., #204, Pacific Palisades CA 90272-2520. (310)459-2834. **Contact:** Julie Popkin. Estab. 1989. Represents 35 clients. 30% of clients are new/unpublished writers. Currently handles: 70% nonfiction books; 30% novels.

- Prior to opening her agency, Ms. Popkin taught at the university level and did freelance editing and writing.

Member Agents: Julie Popkin; Margaret McCord (fiction, memoirs, biography); Linda Schubert (non-fiction).

Represents: Nonfiction books, novels, translations. **Considers these nonfiction areas:** Art/architecture/design; ethnic/cultural interests; government/politics/law; history; philosophy; women's issues/studies (feminist); criticism. **Considers these fiction areas:** Literary; mainstream/contemporary; mystery/suspense.

- This agency specializes in selling book-length mss including fiction and nonfiction. Especially interested in social issues, ethnic and minority subjects, Latin American authors. Does not want to receive New Age, spiritual, romance, science fiction.

How to Contact: Query with SASE. No e-mail or fax queries. Responds in 1 month to queries; 2 months to mss. "Mostly clients find me through guides and personal contacts."

Recent Sales: Sold 8 titles in the last year. *Two Worlds in One*, by Virginia Li (Prometheus); *The Red and the Blacklist*, by Norma Barzman (Nation Books); *Selected Poems*, by P.K. Page (Godine).

Terms: Agent receives 15% commission on domestic sales; 20% commission on foreign sales; 10% commission on dramatic rights sales. Sometimes charges fee if the ms requires extensive copying and mailing.

Writers' Conferences: BEA (Los Angeles, June); Santa Barbara (June).

Reading List: Reads "an assortment of literary journals—*Grand Street, Sewanee Review, Santa Monica Review, The New York Times, New York Review of Books*, book reviews, etc." Looks for "literary quality, unusual work."

Tips: "Keep your eyes on the current market. Publishing responds to changes very quickly and works toward perceived and fresh subject matter often. Historical fiction seems to be rising in interest after a long quiet period."

HELEN F. PRATT INC., 1165 Fifth Ave., New York NY 10029. **Contact:** Helen F. Pratt. Member of AAR.

- This agency did not respond to our request for information. Query before submitting.

Member Agents: Helen F. Pratt, Seamus Mullarkey.

ROBERT PRESKILL LITERARY AGENCY, Lit West Group LLC, 1763 Golden Gate Ave., Suite 10, San Francisco CA 94115. (415)346-9449. Fax: (415)820-7745. E-mail: literaryagent@geocities.com. Website: www.litwest.com. **Contact:** Robert Preskill, Esq. Member of Illinois Bar; Authors Guild. 10% of clients are new/unpublished writers. Currently handles: 50% nonfiction books; 40% novels; 10% story collections.

- Mr. Preskill formerly worked for McGraw-Hill Companies.

Member Agents: Agents of Lit West Group LLC: Robert Preskill (literary fiction, relevant nonfiction by "experts"); Katherine Boyle (pop-culture, psychology, literary fiction); Linda Mead (business, self-help, general nonfiction, selected works of fiction); Nancy Ellis (general nonfiction, reference, self-help, young adult, fiction).

Represents: Nonfiction books, novels, short story collections, novellas. **Considers these nonfiction areas:** Art/architecture/design; biography/autobiography; business/economics; current affairs; government/politics/law; history; how-to; humor/satire; interior design/decorating; language/literature/criticism; memoirs; military/war; money/finance; multicultural; music/dance; nature/environment; popular culture; psychology; self-help/personal improvement; sports; travel; true crime/investigative. **Considers these fiction areas:** Comic books/cartoon; detective/police/crime; literary; thriller.

O→ "RPLA spends extra time editing and reviewing a work once it is chosen. Much of the time we will help chart a course toward publication by assisting with marketing ideas, submitting to literary magazines and other appropriate publications and through pursuit of sub-rights. Regarding fiction, looks for things grounded in personal storytelling, subtle and powerful action, politics, issues that illuminate a deeper layer of imagery; things that take dialog and the negative space of good dialog somewhere beyond the simple experience. There are plenty of stories that pass us by on a daily basis, but we fail to see them. I am interested in those stories in the world as it exists. Does not want fantasy, romance."

How to Contact: Query with SASE. *After* query, send 3 sample chapters with SASE. Considers simultaneous queries. Responds in 1 week to queries; 10 weeks to mss. Returns materials only with SASE. Obtains most new clients through recommendations from others, solicitations.

Recent Sales: Sold 10 titles and sold 2 options on scripts in the last year. *Instant Karma*, by Mark Swartz (City Lights Publishers); *Indigenous*, personal essays by Cris Mazza (City Lights Publishers); *Unititled Sports/Lifestyle Narrative*, by world class athelete Marla Streb (Plume); *Westerfield's Chain*, by Jack Clark (St. Martin's Press); *On the Homefront*, by Jack Clark and Mary Jo Clark (Plume); *Murder for Christmas*, (Morrow); *Esther Stories*, by Peter Orner (Houghton Mifflin); *Small World* (travel), by Brad Herzog (Simon & Schuster). Other clients include Dan Whipple, Robley Wilson, Alvin Greenberg, Robert Goldberg, Alexai Galaviz-Budzlszewski.

Terms: Agent receives 15% commission on domestic sales; 20% commission on foreign sales. Offers written contract; 30-day notice must be given to terminate contract. Charges clients for project related expenses only (such as postage and photocopying).

Writers' Conferences: Maui Writers Conference (Maui HI); Asilomar Writers Conference (Pacific Grove CA); Saroyan Writers Conference (Fresno CA); Willamet Writers Conference (Portland OR).

Tips: "I was trained through the wonderful program at University of Illinois and learned from the writing of Mark Costello, William Gass, William Maxwell, Joy Williams, Grace Paley, Richard Ford, Joan Didion, Alice Munro, Mary Gaitskill, Nathaniel West, Steve Erickson and Thomas McGuane."

AARON M. PRIEST LITERARY AGENCY, 708 Third Ave., 23rd Floor, New York NY 10017. (212)818-0344. Fax: (212)573-9417. E-mail: lchilds@aaronpriest.com. **Contact:** Aaron Priest or Molly Friedrich. Estab. 1974. Member of AAR. Currently handles: 25% nonfiction books; 75% novels.

Member Agents: Lisa Erbach Vance; Paul Cirone; Aaron Priest; Molly Friedrich; Lucy Childs.

Represents: Nonfiction books, novels.

How to Contact: No e-mail or fax queries. Considers simultaneous queries. If interested, will respond within 2 weeks.

Recent Sales: *Bow's Boy*, by Richard Babcock (Scribner); *Of Magic*, by Frances Sherwood (Norton).

Terms: Agent receives 15% commission on domestic sales. Charges for photocopying, foreign postage expenses.

SUSAN ANN PROTTER LITERARY AGENT, 110 W. 40th St., Suite 1408, New York NY 10018. (212)840-0480. **Contact:** Susan Protter. Estab. 1971. Member of AAR. Represents 40 clients. 5% of clients are new/unpublished writers. Works with a very small number of new/previously unpublished authors. Currently handles: 50% nonfiction books; 50% novels; occasional magazine article or short story (for established clients only).

● Prior to opening her agency, Ms. Protter was associate director of subsidiary rights at Harper & Row Publishers.

Represents: Nonfiction books, novels. **Considers these nonfiction areas:** Biography/autobiography; current affairs; health/medicine; memoirs; psychology; science/technology; international. **Considers these fiction areas:** Detective/police/crime; mystery/suspense; science fiction; thriller; no screenplays.

O→ Writers must have book-length project or manuscript that is ready to be sold. Does not want to receive westerns, romance, fantasy, children's books, young adult novels, screenplays, plays, poetry, Star Wars or Star Trek.

How to Contact: Currently looking for limited number of new clients. Send short query with SASE. No unsolicited manuscripts. Responds in 3 weeks to queries; 2 months to mss.

Recent Sales: *As Above, So Below*, by Rudy Rucker; *Write to the Point*, by Salvatore J. Iacone; *A Cat on the Bus*, by Lydia Adamson.

Terms: Agent receives 15% commission on domestic sales; 25% commission on foreign sales; 15% commission on dramatic rights sales. "If we request to see your manuscript, there is a $10 minimum handling fee requested to cover cost of returning materials should they not be suitable." Charges clients for photocopying, messenger, express mail, airmail expenses.

Tips: "Please send neat and professionally organized queries. Make sure to include a SASE or we cannot reply. We receive approximately 400 queries a week and read them in the order they arrive. We usually reply within two weeks to any query. Please, do not call or email queries. If you are sending a multiple query, make sure to note that in your letter. I am looking for something outstanding in a large, difficult market."

QUICKSILVER BOOKS—LITERARY AGENTS, 50 Wilson St., Hartsdale NY 10530-2542. (914)946-8748. Fax: (914)946-8748. Website: www.quicksilverbooks.com. **Contact:** Bob Silverstein. Estab. 1973 as packager; 1987 as literary agency. Represents 50 clients. 50% of clients are new/unpublished writers. Currently handles: 75% nonfiction books; 25% novels.
  • Prior to opening his agency, Mr. Silverstein served as senior editor at Bantam Books and Dell Books/Delacorte Press.
Represents: Nonfiction books, novels. **Considers these nonfiction areas:** Anthropology/archaeology; biography/autobiography; business/economics; child guidance/parenting; cooking/foods/nutrition; current affairs; ethnic/cultural interests; health/medicine; history; how-to; language/literature/criticism; memoirs; nature/environment; New Age/metaphysics; popular culture; psychology; religious/inspirational; science/technology; self-help/personal improvement; sociology; sports; true crime/investigative; women's issues/studies. **Considers these fiction areas:** Action/adventure; glitz; mystery/suspense; thriller.
  ☞ This agency specializes in literary and commercial mainstream fiction and nonfiction (especially psychology, New Age, holistic healing, consciousness, ecology, environment, spirituality, reference, cookbooks, narrative nonfiction). Actively seeking commercial mainstream fiction and nonfiction in most categories. Does not want to receive science fiction, pornography, poetry, or single-spaced manuscripts.
How to Contact: Query with SASE. Authors are expected to supply SASE for return of mss and for query letter responses. No e-mail or fax queries. Considers simultaneous queries. Responds in 2 weeks to queries; 1 month to mss. Returns materials only with SASE. Obtains most new clients through recommendations, listings in sourcebooks, solicitations, workshop participation.
Recent Sales: Sold over 20 titles in the last year. *Pictures from the Heart—A Tarot Dictionary*, by Sandra Thurmon, Ed.D. (St. Martin's); *Quit Bein' a Girl*, Lois Frankel, Ph.D. (Warner Books); *Look Great At Any Age*, by Brad Schoenfeld (Prentice Hall); *Every Woman's Yoga*, by Jaime Stover Schmitt (Prima).
Terms: Agent receives 15% commission on domestic sales; 20% commission on foreign sales. Offers written contract. Charges clients for photocopying of mss and proposals, but prefers authors provide actual copies; foreign mailings of books and mss.
Writers' Conferences: National Writers Union Conference (Dobbs Ferry NY, April).
Tips: "Write what you know. Write from the heart."

SUSAN RABINER, LITERARY AGENT, INC., 240 W. 35 St., Suite 500, New York NY 10001-2506. (212)279-0316. Fax: (212)279-0932. E-mail: susan@rabiner.net. **Contact:** Susan Rabiner.
  • Prior to becoming an agent, Susan Rabiner was editorial director of Basic Books, then the serious nonfiction division of HarperCollins Publishers. She is the co-author of *Thinking Like Your Editor: How to Write Great Serious Nonfiction and Get it Published* (W.W. Norton).
Member Agents: Susan Rabiner, Susan Arellano.
Represents: Nonfiction books, textbooks. **Considers these nonfiction areas:** Biography; business; education; history; psychology; science.
  ☞ Does not want to receive fiction, personal memoirs, self-help.
How to Contact: Submit outline/proposal, SASE. Accepts e-mail queries. No fax queries. Considers simultaneous queries. Responds in 3 weeks to queries. Returns materials only with SASE. Obtains most new clients through recommendations from others.
Recent Sales: Sold 10-20 titles in the last year. *To the Tower of Babel: How Children Learn by Speak*, by Charles Yang (Scribner); *Trapped*, by Elizabeth Warren and Amelia Tyagi Warren (Basic Books); *Icebound*, by Gay & Laney Salisbury (W.W. Norton); *Honor Killing*, by David Stannard (Viking-Penguin). Other clients include Iris Chang, author of *The Rape of Nanking*; Lawrence Krauss, author of *The Physics of Star Trek*; Daniel Schacter, author of *Searching for Memory*; Herbert Bix, author of *Hirohito and the Making of Modern Japan*; Bruce Tulgan, *Winning the Talent Wars*; Stephanie Coontz, author of *The Way We Never Were*.
Terms: Agent receives 15% commission on domestic sales; 20% commission on foreign sales. Offers written contract; 30-day notice must be given to terminate contract. Charges clients for postage to foreign publishers.

[N] CHARLOTTE CECIL RAYMOND, LITERARY AGENT, 32 Bradlee Rd., Marblehead MA 01945. **Contact:** Charlotte Cecil Raymond. Estab. 1983. Currently handles: 90% nonfiction books; 10% novels.
Represents: Nonfiction books. **Considers these nonfiction areas:** Biography/autobiography; current affairs; ethnic/cultural interests (cultural, gender interests); history; nature/environment; psychology; sociology.
  ☞ Does not want to receive self-help/personal improvement, science fiction, fantasy, young adult, poetry, screenplays.
How to Contact: Query with SASE, submit proposal package, outline. Responds in 2 weeks to queries; 6 weeks to mss.
Terms: Agent receives 15% commission on domestic sales. 100% of business is derived from commissions on ms sales.

HELEN REES LITERARY AGENCY, 123 N. Washington St., 2nd Floor, Boston MA 02114. (617)723-5232, ext. 233 or 222. **Contact:** Joan Mazmanian, Ann Collette, Barbara Rifkind. Estab. 1981. Member of AAR. Represents 50 clients. 50% of clients are new/unpublished writers. Currently handles: 60% nonfiction books; 40% novels.

Member Agents: Joan Mazmanian; Ann Collette (literary fiction, women's studies, health, biography, history); Barbara Rifkind (business, money/finance/economics, government/politics/law, contemporary issues).

Represents: Nonfiction books, novels. **Considers these nonfiction areas:** Biography/autobiography; business/economics; current affairs; government/politics/law; health/medicine; history; money/finance; women's issues/studies. **Considers these fiction areas:** Contemporary issues; historical; literary; mainstream/contemporary; mystery/suspense; thriller.

O—¬ This agency specializes in general nonfiction, health, business, world politics, autobiographies, psychology, women's issues.

How to Contact: Query with SASE, outline, 2 sample chapter(s). No e-mail or fax queries. Responds in 2 weeks to queries; 3 weeks to mss. Obtains most new clients through recommendations from others, solicitations, conferences.

Recent Sales: Sold 26 titles in the last year. *Interpreting the Declaration of Independence*, by Alan Dershowitz (Wiley); *Why Should Anyone Be Led By You*, by Rob Goffee and Gareth Jones (Harvard Business School Press); *Killing Time*, by Elise Title (St. Martin's Press).

Terms: Agent receives 15% commission on domestic sales; 20% commission on foreign sales.

JODY REIN BOOKS, INC., 7741 S. Ash Court, Littleton CO 80122. (303)694-4430. Fax: (303)694-0687. E-mail: jodyrein@jodyreinbooks.com. Website: JodyReinBooks.com. **Contact:** Winnefred Dollar. Estab. 1994. Member of AAR, Authors Guild. Currently handles: 80% nonfiction books; 20% novels.

● Prior to opening her agency, Jody Rein worked for 13 years as an acquisitions editor for Contemporary Books, Bantam/Doubleday/Dell and Morrow/Avon.

Member Agents: Jody Rein; Alexandra Philippe (screenwriting); Mary Cullens.

Represents: Nonfiction books (primarily narrative and commercial nonfiction), novels (select literary novels, commercial mainstream and mystery), movie scripts (some). **Considers these nonfiction areas:** Business/economics; child guidance/parenting; creative nonfiction; current affairs; ethnic/cultural interests; government/politics/law; health/medicine; history; how-to; humor/satire; music/dance; nature/environment; popular culture; psychology; religious/inspirational; science/technology; self-help/personal improvement; sociology; theater/film; women's issues/studies. **Considers these fiction areas:** Literary; mainstream/contemporary; mystery/suspense.

O—¬ This agency specializes in commercial and narrative nonfiction.

How to Contact: Query with SASE. No e-mail or fax queries. Considers simultaneous queries. Responds in 6 weeks to queries; 2 months to mss. Obtains most new clients through recommendations from others.

Recent Sales: *8 Simple Rules for Dating My Daughters*, by Bruce Cameron (Workman); *Think Like a Genius*, by Todd Siler (Bantam); *The ADDed Dimension*, by Kate Kelly (Scribner); *Picasso's War*, by Russell Martin (Dutton); *The Lakota Way*, by Joseph Marshall III (Viking Penguin); *Skeletons on the Zaharah*, by Dean King (Little, Brown).

Terms: Agent receives 15% commission on domestic sales; 25% commission on foreign sales. Offers written contract. Charges clients for express mail, overseas expenses, photocopying ms.

Tips: "Do your homework before submitting. Make sure you have a marketable topic and the credentials to write about it. Well-written books on exciting nonfiction topics that have broad appeal. Novels written by authors who have spent years developing their craft. Authors must be well established in their fields and have strong media experience."

JODIE RHODES LITERARY AGENCY, 8840 Villa La Jolla Dr., Suite 315, La Jolla CA 92037-1957. (858)625-0544. Fax: (858)625-0544. **Contact:** Jodie Rhodes, president. Estab. 1998. Member of AAR. Represents 50 clients. 60% of clients are new/unpublished writers. Currently handles: 60% nonfiction books; 35% novels; 5% middle to young adult books.

● Prior to opening her agency, Ms. Rhodes was a university level creative writing teacher, workshop director, published novelist and Vice President Media Director at the N.W. Ayer Advertising Agency.

Member Agents: Jodie Rhodes, president; Clark McCutcheon (fiction); Bob McCarter (nonfiction).

Represents: Nonfiction books, novels, juvenile books. **Considers these nonfiction areas:** Biography/autobiography; child guidance/parenting; ethnic/cultural interests; government/politics/law; health/medicine; history; memoirs; military/war; science/technology; women's issues/studies. **Considers these fiction areas:** Contemporary issues; ethnic; family saga; historical; juvenile; literary; mainstream/contemporary; mystery/suspense; thriller; young adult; women's.

O—¬ Actively seeking "writers passionate about their books with a talent for richly textured narrative, an eye for details, and a nose for research." Nonfiction writers must have recognized credentials and expert knowledge of their subject matter. Does not want to receive erotica, horror, fantasy, romance, science fiction.

How to Contact: Query with brief synopsis, first 30 to 50 pages and SASE. No e-mail or fax queries. Considers simultaneous queries. Responds in 10 days to queries. Returns materials only with SASE. Obtains most new clients through recommendations from others, agent sourcebooks.

insider report

The way to an agent's heart

Jodie Rhodes has been a literary agent for four years, but is certainly no newcomer to the publishing industry. She's a published novelist who has also been an editor, creative writing teacher, and advertising executive. She also writes columns for writers' magazines, gives seminars at The Learning Annex, and conducts writers' workshops. Rhodes has an impressive track record of sales and is known for nurturing writers with publishing potential.

Jodie Rhodes

What first drew you to agenting?
Indignation, actually. I'd been doing workshops and heard these horror stories about how agents treated new writers. I decided to become an agent who'd be an advocate for new writers and give them a helping hand. I admit I was a bit naïve in those days. I couldn't understand why agents wouldn't at least take a moment to write a little personal note, a helpful critique tip for writers. Now that I know the volume of mail we all get, I realize agents would be hard pressed to perform that courtesy. [However,] I continue to send personal handwritten notes to writers who clearly have talent and a book with potential.

What qualifications do you have for a manuscript before you'll consider offering to represent it?
It must make my eyes light up. It must speak to me in some way, say things that intrigue me, that I want to learn, that I care about. It's like a blind date. Either the chemistry is there or it isn't. I should add that first it must pass the acid test of writing skill. I can tell in the opening paragraph on page one if the writer has talent.

Does the personality of a writer affect your decision to take him on as a client?
Absolutely! All my writers are my friends. I know about their lives, their families, their problems and struggles. It takes enormous energy and dedication to properly market a writer. So I have to care about them. An arrogant writer, a writer that nags you and calls all the time, an inconsiderate, demanding or rude writer, they could have ten bestsellers to offer me and I wouldn't represent them.

In what ways can working with a smaller, newer agency such as yours be an advantage to writers?
In my opinion, the best agent a new unpublished writer can find is an agent who's been in business less than five years and has had impressive successes—by that, I mean sold at least 12-15 books with at least 4-6 to the giant New York houses. They should have sold a variety of books (novels, narrative nonfiction, hard nonfiction, etc.), and had some significant advances.

At this stage we're still hungry, still very much in the growing stage, ready to focus all our energy on every writer we represent. For example, when I sign a writer and they send me the final edited version of their manuscript or proposal, within one week it's on its way to editors. Large agencies often take [longer].

Also in large agencies the new writer is the small fish in the big pond and unless they have a very hot property, they're not going to be a priority. The other thing is as agencies grow, they build a stable of established writers who turn out a book every year or so that sells with very little effort because they already have an audience base. We have to work 100 times harder to sell a new writer.

You've also been a tenacious advocate for your writers, continually submitting manuscripts after rounds of rejections. Please tell a recent success story where this paid off.

I'm glad you asked that because it allows me to tell you two important ways I help writers get published. I constantly receive submissions for novels by writers with fascinating backgrounds in medicine, various science fields and technology. Recently I received one from a pediatric opthamologist, clinical professor at the Jules Stein Eye Institute and Medical Consultant to the Los Angeles Unified School District.

I could tell immediately the novel wouldn't sell, so I wrote and asked him if he'd ever considered writing a parenting book on eye care for children. He wrote back that he actually had thought about it. In no time at all, I'd sent him the proper format for a proposal and then I worked hard with him in writing it, did a fair amount of editing, finally said it was ready and launched my e-mail marketing pitch.

Everything was right about this, as far as I was concerned. The author's credentials couldn't be better. He had a very warm, accessible writing style. And he had very important things to say.

I went to eight key health/parenting editors. To my horror, only two asked for the book. I couldn't believe it. I dug deeper and sent out another eight pitches. Only one replied. Sweating now, I went through *Publishers Weekly* for every publisher who handled health, medicine and parenting books. I went places I'd never been before and had my memory jarred that Random House had acquired Prima.

I finally got nine editors who wanted to see it. One said she'd be interested if he'd rewrite it focusing only on the connection between eye problems and learning problems. After several weeks, I had five rejections for reasons that stunned me. Nobody believed parents were concerned enough about their kids' eyes to buy a book. They just sent them to a doctor for checkups.

We were getting nowhere. So I sent an e-mail alert, telling the editors who still hadn't replied that I had an interested editor with a conditional offer based on the author revising the proposal and where did they stand?

All replied in five minutes. None had gotten around to reading it and promised to do so as soon as possible. My extra research paid off. Alice Feinstein, editorial director for Random House's health imprint Prima read the proposal Monday morning and called me with a terrific offer—a handsome five figure advance—at noon. They're going to support it with an incredible three month marketing promotion plan and are interested in new books by the author.

What can a writer do to make a query letter stand out in a professional manner?

Be professional up front. Writers should create their own letterhead, type a crisp, clean, error-free letter, address it to the contact person at the agency (not sir, madam, agent, to whom it may concern) and use short paragraphs. Next, tell us something that intrigues us in strong simple language. In one short paragraph give a picture of the protagonist, the plot and the conflict that drives it.

What query faux pas turn you off?

Sure death is to praise your book, telling us it's original, unique, provocative, compelling, haunting, spellbinding, memorable, heartrending, etc. This garbage spews forth from 95 percent of query letters. Comparing your book to bestsellers by celebrity authors is another fatal error, informing us how much your friends and family loved it, and addressing us by our first names. Long rambling paragraphs turn us off and stop us from reading. I can't tell you how many writers' query letters consist of a one-page-long unbroken paragraph.

Should an author submit multiple queries, and should he admit it if he does?

Writers who don't make multiple submissions put themselves at a terrible disadvantage. To sell your house, you get an agent who puts it into their multiple listings. Personally I don't think writers should state this if it's a multiple query letter. Every time I read that, it feels like a threat for me to get on the ball and respond quickly. When writers don't mention the matter, I know they've sent out multiple queries.

The time to tell agents of other agent contacts is when an agent asks to see either part or all of the manuscript. A writer should absolutely inform other agents of this.

Are you looking for any specific types of literature right now more than others?

I'm enormously interested in multicultural books, both fiction and nonfiction, as well as African American literature. The publishing industry has been hopelessly behind in realizing what a huge Spanish reading audience exists in this country. However, they are finally beginning to get the picture. Books about Asia and, increasingly, books about Eastern Europe and the Middle East are also in demand. A tremendous market exists for popular science books by authors with strong credentials and impressive academic and research backgrounds. Legal thrillers and true crime books are always in vogue. Parenting books continue to be hot, but you have to present something new and important and have the credentials to back it up.

Any other tips for writers?

Your fellow writers are your competition. There are writers out there who've spent years researching their book, and that marvelous stamp of authenticity shows. If you've spent all your time writing and no time researching, you're setting yourself up for rejection.

Do not write in the dark. Every writer needs an objective eye to view their work. Get knowledgeable, professional editorial guidance and never count on what your friends, family and friendly writer groups tell you.

People will tell you the key to success is perseverance. Wrong. I know all too many writers who've persevered for years and will always be rejected. That's because they think it's their book that's wrong and so write another, and when that's rejected, write another. They don't understand it's their writing that's being rejected because they carry every mistake with them to the new book. The key to success is *enlightened* perseverance. Find out why you're getting rejected. Until you find out and fix it, you'll never be published.

—Rachel Vater

Recent Sales: Sold 32 titles in the last year. *Odyssey of Healing*, by Aaron Filler (Oxford University Press); *Living in a Black and White World*, by Ann Pearlman (John Wiley & Sons); *Like Sound Through Water*, by Karen Foli (Simon & Schuster); *Eyes of a Child*, by Robert Clark (Random House); *Dying to be Thin*, by Tara and Linda Rio (Rodale); *Sapphire's Grave*, by Hilda Highgate (Doubleday).

Terms: Agent receives 15% commission on domestic sales; 20% commission on foreign sales. Offers written contract; 30-day notice must be given to terminate contract. Charges clients for fax, photocopying, phone calls and postage. "Charges are itemized and approved by writers upfront."

Writers' Conferences: Southern California Writers Conference (San Diego, mid-February); SDSU Writers Conference (San Diego, mid-January); Los Angeles Writers' Conference (Los Angeles, mid-October).

Tips: "Think your book out before you write it. Do your research, know your subject matter intimately, write vivid specifics, not bland generalities. Care deeply about your book. Don't imitate other writers. Find your own voice. We never take on a book we don't believe in, and we go the extra mile for our writers. We welcome talented new writers. We hold monthly weekend clinics on how to write a query letter and weekly writing workshops for area writers."

ANGELA RINALDI LITERARY AGENCY, P.O. Box 7877, Beverly Hills CA 90212-7877. (310)842-7665. Fax: (310)837-8143. E-mail: info@rinaldiliterary.com. **Contact:** Angela Rinaldi. Estab. 1994. Member of AAR. Represents 50 clients. Currently handles: 50% nonfiction books; 50% novels.

● Prior to opening her agency, Ms. Rinaldi was an editor at New American Library, Pocket Books and Bantam, and the Manager of Book Development for *The Los Angeles Times*.

Represents: Nonfiction books, novels, TV and motion picture rights for clients only. **Considers these nonfiction areas:** Biography/autobiography; business/economics; child guidance/parenting; current affairs; health/medicine; money/finance; popular culture; psychology; self-help/personal improvement; sociology; true crime/investigative; women's issues/studies. **Considers these fiction areas:** Literary; mainstream/contemporary.

O➤ Actively seeking commercial and literary fiction. Does not want to receive scripts, category romances, children's books, westerns, science fiction/fantasy and cookbooks.

How to Contact: For fiction: Send the first 3 chapters, brief synopsis, SASE. For nonfiction: Query with SASE first or send outline/proposal, SASE. Do not send metered mail as SASE. Considers simultaneous queries. Please advise if this is a multiple submission. Responds in 6 weeks to queries. Returns materials only with SASE.

Recent Sales: *Stepwives: Ten Steps to Help Ex-wives and Stepmothers*, by Lynne Oxhorn, Louise Oxhorn, and Marjorie Krausz (Simon & Schuster); *Zen Golf: Mastering the Mental Game*, by Dr. Joseph Parent (Doubleday); *Who Moved My Cheese?*, by Dr. Spencer Johnson (Putnam); *Breach of Confidence*, by Eben Paul Perison (NAL/ Signet).

Terms: Agent receives 15% commission on domestic sales; 20% commission on foreign sales. Offers written contract. Charges clients for photocopying if client doesn't supply copies for submission.

ANN RITTENBERG LITERARY AGENCY, INC., 1201 Broadway, Suite 708, New York NY 10001. (212)684-6936. Fax: (212)684-6929. **Contact:** Ann Rittenberg, president. Associate: Susannah Susman. Estab. 1992. Member of AAR. Represents 35 clients. 40% of clients are new/unpublished writers. Currently handles: 50% nonfiction books; 50% novels.

Represents: Nonfiction books, novels. **Considers these nonfiction areas:** Biography/autobiography; gardening; history (social/cultural); memoirs; travel; women's issues/studies. **Considers these fiction areas:** Literary.

O➤ This agent specializes in literary fiction and literary nonfiction.

How to Contact: Submit outline, 3 sample chapter(s), SASE. Considers simultaneous queries. Responds in 6 weeks to queries; 2 months to mss. Obtains most new clients through referrals from established writers and editors.

Recent Sales: Sold 20 titles in the last year. *The New York Night*, by Mark Caldwell (Scribner 2003); *Seven Blessings*, by Ruchama King (St. Martin's Press 2003); *Sweet Dream Baby*, by Sterling Watson (Sourcebooks 2002).

Terms: Agent receives 15% commission on domestic sales; 20% commission on foreign sales. Offers written contract. Charges clients for photocopying only.

RIVERSIDE LITERARY AGENCY, 1052 Weatherhead Hollow, Guilford VT 05301. (802)257-2677. Fax: (802)257-8907. E-mail: rivlit@sover.net. **Contact:** Susan Lee Cohen. Estab. 1991. Represents 40 clients. 20% of clients are new/unpublished writers.

Represents: Nonfiction books (adult), novels (adult), very selective.

How to Contact: Query with SASE, outline. Accepts e-mail queries. No fax queries. Considers simultaneous queries. Responds in 1 month to queries. Obtains most new clients through referrals.

Recent Sales: Sold 14 titles in the last year. *Letters to a Young Therapist*, by Mary Pipher, Ph.D. (Basic Books); *Mindfulness and Money*, by Kulananda and Dominic Houlder (Broadway).

Terms: Agent receives 15% commission on domestic sales. Offers written contract. Charges clients for foreign postage, photocopying large manuscripts, express mail deliveries, etc.

Making a personal life public

Ann Pearlman has lived an extraordinary life—the stuff of films. Whether the subject matter is poverty, racism, gang warfare, psychology or even the inside world of pro football, her list of qualifications for writing on the topic is a mile long. From her beginnings as the privileged daughter of the Jewish intellectual class, Pearlman went on archeological digs, worked with prostitutes in London and spent time in Paris with exiles from communist Europe. After receiving her Master's degree from Case Western University, she worked in school systems, protective services, a women's prison, a children's guidance clinic and even helped run a poverty program for the city of Cincinnati before starting her private practice as a psychotherapist, which she continues to this day.

Ann Pearlman

Pearlman's book *Keep the Home Fires Burning: How to Have an Affair with Your Spouse*, published in 1985, garnered her two appearances on both *Oprah* and the *Sally Jessy Raphael* television shows. Ironically, she would later find that her husband of thirty years had been unfaithful. The marriage ended in divorce and to extradite herself from her feelings, she began journaling. Late at night with the monitor turned off, she typed on her computer and *Infidelity: A Memoir*, was the result. Between drafts, she began dealing with childhood memories of her father's adultery. At the end of several years, she had a strong draft. Her main motivation had changed from working out feelings to exploring the subject of adultery and the dilemma it presents to us as human beings.

As Pearlman proceeded with the writing and publishing of the book, she would have to face the response of her family, including her ex-husband. "I encouraged my children to read *Infidelity* before I did the final version wanting their feedback as well as wanting to discuss any issues the book may have evoked. I gave a copy of the book, once it was in galleys, to my ex-husband telling him that if he had objections I would consider making changes. He called that night saying the book was an absolute page-turner. He went on to say that what was in the book was an artistic judgement of mine and he would not interfere."

Writing *Infidelity* was not only about telling her own story and working through a painful loss but also about telling the truth in hopes that others who identify might benefit. Pearlman believes in facing the truth and, as a therapist, understands the healthful, helpful benefits of telling each other about our real lives. "I listen to people discuss their feelings and difficult events every day. Therapists know a family is as sick as the secrets it keeps. There is no point in writing if the writer isn't as honest as possible."

The book would be a kick-off for literary agent Jodie Rhodes' career. She had opened her own agency and was beginning to second-guess the endeavor when she first heard from Pearlman. "This brilliant manuscript titled *Infidelity* showed up in a pile of other submissions. I read it nonstop, hardly able to believe my eyes at the power and grace of this writer named Ann

Pearlman," Rhodes exclaims. Rhodes enthusiastically shopped the book and it went on to be published in hardcover by MacAdam Cage and trade paper by Broadway, who paid $250,000 in a heated auction for the rights. Later, London powerhouse Hodder Stoughton bought UK and Commonwealth rights, where it was serialized in the *LondonObserver's Sunday* magazine and in Sydney, Australia's Morning Herald Sunday magazine. Lion's Gate optioned the movie rights. But it didn't happen for Pearlman on the first try. She received more than thirty rejections before making her connection with Rhodes. It proved a blessed connection for them both. "Ann Pearlman will always be a very special writer to me," agent Jodie Rhodes says. "I probably wouldn't be an agent today if it weren't for her."

Writing on infidelity would not be Ann Pearlman's last foray into the deep waters of personal experience and social ills. As a social worker and therapist, she has for many years seen the damage of racism in the civil rights movement, universities, city governments, professional sports, ghettos, prisons and hospitals. She has also experienced it firsthand. Her new book, *Living in a Black and White World*, addresses racism, the most divisive issue in our country, in a way that's never been presented before: from the perspective of a white woman.

Pearlman has lived in both black and white worlds. She is white, her former husband, a professional football player, is black, and she is mother to adopted and natural biracial children. Married to a black man, she experienced the impact of race and the cultural differences. "I was accepted into a rich black culture during an era of limitless hope and change," she confides. "That acceptance contrasted with my liberal parents' anxiety about my relationship." From its start, her interracial relationship brought threat, even from within her own family. Her father tried to have her boyfriend arrested for dating her because he was black. She was also verbally abused and threatened with rape by whites for being with a black man. She even saw a very close white friend murdered for loving a Black Panther.

Because of her intimate relationships, she has seen racism infect the spirits and psyches of both blacks and whites. When asked whether she is concerned about fallout from writing such a highly charged, almost-taboo subject, Pearlman says, "*Living in Black and White World* will not be a politically correct book. I have seen political correctness redefined as quickly as the current term to describe black people from colored to Negro to black to Afro-American to African-American. Speaking the truth as I see it may be helpful; careful platitudes are not. Portraying events in my life and how they felt, tasted, and smelled lets others into my world and adds to our examination and understanding of race. Preconceived ideas about people tumble down with knowledge."

Pearlman's vocation as a social worker and psychotherapist has afforded her additional views of racism in America and its changes over time. There have been some vast improvements in the lives of African-Americans, she observes. "There's a larger black middle class; white people have become more accepting in their expressed attitudes toward blacks. Yet, forty-five percent of whites and sixty-six percent of blacks say relations between the races will always be a problem. According to statistics from 1999, our overall rate of poverty is twelve percent, yet twenty four percent of blacks live in poverty with the concomitant threefold increase of mental disorder and distress. So, in spite of our progress, racism remains a cancer that threatens to weaken all of us."

It could be considered that Pearlman has put herself back in the line of fire by writing on such a controversial topic. But her motivation for writing *Black and White* is simple. She hopes to be part of the change in this country's problem of racism. "There is still no level playing field in this country. Every day, black people are unsure if reactions to them are a result of race or their talents and character. White people are by and large oblivious to this dynamic. Or in denial regarding their complicity in it. On the other hand, many blacks struggle with the incorporation of racial self-hatred that is the end result of racism. I'm hopeful that this book may help. My experiences and those of my children will augur some circumstances for future families. This story is my family's story; it is also America's story." *Living in a Black and White World* quickly sold, with the help of Pearlman's agent Jodie Rhodes, and will be published by Wiley in the spring of 2003.

Asked about the challenges of divulging personal feelings and experiences in a literary work, Pearlman responds, "It's really no different than writing anything. We always incorporate our feelings, one way or another, and regardless of how well we disguise them, incorporate our experiences. My fiction utilized my feelings, experiences, and fantasies. Writing a memoir, particularly one which uses fictive techniques (setting scenes, dialogue, using the present tense for past events) seemed like an easy slide. I just had to edit out the fantasy. Truth is, after all, only as we experience it, interpret it. Like the movie, *Rashomon*, each of us has our unique viewpoint of the same events."

Pearlman contends that her success as a writer has not changed her. "I still work as a psychotherapist, I still write every day from 8 a.m. until noon, I still don't have absolute security that every one of my books will be published. On the other hand, I'd been writing fiction for over a decade and there were times when I thought I was nuts— sitting around in a bathrobe giving myself carpal tunnel syndrome. Now, my writing seems legitimatized."

It is always hard to translate a life into a book, and not everyone is willing to make public his or her most personal experience. Ann Pearlman has encountered great personal challenges yet faced them down with the creative and productive response of writing and, at the same time, continued to be an advocate for others. Her life is a tribute to acceptance and perseverance, and her books bring home the power and best use of the written word.

—*Terri See*

RLR ASSOCIATES, LTD., 7 W. 51st St., New York NY 10019. (212)541-8641. Fax: (212)541-6052. Website: www.rlrassociates.net/literary. **Contact:** Jennifer Unter, Ezra Fitz. Represents 50 clients. 25% of clients are new/unpublished writers. Currently handles: 70% nonfiction books; 25% novels; 5% story collections.
Member Agents: Jennifer Unter, Ezra Fitz.
Represents: Nonfiction books, novels, short story collections, scholarly books. **Considers these nonfiction areas:** Animals; anthropology/archaeology; art/architecture/design; biography/autobiography; business/economics; child guidance/parenting; cooking/foods/nutrition; current affairs; education; ethnic/cultural interests; gay/lesbian issues; government/politics/law; health/medicine; history; humor/satire; interior design/decorating; language/literature/criticism; memoirs; money/finance; multicultural; music/dance; nature/environment; photography; popular culture; psychology; religious/inspirational; science/technology; self-help/personal improvement; sociology; sports; translation; travel; true crime/investigative; women's issues/studies. **Considers these fiction areas:** Action/adventure; comic books/cartoon; contemporary issues; detective/police/crime; ethnic; experimental; family saga; feminist; gay/lesbian; historical; horror; humor/satire; literary; mainstream/contemporary; multicultural; mystery/suspense; sports; thriller.

○─ "We provide a lot of editorial assistance to our clients and have connections." Actively seeking fiction (all types except for romance and fantasy), current affairs, history, art, popular culture, health, business. Does not want to receive romance or fantasy; screenplays.
How to Contact: Query with SASE. Does not accept e-mail queries. Considers simultaneous queries. Responds in 5 weeks to queries; 5 weeks to mss. Returns materials only with SASE. Obtains most new clients through recommendations from others.
Recent Sales: Sold 20 titles in the last year. Other clients include Shelby Foote, The Grief Recovery Institute, Don Wade, Don Zimmer, The Knot.com, David Plowder, PGA of America, Danny Peary, Jahnna Beecham & Malcolm Hillgartner.

Terms: Agent receives 15% commission on domestic sales; 20% commission on foreign sales. Offers written contract.

Tips: "Please check out our website for more details on our agency. No e-mail submissions please."

B.J. ROBBINS LITERARY AGENCY, 5130 Bellaire Ave., North Hollywood CA 91607-2908. (818)760-6602. Fax: (818)760-6616. E-mail: robbinsliterary@aol.com. **Contact:** (Ms.) B.J. Robbins. Estab. 1992. Member of Board of Directors, PEN American Center West. Represents 40 clients. 50% of clients are new/unpublished writers. Currently handles: 50% nonfiction books; 50% novels.

Member Agents: Rob McAndrews (commercial fiction).

Represents: Nonfiction books, novels. **Considers these nonfiction areas:** Biography/autobiography; child guidance/parenting; current affairs; ethnic/cultural interests; health/medicine; how-to; humor/satire; memoirs; music/dance; popular culture; psychology; self-help/personal improvement; sociology; sports; theater/film; true crime/investigative; women's issues/studies. **Considers these fiction areas:** Contemporary issues; detective/police/crime; ethnic; literary; mainstream/contemporary; mystery/suspense; sports; thriller.

How to Contact: Submit 3 sample chapter(s), outline/proposal, SASE. No e-mail or fax queries. Considers simultaneous queries. Responds in 2 weeks to queries; 6 weeks to mss. Returns materials only with SASE. Obtains most new clients through conferences, referrals.

Recent Sales: Sold 15 titles in the last year. *Please, Please, Please*, by Renee Swindle (Dial Press); *Katie.com*, by Katherine Tarbox (Dutton); *Quickening*, by Laura Catherine Brown (Random House/Ballantine); *Snow Mountain Passage*, by James D. Houston (Knopf); *The Last Summer*, by John Hough, Jr. (Simon & Schuster).

Terms: Agent receives 15% commission on domestic sales; 20% commission on foreign sales. Offers written contract; 3-month notice must be given to terminate contract. 100% of business is derived from commissions on ms sales. Charges clients for postage and photocopying only. Writers charged for fees only after the sale of ms.

Writers' Conferences: Squaw Valley Fiction Writers Workshop (Squaw Valley CA, August); Maui Writers Conference (Maui HI); SDSU Writers Conference (San Diego CA, January).

THE ROBBINS OFFICE, INC., 405 Park Ave., New York NY 10022. (212)223-0720. Fax: (212)223-2535. **Contact:** Kathy P. Robbins, owner.

Member Agents: David Halpern, Sandy Bontemps (foreign rights).

Represents: Nonfiction books, novels. **Considers these nonfiction areas:** Biography/autobiography; government/politics/law (political commentary); language/literature/criticism (criticism); memoirs; investigative journalism. **Considers these fiction areas:** Literary; mainstream/contemporary (commercial); poetry.

  O— This agency specializes in selling serious nonfiction, commercial and literary fiction.

How to Contact: Accepts submissions by referral only.

Recent Sales: *Loose Lips*, by Claire Berlinski (Random House); *Me Times Three*, by Alex Witchel (Knopf); *The Natural*, by Joe Klein (Doubleday).

Terms: Agent receives 15% commission on domestic sales; 15% commission on foreign sales; 15% commission on dramatic rights sales. Bills back specific expenses incurred in doing business for a client.

LINDA ROGHAAR LITERARY AGENCY, INC., 133 High Point Dr., Amherst MA 01002. (413)256-1921. Fax: (413)256-2636. E-mail: lroghaar@aol.com. Website: www.lindaroghaar.com. **Contact:** Linda L. Roghaar. Estab. 1996. Represents 50 clients. 40% of clients are new/unpublished writers. Currently handles: 90% nonfiction books; 10% novels.

  ● Prior to opening her agency, Ms. Roghaar worked in retail bookselling for 5 years and as a publishers' sales rep for 15 years.

Represents: Nonfiction books, novels. **Considers these nonfiction areas:** Animals; anthropology/archaeology; biography/autobiography; education; history; nature/environment; popular culture; religious/inspirational; self-help/personal improvement; women's issues/studies. **Considers these fiction areas:** Mystery/suspense (amateur sleuth, cozy, culinary, malice domestic).

How to Contact: Query with SASE. Accepts e-mail queries. No fax queries. Considers simultaneous queries and submissions. Responds in 2 months to queries; 4 months to mss.

Recent Sales: *Refrigerator Rights*, by Dr. Will Miller (Penguin Putnam/Perigee); *White China*, by Molly Wolf (Jossey-Bass); *Crooked Heart*, by Cristina Sumners (Bantam); *All Natural Knitting from the Green Mountain Spinnery* (Countryman/W.W. Norton).

Terms: Agent receives 15% commission on domestic sales; negotiable commission on foreign sales. Offers written contract, binding for negotiable time.

THE ROSENBERG GROUP, 23 Lincoln Avenue, Marblehead MA 01945. (781)990-1341. Fax: (781)990-1344. Website: www.rosenberggroup.com. **Contact:** Barbara Collins Rosenberg. Estab. 1998. Member of AAR, recognized agent of the RWA. Represents 32 clients. Currently handles: 30% nonfiction books; 30% novels; 10% scholarly books; 30% textbooks.

  ● Prior to becoming an agent, Barbara was a senior editor for Harcourt.

Member Agents: Barbara Collins Rosenberg

Represents: Nonfiction books, novels, textbooks. **Considers these nonfiction areas:** Current affairs; memoirs; popular culture; psychology; women's issues/studies; women's health; food/wine/beverages; autobiography. **Considers these fiction areas:** Literary; romance; women's.

> O—¬ "Barbara is well-versed in the romance market (both category and single title). She is a frequent speaker at romance conferences. Actively seeking romance category or single title in contemporary "chick-lit," romantic suspense and the historical sub-genres. Does not want to receive time-travel, paranormal, or inspirational/spiritual romances.

How to Contact: Query with SASE. No e-mail or fax queries. Responds in 2 weeks to queries; 6 weeks to mss. Returns materials only with SASE. Obtains most new clients through recommendations from others and conferences.

Recent Sales: Sold 32 titles in the last year. *Dark of Night*, by Dee Davis (Ballantine); *The Lively Shadow*, by Donald Murray (Ballantine); *8 Weeks to a Healthy Dog*, by Shawn Messonnier D.V.M. (Rodale); *Not Your Mother's Mid-Life*, by Marilyn Kentz and Nancy Alspaugh (Andrews McMeel); *Private Maneuvers*, by Cathy Mann (Harlequin).

Terms: Agent receives 15% commission on domestic sales; 15% commission on foreign sales. Offers written contract; 30-day notice must be given to terminate contract. Postage and photocopying limit of $350 per year.

Writers' Conferences: Central Ohio Fiction Writer's Conference (Columbus OH, October); Fun in the Sun Conference (Fort Lauderdale, FL, February 2003).

⊘ RITA ROSENKRANZ LITERARY AGENCY, 440 West End Ave., Suite 15D, New York NY 10024. (212)873-6333. **Contact:** Rita Rosenkranz. Estab. 1990. Member of AAR. Represents 30 clients. 20% of clients are new/unpublished writers. Currently handles: 98% nonfiction books; 2% novels.

• Prior to opening her agency, Rita Rosenkranz worked as an editor in major New York publishing houses.

Represents: Nonfiction books. **Considers these nonfiction areas:** Animals; anthropology/archaeology; art/architecture/design; biography/autobiography; business/economics; child guidance/parenting; computers/electronic; cooking/foods/nutrition; crafts/hobbies; current affairs; ethnic/cultural interests; gay/lesbian issues; government/politics/law; health/medicine; history; how-to; humor/satire; interior design/decorating; language/literature/criticism; military/war; money/finance; music/dance; nature/environment; New Age/metaphysics; photography; popular culture; psychology; religious/inspirational; science/technology; self-help/personal improvement; sports; theater/film; women's issues/studies.

> O—¬ "This agency focuses on adult nonfiction. Stresses strong editorial development and refinement before submitting to publishers, and brainstorms ideas with authors." Actively seeking authors "who are well paired with their subject, either for professional or personal reasons."

How to Contact: Submit proposal package, outline, SASE. No e-mail or fax queries. Considers simultaneous queries. Responds in 2 weeks to queries. Obtains most new clients through solicitations, conferences, word of mouth.

Recent Sales: Sold 35 titles in the last year. *Saving Beauty from the Beast: How to Protect Your Daughter from an Unhealty Relationship*, by Vicki Crompton and Ellen Kessner (Little, Brown); *My Mother's Charms: Timeless Gifts of Family Wisdom*, by Kathleen Oldford (Harper San Francisco).

Terms: Agent receives 15% commission on domestic sales; 20% commission on foreign sales. Offers written contract, binding for 3 years; 60-day written notice must be given to terminate contract. 100% of business is derived from commissions on ms sales. Charges clients for photocopying. Makes referrals to editing service.

Tips: "Identify the current competition for your project to make sure the project is valid. A strong cover letter is very important."

⊘ ROSENSTONE/WENDER, 3 E. 48th St., 10th floor, New York NY 10017. Member of AAR.

• This agency did not respond to our request for information. Query before submitting.

Member Agents: Howard Rosenstone (literary, adult, dramatic); Phyllis Wender (literary, adult, dramatic); Sonia Pabley; Ronald Gwiazda; Susan Perlman Cohen.

◖ THE GAIL ROSS LITERARY AGENCY, 1666 Connecticut Ave. NW, #500, Washington DC 20009. (202)328-3282. Fax: (202)328-9162. E-mail: jennifer@gailross.com. Website: www.gailross.com. **Contact:** Jennifer Manguera. Estab. 1988. Member of AAR. Represents 200 clients. 75% of clients are new/unpublished writers. Currently handles: 95% nonfiction books; 5% novels.

Member Agents: Gail Ross.

Represents: Nonfiction books, novels. **Considers these nonfiction areas:** Anthropology/archaeology; biography/autobiography; business/economics; education; ethnic/cultural interests; gay/lesbian issues; government/politics/law; health/medicine; money/finance; nature/environment; psychology; religious/inspirational; science/technology; self-help/personal improvement; sociology; sports; true crime/investigative. **Considers these fiction areas:** Literary.

> O—¬ This agency specializes in adult trade nonfiction.

How to Contact: Query with SASE. Considers simultaneous queries. Responds in 1 month to queries. Obtains most new clients through recommendations from others.

Recent Sales: Sold 50 titles in the last year. This agency prefers not to share information on specific sales.

Terms: Agent receives 15% commission on domestic sales; 25% commission on foreign sales. Charges for office expenses (i.e., postage, copying).

☑ ◖ ◎ **CAROL SUSAN ROTH, LITERARY REPRESENTATION, (Specialized: health, business, spirituality, self-help)**, PO Box 620337, Woodside CA 94062. (650)323-3795. E-mail: carol@authorsbest.com. **Contact:** Carol Susan Roth. Estab. 1995. Represents 40 clients. 50% of clients are new/unpublished writers. Currently handles: 100% nonfiction books.
- Prior to becoming an agent, Ms. Roth was trained as a psychotherapist and worked as a motivational coach, conference producer and promoter for bestselling authors (e.g. Scott Peck, Bernie Siegal, John Gray) and the Heart of Business conference.

Represents: Nonfiction books. **Considers these nonfiction areas:** Business/economics; health/medicine; money/finance (personal finance/investing); New Age/metaphysics; religious/inspirational; self-help/personal improvement; spirituality.

> O➘ This agency specializes in spirituality, health, personal growth, personal finance, business. Actively seeking previously published authors—experts in health, spirituality, personal growth, business. Does not want to receive fiction.

How to Contact: Submit proposal package, SASE. Accepts e-mail queries, no attachments. Considers simultaneous queries. Responds in 1 week to queries. Returns materials only with SASE. Obtains most new clients through recommendations from others, solicitations.

Recent Sales: Sold 15 titles in the last year. *Two Questions*, by Michael Ray (Scribner); *The Chiropractic Way*, by Michael Lenaaz (Bantam).

Terms: Agent receives 15% commission on domestic sales; 15% commission on foreign sales. Offers written contract, binding for 3 years; 60-day notice must be given to terminate contract. This agency "asks the client to provide postage and do copying." Offers a proposal development and marketing consulting service on request. Service is separate from agenting services.

Writers' Conferences: Maui Writer's Conference (Maui HI, September).

Reading List: Reads *Yoga Journal, New Age, People, Men's Health, Inquiring Mind, Fast Company,* and *Red Herring* to find new clients. Looks for "ability to write and self-promote."

Tips: "Have charisma, content, and credentials—solve an old problem in a new way. I prefer clients with extensive seminar and media experience."

◖ **JANE ROTROSEN AGENCY LLC**, 318 E. 51st St., New York NY 10022. (212)593-4330. Fax: (212)935-6985. E-mail: firstinitiallastname@janerotrosen.com. Estab. 1974. Member of AAR, Authors Guild. Represents over 100 clients. Currently handles: 30% nonfiction books; 70% novels.

Member Agents: Jane R. Berkey; Andrea Cirillo; Annelise Robey; Margaret Ruley; Kara Cesare (director of English-language sub-rights); Perry Gordijn (director of translation rights).

Represents: Nonfiction books, novels. **Considers these nonfiction areas:** Biography/autobiography; business/economics; child guidance/parenting; cooking/foods/nutrition; current affairs; health/medicine; how-to; humor/satire; money/finance; nature/environment; popular culture; psychology; self-help/personal improvement; sports; true crime/investigative; women's issues/studies. **Considers these fiction areas:** Action/adventure; detective/police/crime; family saga; historical; horror; mainstream/contemporary; mystery/suspense; romance; thriller; women's.

How to Contact: Query with SASE. By referral only. No e-mail or fax queries. Responds in 2 months to mss. Responds in 2 weeks (to writers who have been referred by a client or colleague). Returns materials only with SASE.

Recent Sales: Sold 140 titles in the last year. This agency prefers not to share information on specific sales.

Terms: Agent receives 15% commission on domestic sales; 20% commission on foreign sales. Offers written contract, binding for 3-5 years; 60-day notice must be given to terminate contract. Charges clients for photocopying, express mail, overseas postage, book purchase.

☑ ◖ **THE DAMARIS ROWLAND AGENCY**, 5 Peter Cooper Road, Apt. 13H, New York NY 10010. (212)475-8942. Fax: (212)358-9411. **Contact:** Damaris Rowland or Steve Axelrod. Estab. 1994. Member of AAR. Represents 50 clients. 10% of clients are new/unpublished writers. Currently handles: 25% nonfiction books; 75% novels.

Represents: Novels. **Considers these fiction areas:** Historical; literary; mainstream/contemporary; romance (contemporary, gothic, historical, regency); commercial.

> O➘ This agency specializes in women's fiction. Submit query with SASE.

How to Contact: Submit query with SASE. Responds in 6 weeks to queries. Obtains most new clients through recommendations from others, solicitations, conferences.

IF YOU'RE LOOKING for a particular agent, check the Agents Index to find the specific agency where the agent works. Then check the listing for that agency in the appropriate section.

Recent Sales: *The Next Accident*, by Lisa Gardner; *To Trust a Stranger*, by Karen Robard; *Nursing Homes*, by Peter Silin.

Terms: Agent receives 15% commission on domestic sales; 20% commission on foreign sales. Offers written contract; 30-day notice must be given to terminate contract. Charges only if extraordinary expenses have been incurred, e.g., photocopying and mailing 15 mss to Europe for a foreign sale.

Writers' Conferences: Novelists Inc. (Denver, October); RWA National (Texas, July); Pacific Northwest Writers Conference.

THE PETER RUBIE LITERARY AGENCY, 240 W. 35th St., Suite 500, New York NY 10001. (212)279-1776. Fax: (212)279-0927. E-mail: peterrubie@prlit.com. Website: www.prlit.com. **Contact:** Peter Rubie or June Clark. Estab. 2000. Member of AAR. Represents 130 clients. 30% of clients are new/unpublished writers.

- Prior to opening his agency, Mr. Rubie was a founding partner at Perkins, Rubie & Associates and the fiction editor at Walker and Co.

Member Agents: June Clark (New Age, pop culture, gay issues); Peter Rubie (crime, science fiction, fantasy, literary fiction, thrillers, narrative nonfiction, history, commercial science, music).

Represents: Nonfiction books, novels. **Considers these nonfiction areas:** Cooking/foods/nutrition; creative nonfiction; current affairs; ethnic/cultural interests; music/dance; popular culture; science/technology; theater/film; commercial academic material; TV. **Considers these fiction areas:** Action/adventure; detective/police/crime; ethnic; fantasy; gay/lesbian; historical; literary; science fiction; thriller.

How to Contact: Query with SASE. Accepts e-mail queries. No fax queries. Responds in 2 months to queries; 3 months to mss. Returns materials only with SASE. Obtains most new clients through recommendations from others.

Recent Sales: Sold 30 titles in the last year. *The Emperor and the Wolf*, by Stuart Galbraith (Faber and Faber); *Unfinished Business*, by Harlon Ullman (Kensington); *No One Left Behind*, by Amy Yarsinske (Dutton/Signet); *Toward Rational Exuberance* (Farrar, Straus & Giroux); *On Night's Shore*, by Randall Silvis (St. Martin's Press); *Jewboy*, by Allan Kauffman (Fromm); *Einstein's Refrigerator*, by Steve Silverman (Andrews McMeel); *Hope's End*, by Stephen Chambers (TOR).

Terms: Agent receives 15% commission on domestic sales; 20% commission on foreign sales. Offers written contract. Charges clients for photocopying and some foreign mailings.

Tips: "We look for writers who are experts and have an outstanding prose style. Be professional. Read *Publishers Weekly* and genre-related magazines. Join writers' organizations. Go to conferences. Know your market, and learn your craft. Read Rubie's books *The Elements of Storytelling* (Wiley) and *The Writer's Market FAQs* (Writer's Digest Books). Go to our website for up-to-date information on clients and sales."

RUSSELL & VOLKENING, 50 W. 29th St., #7E, New York NY 10001. (212)684-6050. Fax: (212)889-3026. **Contact:** Timothy Seldes. Estab. 1940. Member of AAR. Represents 140 clients. 20% of clients are new/unpublished writers. Currently handles: 45% nonfiction books; 50% novels; 3% story collections; 2% novellas.

Member Agents: Timothy Seldes (nonfiction, literary fiction).

Represents: Nonfiction books, novels, short story collections, novellas. **Considers these nonfiction areas:** Anthropology/archaeology; art/architecture/design; biography/autobiography; business/economics; cooking/foods/nutrition; creative nonfiction; current affairs; education; ethnic/cultural interests; gay/lesbian issues; government/politics/law; health/medicine; history; language/literature/criticism; military/war; money/finance; music/dance; nature/environment; photography; popular culture; psychology; science/technology; sociology; sports; theater/film; true crime/investigative; women's issues/studies. **Considers these fiction areas:** Action/adventure; detective/police/crime; ethnic; literary; mainstream/contemporary; mystery/suspense; picture books; sports; thriller.

○─ This agency specializes in literary fiction and narrative nonfiction.

Recent Sales: *Back when We Were Grownups*, by Anne Tyler (Knopf); *Warriors of God*, by James Reston Jr. (Doubleday); *No Certain Rest*, by Jim Lehrer (Random House).

Terms: Agent receives 15% commission on domestic sales; 20% commission on foreign sales. Charges clients for "standard office expenses relating to the submission of materials of an author we represent, e.g., photocopying, postage."

Tips: "If the query is cogent, well-written, well-presented and is the type of book we'd represent, we'll ask to see the manuscript. From there, it depends purely on the quality of the work."

REGINA RYAN PUBLISHING ENTERPRISES, INC., 251 Central Park W., 7D, New York NY 10024. (212)787-5589. Fax: (212)787-0243. E-mail: rryanbooks@aol.com. **Contact:** Regina Ryan. Estab. 1976. Currently handles: 90% nonfiction books; 5% novels; 5% juvenile books.

- Prior to becoming an agent, Ms. Ryan was an editor at Alfred A. Knopf, editor-in-chief of Macmillan Adult Trade, and a book producer.

Represents: Nonfiction books, novels, short story collections, juvenile books.

How to Contact: Query with SASE or by e-mail at queryrryanbooks@aol.com. Considers simultaneous queries. Responds in 1 month to queries; 6 weeks to mss. Returns materials only with SASE. Obtains most new clients through recommendations from others.

Recent Sales: *Thomas Eakins*, by William I. Homer (Abbeville Press); *How to Build Your Child's Emotional Life*, by Paul Holinger, M.D. (Pocket Books); *We Rode the Orphan Trains*, by Andrea Warren (Houghton Mifflin); *The Uncollected Prose of Dorothy West*, by Lionel Bascon (St. Martin's Press).
Terms: Agent receives 15% commission on domestic sales; 15% commission on foreign sales. Offers written contract; 1-month negotiable notice must be given to terminate contract. Charges clients for all out of pocket expenses, such as long distance, messengers, freight, copying, "if it's more than just a nominal amount."
Tips: "Please send an analysis of the competition. This is essential on nonfiction projects. A sample chapter or two is helpful."

THE SAGALYN AGENCY, 7201 Wisconsin Ave., Suite 675, Bethesda MD 20814. (301)718-6440. Fax: (301)718-6444. E-mail: agency@Sagalyn.com. Website: Sagalyn.com. **Contact:** Raphael Sagalyn. Estab. 1980. Member of AAR. Currently handles: 75% nonfiction books; 25% novels.
Represents: Nonfiction books (history, science, business).
  ○━ Does not want to receive stage plays, screenplays, poetry, science fiction, romance, children's books or young adult books.
How to Contact: No fax queries. Accepts e-mail queries, no attachments. Responds in 6 weeks to queries.
Recent Sales: See website for sales information.
Tips: "We receive between 1,000-1,200 queries a year, which in turn lead to two or three new clients."

VICTORIA SANDERS & ASSOCIATES, 241 Avenue of the Americas, New York NY 10014-4822. (212)633-8811. Fax: (212)633-0525. E-mail: queriesvsa@hotmail.com. Website: www.victoriasanders.com. **Contact:** Victoria Sanders or Diane Dickensheid. Estab. 1993. Member of AAR; signatory of WGA. Represents 75 clients. 25% of clients are new/unpublished writers. Currently handles: 50% nonfiction books; 50% novels.
Member Agents: Imani Wilson (assistant literary agent).
Represents: Nonfiction books, novels. **Considers these nonfiction areas:** Biography/autobiography; current affairs; ethnic/cultural interests; gay/lesbian issues; government/politics/law; history; humor/satire; language/literature/criticism; music/dance; popular culture; psychology; theater/film; translation; women's issues/studies. **Considers these fiction areas:** Action/adventure; contemporary issues; ethnic; family saga; feminist; gay/lesbian; literary; thriller.
How to Contact: Query with SASE. Accepts e-mail queries. No fax queries. Considers simultaneous queries. Responds in 3 weeks to queries; 1 month to mss. Returns materials only with SASE. Obtains most new clients through recommendations from others, or "I find them through my reading and pursue."
Recent Sales: Sold 11 titles in the last year. *Field Hand*, by Karen R. Good (Crown); *Language of Sisters*, by Amy Yurk (Nal/Dutton).
Terms: Agent receives 15% commission on domestic sales; 20% commission on foreign sales. Offers written contract. Charges for photocopying mss, messenger, express mail and extraordinary fees. If in excess of $100, client approval is required.
Tips: "Limit query to letter, no calls, and give it your best shot. A good query is going to get a good response."

SANDUM & ASSOCIATES, 144 E. 84th St., New York NY 10028-2035. (212)737-2011. Fax: (on request). **Contact:** Howard E. Sandum, managing director. Estab. 1987. Represents 35 clients. 20% of clients are new/unpublished writers. Currently handles: 80% nonfiction books; 20% novels.
Represents: Nonfiction books, novels (literary). **Considers these fiction areas:** Literary.
  ○━ This agency specializes in general nonfiction.
How to Contact: Query with proposal, sample pages and SASE. Do not send full ms unless requested. Responds in 2 weeks to queries.
Terms: Agent receives 15% commission on domestic sales; adjustable commission on foreign sales; adjustable commission on dramatic rights sales. Charges clients for photocopying, air express, long-distance telephone/fax.

SCHERF, INC. LITERARY PROPERTIES, P.O. Box 80180, Las Vegas NV 89180-0180. (702)243-4895. Fax: (702)243-7460. E-mail: ds@scherf.com. Website: www.scherf.com/literarymanagement.htm. **Contact:** Dietmar Scherf. Estab. 1999. Currently handles: 10% nonfiction books; 80% novels; 10% novellas.
  ● Prior to opening his agency, Mr. Scherf wrote several nonfiction books, and has been a publisher and editor since 1983. He is also CEO of Scherf Music and Scherf Films.
Member Agents: Mr. Dietmar Scherf (fiction/nonfiction).
Represents: Nonfiction books, novels, novellas. **Considers these nonfiction areas:** Business/economics; how-to; money/finance; popular culture; psychology; religious/inspirational; self-help/personal improvement; true crime/investigative. **Considers these fiction areas:** Action/adventure; literary; mainstream/contemporary; mystery/suspense; thriller.
  ○━ No longer accepting unsolicited queries/submissions. Does not want to receive gay, lesbian, erotica, or anything with foul language.
How to Contact: Query with SASE. No e-mail or fax queries. Considers simultaneous queries. Responds in 2 months to queries; 3 months to mss. Returns materials only with SASE. Obtains most new clients through recommendations from others, writing contests.
Recent Sales: Sold 1 title in the last year. *The Consultant*, by Alec Donzi.

Terms: Agent receives 10-15% commission on domestic sales; 15-20% (depending if new or established author) commission on foreign sales. Offers written contract, binding for variable term; 30-day notice must be given to terminate contract. Charges clients for postage, photocopying. Writers reimbursed for office fees after the sale of ms. May refer new writers to editing service. 0% of business is derived from referrals.

Tips: "Write the best manuscript, and polish it to the max. Write about a story that you love and are enthusiastic about. Learn good writing skills through books, seminars/courses, etc., especially regarding characterization, dialogue, plot, etc. in respect to novels. Know your competition well, and read books from authors that may fall into your category. For novels, your manuscript should have 90,000 to 120,000 words. In nonfiction, do the best research on your subject and be different from your competition with a new approach. While artists are creative individuals, and the business aspect should not be their primary concern when creating a work, the reality of things is that publishing is a business, and publishers look at the commercial potential of each work so they can continue to publish books."

SCHIAVONE LITERARY AGENCY, INC., 236 Trails End, West Palm Beach FL 33413-2135. (561)966-9294. Fax: (561)966-9294. E-mail: profschia@aol.com. Website: www.freeyellow.com/members8/schiavone/index.html. **Contact:** James Schiavone, Ed.D. Estab. 1996. Member of National Education Association. Represents 40 clients. 2% of clients are new/unpublished writers. Currently handles: 50% nonfiction books; 49% novels; 1% textbooks.

- Prior to opening his agency, Dr. Schiavone was a full professor of development skills at the City University of New York and author of 5 trade books and 3 textbooks.

Represents: Nonfiction books, novels, juvenile books, scholarly books, textbooks, movie scripts, feature film, TV movie of the week. **Considers these nonfiction areas:** Animals; anthropology/archaeology; biography/autobiography; child guidance/parenting; current affairs; education; ethnic/cultural interests; gay/lesbian issues; government/politics/law; health/medicine; history; how-to; humor/satire; juvenile nonfiction; language/literature/criticism; military/war; nature/environment; popular culture; psychology; science/technology; self-help/personal improvement; sociology; true crime/investigative. **Considers these fiction areas:** Contemporary issues; ethnic; family saga; historical; horror; humor/satire; juvenile; literary; mainstream/contemporary; science fiction; young adult.

  - ☞ This agency specializes in celebrity biography and autobiography. "We have a management division that handles motion picture and TV rights." Actively seeking serious nonfiction, literary fiction and celebrity biography. Does not want to receive poetry.

How to Contact: Query with SASE. Considers one page e-mail queries with no attachments. Does not accept phone or fax queries. Considers simultaneous queries. Responds in 2 weeks to queries; 6 weeks to mss. Returns materials only with SASE. Obtains most new clients through recommendations from others, solicitations, conferences.

Terms: Agent receives 15% commission on domestic sales; 20% commission on foreign sales. Offers written contract, binding for project period; written notice must be given to terminate contract. Charges clients for long distance, photocopying, postage, special handling. Dollar amount varies with each project depending on level of activity.

Writers' Conferences: Key West Literary Seminar (Key West FL, January); South Florida Writer's Conference (Miami FL, May).

Tips: "I prefer to work with established authors published by major houses in New York. I will consider marketable proposals from new/previously unpublished writers."

SUSAN SCHULMAN, A LITERARY AGENCY, (Specialized: health, business, public policy, self-help, women's issues), 454 W. 44th St., New York NY 10036-5205. (212)713-1633/4/5. Fax: (212)586-8830. E-mail: schulman@aol.com. Website: www.susanschulmanagency.com. **Contact:** Susan Schulman, president. Estab. 1979. Member of AAR, Dramatists Guild, Women's Media Group; signatory of WGA. 10-15% of clients are new/unpublished writers. Currently handles: 70% nonfiction books; 20% novels; 10% stage plays.

Member Agents: Susan Schulman (self-help, health, business, spirituality); Christine Morin (children's books, ecology, natural sciences and business books); Bryan Leifert (plays and pitches for films).

Represents: Nonfiction books, novels. **Considers these nonfiction areas:** Anthropology/archaeology; biography/autobiography; child guidance/parenting; current affairs; education; ethnic/cultural interests; gay/lesbian issues; government/politics/law; health/medicine; history; how-to; juvenile nonfiction; money/finance; music/dance; nature/environment; New Age/metaphysics; popular culture; psychology; religious/inspirational; self-help/personal improvement; sociology; theater/film; translation; true crime/investigative; women's issues/studies. **Considers these fiction areas:** Contemporary issues; detective/police/crime; gay/lesbian; historical; literary; mainstream/contemporary; mystery/suspense; young adult. **Considers these script subject areas:** Comedy; contemporary issues; detective/police/crime; feminist; historical; mainstream; mystery/suspense; psychic/supernatural; religious/inspirational; teen.

  - ☞ This agency specializes in books for, by and about women's issues including family, careers, health and spiritual development, business and sociology, history and economics, government and public policy. Emphasizing contemporary women's fiction and nonfiction books of interest to women.

How to Contact: Query with SASE, outline/proposal. Accepts e-mail and fax queries. Considers simultaneous queries. Responds in 1 week to queries; 6 weeks to mss. Returns materials only with SASE.

Recent Sales: Sold 30 titles in the last year. *God Is No Laughing Matter*, by Julia Cameron (Putnam); *Corporate Irresponsibility*, (Yale). ***Movie/TV MOW script(s) optioned/sold:*** *In the Skin of a Lion*, by Michael Ondaatje (Serendipity Parent Productions); *Holes*, by Louis Sachar (Phoenix Pictures); *Sideways Stories from Wayside School*, by Louis Sachar (Len Oliver Productions).

Terms: Agent receives 15% commission on domestic sales; 7½-10% (plus 7½-10% to co-agent) commission on foreign sales; 10-20% commission on dramatic rights sales. Charges client for special messenger or copying services, foreign mail and any other service requested by client.

■ LAURENS R. SCHWARTZ AGENCY, 5 E. 22nd St., Suite 15D, New York NY 10010-5325. (212)228-2614. **Contact:** Laurens R. Schwartz. Estab. 1984. Represents 100 clients.

Represents: Nonfiction books, novels, general mix of nonfiction and fiction. Also handles movie and TV tie-ins, licensing and merchandising.

How to Contact: Query with SASE. No unsolicited mss. Responds in 1 month to queries. "Have had 18 best-sellers."

Terms: Agent receives 15% commission on domestic sales; 25% commission on foreign sales. "No client fees except for photocopying, and that fee is avoided by an author providing necessary copies or, in certain instances, transferring files on diskette or by e-mail attachment." Where necessary to bring a project into publishing form, editorial work and some rewriting provided as part of service. Works with authors on long-term career goals and promotion.

Tips: "I do not like receiving mass mailings sent to all agents. I am extremely selective—only take on one to three new clients a year. Do not send everything you have ever written. Choose one work and promote that. Always include a SASE. Never send your only copy. Always include a background sheet on yourself and a one-page synopsis of the work (too many summaries end up being as long as the work)."

◆ SCOVIL CHICHAK GALEN LITERARY AGENCY, 381 Park Ave. South, Suite 1020, New York NY 10016. (212)679-8686. Fax: (212)679-6710. E-mail: mailroom@scglit.com. **Contact:** Russell Galen. Estab. 1993. Member of AAR. Represents 300 clients. Currently handles: 70% nonfiction books; 30% novels.

Member Agents: Russell Galen; Jack Scovil; Anna Ghosh.

How to Contact: Accepts e-mail and fax queries. Considers simultaneous queries.

Recent Sales: Sold 100 titles in the last year. *Across the Black Waters*, by Minai Hajratwala (Houghton Mifflin); *The Secret*, by Walter Anderson (HarperCollins); *The Pillars of Creation*, by Terry Goodkind (Tor); *In The Hand of Dante*, by Nick Tosches (Little, Brown).

Terms: Charges clients for photocopying and postage.

⑤ ◆ SEBASTIAN LITERARY AGENCY, The Towers, 172 E. Sixth St., #2005, St. Paul MN 55101. (651)224-6670. Fax: (651)224-6895. E-mail: harperlb@aol.com (query only—no attachments). **Contact:** Laurie Harper. Estab. 1985. Member of AAR, Authors Guild. Represents 50 clients.

- Prior to becoming an agent, Laurie Harper was owner of a small regional publishing company selling mainly to retail bookstores, including B. Dalton and Waldenbooks. She was thus involved in editing, production, distribution, marketing and promotion. She came to publishing with a business and finance background, including eight years in banking.

Represents: Trade nonfiction, select literary fiction. **Considers these nonfiction areas:** Business/economics; creative nonfiction; current affairs; health/medicine; history (popular); money/finance; psychology; science/technology (popular); self-help/personal improvement; sociology; women's issues/studies; consumer reference.

- Ms. Harper is known for working closely with her authors to plan and execute individual short-term and long-term goals. "A successful publishing experience is dependent upon closely coordinated efforts between the writer, the agent, the editor, the publisher's marketing group and sales force, and the booksellers. I give my authors as much advance information as possible so they can work most effectively with the publisher. An author needs every advantage he or she can have, and working closely with the agent can be one of those advantages." Does not want to receive scholarly work, screenplays, children's or young adult work.

How to Contact: Taking new clients selectively; mainly by referral. Considers simultaneous queries. Responds in 3 weeks to queries; 6 weeks to mss. Obtains most new clients through "referrals from authors and editors, but some at conferences and some from unsolicited queries from around the country."

Recent Sales: Sold 25 titles in the last year. *Bald in the Land of Big Hair*, by Joni Rodgers (HarperCollins); *Short Cycle Selling*, by James Kasper (McGraw-Hill); *Two in the Field*, by Darryl Brock (NAL/Dutton); *For All We Know*, by Peter S. Beagle (Simon & Schuster); *Latticework: The New Investing*, by Robert Hagstrom (Texere Pub).

Terms: Agent receives 15% commission on domestic sales; 20% commission on foreign sales. Offers written contract. Charges clients a one-time $100 administration fee and charges for photocopies of ms for submission to publisher.

Writers' Conferences: ASJA; various independent conferences throughout the country.

⬤ **SEDGEBAND LITERARY ASSOCIATES**, 7312 Martha Lane, Fort Worth TX 76112. (817)496-3652. Fax: (425)952-9518. E-mail: queries@sedgeband.com. Website: www.sedgeband.com. **Contact:** David Duperre or Ginger Norton. Estab. 1997. 50% of clients are new/unpublished writers. Currently handles: 50% nonfiction books; 50% novels.

Member Agents: David Duperre (literary, scripts, mystery, suspense); Ginger Norton (romance, horror, nonfiction, mainstream/contemporary).

Represents: Nonfiction books, novels, novellas. **Considers these nonfiction areas:** Biography/autobiography; ethnic/cultural interests; history; true crime/investigative. **Considers these fiction areas:** Action/adventure; experimental; horror; literary; mainstream/contemporary; mystery/suspense; romance.

O⤙ This agency is looking for talented writers who have patience and are willing to work hard. Actively seeking new nonfiction writers, some fiction.

How to Contact: Query with SASE. No phone queries accepted. No full mss. Accepts e-mail queries with no attachments; responds in 1 week. Responds in 4 months to written queries. Responds in 4 months to requested mss. Returns materials only with SASE. Obtains most new clients through queries, the Internet, referrals.

Recent Sales: Sold 28 titles in the last year. *The Torso Murders of Victorian London*, (Mcfarland); *Kiss Me, Kat*, (Lionhearted); *Silent Screams* (Gardenia Press).

Terms: Agent receives 15% commission on domestic sales; 20% commission on foreign sales. Offers written contract, binding for 1 year; 30-day written notice must be given to terminate contract. Charges clients for postage, photocopies, long distance calls, etc., "until we make a sale to an established publisher. We do not charge any reading or retainer fees."

Tips: "We care about writers and books, not just money, but we care about the industry as well. We will not represent anyone who might hurt our clients or our reputation. We expect our writers to work hard and to be patient. Do not send a rude query, it will get you nowhere. If we ask to see your book, send it as soon as possible. Don't wait around or ask a bunch of irrelevant questions about movie rights and so forth, *(at this point we haven't even offered to represent you!).* If you can't write a synopsis, don't bother to query us. Don't handwrite your query or send us samples of your writing that are handwritten—we won't read any of it. Be professional."

⬤ **LYNN SELIGMAN, LITERARY AGENT**, 400 Highland Ave., Upper Montclair NJ 07043. (973)783-3631. **Contact:** Lynn Seligman. Estab. 1985. Member of Women's Media Group. Represents 32 clients. 15% of clients are new/unpublished writers. Currently handles: 85% nonfiction books; 10% novels; 5% photography books.

• Prior to opening her agency, Ms. Seligman worked in the subsidiary rights department of Doubleday and Simon & Schuster, and served as an agent with Julian Bach Literary Agency (now IMG Literary Agency).

Represents: Nonfiction books, novels. **Considers these nonfiction areas:** Anthropology/archaeology; art/architecture/design; biography/autobiography; business/economics; child guidance/parenting; cooking/foods/nutrition; current affairs; education; ethnic/cultural interests; government/politics/law; health/medicine; history; how-to; humor/satire; interior design/decorating; language/literature/criticism; money/finance; music/dance; nature/environment; photography; popular culture; psychology; science/technology; self-help/personal improvement; sociology; theater/film; true crime/investigative; women's issues/studies. **Considers these fiction areas:** Detective/police/crime; ethnic; fantasy; feminist; gay/lesbian; historical; horror; humor/satire; literary; mainstream/contemporary; mystery/suspense; romance (contemporary, gothic, historical, regency); science fiction.

O⤙ This agency specializes in "general nonfiction and fiction. I do illustrated and photography books and represent several photographers for books." This agency does not handle children or young adult books.

How to Contact: Query with SASE, 1 sample chapter(s), outline/proposal. Prefers to read materials exclusively. No e-mail or fax queries. Considers simultaneous queries. Responds in 2 weeks to queries; 2 months to mss. Returns materials only with SASE. Obtains most new clients through referrals from other writers or editors.

Recent Sales: Sold 10 titles in the last year. *Big Fat Lies*, by Dr. Glen Gaesser (Gurze Books); *Watching Weddings*, by Carol McD. Wallace (Penguin Putnam); *A Gentleman at Heart*, by Barbara Pierre (Kensington).

Terms: Agent receives 15% commission on domestic sales; 25% commission on foreign sales. Charges clients for photocopying, unusual postage or telephone expenses (checking first with the author), express mail.

⬤ **EDYTHIA GINIS SELMAN AGENCY**, 14 Washington Place, New York NY 10003. Member of AAR.

• This agency did not respond to our request for information. Query before submitting.

Member Agents: Edythea Ginis Selman; Richard Selman (associate member).

$ ⬤ **THE SEYMOUR AGENCY**, 475 Miner St., Canton NY 13617. (315)386-1831. Fax: (315)386-1037. E-mail: marysue@slic.com. Website: www.theseymouragency.com. **Contact:** Mary Sue Seymour. Estab. 1992. Represents 75 clients. 20% of clients are new/unpublished writers. Currently handles: 50% nonfiction books; 50% novels.

• Ms. Seymour is a retired New York State certified teacher.

Represents: Nonfiction books, novels (romance). **Considers these nonfiction areas:** Agriculture/horticulture; Americana; animals; anthropology/archaeology; art/architecture/design; biography/autobiography; business/economics; child guidance/parenting; computers/electronic; cooking/foods/nutrition; crafts/hobbies; creative nonfiction; current affairs; education; ethnic/cultural interests; gardening; government/politics/law; health/medicine;

history; how-to; interior design/decorating; juvenile nonfiction; language/literature/criticism; memoirs; military/war; money/finance; multicultural; music/dance; nature/environment; philosophy; photography; popular culture; psychology; recreation; religious/inspirational; science/technology; self-help/personal improvement; sex; sociology; sports; theater/film; travel; true crime/investigative; women's issues/studies; young adult. **Considers these fiction areas:** Romance (contemporary, gothic, historical, medieval, regency, etc.); westerns/frontier.

Actively seeking nonfiction and well-written romance. Does not want to receive screenplays, short stories, poetry, general novels.

How to Contact: Query with SASE, synopsis, first 50 pages for romance. Accepts e-mail queries. No fax queries. Considers simultaneous queries. Responds in 1 month to queries; 3 months to mss. Returns materials only with SASE.

Recent Sales: *The Everything Golf Instruction Book* , by Rob Plumer, Ph.D. (Adams Media Corp.); *Heart of a Hunter*, by Betty Davidson (Berkley); *Weddings on a Budget*, by Barbara Cameron (Adams Media Corp.).

Terms: Agent receives 15% commission on domestic sales; 20% commission on foreign sales. Offers written contract, binding for 1 year; Takes 12½% of published author. This agency charges unpublished authors $4.97 for sending out a copy of a manuscript; writers reimbursed for office fees after the sale of ms.

Writers' Conferences: RWA conferences.

Tips: "Send query, synopsis and first 50 pages. If you don't hear from us, you didn't send a SASE. We are looking for nonfiction and romance—women in jeopardy, suspense, contemporary, historical, regency and any well-written fiction and nonfiction by credentialed authors."

THE ROBERT E. SHEPARD AGENCY, 4111 18th St., Suite 3, San Francisco CA 94114-2441. (415)255-1097. E-mail: query@shepardagency.com. Website: www.shepardagency.com. **Contact:** Robert Shepard. Estab. 1994. Member of Authors Guild (associate). Represents 30 clients. 25% of clients are new/unpublished writers. Currently handles: 90% nonfiction books; 10% scholarly books.

- Prior to opening his agency, Mr. Shepard "spent eight and a half years in trade publishing (both editorial and sales/marketing management). I also consulted to a number of major publishers on related subjects."

Represents: Nonfiction books, scholarly books (appropriate for trade publishers). **Considers these nonfiction areas:** Business/economics; current affairs; ethnic/cultural interests; gay/lesbian issues; government/politics/law; history; money/finance; popular culture; science/technology; sociology; sports; women's issues/studies.

This agency specializes in nonfiction, particularly key issues facing society and culture. Other specialties include personal finance, business, gay/lesbian subjects. Actively seeking "works by experts recognized in their fields whether or not they're well-known to the general public and books that offer fresh perspectives or new information even when the subject is familiar." Does not want to receive autobiography, highly visual works, fiction.

How to Contact: Query with SASE. E-mail queries encouraged. Fax and phone queries strongly discouraged. Considers simultaneous queries. Responds in 1 month to queries; 6 weeks to mss. Returns materials only with SASE. Obtains most new clients through recommendations from others, solicitations.

Recent Sales: Sold 10 titles in the last year. Recent titles include the bestselling *Word Freak: Heartbreak, Triumph, Genius, and Obsession in the World of Competitive Scrabble Players*, by Stefan Fatsis (Houghton Mifflin HC, Penguin PB); *Wine & War: The French, the Nazis, and the Battle for France's Greatest Treasure*, by Don and Petie Kladstrup (Broadway Books); *Talking Money*, by Jean Chatzky (Warner Books).

Terms: Agent receives 15% commission on domestic sales; 20% commission on foreign sales. Offers written contract, binding for term of project or until canceled; 30-day notice must be given to terminate contract. Charges clients "actual expenses for phone/fax, photocopying, and postage only if and when project sells, against advance."

Reading List: Reads *Chronicle of Higher Education*, "certain professional publications and a wide range of periodicals" to find new clients. Looks for "a fresh approach to traditional subjects or a top credential in an area that hasn't seen too much trade publishing in the past. And, of course, superb writing."

Tips: "We pay attention to detail. We believe in close working relationships between author and agent and between author and editor. Regular communication is key. Please do your homework! There's no substitute for learning all you can about similar or directly competing books and presenting a well-reasoned competitive analysis. Don't work in a vacuum; visit bookstores, and talk to other writers about their own experiences."

WENDY SHERMAN ASSOCIATES, INC., 450 Seventh Ave., Suite 3004, New York NY 10123. (212)279-9027. Fax: (212)279-8863. E-mail: wendy@wsherman.com. **Contact:** Wendy Sherman. Estab. 1999. Member of AAR. Represents 30 clients. 30% of clients are new/unpublished writers. Currently handles: 50% nonfiction books; 50% novels.

- Prior to becoming an agent, Ms. Sherman worked for Aaron Priest agency and was vice president, executive director of Henry Holt, associate publisher, subsidary rights director, sales and marketing director.

Member Agents: Jessica Lichtenstein (general nonfiction, suspense fiction); Wendy Sherman.

Represents: Nonfiction books, novels. **Considers these nonfiction areas:** Psychology; narrative nonfiction, practical. **Considers these fiction areas:** Literary; women's.

○→ "We specialize in developing new writers as well as working with more established writers. My experience as a publisher has proven to be a great asset to my clients."

How to Contact: Query with SASE, or send outline/proposal, 1 sample chapter. All unsolicited mss returned unopened. Considers simultaneous queries. Prefers to read ms exclusively. Responds in 1 month to queries. Returns materials only with SASE. Obtains most new clients through recommendations from others.

Recent Sales: Sold 15 titles in the last year. *Real Love*, by Greg Baer, Ph.D. (Penguin Putnam); *The Cloud Atlas*, by Liam Callanan (Delacorte). Other clients include D.W. Buffa, Nani Power, Sarah Stonich, Alan Eisenstock, Howard Bahr, Lundy Bancroft, Lise Friedman, Tom Schweich, Suzanne Chazin.

Terms: Agent receives 15% commission on domestic sales; 20% commission on foreign sales. Offers written contract. Charges for photocopying of ms, messengers, express mail services, etc. (reasonable, standard expenses).

THE SHUKAT COMPANY LTD., 340 W. 55th St., Suite 1A, New York NY 10019-3744. (212)582-7614. Fax: (212)315-3752. **Contact:** Maribel Rivas, Lysna Scriven-Marzani, Scott Shukat. Estab. 1972. Member of AAR. Currently handles: dramatic works.

How to Contact: Query with SASE, outline/proposal or 30 pages. Include bio, credit and synopsis.

ROSALIE SIEGEL, INTERNATIONAL LITERARY AGENCY, INC., 1 Abey Dr., Pennington NJ 08534. (609)737-1007. Fax: (609)737-3708. **Contact:** Rosalie Siegel. Estab. 1977. Member of AAR. Represents 35 clients. 10% of clients are new/unpublished writers. Currently handles: 45% nonfiction books; 45% novels; 10% young adult books and short story collections for current clients.

Represents: Nonfiction books, novels, short story collections, young adult books.

○→ This agency specializes in foreign authors, especially French, though diminishing.

How to Contact: Obtains most new clients through referrals from writers and friends.

Terms: Agent receives 15% commission on domestic sales; 20% commission on foreign sales. Offers written contract; 60-day notice must be given to terminate contract. Charges clients for photocopying.

JEFFREY SIMMONS LITERARY AGENCY, 10 Lowndes Square, London SWIX 9HA, England. (020)7235 8852. Fax: (020)7235 9733. **Contact:** Jeffrey Simmons. Estab. 1978. Represents 43 clients. 40% of clients are new/unpublished writers. Currently handles: 60% nonfiction books; 40% novels.

● Prior to becoming an agent, Mr. Simmons was a publisher and he is also an author.

Represents: Nonfiction books, novels. **Considers these nonfiction areas:** Biography/autobiography; current affairs; government/politics/law; history; language/literature/criticism; memoirs; music/dance; popular culture; sociology; sports; theater/film; translation; true crime/investigative. **Considers these fiction areas:** Action/adventure; confession; detective/police/crime; family saga; literary; mainstream/contemporary; mystery/suspense; thriller.

○→ This agency seeks to handle good books and promising young writers. "My long experience in publishing and as an author and ghostwriter means I can offer an excellent service all around, especially in terms of editorial experience where appropriate." Actively seeking quality fiction, biography, autobiography, showbiz, personality books, law, crime, politics, world affairs. Does not want to receive science fiction, horror, fantasy, juvenile, academic books, specialist subjects (i.e., cooking, gardening, religious).

How to Contact: Submit sample chapter, outline/proposal, IRCs if necessary, SASE. Prefers to read materials exclusively. Responds in 1 week to queries; 1 month to mss. Obtains most new clients through recommendations from others, solicitations.

Recent Sales: Sold 16 titles in the last year. *War of the Windsors*, by Picknett, Prince and Prior (Mainstream); *Town Without Pity*, by Don Hale (Century); *Only Fools and Horses*, by Richard Webber (Orion).

Terms: Agent receives 10-15% commission on domestic sales; 15% commission on foreign sales. Offers written contract, binding for lifetime of book in question or until it goes out of print.

Tips: "When contacting us with an outline/proposal, include a brief biographical note (listing any previous publications, with publishers and dates). Preferably tell us if the book has already been offered elsewhere."

EVELYN SINGER LITERARY AGENCY INC., P.O. Box 594, White Plains NY 10602-0594. (914)948-5565. **Contact:** Evelyn Singer. Estab. 1951. Represents 20 clients.

● Prior to opening her agency, Ms. Singer served as an associate in the Jeanne Hale Literary Agency.

Represents: Nonfiction books (trade books only), novels, juvenile books (for over 4th grade reading level). **Considers these nonfiction areas:** Anthropology/archaeology; biography/autobiography; business/economics; child guidance/parenting; current affairs; ethnic/cultural interests; government/politics/law; health/medicine; how-to; juvenile nonfiction; money/finance; nature/environment; psychology; religious/inspirational; science/technology; self-help/personal improvement; women's issues/studies. **Considers these fiction areas:** Contemporary issues; ethnic; feminist; historical; literary; mainstream/contemporary; mystery/suspense; regional; thriller.

○→ This agency specializes in nonfiction (adult/juvenile, adult suspense). Does not want to receive textbooks.

How to Contact: Query with SASE. No e-mail or fax queries. Responds in 3 weeks to queries; 2 months to mss. Returns materials only with SASE. Obtains most new clients through recommendations only.

Recent Sales: Sold 4 titles in the last year. *Return of Gabriel*, by John Armistead (Milkweed); *Cross and Switchblade*, by David Wilkerson with John and Elizabeth Sherrill (Blackstone Audio Books).

Terms: Agent receives 15% commission on domestic sales; 20% commission on foreign sales. Offers written contract, binding for 3 years. Charges clients for long-distance phone calls, overseas postage ("authorized expenses only") after sale of ms.

Tips: "I am accepting very few writers. Writers must have earned at least $20,000 from freelance writing. SASE must accompany all queries and material for reply and or return of ms. Enclose biographical material and double-spaced book outline or chapter outline. List publishers queried, publication credits and length of book in pages or words."

IRENE SKOLNICK LITERARY AGENCY, 22 W. 23rd St., 5th Floor, New York NY 10010. (212)727-3648. Fax: (212)727-1024. E-mail: sirene35@aol.com. **Contact:** Irene Skolnick. Estab. 1993. Member of AAR. Represents 45 clients. 75% of clients are new/unpublished writers.

Member Agents: Irene Skolnick; Laura Friedman Williams.

Represents: Nonfiction books (adult), novels (adult). **Considers these nonfiction areas:** Biography/autobiography; current affairs; cultural history. **Considers these fiction areas:** Contemporary issues; literary; mainstream/contemporary.

How to Contact: Query with SASE, outline, sample chapter(s). Accepts e-mail and fax queries. Prefers to read materials exclusively. Responds in 1 month to queries. Returns materials only with SASE.

Recent Sales: *Paradise Park*, by Allegra Goodman (Dial); *Fraud*, by David Rakoff (Doubleday); *Taking Lives*, by Michael Pye; *George Sand: A Woman's Life Writ Large*, by Belinda Jack; *The Temple of Optimism*, by James Fleming.

Terms: Agent receives 15% commission on domestic sales; 20% commission on foreign sales. Sometimes offers criticism service; Charges for international postage, photocopying over 40 pages.

BEVERLEY SLOPEN LITERARY AGENCY, 131 Bloor St. W., Suite 711, Toronto Ontario M5S 1S3, Canada. (416)964-9598. Fax: (416)921-7726. E-mail: slopen@inforamp.net. Website: www.slopenagency.on.ca. **Contact:** Beverley Slopen. Estab. 1974. Represents 60 clients. 40% of clients are new/unpublished writers. Currently handles: 60% nonfiction books; 40% novels.

● Prior to opening her agency, Ms. Slopen worked in publishing and as a journalist.

Represents: Nonfiction books, novels, scholarly books, textbooks (college). **Considers these nonfiction areas:** Anthropology/archaeology; biography/autobiography; business/economics; current affairs; psychology; sociology; true crime/investigative; women's issues/studies. **Considers these fiction areas:** Literary; mystery/suspense.

O╼ This agency has a "strong bent towards Canadian writers." Actively seeking "serious nonfiction that is accessible and appealing to the general reader." Does not want to receive fantasy, science fiction or children's.

How to Contact: Query with SAE and IRCs. Returns materials only with SASE (Canadian postage). Accepts short e-mail queries. Considers simultaneous queries. Responds in 2 months to queries.

Recent Sales: Sold 25 titles in the last year. *Baroque-a-nova*, by Kevin Chong (Penguin Putnam); *The Rescue of Jerusalem*, by Henry T. Aubin (Doubleday Canada, Soho Press US); *Midnight Cab*, by James W. Nichol (Knopf Canada); *Fatal Passage*, by Ken McGoogan (Carroll & Graf US, Bantam Press UK). Other clients include historians Modris Eksteins, Michael Marrus, Timothy Brook, critic Robert Fulford, novelists Donna Morrissey (*Kit's Law* and *Downhill Chance*), Howard Engel, Morley Torgov.

Terms: Agent receives 15% commission on domestic sales; 10% commission on foreign sales. Offers written contract, binding for 2 years; 90-day notice must be given to terminate contract.

Tips: "Please no unsolicited manuscripts."

ROBERT SMITH LITERARY AGENCY LTD., 12 Bridge Wharf, 156 Caledonian Road, London NI 9UU, England. (020) 7278 2444. Fax: (020) 7833 5680. E-mail: robertsmith.literaryagency@virgin.net. **Contact:** Robert Smith. Estab. 1997. Member of Association of Authors' Agents. Represents 25 clients. 10% of clients are new/unpublished writers. Currently handles: 80% nonfiction books; 20% syndicated material.

● Prior to becoming an agent, Mr. Smith was a book publisher.

Member Agents: Robert Smith (all nonfiction); Renuka Harrison (mind/body/spirit).

Represents: Nonfiction books, syndicated material. **Considers these nonfiction areas:** Biography/autobiography; cooking/foods/nutrition; health/medicine; memoirs; music/dance; New Age/metaphysics; popular culture; self-help/personal improvement; theater/film; true crime/investigative.

O╼ This agency offers clients full management service in all media. Clients are not necessarily book authors. "Our special expertise is in placing newspaper series internationally." Actively seeking autobiographies.

How to Contact: Submit outline/proposal, IRCs if necessary, SASE. Prefers to read materials exclusively. Accepts e-mail and fax queries. Responds in 1 week to queries. Returns materials only with SASE. Obtains most new clients through recommendations from others, direct approaches to prospective authors.

Recent Sales: Sold 25 titles in the last year. *The Truth At Last*, by Christine Keeler (Sidgwick & Jackson/Macmillan); *Princess Margaret*, by Christopher Warwick (Andre Deutsch); *Presenting on Television*, by Joanne Zorian-Lynn (A&C Black); *Ron Kray*, by Laurie O'Leary (Headline); *The Ultimate Jack the Ripper Sourcebook*, by Stewart Evans and Keith Skinner (Constable Robinson). ***Movie/TV MOW script(s) optioned/sold:*** *The Guv'nor*, by Lenny McLean and Peter Gerrard (Arrival Films). Other clients include Neil & Christine Hamilton, James Haspiel, Geoffrey Guiliano, Norman Parker, Mike Reid, Rochelle Morton, Reg Kray, Julie Chrystyn.

Terms: Agent receives 15% commission on domestic sales; 20% commission on foreign sales. Offers written contract, binding for 3 months; 3-month notice must be given to terminate contract. Charges clients for couriers, photocopying and postage, overseas mailings of mss, subject to client authorization.

⊘ SMITH-SKOLNIK LITERARY MANAGEMENT, 303 Walnut St., Westfield NJ 07090. Member of AAR.
- This agency specializes in literary fiction. Query with SASE before submitting.

◖ MICHAEL SNELL LITERARY AGENCY, P.O. Box 1206, Turo MA 02666-1206. (508)349-3718. **Contact:** Michael Snell. Estab. 1978. Represents 200 clients. 25% of clients are new/unpublished writers. Currently handles: 90% nonfiction books; 10% novels.
- Prior to opening his agency, Mr. Snell served as an editor at Wadsworth and Addison-Wesley for 13 years.

Member Agents: Michael Snell (business, management, computers); Patricia Smith (nonfiction, all categories).
Represents: Nonfiction books. **Considers these nonfiction areas:** Agriculture/horticulture; Americana; animals; anthropology/archaeology; art/architecture/design; biography/autobiography; business/economics; child guidance/parenting; computers/electronic; cooking/foods/nutrition; crafts/hobbies; creative nonfiction; current affairs; education; ethnic/cultural interests; gardening; gay/lesbian issues; government/politics/law; health/medicine; history; how-to; humor/satire; interior design/decorating; juvenile nonfiction; language/literature/criticism; memoirs; military/war; money/finance; multicultural; music/dance; nature/environment; New Age/metaphysics; philosophy; photography; popular culture; psychology; recreation; regional; religious/inspirational; science/technology; self-help/personal improvement; sex; sociology; software; spirituality; sports; theater/film; translation; travel; true crime/investigative; women's issues/studies; young adult.
- ⌐ This agency specializes in how-to, self-help and all types of business and computer books, from low-level how-to to professional and reference. Especially interested in business, health, law, medicine, psychology, science, women's issues. Actively seeking "strong book proposals in any nonfiction area where a clear need exists for a new book. Especially self-help, how-to books on all subjects, from business to personal well-being." Does not want to receive "complete manuscripts; considers proposals only. No fiction. No children's books."

How to Contact: Query with SASE. Prefers to read materials exclusively. Responds in 1 week to queries; 2 weeks to mss. Obtains most new clients through queries, word-of-mouth, *LMP* and *Guide to Literary Agents*.
Recent Sales: Sold 36 titles in the last year. *Fit and Fat*, by Sally Edwards (Macmillan); *How to Say It to Your Dog*, by Janine Adams (Prentice-Hall); *Do-It-Yourself Advertising*, by Eha Hahn (Wiley); *Pain Relief for Life*, by Al Skribish (Catur/New Page).
Terms: Agent receives 15% commission on domestic sales; 15% commission on foreign sales.
Tips: "Send a half- to full-page query, with SASE. Brochure 'How to Write a Book Proposal' available on request and SASE. We suggest prospective clients read Michael Snell's book, *From Book Idea to Bestseller* (Prima, 1997)."

◖ SOBEL WEBER ASSOCIATES, 146 E. 19th St., New York NY 10003. (212)420-8585. Fax: (212)505-1017. Website: www.sobelweber.com. **Contact:** Nat Sobel, Judith Weber. Represents 125 clients. 15% of clients are new/unpublished writers.
- ⌐ "We edit every book before submitting it to publishers, even those books under contract. For fiction, that may mean two or three drafts of the work. We are less interested in previously published authors than in pursuing new talent wherever we find it."

⊘ ELYSE SOMMER, 11034 73rd Rd., P.O. Box 1133, Forest Hills NY 11375. (718)263-2668. **Contact:** Elyse Sommer. Estab. 1952. Member of AAR.
Represents: Nonfiction books, novels (some mystery but no science fiction), juvenile books (no pre-school).
- ⌐ Specializes in nonfiction: reference books, dictionaries, popular culture.

◖ SPECTRUM LITERARY AGENCY, 320 Central Park W., Suite 1-D, New York NY 10025. Website: www.spectrumliteraryagency.com. **Contact:** Eleanor Wood, president. Represents 80 clients. Currently handles: 10% nonfiction books; 90% novels.
Member Agents: Lucienne Diver.

FOR EXPLANATIONS OF THESE SYMBOLS, SEE THE INSIDE FRONT AND BACK COVERS OF THIS BOOK

Represents: Nonfiction books, novels. **Considers these nonfiction areas:** Considers select nonfiction. **Considers these fiction areas:** Fantasy; historical; mainstream/contemporary; mystery/suspense; romance; science fiction.

How to Contact: Query with SASE. No e-mail or fax queries. Prefers to read materials exclusively. Responds in 2 months to queries. Obtains most new clients through recommendations from authors and others.

Recent Sales: Sold over 100 titles in the last year. This agency prefers not to share information on specific sales.

Terms: Agent receives 15% commission on domestic sales. Deducts for photocopying and book orders.

THE SPIELER AGENCY, 154 W. 57th St., 13th Floor, Room 135, New York NY 10019. (212)757-4439. Fax: (212)333-2019. E-mail: spielerlit@aol.com. **Contact:** Ada Muellner. Spieler Agency West, 4096 Piedmont Ave., Oakland CA 94611. **Contact:** Victoria Shoemaker. Estab. 1981. Represents 160 clients. 2% of clients are new/unpublished writers.

● Prior to opening his agency, Mr. Spieler was a magazine editor.

Member Agents: Joe Spieler; John Thornton (nonfiction); Lisa M. Ross (fiction/nonfiction); Deidre Mullane; Eric Myers. Spieler Agency West (Oakland, CA): Victoria Shoemaker.

Represents: Nonfiction books, literary fiction, children's books. **Considers these nonfiction areas:** Biography/autobiography; business/economics; child guidance/parenting; cooking/foods/nutrition; current affairs; gay/lesbian issues; government/politics/law; history; memoirs; money/finance; music/dance; nature/environment (environmental issues); sociology; theater/film; travel; women's issues/studies. **Considers these fiction areas:** Family saga; feminist; gay/lesbian; humor/satire; literary.

How to Contact: Query with SASE. Prefers to read materials exclusively. No e-mail or fax queries. Considers simultaneous queries. Responds in 2 weeks to queries; 5 weeks to mss. Returns materials only with SASE. Obtains most new clients through recommendations and occasionally through listing in *Guide to Literary Agents*.

Recent Sales: *A Needle to the Heart: Special Military Operations from the Heroic to the Nuclear Age*, by Derek Leebaert (Little, Brown); *Biography of Yasir Arafat*, by Barry Rubin and Judith Colp Rubin (Palgrave/St. Martin's); *One Market Under God*, by Tom Frank (Doubleday).

Terms: Agent receives 15% commission on domestic sales. Charges clients for messenger bills, photocopying, postage.

Writers' Conferences: London Bookfair.

PHILIP G. SPITZER LITERARY AGENCY, 50 Talmage Farm Lane, East Hampton NY 11937. (631)329-3650. Fax: (631)329-3651. E-mail: spitzer516@aol.com. **Contact:** Philip Spitzer. Estab. 1969. Member of AAR. Represents 60 clients. 10% of clients are new/unpublished writers. Currently handles: 50% nonfiction books; 50% novels.

● Prior to opening his agency, Mr. Spitzer served at New York University Press, McGraw-Hill and the John Cushman Associates literary agency.

Represents: Nonfiction books, novels. **Considers these nonfiction areas:** Biography/autobiography; business/economics; current affairs; ethnic/cultural interests; government/politics/law; health/medicine; history; language/literature/criticism; military/war; music/dance; nature/environment; popular culture; psychology; sociology; sports; theater/film; true crime/investigative. **Considers these fiction areas:** Contemporary issues; detective/police/crime; literary; mainstream/contemporary; mystery/suspense; sports; thriller.

O─ This agency specializes in mystery/suspense, literary fiction, sports, general nonfiction (no how-to).

How to Contact: Query with SASE, outline, 1 sample chapter(s). Responds in 1 week to queries; 6 weeks to mss. Obtains most new clients through recommendations from others.

Recent Sales: *Chasing the Dime*, by Michael Connelly (Little, Brown); *White Doves at Morning*, by James Lee Burke (Simon & Schuster); *Eleanora Duse*, by Helen Sheehy (Knopf); *Air Burial*, by Jean Shields (Carroll & Graff).

Terms: Agent receives 15% commission on domestic sales; 20% commission on foreign sales. Charges clients for photocopying.

Writers' Conferences: BEA.

NANCY STAUFFER ASSOCIATES, P.O. Box 1203, Darien CT 06820. (203)655-3717. Fax: (203)655-3704. E-mail: nanstauf@earthlink.net. **Contact:** Nancy Stauffer Cahoon. Estab. 1989. Member of the Authors Guild. 10% of clients are new/unpublished writers. Currently handles: 15% nonfiction books; 85% novels.

Represents: Nonfiction books, novels (literary fiction). **Considers these nonfiction areas:** Biography/autobiography; creative nonfiction; current affairs; ethnic/cultural interests. **Considers these fiction areas:** Contemporary issues; literary; mainstream/contemporary; regional.

How to Contact: Obtains new clients through referrals from existing clients.

Recent Sales: *American Coyote*, by Sherman Alexie (Grove/Atlantic); *No Enemy But Time*, by William C. Harris (St. Martin's Press); *The Fruit of Stone*, by Mark Spragg (Riverhead Books).

Terms: Agent receives 15% commission on domestic sales; 20% commission on foreign sales; 20% commission on dramatic rights sales.

Writers' Conferences: Writers At Work and Entrada; Radcliffe Publishing Course.

⬤ STEELE-PERKINS LITERARY AGENCY, 26 Island Lane, Canandaigua NY 14424. (716)396-9290. Fax: (716)396-3579. E-mail: pattiesp@aol.com. **Contact:** Pattie Steele-Perkins. Member of AAR, RWA. Currently handles: 100% Romance and mainstream women's fiction.
Represents: Novels. **Considers these fiction areas:** Mainstream/contemporary; multicultural; romance; women's.
○﹁ Actively seeking romance, women's fiction and multicultural works.
How to Contact: Submit outline, 3 sample chapter(s), SASE. Considers simultaneous queries. Responds in 6 weeks to queries. Returns materials only with SASE. Obtains most new clients through recommendations from others, queries/solicitations.
Recent Sales: This agency prefers not to share information on specific sales.
Terms: Agent receives 15% commission on domestic sales. Offers written contract, binding for 1 year; 30-day notice must be given to terminate contract.
Writers' Conferences: National Conference of Romance Writers of America; Book Expo America Writers' Conferences.
Tips: "Be patient. E-mail rather than call. Make sure what you are sending is the best it can be."

⬤ STERLING LORD LITERISTIC, INC., 65 Bleecker St., New York NY 10012. (212)780-6050. Fax: (212)780-6095. **Contact:** Philippa Brophy. Estab. 1952. Signatory of WGA. Represents 600 clients. Currently handles: 50% nonfiction books; 50% novels.
Member Agents: Peter Matson; Sterling Lord; Philippa Brophy; Chris Calhoun; Charlotte Sheedy; George Nicholson; Neeti Madan; Jim Rutman; Claudia Cross; Laurie Liss.
Represents: Nonfiction books, novels, literary value considered first.
How to Contact: Query with SASE. Responds in 1 month to mss. Obtains most new clients through recommendations from others.
Recent Sales: This agency prefers not to share information on specific sales. Other clients include Kent Haruf, Dick Fancis, Mary Gordon, Sen. John McCain, Simon Winchester, James McBride, Billy Collins.
Terms: Agent receives 15% commission on domestic sales; 20% commission on foreign sales. Offers written contract. Charges clients for photocopying.

⬤ STERNIG & BYRNE LITERARY AGENCY, 3209 S. 55, Milwaukee WI 53219-4433. (414)328-8034. Fax: (414)328-8034. E-mail: jackbyrne@hotmail.com. Website: www.sff.net/people/jackbyrne. **Contact:** Jack Byrne. Estab. 1950s. Member of SFWA, MWA, SCBWI. Represents 30 clients. 10% of clients are new/unpublished writers. Accepting few new clients. Currently handles: 5% nonfiction books; 85% novels; 10% juvenile books.
Member Agents: Jack Byrne.
Represents: Nonfiction books, novels, juvenile books. **Considers these fiction areas:** Fantasy; horror; mystery/suspense; science fiction.
○﹁ "Our client list is comfortably full and our current needs are therefore quite limited." Strong preference given to established writers. Does not want to receive romance, poetry, textbooks, highly specialized nonfiction.
How to Contact: Query with SASE. Accepts e-mail queries, no attachments. Responds in 3 weeks to queries; 3 months to mss. Returns materials only with SASE.
Recent Sales: Sold 11 titles in the last year. *Across the Plains in the Donner Party*, by Karen Zeinert (Zander); *Three Hands for Scorpio*, by Andre Norton (TOR); *The Duke's Balad* and *Silver May Tarnish*, by Andre Norton and Lyn McConchie (TOR); *Carnam's Castle*, by Betty Ren Wright (Holiday House). Other clients include Jane Routley, Lael Littke, Sasha Miller, John C. Wright.
Terms: Agent receives 15% commission on domestic sales; 20% commission on foreign sales. Offers written contract; 60-day notice must be given to terminate contract.
Reading List: Reads *Publishers Weekly*, *Science Fiction Chronicles*, etc. to find new clients. Looks for "whatever catches my eye."
Tips: "Don't send first drafts; have a professional presentation...including cover letter; know your field. Read what's been done...good and bad."

Ⓝ STIMOLA LITERARY STUDIO, 210 Crescent Ave., Leonia NJ 07605. E-mail: ctrystudio@aol.com. **Contact:** Rosemary B. Stimola. Member of AAR.
● This agency did not respond to our request for information. Query before submitting.
Member Agents: Rosemary B. Stimola (literary, childrens).

⬤ ROBIN STRAUS AGENCY, INC., 229 E. 79th St., New York NY 10021. (212)472-3282. Fax: (212)472-3833. E-mail: springbird@aol.com. **Contact:** Ms. Robin Straus. Estab. 1983. Member of AAR. Currently handles: 65% nonfiction books; 35% novels.
● Prior to becoming an agent, Robin Straus served as a subsidary rights manager at Random House and Doubleday and worked in editorial at Little, Brown.
Represents: Nonfiction books, novels. **Considers these nonfiction areas:** Animals; anthropology/archaeology; art/architecture/design; biography/autobiography; child guidance/parenting; cooking/foods/nutrition; current af-

fairs; ethnic/cultural interests; government/politics/law; health/medicine; history; language/literature/criticism; music/dance; nature/environment; popular culture; psychology; sociology; theater/film; women's issues/studies. **Considers these fiction areas:** Contemporary issues; family saga; historical; literary; mainstream/contemporary.

➔ This agency specializes in high quality fiction and nonfiction for adults (no genre fiction; no screenplays; no books for children). Takes on very few new clients.

How to Contact: For nonfiction: Query with proposal and sample pages. For fiction: Query with brief synopsis and opening chapter or 2. Responds and returns materials only with SASE. We do not download **any** submissions. Responds in 1 month to queries; 1 month to mss. Obtains most new clients through recommendations from others.

Recent Sales: This agency prefers not to share information on specific sales.

Terms: Agent receives 15% commission on domestic sales; 20% commission on foreign sales. Offers written contract. Charges for "photocopying, express mail services, messenger and foreign postage, etc. as incurred."

⊘ GUNTHER STUHLMANN, AUTHOR'S REPRESENTATIVE, P.O. Box 276, Becket MA 01223-0276. Estab. 1954.

● This agency did not respond to our request for information. Query before submitting.

◍ SUITE A MANAGEMENT TALENT & LITERARY AGENCY, (formerly Robinson Talent and Literary Management), 1101 S. Robertson Blvd., Suite 210, Los Angeles CA 90035. (310)278-0801. Fax: (310)278-0807. E-mail: suite-a@juno.com. **Contact:** Lloyd Robinson. Estab. 1996. Member of DGA; signatory of WGA. Represents 76 clients. 10% of clients are new/unpublished writers. Currently handles: 15% novels; 40% movie scripts; 40% TV scripts; 5% stage plays.

● See the expanded listing for this agency in Script Agents.

⊕ ⊘ THE SUSIJN AGENCY, 820 Harrow Road, London NW10 5JU, England. (020) 8968 7435. Fax: 0044 (207)580-8626. E-mail: info@thesusijnagency.com. Website: www.thesusijnagency.com. **Contact:** Laura Susijn. Estab. 1998. Currently handles: 15% nonfiction books; 85% novels.

● Prior to becoming an agent, Ms. Susijn was a rights director at Sheil Land Associates and at Fourth Estate Ltd.

Member Agents: Laura Susijn.

Represents: Nonfiction books, novels. **Considers these nonfiction areas:** Biography/autobiography; memoirs; multicultural; popular culture; science/technology; travel. **Considers these fiction areas:** Literary.

➔ This agency specializes in international works, selling world rights, representing non-English language writing as well as English. Emphasis on cross-cultural subjects. Self-help, romance, sagas, science fiction, screenplays.

How to Contact: Submit outline, 2 sample chapter(s). Accepts e-mail and fax queries. Considers simultaneous queries. Responds in 2 months to queries. Returns materials only with SASE. Obtains most new clients through recommendations from others, via publishers in Europe and beyond.

Recent Sales: Sold 120 titles in the last year. *Gone*, by Helena Echlin (Secker and Warburg, UK); *Daalder*, by Philibert Schogt (4 Walls 8 Windows); *Prisoner in a Red Rose Chain*, by Jeffrey Moore (Weidenfeld & Nicholson); *Smell*, by Radhika Jha (Quartet Books); *The Formula One Fanatic*, by Koen Vergeer (Bloomsbury); *A Mouthful of Glass*, by Henk Van Woerden (Granta); *Fragile Science*, by Robin Baker (Macmillan); *East of Acre Lane*, by Alex Wheatle (Fourth Estate). Other clients include Vassallucci, Podium, Atlas, De Arbeiderspers, Tiderne Skifter, MB Agency, Van Oorschot.

Terms: Agent receives 15% commission on domestic sales; 15-20% commission on foreign sales. Offers written contract; 6-week notice must be given to terminate contract. Charges clients for photocopying, buying copies only if sale is made.

◍ THE SWAYNE AGENCY LITERARY MANAGEMENT & CONSULTING, INC., 7 Penn Plaza, 16th Floor, New York NY 10001. (212)391-5438. E-mail: mgray@swayneagency.com. Website: www.swayneagency.com. Estab. 1997. Represents 125 clients. Currently handles: 90% nonfiction books; 10% fiction.

Member Agents: Susan Barry (science, business, business narrative, finance, memoir, narrative nonfiction and sports); Lisa Swayne (business, business narrative, narrative nonfiction, literary fiction, women's health and spirituality).

Represents: Nonfiction books. **Considers these nonfiction areas:** Business/economics; computers/electronic; current affairs; ethnic/cultural interests; how-to; popular culture; women's issues/studies.

➔ This agency specializes in authors who participate in multimedia: book publishing, radio, movies and television, and information technology. Does not want to receive westerns, romance novels, science fiction, children's books.

How to Contact: Query with SASE, proposal package, outline. No fax queries. Accepts e-mail queries, no attachments. Considers simultaneous queries. Responds in 6 weeks to mss. Obtains most new clients through recommendations from colleagues and clients.

Recent Sales: *Nader*, by Justin Martin (Perseus Books); *Bloodhighways*, by Adam Penenberg (HarperCollins); *Into the Hearts and Minds*, by Charles Grantham (John Wiley & Sons/Gartner Press); *The Complete Idiots Guide to Infectious Diseases*, by David Perlan and Ann Cohen (Alpha Books/MacMillan); *Killing Time With Strangers*, W.S. Penn (University of Arizona Press).
Terms: Agent receives 15% commission on domestic sales; 20% commission on foreign sales. Offers written contract, binding for 1 year; 60-day notice must be given to terminate contract.
Reading List: Reads *Harpers*, *New York Times*, *Business Week*, *Wall Street Journal*, *New York Observer*, *Forbes*, *Fortune*.

[N] ROBERT E. TABIAN/LITERARY AGENT, 31 E. 32nd St., Suite 300, New York NY 10016. Estab. 1992.
● Prior to opening his agency, Mr. Tabian was a former vice president, subsidiary rights, of The Putnam Publishing Group.
Represents: Nonfiction books; novels. **Considers these nonfiction areas:** business/economics; health/medicine; history; how-to (by credentialed professionals); multicultural; popular culture; psychology; science/technology; narrative nonfiction; diet and exercise. **Considers these fiction areas:** literary; mainstream/contemporary; mystery; thriller; women's.
Writer's Conferences: SDSU Writers Conference (San Diego, January).
Tips: Agency represents titles published by Putnam, Viking/Penguin, Simon & Schuster, Pocket Books, HarperCollins, William Morrow, Random House, Broadway, Warner and Hyperion among others.

[M] THE JOHN TALBOT AGENCY, INC., 540 W. Boston Post Rd., PMB 266, Mamaroneck NY 10543-3437. (914)381-9463. Website: www.johntalbotagency.com. **Contact:** John Talbot. Estab. 1998. Member of Authors Guild. Represents 50 clients. 15% of clients are new/unpublished writers. Currently handles: 35% nonfiction books; 65% novels.
● Prior to becoming an agent, Mr. Talbot was a book editor at Simon & Schuster and Putnam Berkley.
Represents: Nonfiction books, novels. **Considers these nonfiction areas:** General and narrative nonfiction. **Considers these fiction areas:** Literary; mystery/suspense.
○➔ This agency specializes in commercial suspense and literary fiction "by writers who are beginning to publish in magazines and literary journals." Also narrative nonfiction, especially outdoor adventure and spirituality. Does not want to receive children's books, science fiction, fantasy, westerns, poetry, screenplays.
How to Contact: Query with SASE. Accepts e-mail queries. No fax queries. Considers simultaneous queries. Responds in 1 month to queries; 2 months to mss. Obtains most new clients through referrals. See website for updates.
Recent Sales: Sold 30 titles in the last year. *The Edge of Justice*, by Clinton McKinzie (Delacorte/Dell); *Crush Depth*, by Joe Buff (Morrow); *Burden*, by Tony Walters (St. Martin's Press); *Around Again*, by Suzanne Strempek Shea (Pocket Books). Other clients include Doris Meredith, Peter Telep, Clarence Major.
Terms: Agent receives 15% commission on domestic sales; 20% commission on foreign sales. Offers written contract; 60-day notice must be given to terminate contract. Charges clients for photocopying, overnight delivery, additional copies of books needed for use in sale of subsidiary rights, and fees incurred for submitting mss or books overseas.

[M] TALESMYTH ENTERTAINMENT, INC., 312 St. John St., Suite #69, Portland ME 04102. (207)879-0307. Fax: (207)775-1067. E-mail: talesmyth@hotmail.com. **Contact:** Thomas Burgess. Estab. 2000. Signatory of WGA. Represents 5 clients. 100% of clients are new/unpublished writers. Currently handles: 10% novels; 10% story collections; 80% movie scripts.
● See the expanded listing for this agency in Script Agents.

[M] ROSLYN TARG LITERARY AGENCY, INC., 105 W. 13th St., New York NY 10011. (212)206-9390. Fax: (212)989-6233. E-mail: roslyntarg@aol.com. **Contact:** Roslyn Targ. Estab. 1945. Member of AAR. Represents 100 clients.
Member Agents: Roslyn Targ.
How to Contact: Query with SASE, outline/proposal, curriculum vitae. Accepts e-mail queries. Prefers to read materials exclusively. No mss without query first. Obtains most new clients through recommendations from others, solicitations.
Terms: Agent receives 15% commission on domestic sales; 20% commission on foreign sales. Charges standard agency fees (bank charges, long distance, postage, photocopying, shipping of books, overseas long distance and shipping, etc.).
Tips: "This agency reads on an exclusive basis only."

[M] [$] PATRICIA TEAL LITERARY AGENCY, 2036 Vista Del Rosa, Fullerton CA 92831-1336. Phone/fax: (714)738-8333. **Contact:** Patricia Teal. Estab. 1978. Member of AAR. Represents 60 clients. Currently handles: 10% nonfiction books; 90% novels.

Represents: Nonfiction books, novels. **Considers these nonfiction areas:** Animals; biography/autobiography; child guidance/parenting; health/medicine; how-to; psychology; self-help/personal improvement; true crime/investigative; women's issues/studies. **Considers these fiction areas:** Glitz; mainstream/contemporary; mystery/suspense; romance (contemporary, historical).

O➔ This agency specializes in women's fiction and commercial how-to and self-help nonfiction. Does not want to receive poetry, short stories, articles, science fiction, fantasy, regency romance.

How to Contact: *Published authors only.* Query with SASE. No e-mail or fax queries. Considers simultaneous queries. Responds in 10 days to queries; 6 weeks to mss. Returns materials only with SASE. Obtains most new clients through conferences, recommendations from authors and editors.

Recent Sales: Sold 20 titles in the last year. *The Black Sheep's Baby*, by Kathleen Creighton (Silhouette); *Man with a Message*, by Muriel Jensen (Harlequin).

Terms: Agent receives 10-15% commission on domestic sales; 20% commission on foreign sales. Offers written contract, binding for 1 year. Charges previously unpublished clients $35 for postage and phone calls.

Writers' Conferences: Romance Writers of America conferences; California State University (San Diego, January); Asilomar (California Writers Club); BEA (Chicago June); Bouchercon; Hawaii Writers Conference (Maui).

Reading List: Reads *Publishers Weekly*, *Romance Report* and *Romantic Times* to find new clients. "I read the reviews of books and excerpts from authors' books."

Tips: "Include SASE with all correspondence."

🅰 ◎ ANN TOBIAS—A LITERARY AGENCY FOR CHILDREN'S BOOKS, (Specialized: children's books), 520 E. 84th St., Apt. 4L, New York NY 10028. **Contact:** Ann Tobias. Estab. 1988. Represents 25 clients. 50% of clients are new/unpublished writers. Currently handles: 100% juvenile books.

● Prior to opening her agency, Ms. Tobias worked as a children's book editor at Harper, William Morrow, Scholastic.

Represents: Juvenile books. **Considers these nonfiction areas:** Juvenile nonfiction; young adult. **Considers these fiction areas:** Picture books; poetry (for children); young adult; illustrated mss; mid-level novels.

O➔ This agency specializes in books for children. Actively seeking material for children.

How to Contact: Send entire ms for picture books; 30 pages and synopsis for longer work, both fiction and nonfiction. No phone queries. All queries must be in writing and accompanied by a SASE. No e-mail or fax queries. Considers simultaneous queries. Responds in 2 months to mss. Returns materials only with SASE. Obtains most new clients through recommendations from editors.

Recent Sales: Sold 23 titles in the last year. This agency prefers not to share information on specific sales.

Terms: Agent receives 15% commission on domestic sales; 20% commission on foreign sales. No written contract. Charges clients for photocopying, overnight mail, foreign postage, foreign telephone.

Reading List: Reads *Horn Book, Bulletin for the Center of the Book* and *School Library Journal*. "These are review media and they keep me up to date on who is being published and by what company."

Tips: "Read at least 200 children's books in the age group and genre in which you hope to be published. Follow this by reading another 100 children's books in other age groups and genres so you will have a feel for the field as a whole."

🅽 🅰 TRACE INC., THE TRACY SHERROD LITERARY AGENCY, 511 Avenue of Americas, #109, New York NY 10011, USA. (212)369-6785. **Contact:** Tracy Sherrod. Estab. 2002.

● Prior to becoming an agent, Tracy Sherrod was an editor with Pocket Books, a division of Simon & Schuster.

Represents: Nonfiction books, novels. **Considers these nonfiction areas:** Business/economics; health/medicine; multicultural; self-help/personal improvement; spirituality. **Considers these fiction areas:** Literary; multicultural; commercial women's fiction.

🅰 SUSAN TRAVIS LITERARY AGENCY, 1317 N. San Fernando Blvd., Suite 175, Burbank CA 91504. (818)557-6538. Fax: (818)557-6549. **Contact:** Susan Travis. Estab. 1995. Represents 10 clients. 60% of clients are new/unpublished writers. Currently handles: 90% nonfiction books; 10% novels.

● Prior to opening her agency, Ms. Travis served as an agent with the McBride Agency and prior to that worked in the Managing Editors Department of Ballantine Books.

Represents: Nonfiction books. **Considers these nonfiction areas:** Child guidance/parenting; cooking/foods/nutrition; ethnic/cultural interests; health/medicine; how-to; psychology; self-help/personal improvement; women's issues/studies.

O➔ This agency specializes in mainstream nonfiction. Actively seeking cookbooks. Does not want to receive science fiction, poetry or children's books.

How to Contact: Query with SASE, or may submit detailed nonfiction proposal with sample chapters. Must include SASE for response. Responds in 1 month to queries; 6 weeks to mss. Obtains most new clients through recommendations from existing clients, and mss requested from query letters.

Recent Sales: This agency prefers not to share information on specific sales.

Terms: Agent receives 15% commission on domestic sales; 20% commission on foreign sales. Offers written contract, binding for 1 year; 60-day notice must be given to terminate contract. 100% of business is derived from commissions on ms sales. Charges clients for photocopying of mss and proposals if copies not provided by author.

⬛ ◎ SCOTT TREIMEL NY, (Specialized: children's books), 434 Lafayette St., New York NY 10003. (212)505-8353. Fax: (212)505-0664. E-mail: st.ny@verizon.net. **Contact:** Scott Treimel, Annie Holub. Estab. 1995. Member of AAR. Represents 38 clients. 15% of clients are new/unpublished writers. Currently handles: 100% juvenile books.

• Prior to becoming an agent, Mr. Treimel was an assistant at Curtis Brown, Ltd. (for Marilyn E. Marlow); a rights agent for Scholastic, Inc.; a book packager and rights agent for United Feature Syndicate; a freelance editor and a rights consultant for HarperCollins Children's Books; and the founding director of Warner Bros. Worldwide Publishing.

Member Agents: Ari Hopkins (general/children's, all categories).

Represents: Children's book authors and illustrators. **Considers these nonfiction areas:** Agriculture/horticulture; Americana; animals; anthropology/archaeology; art/architecture/design; biography/autobiography; creative nonfiction; current affairs; education; ethnic/cultural interests; gardening; gay/lesbian issues; government/politics/law; history; humor/satire; juvenile nonfiction; language/literature/criticism; memoirs; military/war; multicultural; music/dance; philosophy; photography; popular culture; recreation; regional; science/technology; sex; sociology; sports; theater/film; translation; true crime/investigative; women's issues/studies; young adult. **Considers these fiction areas:** Action/adventure; comic books/cartoon; contemporary issues; detective/police/crime; ethnic; experimental; family saga; fantasy; feminist; gay/lesbian; historical; horror; humor/satire; juvenile; literary; mainstream/contemporary; military/war; multicultural; multimedia; mystery/suspense; picture books; plays; poetry; poetry in translation; psychic/supernatural; regional; science fiction; sports; thriller; translation; westerns/frontier; young adult; (all categories excluding religion and crafts).

○━ This agency specializes in children's books: tightly focused segments of the trade and educational markets. Interested in seeing author-illustrators, first chapter books, middle-grade fiction and young adult fiction.

How to Contact: Query with SASE. For longer work, send synopsis and first two chapters. Replies only to materials sent with SASE. No fax queries. Obtains most new clients through recommendations from others, solicitations.

Recent Sales: Sold 19 titles in the last year. *Tribes*, by Arthur Slade (Harper Collins Canada and Random House); *Look What the Cat Dragged In*, by Gary Hogg (Dutton). Also sold books to Harper, Dutton, Clarion, Random House, Roaring Brook Press, etc.

Terms: Agent receives 15-20% commission on domestic sales; 20-25% commission on foreign sales. Offers verbal or written contract, "binding on a book contract by contract basis." Charges clients for photocopying, overnight/express postage, messengers, and books ordered to sell foreign, film, etc. rights.

Writers' Conferences: Can You Make a Living from Children's Books, Society of Children's Book Writers & Illustrators (Los Angeles, August); Society of Children's Book Writers & Illustrators (Los Angeles, August); "Understanding Book Contracts," SCBWI (Watertown NY); "Creating Believable Teen Characters," SCBWI; Picture Book Judge for Tassie Walden Award; New Voices in Children's Literature; "Craft, Craft and More Craft" SCBWI; "Understanding Book Contracts" SCBWI; The Professionals Panel.

Tips: "Keep your cover letters short and be sure to include your publishing credits. Manuscripts and illustration samples received without a SASE will be recycled on receipt."

◖ 2M COMMUNICATIONS LTD., 121 W. 27 St., #601, New York NY 10001. (212)741-1509. Fax: (212)691-4460. E-mail: morel@bookhaven.com. **Contact:** Madeleine Morel. Estab. 1982. Represents 50 clients. 20% of clients are new/unpublished writers. Currently handles: 100% nonfiction books.

• Prior to becoming an agent, Madeleine Morel worked at a publishing company.

Represents: Nonfiction books. **Considers these nonfiction areas:** Biography/autobiography; child guidance/parenting; ethnic/cultural interests; gay/lesbian issues; health/medicine; memoirs; music/dance; self-help/personal improvement; theater/film; travel; women's issues/studies.

○━ This agency specializes in adult nonfiction.

How to Contact: Query with SASE, submit outline, 3 sample chapter(s). Accepts e-mail queries. Considers simultaneous queries. Responds in 1 week to queries; 1 month to mss. Obtains most new clients through recommendations from others, solicitations.

Recent Sales: Sold 10 titles in the last year. *Botox*, by Terri Malloy (Berkley); *Patriotic Songs*, by Ace Collins (Harper/Collins).

ALWAYS INCLUDE a self-addressed, stamped envelope (SASE) for reply or return of your query or manuscript.

insider report

What do publishers want?
This editor-turned-agent knows!

With graduation looming, Tracy Sherrod was hanging around her dormitory at James Madison College, a residential unit within Michigan State University. A roommate asked her what she planned to do with her life.

"I don't really know. I like books and I like the books that this company publishes," Sherrod replied, waving a copy of a book from Feminist Press.

Her friend said, "Call that company up and ask them for a job."

Sherrod made that call. And guess what? Feminist Press gave her a job over the phone.

Fifteen years later, Sherrod recalls those days with laughter in her voice. "Now anybody else would have been suspicious,

Tracy Sherrod

right? But me, coming from Michigan, I'm like, 'Okay, I got a job.' I moved to New York with sixty-three dollars, like an idiot. I was only making fifty dollars a week at Feminist Press because what I really got was an internship. A couple nights I wound up sleeping at the office. Thank goodness they hired me on full-time after three weeks."

That proved to be the first in a string of publishing jobs for Sherrod as she climbed the professional ladder. Finally, last year, she opened her own literary agency Trace Inc., The Tracy Sherrod Literary Agency.

Ironically, one of her early jobs was with another agent, Marie Brown Literary Services. She stayed there only about a year and a half before moving back to the publishing side.

"I was too young to be an agent back then," Sherrod says with absolute candor. "I was only twenty-one and there I was trying to be an agent. I had a really good eye for writers to go after and they've all since published books and done well. But I didn't have professional courage in a way. I was dealing with people like Cornel West and Dr. James Washington. But, at that age, I just didn't know how I could help them. I was intimidated."

She went over to publisher Henry Holt as an editorial assistant. She quickly proved that she brought her good eye for people with her. The first book she acquired for Holt was about winning scholarship money for college. Sherrod bought it for $8,000.00 and it wound up selling 40,000 copies. Ironically, she purchased it from Marie Brown, her old agency.

Among her other successes in her six years in the editorial department at Holt were *Still Life in Harlem* by Eddy L. Harris, a *New York Times* notable book of the year, and a book by Reggie Wells, Oprah Winfrey's make-up artist.

Her last job on the publisher's side of the desk was at Pocket Books Division of Simon and Schuster, where she spent four years. Sherrod built a solid clientele of black celebrity authors at Pocket Books. "I published Tupac Shakur's poetry which sold over 270,000 copies. I worked with comedian Bernie Mac and journalist Darrell Dawsey." Among other celebrities, Sherrod has worked with Sister Souljah and rapper turned pastor Mason Betha. She is proud of her association with Zane, a writer Sherrod is convinced is positioned to become a best-selling author. Rosalyn McMillan (Terry's McMillan's sister) and bell hooks are among other prominent authors with whom she has developed relationships. After years of publishing experience, Sherrod began to formulate a vision for multicultural publishing, a vision she felt that she could fulfill more expeditiously as an agent than as an editor. "I enjoyed huge successes at Pocket Books but, as an editor, I was limited in the number of books I could do each year. As an agent, I'm able to handle and promote more books than an editor."

"Promote" is a key component in Sherrod's strategy as an agent. She has expanded the role of her new agency beyond acting as an intermediary between author and publisher in the sales process. She believes it is vital that authors help market and promote their books after publication and she stands prepared to help with that task.

One of Sherrod's partners, Tony Clark, is in charge of the marketing services the agency offers to their authors after publication. "We work closely with the publishers and ask our authors to set aside a portion of their advances to supplement the publisher's marketing budget. Authors have to invest back in their careers if they intend to have careers. What a lot of people don't realize is that publishers' marketing budgets are cut every single year but the demand for the amount of money coming in goes up every single year. So authors have to be more responsible for the marketing of their books."

Sherrod's agency also has a service called "Temporary On-Call Personal Assistant," which, for a fee, helps authors with a wide range of practical tasks from mail pick-up or package delivery to helping with unique situations. "For instance, one author called me when she had to enter five thousand names in her personal data base so that she could use them for announcements about her public readings and such. We lined up someone to do that."

Is she intimidated as an agent this time around? Hardly.

"I know the business inside and out. I know what editors are looking for. I know what editor's lives are like and how busy they are. I know how to make things easier for editors to respond. I can see where fiction is going and where non-fiction is going. I know what's working and not working. I know how important it is to be ahead of trend, not to follow it."

Among her hunches is that purely entertainment fiction will diminish in favor of fiction that enriches our lives. Romantic comedies will soon take a backseat to more profound subjects. She points to *Bridget Jones's Diary* as an example of the soon-to-be passe brand of fiction and *Cane River* by Lalita Tademy as the emerging model.

Her nonfiction model follows the same path. "I see more books about a better quality of life. More self-help that's spiritual in nature. Definitely. Books with a religious angle are really going to take off."

Her vision for multicultural publishing falls in line with her predictions for trends in fiction and non-fiction. "I see a lot more serious multicultural literature—books that are emotionally enriching and spiritual. It's not as if black literature is now somehow lesser than general mainstream literature in terms of quality. It's equal across the board with junk and good stuff in both marketplaces." Still, Sherrod predicts that more multicultural literature will be published that is so enriching that it draws readers from diverse backgrounds.

As an agent, Sherrod is looking for literary fiction, commercial women's fiction, spiritual nonfiction, business nonfiction and health nonfiction, especially alternative health books. Any of the aforementioned categories that add a spiritual twist are sure to grab her attention.

While her career has been marked by success in multicultural publishing, she is quick to point out that she is interested in any book that grabs her talent-seeking eye. "White authors may think that a black agent can't sell their work as well. That's not true. I've worked well with white authors. I edited Melanie Rae Thon, from Salt Lake City, a white author who didn't sell well but won several awards. She's as good a writer as Toni Morrison. I've never loved a writer more because this woman is a genius. But, it doesn't matter if you're a genius if your books don't sell well."

She is so impressed by Thon that she lists Thon's collection of stories, *First, Body* among her personal all-time favorite books along with *Immortality* by Milan Kundera, *Sula* by Toni Morrison, and *The Fire Next Time* by James Baldwin.

Sherrod is happy to pass along advice about how writers stand a better chance of catching that talent-seeking eye of hers. "Think only about writing. Don't think about getting published. Don't think about what the reader will think about your writing. Think only about the story you have to tell. Surround yourself with other writers and people whose writing you admire. Read everything you can about writing and read, read, read, read, read. Because one thing is for sure, an editor can pick up a manuscript and tell for sure whether that writer is a reader. Typically, if you're not a reader, it's very unlikely that you'll be a solidly published writer. Live the words and not the fantasy. So many people have this dream where they're writing in the middle of nowhere and, one day, they're going to be called Emily Dickinson. That's not true. You have to work at being a writer, and I don't mean acting like one. I mean sitting down and facing those words and struggling with them every single day."

—W.E. Reinka

Terms: Agent receives 15% commission on domestic sales; 20% commission on foreign sales. Offers written contract, binding for 2 years. Charges clients for postage, photocopying, long distance calls, faxes.

 UNITED TRIBES, 240 W. 35th St., Suite 500, New York NY 10001. (212)534-7646. E-mail: janguerth@aol.com. Website: www.unitedtribes.com. **Contact:** Jan-Erik Guerth. Estab. 1998. Currently handles: 100% nonfiction books.

• Prior to becoming an agent, Mr. Guerth was a comedian, journalist, radio producer and film distributor.

Represents: Nonfiction books. **Considers these nonfiction areas:** Anthropology/archaeology; art/architecture/design; biography/autobiography; business/economics; child guidance/parenting; cooking/foods/nutrition; current affairs; education; ethnic/cultural interests; gay/lesbian issues; government/politics/law; health/medicine; history; how-to; language/literature/criticism; memoirs; money/finance; music/dance; nature/environment; popular culture; psychology; religious/inspirational; science/technology (popular); self-help/personal improvement; sociology; theater/film; translation; women's issues/studies.

    O– This agency represents secular spirituality and serious nonfiction; and ethnic, social, gender and cultural issues, comparative religions, self-help and wellness, science and arts, history and politics, nature and travel, and any fascinating future trends.

How to Contact: Submit outline, résumé, SASE. Agent prefers email queries. Considers simultaneous queries. Responds in 1 month to queries. Returns materials only with SASE. Obtains most new clients through recommendations from others, solicitations, conferences.

Recent Sales: *Squatting in the City of Tomorrow*, by Robert Neuwirth (Routledge); *The Green Desert*, by Rita Winters (Wildcat Canyon Press).

Terms: Agent receives 15% commission on domestic sales; 20% commission on foreign sales.

THE RICHARD R. VALCOURT AGENCY, INC., (Specialized: government issues), 177 E. 77th St., PHC, New York NY 10021-1934. Phone/fax: (212)570-2340. **Contact:** Richard R. Valcourt, president. Estab. 1995. Represents 25 clients. 20% of clients are new/unpublished writers. Currently handles: 100% nonfiction books.

• Prior to opening his agency, Mr. Valcourt was a journalist, editor and college political science instructor. He is also editor-in-chief of the International Journal of Intelligence and faculty member at American Military University in Virginia.

Represents: Scholarly books.

O⊸ This agency specializes in intelligence and other national security affairs. Represents exclusively academics, journalists and professionals in the categories listed.

How to Contact: Query with SASE. Prefers to read materials exclusively. No e-mail or fax queries. Responds in 1 week to queries; 1 month to mss. Returns materials only with SASE. Obtains most new clients through recommendations from others.

Terms: Agent receives 15% commission on domestic sales; 20% commission on foreign sales. Offers written contract. Charges clients for excessive photocopying, express mail, overseas telephone expenses.

VAN DER LEUN & ASSOCIATES, 32 Gramercy Park S, Suite 11L, New York NY 10003. (212)982-6165. Website: www.publishersmarketplace.com/pvanderleun. **Contact:** Patricia Van der Leun, president. Estab. 1984. Represents 30 clients. Currently handles: 75% nonfiction books; 25% novels.

• Prior to becoming an agent, Ms. van der Leun was a professor of Art History.

Represents: Nonfiction books, novels, illustrated books. **Considers these nonfiction areas:** Art/architecture/design (art history); biography/autobiography; cooking/foods/nutrition (food and wine, cookbooks); creative nonfiction; current affairs; ethnic/cultural interests; gardening; history; memoirs; religious/inspirational; spirituality; sports; travel. **Considers these fiction areas:** Comic books/cartoon; contemporary issues; humor/satire; literary; mainstream/contemporary; multicultural; multimedia; picture books; poetry; poetry in translation; short story collections; translation; women's.

O⊸ This agency specializes in fiction, art history, food and wine, gardening, biography.

How to Contact: Query with letter only, include author bio and SASE. Considers simultaneous queries. Responds in 2 weeks to queries.

Recent Sales: Sold 15 titles in the last year. *Bobbi Brown Beauty Evolution*, by Bobbi Brown (Harper-Collins); *Gone to the Country: Life and Art in the Hamptons*, by Robert Long (Farrar, Straus & Giroux); *The Astronomy Encyclopedia*, by David Darling (John Wiley & Sons).

Terms: Agent receives 15% commission on domestic sales; 25% commission on foreign sales. Offers written contract. Charges clients for postage and photocopying of mss only if excessive.

ANNETTE VAN DUREN AGENCY, 11684 Ventura Blvd., #235, Studio City CA 91604. (818)752-6000. Fax: (818)752-6985. **Contact:** Annette Van Duren or Teena Portier. Estab. 1985. Signatory of WGA. Represents 12 clients. 0% of clients are new/unpublished writers. Currently handles: 10% nonfiction books; 50% movie scripts; 40% TV scripts.

• See the expanded listing for this agency in Script Agents.

VENTURE LITERARY, 8895 Towne Centre Dr., Suite 105, #141, San Diego CA 92122. (619)807-1887. Fax: (561)365-8321. E-mail: agents@ventureliterary.com. Website: www.ventureliterary.com. **Contact:** Frank R. Scatoni. Estab. 1999. Represents 25 clients. 50% of clients are new/unpublished writers. Currently handles: 90% nonfiction books; 10% novels.

• Prior to becoming an agent, Mr. Scatoni worked as an editor at Simon & Schuster.

Member Agents: Frank R. Scatoni (general nonfiction, including biography, memoir, narrative nonfiction, sports and serious nonfiction); Greg Dinkin (general nonfiction/business, gambling).

Represents: Nonfiction books, novels. **Considers these nonfiction areas:** Animals; anthropology/archaeology; biography/autobiography; business/economics; current affairs; ethnic/cultural interests; government/politics/law; history; memoirs; military/war; money/finance; multicultural; music/dance; nature/environment; popular culture; psychology; science/technology; sports; true crime/investigative; gambling. **Considers these fiction areas:** Action/adventure; detective/police/crime; literary; mainstream/contemporary; mystery/suspense; sports; thriller.

O⊸ Specializes in nonfiction, sports, business, natural history, biography, gambling. Actively seeking nonfiction.

How to Contact: Nonfiction: submit proposal with 3 sample chapters; fiction: submit query letter and finished ms. Considers simultaneous queries. Responds in 1 month to queries; 6 months to mss. Returns materials only with SASE. Obtains most new clients through recommendations from others.

Recent Sales: *Gearheads: Inside the World of Robotic Combat*, by Brad Stone (Simon & Schuster); *The Perfect Ride: The Life and Times of a Hall of Fame Jockey*, by Gary Stevens (Kensington Publishing); *The Poker MBA: Winning in Business No Matter What Cards You're Dealt*, by Greg Dinkin and Jeffrey Gitomer (Crown Business); *Brawl: The Fighting World of Mixed Martial Arts*, by Erich Krauss (ECW Press); *Killer Poker*, by John Vorhaus (Kensington); *Act Now! A Step by Step Guide to Becoming a Working Actor*, by Peter Jazwinski (Crown/Three Rivers Press); *Beyond the Shadow of the Senators: Baseball's Fight for Integration*, by Brad Snyder (McGraw-Hill/Contemporary); *Tonight . . . In This Very Ring: A Fan's History of Professional Wrestling*, by Scott Keith (Citadel Press).

Terms: Agent receives 15% commission on domestic sales; 20% commission on foreign sales. Offers written contract. Charges clients for photocopying and postage only.

Writers' Conferences: San Diego State University Writers Conference (San Diego CA); La Jolla Writers Conference (La Jolla CA).

◯ **RALPH VICIANANZA, LTD.**, 111 Eighth Ave., Suite 1501, New York NY 10011. (212)924-7090. Fax: (212)691-9644. Member of AAR. Represents 120 clients. 5% of clients are new/unpublished writers.
Member Agents: Ralph M. Viciananza; Chris Lotts; Chris Schelling.
Represents: Nonfiction books, novels. **Considers these nonfiction areas:** Biography/autobiography; business/economics; history; popular culture; religious/inspirational; science/technology. **Considers these fiction areas:** Fantasy; literary; mainstream/contemporary (popular fiction); multicultural; science fiction; thriller; women's fiction.
    O➤ This agency specializes in foreign rights.
How to Contact: Query with SASE. No unsolicited mss.
Recent Sales: This agency prefers not to share information on specific sales.
Terms: Agent receives 15% commission on domestic sales; 20% commission on foreign sales.

◯ **DAVID VIGLIANO LITERARY AGENCY**, 584 Broadway, Suite 809, New York NY 10012. Member of AAR.
    ● This agency did not respond to our request for information. Query before submitting.

◯ **THE VINES AGENCY, INC.**, 648 Broadway, Suite 901, New York NY 10012. (212)777-5522. Fax: (212)777-5978. E-mail: jv@vinesagency.com. Website: www.vinesagency.com. **Contact:** James C. Vines, Paul Surdi, Ali Ryan, Gary Neuwirth. Estab. 1995. Member of Author's Guild; signatory of WGA. Represents 52 clients. 20% of clients are new/unpublished writers. Currently handles: 50% nonfiction books; 50% novels.
    ● Prior to opening his agency, Mr. Vines served as an agent with the Virginia Barber Literary Agency.
Member Agents: James C. Vines (quality and commercial fiction and nonfiction); Gary Neuwirth; Paul Surdi (women's fiction, ethnic fiction, quality nonfiction); Ali Ryan (women's fiction and nonfiction, mainstream).
Represents: Nonfiction books, novels, feature film, TV scripts. **Considers these nonfiction areas:** Biography/autobiography; business/economics; current affairs; ethnic/cultural interests; history; how-to; humor/satire; memoirs; military/war; money/finance; nature/environment; New Age/metaphysics; photography; popular culture; psychology; religious/inspirational; science/technology; self-help/personal improvement; sociology; spirituality; sports; translation; travel; true crime/investigative; women's issues/studies. **Considers these fiction areas:** Action/adventure; contemporary issues; detective/police/crime; ethnic; experimental; family saga; feminist; gay/lesbian; historical; horror; humor/satire; literary; mainstream/contemporary; mystery/suspense; occult; psychic/supernatural; regional; romance (contemporary, historical); science fiction; sports; thriller; westerns/frontier; women's. **Considers these script subject areas:** Action/adventure; comedy; detective/police/crime; ethnic; experimental; feminist; gay/lesbian; historical; horror; mainstream; mystery/suspense; romantic comedy; romantic drama; science fiction; teen; thriller; western/frontier.
    O➤ This agency specializes in mystery, suspense, science fiction, women's fiction, ethnic fiction, mainstream novels, screenplays, teleplays.
How to Contact: Submit outline, 3 sample chapter(s), SASE. Accepts e-mail and fax queries. Considers simultaneous queries. Responds in 2 weeks to queries; 1 month to mss. Returns materials only with SASE. Obtains most new clients through query letters, recommendations from others, reading short stories in magazines, soliciting conferences.
Recent Sales: Sold 48 titles and sold 5 scripts in the last year. *Intraface*, by Christine Moriarty (Bantam Dell); *The Surrendered Single*, by Laura Doyle (Simon & Schuster); *America the Beautiful*, by Moon Unit Zappa (Scribner); *The Power of the Dog*, by Don Winslow; *Getting Our Breath Back*, by Shawne Johnson (Dutton); *This Bitter Earth*, by Bernice McFadden (Plume).
Terms: Agent receives 15% commission on domestic sales; 25% commission on foreign sales. Offers written contract, binding for 1 year; 30-day notice must be given to terminate contract. 100% of business is derived from commissions on ms sales. Charges clients for foreign postage, messenger services, photocopying.
Writers' Conferences: Maui Writer's Conference.
Tips: "Do not follow up on submissions with phone calls to the agency. The agency will read and respond by mail only. Do not pack your manuscript in plastic 'peanuts' that will make us have to vacuum the office after opening the package containing your manuscript. Always enclose return postage."

◯ **MARY JACK WALD ASSOCIATES, INC.**, 111 E. 14th St., New York NY 10003. (212)254-7842. **Contact:** Danis Sher. Estab. 1985. Member of AAR, Authors Guild, SCBWI. Represents 35 clients. 5% of clients are new/unpublished writers. Currently handles: nonfiction books; novels; story collections; novellas; juvenile books.
    ● This agency is not accepting mss at this time.
Member Agents: Mary Jack Wald; Danis Sher; Lynne Rabinoff (assoc. for foreign rights); Alvin Wald.
Represents: Nonfiction books, novels, short story collections, novellas, juvenile books, movie scripts, TV scripts. **Considers these nonfiction areas:** Biography/autobiography; current affairs; ethnic/cultural interests; history; juvenile nonfiction; language/literature/criticism; music/dance; nature/environment; photography; sociol-

ogy; theater/film; translation; true crime/investigative. **Considers these fiction areas:** Action/adventure; contemporary issues; detective/police/crime; ethnic; experimental; family saga; feminist; gay/lesbian; glitz; historical; juvenile; literary; mainstream/contemporary; mystery/suspense; picture books; thriller; young adult; satire.

   O→ This agency specializes in literary works, juvenile.

How to Contact: Not accepting new clients at this time.

Recent Sales: *Duck Feet, Cow Socks, and Horseshoes*, by Baxter Black.

Terms: Agent receives 15% commission on domestic sales; 15-30% commission on foreign sales. Offers written contract, binding for 1 year.

WALES, LITERARY AGENCY, INC., P.O. Box 9428, Seattle WA 98109-0428. (206)284-7114. E-mail: waleslit@aol.com. **Contact:** Elizabeth Wales, Meg Lemke. Estab. 1988. Member of AAR, Book Publishers' Northwest. Represents 65 clients. 10% of clients are new/unpublished writers. Currently handles: 60% nonfiction books; 40% fiction.

   • Prior to becoming an agent, Ms. Wales worked at Oxford University Press and Viking Penguin.

Member Agents: Elizabeth Wales; Meg Lemke.

Represents: Nonfiction books (narrative), novels. **Considers these nonfiction areas:** Animals; biography/autobiography; current affairs; ethnic/cultural interests; gay/lesbian issues; history; memoirs; multicultural; nature/environment; popular culture; science/technology; travel; women's issues/studies; open to creative or serious treatments of almost any nonfiction subject. **Considers these fiction areas:** Contemporary issues; ethnic; feminist; gay/lesbian; literary; mainstream/contemporary; multicultural; regional.

   O→ This agency specializes in mainstream nonfiction and fiction, as well as narrative and literary fiction.

How to Contact: Query with cover letter, writing sample (no more than 30 pages) and SASE. No phone or fax queries. Prefers regular mail queries, but accepts one-page e-mail queries with no attachments. Considers simultaneous queries. Responds in 3 weeks to queries; 6 weeks to mss. Returns materials only with SASE.

Recent Sales: Sold 15 titles in the last year. *Fateful Harvest*, by Duff Wilson (HarperCollins); *Midnight to the North*, by Sheila Nickerson (Tarcher Penguin Putnam); *Fifth Life of the CatWoman*, by Kathleen Dexter (Berkley Penguin Putnam); *Rides: An AutoBiography*, by K. Lake (Algonquin).

Terms: Agent receives 15% commission on domestic sales; 20% commission on foreign sales. Offers written contract, binding for book-by-book basis. "We make all our income from commissions. We offer editorial help for some of our clients and help some clients with the development of a proposal, but we do not charge for these services. We do charge clients, after a sale, for express mail, manuscript photocopying costs, foreign postage."

Writers' Conferences: Pacific NW Writers Conference (Seattle, July); Writers at Work (Salt Lake City); Writing Rendezvous (Anchorage).

Tips: "Especially encourages writers living in the Pacific Northwest, West Coast, Alaska and Pacific Rim countries to submit work."

T. C. WALLACE, LTD., 425 Madison Ave., New York NY 10017. **Contact:** Thomas C. Wallace. Member of AAR.

   • This agency did not respond to our request for information. Query before submitting.

JOHN A. WARE LITERARY AGENCY, 392 Central Park West, New York NY 10025-5801. (212)866-4733. Fax: (212)866-4734. **Contact:** John Ware. Estab. 1978. Represents 60 clients. 40% of clients are new/unpublished writers. Currently handles: 75% nonfiction books; 25% novels.

   • Prior to opening his agency, Mr. Ware served as a literary agent with James Brown Associates/Curtis Brown, Ltd. and as an editor for Doubleday & Company.

Represents: Nonfiction books, novels. **Considers these nonfiction areas:** Animals; anthropology/archaeology; biography/autobiography; current affairs; health/medicine (academic credentials required); history (including oral history, Americana and folklore); language/literature/criticism; music/dance; nature/environment; popular culture; psychology (academic credentials required); science/technology; sports; travel; true crime/investigative; women's issues/studies; social commentary; investigative journalism; 'bird's eye' views of phenomena. **Considers these fiction areas:** Detective/police/crime; mystery/suspense; thriller; accessible literate noncategory fiction.

How to Contact: Query by letter only first, including SASE. No e-mail or fax queries. Considers simultaneous queries. Responds in 2 weeks to queries.

Recent Sales: *Miracles at the Jesus Oak*, by Craig Harline (Doubleday); *Life Science*, by Elise Blackwell (Little, Brown); *An Unreturned Pilgrim: Biography of Bishop James A. Pike*, by David Robertson (Knopf). Other clients include Travis Hugh Culley, Jon Krakauer, Jack Womack, David Robertson, Jennifer Niven and Nancy E. Turner.

Terms: Agent receives 15% commission on domestic sales; 20% commission on foreign sales; 15% commission on dramatic rights sales. Charges clients for messenger service, photocopying.

Tips: "Writers must have appropriate credentials for authorship of proposal (nonfiction) or manuscript (fiction); no publishing track record required. Open to good writing and interesting ideas by new or veteran writers."

HARRIET WASSERMAN LITERARY AGENCY, 137 E. 36th St., New York NY 10016. Member of AAR.

   • This agency did not respond to our request for information. Query before submitting.

◉ WATERSIDE PRODUCTIONS, INC., 2191 San Elijo Ave., Cardiff-by-the-Sea CA 92007. (760)632-9190. Fax: (760)632-9295. E-mail: admin@waterside.com. Website: www.waterside.com. **Contact:** Matt Wagner, Margot Maley Hutchison, David Fugate. President: Bill Gladstone. Estab. 1982. Represents 300 clients. 20% of clients are new/unpublished writers. Currently handles: 100% nonfiction books.

Member Agents: Bill Gladstone (trade computer titles, business); Margot Maley (trade computer titles, nonfiction); Matthew Wagner (trade computer titles, nonfiction); Carole McClendon (trade computer titles); David Fugate (trade computer titles, business, general nonfiction, sports books); Christopher Van Buren (trade computer titles, spirituality, self-help); Christian Crumlish (trade computer titles); Carole McClendon, Christian Crumlish, Danielle Jatlow, Neil Gudovitz, Jawahara K. Saidullah, Penny C. Sansevieri, Kimberly Valentini.

Represents: Nonfiction books. **Considers these nonfiction areas:** Art/architecture/design; biography/autobiography; business/economics; child guidance/parenting; computers/electronic; ethnic/cultural interests; health/medicine; humor/satire; money/finance; nature/environment; popular culture; psychology; sociology; sports.

How to Contact: Prefers to read materials exclusively. Query with outline/proposal and SASE. Considers simultaneous queries. Responds in 2 weeks to queries; 2 months to mss. Obtains most new clients through recommendations from others.

Recent Sales: *Dan Gookin's Naked Windows*, by Dan Gookin (Sybex); *Battlebots: The Official Guide*, by Mark Clarkson (Osborne McGraw-Hill); *Opening the XBOX: Inside Microsoft's Effort to Unleash an Entertainment Revolution*, by Dean Takahashi (Prima); *Just For Fun*, by Linus Torvalds and David Diamond (HarperCollins); *Photoshop Restoration and Retouching*, by Katrin Eismann (Que Publishing); *Action Script: The Definitive Guide*, by Colin Moock (O'Reily & Associates); *Flash Cartooning*, by Mark Clarkson (Hungry Minds); *Mastering XML*, by Chuck White, et al. (Sybex); *1001 VisualC++ Programming Tips*, by Charles Wright; *Kris Jamsa's Starting with Visual C++*, by Charles Wright (Prima Publishing); *Kris Jamsa's Starting with Microsoft Visual Basic*, by Rob Francis (Prima Publishing); *Easy Web Graphics*, by Julie Adair King (Microsoft Press); *Dreamweaver 4 Magic*, by Al Sparber (New Riders); *The Complete Guide to Client/Server Programming*, by Eric J. Johnson (Prentice-Hall PTR).

Writers' Conferences: "We host the Waterside Publishing Conference each spring in San Diego. Please check our website at www.waterside.com for details."

Tips: "For new writers, a quality proposal and a strong knowledge of the market you're writing for goes a long way towards helping us turn you into a published author."

◉ WATKINS LOOMIS AGENCY, INC., 133 E. 35th St., Suite 1, New York NY 10016. (212)532-0080. Fax: (212)889-0506. **Contact:** Katherine Fausset. Estab. 1908. Represents 150 clients.

Member Agents: Gloria Loomis (president); Katherine Fausset (agent).

Represents: Nonfiction books, novels, short story collections. **Considers these nonfiction areas:** Art/architecture/design; biography/autobiography; current affairs; ethnic/cultural interests; history; nature/environment; popular culture; science/technology; true crime/investigative; journalism. **Considers these fiction areas:** Literary.

    O— This agency specializes in literary fiction, nonfiction.

How to Contact: Query with SASE, by standard mail only. Responds in 1 month to queries.

Recent Sales: This agency prefers not to share information on specific sales. Clients include Walter Mosley and Cornel West.

Terms: Agent receives 15% commission on domestic sales; 20% commission on foreign sales.

◉ SANDRA WATT & ASSOCIATES, 1750 N. Sierra Bonita, Hollywood CA 90045-2423. (323)874-0791. E-mail: rondvart@aol.com. Estab. 1977. Represents 55 clients. 15% of clients are new/unpublished writers. Currently handles: 40% nonfiction books; 60% novels.

    ● Prior to opening her agency, Ms. Watt was vice president of an educational publishing company.

Member Agents: Sandra Watt (scripts, nonfiction, novels).

Represents: Nonfiction books, novels. **Considers these nonfiction areas:** Agriculture/horticulture; animals; anthropology/archaeology; art/architecture/design; crafts/hobbies; current affairs; how-to; humor/satire; language/literature/criticism; memoirs; nature/environment; New Age/metaphysics; popular culture; psychology; religious/inspirational; self-help/personal improvement; sports; travel; true crime/investigative; women's issues/studies; reference. **Considers these fiction areas:** Contemporary issues; detective/police/crime; family saga; mainstream/contemporary; mystery/suspense; regional; religious/inspirational; thriller; young adult; women's mainstream novels.

    O— This agency specializes in "books to film" and scripts: film noir, family, romantic comedies, books, women's fiction, young adult, mystery, commercial nonfiction. Does not want to receive "first 'ideas' for finished work."

How to Contact: Query with SASE. Accepts e-mail and fax queries. Considers simultaneous queries. Responds in 2 weeks to queries; 2 months to mss. Returns materials only with SASE. Obtains most new clients through recommendations from others, referrals and "from wonderful query letters. Don't forget the SASE!"

Terms: Agent receives 15% commission on domestic sales; 25% commission on foreign sales. Offers written contract, binding for 1 year. Charges clients one-time nonrefundable marketing fee of $100 for unpublished authors.

☑ ◪ **WAXMAN LITERARY AGENCY**, 80 Fifth Ave., New York NY 10003. (212)262-2388. Fax: (212)262-0119. Website: www.waxmanagency.com. Estab. 1997. Member of AAR. Represents 60 clients. 50% of clients are new/unpublished writers. Currently handles: 60% nonfiction books; 40% novels.   *poss.*
- Prior to opening his agency, Mr. Waxman was an editor for five years at HarperCollins.

Member Agents: Scott Waxman (all categories of nonfiction, commercial fiction).

Represents: Nonfiction books, novels. **Considers these nonfiction areas:** Business/economics; ethnic/cultural interests; health/medicine; history; money/finance; religious/inspirational; sports. **Considers these fiction areas:** Literary.

○━ "We are interested in literary fiction with commercial appeal."

How to Contact: Query through Web site. All unsolicited mss returned unopened. Considers simultaneous queries. Responds in 2 weeks to queries; 6 weeks to mss. Returns materials only with SASE. Obtains most new clients through recommendations from others, solicitations, conferences.

Terms: Agent receives 15% commission on domestic sales; 25% commission on foreign sales. Offers written contract; 60-day notice must be given to terminate contract. Charges for photocopying, express mail, fax, international postage, book orders; refers to editing services for clients only. 0% of business is derived from editing services.

◪ **WECKSLER-INCOMCO**, 170 West End Ave., New York NY 10023. (212)787-2239. Fax: (212)496-7035. **Contact:** Sally Wecksler. Estab. 1971. Represents 25 clients. 50% of clients are new/unpublished writers. Currently handles: 60% nonfiction books; 15% novels; 25% juvenile books.
- Prior to becoming an agent, Ms. Wecksler was an editor at *Publishers Weekly*; publisher with the international department of R.R. Bowker; and international director at Baker & Taylor.   *no*

Member Agents: Joann Amparan (general, children's books); Sally Wecksler (general, foreign rights/co-editions, fiction, illustrated books, children's books, business).

Represents: Nonfiction books, novels, juvenile books. **Considers these nonfiction areas:** Art/architecture/design; biography/autobiography; business/economics; creative nonfiction; current affairs; history; juvenile nonfiction; music/dance; nature/environment; photography; theater/film. **Considers these fiction areas:** Contemporary issues; historical; juvenile; literary; mainstream/contemporary; picture books.

○━ This agency specializes in nonfiction with illustrations (photos and art). Actively seeking "illustrated books for adults or children with beautiful photos or artwork." Does not want to receive "science fiction or books with violence."

How to Contact: Query with SASE, outline, author bio. Responds in 1 month to queries; 2 months to mss. Obtains most new clients through recommendations from others, solicitations.

Recent Sales: Sold 11 titles in the last year. *What Every Successful Woman Knows*, by William J. Morin (McGraw-Hill); *Total Career Fitness* (Jossey-Bass).

Terms: Agent receives 15% commission on domestic sales; 20% commission on foreign sales. Offers written contract, binding for 3 years.

Tips: "Make sure a SASE is enclosed. Send three chapters and outline, clearly typed or word processed, double-spaced, written with punctuation and grammar in approved style. No presentations by fax or e-mail. Prefers writers who have had something in print."

◪ **THE WENDY WEIL AGENCY, INC.**, 232 Madison Ave., Suite 1300, New York NY 10016. Member of AAR.
- This agency did not respond to our request for information. Query before submitting.

Member Agents: Wendy Weil; Emily Forland (associate member).

◪ **CHERRY WEINER LITERARY AGENCY**, 28 Kipling Way, Manalapan NJ 07726-3711. (732)446-2096. Fax: (732)792-0506. E-mail: cherry8486@aol.com. **Contact:** Cherry Weiner. Estab. 1977. Represents 40 clients.   *no*
10% of clients are new/unpublished writers. Currently handles: 10-20% nonfiction books; 80-90% novels.
- This agency is currently not looking for new clients except by referral or by personal contact at writers' conferences.

Represents: Nonfiction books, novels. **Considers these nonfiction areas:** Self-help/personal improvement; sociology. **Considers these fiction areas:** Action/adventure; contemporary issues; detective/police/crime; family saga; fantasy; glitz; historical; mainstream/contemporary; mystery/suspense; psychic/supernatural; romance; science fiction; thriller; westerns/frontier.

○━ This agency specializes in science fiction, fantasy, westerns, mysteries (both contemporary and historical), historical novels, Native American works, mainstream, all the genre romances.

How to Contact: Query with SASE. Prefers to read materials exclusively. No e-mail or fax queries. Responds in 1 week to queries; 2 months to mss. Returns materials only with SASE.

CONTACT THE EDITOR of *Guide to Literary Agents* by e-mail at literaryagents @fwpubs.com with your questions and comments.

Recent Sales: Sold 40 titles in the last year. *Earthborn*, by Paul Collins (Tor).

Terms: Agent receives 15% commission on domestic sales; 15% commission on foreign sales. Offers written contract. Charges clients for extra copies of mss "but would prefer author do it"; 1st class postage for author's copies of books; Express Mail for important document/manuscripts.

Writers' Conferences: Western writers convention; science fiction conventions; fantasy conventions.

Tips: "Meet agents and publishers at conferences. Establish a relationship, then get in touch with them reminding them of meetings and conference."

THE WEINGEL-FIDEL AGENCY, 310 E. 46th St., 21E, New York NY 10017. (212)599-2959. **Contact:** Loretta Weingel-Fidel. Estab. 1989. Currently handles: 75% nonfiction books; 25% novels.
- Prior to opening her agency, Ms. Weingel-Fidel was a psychoeducational diagnostician.

Represents: Nonfiction books, novels. **Considers these nonfiction areas:** Art/architecture/design; biography/autobiography; memoirs; music/dance; psychology; science/technology; sociology; women's issues/studies; investigative. **Considers these fiction areas:** Literary; mainstream/contemporary.
- This agency specializes in commercial, literary fiction and nonfiction. Actively seeking investigative journalism. Does not want to receive genre fiction, self-help, science fiction, fantasy.

How to Contact: Referred writers only. No unsolicited mss.

Recent Sales: *The New Rabbi*, by Stephen Fried (Bantam); *Love, Greg & Lauren*, by Greg Manning (Bantam); *The V Book*, by Elizabeth G. Stewart, M.D. and Paula Spencer (Bantam).

Terms: Agent receives 15% commission on domestic sales; 20% commission on foreign sales. Offers written contract, binding for 1 year; automatic renewal. Bills sent back to clients all reasonable expenses such as UPS, express mail, photocopying, etc.

Tips: "A very small, selective list enables me to work very closely with my clients to develop and nurture talent. I only take on projects and writers about which I am extremely enthusiastic."

TED WEINSTEIN LITERARY MANAGEMENT, 287 Duncan St., San Francisco CA 94131-2019. E-mail: query@twliterary.com. Website: www.twliterary.com. **Contact:** Ted Weinstein. Estab. 2001. Represents 20 clients. 75% of clients are new/unpublished writers. Currently handles: 100% nonfiction books.
- Prior to becoming an agent, Mr. Weinstein was the VP of marketing and business development at Nolo Press, head of licensing and electronic publishing at Miller Freeman Publishing, and a freelance journalist.

Represents: Nonfiction books. **Considers these nonfiction areas:** Biography/autobiography; business/economics; current affairs; government/politics/law; health/medicine; history; popular culture; science/technology; self-help/personal improvement; travel; environment, lifestyle.

How to Contact: Submit proposal package, outline, 1 sample chapter(s). See website for detailed submission guidelines. Considers simultaneous queries. Returns materials only with SASE. Obtains most new clients through recommendations from others.

Recent Sales: *Paris in Mind*, by Jennifer Lee (Vintage/Random House); *Skeptics Dictionary*, by Robert Carroll (John Wiley & Sons).

Terms: Agent receives 15% commission on domestic sales; 20-30% commission on foreign sales. Offers written contract, binding for 1 year, 60 days, termination thereafter. Charges clients for photocopying and express shipping. Writers reimbursed after the sale of ms. 0% of business is derived from reading or criticism fees.

RHODA WEYR AGENCY, 151 Bergen St., Brooklyn NY 11217. **Contact:** Rhoda A. Weyr, president. Estab. 1983. Member of AAR. This agency is not taking on new clients.

LYNN WHITTAKER, LITERARY AGENT, Graybill & English, LLC, 1920 N St. NW, Suite 620, Washington DC 20036-1619. (202)861-0106, ext. 37. Fax: (202)457-0662. E-mail: lynnwhittaker@aol.com. Website: www.graybillandenglish.com. Estab. 1998. Member of AAR. Represents 24 clients. 10% of clients are new/unpublished writers. Currently handles: 85% nonfiction books; 15% novels.
- Prior to becoming an agent, Ms. Whittaker was an editor, owner of a small press, and taught at the college level.

Represents: Nonfiction books, novels, short story collections. **Considers these nonfiction areas:** Animals; biography/autobiography; current affairs; ethnic/cultural interests; gay/lesbian issues; history; language/literature/criticism; memoirs; money/finance; multicultural; nature/environment; popular culture; science/technology; sports; travel; women's issues/studies. **Considers these fiction areas:** Detective/police/crime; ethnic; experimental; feminist; historical; literary; multicultural; mystery/suspense; sports.
- "As a former editor, I especially enjoy working closely with writers to develop and polish their proposal and manuscripts." Actively seeking literary fiction, sports, history, creative nonfiction of all kinds, nature and science, ethnic/multicultural, women's stories & issues. Does not want to receive romance/women's commercial fiction, children's/young adult, religious, fantasy/horror.

How to Contact: Query with SASE, submit proposal package, outline, 2 sample chapter(s). Responds in 2 weeks to queries; 1 month to mss. Returns materials only with SASE. Obtains most new clients through recommendations from others.

Recent Sales: *Never Say Never: When Others Say You Can't and You Know You Can*, by Phyllis George (McGraw-Hill); *The Art of Death*, by Sarah Stewart Taylor (St. Martin's); *20 Seasons in the Sun: My Baseball*

Life in Pictures, by Carl Ripken Jr. and Jerry Wachter (Morrow). Other clients include Leonard Shapiro, John Tallmadge, Dorothy Sucher, James McGregor Burns, American Women in Radio and Television (AWRT), Maniza Naqui, Chris Palmer.
Terms: Agent receives 15% commission on domestic sales; 20% commission on foreign sales. Offers written contract; 30-day notice must be given to terminate contract. Direct expenses for photocopying of proposals and mss, UPS/FedEx.
Writers' Conferences: Creative Nonfiction Conference, (Goucher College MD, August); Washington Independent Writers, (Washington DC, May); Hariette Austin Writers Conference, (Athens GA, July).

◉ **WIESER & WIESER, INC.**, 25 E. 21 St., 6th Floor, New York NY 10010. (212)260-0860. **Contact:** Olga Wieser. Estab. 1975. 30% of clients are new/unpublished writers. Currently handles: 50% nonfiction books; 50% novels.
Member Agents: Jake Elwell (history, military, mysteries, romance, sports, thrillers); Olga Wieser (psychology, fiction, pop medical, literary fiction).
Represents: Nonfiction books, novels. **Considers these nonfiction areas:** Business/economics; cooking/foods/nutrition; current affairs; health/medicine; history; money/finance; nature/environment; psychology; sports; true crime/investigative. **Considers these fiction areas:** Contemporary issues; detective/police/crime; historical; literary; mainstream/contemporary; mystery/suspense; romance; thriller.
  O⚲ This agency specializes in mainstream fiction and nonfiction.
How to Contact: Query with outline/proposal and SASE. Responds in 2 weeks to queries. Obtains most new clients through queries, authors' recommendations and industry professionals.
Recent Sales: *Mary: The Chosen One*, by Roberta Kells Dorr (Revell); *Eddie Rickenbacker*, by H. Paul Jeffers (Presidio); *Sea of Grey*, by Dewey Lambdin (St. Martin's Press); *The Voyage of the Hunley*, by Edwin P. Hoyt (Burford Books); *Cyclops*, by Jim DeFelice (Pocket); *Skyhook*, by John Nance (Putnam).
Terms: Agent receives 15% commission on domestic sales; 20% commission on foreign sales. Offers written contract. Charges clients for photocopying and overseas mailing.
Writers' Conferences: BEA; Frankfurt Book Fair.

◉ **WITHERSPOON ASSOCIATES, INC.**, 235 E. 31st St., New York NY 10016. (212)889-8626. **Contact:** David Forrer. Estab. 1990. Represents 150 clients. 20% of clients are new/unpublished writers. Currently handles: 50% nonfiction books; 45% novels; 5% story collections.
  • Prior to becoming an agent, Ms. Witherspoon was a writer and magazine consultant.
Member Agents: Maria Massie; Kimberly Witherspoon; David Forrer; Alexis Hurley.
Represents: Nonfiction books, novels. **Considers these nonfiction areas:** Anthropology/archaeology; biography/autobiography; business/economics; current affairs; ethnic/cultural interests; gay/lesbian issues; government/politics/law; health/medicine; history; memoirs; money/finance; music/dance; science/technology; self-help/personal improvement; theater/film; travel; true crime/investigative; women's issues/studies. **Considers these fiction areas:** Contemporary issues; detective/police/crime; ethnic; family saga; feminist; gay/lesbian; historical; literary; mainstream/contemporary; mystery/suspense; thriller.
How to Contact: Query with SASE. Prefers to read materials exclusively. No unsolicited mss. Considers simultaneous queries. Responds in 6 weeks to queries. Obtains most new clients through recommendations from others, solicitations, conferences.
Recent Sales: This agency prefers not to share information on specific sales.
Terms: Agent receives 15% commission on domestic sales; 20% commission on foreign sales. Offers written contract. Office fees are deducted from author's earnings.
Writers' Conferences: BEA (Chicago, June); Frankfurt (Germany, October).

◙ **AUDREY A. WOLF LITERARY AGENCY**, 1001 Connecticut Ave. NW, Washington DC 20036. Member of AAR.
  • This agency did not respond to our request for information. Query before submitting.

◐ **THE WONDERLAND PRESS, INC.**, 160 Fifth Ave., Suite 625, New York NY 10010-7003. (212)989-2550. E-mail: litraryagt@aol.com. **Contact:** John Campbell. Estab. 1985. Member of the American Book Producers Association. Represents 32 clients. Currently handles: 90% nonfiction books; 10% novels.
  • The Wonderland Press is also a book packager and "in a position to nurture strong proposals all the way from concept through bound books."
Represents: Nonfiction books, novels. **Considers these nonfiction areas:** Art/architecture/design; biography/autobiography; ethnic/cultural interests; health/medicine; history; how-to; interior design/decorating; language/literature/criticism; photography; popular culture; psychology; self-help/personal improvement. **Considers these fiction areas:** Action/adventure; literary; thriller.
  O⚲ This agency specializes in high-quality nonfiction, illustrated, reference, how-to and entertainment books. Does not want to receive poetry, memoir, children's fiction or category fiction.
How to Contact: Submit proposal package, outline, SASE. Prefers to read materials exclusively. Accepts e-mail and fax queries. Responds in 5 days to queries; 2 weeks to mss. Obtains most new clients through recommendations from others, solicitations.

Recent Sales: Sold 38 titles in the last year. *Nude Body Nude*, by Howard Schatz (HarperCollins); *The Essential Dale Chihuly* (Abrams).

Terms: Agent receives 15% commission on domestic sales. Offers written contract; 30- to 90-day notice must be given to terminate contract. Offers criticism service, included in 15% commission; charges clients for photocopying, long-distance telephone, overnight express-mail, messengering.

Tips: "We welcome submissions from new authors, but proposals must be unique, of high commercial interest and well-written. Follow your talent. Write with passion. Know your market. Submit polished work instead of apologizing for its mistakes, typos, incompleteness, etc. We want to see your best work."

ANN WRIGHT REPRESENTATIVES, 165 W. 46th St., Suite 1105, New York NY 10036-2501. (212)764-6770. Fax: (212)764-5125. E-mail: annwrightlit@aol.com. **Contact:** Dan Wright. Estab. 1961. Signatory of WGA. Represents 23 clients. 30% of clients are new/unpublished writers. Currently handles: 50% novels; 40% movie scripts; 10% TV scripts.

● See the expanded listing for this agency in Script Agents.

WRITERS HOUSE, 21 W. 26th St., New York NY 10010. (212)685-2400. Fax: (212)685-6550. Estab. 1974. Member of AAR. Represents 440 clients. 50% of clients are new/unpublished writers. Currently handles: 25% nonfiction books; 40% novels; 35% juvenile books.

Member Agents: Albert Zuckerman (major novels, thrillers, women's fiction, important nonfiction); Amy Berkower (major juvenile authors, women's fiction, art and decorating, psychology); Merrilee Heifetz (quality children's fiction, science fiction and fantasy, popular culture, literary fiction); Susan Cohen (juvenile and young adult fiction and nonfiction, Judaism, women's issues); Susan Ginsburg (serious and popular fiction, true crime, narrative nonfiction, personality books, cookbooks); Michele Rubin (serious nonfiction); Robin Rue (commercial fiction and nonfiction, YA fiction); Jennifer Lyons (literary, commercial fiction, international fiction, nonfiction and illustrated); Jodi Reamer (juvenile and young adult fiction and nonfiction, adult commercial fiction, popular culture); Simon Lipskar (literary and commercial fiction, narrative nonfiction); Nicole Pitesa (juvenile and young adult fiction, literary fiction); Steven Malk (juvenile and young adult fiction and non-fiction).

Represents: Nonfiction books, novels, juvenile books. **Considers these nonfiction areas:** Animals; art/architecture/design; biography/autobiography; business/economics; child guidance/parenting; cooking/foods/nutrition; health/medicine; history; interior design/decorating; juvenile nonfiction; military/war; money/finance; music/dance; nature/environment; psychology; science/technology; self-help/personal improvement; theater/film; true crime/investigative; women's issues/studies. **Considers these fiction areas:** Action/adventure; comic books/cartoon; confession; contemporary issues; detective/police/crime; erotica; ethnic; experimental; family saga; fantasy; feminist; gay/lesbian; glitz; gothic; hi-lo; historical; horror; humor/satire; juvenile; literary; mainstream/contemporary; military/war; multicultural; multimedia; mystery/suspense; New Age; occult; picture books; plays; poetry; poetry in translation; psychic/supernatural; regional; religious/inspirational; romance; science fiction; short story collections; spiritual; sports; thriller; translation; westerns/frontier; young adult; women's.

O─ This agency specializes in all types of popular fiction and nonfiction. Does not want to receive scholarly, professional, poetry, plays or screenplays.

How to Contact: Query with SASE. No e-mail or fax queries. Responds in 1 month to queries. Obtains most new clients through recommendations from others.

Recent Sales: Sold 200-300 titles in the last year. *Next*, by Michael Lewis (Norton); *The Art of Deception*, by Ridley Pearson (Hyperion); *Report from Ground Zero*, by Dennis Smith (Viking); *The Villa*, by Nora Roberts (Penguin/Putnam); *Captain Underpants*, by Dan Pilkey (Scholastic). Other clients include Francine Pascal, Ken Follett, Stephen Hawking, Neil Gaiman and Laurel Hamilton.

Terms: Agent receives 15% commission on domestic sales; 20% commission on foreign sales. Offers written contract, binding for 1 year. Agency charges fees for copying manuscripts and proposals and overseas airmail of books.

Tips: "Do not send mss. Write a compelling letter. If you do, we'll ask to see your work."

WRITERS' PRODUCTIONS, P.O. Box 630, Westport CT 06881-0630. (203)227-8199. Fax: (203)227-6349. E-mail: dlm67@worldnet.att.net. **Contact:** David L. Meth. Estab. 1982. Represents 25 clients. Currently handles: 40% nonfiction books; 60% novels.

● "I am not taking on new clients at this time."

Represents: Nonfiction books, novels, literary quality fiction.

How to Contact: No new clients accepted at this time. No e-mail or fax queries. Obtains most new clients through recommendations from others.

Recent Sales: This agency prefers not to share information on specific sales.

Terms: Agent receives 15% commission on domestic sales; 25% commission on foreign sales. Offers written contract. Charges clients for electronic transmissions, long-distance phone calls, express or overnight mail, courier service, etc.

Tips: "Send only your best, most professionally prepared work. Do not send it before it is ready. We must have SASE for all correspondence and return of manuscripts. Do not waste time sending work to agencies or editors who are not accepting new clients."

WRITERS' REPRESENTATIVES, INC., 116 W. 14th St., 11th Floor, New York NY 10011-7305. (212)620-0023. E-mail: transom@writersreps.com. Website: www.writersreps.com. **Contact:** Glen Hartley or Lynn Chu. Estab. 1985. Represents 130 clients. 5% of clients are new/unpublished writers. Currently handles: 90% nonfiction books; 10% novels.
• Prior to becoming agents, Ms. Chu was a lawyer, and Mr. Hartley worked at Simon & Schuster, Harper & Row and Cornell University Press.
Member Agents: Lynn Chu; Glen Hartley; Catharine Sprinkel.
Represents: Nonfiction books, novels. **Considers these fiction areas:** Literary.
　O→ This agency specializes in serious nonfiction. Actively seeking serious nonfiction and quality fiction. Does not want to receive motion picture/television screenplays.
How to Contact: Query with SASE. Accepts e-mail queries, but no attachments. Considers simultaneous queries. Obtains most new clients through "recommendations from our clients."
Recent Sales: Sold 30 titles in the last year. *The Shield of Achilles*, by Philip Bobbitt; *Sisters of Salome*, by Toni Bentley; *World on Fire*, by Amy Chua; *Genius*, by Harold Bloom.
Terms: Agent receives 15% commission on domestic sales; 20% commission on foreign sales.
Tips: "Always include a SASE. That will ensure a response from the agent and the return of material submitted."

WYLIE-MERRICK LITERARY AGENCY, 1138 S. Webster St., Kokomo IN 46902-6357. (765)459-8258 or (765)457-3783. E-mail: smartin@wylie-merrick.com; rbrown@wylie-merrick.com. Website: www.wylie-merrick.com. **Contact:** S.A. Martin, Robert Brown. Estab. 1999. Member of SCBWI. Currently handles: 25% nonfiction books; 25% novels; 50% juvenile books.
• Ms. Martin holds a Master's degree in Language Education and is a writing and technology curriculum specialist.
Member Agents: S.A. Martin (juvenile/middle grade/young adult); Robert Brown (adult fiction/nonfiction, young adult).
Represents: Nonfiction books (adult and juvenile), novels (adult and juvenile), juvenile books. **Considers these nonfiction areas:** How-to; juvenile nonfiction; self-help/personal improvement. **Considers these fiction areas:** Action/adventure; contemporary fantasy; historical; mystery/suspense; picture books; religious/inspirational; romance; science fiction; thriller; young adult (middle grade).
　O→ This agency specializes in children's and young adult literary as well as mainstream adult fiction. Actively seeking middle-grade/young adult fiction and nonfiction, picture books, adult fiction and nonfiction.
How to Contact: Query with SASE, include first 10 pages for novels, complete mss for picturebooks. No e-mail or fax queries. Considers simultaneous queries. Responds in 1 month to queries; 3 months to mss. Returns materials only with SASE. Obtains most new clients through recommendations from others, queries and conferences.
Recent Sales: Sold 1 currently, 2 pending titles in the last year. *Full Court Pressure*, by Jon Ripslinger (Roaring Brook).
Terms: Agent receives 15% commission on domestic sales; 20% commission on foreign sales. Offers written contract. Charges clients for postage, photocopying, handling.
Tips: "We work with a small, select group of writers. We are highly selective when considering new clients, so your work must be the best it can possibly be for us to consider it. We only work with serious professionals who know their craft and the publishing industry. Anything less we reject."

ZACHARY SHUSTER HARMSWORTH, 1776 Broadway, Suite 1405, New York NY 10019. (212)765-6900. Fax: (212)765-6490. E-mail: e.harmsworth@zshliterary.com. Website: www.zshliterary.com. Also: Boston Office: 729 Boylston St., 5th Floor. Phone: (617)262-2400, Fax: (617)262-2468. **Contact:** Esmond Harmsworth; Scott Gold (NY). Estab. 1996. Represents 125 clients. 20% of clients are new/unpublished writers. Currently handles: 45% nonfiction books; 45% novels; 5% story collections; 5% scholarly books.
• "Our principals include two former publishing and entertainment lawyers, a journalist and an editor/agent." Lane Zachary was an editor at Random House before becoming an agent.
Member Agents: Esmond Harmsworth (commercial and literary fiction, history, science, adventure); Todd Shuster (narrative and prescriptive nonfiction, biography, memoirs); Lane Zachary (biography, memoirs, literary fiction); Jennifer Gates (literary fiction, nonfiction).
Represents: Nonfiction books, novels. **Considers these nonfiction areas:** Animals; biography/autobiography; business/economics; current affairs; gay/lesbian issues; government/politics/law; health/medicine; history; how-to; language/literature/criticism; memoirs; money/finance; music/dance; psychology; science/technology; self-help/personal improvement; sports; true crime/investigative; women's issues/studies. **Considers these fiction areas:** Contemporary issues; detective/police/crime; ethnic; feminist; gay/lesbian; historical; literary; mainstream/contemporary; mystery/suspense; thriller.

FOR INFORMATION ON THE CONFERENCES agents attend, refer to the **Writers' Conferences** section in this book.

O— This agency specializes in journalist-driven narrative nonfiction, literary and commercial fiction. Actively seeking narrative nonfiction, mystery, commercial and literary fiction, memoirs, history, biographies. Does not want to receive poetry.

How to Contact: Query with SASE, submit 50 page sample of ms. No e-mail or fax queries. Considers simultaneous queries. Responds in 3 months to mss. Obtains most new clients through recommendations from others, solicitations, conferences.

Recent Sales: Sold 40-50 titles in the last year. *All Kinds of Minds*, by Mel Levine (Simon & Schuster) #1 New York Times bestseller. Other clients include Leslie Epstein, David Mixner.

Terms: Agent receives 15% commission on domestic sales; 20% commission on foreign sales. Offers written contract, binding for 1 work only; 30-day notice must be given to terminate contract. Charges clients for postage, copying, courier, telephone. "We only charge expenses if the manuscript is sold."

Tips: "We work closely with all our clients on all editorial and promotional aspects of their works."

N **THE ZACK COMPANY, INC.**, 243 West 70th Street, Suite 8D, New York NY 10023-4366. Website: www.zackcompany.com. **Contact:** Andrew Zack. Estab. 1996. Member of AAR, The Authors Guild, MWA, SFWA. Represents 40 clients.

● Mr. Zack has been an agent since 1993. Prior to agenting, he was an editor for the Berkley Publishing Group and has also worked with Simon & Schuster, Warner Books and other publishers.

Represents: Nonfiction books, novels. **Represents these fiction areas:** commercial fiction, thrillers, mystery/crime, action (*not* action adventure), science fiction, fantasy, historical fiction (no westerns), horror. **Represents these nonfiction areas:** politics/current affairs, science/technology, natural sciences, business, biography/autobiography/memoir, personal finance/investing, parenting, history (particularly military and intelligence services history), health/medicine, relationship books.

O— Does not want to receive women's fiction, romance, westerns, short story collections, screenplays, genre horror, gay or lesbian, humor, religious, poetry, children's books, novels under 65,000 words, previously self-published books selling under 20,000 copies.

How to Contact: Query with SASE. No fax or e-mail queries. Responds only if interested. Do not send queries by certified mail, no sample chapters unless requested.

Tips: "Nonfiction must be written by a qualified expert in the field."

N **SUSAN ZECKENDORF ASSOC. INC.**, 171 W. 57th St., New York NY 10019. (212)245-2928. **Contact:** Susan Zeckendorf. Estab. 1979. Member of AAR. Represents 15 clients. 25% of clients are new/unpublished writers. Currently handles: 50% nonfiction books; 50% novels.

● Prior to opening her agency, Ms. Zeckendorf was a counseling psychologist.

Represents: Nonfiction books, novels. **Considers these nonfiction areas:** Biography/autobiography; child guidance/parenting; health/medicine; history; music/dance; psychology; science/technology; sociology; women's issues/studies. **Considers these fiction areas:** Detective/police/crime; ethnic; historical; literary; mainstream/contemporary; mystery/suspense; thriller.

O— Actively seeking mysteries, literary fiction, mainstream fiction, thrillers, social history, parenting, classical music, biography. Does not want to receive science fiction, romance. "No children's books."

How to Contact: Query with SASE. No e-mail or fax queries. Considers simultaneous queries. Responds in 10 days to queries; 3 weeks to mss. Returns materials only with SASE.

Recent Sales: Sold 2 titles in the last year. *How to Write a Damn Good Mystery*, by James N. Frey (St. Martin's); *Moment of Madness*, by Una-Mary Parker (Headline).

Terms: Agent receives 15% commission on domestic sales; 20% commission on foreign sales. Charges for photocopying, messenger services.

Writers' Conferences: Central Valley Writers Conference; The Tucson Publishers Association Conference; Writer's Connection; Frontiers in Writing Conference (Amarillo TX); Golden Triangle Writers Conference (Beaumont TX); Oklahoma Festival of Books (Claremont OK); Mary Mount Writers Conference.

Tips: "We are a small agency giving lots of individual attention. We respond quickly to submissions."

Script Agents

Making it as a screenwriter takes time. For starters, a good script takes time. It takes time to write. It takes time to rewrite. It takes time to write the four or five scripts that precede the really great one. The learning curve from one script to the next is tremendous, and you'll probably have a drawer full of work before you're ready to approach an agent. Your talent has to show on the page, and the page has to excite people.

You'll need both confidence and insecurity at the same time. Confidence to enter the business at all. For a twenty-two-week season, a half-hour sitcom buys two freelance scripts. There are less than 300 network television movies and less than 100 big screen feature films produced each year. Nevertheless, in recent years the number of cable channels buying original movies has grown, independent film houses have sprouted up all over the country, and more studios are buying direct to video scripts—all of which offer a wide range of opportunities for emerging scriptwriters. If you're good and you persevere, you will find work.

Use your insecurity to spur you and your work on to become better. Accept that, at the beginning, you know little. Then go out and learn. Read all the books you can find on scriptwriting, from format to dramatic structure. Learn the formulas, but don't become formulaic. Observe the rules, but don't be predictable. Absorb what you learn, and make it your own.

And finally, you'll need a good agent. In this book we call agents handling screenplays or teleplays script agents, but in true West Coast parlance they are literary agents, since they represent writers as opposed to actors or musicians. Most studios, networks, and production companies will return unsolicited manuscripts unopened for legal protection. An agent has the entree to get your script on the desk of a story analyst or development executive.

The ideal agent understands what a writer writes, is able to explain it to others, and has credibility with individuals who are in a position to make decisions. An agent sends out material, advises what direction a career should take, and makes the financial arrangements. And how do you get a good agent? By going back to the beginning—great scripts.

THE SPEC SCRIPT

There are two sides to an agent's representation of a scriptwriter: finding work on an existing project and selling original scripts. Most writers break in with scripts written on "spec," that is, on speculation without a specific sale in mind. A spec script is a calling card that demonstrates skills, and gets your name and abilities before influential people. Movie spec scripts are always original, not for a sequel. Spec scripts for TV are always based on existing TV shows, not for an original concept.

More often than not, a spec script will not be made. An original movie spec can either be "optioned" or "bought" outright, with the intention of making a movie, or it can attract rewrite work on a script for an existing project. For TV, on the basis of the spec script, a writer can be invited in to pitch five or six ideas to the producers. If an idea is bought, the writer is paid to flesh out the story to an outline. If that is acceptable, the writer can be commissioned to write the script.

At that point the in-house writing staff comes in, and in a lot of cases, rewrites the script. But it's a sale, and the writer receives the residuals every time that episode is shown anywhere in the world. The goal is to sell enough scripts so you are invited to join the writing staff.

What makes a good spec script? Good writing for a start. Write every single day. Talk to as many people you can find who are different from you. Take an acting class to help you really hear dialogue. Take a directing class to see how movies are put together. If you are just getting started, working as an assistant to an established screenwriter can be beneficial. You get excellent experience, and as your name becomes attached to scripts, you'll have more assets to bring with you as you start to approach agents.

Learn the correct dramatic structure, and internalize those rules. Then throw them away and write intuitively. The three-act structure is basic and crucial to any dramatic presentation. Act 1—get your hero up a tree. Act 2—throw a rock at him. Act 3—get him down. Some books will tell you that certain events have to happen by a certain page. What they're describing is not a template but a rhythm. Good scriptwriting is good storytelling.

Spec scripts for movies

If you're writing for movies, explore the different genres until you find one you feel comfortable writing. Read and study scripts for movies you admire to find out what makes them work. Choose a premise for yourself, not "the market." What is it you care most about? What is it you know the most about? Write it. Know your characters and what they want. Know what the movie is about, and build a rising level of tension that draws the reader in and makes her care about what happens.

For feature films, you'll need two or three spec scripts, and perhaps a few long-form scripts (miniseries, movies of the week or episodics) as well. Your scripts should depict a layered story with characters who feel real, each interaction presenting another facet of their personalities.

Although you should write from your heart, keep in mind that Hollywood follows trends like no other industry. A script on a hot topic means more money for the studio. Current big genres are teen movies with edge, *Sixth Sense*-type thrillers, family-oriented stories, and real-life dramas. Instead of trying to write to a trend, use your stellar script to start one of your own.

Spec scripts for TV

If you want to write for TV, watch a lot of it. Tape several episodes of a show, and analyze them. Where do the jokes fall? Where do the plot points come? How is the story laid out? Read scripts of a show to find out what professional writers do that works. (Script City, (800)676-2522, and Book City, (800)4-CINEMA, have thousands of movie and TV scripts for sale.)

Your spec script will demonstrate your knowledge of the format and ability to create believable dialogue. Choosing a show you like with characters you're drawn to is important. Current hot shows for writers include *Smallville*, *Gilmore Girls*, *Law and Order*, and *Will & Grace*. Newer shows may also be good bets, such as *Alias* and *Six Feet Under*. If a show has been on three or more years, a lot of story lines have already been done, either on camera or in spec scripts. Your spec should be for today's hits, not yesterday's.

Television shows where the cast is predominantly composed of teenagers continue to be extremely popular. Shows like *Buffy the Vampire Slayer* and *Dawson's Creek* appealed so strongly to both adult and teen audiences that almost every network raced to add similar shows to their fall lineup. Animated sitcoms like *The Simpsons*, which are aimed at adult audiences, also remain favorites. Most networks now have animated shows in prime-time slots.

You probably already want to write for a specific program. Paradoxically, to be considered for that show your agent will submit a spec script for a different show, because—to protect themselves from lawsuits—producers do not read scripts written for their characters. So pick a show similar in tone and theme to the show you really want to write for. If you want to write for *Everybody Loves Raymond*, submit a spec script for *King of Queens*. The hour-long dramatic shows are more individual in nature. You practically would have had to attend med school to write for *ER*, but *Law and Order* and *CSI* have a number of things in common that would make them good specs for one another. Half-hour shows generally have a writing staff and only occasionally buy freelance scripts. Hour-long shows are more likely to pick up scripts written by freelancers.

In writing a spec script, you're not just writing an episode. You're writing an *Emmy-winning* episode. You are not on staff yet; you have plenty of time. Make this the episode the staff writers wish they had written. But at the same time, certain conventions must be observed. The regular characters always have the most interesting story line. Involve all the characters in the episode. Don't introduce important new characters.

SELLING YOURSELF TO THE SALESPEOPLE

Scriptwriting is an art and craft. Marketing your work is salesmanship, and it's a very competitive world. Read the trades, attend seminars, stay on top of the news. Make opportunities for yourself.

But at the same time, your writing side always has to be working, producing pages for the selling side to hawk. First you sell yourself to an agent. Then the agent sells herself to you. If you both feel the relationship is mutually beneficial, the agent starts selling you to others.

All agents are open to third-party recommendations, referrals from a person whose opinion is trusted. To that end, you can pursue development people, producers' assistants, anyone who will read your script. Mail room employees at the bigger agencies are agents in training. They're looking for the next great script that will earn them a raise and a promotion to the next rung.

The most common path, however, is through a query letter. In one page you identify yourself, what your script is about and why you're contacting this particular agent. Show that you've done some research, and make the agent inclined to read your script. Find a connection to the agent like "we both attended the same college," or mention recent sales you know through your reading the agent has made. Give a three- or four-line synopsis of your screenplay, with some specific plot elements, not just a generic premise. You can use comparisons as shorthand. *Men in Black* could be described as "*Ghostbusters* meets *Alien*," and lets the reader into the story quickly through something she's familiar with already. Be sure to include your name, return address, and telephone number in your letter, as well as a SASE. If the response is positive, the agent probably will want to contact you by phone to let you know of her interest, but she will need the SASE to send you a release form that must accompany your script.

Your query might not be read by the agent but by an assistant. That's okay. There are few professional secretaries in Hollywood, and assistants are looking for material that will earn them the step up they've been working for.

To be taken seriously, your script must be presented professionally. You must follow predetermined script formats. Few agents have time to develop talent. A less than professional script will be read only once. If it's not ready to be seen, you may have burned that bridge. Putting the cart before the horse, or the agent before the script, will not get you to where you want to go.

Read everything you can about scripting and the industry. As in all business ventures, you must educate yourself about the market to succeed. There are a vast number of books to read. Samuel French Bookstores [(323)876-0570] offer an extensive catalog of books for scriptwriters. *From Script to Screen*, by Linda Seger and Edward Jay Whetmore, J. Michael Straczynski's *The Complete Book of Scriptwriting* and Richard Walter's *Screenwriting* are highly recommended books on the art of scriptwriting. Study the correct format for your type of script. Cole and Haag's *Complete Guide to Standard Script Formats* is a good source for the various formats. Newsletters such as *Hollywood Scriptwriter* are good sources of information. Trade publications such as *The Hollywood Reporter*, *Premiere*, *Variety* and *Written By* are invaluable as well. A number of smaller magazines have sprung up in the last few years, including *Script Magazine* and *New York Screenwriter*.

Top 11 Screenwriting Mistakes, and How to Avoid Them

BY RICHARD KREVOLIN

As a story consultant and teacher, I read hundreds of scripts a year. As a result of spending so much time wading through screenplays, certain trends inevitably become apparent. In fact, after a while, you come to see that certain mistakes, certain definite blunders appear over and over again in almost every script. To save you many, many hours of time, pain and suffering, here is an outline of the 11 biggest mistakes screenwriters make and how you can avoid them.

1. The premise is not compelling enough.

I don't care how well you write, if you are trying to break into Hollywood with your screenplay, you need to write a movie with a compelling premise.

Scripts—for better or worse—are not sold on writing quality; they are sold on ideas, concepts and premises. Hence, yours better be something that makes other people say, "Wow, that would make an amazing film!" Like it or not, the people who are going to try to sell your film are going to use a single sentence to do so. Thus, you've got to make that sentence rock!

2. The main characters are unlikable.

Most people don't identify with the rich, the mean, the stupid. So, in general, main characters tend to be well-meaning members of the working class trying to better themselves. Think about it. Yes, Julia Roberts once played a movie star in *Notting Hill* (but she was an unloved, misunderstood, innocent movie star); however, think of her other roles—a single mother/paralegal (*Erin Brockovich*), a streetwalker (*Pretty Woman*), a hair stylist (*Runaway Bride*), etc. If your protagonist must be wealthy, a gangster, a cheat or some type of inherently unsympathetic person, make sure that he or she has lots of redeeming qualities: kindness, amiability, gentleness, humor, compassion, or eccentricity.

The only other way to go with your script is to have your rich, mean, unsympathetic protagonist become an underdog very quickly who is stripped of his ranks a la Scrooge and then, instantly he's become one of us and entirely more engaging. Then the rest of the story is about him becoming a better person, and how can we not like that? In the end, remember, Hollywood storytelling is a great democratic art. It must appeal to millions of people and let's be honest, most of them don't like their jobs, their bodies, their income levels, etc. Hence, we see the predominance of the escapist fantasy of Hollywood tales that feature regular Joes and Janes who break through the system and win—unlike what happens to most people. You are the dream weaver and always keep that in mind, please.

RICHARD KREVOLIN *has served as a professor of screenwriting at USC Film School since 1988 and is the author of* Screenwriting From the Soul. *He has a new book coming out in 2003 called* How to Adapt Anything Into a Screenplay *(Wiley & Sons). He can be reached at Krevolin@usc.edu. His Website is www.rcf.usc.edu/~krevolin.*

3. Too many characters are introduced too quickly.

Reading the first few pages of many scripts can be a bewildering experience filled with long hours of flipping pages back and forth. This is a direct result of way too many characters introduced in the first several pages. The human mind can only process so much. You as the author may be familiar with all the people who populate your story, but the reader is not. Relax there, Speedy, and slowly introduce the main character. Then have other characters introduced through his eyes, his experiences. The rest of the characters are supporting cast members. I want to start with the main character, follow him and end with him. As you need to, have him meet the rest of the players and we will slowly assimilate all the people we need to know.

4. There's too little at stake.

This may be the most common problem in screenwriting. What is at stake? I am always screaming at my students, "WHO CARES? RAISE THE STAKES!" There must be clarity as to what is at stake and what will happen if the main character fails to achieve his or her goals. Whether it's the end of the world or the end of a relationship, if you don't show magnitude the audience will not care deeply about the outcome.

5. It's missing a constant sense of danger or tension.

In many scripts I read, there seems to be an awful lot of people sitting around gabbing and the story never seems to go anywhere. From the get-go, the story needs to build. Then as it builds, the tension constantly needs to increase and a sense of threat needs to be present. Heck, what page does your inciting incident occur? The later it occurs, the sooner you'll need to go back and rewrite.

Think about this: Something important, or as William Goldman calls it, "a whammo!," needs to happen every 10 pages. Every 10 pages, something needs to reignite the flame.

Have you seen *Behind Enemy Lines*? In this film, we keep thinking things can't get worse for the Owen Wilson character, but of course, they do. And, of course, as the movie moves forward, we realize that it is just not one man's life that is at stake, but in fact, he is involved in a situation that could conceivably ignite World War III.

6. The dialogue is unrealistic and overwritten.

People rarely say what they're really thinking. When they do, it's filtered, candy-coated, homogenized and pared down to elicit a desired response. More aptly put, people say the things they say to get what they want.

This is especially true in film. All the genuine moments involving the dialogue in your story have one thing in common: they're short. The logic here is simple. The less time it takes to make your point, the more clear it will be. It forces the reader to notice. A slow rain inconveniences people, but a flash flood gets their attention. Keeping that in mind, remember that the dialogue can't be too on-the-nose. Dialogue is a subtle business; be a little softer on the keys.

One more quickie on dialogue: Don't ever ask yourself, "Would a person actually say this?" Ask yourself, "Given everything we know about this character, the world he lives in, and events that have occurred thus far, would he say this?" People don't go to the movies to hear the same conversations they hear every day; they go to hear the catchy, punchy, subtle or silky sweet lines that make movies quotable.

7. The script looks unprofessional.

These days with spell check and the rest, there just is no excuse for typos. I can't stress how important it is to read your script thoroughly before you send it out. Studio and agency readers go through hundreds of scripts every year, but believe me, they always notice an overabundance of typographical errors. Also, avoid formatting errors. You don't necessarily need expensive software, but your script better stick to basic format.

The most important thing is that you need to CAPITALIZE THE NAME OF EVERY CHARACTER. No matter how incidental. Everyone from ERIC to JANE to A GARBAGE MAN, everyone. In addition, pay close attention to your slug lines. If the camera needs to move to a different location, you need a new slug line.

You should never have a paragraph that exceeds five lines. In most cases, they should be somewhere between one and three lines long. Sometimes it just takes breaking up some of the larger paragraphs; other times you'll have to pare the larger ones down to one or two lines.

CAPITALIZE ANY IMPORTANT PROPS OR SOUNDS. Explosions, guns firing, cars crashing, anything you want to stand out. The same goes for props, anything you want or need the reader to remember, CAPITALIZE IT.

8. The rules of the world are undefined.

In your movie, you need to define your world early on and be consistent from then on. In other words, if you are writing a science fiction pic that takes place in the future, we need to see how people dress, relate, transport themselves, etc. from the get-go and that cannot be altered halfway through your story. When ET flies at the end of that film, it is surprising, but it is not inconsistent with what we've seen up to then. Consistency is the key to defining what is and is not possible in your world even if that world is different than the one we live in.

9. The antagonist lacks a clear master plan.

Many times, we will take the time to clarify the goals, needs and desires of our main character, but we'll fail to clarify the same for our antagonist. Your story is only as good as your baddie, so don't forget to flesh him out.

Many stories with problems result from antagonist issues. If you know the complete agenda of the bad guy, what he is trying to achieve and why, you can then plan the story accordingly. This will provide relief in the third act and you can move backwards to make the rest work as well.

10. The genre of the film is poorly defined.

The genre must be clear from the beginning or your script just won't be marketable.

There is no room for a historical romantic comedic teen movie. Know what genre your picture is and abide by the rules of that genre. In a comedy, you can't have people dying all over the place. Unless of course it is a black comedy in which the comedy comes out of *funny* deaths. The key thing here is that you must know exactly how far you can go within your genre. The tone must be nailed and must be consistently followed throughout the story.

11. The ending is inconsistent with the theme.

Be very, very careful when you get close to the end. The end must be bigger than all the rest of the film. It must come as the most emotionally powerful moment of your film or else you're dead. And no matter what, the way you choose to end your film dictates the theme of your tale. A comedy entails big laughs at the climax and in keeping with that, a happy ending.

Romantic comedies entail the lovers getting together. Not in the way we expected, but still they must get together-at least in classic romantic comedies. Some modern romantic comedies like *My Best Friend's Wedding* break this rule and in fact, most of the people I know felt more than a little betrayed by this film.

There you have it. The biggest and most frequent mistakes clearly laid out so you can spot them and from now on, avoid them. It's a minefield out there. Be careful and be smart. I love you all and I mean that.

A Screenwriter's Checklist

Is your premise compelling?
Are your main characters likeable?
Have you slowly introduced the characters through the main character's eyes?
Is there enough at stake?
Is there a constant sense of danger or tension?
Is your dialogue realistic?
Does your script look professional?
Have you defined the rules of your world?
Does your antogonist have a clear master plan?
Is the genre of the film clearly defined?
Is your ending consistent with your theme?

The Screenwriter's Union: The Writer's Guild of America

BY JOHN MORGAN WILSON

The eight-thousand-member Writers Guild of America, with branches on West and East Coasts, is a labor union that represents film and TV writers as well as writers in other new, emerging technologies.

The WGA has its origins in the Screen Writers Guild, a social club formed in 1921 by motion picture writers. In the 1930s, its members began to address such issues as the protection of writers' rights and economic conditions.

Following the 1937 Supreme Court decision upholding the constitutionality of the National Labor Relations Act, the guild became certified as the collective bargaining agent of all motion picture writers and began collective bargaining with producers in 1939. Over the next fifteen years, the guild went through various organizational changes and became affiliated with guilds representing writers in other mediums, such as radio and television. It finally set up dual branches in 1954, as the Writers Guild of America, west, and the Writers Guild of America, East, with the Mississippi River serving as the jurisdictional dividing line.

The WGA is an extremely active and powerful organization that at times has gone on strike against producers over wages and other issues, forcing producers to the negotiating table. It is considered to have one of the most attractive wage and benefits packages among the entertainment industry unions. WGA wage minimums are based on such factors as the length, format (half hour, hour and so on), medium of distribution (network, syndication, cable, feature film), budget range and other factors; the breakdown is complicated. If you need current minimums for your research, contact the WGA.

Among the other WGA member services are the monitoring, collection and distribution of millions of dollars of residuals (payments for the reuse of film and TV programs) annually; the determination of writing credits for feature films and TV shows; and the enforcement of rights set forth in labor agreements with production companies, as well as individual contracts. The WGA also sponsors many writer-related events throughout the year, including seminars and panel discussions, and actively works on behalf of writers in the areas of legislation, international agreements and public relations.

There is a common misconception that a writer must be a member of the WGA to sell a screenplay or work within the industry. This is not the case; virtually every day, non-WGA writers sell or option scripts or get hired for writing assignments or staff jobs. To qualify for membership, a writer must earn twenty-four units of credit during a three-year period, based on work completed under contract or upon the sale or licensing of original written material with a

JOHN MORGAN WILSON *has been a freelance reader for* Showtime, *acquisitions coordinator for Viacom Enterprises, news editor and segment producer for Fox Entertainment News, and writer or writer-producer of more than 60 documentary and reality-based TV episodes, including the Discover Channel's "Hollywood's Greatest Stunts." Wilson is also an award-winning reporter and author of the Benjamin Justice Mystery series. This article is an excerpt from his book* Inside Hollywood, *copyright © 1998 by John Morgan Wilson. Used with permission of Writer's Digest Books, an imprint of F&W Publications, Inc. Visit your local bookseller or call 1-800-448-0915 to obtain your copy.*

company that has signed a WGA Collective Bargaining Agreement. For example, the sale of a feature length screenplay to a guild signatory company is worth twenty-four units, a rewrite earns twelve units, a polish three units and so on.

Membership in the guild hardly guarantees wealth and success. Only one percent of the WGA's membership, for example, consistently earns more than a million dollars a year, and half the active members make less than $75,000 annually. Many members make only a marginal living, if that.

Among the WGA's other services, available to both members and nonmembers:

- A script registration service that provides a dated record of the writer's claim to authorship of a particular piece of material should any issues arise concerning ownership or originality. The Writer's Guild of America, west (WGAw) registers some thirty thousand scripts and treatments each year; members, $10 per registration; nonmembers, $20 (323/782-4540). Writers may also register their scripts via the WGA Website: www.wga.org.
- A variety of programs designed to encourage access and career opportunities for writers who are African-American, Latino, Asian/Pacific Islander, American Indian, women, over forty, disabled or freelance (323/782-4648).
- An agency list to assist writers in contacting literary agents who have signed the WGA Agency Agreement (cost by mail, $2.50; 323/782-4502) or available free on their website.
- The James R. Webb Memorial Library, which houses a large collection of scripts, video-tapes, books, photos and other items related to the screenwriting trade, is open to the public for research purposes Monday to Friday, 10 A.M. to 5 P.M. (closed for lunch 12:30 to 1:30 P.M.). Located at the new WGAw headquarters (see address below) (323/782-4544).
- A monthly magazine, *Written By*, which includes interviews with noted member screen-writers, writing tips, guild news and other features of interest to scriptwriters. (For subscription information, call the toll-free number: 888-WRITNBY).
- A website (http://www.wga.org) with WGA news, writing tips, interviews and so on.
- For a free WGA general information booklet, which includes a list of other WGA informational publications and their prices, as well as details on all of the above subject areas, contact the WGAw, 7000 West Third St., Los Angeles, CA 90048/ (323/782-4803).

Synopsis and Treatments

BY PAMELA WALLACE

A treatment, which is another word for synopsis, is the backbone of your screenplay. It's your blueprint, just like the blueprint a builder follows in building a house. It keeps you focused and prevents you from wandering off the spine of the story. Simply put, a treatment is a narrative account of your story, written in present tense. For example, a treatment might begin: "A teenage boy in a battered old car pulls up to the curb at a middle-class, suburban house. He leaps out, races to the front door, and desperately pounds on it, screaming, 'Jody, it's me! Let me in!' A beat, then a rather plain teenage girl throws open the door and stares in shock at the boy." Notice that it's important to put as much emotion and sense of action into a treatment as possible. It should be a concise but entertaining read, especially if someone is going to read it before looking at your script.

Aside from coming up with a very good, very commercial idea in the first place, the treatment is the hardest part of the writing process. In it, you lay out the story—the plot and the characters and their arcs. Of the total creative effort involved in completing a screenplay, roughly 75 percent or more goes into working out the story. Who are the main characters? What do they want? Why do they want it? How do they set about accomplishing their goals? What stops them? What are the consequences of their success or failure?

There is a famous story about Agatha Christie, the most successful mystery writer of all time, many of whose books were made into movies. She was walking in her garden with a friend, deep in thought. Suddenly, she exclaimed, "I've just finished my new book!" Her friend asked, "May I read it?" Ms. Christie replied, "Oh, I haven't written it yet." She had simply done the hardest part—figuring out how the story would play out.

Before you can get to where Dame Agatha was at the end of that walk in the garden, you must first determine what kind of movie you want your story to fit into. You've written a logline, encapsulating the essence of your story. But what approach do you want to take? Is this a serious drama? A broad comedy? The same idea can be developed in any of those genres. For instance, the teen movie *Clueless* was a young, hip romantic comedy take on Jane Austen's classic English novel, *Emma*. Same story, very different approach.

Once you've got your logline and genre, you may still be a little confused as to which aspect of the story to focus on. For instance, in *Witness* we had many choices. We could have focused on police corruption, the relationship between the two cops who were partners, the interaction of the Amish with the outer world, the religious beliefs of the Amish or any number of other things. But from the inception of the idea, I wanted this to be a romantic story. I felt that the

PAM WALLACE *began writing screenplays in the mid-1980s and in 1985 she won an academy award for co-writing the movie* Witness. *She has written or co-written several other films, including the award-winning HBO film* If These Walls Could Talk *and movies of the week for CBS and ABC. She has published over 25 novels, several of which have been optioned or produced as movies of the week, miniseries or made-for-cable movies. She lives in Fresno, California. This article is an excerpt from her book* You can Write a Movie, *copyright © 2000 by Pamela Wallace. Used with permission of Writer's Digest Books, an imprint of F&W Publications, Inc. Visit your local bookseller or call 1-800-448-0915 to obtain your copy.*

wide gulf between the Amish and the outside world provided a perfect barrier to keep two people who love each other from getting together. Because it's so hard to come up with a fresh conflict in a love story, that was too good a dramatic opportunity to pass up.

Deciding to make it a love story determined the form of the movie. It meant the plot would focus on the developing relationship between the hero and heroine. And the subplot, of course, concerned the heroine's son who witnesses a murder.

If you give ten different writers the same logline, they will come up with ten different approaches to the story. Each will bring his own feelings, interests and unique perspective to it. A concept that strikes one writer as a perfect vehicle for hilarious comedy appears to another to be ripe for development as a serious drama.

In a treatment, you structure the plot and develop the characters of your movie. Structure determines what happens and when it happens. It is defined by the protagonist's goal. It begins with the initial setup, where you establish the main characters, what the movie's about and what's at stake. It moves on to the inciting incident, which launches the real story. The protagonist finds himself in a new situation, with a change of plans. He makes progress toward his goal, despite serious obstacles and complications. Approximately halfway through the movie, the stakes are raised—more is at stake than the protagonist originally conceived. There is a major setback (the "all is lost" moment), followed by a renewed determination by the protagonist to achieve his goal. His efforts culminate in the climax, where he succeeds or fails. At the end there's a very brief resolution.

In your treatment, you should know key things about your main characters, especially the protagonist. Usually the protagonist has a wound (either inner or outer), that is an unresolved source of deep pain, and generally precedes the events of the movie. For instance, in *Message in a Bottle* (based on the best-selling novel by Nicholas Sparks), Kevin Costner's character is mourning the loss of his beloved wife, who has been dead for two years. His attachment to her prevents him from fully accepting the love offered by Robin Wright Penn's character.

The protagonist in any movie must deal with a deep emotional fear. His inner conflict stems from the fact that this fear is an obstacle to fulfillment. Unless the protagonist can resolve this fear, he won't achieve his goal.

A good treatment usually will resemble the following structure.

Act One: This begins with a strong establishing scene, preferably a "hook" that immediately captures the audience's interest. The hero or heroine is introduced in an interesting way, as is the villain or antagonistic force (for instance, tornadoes in *Twister*). The problem is set before the hero, who accepts the challenge, often with serious reluctance or misgivings.

Act Two: This is the backstory explaining the hero's background or the events preceding the beginning of the movie. The hero is in some way attacked or challenged. There are scenes developing the subplot and dealing with the theme. In a romantic story, there will be romantic interludes. The hero will come up against the villain, and at the end of the act, the hero will appear to be defeated, his goal out of reach.

Act Three: The first part of this act is preparation of the plan the hero has come up with to save the day. The middle part of the act is implementing that plan. And the final part of the act is the climax, the ultimate confrontation between hero and villain, followed by a brief resolution scene.

In working on a treatment, a great place to begin is with the ending. Until you know the ending, you can't write your script. (Some writers disagree with this, and love to discover how the story will play out as they write it. Exceptionally talented or very experienced writers will find this easier to do than will novice writers.) Everything in your movie should lead up to the ending.

In general, Act One should have six to ten scenes to set up the main characters and establish what the story is about. Act Two should be approximately fifteen to thirty scenes, focusing on character development, and introducing complications that create barriers to the protagonist achieving his goal. And Act Three should have anywhere from three to ten scenes that show the climax of the story, and a brief epilogue that in some way suggests the future of the protagonist.

The step outline

A good way to begin a treatment is with a step outline. This is a scene outline that describes step by step what happens in each scene in just a sentence or two. It shows the order of the scenes and the action that happens in each one. The step outline points toward the direction of your screenplay and helps you decide which sequence, or order of scenes, will be the most dramatic.

Writers commonly use several ways to do a step outline. One is to write a description of each scene on a note card, then lay out the cards in order (perhaps pinning them to a bulletin board). Many writers like to do this because it's easy to move the cards around and change scenes from one act to another. Some writers even use different colored cards for each scene.

Another way is to list the scenes in sequential order on a legal tablet, numbering them as you go. Or you may take a large sheet of paper, divide it into three separate sections, and briefly outline the scenes to go in each section.

Remember that every scene you include must relate to the spine of the story. Scenes that are not absolutely necessary shouldn't be included. If you're confused about whether a scene is necessary, ask yourself two questions: Does the scene contribute to the development of character? Does it move the story forward? If the answer to both these questions is "no," then the scene should be thrown out. Doing this will ensure that you have a fast-paced, tightly constructed story.

Also, scenes should be organized in a rising sequence, with each scene heightening the tension of the story.

Whatever method you choose is purely a matter of personal choice. The purpose of all these methods is to help you create the best structure for your screenplay, with each scene moving in a cause-and-effect manner toward an exciting and fulfilling climax.

The treatment

Once you've done a step outline, you're ready to write the actual treatment, a detailed narrative account of your story. The only hard and fast rules about treatments are that they should be double-spaced and written in present tense. The length is flexible, but nowadays, short treatments between five to ten pages are considered best. A good, thorough treatment could almost be shot as a movie. All it's lacking is dialogue.

If you're writing the treatment for yourself, and not as a sales tool to show a prospective buyer, it isn't essential to write it in an exciting and colorful style. But if you're going to show it to a producer or studio or network executive, approach it as if you're writing the Great American Short Story. It should be vivid and emotional, and not only hold the reader's interest but get her excited about the movie that could be made from it. Use strong prose with highly descriptive passages and active as opposed to passive verbs. For example, don't describe your protagonist as poorly dressed; say his clothes hang in filthy tatters.

Don't forget to write visually. Picture each scene in your mind as if you're seeing it on a movie screen.

After you've written your treatment, ask yourself the following questions.

- Does your main character change his basic approach to dealing with the problem at the heart of the story? (Example: the Humphrey Bogart character in *Casablanca*, who goes from determined noninvolvement to passionate partisanship.)
- Or (which is more rare), does your main character remain steadfast in the face of overwhelming problems? (Example: the Harrison Ford character in *The Fugitive*.)
- Does he grow by losing a negative character trait and/or gaining a positive one? (Example:

Robert De Niro becoming less focused on appearing macho and more in touch with his emotions in *Analyze This*.)

- Does your hero or heroine resolve his personal problems? (Example: Robin Williams, who combats his suicidal depression by helping people in *Patch Adams*.)
- Does your protagonist achieve the story goal (which happens in most commercial films)?
- Or, does your protagonist fail in achieving the goal, but accomplish something worthwhile nonetheless (which happens in many "tearjerkers," like *Stepmom*)?

Once you have a well worked out treatment, writing the screenplay will be relatively simple.

Fatal Flaws

In doing a treatment, you have an opportunity to find out what's wrong with your story before you actually write the screenplay. You'll be able to tell if you've made the following fatal errors that can prevent even an interesting script from selling:

- A slow setup that doesn't capture the audience's attention quickly enough.
- A confusing beginning that doesn't make it clear to the audience what kind of movie this is, who the protagonist is and what's at stake.
- A sagging middle—a boring Act Two that doesn't have enough twists and turns, barriers and complications, to hold the audience's interest.
- An abrupt ending that feels as if the writer simply got tired of the story and wrapped it up in a hurry.
- A cliched story that has nothing new or fresh about it. This is the "we've seen it before" syndrome.
- Too many intrusive flashbacks that keep stopping the momentum of the story.
- A reliance on voice-overs to get across information, instead of finding a way to show this information through action or dialogue. Show don't tell.
- Too many warring elements. The writer has thrown in everything he can think of in an effort to make the story exciting. Because so much is going on, none of it is very well developed.
- A reliance on lengthy dialogue, as opposed to action or visual elements.

Script Agents:
Nonfee-charging and Fee-charging

This section contains agents who sell feature film scripts, television scripts, and theatrical stage plays. The listings in this section differ slightly from those in the literary agent sections. Nonfee-charging and fee-charging script agencies are listed together. Fee-charging script agents are indicated by a clapper (🎬) symbol. A breakdown of the types of scripts each agency handles is included in the listing.

Many of the script agents listed here are signatories to the Writers Guild of America Artists' Manager Basic Agreement. They have paid a membership fee and agreed to abide by the WGA's standard code of behavior. Agents who are WGA signatories are not permitted to charge a reading fee to WGA members, but are allowed to do so to nonmembers. They are permitted to charge for critiques and other services, but they may not refer you to a particular script doctor. Enforcement is uneven, however. Although a signatory can, theoretically, be stripped of its signatory status, this rarely happens.

A few of the listings in this section are actually management companies. The role of managers is quickly changing in Hollywood—they were once only used by actors, or "talent," and the occasional writer. Now many managers are actually selling scripts to producers.

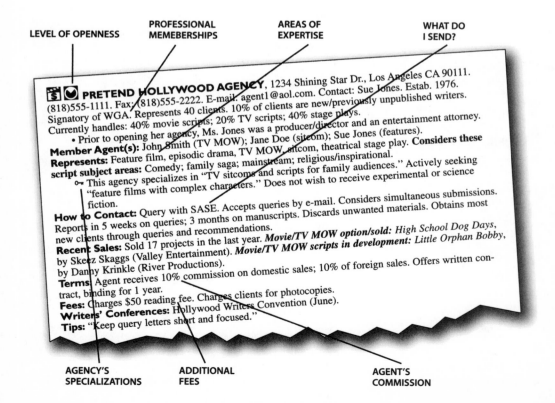

LEVEL OF OPENNESS PROFESSIONAL MEMEBERSHIPS AREAS OF EXPERTISE WHAT DO I SEND?

🎬 📧 **PRETEND HOLLYWOOD AGENCY**, 1234 Shining Star Dr., Los Angeles CA 90111. (818)555-1111. Fax: (818)555-2222. E-mail: agent1@aol.com. Contact: Sue Jones. Estab. 1976. Signatory of WGA. Represents 40 clients. 10% of clients are new/previously unpublished writers. Currently handles: 40% movie scripts; 20% TV scripts; 40% stage plays.
• Prior to opening her agency, Ms. Jones was a producer/director and an entertainment attorney.
Member Agent(s): John Smith (TV MOW); Jane Doe (sitcom); Sue Jones (features).
Represents: Feature film, episodic drama, TV MOW, sitcom, theatrical stage play. **Considers these script subject areas:** Comedy; family saga; mainstream; religious/inspirational.
⚬ This agency specializes in "TV sitcoms and scripts for family audiences." Actively seeking "feature films with complex characters." Does not wish to receive experimental or science fiction.
How to Contact: Query with SASE. Accepts queries by e-mail. Considers simultaneous submissions. Reports in 5 weeks on queries; 3 months on manuscripts. Discards unwanted materials. Obtains most new clients through queries and recommendations.
Recent Sales: Sold 17 projects in the last year. *Movie/TV MOW option/sold: High School Dog Days,* by Skeez Skaggs (Valley Entertainment). *Movie/TV MOW scripts in development: Little Orphan Bobby,* by Danny Krinkle (River Productions).
Terms: Agent receives 10% commission on domestic sales; 10% of foreign sales. Offers written contract, binding for 1 year.
Fees: Charges $50 reading fee. Charges clients for photocopies.
Writers' Conferences: Hollywood Writers Convention (June).
Tips: "Keep query letters short and focused."

AGENCY'S SPECIALIZATIONS ADDITIONAL FEES AGENT'S COMMISSION

Quick Reference Icons

At the beginning of some listings, you will find one or more of the following symbols for quick identification of features particular to that listing.

- **N** Agency new to this edition.
- ✓ Change in address, contact information or phone number from last year's edition.
- **$** Fee-charging script agent.
- ▣ Agents who make sales to electronic publishers.
- ⬍ Canadian agency.
- 🌐 International agency.

Level of Openness

Each agency has an icon indicating its openness to submissions. Before contacting any agency, check the listing to make sure it is open to new clients.

- ☐ Newer agency actively seeking clients.
- ☑ Agency seeking both new and established writers.
- ◐ Agency prefers to work with established writers, mostly obtains new clients through referrals.
- ◎ Agency handling only certain types of work or work by writers under certain circumstances.
- ⊘ Agency not currently seeking new clients. We include these agencies to let you know they are currently not open to new clients. *Unless you have a strong recommendation from someone well-respected in the field, our advice is to avoid approaching these agents.*

It's a good idea to register your script before sending it out, and the WGA offers a registration service to members and nonmembers alike. Membership in the WGA is earned through the accumulation of professional credits and carries a number of significant benefits. Write the Guild for more information on specific agencies, script registration, and membership requirements, or visit their website at www.wga.org.

Like the literary agents listed in this book, some script agencies ask that clients pay for some or all of the office fees accrued when sending out scripts. Some agents ask for a one-time "handling" fee up front, while others deduct office expenses after a script has been sold. Always have a clear understanding of any fee an agent asks you to pay.

Canadian and International agents are included in this section. Canadian agents have a (⬍) preceding their listing, while International agents have a (🌐) preceding their listing. Remember to include an International Reply Coupon (IRC) with your self-addressed envelope when contacting Canadian and International agents.

When reading through this section, keep in mind the following information specific to the script agent listings:

SUBHEADS

Each listing is broken down into subheads to make locating specific information easier. In the first section, you'll find contact information for each agency. You'll also learn if the agent is a WGA signatory or a member of any other professional organizations. (An explanation of all organizations' acronyms is available on page 319.) Further information is provided which indicates an agency's size, its willingness to work with a new or previously unpublished writer, and a percentage breakdown of the general types of scripts the agency will consider.

Member Agents: Agencies comprised of more than one agent list member agents and their

individual specialties to help you determine the most appropriate person for your query letter.
Represents: Make sure you query only agents who represent the type of material you write. To help you narrow your search, we've included an **Agents Specialties Index** and the **Script Agents Format Index** in the back of the book.

☞ Look for the key icon to quickly learn an agent's areas of specializations and individual strengths. Agents also mention here what specific areas they are currently seeking as well as subjects they do *not* wish to receive.

How to Contact: Most agents open to submissions prefer initially to receive a query letter briefly describing your work. Script agents usually discard material sent without a SASE. Here agents also indicate if they accept queries by fax or e-mail, if they consider simultaneous submissions, and their preferred way of meeting new clients.

Recent Sales: Reflecting the different ways scriptwriters work, agents list scripts optioned or sold, and scripting assignments procured for clients. The film industry is very secretive about sales, but you may be able to get a list of clients or other references upon request—especially if the agency is interested in representing your work.

Terms: Most agents' commissions range from 10 to 15 percent, and WGA signatories may not earn over 10 percent from WGA members.

Fees: Agencies who charge some type of fee (for reading, critiques, consultations, promotion, marketing, etc.) are indicated with a clapper (🎬) symbol by their name. Also listed here are any additional office fees the agent asks the client to pay.

Writers' Conferences: For screenwriters unable to move to Los Angeles, writers' conferences provide another venue for meeting agents. For more information about a specific conference, check the **Writers' Conferences** section starting on page 283.

Tips: Agents offer advice and additional instructions for writers looking for representation.

SPECIAL INDEXES

Additional Script Agents: Many script agents are also interested in book manuscripts; many literary agents will also consider scripts. Agents who primarily sell books but also handle at least 10 to 15 percent scripts appear among the listings in this section, with the contact information, breakdown of work currently handled and a note to check the full listing in either the Nonfee-charging or Fee-charging sections. Those literary agents who sell mostly books and less than 10 to 15 percent scripts do not appear in this section. Complete listings for these agents appear in the Nonfee-charging section.

Agents Specialties Index: In the back of the book on page 324 is an index divided into various subject areas specific to scripts, such as mystery, romantic comedy, and teen. This index should help you compose a list of agents specializing in your areas. Cross-referencing categories and concentrating on agents interested in two or more aspects of your manuscript might increase your chances of success. Agencies open to all categories are grouped under the subject heading "open."

Script Agents Format Index: Following the **Agents Specialties Index** is an index organizing agents according to the script types they consider: such as TV movie of the week (MOW), sitcom, or episodic drama.

Agencies Indexed by Openness to Submissions: This index lists agencies according to their receptivity to new clients.

Geographic Index: For writers looking for an agent close to home, this index lists agents state-by-state.

Agents Index: Often you will read about an agent who is an employee of a larger agency and you may not be able to locate her business phone or address. Starting on page 377 is a list of agents' names in alphabetical order along with the name of the agency they work for. Find the name of the person you would like to contact and then check the agency listing.

Listing Index: This index lists all agencies, independent publicists, and writers' conferences listed in the book.

For More Information

For more information on approaching agents, read "Basics of Contacting a Literary Agent" starting on page 36. Also, take note of the articles dealing specifically with contacting—and working with—script agents that start on page 201.

SCRIPT AGENTS

ABOVE THE LINE AGENCY, 9200 Sunset Blvd., #804, Los Angeles CA 90069. (310)859-6115. Fax: (310)859-6119. **Contact:** Bruce Bartlett. Owner: Rima Bauer Greer. Estab. 1994. Signatory of WGA. Represents 35 clients. 10% of clients are new/unpublished writers. Currently handles: 95% movie scripts; 5% TV scripts.
  • Prior to opening her agency, Ms. Greer served as president with Writers & Artists Agency.
Represents: Feature film, TV movie of the week. **Considers these script subject areas:** Cartoon/animation; writers and directors.
How to Contact: Query with SASE. This agency does not guarantee a response.
Recent Sales: *Movie/TV MOW script(s) optioned/sold: The Authority*, Marcom and Hollaway (Disney); *Time Line*, Frank Cappello (Paramount); *Red Mars*, Greg Widen (Sci Fi Channel).
Terms: Agent receives 10% commission on domestic sales; 10% commission on foreign sales.

ABRAMS ARTISTS AGENCY, 275 Seventh Ave., 26th Floor, New York NY 10001. (646)486-4600. Fax: (646)486-2358. **Contact:** Jack Tantleff. Estab. 1986. Member of AAR; signatory of WGA.
Member Agents: Jack Tantleff (theater, TV, film); Charmaine Ferenczi (theater); John Santoianni (TV, film, theater).
Represents: Feature film, episodic drama, sitcom, animation (TV), soap opera, musical. **Considers these script subject areas:** Comedy; contemporary issues; mainstream; mystery/suspense; romantic comedy; romantic drama.
  O—┐ This agency specializes in theater, film, TV.
How to Contact: Query with SASE, outline. Returns material only with SASE.
Recent Sales: This agency prefers not to share information on specific sales.
Terms: Agent receives 10% commission on domestic sales; 10% commission on foreign sales; 10% commission on dramatic rights sales.

ACME TALENT & LITERARY, 4727 Wilshire, #333, Los Angeles CA 90010. (323)954-2263. Fax: (323)954-2262. 875 Ave. of the Americas, Suite 2108, New York NY 10001. (212)328-0388. Fax: (212)328-0391. **Contact:** Lisa Lindo. Estab. 1993. Signatory of WGA. Represents 50 clients. Currently handles: movie scripts; TV scripts; Internet rights, video game rights, comic book rights.
Member Agents: Lisa Lindo (feature film specs); Mickey Freiberg (books, film scripts); Kevin Cleary (film, comic books); Leo Bookman (film); Josh Morris (film, video games, comic books); "also additional agents handling talent in Los Angeles and in New York."
Represents: Feature film. **Considers these script subject areas:** Action/adventure; biography/autobiography; cartoon/animation; comedy; contemporary issues; detective/police/crime; erotica; ethnic; experimental; family saga; fantasy; feminist; gay/lesbian; glitz; historical; horror; juvenile; mainstream; multicultural; multimedia; mystery/suspense; psychic/supernatural; regional; religious/inspirational; romantic comedy; romantic drama; science fiction; sports; teen; thriller; western/frontier;
  O—┐ This agency specializes in "feature films, completed specs or pitches by established produced writers and new writers." Actively seeking great feature scripts. No unsolicited material.
How to Contact: Query with SASE. No e-mail or fax queries. Considers simultaneous queries. Responds in 2 weeks to queries. Returns materials only with SASE. Obtains most new clients through recommendations from established industry contacts, production companies of note, and reputable entertainment attorneys.
Recent Sales: Sold over 10 scripts in the last year. "Since the beginning of this year, Acme has become a major player in the Internet/original content world of dot coms with websodes on several sites. Gaming division, Acme Interactive, is the newest division of the company handling videogames and game developers. Paramount's *Save the Last Dance* was sold by Acme."
Terms: Agent receives 10% commission on domestic sales; 10% commission on foreign sales. Offers written contract, binding for 2 years.

Tips: "We are very hands-on, work developmentally with specs in progress. Individual attention due to low number of clients. All sales have been major 6-7 figures. Call, e-mail with any questions."

THE AGENCY, 1800 Avenue of the Stars, Suite 1114, Los Angeles CA 90067-4206. (310)551-3000. **Contact:** Jerry Zeitman. Estab. 1984. Signatory of WGA. Represents 300 clients. No new/previously unpublished writers. Currently handles: 45% movie scripts; 45% TV scripts; 10% syndicated material.
Represents: Feature film, TV movie of the week, episodic drama, sitcom, animation, miniseries. **Considers these script subject areas:** Action/adventure; cartoon/animation; comedy; contemporary issues; detective/police/crime; ethnic; family saga; fantasy; historical; horror; juvenile; mainstream; mystery/suspense; psychic/supernatural; romantic comedy; romantic drama; science fiction; teen; thriller; western/frontier; women's issues; military/war.
    O— This agency specializes in TV and motion pictures.
How to Contact: Query with SASE. Responds to queries in 2 weeks, if interested. Obtains most new clients through recommendations from others.
Recent Sales: This agency prefers not to share information on specific sales.
Terms: Agent receives 10% commission on domestic sales; 10% commission on foreign sales. Offers written contract, binding for 2 years.

ALLRED AND ALLRED, LITERARY AGENTS, 7834 Alabama Ave., Canoga Park CA 91304-4905. (818)346-4313. **Contact:** Robert Allred. Estab. 1991. Represents 5 clients. 100% of clients are new/unpublished writers.
    • See the expanded listing for this agency in Literary Agents.

THE ALPERN GROUP, 15645 Royal Oak Rd., Encino CA 91436. (818)528-1111. Fax: (818)528-1110. **Contact:** Jeff Alpern. Estab. 1994. Represents 50 clients. 10% of clients are new/unpublished writers. Currently handles: 30% movie scripts; 60% TV scripts; 10% stage plays.
    • Prior to opening his agency, Mr. Alpern was an agent with William Morris.
Member Agents: Jeff Alpern (president), Liz Wise, Jeff Aghassi.
Represents: Movie scripts, feature film, TV scripts, TV movie of the week, episodic drama, miniseries. **Considers these script subject areas:** Action/adventure; biography/autobiography; cartoon/animation; comedy; contemporary issues; detective/police/crime; erotica; ethnic; experimental; family saga; fantasy; feminist; gay/lesbian; glitz; historical; horror; juvenile; mainstream; multicultural; multimedia; mystery/suspense; psychic/supernatural; regional; religious/inspirational; romantic comedy; romantic drama; science fiction; sports; teen; thriller; western/frontier.
How to Contact: Query with SASE. Responds in 1 month to queries.
Terms: Agent receives 10% commission on domestic sales. Offers written contract.

MICHAEL AMATO AGENCY, 1650 Broadway, Suite 307, New York NY 10019. (212)247-4456 or (212)247-4457. Fax: (212)664-0641. Website: www.amatoagency.tvheaven.com. **Contact:** Michael Amato. Estab. 1970. Member of SAG, AFTRA. Represents 6 clients. 2% of clients are new/unpublished writers.
Represents: Feature film, TV movie of the week, episodic drama, animation, documentary, miniseries. **Considers these script subject areas:** Action/adventure.
    O— This agency specializes in action/adventure scripts.
How to Contact: Query with SASE. Responds in 1 month to queries. Obtains most new clients through recommendations from others.
Recent Sales: This agency prefers not to share information on specific sales.

MARCIA AMSTERDAM AGENCY, 41 W. 82nd St., New York NY 10024-5613. (212)873-4945. **Contact:** Marcia Amsterdam. Estab. 1970. Signatory of WGA. Currently handles: 15% nonfiction books; 70% novels; 5% movie scripts; 10% TV scripts.
    • See the expanded listing for this agency in Literary Agents.

BASKOW AGENCY, 2948 E. Russell Rd., Las Vegas NV 89120. (702)733-7818. Fax: (702)733-2052. E-mail: jaki@baskow.com. **Contact:** Jaki Baskow. Estab. 1976. Represents 8 clients. 40% of clients are new/unpublished writers. Currently handles: 5% nonfiction books; 5% novels; 20% movie scripts; 70% TV scripts.

THE PUBLISHING FIELD is constantly changing! Agents often change addresses, phone numbers, or even companies. If you're still using this book and it is 2004 or later, buy the newest edition of *Guide to Literary Agents* at your favorite bookstore or order directly from Writer's Digest Books at (800)448-0915.

Member Agents: Crivolus Sarulus (scripts), Jaki Baskow.
Represents: Feature film, TV movie of the week, episodic drama, sitcom, documentary, miniseries, variety show. **Considers these script subject areas:** Action/adventure; biography/autobiography; comedy; contemporary issues; family saga; glitz; mystery/suspense; religious/inspirational; romantic comedy; romantic drama; science fiction (juvenile only); thriller.

O→ Actively seeking unique scripts/all-American true stories, kids projects and movies of the week. Does not want to receive heavy violence.

How to Contact: Submit outline, proposal and treatments. Accepts e-mail and fax queries. Responds in 1 month to queries. Obtains most new clients through recommendations from others.
Recent Sales: Sold 3 movie/TV MOW scripts in the last year. *Malpractice*, by Larry Leirketen (Blakely); *Angel of Death*, (CBS). Other clients include Cheryl Anderson, Camisole Prods, Michael Store.
Terms: Agent receives 10% commission on domestic sales; 10% commission on foreign sales. Offers written contract.

⌀ BEACON ARTISTS AGENCY, 630 Ninth Ave., Suite 215, New York NY 10036. **Contact:** Patricia McLaughlin. Member of AAR.

● This agency did not respond to our request for information. Query before submitting.

◉ BERMAN BOALS AND FLYNN INC., 208 W. 30th St., #401, New York NY 10001. (212)868-1068.
Contact: Judy Boals or Jim Flynn. Estab. 1995. Member of AAR; signatory of WGA. Represents 35 clients.
Represents: Feature film, TV scripts, stage plays.

O→ This agency specializes in dramatic writing for stage, film, TV.

How to Contact: Query with SASE. Obtains most new clients through recommendations from others.
Recent Sales: This agency prefers not to share information on specific sales.
Terms: Agent receives 10% commission on domestic sales.

◉ THE BOHRMAN AGENCY, 8899 Beverly Blvd., Suite 811, Los Angeles CA 90048. (310)550-5444.
Fax: (310)550-5445. **Contact:** Michael Hruska, Caren Bohrman. Signatory of WGA.
Represents: Novels, feature film, TV scripts. **Considers these script subject areas:** Action/adventure; biography/autobiography; cartoon/animation; comedy; contemporary issues; detective/police/crime; erotica; ethnic; experimental; family saga; fantasy; feminist; gay/lesbian; glitz; historical; horror; juvenile; mainstream; multicultural; multimedia; mystery/suspense; psychic/supernatural; regional; religious/inspirational; romantic comedy; romantic drama; science fiction; sports; teen; thriller; western/frontier.
How to Contact: Query with SASE. No unsolicited mss. Obtains most new clients through recommendations from others.
Recent Sales: This agency prefers not to share information on specific sales.

🌐 ◉ ALAN BRODIE REPRESENTATION, 211 Piccadilly, London W1J 9HF, England. 0207-917-2871.
Fax: 0207-917-2872. E-mail: info@alanbrodie.com. Website: www.alanbrodie.com. **Contact:** Alan Brodie, Sarah McNair or Ali Howarth. Member of PMA. 10% of clients are new/unpublished writers.
Member Agents: Alan Brodie (theater, film, TV); Sarah McNair (theater); Ali Howarth (new writing—theater and TV).

O→ This agency specializes in stage, film and television.

How to Contact: All unsolicited mss returned unopened. North American writers are only accepted in exceptional circumstances. Accepts e-mail and fax queries. Obtains most new clients through recommendations from others.
Recent Sales: This agency prefers not to share information on specific sales.
Terms: Agent receives 10-15% commission on domestic sales. Charges clients for photocopying and courier mail.
Tips: "Biographical details can be helpful. Generally only playwrights whose work has been performed will be considered, provided they come recommended by an industry professional."

◖ CURTIS BROWN LTD., 10 Astor Place, New York NY 10003-6935. (212)473-5400. Fax: (212)473-5400. 1750 Montgomery St., San Francisco CA 94111. (415)954-8566. **Contact:** Peter L. Ginsberg, president.
Contact: Perry Knowlton, chairman emeritas; Timothy Knowlton, CEO. Queries to Blake Peterson.

● See the expanded listing for this agency in Literary Agents.

◉ DON BUCHWALD & ASSOCIATES, INC., 6500 Wilshire Blvd., Suite 2200, Los Angeles CA 90048.
(323)655-7400. Fax: (323)655-7470. Website: www.buchwald.com. Estab. 1977. Signatory of WGA. Represents 50 clients.
Represents: Movie scripts, feature film, TV scripts, TV movie of the week, episodic drama, sitcom, documentary, miniseries.

O→ This agency represents talent and literary clients.

How to Contact: Query with SASE. Considers simultaneous queries. Obtains most new clients through recommendations from others.

KELVIN C. BULGER AND ASSOCIATES, 11 E. Adams St., Suite 604, Chicago IL 60603. (312)692-1002. Fax: (312)692-1002. E-mail: kcbwoi@aol.com. **Contact:** Melanie Barnes-Zeleke. Estab. 1992. Signatory of WGA. Represents 25 clients. 90% of clients are new/unpublished writers. Currently handles: 75% movie scripts; 25% TV scripts.
Member Agents: Kelvin C. Bulger, Melanie Barnes-Zeleke, Baku Talbert.
Represents: Feature film, TV movie of the week, documentary, syndicated material. **Considers these script subject areas:** Action/adventure; cartoon/animation; comedy; contemporary issues; ethnic; family saga; religious/inspirational.
How to Contact: Query with SASE. Include one page logline, one page plot synopsis beginning, middle and end, and first 10 pages of your screenplay. Accepts e-mail and fax queries. Considers simultaneous queries. Responds in 3 weeks to queries; 2 months to mss. Returns materials only with SASE. Obtains most new clients through recommendations from others, solicitations.
Recent Sales: This agency prefers not to share information on specific sales.
Terms: Agent receives 10% commission on domestic sales; 10% commission on foreign sales. Offers written contract, binding for 6-12 months.
Tips: "Proofread before submitting to agent. We only reply to letters of inquiry if SASE is enclosed."

CEDAR GROVE AGENCY ENTERTAINMENT, P.O. Box 1692, Issaquah WA 98027-0068. (425)837-1687. E-mail: cedargroveagency@juno.com. Website: freeyellow.com/members/cedargrove/index.html. **Contact:** Renee MacKenzie, Samantha Powers. Estab. 1995. Member of Cinema Seattle. Represents 7 clients. 100% of clients are new/unpublished writers. Currently handles: 90% movie scripts; 10% TV scripts.
• Prior to becoming agents, Ms. Taylor worked for the stock brokerage firm, Morgan Stanley Dean Witter; Ms. Powers was a customer service/office manager; Ms. MacKenzie was an office manager and recently a Production Manager.
Member Agents: Amy Taylor (Senior Vice President, Motion Picture Division), Samantha Powers (Executive Vice President, Motion Picture Division), Renee MacKenzie (Story Editor).
Represents: Feature film, TV movie of the week, sitcom. **Considers these script subject areas:** Action/adventure; biography/autobiography; comedy; detective/police/crime; family saga; juvenile; mystery/suspense; romantic comedy; science fiction; sports; thriller; western/frontier.
➩ Cedar Grove Agency Entertainment was formed in the Pacific Northwest to take advantage of the rich and diverse culture as well as the many writers who reside there. Does not want period pieces, horror genres, children's scripts dealing with illness, or scripts with excessive substance abuse.
How to Contact: Query with SASE, 1-page synopsis. No phone calls please. No attachments if emailed. Accepts e-mail and fax queries. Responds in 10 days to queries; 2 months to mss. Obtains most new clients through referrals and website.
Recent Sales: This agency prefers not to share information on specific sales.
Terms: Agent receives 10% commission on domestic sales. Offers written contract, binding for 6-12 months; 30-day notice must be given to terminate contract.
Tips: "We focus on finding that rare gem, the undiscovered, multi-talented writer, no matter where they live. Write, write, write! Find time everyday to write. Network with other writers when possible, and write what you know. Learn the craft through books. Read scripts of your favorite movies. Enjoy what you write!"

CHADWICK & GROS LITERARY AGENCY, Garden District Branch, Belleview Drive, Palazzo 226, Baton Rouge LA 70806-5049. (225)338-9521. Fax: (225)338-9521. E-mail: apiazza@peoplepc.com or cguk@peoplepc.com. Website: colorpro.com/chadwick-gros/. **Contact:** Tony Seigan, associate director/overseas officer; Anna Piazza, director. Estab. 1998. Represents 30 clients. 95% of clients are new/unpublished writers. Currently handles: 90% movie scripts; 10% TV scripts.
• Prior to becoming an agent, Ms. Piazza was a talent scout for Rinehart & Associates.
Member Agents: Anna Piazza (director), Tony Seigan (associate director/overseas officer), David J. Carubba (business manager), C.J. Myerson (president of Institute of Baton Rouge Oxford Writers [I-BROWS] Colony), Theron T. Jacks (business advisor).
Represents: Feature film, TV movie of the week, sitcom. **Considers these script subject areas:** Action/adventure; biography/autobiography; comedy; detective/police/crime; family saga; juvenile; mystery/suspense; romantic comedy; science fiction; sports; thriller; western/frontier.
➩ Actively seeking "good attitudes; tough-minded, sure-footed, potential pros." This agency will not be signing new clients until July 2007. "Presently, our plate is full."
How to Contact: Query with SASE, 1-page synopsis. Accepts queries during February, July and October, but will not be signing new clients until July 2007. Considers simultaneous queries. Responds in 10 days to queries; 2 months to mss. Returns materials only with SASE. Obtains most new clients through recommendations from others, website.
Recent Sales: Sold 17 scripts in the last year. *Carrot Tips*, by J. Seivers (Generation X); *The Author*; *The Ouida Link*; *WhorehouseRoux*; *The Fine and the Wicked*, by Sam Goldwyn, Jr.

Terms: Agent receives 10% commission on domestic sales; 15% commission on foreign sales. Offers written contract, binding for 1-2 years; 6-month notice must be given to terminate contract. Charges clients for all communications with C&G—phone, fax, postage and handling that is, office expenses, postage, photocopying, but *no marketing fee.*

Tips: "Be most businesslike when you tap on an agency's door. Agencies are business offices, and every exchange costs money, time, effort, grief or joy."

☑ **CIRCLE OF CONFUSION LTD.**, 107-23 71st Road, Suite 30, Forest Hills NY 11375. E-mail: circlequeri es@aol.com. **Contact:** Shelly Narine. Estab. 1990. Signatory of WGA. Represents 30 clients. 40% of clients are new/unpublished writers. Currently handles: 95% movie scripts, 5% other.

Member Agents: Lawrence Mattis; Trisha Smith

Represents: Nonfiction books, novels, novellas, feature film, TV scripts. **Considers these nonfiction areas:** Agriculture/horticulture; Americana; animals; anthropology/archaeology; art/architecture/design; biography/autobiography; business/economics; child guidance/parenting; computers/electronic; cooking/foods/nutrition; crafts/hobbies; creative nonfiction; current affairs; education; ethnic/cultural interests; gardening; gay/lesbian issues; government/politics/law; health/medicine; history; how-to; humor/satire; interior design/decorating; juvenile nonfiction; language/literature/criticism; memoirs; military/war; money/finance; multicultural; music/dance; nature/environment; New Age/metaphysics; philosophy; photography; popular culture; psychology; recreation; regional; religious/inspirational; science/technology; self-help/personal improvement; sex; sociology; software; spirituality; sports; theater/film; translation; travel; true crime/investigative; women's issues/studies; young adult. **Considers these fiction areas:** Action/adventure; comic books/cartoon; confession; contemporary issues; detective/police/crime; erotica; ethnic; experimental; family saga; fantasy; feminist; gay/lesbian; glitz; gothic; hi-lo; historical; horror; humor/satire; juvenile; literary; mainstream/contemporary; military/war; multicultural; multimedia; mystery/suspense; New Age; occult; picture books; plays; poetry; poetry in translation; psychic/supernatural; regional; religious/inspirational; romance; science fiction; short story collections; spiritual; sports; thriller; translation; westerns/frontier; young adult; women's. **Considers these script subject areas:** Action/adventure; biography/autobiography; cartoon/animation; comedy; contemporary issues; detective/police/crime; erotica; ethnic; experimental; family saga; fantasy; feminist; gay/lesbian; glitz; historical; horror; juvenile; mainstream; multicultural; multimedia; mystery/suspense; psychic/supernatural; regional; religious/inspirational; romantic comedy; romantic drama; science fiction; sports; teen; thriller; western/frontier.

○━ Specializes in screenplays for film and TV.

How to Contact: Query with SASE. Responds in 1 month to queries; 2 months to mss. Obtains most new clients through recommendations from others, solicitations, writing contests and queries.

Recent Sales: *Movie/TV MOW script(s) optioned/sold: The Matrix*, by Wachowski Brothers (Warner Brothers); *Ghosts of October*, by Chabot/Peterka (Dreamworks); *Blood of the Gods*, by Jaswinski (Warner Brothers); *Droid*, by Massa (Warner Brothers); *Extinction*, by Herkrom and Leone (Sony); *Motor City*, by Miro & Bernard.

Terms: Agent receives 10% commission on domestic sales; 10% commission on foreign sales. Offers written contract, binding for 1 year.

Tips: "We look for writing that shows a unique voice, especially one which puts a fresh spin on commercial Hollywood genres."

☑ ◐ **CLIENT FIRST-A/K/A LEO P. HAFFEY AGENCY**, P.O.Box 128049, Nashville TN 37212-8049. (615)463-2388. E-mail: c1st@nashville.net. Website: www.c-1st.com. **Contact:** Robin Swensen. Estab. 1990. Signatory of WGA. Represents 21 clients. 25% of clients are new/unpublished writers. Currently handles: 40% novels; 60% movie scripts.

Member Agents: Leo Haffey (attorney/agent in the motion picture industry).

Represents: Nonfiction books (self-help), novels, short story collections, novellas, feature film, animation. **Considers these script subject areas:** Action/adventure; cartoon/animation; comedy; contemporary issues; detective/police/crime; family saga; historical; mystery/suspense; romantic drama (contemporary, historical); science fiction; sports; thriller; western/frontier.

○━ This agency specializes in movie scripts and novels for sale to motion picture industry.

How to Contact: Query with SASE, synopsis, treatment or summary. Do not send scripts/screenplays unless requested. Considers simultaneous queries. Responds in 1 week to queries; 2 months to mss. Returns materials only with SASE. Obtains most new clients through recommendations from others.

Recent Sales: This agency prefers not to share information on specific sales.

Terms: Offers written contract, binding for negotiable length of time.

Tips: "The motion picture business is a numbers game like any other. The more you write the better your chances are of success. Please send a SASE along with your query letter."

◐ **COMMUNICATIONS AND ENTERTAINMENT, INC.**, 2851 South Ocean Blvd., #5K, Boca Raton FL 33432-8407. (561)391-9575. Fax: (561)391-7922. E-mail: jlbearde@bellsouth.net. **Contact:** James L. Bearden. Estab. 1989. Represents 10 clients. 50% of clients are new/unpublished writers. Currently handles: 10% novels; 5% juvenile books; 40% movie scripts; 40% TV scripts.

● Prior to opening his agency, Mr. Bearden worked as a producer/director and an entertainment attorney.

Member Agents: James Bearden (TV/film); Roslyn Ray (literary).

Represents: Novels, juvenile books, movie scripts, TV scripts, syndicated material. **Considers these nonfiction areas:** History; music/dance; theater/film. **Considers these fiction areas:** Action/adventure; comic books/cartoon; fantasy; historical; mainstream/contemporary; science fiction; thriller.
How to Contact: For scripts, query with SASE. For books, query with outline/proposal or send entire ms. Responds in 1 month to queries; 3 months to mss. Obtains most new clients through recommendations from others.
Recent Sales: This agency prefers not to share information on specific sales.
Terms: Agent receives 10% commission on domestic sales; 5% commission on foreign sales. Offers written contract, binding time for varies with project.
Tips: "Be patient."

COMMUNICATIONS MANAGEMENT ASSOCIATES, 1129 Sixth Ave., #1, Rockford IL 61104-3147. Fax: (815)964-3061. **Contact:** Thomas R. Lee. Estab. 1989. Represents 30 clients. 50% of clients are new/unpublished writers. Currently handles: 5% nonfiction books; 10% novels; 80% movie scripts; 5% TV scripts.
Member Agents: Jack Young.
Represents: Novels, short story collections, novellas, juvenile books, scholarly books, poetry books, feature film, TV movie of the week, animation, documentary, miniseries. **Considers these fiction areas:** Action/adventure (adventure); detective/police/crime; erotica; fantasy; historical; horror; juvenile; mainstream/contemporary; mystery/suspense; picture books; romance (historical, regency); science fiction; thriller; westerns/frontier; young adult. **Considers these script subject areas:** Action/adventure; biography/autobiography; cartoon/animation; comedy; contemporary issues; detective/police/crime; erotica; fantasy; historical; horror; juvenile; mainstream; psychic/supernatural; religious/inspirational; romantic comedy; romantic drama; science fiction; teen; thriller; western/frontier.
O➡ This agency specializes in research, editing and financing.
How to Contact: Query with SASE, proposal package, outline, 3 sample chapter(s). Discards unwanted material. Accepts fax queries. Considers simultaneous queries. Obtains most new clients through recommendations from others.
Recent Sales: Sold 2 scripts in the last year. Send query for list of credits.
Terms: Agent receives 10% commission on domestic sales; 15% commission on foreign sales. Offers written contract, binding for 2-4 months; 60 days notice must be given to terminate contract. Charges clients for postage, photocopying and office expenses.
Writers' Conferences: BEA.
Tips: "Don't let greed or fame-seeking, or anything but a sincere love of writing push you into this business."

THE COPPAGE COMPANY, 5411 Camellia Ave., North Hollywood CA 91601. (818)980-8806. Fax: (818)980-8824. **Contact:** Judy Coppage. Estab. 1985. Signatory of WGA; Member of DGA, SAG, AFTRA.
Represents: Feature film, TV scripts (original).
O➡ This agency specializes in "writers who also produce, direct and act."
How to Contact: Obtains most new clients through recommendation only.
Recent Sales: This agency prefers not to share information on specific sales.

CREATIVE ARTIST'S AGENCY, 9830 Wilshire Blvd., Beverly Hills CA 90212. One of the most powerful agencies, this agency accepts established screenwriting professionals only. Some of their clients include Tom Hanks, Russell Crowe, Tom Cruise, Steven Spielberg, Gwyneth Paltrow. To catch the attention of this agency, newer screenwriters require a strong referral by someone the agent knows personally, a face-to-face pitch at a conference one of the agents attends, or the top award in one of the most prestigious competitions. Does not accept queries or unsolicited scripts.

DOUROUX & CO., 445 S. Beverly Dr., Suite 310, Beverly Hills CA 90212. E-mail: douroux@relaypoint.n et. Website: www.relaypoint.net/~douroux. **Contact:** Michael E. Douroux. Estab. 1985. Member of DGA; signatory of WGA. 20% of clients are new/unpublished writers. Currently handles: 50% movie scripts; 50% TV scripts.
Member Agents: Michael E. Douroux (chairman/CEO).
Represents: Movie scripts, feature film, TV scripts, TV movie of the week, episodic drama, sitcom, animation. **Considers these script subject areas:** Action/adventure; comedy; detective/police/crime; family saga; fantasy; historical; mainstream; mystery/suspense; romantic comedy; romantic drama; science fiction; thriller; western/frontier.
How to Contact: Query with SASE or by e-mail. Considers simultaneous queries.
Recent Sales: This agency prefers not to share information on specific sales.
Terms: Agent receives 10% commission on domestic sales. Offers written contract, binding for 2 years. Charges for photocopying only.

DRAMATIC PUBLISHING, (Specialized: theatrical works), 311 Washington St., Woodstock IL 60098. (815)338-7170. Fax: (815)338-8981. E-mail: plays@dramaticpublishing.com. Website: www.dramaticpub lishing.com. **Contact:** Linda Habjan. Estab. 1885. Currently handles: 2% textbooks; 98% stage plays.

Represents: Stage plays.

    O→ This agency specializes in a full range of stage plays, musicals, adaptations, and instructional books about theater.

How to Contact: Submit complete ms, SASE. Responds in 10-12 months to mss.

Recent Sales: This agency prefers not to share information on specific sales.

ⓔ ENDEAVOR, 9701 Wilshire Blvd., 10th Floor, Beverly Hills CA 90212. One of the most powerful agencies, this agency accepts established screenwriting professionals only. Some of their clients include Drew Barrymore, Estelle Warren, Ben Affleck. To catch the attention of this agency, newer screenwriters require a strong referral by someone the agent knows personally, a face-to-face pitch at a conference one of the agents attends, or the top award in one of the most prestigious competitions. Does not accept queries or unsolicited scripts.

ⓜ EPSTEIN-WYCKOFF-CORSA-ROSS AND ASSOCIATES, 280 S. Beverly Dr., #400, Beverly Hills CA 90212-3904. (310)278-7222. **Contact:** Brett Carducci. Estab. 1993. Signatory of WGA. Represents 15 clients. Currently handles: 60% movie scripts; 30% TV scripts; 2% stage plays.

Member Agents: Craig Wyckoff (talent); Gary Epstein (talent).

Represents: Feature film, TV movie of the week, episodic drama, sitcom, animation, miniseries, soap opera, stage plays. **Considers these script subject areas:** Action/adventure; comedy; contemporary issues; detective/police/crime; erotica; family saga; feminist; gay/lesbian; historical; juvenile; mainstream; mystery/suspense; romantic comedy; romantic drama; teen; thriller.

    O→ This agency specializes in features, TV, and stage plays.

How to Contact: Obtains most new clients through recommendations from others.

Recent Sales: This agency prefers not to share information on specific sales.

Terms: Agent receives 15% commission on domestic sales; 20% commission on foreign sales; 10% commission on dramatic rights sales. Offers written contract, binding for 1 year.

ⓔ FEIGEN/PARRENT LITERARY MANAGEMENT, 10158 Hollow Glen Circle, Bel Air CA 90077-2112. (310)271-4722. Fax: (310)274-0503. E-mail: feigenparrentlit@aol.com. **Contact:** Brenda Feigen, Joanne Parrent. Estab. 1995. Member of PEN USA West, Authors Guild, LA County Bar Association. Represents 35-40 clients. 20-30% of clients are new/unpublished writers. Currently handles: 40% nonfiction books; 30% novels; 25% movie scripts; 5% TV scripts.

    • See the expanded listing for this agency in the Literary Agents section.

ⓔ FILMWRITERS LITERARY AGENCY, 4932 Long Shadow Dr., Midlothian VA 23112. (804)744-1718. **Contact:** Helene Wagner. Signatory of WGA. Currently not accepting clients.

    • Prior to opening her agency, Ms. Wagner was director of the Virginia Screenwriter's Forum for 7 years and taught college level screenwriting classes. "As a writer myself, I have won or been a finalist in most major screenwriting competitions throughout the country and have a number of my screenplays optioned. Through the years I have enjoyed helping and working with other writers. Some have gone on to have their movies made, their work optioned, and won national contests."

Represents: Feature film, TV movie of the week, miniseries. **Considers these script subject areas:** Action/adventure; comedy; contemporary issues; detective/police/crime; historical; juvenile; mystery/suspense; psychic/supernatural; romantic comedy; romantic drama; teen; thriller.

    O→ This agency does not accept unsolicited queries.

How to Contact: No e-mail or fax queries. "Obtains new clients only through recommendations from those known to me in the industry."

Recent Sales: *Movie/TV MOW script(s) optioned/sold: Woman of His Dreams*, by Jeff Rubin (Ellenfreyer Productions).

Terms: Agent receives 10% commission on domestic sales; 10% commission on foreign sales. Offers written contract. Clients supply photocopying and postage. Writers reimbursed for office fees after the sale of ms.

Tips: "Professional writers should wait until they have at least four drafts done before they send out their work because they know it takes that much hard work to make a story and characters work. Show me something I haven't seen before with characters that I care about, that jump off the page. I not only look at writer's work, I look at the writer's talent. If I believe in a writer, even though a piece may not sell, I'll stay with the writer and help nurture that talent which a lot of the big agencies won't do."

ⓜ FITZGERALD LITERARY MANAGEMENT, 84 Monte Alto Rd., Santa Fe NM 87505. Phone/fax: (505)466-1186. **Contact:** Lisa FitzGerald. Estab. 1994. Represents 12 clients. 75% of clients are new/unpublished writers. Currently handles: 15% film rights novels; 85% movie scripts.

    • Prior to opening her agency, Ms. FitzGerald headed development at Universal Studios for Bruce Evans and Raynold Gideon, Oscar-nominated writer-producers. She also served as Executive Story Analyst at CBS, and held positions at Curtis Brown Agency in New York and Adams, Ray & Rosenberg Talent Agency in Los Angeles.

Represents: Novels, feature film, TV movie of the week. **Considers these fiction areas:** Juvenile; mainstream/contemporary (novels with film potential); young adult. **Considers these script subject areas:** Action/adventure;

insider report

Eric Wald:
Sharing a *View From the Top*

Eric Wald first became interested in pursuing screenwriting in college. "I made a few short films back then, which I really enjoyed," he says. After graduation, Wald continued to write screenplays while working as a ghostwriter for a food and wine critic.

Then, in a serendipitous move, Wald attended a weekend seminar led by Richard Walter, the chair of the UCLA screenwriting department. "As part of the deal, [Walter] agrees to read and give feedback on one of your scripts," Wald explains. "He liked the script I submitted, and I developed a relationship with him through that." Wald then applied to the UCLA MFA program and was accepted for the fall of 1998.

His dedication to writing and rewriting paid off, and Wald made his first screenplay sale, *View From the Top*, to Miramax Films. Once the wheels were set in motion, they didn't stop until Wald had an agent, a sale, and a production credit.

Produced by Brillstein-Grey Entertainment, *View From the Top* is scheduled for release in January 2003, starring Gwyneth Paltrow as the lead character Donna, a woman determined to become a first class international flight attendant. Christina Applegate plays her rival Christine.

Here, Wald shares his insights on the writing process, explains how he made his sale, and offers tips for new screenwriters.

How did you come up with the idea for *View From the Top*? **What was your inspiration behind the main character Donna?**
A friend of mine worked for American Airlines as a ticketing agent. She was sent to the American Learning Center in Dallas, Texas, which is this huge campus where every American Airlines employee is sent. She described this place where you could walk down a hallway, open a doorway, and all of a sudden you're in an airplane cabin. She also described some of the classes she had to take, and I just knew there was a movie idea in there somewhere. At the same time I had ideas for the characters separately, and everything fit together nicely. I spent about six months taking notes, interviewing flight attendants, and doing research before I actually got into the writing.

How did you come up with Donna's rival?
Initially, the rival character Christine had a much smaller role. I believe in rewriting massively, so the story emerged after I did all the rewriting, draft after draft. It developed the conflicts between characters and hammered out their motivations.

What kind of organizational method do you use?
For original ideas, I spend a lot of time just taking notes, whether it's something as simple as a line of dialogue or a character name, and I try to accumulate a lot of background on the characters. Then I start working on a fairly detailed treatment, usually about eight to ten pages.

I lay out the basic story—so I know where it's headed—and as many of the story beats as possible. From that treatment I get a first draft done, no matter how bad. I have friends who start scripts they never finish. Sometimes it's not a bad thing to give up on a script that's not working. But if it's an idea you really believe in, it's important to lay down that first draft and give yourself something to work from. Don't write 30 pages and keep going back and editing, because then you'll never finish.

How did you catch an agent's interest?

I'd written about a dozen scripts before I came to UCLA. I had already started *View From the Top* and continued to develop it during my first quarter. I entered it in the year-end student showcase. I didn't win the contest, but one of the judges was a woman named Laura Hopper, who worked at Brillstein-Grey. She liked the script, brought me in for a meeting, and said they were interested in getting the script set up. So they sent the script around to the big five agencies. I got an immediate response from CAA and Endeavor, and I decided to sign with CAA.

What were your reasons for choosing CAA?

In the meeting, they seemed really professional and well-organized. They didn't want to go out with it right away, but they wanted me to polish it a little more. It showed me that they had a vision and a professional approach for the script.

Should writers try to actively find an agent?

Once a writer has a body of work, and has a few scripts ready to be submitted to the industry, it's critical to have an agent. I know some people who work with managers too. You definitely need someone representing you who is plugged into the industry, knows where to send your script, and will negotiate the deal if you get to that point.

How quickly did CAA end up selling your script?

I spent about a month and a half rewriting it. A week before it was ready, Brad Grey signed a deal with Miramax, so they decided to give the script to Miramax on a first-look basis. It actually went to Harvey Weinstein on a Tuesday night. He read it in 45 minutes and called at nine the next morning saying he wanted to buy it. It happened pretty fast. Obviously it helped that it went to the head of Miramax, someone capable of making a decision right away.

What was your favorite part of the process?

I loved writing the first draft, which is always fun. No one's there editing you while you explore the characters and find your story, so that was a great experience. And it was satisfying when it did eventually sell. That was certainly a very exciting day! I also enjoyed all the rewrites, to see the script take shape and get better and better and funnier and funnier.

What are some of the frustrations you encountered?

Once the project started moving towards production, the studio hired several other writers to re-work the script. I guess they were trying to take it in a more commercial direction. I realize this happens to most first-time writers, but it's still difficult to watch your script change. Then again, if I didn't want them to change it, I shouldn't have sold it!

Are there any scenes that were cut from your original script that you particularly miss?

I had a scene where Donna's having sex in an airplane lavatory, and the guy she's with keeps hitting the latch on the door. There's a cut to the outside of the door and it keeps flashing "occupied, vacant, occupied, vacant." (laughs) It's one of my favorite moments, but I don't know if that's still in there.

Do you have any advice for newer scriptwriters about craft?

One thing I find in a lot of scripts I read is that the dialogue or situations feel false. Characters don't talk the way people talk, and I just don't buy it. Or they'll do things that don't make sense to me on a gut level. I also find a lot of characters sound the same, instead of each character having a distinct voice. One other thing—and specifically Richard Walter was really great about encouraging this: try to make your writing as economical as possible. There tends to be either too much description or too much chit chat in dialogue, and it's not advancing the story or plot as it should.

Do you have any general advice for screenwriters?

Don't try to rush into the business aspect of it until you've built up a body of work. I know it's tempting to write one script and come to LA to try to sell it, but you're better off if you learn the craft, write a couple scripts, and build up a small body of work. It helps to write away from LA at first. You tend to run out of ideas when everyone you know is talking about movies and writing movies.

What are you working on now?

I actually just started a job this week doing a remake of an RKO Pictures movie called *Mr. Blandings Builds His Dream House*, which is an old Cary Grant movie. It had been loosely remade in the 80s as *The Money Pit*, which was the broader version and we're trying to go back more to the spirit of the original script. There's already a director attached, Steve Carr, who directed *Dr. Dolittle 2*.

Having a director attached increases the chance of it getting produced?

It certainly helps. But it's always a long-shot. A lot of writers have very full careers in Hollywood without actually having a movie made. There are so many factors against you. I got spoiled—the first thing I sold got made.

What kind of work would you like to do in the future?

I'm realistic about it. I know most writers in Hollywood don't have great career longevity. So I've enjoyed what I've accomplished already and hopefully I can keep writing for a few more years. Ideally, if I have enough success, I would like to do original scripts that capture a personal vision, and movies that I'd like to see. Maybe the way to accomplish that ultimately is to try directing a little further down the line.

What makes a script marketable?

It's important that people write stuff they believe in and would want to see, that they don't just go for the commercial home run. One thing a lot of people said about the script for *View*

From the Top was they felt like it had an original voice they hadn't heard before. You have to remember that producers and development people at studios are taking home a stack of scripts to read every weekend. If there's one with a unique voice [it stands out]. It also helps to have a great lead character that a movie star would want to play.

Any general advice about the profession?

It's a difficult profession. A lot of your success is dependent upon other people, and I think that's why a lot of writers tend to be neurotic and frustrated. It's hard not to think about the business side of things, but I try to take pride in the work itself. That's the one thing you do have control over.

With success depending on other people, does a writer need to present himself well socially?

That's critical! In fact, when I met with CAA, that was a big factor in their decision to sign me. They want to see how well you do in a room, how you carry yourself and if you're able to act in a professional manner. Because so much of whether you get hired on assignment is based upon how good you are in these meetings, how you're able to present yourself and articulate your ideas.

Did you find these meetings awkward at first?

I still do. It's amazing to see the way these pitch meetings can go. You can be in the meeting, and it's going fine. You've practised everything, hopefully rehearsed as much as possible. And then, the executive will come up with one question that derails the whole pitch and all the energy goes out of the room, and that's it, you're done. (laughs)

Any other tips for writers?

If you're writing full time, get dressed for work every morning. Don't write in your pajamas. (laughs) You'll take it more seriously if you think of it as a job.

I set a goal for each day, maybe around three to five pages, and once I do that, I turn off the computer, stop thinking about it, and do something else. Then I start fresh the next day. People can become so obsessed they forget to live, and that ultimately affects their writing. So you want to strike a healthy balance.

—*Rachel Vater*

biography/autobiography; comedy; contemporary issues; detective/police/crime; erotica; ethnic; family saga; fantasy; historical; horror; juvenile; mainstream; mystery/suspense; psychic/supernatural; romantic comedy; romantic drama; science fiction; sports; teen; thriller; western/frontier;

○➞ This agency specializes in screenwriters and selling film rights to novels. Actively seeking mainstream feature film scripts. Does not want to receive true stories.

How to Contact: We are not accepting new clients except by referral.

Recent Sales: Sold 7 titles and sold 5 scripts in the last year.

Terms: Agent receives 15% commission on domestic sales. Offers written contract, binding for 1-2 years. Charges clients for photocopying and postage.

Tips: "Know your craft. Read produced screenplays. Enter screenplay contests. Educate yourself on the business in general (read *The Hollywood Reporter* or *Daily Variety*). Learn how to pitch. Keep writing and don't be afraid to get your work out there."

B.R. FLEURY AGENCY, P.O. Box 149352, Orlando FL 32814-9352. (407)895-8494. Fax: (407)898-3923. E-mail: brfleuryagency@yahoo.com. **Contact:** Blanche or Margaret. Estab. 1994. Signatory of WGA. Currently handles: 30% nonfiction books; 60% novels; 10% movie scripts.

● See expanded listing for this agency in Literary Agents.

THE BARRY FREED CO., 2040 Ave. of the Stars, #400, Los Angeles CA 90067. (310)277-1260. Fax: (310)277-3865. E-mail: blfreed@aol.com. **Contact:** Barry Freed. Signatory of WGA. Represents 15 clients. 95% of clients are new/unpublished writers. Currently handles: 100% movie scripts.

● Prior to opening his agency, Mr. Freed worked for ICM.

Represents: Feature film, TV movie of the week. **Considers these script subject areas:** Action/adventure; comedy; contemporary issues; detective/police/crime; ethnic; family saga.

○➞ Actively seeking adult drama, comedy, romantic comedy. Does not want to receive period, science fiction.

How to Contact: Query with SASE. Prefers to read materials exclusively. Accepts e-mail and fax queries. Responds in 3 months to mss. Responds immediately to queries. Obtains most new clients through recommendations from others.

Recent Sales: This agency prefers not to share information on specific sales.

Terms: Offers written contract, binding for 2 years.

Tips: "Our clients are a highly qualified, small roster of writers who write comedy, action adventure/thrillers, adult drama, romantic comedy."

ROBERT A. FREEDMAN DRAMATIC AGENCY, INC., 1501 Broadway, Suite 2310, New York NY 10036. (212)840-5760. **Contact:** Robert A. Freedman. Estab. 1928. Member of AAR; signatory of WGA.

● Mr. Freedman has served as vice president of the dramatic division of AAR.

Member Agents: Robert A. Freedman, president; Selma Luttinger, vice president; Marta Praeger (stage plays) and Robin Kaver (movie and TV scripts), associates.

Represents: Movie scripts, TV scripts, stage plays.

○➞ This agency works with both established and new authors. Specializes in plays, movie scripts and TV scripts.

How to Contact: Query with SASE. All unsolicited mss returned unopened. Responds in 2 weeks to queries; 3 months to mss.

Recent Sales: "We will speak directly with any prospective client concerning sales that are relevant to his/her specific script."

Terms: Agent receives 10% commission on domestic sales. Charges clients for photocopying.

SAMUEL FRENCH, INC., 45 W. 25th St., New York NY 10010-2751. (212)206-8990. Fax: (212)206-1429. E-mail: samuelfrench@earthlink.net. Website: www.samuelfrench.com. **Contact:** Lawrence Harbison, senior editor. Estab. 1830. Member of AAR.

Member Agents: Alleen Hussung; Brad Lorenz; Linda Kirland; Charles R. Van Nostrand.

Represents: Theatrical stage plays, musicals. **Considers these script subject areas:** Comedy; contemporary issues; detective/police/crime; ethnic; fantasy; horror; mystery/suspense; thriller.

○➞ This agency specializes in publishing plays which they also license for production.

How to Contact: Query with SASE, or submit complete ms to Lawrence Harbison. Accepts e-mail and fax queries. Considers simultaneous queries. Responds in 8 months to mss. Responds immediately to queries.

Recent Sales: This agency prefers not to share information on specific sales.

Terms: Agent receives variable commission on domestic sales.

THE GAGE GROUP, 14724 Ventura Blvd., Suite 505, Sherman Oaks CA 91403. (818)905-3800. Fax: (818)905-3322. E-mail: gagegroupla@yahoo.com. Estab. 1976. Member of DGA; signatory of WGA. Represents 34 clients.

Member Agents: Jonathan Westover (head of department/ feature); Sharon Moist (television).

Represents: Movie scripts, feature film, TV scripts, theatrical stage play. **Considers these script subject areas:** Action/adventure; biography/autobiography; cartoon/animation; comedy; contemporary issues; detective/police/

crime; erotica; ethnic; experimental; family saga; fantasy; feminist; gay/lesbian; glitz; historical; horror; juvenile; mainstream; multicultural; multimedia; mystery/suspense; psychic/supernatural; regional; religious/inspirational; romantic comedy; romantic drama; science fiction; sports; teen; thriller; western/frontier; considers all script subject areas.
How to Contact: Query with SASE. Accepts queries by e-mail. Considers simultaneous queries and submissions. Responds in 1 month to queries; 1 month to mss.
Recent Sales: This agency prefers not to share information on specific sales.
Terms: Agent receives 10% commission on domestic sales; 10% commission on foreign sales. Agency charges clients the cost of copying the script.

THE LAYA GELFF LITERARY AND TALENT AGENCY, 16133 Ventura Blvd., Suite 700, Encino CA 91436. (818)996-3100. Estab. 1985. Signatory of WGA. Represents many clients. Currently handles: 50% movie scripts; 45% TV scripts; 5% book mss.
Represents: Feature film, TV scripts.
   This agency specializes in TV and film scripts; WGA members preferred. "Also represents writers to publishers." Does not represent sitcoms for TV.
How to Contact: Query with SASE. Must include SASE for reply. Considers simultaneous queries. Responds in 5 weeks to queries; 5 weeks to mss. Obtains most new clients through recommendations from others.
Recent Sales: This agency prefers not to share information on specific sales.
Terms: Agent receives 10% commission on domestic sales; 10% commission on foreign sales. Offers written contract. Charges reading fee for book representation only, as well as postage and copying.
Tips: WGA members preferred.

GRAHAM AGENCY, 311 W. 43rd St., New York NY 10036. **Contact:** Earl Graham. Estab. 1971. Represents 40 clients. 30% of clients are new/unpublished writers. Currently handles: movie scripts; stage plays.
Represents: Feature film, theatrical stage play.
   This agency specializes in playwrights and screenwriters only. "We're interested in commercial material of quality." Does not want to receive one-acts or material for children.
How to Contact: Query with SASE. No e-mail or fax queries. Responds in 3 months to queries; 6 weeks to mss. Obtains most new clients through recommendations from others, solicitations.
Recent Sales: This agency prefers not to share information on specific sales.
Terms: Agent receives 10% commission on dramatic rights sales.
Tips: "Write a concise, intelligent letter giving the gist of what you are offering."

GRANT, SAVIC, KOPALOFF & ASSOCIATES, (formerly Soloway Grant Kopaloff & Associates), 414 Wilshire Blvd., Los Angeles CA 90048. (323)782-1854. Fax: (323)782-1877. E-mail: sgkassoc@pacbell.net. **Contact:** Don Kopaloff. Estab. 1976. Signatory of WGA; AFF, DGA.
Member Agents: Arnold Soloway; Susan Grant; Don Kopaloff.
Represents: Movie scripts, TV scripts. **Considers these script subject areas:** Action/adventure; biography/autobiography; cartoon/animation; comedy; contemporary issues; detective/police/crime; erotica; ethnic; experimental; family saga; fantasy; feminist; gay/lesbian; glitz; historical; horror; juvenile; mainstream; multicultural; multimedia; mystery/suspense; psychic/supernatural; regional; religious/inspirational; romantic comedy; romantic drama; science fiction; sports; teen; thriller; western/frontier.
How to Contact: Query with SASE. After query letter is accepted, writer must sign release. Not accepting unsolicited mss. Responds in 1 month to queries.
Recent Sales: This agency prefers not to share information on specific sales.
Terms: Agent receives 10% commission on domestic sales; 10% commission on foreign sales. May make referrals to freelance editors. Use of editors does not ensure representation. 0% of business is derived from referrals to editing service.
Tips: "Advise against 'cutsie' inquiry letters."

THE SUSAN GURMAN AGENCY, 865 West End Ave., #15A, New York NY 10025-8403. (212)749-4618. Fax: (212)864-5055. E-mail: gurmanagency@earthlink.net. **Contact:** Susan Gurman. Estab. 1993. Signatory of WGA. 28% of clients are new/unpublished writers. Currently handles: 70% movie scripts; 30% stage plays.
Member Agents: Gail Eisenberg (associate agent); Susan Gurman.
Represents: Feature film, TV movie of the week, theatrical stage play. **Considers these nonfiction areas:** Biography/autobiography; true crime/investigative. **Considers these fiction areas:** Action/adventure (adventure);

CHECK THE AGENT SPECIALTIES INDEX to find agents who are interested in your specific nonfiction or fiction subject area.

detective/police/crime; family saga; fantasy; horror; literary; mainstream/contemporary; mystery/suspense; picture books; thriller. **Considers these script subject areas:** Comedy; detective/police/crime; family saga; horror; mainstream; mystery/suspense; romantic comedy; romantic drama; thriller; true stories.

○→ This agency specializes in referred screenwriters and playwrights.

How to Contact: No e-mail or fax queries. Considers simultaneous queries. Responds in 2 weeks to queries; 2 months to mss. Obtains most new clients through recommendations from others.

Recent Sales: Sold 10 scripts in the last year. This agency prefers not to share information on specific sales.

Terms: Agent receives 10% commission on domestic sales; 10% commission on foreign sales.

H.W.A. TALENT REPRESENTATIVES, 3500 W. Olive Ave., Suite 1400, Burbank CA 91505. (818)972-4310. Fax: (818)972-4313. **Contact:** Kimber Wheeler. Estab. 1985. Signatory of WGA. 60% of clients are new/unpublished writers. Currently handles: 10% novels; 90% movie scripts.

Represents: Novels, movie scripts, TV scripts. **Considers these script subject areas:** Action/adventure; comedy; contemporary issues; ethnic; family saga; fantasy; feminist; horror; mystery/suspense; psychic/supernatural; romantic comedy; romantic drama; science fiction; sports; thriller.

How to Contact: Query with SASE, outline/proposal.

Recent Sales: This agency prefers not to share information on specific sales.

Terms: Agent receives 10% commission on domestic sales. Offers written contract, binding for 1 year; WGA rules on termination apply.

Tips: "A good query letter is important. Use any relationship you have in the business to get your material read."

HART LITERARY MANAGEMENT, 3541 Olive St., Santa Ynez CA 93460. (805)686-7912. E-mail: hartliteraryagency@hotmail.com. Website: www.hartliterary.com. **Contact:** Susan Hart. Estab. 1997. Signatory of WGA. Represents 25 clients. 95% of clients are new/unpublished writers. Currently handles: 100% movie scripts.

● Prior to opening the agency, Ms. Hart was a screenwriter.

Represents: Movie scripts, feature film, TV movie of the week, mostly PG-13. **Considers these script subject areas:** Biography/autobiography; family saga; horror; juvenile; mainstream; science fiction; teen.

How to Contact: Query with SASE. Accepts e-mail queries. No fax queries. Considers simultaneous queries. Responds in 2 weeks to queries. Returns materials only with SASE. Obtains most new clients through solicitations.

Recent Sales: Sold 1 script in the last year. *Annus Horribilis (My Horrible Year)*, by J. McIluaine (Millbrook Farm Productions/Showtime); *Encrypt*, by Richard Taylor (USA Cable).

Terms: Agent receives 10% domestic or worldwide sales on gross income written any source from the screenplays commission on domestic sales. Offers written contract, binding for 1 year but may be cancelled at any time by both parties in writing. Charges clients for photocopies and postage; $6.50 domestic, $10 Canadian and $12 international (currently). This is the same as WGA requirement that screenwriters send copies of all screenplays to their agents and is cheaper than that in most cases.

Tips: "I want a great story spell-checked, formatted, and "typed" in industry standard 12 point Courier or Courier New only, between 95-120 pages maximum. No overt gore, sex, violence. See website for genres I may look at."

CAROLYN HODGES AGENCY, 1980 Glenwood Dr., Boulder CO 80304-2329. (303)443-4636. Fax: (303)443-4636. E-mail: hodgesc@earthlink.net. **Contact:** Carolyn Hodges. Estab. 1989. Signatory of WGA. Represents 15 clients. 75% of clients are new/unpublished writers. Currently handles: 15% movie scripts; 45% TV scripts.

● Prior to opening her agency, Ms. Hodges was a freelance writer and founded the Writers in the Rockies Screenwriting Conference.

Represents: Feature film, TV movie of the week. **Considers these script subject areas:** Comedy (light, black); romantic comedy; thriller (suspense, psychological).

○→ This agency represents screenwriters for film and TV MOW. Does not want TV sitcom, drama or episodics.

How to Contact: Query with SASE. Accepts e-mail and fax queries. Considers simultaneous queries. Responds in 1 week to queries; 10 weeks to mss. Returns materials only with SASE. Obtains most new clients through recommendations from others.

Recent Sales: Available upon request.

Terms: Agent receives 10% commission on domestic sales; 10% commission on foreign sales. Offers written contract. No charge for criticism. "I always try to offer concrete feedback, even when rejecting a piece of material."

Tips: "Become proficient at your craft. Attend all workshops accessible to you. READ all the books applicable to your area of interest. READ as many 'produced' screenplays as possible. Live a full, vital and rewarding life so your writing will have something to say. Get involved in a writer's support group. Network with other writers. Receive 'critiques' from your peers and consider merit of suggestions. Don't be afraid to re-examine your perspective. Do yourself a favor and don't submit the 'first draft' of 'first script' to agents. Immature writing is obvious and will hurt your chance of later submissions."

BARBARA HOGENSON AGENCY, 165 West End Ave., Suite 19-C, New York NY 10023. (212)874-8084. Fax: (212)362-3011. **Contact:** Barbara Hogenson. Estab. 1994. Member of AAR; signatory of WGA. Represents 60 clients. 5% of clients are new/unpublished writers. Currently handles: 35% nonfiction books; 15% novels; 50% stage plays.

• Prior to opening her agency, Ms. Hogenson was with the prestigious Lucy Kroll Agency for 10 years.

Represents: Nonfiction books, novels, theatrical stage play. **Considers these nonfiction areas:** Biography/autobiography; history; interior design/decorating; music/dance; popular culture; theater/film. **Considers these fiction areas:** Action/adventure; detective/police/crime; ethnic; historical; humor/satire; literary; mainstream/contemporary; mystery/suspense; romance (contemporary); thriller.

How to Contact: Query with SASE, outline. No unsolicited mss. Responds in 1 month to queries. Obtains most new clients through recommendations from others.

Recent Sales: *Letters*, by Harrison Kinney and Rosemary Thurber. **Book Sales:** *Peter Loon*, by Van Reid; *Life Lessons*, by Elizabeth Kubler-Ross.

Terms: Agent receives 15% commission on domestic sales; 20% commission on foreign sales; 10% commission on dramatic rights sales. Offers written contract.

HUDSON AGENCY, 3 Travis Lane, Montrose NY 10548. (914)737-1475. Fax: (914)736-3064. Website: www.hudsonagency.net.

Tips: Check out our website for our staff member list, the appropriate e-mail addresses to send queries to, or view our client list. We specialize in features of all genres and animation but will not handle anything associated with the occult or anything containing gratuitous violence, sex or language."

INTERNATIONAL CREATIVE MANAGEMENT, 40 W. 57th St., New York NY 10019. and 8942 Wilshire Blvd., Beverly Hills CA 90211. Member of AAR; signatory of WGA. One of the most powerful script agencies, this agency accepts established screenwriting professionals only. Some of their clients include Jennifer Lopez, Cameron Diaz, Jodie Foster, Mel Gibson, Denzel Washington, Michell Pfeiffer. To catch the attention of this agency, newer screenwriters require a strong referral by someone the agent knows personally, a fact-to-face pitch at a conference one of the agents attends, or the top award in one of the most prestigious competitions. Does not accept queries or unsolicited scripts.

INTERNATIONAL LEONARDS CORP., 3612 N. Washington Blvd., Indianapolis IN 46205-3534. (317)926-7566. **Contact:** David Leonards. Estab. 1972. Signatory of WGA. Currently handles: 50% movie scripts; 50% TV scripts.

Represents: Feature film, TV movie of the week, sitcom, animation, variety show. **Considers these script subject areas:** Action/adventure; cartoon/animation; comedy; contemporary issues; detective/police/crime; horror; mystery/suspense; romantic comedy; science fiction; sports; thriller.

How to Contact: All unsolicited mss returned unopened.

Recent Sales: This agency prefers not to share information on specific sales.

Terms: Agent receives 10% commission on domestic sales; 10% commission on foreign sales. Offers written contract, binding for WGA standard terms, which vary.

JARET ENTERTAINMENT, 6973 Bird View Ave., Malibu CA 90265. (310) 589-9600. Fax: (310) 589-9602. E-mail: info@jaretentertainment.com. Website: www.Jaretentertainment.com. **Contact:** Nathan Santell. Represents 20 clients. 70% of clients are new/unpublished writers. Currently handles: 75% movie scripts; 25% TV scripts.

Member Agents: Nathan Santell (story editor/senior assistant/junior manager).

Represents: Movie scripts, TV scripts, TV movie of the week, animation. **Considers these script subject areas:** Action/adventure; biography/autobiography; cartoon/animation; comedy; mystery/suspense; psychic/supernatural; romantic comedy; romantic drama; science fiction; sports; thriller.

○━ This management company specializes in creative, out-of-the-box thinking. "We're willing to take a chance on well-written materials." Actively seeking "high concept, science fiction, thrillers, mysteries and smart romantic comedies." Does not want "any projects with unnecessary violence, westerns, or anything you've seen before—studio programmers, black comedy or period pieces that drag out and are boring."

How to Contact: Query with SASE. Discards unwanted material. Accepts e-mail and fax queries. Considers simultaneous queries. Obtains most new clients through recommendations from others.

Recent Sales: Sold 5 scripts in the last year. *Bumper to Bumper*, (Fox); *The Fraud Prince*, (Warner Brothers). *Scripting Assignment(s): Girl in the Curl*, (Paramount).

Terms: Agent receives 10% commission on domestic sales. Offers written contract, binding for 10-24 months.

LESLIE KALLEN AGENCY, 15760 Ventura Blvd., Suite #700, Encino CA 91436. (818)906-2785. Fax: (818)906-8931. Website: www.lesliekallen.com. Estab. 2001.

Represents: Feature film, TV movie of the week.

○━ This agency specializes in feature film, gamers, animators and MOWs.

How to Contact: Referral only.

Recent Sales: This agency prefers not to share information on specific sales.
Terms: Agent receives 10% commission on domestic sales.

⊘ THE JOYCE KETAY AGENCY, 1501 Broadway, Suite 1908, New York NY 10036. (212)354-6825. Fax: (212)354-6732. **Contact:** Joyce Ketay, Carl Mulert. Signatory of WGA.
Member Agents: Joyce Ketay; Carl Mulert.
Represents: Feature film, TV movie of the week, episodic drama, sitcom, theatrical stage play. **Considers these script subject areas:** Action/adventure; comedy; contemporary issues; detective/police/crime; ethnic; experimental; family saga; fantasy; feminist; gay/lesbian; glitz; historical; juvenile; mainstream; mystery/suspense; psychic/supernatural; romantic comedy; romantic drama; thriller; western/frontier.
    ☞ This agency specializes in playwrights and screenwriters only. Does not want to receive novels.
Recent Sales: This agency prefers not to share information on specific sales.

◎ PAUL KOHNER, INC., (Specialized: film rights), 9300 Wilshire Blvd., Suite 555, Beverly Hills CA 90212-3211. (310)550-1060. **Contact:** Stephen Moore. Estab. 1938. Member of ATA; signatory of WGA. Represents 150 clients. 10% of clients are new/unpublished writers.
Represents: Feature film, TV movie of the week, episodic drama, sitcom, animation, documentary, miniseries, soap opera, variety show, stage plays, film/TV rights to published books. **Considers these script subject areas:** Action/adventure; comedy; family saga; historical; mainstream; mystery/suspense; romantic comedy; romantic drama.
    ☞ This agency specializes in film and TV rights sales and representation of film and TV writers.
Recent Sales: This agency prefers not to share information on specific sales.
Terms: Agent receives 10% commission on domestic sales; 10% commission on foreign sales. Offers written contract, binding for 1-3 years. "We charge clients for copying manuscripts or scripts for submission unless a sufficient quantity is supplied by the author."

🄽 ⊘ OTTO R. KOZAK LITERARY & MOTION PICTURE AGENCY, P.O. Box 152, Long Beach NY 11561. Fax: (516)371-2329. E-mail: literaryagent1@aol.com. Website: www.internationalliteraryagent.com. **Contact:** Robert Kozak, marketing associate. Signatory of WGA. Represents 118 clients. 75% of clients are new/unpublished writers. 75% movie scripts, 25% TV scripts.
    ● Prior to becoming an agent Mr. Kozak was a film importer (Europe), distributor for an art circuit moviehouse.
Member Agents: Yitka Kozak (script story analyst).
Represents: Biography/autobiography, contemporary issues, feminist, historical, religious/inspirational, teen. Contacts in Europe—to place scripts with production companies. Robert Kozak has sales/marketing experience in the finance field; Yitka Kozak worked as a script/story analyst for AVCO Embassy Pictures for 5 years. We guide novices to realistic expectations; provide advice on proper script form, script self-evaluation. Actively seeking socially relevant material; female issues/audience oriented.
How to Contact: Query with SASE. Will ask for outline, synopsis, treatment based on query. Accepts queries by e-mail. Consider simultaneous queries and submissions. Responds in 3 weeks to queries; 3 months to screenplays. Return only with SASE. Obtains most new clients through recommendations from others.
Recent Sales: Sold 2 script projects last year. Optioned 5 script projects last year. This agency prefers not to share information on specific sales.
Terms: Standard 10% commission.
Tips: "I do not handle any mss (novels). Writers must include SASE for response."

⊘ EDDIE KRITZER PRODUCTIONS, 8484 Wilshire Blvd., Suite 205, Beverly Hills CA 90211. (323)655-5696. Fax: (323)655-5173. E-mail: producedby@aol.com. Website: www.eddiekritzer.com. **Contact:** Larisa Wain, executive story editor. Estab. 1995. Represents 20 clients. 50% of clients are new/unpublished writers. Currently handles: 25% nonfiction books; 5% novels; 10% movie scripts; 15% TV scripts; 1% stage plays; 1% syndicated material.
    ● See the expanded listing for this agency in Literary Agents.

⊘ THE CANDACE LAKE AGENCY, 9200 Sunset Blvd., Suite 820, Los Angeles CA 90069. (310)247-2115. Fax: (310)247-2116. E-mail: clagency@bwkliterary.com. **Contact:** Candace Lake. Estab. 1977. Signatory of WGA. 50% of clients are new/unpublished writers. Currently handles: 20% novels; 40% movie scripts; 40% TV scripts.
Member Agents: Candace Lake (president/agent); Richard Ryba (agent); Steven Day Clark (assistant).
Represents: Novels, feature film, TV movie of the week, episodic drama. **Considers these fiction areas:** Action/adventure; comic books/cartoon; confession; contemporary issues; detective/police/crime; ethnic; family saga; fantasy; feminist; gay/lesbian; glitz; gothic; hi-lo; historical; horror; humor/satire; juvenile; literary; mainstream/contemporary; military/war; multicultural; multimedia; mystery/suspense; New Age; occult; picture books; plays; psychic/supernatural; regional; religious/inspirational; romance; science fiction; spiritual; sports; thriller; translation; westerns/frontier; young adult. **Considers these script subject areas:** Action/adventure; biography/autobiography; cartoon/animation; comedy; contemporary issues; detective/police/crime; ethnic; fam-

ily saga; fantasy; feminist; gay/lesbian; glitz; historical; horror; juvenile; mainstream; multicultural; multimedia; mystery/suspense; psychic/supernatural; regional; religious/inspirational; romantic comedy; romantic drama; science fiction; sports; teen; thriller; western/frontier.

O— This agency specializes in screenplay and teleplay writers.

How to Contact: Query with SASE. No unsolicited material. Considers simultaneous queries. Responds in 1 month to queries; 3 months to mss. Returns materials only with SASE. Obtains most new clients through recommendations from others.

Recent Sales: This agency prefers not to share information on specific sales.

Terms: Agent receives 10% commission on domestic sales; 10% commission on foreign sales. Offers written contract, binding for 2 years.

THE LANTZ OFFICE, 200 W. 57th St., Suite 503, New York NY 10019. **Contact:** Robert Lantz. Member of AAR.

• This agency did not respond to our request for information. Query before submitting.

LARCHMONT LITERARY AGENCY, 444 N. Larchmont Blvd., Suite 200, Los Angeles CA 90004. (323)856-3070. E-mail: agency@larchmontlit.com. **Contact:** Joel Millner or Greg Lewis. Estab. 1998. Member of DGA; signatory of WGA. Currently handles: 5% novels; 90% movie scripts; 5% TV scripts.

• Prior to becoming an agent, Mr. Millner attended NYU Film School and participated in The William Morris agent training program.

Represents: Novels, movie scripts, feature film. **Considers these fiction areas:** Action/adventure; fantasy; historical; horror; humor/satire; juvenile; literary; mainstream/contemporary; mystery/suspense; romance; science fiction; sports; thriller. **Considers these script subject areas:** Action/adventure; biography/autobiography; cartoon/animation; comedy; contemporary issues; detective/police/crime; fantasy; historical; horror; mainstream; mystery/suspense; psychic/supernatural; romantic comedy; romantic drama; science fiction; sports; thriller.

O— This agency specializes in feature writers and feature writer/directors. "We maintain a small, highly selective client list and offer a long-term career management style of agenting that larger agencies can't provide." Actively seeking spec feature scripts or established feature writers.

How to Contact: Query with SASE. Prefers to read materials exclusively. Responds in 2 weeks to queries. Obtains most new clients through recommendations from others.

Recent Sales: This agency prefers not to share information on specific sales.

Terms: Agent receives 10% commission on domestic sales. No written contract.

Writers' Conferences: NYU Film School (Los Angeles, June), UCLA, USC.

Tips: "Please do not send a script until it is in its best possible draft."

LEGACIES, 501 Woodstork Circle, Bradenton FL 34209-7393. (941)792-9159. Fax: (941)795-0552. **Contact:** Marcy Ann Amato, executive director. Estab. 1993. Member of Florida Motion Picture & Television Association, Board of Talent Agents, Dept. of Professional Regulations License No. TA 0000404; signatory of WGA. 50% of clients are new/unpublished writers. Currently handles: 10% novels; 80% movie scripts; 10% stage plays.

Represents: Feature film. **Considers these script subject areas:** Comedy; contemporary issues; family saga; feminist; historical.

O— This agency specializes in screenplays.

How to Contact: Query with SASE. Considers simultaneous queries. Responds in 2 weeks to queries; 6 weeks to mss.

Recent Sales: *Death's Parallel*, by Dr. Oakley Jordan (Rainbow Books). *Movie/TV MOW script(s) optioned/sold: A Bench On Which To Rest*, by Maria Phillips; *Progress of the Sun*, by Patricia Friedberg; *Elsie Venner*, by Raleigh Marcell.

Terms: Agent receives 10% commission on domestic sales; 15% commission on foreign sales. Offers written contract.

Tips: "New writers should purchase script writing computer programs, or read and apply screenplay format before submitting."

PAUL S. LEVINE LITERARY AGENCY, 1054 Superbra Ave., Venice CA 90291-3940. (310)450-6711. Fax: (310)450-0181. E-mail: pslevine@ix.netcom.com. Website: www.netcom.com/~pslevine/lawliterary.html. **Contact:** Paul S. Levine. Estab. 1996. Member of the State Bar of California. Represents over 100 clients. 75% of clients are new/unpublished writers. Currently handles: 30% nonfiction books; 30% novels; 10% movie scripts; 30% TV scripts.

• See the expanded listing for this agency in Literary Agents.

LIVINGSTON COOKE, 457A Danforth Ave., Suite 201, Toronto Ontario M4K 1P1, Canada. (416)406-3390. Fax: (416)406-3389. E-mail: livcooke@idirect.ca. **Contact:** Elizabeth Griffen. Estab. 1992. Represents 200 clients. 30% of clients are new/unpublished writers. Currently handles: 50% nonfiction books; 30% novels; 10% movie scripts; 10% TV scripts.

• See the expanded listing for this agency in Literary Agents.

THE LUEDTKE AGENCY, 1674 Broadway, Suite 7A, New York NY 10019. (212)765-9564. Fax: (212)765-9582. **Contact:** Elaine Devlin. Estab. 1997. Signatory of WGA. Represents 35 clients. 20% of clients are new/unpublished writers. Currently handles: 70% movie scripts; 10% TV scripts; 20% stage plays.

● Prior to becoming an agent, Penny Luedtke was in classical music management; Elain Devlin was in film development, story editing; Marcia Weiss was an attorney, owner of a music agency.

Member Agents: Penny Luedtke (primarily represents talent, some special project writers); Elaine Devlin (screenwriters, playwrights); Marcia Weiss (screenwriters, television writers).

Represents: Movie scripts, feature film, TV scripts, TV movie of the week, sitcom, miniseries, soap opera, theatrical stage play, stage plays. **Considers these script subject areas:** Action/adventure; biography/autobiography; cartoon/animation; comedy; contemporary issues; detective/police/crime; ethnic; family saga; fantasy; feminist; gay/lesbian; historical; horror; juvenile; mainstream; multicultural; multimedia; mystery/suspense; psychic/supernatural; regional; religious/inspirational; romantic comedy; romantic drama; science fiction; sports; teen; thriller; western/frontier.

○━ "We are a small shop and like it that way. We work closely with our writers developing projects and offer extensive editorial assistance." Actively seeking well-written material. Does not want any project with graphic or explicit violence against women or children.

How to Contact: Query with SASE. No e-mail or fax queries. Considers simultaneous queries. Responds in 1 month to queries; 3 months to mss. Returns materials only with SASE. Obtains most new clients through recommendations from others.

Recent Sales: This agency prefers not to share information on specific sales.

Terms: Agent receives 10% commission on domestic sales; 15% commission on foreign sales. Offers written contract, binding for WGA standard terms. Charges clients expenses for couriers, messengers, international telephone and photocopying.

THE MANAGEMENT COMPANY, 1337 Ocean Ave., Suite F, Santa Monica CA 90401. (310)990-5602. **Contact:** Tom Klassen. Represents 15 clients.

● Prior to starting his agency Mr. Klassen was an agent with International Creative Management (ICM).

Member Agents: Tom Klasen; F. Miguel Valenti; Helene Taber; Paul Davis; Steve Gamber.

Represents: Feature film (scripts), TV scripts, episodic drama, sitcom, miniseries.

○━ Actively seeking "studio quality action-drama scripts and really good comedies." Does not want horror scripts.

How to Contact: Submit query letter with synopsis. No e-mail or fax queries. Responds in 3 weeks to queries. Returns materials only with SASE. Obtains most new clients through recommendations from others, conferences.

Recent Sales: Sold 8 scripts in the last year.

Terms: Agent receives 10% commission on domestic sales; 10% commission on foreign sales. Offers written contract, binding for 2 years.

Writers' Conferences: Sundance Film Festival; New York Film Festival; Telluride; Atlanta; Chicago; Minnesota.

Tips: "We only accept query letters with a short, one-page synopsis. We will request full manuscript with a SASE if interested. We rarely take on nonreferred material, but do review query letters and occasionally take on new writers. We have done very well with those we have taken on."

MANUS & ASSOCIATES LITERARY AGENCY, INC., 145 Park Ave., New York NY 10022. NY (212)644-8020; CA (650)470-5151. Fax: NY (212)644-3374; CA (650)470-5159. Also: 375 Forest Ave., Palo Alto CA 94301 **Contact:** Janet Manus (New York); Jillian Manus (California). Estab. 1985. Member of AAR. Represents 75 clients. 15% of clients are new/unpublished writers. Currently handles: 60% nonfiction books; 30% novels; 10% juvenile books; (sells 40% of material into TV/film markets).

● See the expanded listing for this agency in the Literary Agents section.

ELISABETH MARTON AGENCY INC., One Union Square West, Suite 612, New York NY 10003-3303. Fax: (212)691-9061. E-mail: info@martonagency.com. **Contact:** Elisabeth Marton. Member of AAR.

Member Agents: Elisabeth Marton; Tonda Marton; Anne Reingold.

○━ This agency specializes in foreign language licensing.

FOR EXPLANATIONS OF THESE SYMBOLS, SEE THE INSIDE FRONT AND BACK COVERS OF THIS BOOK

N ⊘ HELEN MERRILL, LTD., 295 Lafayatte St., Suite 915, New York NY 10012-2700. **Contact:** Patrick Herold. Member of AAR.
Member Agents: Patrick Herold (associate member).

⊘ THE STUART M. MILLER CO., 11684 Ventura Blvd., #225, Studio City CA 91604-2699. (818)506-6067. Fax: (818)506-4079. E-mail: smmco@aol.com. **Contact:** Stuart Miller. Estab. 1977. Signatory of WGA; Signatory of DGA. Currently handles: 50% movie scripts; 40% multimedia; 10% books.
Represents: Nonfiction books, novels, movie scripts. **Considers these nonfiction areas:** Biography/autobiography; computers/electronic; current affairs; government/politics/law; health/medicine; history; how-to; memoirs; military/war; self-help/personal improvement; true crime/investigative. **Considers these fiction areas:** Action/adventure; detective/police/crime; historical; literary; mainstream/contemporary; mystery/suspense; science fiction; sports; thriller. **Considers these script subject areas:** Action/adventure; biography/autobiography; cartoon/animation; comedy; contemporary issues; detective/police/crime; family saga; historical; mainstream; multimedia; mystery/suspense; romantic comedy; romantic drama; science fiction; sports; teen; thriller.
How to Contact: Query with SASE, 2-3 page narrative and outline/proposal. Accepts e-mail and fax queries. Considers simultaneous queries. Responds in 3 days to queries; 6 weeks to mss. Returns materials only with SASE.
Recent Sales: This agency prefers not to share information on specific sales.
Terms: Agent receives 10% for movie/TV commission on domestic sales; 15-25% for books commission on foreign sales. Offers written contract, binding for 2 years; WGA standard notice must be given to terminate contract.
Tips: "Always include SASE, e-mail address, or fax number with query letters. Make it easy to respond."

◖ MONTEIRO ROSE AGENCY, 17514 Ventura Blvd., Suite 205, Encino CA 91316. (818)501-1177. Fax: (818)501-1194. Website: www.monteiro-rose.com. **Contact:** Candy Monteiro. Estab. 1987. Signatory of WGA. Represents 50 clients. Currently handles: 40% movie scripts; 20% TV scripts; 40% animation.
Member Agents: Candace Monteiro (literary); Fredda Rose (literary); Milissa Brockish (literary); Jason Davis (literary).
Represents: Feature film, TV movie of the week, episodic drama, animation. **Considers these script subject areas:** Action/adventure; cartoon/animation; comedy; contemporary issues; detective/police/crime; ethnic; family saga; historical; juvenile; mainstream; mystery/suspense; psychic/supernatural; romantic comedy; romantic drama; science fiction; teen; thriller.
　　०┐ This agency specializes in scripts for animation, TV and film.
How to Contact: Query with SASE. Responds in 1 week to queries; 2 months to mss. Returns materials only with SASE. Obtains most new clients through recommendations from others, solicitations.
Recent Sales: This agency prefers not to share information on specific sales.
Terms: Agent receives 10% commission on domestic sales. Offers written contract, binding for 2 years; 90-day notice must be given to terminate contract. Charges for photocopying.
Tips: "It does no good to call and try to speak to an agent before they have read your material, unless referred by someone we know. The best and only way, if you're a new writer, is to send a query letter with a SASE. If agents are interested, they will request to read it. Also enclose a SASE with the script if you want it back."

⊘ WILLIAM MORRIS, 1325 Avenue of the Americas, New York NY 10019. Member of AAR. One of the most powerful agencies, this agency accepts established writing professionals only. Some of their clients include Kirsten Dunst, Leonardo DiCaprio, Bruce Willis, Tom Clancy, Dean Koontz, Jackie Collins. To catch the attention of this agency, newer writers require a strong referral by someone the agent knows personally, a face-to-face pitch at a conference one of the agents attends, or the top award in one of the most prestigious competitions. Does not accept queries or unsolicited scripts.

⊘ DEE MURA ENTERPRISES, INC., 269 W. Shore Dr., Massapequa NY 11758-8225. (516)795-1616. Fax: (516)795-8757. E-mail: samurai5@ix.netcom.com. **Contact:** Dee Mura, Frank Nakamura. Estab. 1987. Signatory of WGA. 50% of clients are new/unpublished writers.
　　● See the expanded listing for this agency in the Literary Agents section.

◖ NIAD MANAGEMENT, 3465 Coy Dr., Sherman Oaks CA 91423. (818)981-2505. Fax: (818)386-2082. E-mail: query@niadmanagement.com. Website: www.niadmanagement.com. Estab. 1997. Represents 20 clients. 2% of clients are new/unpublished writers. Currently handles: 1% novels; 98% movie scripts; 1% stage plays.
Represents: Movie scripts, feature film, TV movie of the week, miniseries, stage plays. **Considers these nonfiction areas:** Biography/autobiography. **Considers these fiction areas:** Action/adventure; detective/police/crime; family saga; literary; mainstream/contemporary; multicultural; mystery/suspense; psychic/supernatural; romance; thriller. **Considers these script subject areas:** Action/adventure; biography/autobiography; comedy; contemporary issues; detective/police/crime; ethnic; family saga; historical; horror; mainstream; multicultural; mystery/suspense; psychic/supernatural; romantic comedy; romantic drama; sports; teen; thriller.

How to Contact: Query with SASE. Accepts e-mail and fax queries. Considers simultaneous queries. Responds in 1 week to queries; 3 months to mss. Returns materials only with SASE. Obtains most new clients through recommendations from others.
Recent Sales: Sold 5 scripts in the last year. *The Dan Gable Story*, by Lee Zlotoff (Charles Hirschorn/Disney); *Insider Trading*, by Claudia Salter (USA Network); *Killing the People Upstairs*, by Bruce Griffiths (Max Media). Other clients include Neil Cohen, Julian Grant, Susan Sandler, Michael Lazarou, Jim McGlynn, Don Most, Fernando Fragata.
Terms: Agent receives 15% commission on domestic sales. Offers written contract, binding for 1 year; 30-day notice must be given to terminate contract.

OMNIQUEST ENTERTAINMENT, 843 Berkeley St., Santa Monica CA 90403-2503. (310)453-6549. Fax: (310)453-2523. E-mail: info@omniquestmedia.com. Website: www.omniquestmedia.com. **Contact:** Michael Kaliski. Estab. 1997. Currently handles: 5% novels; 5% juvenile books; 40% movie scripts; 20% TV scripts; 10% multimedia; 15% stage plays.
Member Agents: Michael Kaliski; Traci Belushi.
Represents: Novels, short story collections, novellas, movie scripts, feature film, TV scripts, TV movie of the week, episodic drama, sitcom, miniseries, syndicated material, stage plays. **Considers these fiction areas:** Action/adventure; detective/police/crime; experimental; family saga; fantasy; literary; psychic/supernatural; romance; science fiction; thriller. **Considers these script subject areas:** Action/adventure; biography/autobiography; comedy; contemporary issues; detective/police/crime; experimental; family saga; fantasy; historical; mainstream; multimedia; mystery/suspense; psychic/supernatural; romantic comedy; romantic drama; science fiction; thriller.
  O┅ Actively seeking books that can be adapted for film and scripts.
How to Contact: Query with SASE, or send outline and 2-3 sample chapters. Accepts e-mail and fax queries. Considers simultaneous queries. Returns materials only with SASE. Obtains most new clients through recommendations from others.
Recent Sales: This agency prefers not to share information on specific sales.
Terms: Agent receives 15% commission on domestic sales; 15% commission on foreign sales. Offers written contract.

FIFI OSCARD AGENCY, INC., 24 W. 40th St., New York NY 10018. **Contact:** Ivy Fischer Stone. Estab. 1956. Member of AAR; signatory of WGA. Represents 108 clients. 5% of clients are new/unpublished writers. Currently handles: 60% nonfiction books; 10% novels; 30% stage plays.
  • See the expanded listing for this agency in the Literary Agents section.

DOROTHY PALMER, 235 W. 56 St., New York NY 10019. (212)765-4280. Fax: (212)977-9801. Estab. 1990. Signatory of WGA. Represents 12 clients. 0% of clients are new/unpublished writers. Currently handles: 70% movie scripts; 30% TV scripts.
  • In addition to being a literary agent, Ms. Palmer has worked as a talent agent for 30 years.
Represents: Feature film, TV movie of the week, episodic drama, sitcom, miniseries. **Considers these script subject areas:** Action/adventure; comedy; contemporary issues; detective/police/crime; family saga; feminist; mainstream; mystery/suspense; romantic comedy; romantic drama; thriller.
  O┅ This agency specializes in screenplays, TV. Actively seeking successful, published writers (screenplays only). Does not want to receive work from new or unpublished writers.
How to Contact: Query with SASE. Prefers to read materials exclusively. Published writers *only*. Returns materials only with SASE. Obtains most new clients through recommendations from others.
Recent Sales: This agency prefers not to share information on specific sales.
Terms: Agent receives 10% commission on domestic sales; 10% commission on foreign sales. Offers written contract, binding for 1 year. Charges clients for postage, photocopies.
Tips: "Do *not* telephone. When I find a script that interests me, I call the writer. Calls to me are a turn-off because they cut into my reading time."

BARRY PERELMAN AGENCY, 1155 N. Laceniga, #508, W. Hollywood CA 90069. (310)659-1122. Fax: (310)659-1122. Estab. 1982. Member of DGA; signatory of WGA. Represents 40 clients. 15% of clients are new/unpublished writers. Currently handles: 100% movie scripts.
Member Agents: Barry Perelman (motion picture/packaging).
Represents: Movie scripts. **Considers these script subject areas:** Action/adventure; biography/autobiography; contemporary issues; detective/police/crime; historical; horror; mystery/suspense; romantic comedy; romantic drama; science fiction; thriller.
  O┅ This agency specializes in motion pictures/packaging.
How to Contact: Query with SASE, proposal package, outline. Responds in 1 month to queries. Obtains most new clients through recommendations from others, solicitations.
Recent Sales: This agency prefers not to share information on specific sales.
Terms: Agent receives 10% commission on domestic sales; 10% commission on foreign sales. Offers written contract, binding for 1-2 years. Charges clients for postage and photocopying.

☑ ◐ **STEPHEN PEVNER, INC.**, 382 Lafayette St., 8th Floor, New York NY 10003. (212)496-0474. Fax: (212)529-3692. E-mail: spevner@aol.com. **Contact:** Stephen Pevner. Estab. 1991.
  ● See the expanded listing for this agency in Literary Agents.

◐ **A PICTURE OF YOU**, 1176 Elizabeth Dr., Hamilton OH 45013-3507. (513)863-1108. Fax: (513)863-1108. E-mail: apoy1@aol.com. **Contact:** Lenny Minelli. Estab. 1993. Signatory of WGA. Represents 45 clients. 50% of clients are new/unpublished writers. Currently handles: 80% movie scripts; 10% TV scripts; 10% syndicated material.
  ● Prior to opening his agency, Mr. Minelli was an actor/producer for 10 years. Also owned and directed a talent agency and represented actors and actresses from around the world.
Member Agents: Michelle Chang (fiction/nonfiction books).
Represents: Nonfiction books, novels, short story collections, novellas, feature film, TV movie of the week, episodic drama, sitcom, animation, documentary, miniseries, syndicated material. **Considers these nonfiction areas:** Gay/lesbian issues; history; juvenile nonfiction; music/dance; religious/inspirational; self-help/personal improvement; theater/film. **Considers these fiction areas:** Action/adventure; detective/police/crime; erotica; ethnic; family saga; fantasy; gay/lesbian; glitz; historical; horror; literary; mainstream/contemporary; mystery/suspense; religious/inspirational; romance (contemporary, gothic, historical); thriller; westerns/frontier; young adult. **Considers these script subject areas:** Action/adventure; biography/autobiography; cartoon/animation; comedy; contemporary issues; detective/police/crime; erotica; ethnic; experimental; family saga; fantasy; feminist; gay/lesbian; glitz; historical; horror; juvenile; mainstream; multicultural; multimedia; mystery/suspense; psychic/supernatural; regional; religious/inspirational; romantic comedy; romantic drama; science fiction; sports; teen; thriller; western/frontier.
  ⟡ This agency specializes in screenplays and TV scripts.
How to Contact: Query with SASE. Accepts e-mail and fax queries. Considers simultaneous queries. Responds in 3 weeks to queries; 1 month to mss. Obtains most new clients through recommendations from others, solicitations.
Recent Sales: *Lost and Found*, by J.P. Brice; *So Long*, by Patrick Cappella. *Scripting Assignment(s): The Governor*, by Gary M. Cappetta.
Terms: Agent receives 10% commission on domestic sales; 15% commission on foreign sales. Offers written contract, binding for 1 year; 90-day notice must be given to terminate contract. Charges clients for postage/express mail and long distance calls.
Tips: "Make sure that the script is the best it can be before seeking an agent."

▣ ◉ **JIM PREMINGER AGENCY**, 450 N. Roxbury, PH 1050, Beverly Hills CA 90210. (310)860-1116. Fax: (310)860-1117. E-mail: general@premingeragency.com. **Contact:** Joan Turner. Estab. 1980. Member of DGA; signatory of WGA. Represents 75 clients. 20% of clients are new/unpublished writers. Currently handles: 1% nonfiction books; 1% novels; 47% movie scripts; 50% TV scripts; 1% stage plays.
Member Agents: Jim Preminger (television and features); Dean Schramm (features and television); Ryan L. Saul (features and television); Melissa Read (television and features).
Represents: Feature film, TV movie of the week, episodic drama, sitcom, miniseries, Internet.
  ⟡ This agency specializes in representing showrunners for television series, writers for television movies, as well as directors and writers for features.
How to Contact: Obtains most new clients through recommendations from others.
Recent Sales: This agency prefers not to share information on specific sales.
Terms: Agent receives 10% commission on domestic sales; 10% commission on foreign sales.

◎ **THE QUILLCO AGENCY**, 3104 W. Cumberland Court, Westlake Village CA 91362. (805)495-8436. Fax: (805)373-9868. E-mail: quillco2@aol.com. **Contact:** Sandy Mackey (owner). Estab. 1993. Signatory of WGA. Represents 15 clients.
Represents: Feature film, TV movie of the week, animation, documentary.
How to Contact: Prefers to read materials exclusively. Not accepting query letters at this time. Returns materials only with SASE.
Recent Sales: This agency prefers not to share information on specific sales.
Terms: Agent receives 10% commission on domestic sales; 10% commission on foreign sales.

☑ ◉ **DAN REDLER ENTERTAINMENT**, 18930 Ringling St., Tarzana CA 91356. (818)776-0938. **Contact:** Dan Redler. Represents 10 clients. Currently handles: 100% movie scripts.
Represents: Movie scripts, feature film. **Considers these script subject areas:** Action/adventure; biography/autobiography; comedy; contemporary issues; detective/police/crime; ethnic; family saga; fantasy; feminist; historical; horror; juvenile; mainstream; mystery/suspense; psychic/supernatural; romantic comedy; romantic drama; science fiction; sports; teen; thriller.
  ⟡ Actively seeking mainstream and contemporary scripts. Does not want to receive small noncommercial stories.
How to Contact: Query with SASE. Prefers to read materials exclusively. Responds in 6 weeks to queries; 1-3 months to mss. Returns materials only with SASE.

Recent Sales: This agency prefers not to share information on specific sales.
Terms: Agent receives 10% commission on domestic sales; 10% commission on foreign sales. Offers written contract, binding for 2 years. Client must supply all copies of scripts.
Tips: "We offer personal service, in-depth career guidance, and aggressive sales efforts."

◑ MICHAEL D. ROBINS & ASSOCIATES, 23241 Ventura Blvd., #300, Woodland Hills CA 91364. (818)343-1755. Fax: (818)343-7355. E-mail: mdr2@msn.com. **Contact:** Michael D. Robins. Estab. 1991. Member of DGA; signatory of WGA. 10% of clients are new/unpublished writers. Currently handles: 5% nonfiction books; 5% novels; 20% movie scripts; 60% TV scripts; 10% syndicated material.
  • Prior to opening his agency, Mr. Robins was a literary agent at a mid-sized agency.
Represents: Nonfiction books, novels, movie scripts, feature film, TV scripts, TV movie of the week, episodic drama, animation, miniseries, syndicated material, stage plays. **Considers these nonfiction areas:** History; humor/satire; memoirs; military/war; popular culture; science/technology; true crime/investigative; urban lifestyle. **Considers these fiction areas:** Action/adventure; comic books/cartoon; detective/police/crime; family saga; fantasy; gay/lesbian; mainstream/contemporary; westerns/frontier (frontier); young adult. **Considers these script subject areas:** Action/adventure; biography/autobiography; cartoon/animation; comedy; contemporary issues; detective/police/crime; erotica; ethnic; experimental; family saga; fantasy; feminist; gay/lesbian; glitz; historical; horror; juvenile; mainstream; multicultural; multimedia; mystery/suspense; psychic/supernatural; regional; religious/inspirational; romantic comedy; romantic drama; science fiction; sports; teen; thriller; western/frontier.
How to Contact: Query with SASE. Accepts e-mail and fax queries. Considers simultaneous queries. Responds in 1 week to queries; 1 month to mss. Obtains most new clients through recommendations from others.
Recent Sales: This agency prefers not to share information on specific sales.
Terms: Agent receives 10% commission on domestic sales; 10% commission on foreign sales. Offers written contract, binding for 2 years; 4-month notice must be given to terminate contract.

✓ 📄 ◐ JACK SCAGNETTI TALENT & LITERARY AGENCY, 5118 Vineland Ave., #102, North Hollywood CA 91601. (818)762-3871. Fax: (818)761-6629. **Contact:** Jack Scagnetti. Estab. 1974. Member of Academy of Television Arts and Sciences; signatory of WGA. Represents 50 clients. 50% of clients are new/unpublished writers. Currently handles: 20% nonfiction books; 70% movie scripts; 10% TV scripts.
  • Prior to becoming an agent, Mr. Scagnetti wrote nonfiction books and magazine articles on movie stars, sports and health subjects and was a magazine and newspaper editor.
Member Agents: Steven Buchjsbaum (books); Sean Wright (books); David Goldman (script analyst); Andy Rodman (scripts/books).
Represents: Nonfiction books, novels, feature film, TV movie of the week, episodic drama, sitcom, animation (movie), miniseries. **Considers these nonfiction areas:** Biography/autobiography; cooking/foods/nutrition; current affairs; health/medicine; how-to; military/war; music/dance; self-help/personal improvement; sports; true crime/investigative; women's issues/studies. **Considers these fiction areas:** Action/adventure; contemporary issues; detective/police/crime; family saga; historical; mainstream/contemporary; mystery/suspense; picture books; romance (contemporary); sports; thriller; westerns/frontier. **Considers these script subject areas:** Action/adventure; comedy; detective/police/crime; family saga; historical; horror; mainstream; mystery/suspense; romantic comedy; romantic drama; sports; thriller.
  ⚬━ This agency specializes in film books with photographs. Actively seeking books and screenplays. Does not want to receive TV scripts for existing shows.
How to Contact: Query with SASE, outline/proposal. No fax queries. Responds in 1 month to queries; 2 months to mss. Returns materials only with SASE. Obtains most new clients through recommendations from others, solicitations.
Recent Sales: *Kastner's Cutthroats*, (44 Blue Prod.). *Movie/TV MOW scripts in development*: *Pain*, by Charles Pickett (Concorde-New Horizons); *Club Video*, TV series, Actuality Productions (Hearst Entertainment).
Terms: Agent receives 15% commission on domestic sales; 15% commission on foreign sales; 10% commission on dramatic rights sales. Offers written contract, binding for 6 months-1 year. Offers criticism service (books only). "Fee depends upon condition of original copy and number of pages." Charges clients for postage and photocopies.
Tips: "Write a good synopsis, short and to the point and include marketing data for the book."

◑ 📷 SUSAN SCHULMAN, A LITERARY AGENCY, (Specialized: health, business, public policy, self-help, women's issues), 454 W. 44th St., New York NY 10036-5205. (212)713-1633/4/5. Fax: (212)586-8830. E-mail: schulman@aol.com. **Contact:** Susan Schulman, president. Estab. 1979. Member of AAR, Dramatists Guild, Women's Media Group; signatory of WGA. 10-15% of clients are new/unpublished writers. Currently handles: 70% nonfiction books; 20% novels; 10% stage plays.
  • See the expanded listing for this agency in the Literary Agents section.

◑ KEN SHERMAN & ASSOCIATES, 9507 Santa Monica Blvd., Beverly Hills CA 90210. (310)273-3840. Fax: (310)271-2875. **Contact:** Ken Sherman. Estab. 1989. Member of BAFTA, PEN Int'l; signatory of WGA; DGA. Represents approximately 50 clients. 10% of clients are new/unpublished writers. Currently handles: nonfiction books; novels; juvenile books; movie scripts; TV scripts; video games/fiction.

• Prior to opening his agency, Mr. Sherman was with The William Morris Agency, The Lantz Office, and Paul Kohner, Inc.

Represents: Nonfiction books, novels, movie scripts, TV scripts, film, television rights to books and life-rights. **Considers these nonfiction areas:** Agriculture/horticulture; Americana; animals; anthropology/archaeology; art/ architecture/design; biography/autobiography; business/economics; child guidance/parenting; computers/electronic; cooking/foods/nutrition; crafts/hobbies; creative nonfiction; current affairs; education; ethnic/cultural interests; gardening; gay/lesbian issues; government/politics/law; health/medicine; history; how-to; humor/satire; interior design/decorating; juvenile nonfiction; language/literature/criticism; memoirs; military/war; money/finance; multicultural; music/dance; nature/environment; New Age/metaphysics; philosophy; photography; popular culture; psychology; recreation; regional; religious/inspirational; science/technology; self-help/personal improvement; sex; sociology; software; spirituality; sports; theater/film; translation; travel; true crime/investigative; women's issues/studies; young adult. **Considers these fiction areas:** Action/adventure; comic books/cartoon; confession; contemporary issues; detective/police/crime; erotica; ethnic; experimental; family saga; fantasy; feminist; gay/lesbian; glitz; gothic; hi-lo; historical; horror; humor/satire; juvenile; literary; mainstream/contemporary; military/war; multicultural; multimedia; mystery/suspense; New Age; occult; picture books; plays; poetry; poetry in translation; psychic/supernatural; regional; religious/inspirational; romance; science fiction; short story collections; spiritual; sports; thriller; translation; westerns/frontier; young adult. **Considers these script subject areas:** Action/adventure; biography/autobiography; cartoon/animation; comedy; contemporary issues; detective/police/ crime; erotica; ethnic; experimental; family saga; fantasy; feminist; gay/lesbian; glitz; historical; horror; juvenile; mainstream; multicultural; multimedia; mystery/suspense; psychic/supernatural; regional; religious/inspirational; romantic comedy; romantic drama; science fiction; sports; teen; thriller; western/frontier.

0—¬ This agency specializes in solid writers for film TV, books and rights to books for film and TV.

How to Contact: Contact by referral only please. Responds in 1 month to mss and scripts. Obtains most new clients through recommendations from others.

Recent Sales: Sold over 20 scripts in the last year. *Priscilla Salyers Story*, to Andrea Baynes (ABC); *Toys of Glass*, by Martin Booth (ABC/Saban Ent.); *Brazil*, by John Updike (film rights to Glaucia Carmagos); *Fifth Sacred Thing*, by Starhawk (Bantam); *Questions From Dad*, by Dwight Twilly (Tuttle); *Snow Falling on Cedars*, by David Guterson (Universal Pictures); *The Witches of Eastwick-The Musical*, by John Updike (Cameron Macintosh, Ltd.).

Terms: Agent receives 15% commission on domestic sales; 15% commission on foreign book sales; 15% commission on dramatic rights sales; 10% for anything WGA. Offers written contract. Charges clients for reasonable office expenses, postage, photocopying, and other negotiable expenses.

Writers' Conferences: Maui; Squaw Valley; Santa Barbara; Santa Fe; Aspen Institute; Aspen Writers Foundation, etc.

SILVER SCREEN PLACEMENTS, 602 65th St., Downers Grove IL 60516-3020. (630)963-2124. Fax: (630)963-1998. E-mail: silverscreen11@yahoo.com. **Contact:** William Levin. Estab. 1989. Signatory of WGA. Represents 14 clients. 100% of clients are new/unpublished writers. Currently handles: 20% novels; 80% movie scripts.

• Prior to opening his agency, Mr. Levin did product placement for motion pictures/TV.

Member Agents: Paul Martin (sales).

Represents: Novels, movie scripts, feature film. **Considers these nonfiction areas:** Education; juvenile nonfiction; language/literature/criticism. **Considers these fiction areas:** Action/adventure; contemporary issues; detective/police/crime; family saga; fantasy; historical; humor/satire; mainstream/contemporary; mystery/suspense; science fiction; thriller; young adult. **Considers these script subject areas:** Action/adventure; comedy; contemporary issues; detective/police/crime; family saga; fantasy; historical; juvenile; mainstream; mystery/suspense; science fiction; thriller; young adult.

0—¬ Actively seeking screenplays for young adults, 17-30. Does not want horror, religious, X-rated.

How to Contact: Brief query with outline/proposal and SASE. No e-mail or fax queries. Responds in 2 weeks to queries; 2 months to mss. Obtains most new clients through recommendations from others, listings with WGA and *Guide to Literary Agents*.

Recent Sales: Sold 4 options and 3 scripts in the last year. This agency prefers not to share information on specific sales. Other clients include Charles Geier, Robert Smola, Michael Jeffries and Robert Melley.

Terms: Agent receives 15% commission on ms sales; 10% (screenplay/teleplay sales) commission on dramatic rights sales. Offers written contract, binding for 2 years. May make referrals to freelance editors. Use of editors does not ensure representation. 0% of business is derived from referrals to editing service. Fees to representing clients only, maximum of $200 a year for office expenses.

Tips: "Advise against 'cutsie' inquiry letters."

CAMILLE SORICE AGENCY, 13412 Moorpark St., #C, Sherman Oaks CA 91423. **Contact:** Camille Sorice. Estab. 1988. Signatory of WGA.

Represents: Novels, feature film. **Considers these script subject areas:** Action/adventure; comedy; detective/ police/crime; family saga; historical; mystery/suspense; romantic comedy; romantic drama; western/frontier.

How to Contact: Query with SASE, synopsis. Prefers to read materials exclusively. No e-mail or fax queries. Considers simultaneous queries. Responds in 6 weeks to mss.

Recent Sales: This agency prefers not to share information on specific sales.
Tips: "No calls. Query letters accepted."

STEIN AGENCY, 5125 Oakdale Ave., Woodland Hills CA 91364. (818)594-8990. Fax: (818)594-8998. E-mail: mail@thesteinagency.com. **Contact:** Mitchel Stein. Estab. 2000. Signatory of WGA. Represents 60 clients. Currently handles: 20% movie scripts; 80% TV scripts.
Member Agents: Mitchel Stein (TV/motion picture); Jake Friedman (TV/motion picture).
Represents: Movie scripts, TV scripts, episodic drama, sitcom. **Considers these script subject areas:** Action/ adventure; detective/police/crime; family saga; fantasy; mainstream; mystery/suspense; psychic/supernatural; romantic comedy; romantic drama; science fiction; teen; thriller.
How to Contact: Query with SASE. Discards material without SASE. Accepts e-mail and fax queries. Considers simultaneous queries. Responds in 1 week to queries. Returns materials only with SASE. Obtains most new clients through recommendations from others.
Recent Sales: This agency prefers not to share information on specific sales.
Terms: Agent receives 10% commission on domestic sales; 10% commission on foreign sales. Offers written contract.

STONE MANNERS AGENCY, 8436 W. Third St., Suite 740, Los Angeles CA 90048. (323)655-1313. **Contact:** Tim Stone. Estab. 1982. Signatory of WGA. Represents 25 clients.
Represents: Movie scripts, TV scripts. **Considers these script subject areas:** Action/adventure; biography/ autobiography; cartoon/animation; comedy; contemporary issues; detective/police/crime; erotica; ethnic; experimental; family saga; fantasy; feminist; gay/lesbian; glitz; historical; horror; juvenile; mainstream; multicultural; multimedia; mystery/suspense; psychic/supernatural; regional; religious/inspirational; romantic comedy; romantic drama; science fiction; sports; teen; thriller; western/frontier.
How to Contact: Not considering scripts at this time.
Recent Sales: This agency prefers not to share information on specific sales.
Terms: Agent receives 10% commission on domestic sales; 10% commission on foreign sales.

SUITE A MANAGEMENT TALENT & LITERARY AGENCY, (formerly Robinson Talent and Literary Management), 1101 S. Robertson Blvd., Suite 210, Los Angeles CA 90035. (310)278-0801. Fax: (310)278-0807. E-mail: suite-a@juno.com. **Contact:** Lloyd Robinson. Estab. 1996. Member of DGA; signatory of WGA. Represents 76 clients. 10% of clients are new/unpublished writers. Currently handles: 15% novels; 40% movie scripts; 40% TV scripts; 5% stage plays.
• Prior to becoming an agent, Mr. Robinson worked as a manager.
Member Agents: Lloyd Robinson (adaptation of books and plays for development as features or TV MOW); Kevin Douglas (scripts for film and TV); Judy Jacobs (feature development).
Represents: Feature film, TV movie of the week, episodic drama, documentary, miniseries, variety show, stage plays, CD-ROM. **Considers these script subject areas:** Action/adventure; cartoon/animation; comedy; contemporary issues; detective/police/crime; erotica; ethnic; experimental; family saga; fantasy; mainstream; mystery/suspense; psychic/supernatural; religious/inspirational; romantic comedy; romantic drama; science fiction; sports; teen; thriller; western/frontier.
    0→ "We represent screenwriters, playwrights, novelists and producers, directors."
How to Contact: Submit synopsis, outline/proposal, log line. Accepts fax and e-mail queries. Obtains most new clients through recommendations from others.
Recent Sales: This agency prefers not to share information on specific sales or client names.
Terms: Agent receives 10% commission on domestic sales; 10% commission on foreign sales. Offers written contract, binding for 1 year minimum. Charges clients for photocopying, messenger, FedEx, and postage when required.
Tips: "We are a talent agency specializing in the copyright business. Fifty percent of our clients generate copyright-screenwriters, playrights and novelists. Fifty percent of our clients service copyright—producers and directors. We represent produced, published and/or WGA writers who are eligible for staff TV positions as well as novelists and playwrights whose works may be adapted for film on television."

TALENT REPRESENTATIVES, INC., 20 E. 53rd St., New York NY 10022. (212)752-1835. Fax: (212)752-7552. **Contact:** Honey Raider. Estab. 1964. Signatory of WGA. 10% of clients are new writers. Currently handles 10% stage plays, 90% daytime TV.
Member Agents: Richie Kern (playwrights only).
Represents: Considers daytime TV only!
    0→ This agency specializes in daytime TV and young playwrights.
How to Contact: Query with SASE. Considers simultaneous queries. Responds in 3 weeks to queries; 3 months to screenplays. Return only with SASE. Obtains new clients through recommendations from others, readings.
Terms: Agent receives 10% commissions.

TALENT SOURCE, 107 E. Hall St., P.O. Box 14120, Savannah GA 31416-1120. (912)232-9390. Fax: (912)232-8213. E-mail: michael@talentsource.com. Website: www.talentsource.com. **Contact:** Michael L. Shortt. Estab. 1991. Signatory of WGA. 35% of clients are new/unpublished writers. Currently handles: 85% movie scripts; 15% TV scripts.

• Prior to becoming an agent, Mr. Shortt was a television program producer/director.

Represents: Feature film, TV movie of the week, episodic drama, sitcom. **Considers these script subject areas:** Comedy; contemporary issues; detective/police/crime; erotica; family saga; juvenile; mainstream; mystery/suspense; romantic comedy; romantic drama; teen.

O— Actively seeking "character-driven stories (e.g., *Sling Blade*, *Sex Lies & Videotape*)." Does not want to receive "big budget special effects science fiction."

How to Contact: Query with SASE, include a proper synopsis, please see the literary button on our website for complete submission details. No e-mail or fax queries. Responds in 10 weeks to queries. Obtains most new clients through recommendations from others.

Recent Sales: This agency prefers not to share information on specific sales.

Terms: Agent receives 10% commission on domestic sales; 15% commission on foreign sales. Offers written contract.

TALESMYTH ENTERTAINMENT, INC., 312 St. John St., Suite #69, Portland ME 04102. (207)879-0307. Fax: (207)775-1067. E-mail: talesmyth@hotmail.com. **Contact:** Thomas Burgess. Estab. 2000. Signatory of WGA. Represents 7 clients. 100% of clients are new/unpublished writers. Currently handles: 10% novels; 10% story collections; 80% movie scripts.

• Prior to becoming an agent, Mr. Burgess produced short films and managed a restaurant.

Member Agents: Thomas "TJ" Burgess (screenplays/book-length fiction).

Represents: Novels, short story collections, movie scripts, feature film. **Considers these fiction areas:** Action/adventure; detective/police/crime; fantasy; historical; horror; humor/satire; mainstream/contemporary; mystery/suspense; New Age; psychic/supernatural; thriller; westerns/frontier. **Considers these script subject areas:** Action/adventure; comedy; detective/police/crime; fantasy; historical; horror; mystery/suspense; psychic/supernatural; romantic comedy; romantic drama; science fiction; thriller; western/frontier.

O— "As a writer and producer myself I have a keen eye for industry trends and an amazing way to have the right ear hear the right pitch. I work to develop writers to marketable levels as well as represent authors that are ready for publication." Stories must have meaningful character/plot development. Does not want romance, juvenile, children or young adult-oriented stories. Not accepting new clients if not referred by an existing client.

How to Contact: Query with SASE. Talesmyth Entertainment accepts new submissions from July 1-December 31 only. Responds in 1 month to queries; 2 months to mss. Obtains most new clients through recommendations from others, will not be accepting any new clients in 2003. Productivity of current clients does not allow for allocation of resources to "new" clients at this time.

Recent Sales: Clients include Gary Hauger, Kevin Brown, F. Allen Farnham, Christopher Cairnduff, Michael Lewin, Lawrence Climo, MD., and Peter Borregine.

Terms: Agent receives 10% commission on domestic sales; 15% commission on foreign sales. Offers written contract, binding for 1 year; 60-day notice must be given to terminate contract. "Submissions of appropriate genre, if requested, received during our acceptance period, whether accepted or rejected, will receive a one-page critique penned by the agent that reviewed the material. At this time all reviews are completed by T.J. Burgess, president of Talesmyth Entertainment. No fee is charged for this critique."

Tips: "Be sure to submit only your best work for consideration. I don't want to see something you just want to get rid of, because I will probably respond in kind. Be certain that your query does a good job of selling me the story and characters and is not just a playful enticement with a "quirky twist." A solid query should summarize the plot and character development in an interesting fashion in one page or less as well as briefly address your expertise in the area or other relevant facts about the market for the story presented, anything else is a waste of your and my time."

UNITED TALENT AGENCY, 9560 Wilshire Blvd., Suite 500, Beverly Hills CA 90212. One of the most powerful agencies, this agency accepts established screenwriting professionals only. Some of their clients include Elizabeth Hurley, Harrison Ford, Jim Carrey, Ben Stiller. To catch the attention of this agency, newer screenwriters require a strong referral by someone the agent knows personally, a face-to-face pitch at a conference one of the agents attends, or the top award in one of the most prestigious competitions. Does not accept queries or unsolicited scripts.

ANNETTE VAN DUREN AGENCY, 11684 Ventura Blvd., #235, Studio City CA 91604. (818)752-6000. Fax: (818)752-6985. **Contact:** Annette Van Duren or Amy Takahara. Estab. 1985. Signatory of WGA. Represents 12 clients. 0% of clients are new/unpublished writers. Currently handles: 10% novels; 50% movie scripts; 40% TV scripts.

Represents: Feature film, TV movie of the week, episodic drama, sitcom, animation.

How to Contact: Not accepting new clients. Obtains most new clients through recommendations from others.

Recent Sales: This agency prefers not to share information about specific sales.

Terms: Agent receives 10% commission on domestic sales. Offers written contract, binding for 2 years.

VISIONARY ENTERTAINMENT, 8265 Sunset Blvd., #104, Hollywood CA 90046. (323)848-9538. Fax: (323)848-8614. E-mail: tparz@aol.com. **Contact:** Tom Parziale. Represents 50 clients. 20% of clients are new/unpublished writers. Currently handles: 75% movie scripts; 25% TV scripts.
- Prior to becoming an agent, Ms. Hopkins was a studio executive. Visionary Entertainment formerly focused on representing talent and has recently started representing writers as well.

Member Agents: Tom Parziale (actors and writers).

Represents: Novels, movie scripts, feature film, TV scripts, episodic drama, sitcom. **Considers these fiction areas:** Action/adventure; comic books/cartoon; confession; contemporary issues; detective/police/crime; erotica; ethnic; experimental; family saga; fantasy; feminist; gay/lesbian; glitz; gothic; hi-lo; historical; horror; humor/satire; juvenile; literary; mainstream/contemporary; military/war; multicultural; multimedia; mystery/suspense; New Age; occult; picture books; plays; poetry; poetry in translation; psychic/supernatural; regional; religious/inspirational; romance; science fiction; short story collections; spiritual; sports; thriller; translation; westerns/frontier; young adult; women's. **Considers these script subject areas:** Action/adventure; biography/autobiography; cartoon/animation; comedy; contemporary issues; detective/police/crime; erotica; ethnic; experimental; family saga; fantasy; feminist; gay/lesbian; glitz; historical; horror; juvenile; mainstream; multicultural; multimedia; mystery/suspense; psychic/supernatural; regional; religious/inspirational; romantic comedy; romantic drama; science fiction; sports; teen; thriller; western/frontier.

O→ Actively seeking fresh ideas and good writers. Does not want to receive cliched ideas.

How to Contact: Send outline/proposal. Discards unwanted queries and mss. Accepts e-mail and fax queries. Considers simultaneous queries. Responds in 1 month to queries. Obtains most new clients through recommendations from others.

Recent Sales: Sold 4 scripts in the last year. *The Fighting Temptations*, by Elizabeth Hunter (MTV Films Paramount); *Never Been Kissed*, by Scott Murphy (Kushner-Locke); *Ship of Ghouls*, by Jeff Walch (Bandeira/Dreamworks); *How to Lose a Man in Ten Days*, by Michelle Alexander (Paramount).

Terms: Agent receives 15% commission on domestic sales. Offers written contract, binding for 2 years; 60-day notice must be given to terminate contract.

Tips: "Write well, and don't use cliche themes or characters."

WARDLOW AND ASSOCIATES, 1501 Main St., Suite 204, Venice CA 90291. (310)452-1292. Fax: (310)452-9002. E-mail: wardlowaso@aol.com. **Contact:** Jeff Ordway. Estab. 1980. Signatory of WGA. Represents 30 clients. 5% of clients are new/unpublished writers. Currently handles: 50% movie scripts; 50% TV scripts.

Member Agents: David Wardlow (literary, packaging); Jeff Ordway (literary).

Represents: Feature film, TV movie of the week, episodic drama, sitcom, miniseries. **Considers these script subject areas:** Action/adventure; biography/autobiography; cartoon/animation; comedy; contemporary issues; detective/police/crime; erotica; ethnic; experimental; family saga; fantasy; feminist; gay/lesbian; glitz; historical; horror; juvenile; mainstream; multicultural; multimedia; mystery/suspense; psychic/supernatural; regional; religious/inspirational; romantic comedy; romantic drama; science fiction; sports; teen; thriller; western/frontier.

O→ Does not want to receive "new sitcom/drama series ideas from beginning writers."

How to Contact: Query with SASE. Will not read unsolicited screenplays/mss. Accepts e-mail and fax queries. Considers simultaneous queries. Returns materials only with SASE. Obtains most new clients through recommendations from others, solicitations.

Recent Sales: This agency prefers not to share information on specific sales.

Terms: Agent receives 10% commission on domestic sales; 10% commission on foreign sales. Offers written contract, binding for 1 year.

DONNA WAUHOB AGENCY, 3135 Industrial Rd., #204, Las Vegas NV 89109-1122. (702)733-1017. Fax: (702)733-1215. E-mail: dwauhob@aol.com. **Contact:** Donna Wauhob; all literary property must go to Cal Maefield (Director of Lit. Dept.). Represents 7 clients. Currently handles: 60% movie scripts; 40% TV scripts.
- Prior to opening her agency, Ms. Wauhob was a model, secretary, and an AF of M agent since 1968.

Represents: Nonfiction books, novels, short story collections, juvenile books, poetry books, movie scripts, feature film, TV scripts, TV movie of the week, episodic drama, sitcom, animation, miniseries, soap opera, variety show. **Considers these nonfiction areas:** Animals; child guidance/parenting; cooking/foods/nutrition. **Considers these script subject areas:** Action/adventure; cartoon/animation; comedy; detective/police/crime; family saga; juvenile; romantic comedy; romantic drama; teen; thriller; western/frontier.

O→ Actively seeking film and TV scripts, juvenile, teen action, cartoon, comedy, family.

CONTACT THE EDITOR of *Guide to Literary Agents* by e-mail at literaryagents @fwpubs.com with your questions and comments.

How to Contact: Accepts e-mail and fax queries. Considers simultaneous queries. Responds in 2 months to queries.
Recent Sales: This agency prefers not to share information on specific sales.
Terms: Agent receives 10% commission on domestic sales; 10% commission on foreign sales. Offers written contract; 6-month notice must be given to terminate contract.

PEREGRINE WHITTLESEY AGENCY, 345 E. 80 St., New York NY 10021. (212)737-0153. Fax: (212)734-5176. E-mail: pwwagy@aol.com. **Contact:** Peregrine Whittlesey. Estab. 1986. Signatory of WGA. Represents 30 clients. 50% of clients are new/unpublished writers. Currently handles: 10% movie scripts; 90% stage plays.
Represents: Feature film, stage plays.
   O— This agency specializes in playwrights who also write for screen and TV.
How to Contact: Query with SASE. Prefers to read materials exclusively. Accepts e-mail and fax queries. Responds in 1 week to queries; 1 month to mss. Obtains most new clients through recommendations from others.
Recent Sales: Sold 20 scripts in the last year. *Christmas Movie*, by Darrah Cloud (CBS). Productions at Arena Stage in Washinton, New Theatre in Miami, La Jolla Playhouse, Seattle Rep., Oregon Shakespeare Festival, South Coast Rep.
Terms: Agent receives 10% commission on domestic sales; 15% commission on foreign sales. Offers written contract, binding for 2 years.

WINDFALL MANAGEMENT, 4084 Mandeville Canyon Rd., Los Angeles CA 90049-1032. (310)471-6317. Fax: (310)471-4577. E-mail: windfall@deltanet.com. **Contact:** Jeanne Field. Represents 20 clients. Currently handles: 20% novels; 50% movie scripts; 25% TV scripts; 5% stage plays; to the film and TV industry only, not to publishers.
   • Prior to becoming a manager, Ms. Field was a producer in the film and television business.
Represents: Movie scripts, TV scripts, TV movie of the week, documentary, miniseries, theatrical stage play, books to the film industry. **Considers these script subject areas:** Action/adventure; biography/autobiography; comedy; contemporary issues; detective/police/crime; experimental; family saga; fantasy; feminist; gay/lesbian; historical; juvenile; mainstream; multimedia; mystery/suspense; romantic comedy; romantic drama; science fiction; sports; teen; thriller (espionage); western/frontier.
   O— Windfall is a management company representing writers and books to the film and television industry. "We are especially interested in mainstream and independent film writers or playwrights." Actively seeking "well-written material that can be attractive to the entertainment industry"
How to Contact: Query with SASE. All unsolicited mss returned unopened. Considers simultaneous queries. Obtains most new clients through recommendations from others, referrals.
Recent Sales: This agency prefers not to share information on specific sales.
Terms: Offers written contract, binding for 1 year; 60-day notice must be given to terminate contract. Maximum of $150 a year for copying and postage, only for clients who are unproved.
Tips: "Live in either New York or Los Angeles. A writer must be available for meetings."

THE WRIGHT CONCEPT, 1612 W. Olive Ave., Suite 205, Burbank CA 91506. (818)954-8943. Fax: (818)954-9370. Website: www.wrightconcept.com. **Contact:** Marcie Wright, Steven Dowd. Estab. 1985. Signatory of WGA; DGA. Currently handles: 50% movie scripts; 50% TV scripts.
Member Agents: Marcie Wright (TV/movie); Steven Dowd.
Represents: Movie scripts, feature film, TV scripts, TV movie of the week, episodic drama, sitcom, animation, syndicated material, variety show. **Considers these script subject areas:** Action/adventure; teen; thriller.
   O— This agency specializes in TV comedy writers and feature comedy writers.
How to Contact: New clients through recommendations only.
Recent Sales: Sold 10-15 scripts in the last year. *Rule Number Three*, by Robert Kuhn (Fox 2000); *Dead Celebrities*, by Tomas Romero (Top Cow); *Miss America*, by Allen Estrin (Universal); *Some of My Best Friends* (CBS); *The Weakest Link* (NBC); *Here Come The Randalls* (Warner); *Baldo* (Univision); *Los Beltrans* (Telemundo).
Terms: Agent receives 10% commission on domestic sales.
Writers' Conferences: Southwest Writers Workshop (Albuquerque, August); Fade-In Magazine Oscar Conference (Los Angeles, May); Fade-In Magazine Top 100 People in Hollywood (Los Angeles, August); University of Georgia's Harriett Austin Writers Conference; Houston Film Festival; Dallas Screenwriters Association; San Francisco Writers Conference; The American Film Institute.

ANN WRIGHT REPRESENTATIVES, 165 W. 46th St., Suite 1105, New York NY 10036-2501. (212)764-6770. Fax: (212)764-5125. E-mail: annwrightlit@aol.com. **Contact:** Dan Wright. Estab. 1961. Signatory of WGA. Represents 23 clients. 30% of clients are new/unpublished writers. Currently handles: 50% novels; 40% movie scripts; 10% TV scripts.
   • Prior to becoming an agent, Mr. Wright was a writer, producer and production manager for film and television (alumni of CBS Television).

Represents: Novels, feature film, TV movie of the week, episodic drama, sitcom. **Considers these fiction areas:** Action/adventure; detective/police/crime; feminist; gay/lesbian; humor/satire; literary; mainstream/contemporary; mystery/suspense (suspense); romance (contemporary, historical, regency); sports; thriller; westerns/frontier. **Considers these script subject areas:** Action/adventure; comedy; detective/police/crime; gay/lesbian; historical; horror; mainstream; mystery/suspense; psychic/supernatural; romantic comedy; romantic drama; sports; thriller; western/frontier.

O— This agency specializes in "books or screenplays with strong motion picture potential." Prefers to work with published/established authors; works with a small number of new/previously unpublished authors. "Eager to work with any author with material that we can effectively market in the motion picture business worldwide." Actively seeking "strong competitive novelists and screen writers." Does not want to receive fantasy or science fiction projects at this time.

How to Contact: Query with SASE, outline. Prefers to read materials exclusively. Does not read unsolicited mss. Responds in 3 weeks to queries; 4 months to mss. Returns materials only with SASE.

Recent Sales: Sold 6 scripts in the last year. This agency prefers not to share information on specific sales.

Terms: Agent receives 10% commission on domestic sales; 15-20% commission on foreign sales; 20% on packaging projects; 10% commission on dramatic rights sales. Offers written contract, binding for 2 years. Critiques only works of signed clients; charges clients for photocopying expenses.

Tips: "Send a letter with SASE. Something about the work, something about the writer."

WRITER STORE, 2004 Rockledge Rd., Atlanta GA 30324. (404)874-6260. Fax: (404)874-6330. E-mail: writerstore@mindspring.com. **Contact:** Rebecca Shrager or Brenda Eanes. Signatory of WGA. Represents 16 clients. 80% of clients are new/unpublished writers. Currently handles: 10% novels; 90% movie scripts.
Member Agents: Rebecca Shrager; Brenda Eanes.
Represents: Novels, movie scripts, feature film, TV scripts, TV movie of the week, animation, miniseries. **Considers these fiction areas:** Action/adventure; detective/police/crime; family saga; fantasy; glitz; historical; humor/satire; literary; mainstream/contemporary; multicultural; mystery/suspense; New Age; psychic/supernatural; regional; science fiction; sports; thriller. **Considers these script subject areas:** Action/adventure; biography/autobiography; cartoon/animation; comedy; contemporary issues; detective/police/crime; ethnic; family saga; fantasy; glitz; historical; mainstream; multicultural; mystery/suspense; psychic/supernatural; regional; romantic comedy; romantic drama; science fiction; sports; teen; thriller.

O— This agency makes frequent trips to Los Angeles to meet with producers and development directors. "We make it a priority to know what the buyers are looking for. People Store, the sister company of Writer Store, has been in business since 1983 and is one of the oldest, largest, and most well-respected SAG talent agencies in the southeast. Writer Store reaps the benefits of a wide variety of contacts in the industry developed over a number of years by People Store." Actively seeking action-adventure, urban (dramas and comedies), thrillers, GOOD comedies of all types, GOOD science fiction, Native American, MOWs, sports, music related, based on a true story pieces, big budget. Does not want disgusting horror, toilet humor, short stories (unless it'a an anthology), children's books.

How to Contact: Query with SASE, synopsis. Accepts e-mail and fax queries. Considers simultaneous queries. Responds in a few days to queries; 2 months to mss. Returns materials only with SASE. Obtains most new clients through solicitations, closed to submissions until January 2003, unless you are an established writer.

Recent Sales: This agency prefers not to share information on specific sales.

Terms: Agent receives 10% commission on domestic sales; 10% commission on foreign sales. Offers written contract, binding for generally 2 years.

Writers' Conferences: Words Into Pictures (Los Angeles, June).

Tips: "Do not send unsolicited manuscripts. They will not be read. Send brief, concise query letter and synopsis. No pictures please. Be sure you understand the craft of screenwriting and are using the proper format."

WRITERS & ARTISTS AGENCY, 19 W. 44th St., Suite 1000, New York NY 10036. (212)391-1112. Fax: (212)575-6397. West Coast location: 8383 Wilshire Blvd., Suite 550, Beverly Hills CA 90211. (323)866-0900. Fax: (323)866-1899 **Contact:** William Craver, Christopher Till. Estab. 1970. Member of AAR; signatory of WGA. Represents 100 clients.
Represents: Movie scripts, feature film, TV scripts, TV movie of the week, episodic drama, miniseries, stage plays, stage musicals. **Considers these script subject areas:** Action/adventure; biography/autobiography; cartoon/animation; comedy; contemporary issues; detective/police/crime; erotica; ethnic; experimental; family saga;

FOR INFORMATION ON THE CONFERENCES agents attend, refer to the **Writers' Conferences** section in this book.

fantasy; feminist; gay/lesbian; glitz; historical; horror; juvenile; mainstream; multicultural; multimedia; mystery/suspense; psychic/supernatural; regional; romantic comedy; romantic drama; sports; teen; thriller; western/frontier.

How to Contact: Query with SASE, author bio, brief description of the project. No unsolicited mss. Responds in 1 month to queries only when accompanied by SASE. Obtains most new clients through professional recommendation.

Recent Sales: This agency prefers not to share information on specific sales.

Independent Production Companies

New this year, this section contains independent producers who buy feature film scripts. These are smaller production companies with limited budgets, so understand that if you have a science fiction script requiring lots of special effects or an action movie with many locations or special props, your work may not be appropriate for this market, which produces more character-driven stories.

Very few producers will accept unsolicited script submissions, but many are willing to consider a query letter. Your query letter should be no more than a page, including a one paragraph summary of your story and a paragraph to list your credentials as they relate to the subject matter of the script or your writing experience.

Because of the large bulk of mail producers receive, expect that the production company will likely respond only if they are interested in your script. If they do request to see your work, they will most likely send you a release form to sign and submit along with your script. This is a standard practice in the industry, and you should be willing to comply without worries that someone will steal your idea.

However, just as you would when submitting to agents, you should register your script before you send it out. The WGA offers a registration service to members and nonmembers alike. Write the Guild for more information on specific agencies, script registration, and membership requirements, or visit them online at www.wga.org.

Include a self-addressed stamped envelope (SASE) with enough room and postage for your script if you want it returned to you, or a smaller envelope with first class postage if you only want a reply. Allow six weeks from receipt of your manuscript before writing a follow-up letter.

Before you send out a query letter, you should have your script completed in proper screenplay format. Remember to keep the binding simple: two or three brass brads with a plain black or white cover.

It's a good idea to visit the production company's website to get a better feel for the kinds of films they've produced, the current movie or movies in production, and what scripts they're interested in producing next.

Many independent production companies are more willing to work with new writers, and these venues present some of the best opportunities for writers to break into the film industry and get their screenplays produced.

Alternative to Agents: Submitting the Script Yourself

BY J. MICHAEL STRACZYNSKI

Although the rest of this article will examine how to try to sell your script on your own, the importance of an agent—a known person in the Hollywood community who knows your work, respects it and can front it to the rest of our sometimes dysfunctional industry—cannot be overstated. It can save you hideous amounts of time and legwork in selling your script.

A good agent knows what stars have development deals at the studios and can direct a script that's perfect for a given start to that person. A good agent knows what studios have recently acquired the rights to books or stories that might suit your abilities. An agent at this stage of your career can be invaluable in getting you in the door for get-acquainted meetings with execs. You shouldn't always aim for the big agencies either; you can get lost there. And the title of a major agency isn't always the surest indicator of quality. One producer I know is always willing to read scripts by new writers represented by a certain smaller, boutique agency because he knows it's picky about its writer-clients and that whatever comes across his desk from that agency is going to be interesting reading.

SELLING IT YOURSELF

Can you sell your script without an agent? Yes, it's possible. Difficult, but possible. It simply requires patience, persistence, and an adherence to the rough guidelines that follow.

The first thing you'll want to decide is to whom to send your screenplay. Part of this decision is estimating, in your own mind, the approximate budget for the screenplay should it get produced. If it needs only a small cast, simple locations and minimal effects, you could safely classify it as a low-budget film.

This determination will narrow down the process of selecting a likely producer. Most independent producers probably can't handle the overwhelming costs of a huge film. By the same token, you'd have a better chance of placing a low-budget film with an independent producer than with a major studio, at least as of this writing. But considering the success of smaller films like *The Bridges of Madison County* and such notorious big-budget disasters as *Waterworld*, it's likely this trend will reverse itself a little in coming years, and the major studios will soon begin looking for more low-budget films to produce and distribute.

So a low- or medium-budget film gives you greater flexibility, allowing you the choice of approaching either a major studio or an independent producer. Don't cheat your script of what's necessary to tell the story, but don't overly burden your script with unnecessary or excessive

As Creator, Executive Producer and Head Writer for the Emmy-winning series Babylon 5, **J. MICHAEL STRACZYNSKI** *has written over 150 produced television episodes, including half-hour, hour and two-hour programs. He has served as writer/producer on such series as the top-ten rated* Murder, She Wrote, *as well as* The New Twilight Zone, Walker Texas Ranger *and* Jake and the Fatman, *among others. He has also story edited nearly half a dozen animated series, and is the author of numerous plays, radio dramas, nonfiction articles, short stories, and two novels. This article is excerpted from* The Complete Book of Scriptwriting © 1996 by J. Michael Straczynski. Used with permission of Writer's Digest Books, an imprint of F&W Publications, Inc. Visit your local bookseller or call 1-800-448-0915 to obtain your copy.*

production values. It's also easier for a screenwriter who hasn't previously sold a script to sell a low-budget script than a high-budget screenplay, simply because the producer won't risk as much should the film fail to become a big hit. Remember, the more you can minimize the risks of production, the greater the chances of your script being both sold *and* produced.

Your next step is to narrow down the possible alternatives to specific production companies. Pick out a handful of production companies you believe might be appropriate for your screenplay. Rank them in order, from the largest to the smallest company. My personal feeling is that you should market your script on an individual basis or, at most, to two producers simultaneously. Any more than that and you're risking trouble.

Having selected the first producer you intend to approach, make sure you address your letter of inquiry to the story editor rather than simply addressing it to the story department. Even though the story editor may read your letter of inquiry and may even respond personally, if you're an unknown commodity your script will almost always be read first by a reader, who will then decide if it's worth the story editor's time. Yeah, it's profoundly unfair. But it's the nature of the beast.

THE QUERY LETTER

Once you have the story editor's name, write a query letter because an unsolicited script arriving without prior warning is anathema to film producers. Your query letter, like your script, should be spare and to the point. You should state that you are familiar with the films they produce; that you have developed a feature film screenplay that is consistent with their trends in production; that you have followed this development through the synopsis, outline and final screenplay stages; and that the script is currently available for examination.

You should also point out that you own all the rights to the screenplay, that it is an original work (or, if it's based on a true story, that you own all the pertinent rights to that story) and that since it's consistent with popular trends, it will likely be a very commercial property. If you have any special qualifications—a degree in an area touched upon by the script, for instance, or direct access to someone involved in the story on which the script is based—mention them as well. You can indicate in general terms the type of screenplay you have—"It's a mystery thriller with an erotic underpinning that ties into the big controversy about capital punishment and dog training"—but do not include specific, detailed information about the story. This will protect both you and the studio from complications concerning plagiarism.

Conclude by stating that if the story editor would be interested in reading the completed screenplay, you would be pleased to send it along for his examination. Also state that you are happy to enclose a release form with your submission, and if there is a specifically worded release form the company prefers, ask that it be forwarded so you can include it with your submission.

As a rule, your finished query letter should run about a page long, and certainly no more than a page and a half. It should be as tightly and well written as possible. I say this because I've seen a lot of writers who can turn out fantastic scripts but who slapdash off some of the crummiest queries I've ever seen. If you've just spent half a year of your life working on a screenplay, it only makes sense to put a little effort and forethought into your query. You should also be sure to keep a copy of the query for reference in writing future letters to the story editor and so that you can just retype (or print out) another should you need to approach another studio.

For further assistance in writing a query letter, a sample letter is printed here. Needless to say, it should not be copied verbatim. It would cause much concern if story editors in Los Angeles were to suddenly begin getting a series of identical query letters.

FOLLOW-UP

Surprising as it may seem, you probably won't have to wait long for a reply. You'll sometimes get word back from the studio within a few weeks, or maybe as much as a month, after you send

Mr. William Young
Creative Executive
Warner Bros. Pictures
4000 Warner Boulevard
Burbank, California 91522

Dear Mr. Young,

I have recently completed an original screenplay that I believe is consistent with the quality and type of films produced by Warner Bros.

Entitled *The Nightshade Equation*, the screenplay includes many of the elements of supernaturalism that have become popular in recent years, while taking an entirely different approach that has not been previously explored: the relationship between the supernatural and the Internal Revenue Service.

While not a member of the Writers Guild, I have been a freelance writer in other media for several years, and The Nightshade Equation is partly based on actual research that I carried out in the area of the occult and which formed the basis for several articles and short stories that I have published on this area in leading regional magazines. (I still retain all rights to the idea, however.)

I would appreciate the opportunity to submit this screenplay for evaluation by the Warner Bros. Story Department on a purely speculative basis. I will be happy to enclose a standard release form with the submission or if there is an in-house release preferred by Warners, I will sign and enclose that one instead.

Hoping that I shall hear from you soon in this regard, I remain

Most sincerely yours,

A. Nother Writer

off your query. During this period, you can realistically look forward to one of two responses. The first is that they simply cannot look at any script unless it's submitted by an agent. But don't let this discourage you because there are many other producers that don't require an agent. They're not as numerous, but they are there; it just may take you a while to find them.

The second possibility is the sought-after permission to submit your screenplay for review. In this latter case, they may tell you to use your own release form, or they will send one along.

Before sending anything off, however, you should take one more step, largely for your own protection. Register the script with the Writers Guild of America, west. It's unlikely anyone will plagiarize your script, but it's never a bad idea to cover all your bets. The steps for registering a script are simple; just send an unbound copy including the title, your full name, address, phone number and social security number on your cover sheet, and the appropriate fee ($20) to WGAw, Intellectual Property Registry at 7000 West Third Street, Los Angeles, California 90048-4329. The telephone number is (323)782-4500. You may also register your script online at www.wga.org.

With this done, you have the option of including the line *Registered, WGAw* on the title page of your screenplay, directly under the date in the lower left-hand corner, along with the serial number the Guild will have assigned your script.

With your material finally collected and your release form filled in, you can then send the material to the person who responded to your letter. Be sure to refer back to your earlier letter and to having received her responding letter so the secretary who opens all the mail will know your property is not coming in unexpected. You should also write the words *Release Form Enclosed: As Requested* on the outside of your mailing envelope.

Then . . . well, then you wait.

POSSIBLE RESPONSES

The response time can range anywhere from a few weeks to several months. Again, there's always the possibility of flat-out rejection. The production company may decide to option the script for one or two years while deciding whether or not to purchase it outright. An *option* means that they will agree to pay you a certain fee, usually anywhere from $5,000 to $10,000, to hold onto your script during that time while trying to set it up. You, in turn, promise not to market the script elsewhere until the option has expired. During the period covered by the option, you may be asked to rewrite the screenplay for additional money. The production company will use this time to make up its mind once and for all whether to go ahead with the film or not. Once so decided, they'll put together a deal and get the film moving into preproduction.

Finally, they may option to purchase the script outright and move directly into preproduction. If this is the case, you will be offered a flat fee, the possibility of a percentage and possibly a salary for further revisions. It's important to emphasize two points:

First, even though your script may be optioned or even purchased, this does not guarantee production. Many more scripts are purchased each year than are ever produced, and nearly three times as many scripts are optioned annually than are purchased and produced. But having one script optioned or purchased is a vital first step. You may receive an assignment to write another film for the same studio, and your next original treatment will be given even greater consideration.

Second, either of these two occurrences will allow you to join the Writers Guild and to get an agent. I strongly urge anyone who receives any kind of offer whatsoever from a studio to immediately contact an agent. Explain that a deal is already in progress, sign a representation contract and have the agent step in and negotiate the sometimes awesome legal machinations that arise whenever one deals with the film industry.

Two final caveats: Once your script has landed at a major studio and the reader has turned in his or her written analysis (referred to as "coverage"), that coverage almost always remains at the studio indefinitely. What does that mean for you? It means that if the script is deemed poorly written or unproducible, it is effectively dead at that studio for the foreseeable future.

This is compounded by the fact that there are not that many major studios capable of financing big films, even though a smaller production company can sometimes finance its own lower-budget films. This becomes a problem for writers when the independent producer asks for a "free option." A free option means . . . well, it's free—to the producer, anyway—so you give him the right to take your script to the major studios and try to get money for a development deal.

Many beginning writers fall for this ploy. It sounds reasonable. "Listen, I think it's a great script, we have a producer who's dying to do it, I think we can get Stallone, but we need to get a major studio on board for a movie like this. So what I'd like to do is just send it, discreetly, to a couple of people I know at Paramount and Universal. I've already talked to them about it off the record, and they're interested. So what I'd like is a free option for just ninety days while I try to get them onboard. If we wait to do an option here, it'll tie things up for weeks, and the property is hot. Besides, as much as I like it, you're a new writer, and I think the boss'll be more inclined to green light the project if we can get a major to sign on."

And you know what happens then? If you say yes, the script goes to the two major studios, and if for whatever reason they reject it—and sometimes that rejection can have more to do with the indie producer than with your words—the coverage stays at the studio, and you've just lost two of the major venues to get your script produced. If you go to another independent producer, that producer then can't go to Paramount or Universal because it's dead there. You've let someone kill off two of the major opportunities for your work to be produced without even paying you for it.

This, not to put too fine a point on it, is not a good thing.

Insist on an option for money before letting an independent producer take your script to a studio. I don't care how much she wheedles, begs, connives, convinces, persuades, threatens or carries on cranky. I've been down this road, and so have many other writers. It's a dead end. If you fall for it now, it's your own fault.

The second real concern you have to be aware of going in is that once a studio purchases your script, nine times out of ten it will turn around and assign it to another writer to rewrite. That writer may even get more money to rewrite your script than you got to write it. You may end up sharing your writing credit with two, four or even six other writers. And the final product may be *nothing* like what you'd originally written. It's unfortunate, and self-destructive on the part of the studios, and in the long term diffuses the voice of the original writer . . . but it's now so firmly entrenched as studio policy that you have to expect it going in. There are whole lists of writers who do nothing but rewrite other writers. Many of the trades, such as *Daily Variety*, have now begun announcing the name of the rewriter in the same article in which they announce the name of the script purchased and the original writer.

It stinks.

But it's the business.

THE FUTURE OF CINEMA

The next ten years, according to most industry watchers, will see more independent movies, more original movies produced for the burgeoning cable and direct-to-video marketplace, and, of course, the studios will continue to turn out spectacles and dramas of various sizes. All of which will mean a host of continued opportunities for new screenwriters. As the need for feature-length productions increases, so will the demand for scripts, and that means that more scriptwriters than ever before will have the opportunity to make their first big break into showbiz tinsel, troubles, splendor, aggravation and all.

See you at the movies.

You can use a number of other resources to get a list of current film producers who might be interested in your particular script. These publications can be found at well-stocked newsstands and libraries, or ordered on line.

Pacific Coast Studio Directory: This quarterly directory has been called the "bible of the entertainment industry" and contains names, addresses and phone numbers of virtually every production company in Los Angeles and San Francisco and others. Also includes talent agencies, publications, industry craftspeople, the different unions, advertisers and film/television bureaus in each state listed. Subscriptions are $30/year and should be sent to Post Office Box V, Pine Mountain CA 93222-0022 or call (661) 242-2722 or visit www.studio-directory.com.

The Hollywood Reporter Bluebook: This annual volume contains hundreds of listings of different production companies and their needs. It's particularly useful for a scriptwriter, and it makes a good companion volume to the *Pacific Coast Studio Directory*.

Hollywood Creative Directory's Producers: Probably the single most useful directory, and also the most expensive (single issue $59.95). It's nearly impossible to find outside of Los Angeles, but can be ordered by calling (323) 308-3558 or online at www.hcdonline.com.

Independent Production Companies

The following listings are for low- to midsized-budget feature film producers. When reading through this section, keep in mind the following information specific to the independent producer listings:

PRODUCER'S SPECIALIZATIONS

WHAT DO I SEND?

FOR MORE INFORMATION

WHO DO I SEND TO?

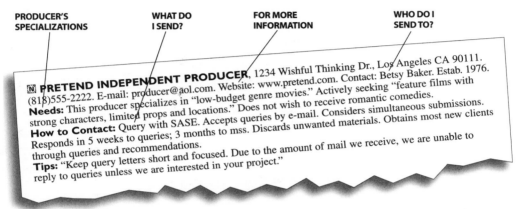

PRETEND INDEPENDENT PRODUCER, 1234 Wishful Thinking Dr., Los Angeles CA 90111. (818)555-2222. E-mail: producer@aol.com. Website: www.pretend.com. Contact: Betsy Baker. Estab. 1976. **Needs:** This producer specializes in "low-budget genre movies." Actively seeking "feature films with strong characters, limited props and locations." Does not wish to receive romantic comedies. **How to Contact:** Query with SASE. Accepts queries by e-mail. Considers simultaneous submissions. Responds in 5 weeks to queries; 3 months to mss. Discards unwanted materials. Obtains most new clients through queries and recommendations. **Tips:** "Keep query letters short and focused. Due to the amount of mail we receive, we are unable to reply to queries unless we are interested in your project."

SUBHEADS

Each listing is broken down into subheads to make locating specific information easier. In the first section, you'll find contact information for each producer. Further information is provided which indicates the producer's specialties, what type of work they're looking for, and how writers should approach them.

Needs: Look here to quickly learn a producer's areas of specializations and individual strengths. Producers also mention what specific areas they are currently seeking as well as subjects they do *not* wish to receive.

How to Contact: Most producers open to submissions prefer initially to receive a query letter briefly describing your work. Producers usually discard material sent without a SASE. Here they also indicate if they accept queries by fax or e-mail, and their preferred way of working with new clients.

Tips: Producers offer advice and additional instructions for writers hoping to break in.

SPECIAL INDEX

Listing Index: This index lists all producers, agencies, independent publicists, and writers' conferences listed in the book.

INDEPENDENT PRODUCERS

N: AXIAL ENTERTAINMENT, 20 W. 21st St., New York NY 10010. E-mail: submissions@axialentertainme nt.com. Website: www.axialentertainment.com. **Executive Producer:** Riaz Patel, CEO. **Contact:** Nora France-scani, director of development (film/theater); David Garfield, director of development (film/TV).
Needs: "Axial is a New York-based production and management company with an unusual model: loosely based on the 'hot house' studio environment of the 1940s, Axial takes writers and film executives—two parties that are often separated by distance and large, heavy, insurmountable barriers—and places them in the same work space. By incubating the development process before it gets to the studios, networks or producers, Axial is exactly the place where chances can be taken on a new writer or a completely original idea. Axial's dynamic creative process is anchored in the weekly Tc (the Tuesday Think Tank meeting). Writers and executives gather together to discuss new story ideas, assess the gaps and gluts in the current marketplace, brainstorm current script road-blocks, and work to make each choice in every story as smart as possible. What are specific studios, networks and theater companies looking for? What kinds of projects are considered out-of-date this month? What are some other ways of getting a character from point A to point B?"
How to Contact: "Unfortunately, Axial Entertainment does not accept any unsolicited materials. If you are interested in submitting, please send an e-mail containing a brief (one page or less) summary of your material at submissions@axialentertainment.com."
Tips: "Axial is not for every writer. The writers who thrive in our environment not only have great talent and express themselves in exciting and dynamic voices, but are highly motivated, prolific, generous with their intelligence, and ego-free about their writing process. At Axial, we specialize in finding original voices (both established and emerging), creating and developing strong, marketable material, and championing that material the entire way from conception to production."

N: BURN PRODUCTIONS, 3800 NE Second Ave., 2nd Floor, Miami FL 331347. Website: www.burnproduc tions.com. "BURN Productions is a film/video production group that specializes in new media for the Internet, broadband and television. The company's mission is to continually create high-quality feature films, shorts and music videos including creative narrative, documentary and experimental styles."

N: BOARDWALK FILMS, E-mail: info@boardwalkfilms.com. Website: www.boardwalkfilms.com. "Board-walk Films is a start-up independent film company with offices in Los Angeles and New York."
Needs: "We want material that's far afield from typical Hollywood studio fare, but we still value a well-told story." The mission of Boardwalk Films is to produce movies that both entertain and challenge viewers. We seek scripts that have a unique point of view or a story that's never been told in quite the same way. Our goal is to find writers with a strong voice whose work should be produced. If you have a script that stands out, we look forward to reading it.
How to Contact: We will not accept unsolicited scripts. E-mail synopsis only to kate@boardwalkfilms.com."

N: CODIKOW FILMS, 8899 Beverly Blvd., Suite 719, Los Angeles CA 90048. (310)246-9388. Fax: (310) 246-9877. E-mail: pitch@codikowfilms.com. Website: www.codikowfilms.com. **Executive Producer:** Stacy Cod ikow. **Contact:** Codikow Story Dept.
Needs: Accepts material for all genres. "Currently searching for a romantic comedy. Codikow Films has been involved in the production of 10 feature films, including *Hollywood Heartbreak* and *Fatal Instinct*. Presently, the company is producing *In Search of Holden Caulfield*. We have an active development slate of projects, ranging from Independent to Studio features."
How to Contact: "Submit a short pitch or synopsis (no more than one 8½ × 11 page). Make sure you include your contact information (name, address, phone, fax and e-mail) as well as the title, genre and logline for your project. Pitches are reviewed each week by the Codikow Story Dept. Because of the volume of material we receive, we can only respond to ideas we are interested in pursuing further. If we find a project interesting, a request for the screenplay will be made by e-mail or phone."
Tips: Stacy Codikow is a member of the Producers Guild of America, the Writers Guild of America, Women in Film, USC Cinema Alumni Association, Cinewoman, AFI 3rd Decade Council, IFP West and has been included in articles written for *The Wall Street Journal*, *New York Times*, Movieline, *Premiere* Magazine, *Scene at the Movies*, *Hollywood Reporter*, *The Daily Variety*, *Screen International*, *The Los Angeles Times*, *Daily News*, *Film & Video* and *Entertainment Today*. She has been featured on the television shows Entertainment Tonight (ET), E!, HBO News, Extra, and Showbiz News (CNN).

N: LEE DANIELS ENTERTAINMENT, 434 Broadway, Suite 402, New York NY 10013. (646)613-1552. Fax: (646)613-1487. Website: www.leedanielsentertainment.com. **Executive Producer:** Lee Daniels. **Contact:** Ebony.
Needs: "We work with all aspects of entertainment, including film, television and theater."
How to Contact: Send query via mail Attn: Ebony or online at www.leedanielsentertainment.com. "All scripts should be registered (WGA, etc.) or copyrighted for your own protection. All scripts should be in standard screenplay format. Include a synopsis, logline and character breakdown (including lead and supporting roles). Do NOT send any extraneous materials."

Tips: Lee Daniels produced *Monster's Ball*. Client list includes Wes Bently (*American Beauty*) and supermodel/ actress Amber Valletta. Past clients include Marianne Jean-Baptiste and Morgan Freeman.

N **ENERGY ENTERTAINMENT**, Website: www.energyentertainment.net. **Executive Producer:** Brooklyn Weaver. Estab. 2001.
How to Contact: Submit query via website. "Energy Entertainment is only accepting electronic query letters, and will not accept unsolicited scripts."
Tips: "Energy Entertainment has a first-look deal with Sony-based Original Film (*Fast and Furious*, *I Know What You Did Last Summer*, *Cruel Intentions*), and *XXX* starring Vin Diesel."

N **GIRLIE GIRL PRODUCTIONS**, 6700 Hillpark Dr., Suite 302, Los Angeles CA 90068-2111. (323)851-1206. Fax: (323)851-1263. E-mail: info@girliegirlproductions.com. Website: www.girliegirlproductions.net. **Executive Producer:** Elizabeth Owen.
Needs: Specializes in the development and production of feature films and documentaries for theatrical release, cable and network television, and ancillary outlets. Also interested in series development for network and cable television. "Currently, Girlie Girl's artistic portfolio includes a wide range of materials from a variety of sources: novels, plays, short stories, published articles, nonfiction works and, of course, screenplays." Current projects include *Dogwalker* (directed by Paul Kobelja, screenplay by Geoffrey Card, based on a short story by Orson Scott Card, co-producer with Fresco Pictures and Paul Kobelja).
How to Contact: "We do not accept unsolicited screenplays. Please submit a one-page cover letter (maximum) by e-mail, mail (include SASE) or fax. Preferred query method is by e-mail (to info@girliegirlproductions.com— no attachments). "If we then want to read your screenplay, a release will be sent the same way you sent us your query. All requested scripts and treatments MUST be accompanied by a signed release, or they will be returned or discarded unread. Finally, please make sure your script is properly formatted. If you don't know what proper format looks like, please find out—before you send your script to us."
Tips: "Just because we're called Girlie Girl Productions doesn't mean we're not interested in stories with male protagonists, but action flicks aren't really our forte (yet!). All we ask for is characters we care about (notice we didn't say 'like') and some intelligent writing. It goes without saying (or at least it should) that every story needs a beginning, a middle and an end. That doesn't mean, of course, that they need necessarily go in that order (*Pulp Fiction* anyone?) but there must be something cohesive there, or it won't be of interest to us."

N **GREY LINE ENTERTAINMENT, INC.**, 115 W. California Blvd., #310, Pasadena CA 91105-3005. E-mail: submissions@greyline.net. Website: www.greyline.net. **Contact:** Sara Miller, submissions coordinator.
Needs: "Grey Line Entertainment is a full-service motion picture production and literary management company. We offer direct management of all services associated with the exploitation of stories. When our clients' motion picture screenplays are ready for the marketplace, Grey Line Entertainment places them directly with studios or with major co-producers who can assist in packaging cast and/or director before approaching financiers (like Warner Bros., New Line, Fox or Disney) or broadcasters (HBO, Showtime, etc.)."
How to Contact: Query via e-mail only to submissions@greyline.net. No attachments. Unsolicited queries OK. "E-mail queries for novels, nonfiction book proposals, screenplays, and treatments should consist of a compelling and business-like letter giving us a brief overview of your story—and a one-sentence pitch. Be sure to include your return address, and a telephone number. Also include relevant background on yourself, including previous publication or production. Allow two weeks for consideration of initial query. No multiple submissions. Treatments and screenplays submitted without a completed and signed Grey Line Submission Form will be discarded. Include SASE for our reply. Submissions without SASE will be discarded. We recommend you register screenplays and treatments with the Copyright Office and/or the Writers Guild of America before submitting your query."
Tips: "Your work must be finished and properly edited before seeking our representation (meaning proofread, spell-checked and rewritten until it's perfect)."

N **GRUENBERG FILMS**, Blankenburger Chaussee 84, D-13125, Berlin Germany. Phone/fax: +49(0)341-2710 319. E-mail: Andreas.Gruenberg@Gruenbergfilm.de. Website: www.gruenbergfilm.de. **Executive Producer:** Andreas Gruenberg.
Needs: Currently seeking: "stories which can be transferred to Germany/Europe or already are located in Germany/Europe and are suitable for television (budget level $1-3 million U.S. dollars); crime-action-comedy located in Berlin with feature film potential; teen-oriented romantic comedies for love stories (both TV/cinema); romantic comedies and melodramas with strong female leads (TV); a Christmas story, packaged or script alone, which could be realized for not more than $3 million U.S. dollars, open for children of 6 and older; and thrillers dealing with diving/divers."
How to Contact: "Interested writers with finished scripts are invited to contact Mr. Andreas Gruenberg at Andreas.Gruenberg@Gruenbergfilm.de. Please send loglines first. We will ask for a one-page synopsis, the script and (if necessary) for additional material if we are interested."

N **JUMPROPE PRODUCTIONS**, 10932 Morrison St., #108, North Hollywood CA 91601. E-mail: submissi on@jumpropeprods.com. Website: www.jumpropeprods.com.

insider report

We're as hungry as the writer is

At some point in time it's bound to happen—you'll sit through a really bad movie and, on the walk through the theater parking lot back to you car, find yourself saying something like, "I could write a better movie than that." Or perhaps you've done just that—you've taken a great idea and turned it into a great film script, and you're waiting by the phone for one of the major studios you sent it to to call you up and tell you that Brad Pitt is excited about working on your film.

The truth, however, is that a screenwriter needs representation to sell his or her movie to a major studio, and it's extremely hard to get a script agent without first having something produced. Independent film production companies, however, provide a way around this vicious circle, as they thrive on fresh, young talent.

Elizabeth Owen

One such company is Girlie Girl Productions, a Los Angeles-based business founded in 1997 by Elizabeth Owen that focuses on narrative features for film and television. "I was an actor until 1997, working steadily in Chicago until I got bored. I had been the manager of a theater company, and had done some theater producing, and knew before I gave up acting that eventually I wanted to move into film," says Owen of how she came to form Girlie Girl. Upon giving up acting, Owen took a look at where her strengths lay, and discovered that they thrust her firmly into the role of "producer." "I love working with writers, love developing material. I love working with actors, and was always very good at pulling different people together and putting them in good working situations—'Hey you, you need to meet this guy,' and, 'You two should work on this project, you'd work well together,' that kind of thing." So she decided to pursue the role of producer, and even lined up an assistant-to-producer job, but was told, " 'Give me six months and I'll get rid of the person I just hired and hire you.' I didn't think that was very nice and I didn't want to wait, so I said, 'I'll just start my own company.' "

Thus Girlie Girl was born in 1997, though it wasn't until 2000 that Owen decided to make it a full-time venture. "Around the same time [that I started Girlie Girl], I was a co-founder and became the executive director of a not-for-profit for filmmakers in Chicago. Most of my time was spent running this not-for-profit, so I ended up focusing very little of my attention on Girlie Girl. At the beginning of 2000, I felt like I had a decision to make, as to whether I would be in the not-for-profit sector for the rest of my life, which I enjoyed and actually really loved, or I was going to start focusing my attention on my own work. I decided to focus on my own work, and that's when I moved out to L.A. and started really developing things."

Owen sees Girlie Girl and other independent production companies as being a good place for writers to get started in the filmmaking industry, and she hopes that her approach reflects that belief. "I come from a theater background, and the people I work with come from theater, publishing, and film, obviously. In the theater world, the writer is at the top of the food chain. It's a complete reverse of the film world. I think I have a certain amount of respect for the writer that a lot of other people don't have. I look at it this way—I'm working with a couple of writers who've made a name for themselves, and I don't have a development deal and have still been able to do that. I think this says something about the way my staff (Lisabeth Laiken, Maaza Mengiste, Joyce San Pedro, Ellen O'Donnell, and Bill Reeves) and I treat writers. I've always tried to go with the notion that this person had an idea, it was their idea and, as much as possible, I want to stick with the person whose vision it was originally and work with them to make something out of it. There are a lot of bad movies out there and most of those movies have like seventeen writer credits on there. It's a joke. That doesn't always mean everything is perfect—obviously, this is a business, but just because it's a business, I don't think you have to be cruel to get things done."

A part of being more writer-focused than major studios is Girlie Girl's willingness to consider first-time writers who aren't yet represented by an agent. "We do accept unsolicited queries. No company that I know of accepts unsolicited submissions—you just can't do it; there are too many legal issues. But we certainly accept query letters and, from there, if we're interested in seeing more, we'll request a script and send a release form. We just want to know a quick pitch—a log line, a quick synopsis, a couple of sentences on the writer, anything of note: Did you win a contest, did the script win a contest, have you had something produced? And if you didn't, don't make things up just to make the letter longer. I'd much rather have a good idea from someone with no background than an okay idea from someone who's won fifteen contests no one's ever heard of." Career writers with a drawer-full of produced scripts don't necessarily have any advantages over the first-time writer, as far as Owen is concerned. "I don't care if they've written one great script or thirty great scripts, a great script is a great script. One guy writes one good script, has no intention of writing another one—if it's a good script, it's a good script, who cares?"

Owen has some technical tips that writers querying her company can use to get a producer's attention. "Do the research, find out what kind of material we're working on. Spell my name right, spell the name of my company right. Don't start your letter with 'Dear Sir'—that is a big turn-off to me. Go to our website—it's really specific. Exactly what we want in a query is on there—just follow the instructions and, if your idea is good, we'll look at your script. We're as hungry as the writer is." Knowing how to properly format a script is another skill that writers should have in order to be taken seriously by a producer. "There are plenty of books out there that can teach you how to properly format a screenplay. Spend the hundred bucks and buy the software. Use the correct font—if you're using a nine-point Helvetica, and your script is 120 pages, your script is probably 160 pages when formatted properly. Learn how to properly put your scripts together—two brads, top and bottom. Don't cut them—if they're too long, fold them. Make it easy on us."

Certain characteristics can make a writer more attractive to a producer, as well. "Someone who's creative, with reasonable expectations, though that doesn't mean short-selling him or herself," says Owen. "Reasonable expectations but still thinking big, because I think a positive attitude is 90 percent of the battle here, somebody who's open to other people's ideas, who listens and wants to be part of a team. I think a lot of people look at the writer-producer relationship as adversarial, but I look at my role as being, in the ideal situation, the one who should be advocating for the writer." Being educated about the business is also important, as it shows a producer you're serious about your craft. "Do your homework—read the trades, know what's being sold, know what's not being sold. Those are all really important things— it's not just about art, it's also about business, and you should educate yourself about both. It doesn't mean you have to completely remove the art from your business, but you should definitely be able to understand the business of your art."

Owen also points to being networked as one of the most important advantages a writer can have. "Anything that puts you in a position to be closer to the industry and closer to people who are working in the industry already is only helpful. There are a lot of online forums, like Done Deal [at www.scriptsales.com], that are great places to meet and network with other writers. Don't be shy—put your stuff out there and get feedback from people who are doing it already."

In the end, of course, the most important thing a writer can do to become a successful screenwriter is to be productive. "The best advice I ever heard was actually from Steven J. Cannell, who said, 'Write every day. Every day, even if it's just for an hour, write every day. If you're a writer, you should be writing.' "

—*Rodney Wilson*

Needs: Looking for feature film scripts. "JRP is looking for screenwriters to work with, NOT material to produce. You can have the greatest idea in the world, but if you can't write, we can't help. We like writers and are willing to work with newcomers should we respond to the material."
How to Contact: Send an e-mail to receive submission instructions via automated reply.
Tips: "We tend not to respond to period pieces and historical epics; stories anchored around the 'based on the true story" mantra; books, novels, treatments, short stories, etc. (if you have a script based on a book, novel, treatment . . . that's another story); or TV scripts/ideas/original shows/ etc.—our focus is on working with feature film screenwriters, so we'd rather see a feature film screenplay."

MAINLINE RELEASING, A Film & TV Production and Distribution Co., 1801 Avenue of the Stars, Suite 1035, Los Angeles CA 90067. (310)286-1001. Fax: (310)286-0530. E-mail: joe@mainlinereleasing.com. Website: www.mainlinereleasing.com. **Contact:** Joseph Dickstein, vice president of acquisitions. Estab. 1997.
Needs: Produces family films, drama, thrillers and erotic features.

NANDAR ENTERTAINMENT GROUP, 1300 N. Cordova, Burbank CA 91505. E-mail: mail@taylorfilm.com. Website: www.taylorfilm.com. **Contact:** Tom Brooks.
Needs: We are accepting all genres for digital and 35mm feature films and shorts for film festivals and theatrical release, except for sexually explicit or pornographic material, which we will neither read nor consider.
How to Contact: "A query letter is preferred—it can be accompanied with a brief synopsis and/or logline as long as it is accompanied with the standard WGA disclosure form filled out and wet-signed, or it will not be looked at. Scripts can be submitted, but will not be returned. I will respond to every submission as long as a SASE is supplied. Send to the attention of the Script Department."
Tips: Does not want to see treatments or synopses of unwritten scripts.

NITE OWL PRODUCTIONS, 126 Hall Rd., Aliquippa PA 15001. (724)775-1993. Fax: (801)881-3017. E-mail: niteowlprods@aol.com. Website: www.niteowlproductionsltd.com. Estab. 2001.
Needs: "We will be producing at least 5 to 10 feature films in the next 2 to 5 years. We are searching for polished, well-structured, well-written and professional-looking screenplays that are essentially ready for production. If your screenplay does not meet these standards, do *not* send us a query for that screenplay. All screenplays must be in English. Provide a working title for your screenplay. All screenplays must be in standard industry format."
How to Contact: "For *all* submissions, send a one page query letter, via e-mail or regular mail. The content of your query letter should be succinct and interesting enough to entice us to ask to see more of the project. Single-space your query letters. If our interest is piqued, we will request the completed synopsis and screenplay. Do *not* send the screenplay to us unless we specifically ask you to do so."
Tips: "*All* submissions MUST include a dated and signed Submission Release Form or they will be discarded immediately. No exceptions. Page length varies according to the format you are submitting. Screenplays that are too long or short may be considered unprofessional. This is especially true for television because a show needs to squeeze into time slots. All full-length feature film screenplays must be between 80 to 130 pages in length. 1 hour television spec scripts need to be 55 to 65 pages in length. No less. No more. A common rule of thumb

says 1 script page equals approximately 1 minute on the television. Do *not* send us computer disks. One hard copy of your screenplay will suffice. Do *not* cheat on your margins. Stay within 1 to 1.25 inches on all sides. If you cheat, we will notice. The industry standard font style and size is Courier 11 to 12 point, but similar fonts are acceptable. Proofread your screenplay thoroughly before submitting to avoid senseless mistakes that might pull your reader's attention from the story, such as typos, punctuation, or grammatical errors. Be certain all of your pages are there and in order. Copyright your script with the U.S. Copyright Office before sending it to us or anyone else. Registration with The Writers Guild of America is also strongly suggested. All screenplays must be firmly bound with a cover page that states the title of work and the author(s) name, address and contact information. Card stock covers are preferred. Send us a COPY of your screenplay, as your materials will *not* be returned to you, regardless of enclosures."

RAINFOREST FILMS, 2141 Powers Ferry Rd., Suite 300, Marietta GA 30067. Fax: (770)953-0848. Website: www.rainforestproductions.com.
Needs: Rainforest's productions include *Pandora's Box*, *Chocolate City* and *Trois*. They have also produced a number of music videos for a variety of artists.
How to Contact: Submit complete ms. "In order to submit a script, a detailed synopsis and signed release form must be included. Any material sent without the accompanying signed release form will be returned unread. Screenplays are sent to our development department where they are reviewed and discussed. Please allow 90 days for written confirmation and response to your work. All material should be marked 'Attn: Screenplay Submissions.' "

VALEO FILMS INC., P.O. Box 5876, Longview TX 75608. (908)797-6489. E-mail: screenplays@valeofilms.com. Website: www.valeofilms.com.
Needs: Currently considering projects "that contain one or more of the following: character or story driven; identifies moral values; romance/love story; educational/documentary; presents the human condition; strong visual imagery; coming of age/learning; or intellectual drama/mystery."
How to Contact: Query by e-mail or regular mail. "We require that you provide us with your name, phone number, address, the title of your work and either a WGA registration number or a copyright number. After receiving this information, we will send you an 'Unsolicited Project Release Letter.' You must then sign and return it with a single copy of your screenplay and/or treatment."
Tips: Does not want "projects that contain the following characteristics: one character saves the world; SFX based; highly action based; extreme and grotesque violence; high sexual content; or strong explicit language. Although we do have a vast array of production resources available to us, VFI is a relatively small production company who prefers to limit the number of projects we have in production. Consequently, we tend to be very selective when it comes to selecting new material."

VINTAGE ENTERTAINMENT, 843 Berkeley St., Santa Monica CA 90403. E-mail: info@GoVintage.com. Website: www.govintage.com. **Executive Producer:** Peter Scott. Estab. 1994. "Vintage Entertainment is a film production and boutique management company located in Santa Monica, California. The management side of the company includes motion picture and TV writers, directors, novelists and new media clientele."
Needs: "Vintage Entertainment intends to find talented artists eager to create the Vintage classics of tomorrow. Artists who embrace change, push the envelope. Artists with unique voices who communicate by instinct, not by formula. We seek artists with talent, passion and craft. We are a small shop. We can't take most clients due to time constraints. We usually say 'no' to artists seeking representation."
How to Contact: Writers who wish to be considered by Vintage Entertainment must first e-mail a succinct logline describing the screenplay they wish to have reviewed. If we have interest in reading your material, we will send you our submission release form via e-mail."
Tips: "Approximately 5% of all artists who approach us get reviewed. In many respects, we are similar to other companies who do what we do—except we don't beat around the bush. We won't regurgitate the stock phrase: 'I'm sorry, we don't accept unsolicited material.' The reality? We don't take material for many reasons, but not that reason. We may have something like it. We may not know how to sell it or make it. We may not like the idea. Whatever we think, you'll hear it. Many artists find our honesty offensive. We accept that risk."

Script Contests

New this year, this section contains script contests. Besides cash awards or other prizes, winning a contest can give you credibility when querying an agent. Especially impressive to agents are winners of the more prestigious contests such as the Nicholl Fellowships in Screenwriting, the Chesterfield Writer's Film Project, or the writing fellowship program sponsored by the Walt Disney Studios and ABC.

Contests can get you recognition from producers or catch the attention of other industry professionals who sponsor or judge the contests. Even making it to the final round of these contests can give you credibility as a screenwriter and should be mentioned in your query letter when you're ready to find an agent. Some contests may even lead directly to representation by an agency as part of the prize package.

Again, it's always a good idea to register your script before submitting it. The WGA offers a registration service to members and nonmembers alike. Membership in the WGA is earned through the accumulation of professional credits and carries a number of significant benefits. Write the Guild for more information on specific agencies, script registration, and membership requirements, or visit them online at www.wga.org.

Contest deadlines, entry fees, and rules may vary from year to year, so it's a good idea to visit the contest's website or send an SASE requesting their rules and regulations before submitting. Contests often require a specific entry form that you may either request by mail or download from their website. Some deadlines are extended at the last minute, so be sure you have the latest information available before entering. You may want those extra weeks to polish your manuscript one last time.

For more listings of screenwriting contests, see www.moviebytes.com or www.scriptsales.com.

N AMERICAN CINEMA FOUNDATION SCREENWRITING COMPETITION, American Cinema Foundation, 9911 W. Pico Blvd., Suite 510, Los Angeles CA 90035. (310)286-9420. Fax: (310)286-7914. E-mail: acinema@cinemafoundation.com. Website: www.cinemafoundation.com. **Contact:** Gary McVey, executive director. Offered annually to elicit scripts suitable for either theatrical or television production and that tell a positive story about specific, fundamental values and their importance to society. **Deadline:** March. Visit website for deadlines and guidelines. Charges $30 fee. **Prize:** $10,000 (first); $5,000 (second); $5,000 (third). Judged by industry professionals. Prominent Hollywood agents will read all winning scripts. Contest open to anyone. One entry per author. Entry must follow contest theme (visit website for current theme). Previous theme was "The Pursuit of Excellence." Winners notified in fall.

N AMERICAN SCREENWRITERS ASSOCIATION/WRITER'S DIGEST INTERNATIONAL SCREENPLAY COMPETITION, 4700 E. Galbraith Rd., Cincinnati OH 45236. (513)531-2690, ext. 1328. E-mail: competitions@fwpubs.com. Website: www.goasa.com. **Contact:** Terri Boes. Offered annually to assist and recognize screenwriters through networking, educational seminars and industry connections. **Deadline:** October15, 2002; October 31, 2002 (late). Charges $40 for ASA members; $50 for nonmembers. $45/$55 (late) after October 15. **Prize:** $2,500 (first); $1,000 (second); $500 (third); $250 (fourth); $100 (fifth). Names and loglines of all winners will be announced to the media and posted on www.asascreenwriters.com and www.writersdigest. com; one year subscription to *Writer's Digest Magazine*; one year membership in the ASA. Competition is judged by professional representatives of the film and screenwriting community. Open to everyone. Scripts must be between 80-120 pages and must be original work not sold or optioned at time of entry.

N THE CHESTERFIELD WRITER'S FILM PROJECT, Paramount Pictures, PMB 544, 1158 26th St., Santa Monica CA 90403. (213)683-3977. E-mail: info@chesterfield-co.com. Website: www.chesterfield-co.com. Offered annually to give fiction, theater, and film writers the opportunity to begin a career in screenwriting. **Deadline:** May 15. Charges $39.50 fee. **Prize:** $20,000 for up to five writers to cover living expenses during their fellowship year in a screenwriting workshop in Los Angeles where writers will be mentored by film professionals and will each write 2 original, feature-length screenplays. Writers are introduced to agents at the end of the year. Winner's scripts are considered under option. Open to any writer of fiction, theater or film. Writers may submit a novel, short story, play or screenplay.

N: THE CYNOSURE SCREENWRITING AWARDS, 3699 Wilshire Blvd., Suite 850, Los Angeles CA 90010. (310)855-8730. E-mail: cynosure@broadmindent.com. Website: www.broadmindent.com. **Co-Director:** Andrea Hamilton. To recognize and award cash prizes to quality concept and character driven screenplays featuring female and minority protagonists. Charges $40 fee (early); $50 fee (late). Offers two $2,000 cash prizes (best script with a female protagonist; best script with a minority, either male or female, protagonist). Open to all writers in any country (written in English only). Scripts must be registered with the WGA or with the US copyright office.

N: THE WALT DISNEY STUDIOS AND ABC ENTERTAINMENT WRITING FELLOWSHIP PROGRAM, 500 S. Buena Vista St., Burbank CA 91521-0705. (818)560-6894. E-mail: abc.fellowships@abc.com. Website: www.abcnewtalent.disney.com. Offered annually. to discover new creative voices and to employ culturally and ethnically diverse talent. **Deadline:** July 6. Finalists notified in winter. Guidelines for SASE, online or by phone. Charges no fee. **Prize:** $50,000 salary for up to 12 writers during Fellowship year. Fellowship winners will work full-time at the Walt Disney Studios and ABC Entertainment beginning in January. Fellows must be willing to relocate to Los Angeles. Acquires rights to all materials written during the term of the Fellowship Program. Open to any writer. Writers must submit application, standard letter agreement, résumé or biography, and a writing sample between June 1st and July 6th. For feature film, writers should submit 100-120 pages or a 2-3 act play. For television, a half-hour or one-hour TV script based on a current prime time TV series or a full-length play. No treatments, outlines, short stories, poems, books, articles, adaptations, musicals or original TV pilots.

N: FILMMAKERS MAGAZINE/THE RADMIN COMPANY SCREENWRITING COMPETITION, Filmmakers Magazine/The Radmin Company, P.O. Box 54050, Irvine CA 92619. E-mail: contest@filmmakers.com. Website: www.filmmakers.com/contests/2002/m.htm. **Contact:** William Masterson. Submissions should be unproduced, unoptioned, unsold. Purpose of contest is to make Hollywood more accessible than ever before to more aspiring screenwriters. **Deadline:** September 10, 2002 (early); January 31, 2003 (final). E-mail or visit website for entry form and guidelines. Charges $38 (by September 10, 2002); $48 (by January 31, 2003). **Prize:** $8,500 in cash and prizes. Top 10 finalists will receive Script Notes and consideration for representation. Top 5 will win free tuition to The Screenwriting Conference in Santa Fe (SCSFe). Top 5 get 5 minutes to pitch their winning scripts to Hollywood producers looking for and accepting scripts written by unproduced/unrepresented writers. Top 5 win live scene readings of their script and get to mingle at social events with invited professional writers, producers and directors at the Screenwriting Conference. Top 50 scripts will be read by the Radmin Company. Top 10 scripts will be read by The Radmin Company, industry professionals, production companies, literary agents. Top 50 scripts will be announced March 3, 2003. Submissions must be full-length film or television movie scripts in any genre. Multiple entries OK. Adaptations from other works OK with writer's written permission to adapt. *Only the title of the script should appear on the front cover.* Writer's name should only appear on entry form. Open to anyone (worldwide).

N: FINAL DRAFT'S "BIG BREAK" INTERNATIONAL SCREENWRITING COMPETITION, Final Draft Software, 16000 Ventura Blvd., Suite 800, Encino CA 91436. (818)995-8995. Fax: (818)995-4422. E-mail: info@finaldraft.com. Website: www.finaldraft.com. Offered annually for a chance to have winner's screenplay read by top industry professionals. Contact contest officials for current deadlines. Visit website for additional guidelines. Charges $50 fee. **Prize:** $10,000, trip to Los Angeles (round-trip coach airfare, 3 nights hotel) and meetings with industry executives (first); $3,000 (second); $1,000 (third). Top 10 winners also receive a) script submission to major Hollywood literary agent; b) Final Draft software; c) one-year subscription to *Creative Screenwriting and Script Magazine;* d) $50 gift card for The Writers Store; e) The Hollywood Creative Directory Producers Guide. Open to anyone. All submissions should be full length, standard industry format and be written in English. Include your name, address, phone number and e-mail address on the title page of your screenplay.

N: GREAT LAKES FILM ASSOCIATION SCREENPLAY COMPETITION, Great Lakes Film Association Screenplay Competition, 100 Nordmere Dr., #9, Edinboro PA 16412. (814)734-6759. E-mail: george@greatlakesfilmfest.com. Website: www.greatlakesfilmfest.com. **Executive Director:** George Woods. Offered annually to unproduced, unoptioned, unsold new and veteran screenwriters to possibly get the break they need. Contact contest officials for current deadlines or visit website. Charges $35 (early); $45 (late). **Prize:** Money, awards, and the top 15 screenplays will be passed along to an industry professional agency. Open to any writer 18 years of age or older. No previous produced film credits. Screenplays must be 80 pages or more. Multiple entries allowed, but each entry must be accompanied by their completed entry from and their own appropriate entry fee.

N: HOLLYWOOD'S NEXT SUCCESS SCREENWRITING CONTEST, 4647 Kingswell Ave., Los Angeles CA 90027. E-mail: hollywoodsns@hotmail.com. Website: www.hollywoodsnextsuccess.com. **Contact:**

Michelle Miller. To recognize writing talent wherever it may be. Visit website for guidelines and entry form. Charges $24 (early); $34 (regular). All winners guaranteed at least 5 requests for their script from agents, producers, studios, etc. Possible immediate option deal or offer of representation. Open to any writer.

N: LIGHTHOUSE SCRIPTS, P.O. Box 551024, Dallas TX 75355-1024. (972)705-9915. E-mail: lighthousesc ripts@prodigy.net. Website: http://pages.prodigy.net/lighthousescripts. **Contact:** T.A. Newton, founder. Submissions required to be unproduced, unoptioned. To give unknown, unproduced writers professional feedback and professional contacts concerning their work. **Deadline:** December 16, 2002. Charges $60. Written critiques. **Prize:** $1,000 (grand prize); $700 (2nd place); $500 (3rd place). Winning scripts and those honorably mentioned will be read by talent agency. Winners and honorable mentions will have their name and script titles published in screenwriting magazines and posted on several industry websites. Open to all writers worldwide—scripts must be written in English, standard industry format and bound. No adaptations. Title page should include author's name, address and telephone number. Do not send original: script will not be returned. If writer is under 10 years of age, script must be submitted by legal guardian. Winners notified March 16, 2003.

N: NEW CENTURY WRITER AWARDS, 32 Alfred St., Suite B, New Haven CT 06512-3927. (203)469-8824. Fax: (203)468-0333. E-mail: newcenturywriter.org. Website: www.newcenturywriter.org. **Contact:** Jason J. Marding, executive director. Offered annually to recognize the quality screenplays, TV scripts, TV movie scripts and musicals of both unpublished and nonproduced writers, as well as writers with few production credits, and to connect these writers with film industry professionals. Visit website for deadlines and guidelines. Charges $30 fee. **Prize:** $3,000 (first place); $1,500 (second place); $500 (third place). Cash awards for remaining top ten scripts. A listing and synopsis of the top ten screenplays is sent to allied production companies. Open to all writers living in any country. Enter one screenplay/stage play/novel/novella (or an excerpt of a novel/novella-in progress) per each $30 entry fee. Seeks character-driven stories for its film art house alliances, and big budget, high concept stories for its Hollywood studio alliances, in all genres. Multiple submissions OK. A single check may accompany multiple submissions. More than one title may be listed on a single application form and release agreement.

N: NICHOLL FELLOWSHIPS IN SCREENWRITING, Academy of Motion Picture Arts and Sciences, 8949 Wilshire Blvd., Beverly Hills CA 90211-1972. (310)247-3000. E-mail: nicholl@oscars.org. Website: www.o scars.org/nicholl. Offered annually. **Deadline:** May 1st. Guidelines for SASE or on website between January and late April. Charges $30 fee. **Prize:** $30,000 for up to five writers. Judged by academy members in the quarter final round. Open to writers who have not earned more than $5,000 for screenwriting. Writers may submit a 100-130 page, original feature film screenplay in standard industry form.

N: PRODUCERS OUTREACH PROGRAM—SCRIPTWRITERS NETWORK, Producers Outreach Program—Scriptwriters Network, 11684 Ventury Blvd., Suite 508, Studio City CA 91604. (303)848-9477. E-mail: thatsarap2001@yahoo.com. Website: www.scriptwritersnetwork.com/prodrech.html. **Contact:** Andrew Pigott, chairman. Offered quarterly to have unagented scripts read by producers/production companies. Charges $30 for Scriptwriters Network members; $60 for WGA members. **Prize:** Guaranteed read by producers/production companies; guaranteed feedback on the writer's work. Must be a member of Scriptwriters Network or WGA (Writers Guild of America). Visit website to join the Scriptwriters Network.

N: SCREENWRITING EXPO SCREENPLAY CONTEST, 6404 Hollywood Blvd., Suite 415, Los Angeles CA 90028. (323)957-1405. Fax: (323)957-1406. E-mail: jim@screenwritingexpo.com. Website: http:// screenwritingexpo.com/competition.html. **Contact:** Jim Mercurio, contest director. Offered for unproduced, un-optioned submissions. Writers of previously produced or optioned material must not have earned more than $8,000 for their or won a fellowship or contest. Offered to reward what Creative Screenwriting has been celebrating for the past 9 years—the art and craft of screenwriting. **Deadline:** August 1 (early); October 1 (final). Visit website for guidelines. Charges $35 (early entry); $40 (regular). Discount for multiple submissions. **Prize:** $5,000 to winner. Other prizes: trips to LA to attend Expo; access to agents, producers and managers; script consultations; software; and magazine subscriptions. Writers who have won a fellowship or contest with a "first look" clause are ineligible. Submissions must be postmarked by October 1, 2002. Screenplays by more than one writer are eligible but only one prize will be given and it will be the winner's responsibility to distribute the prize. Winners notified first week of November 2002. Visit website for further guidelines.

N: SCR(I)PT MAGAZINE'S OPEN DOOR CONTEST, Diversion Films, 5638 Sweet Air Rd., Baldwin MD 21013. (888)245-2228. Fax: (410)592-8062. E-mail: contests@scriptmag.com. Website: www.scriptmag.c om. **Contact:** Marisa Conna, marketing director. To discover, promote, and recognize a talented new screenwriter by awarding them cash and by giving them direct access to companies looking for new material. **Deadline:** August. Visit website for guidelines. Charges $45 (US). **Prize:** $3,000 cash from Scr(i)pt. Notes and consideration for production from Dimension Films, software, books, and more. Open to anyone. Visit website for rules and details.

N: SCRIPT WORLD 2003, Venice Arts and Zeta Entertainment, 8265 Sunset Blvd., Suite 209, W. Hollywood CA 90046. E-mail: contest@scriptworld.info. Website: www.scriptworld.info. **Contact:** Lisa Jones, co-director. The screenwriting competition was established in response to various production companies requesting a conduit in which to identify and mentor new screenwriters. Our goal is to pursue the development of innovative screenwriting programs to support both the local community in Los Angeles and the worldwide community via the Internet. Visit website for deadlines (February, March, April) and guidelines. Charges $40-60, depending on how early you submit ($5 discount for online submissions). **Prize:** $5,000 (first), $1,000 (second) and $500 (third) in cash and prizes plus Final Draft professional screenwriting software. First place also receives directorial and screenwriting seminar tuitions, as well as consideration for option by Zeta Entertainment. One of the top 3 winners will be selected for a Drama Garage Reading. The contest is open to any writer without produced feature film credits.

N: SCRIPTAPALOOZA SCREENWRITING COMPETITION, 7775 Sunset Blvd., Suite 200, Hollywood CA 90046. (323)654-5809. E-mail: info@scriptapalooza.com. Website: www.scriptapalooza.com. **Contact:** Mark Andrushko, president and CEO. Submissions required to be unproduced and unoptioned. Offered with the goal of helping as many writers as possible through the competition. **Deadline:** January 2 ($40); March 1 ($45); May 7 ($50). Visit website for current guidelines. Charges $40-50 fee. **Prize:** $10,000 (first); top 13 scriptwriters receive software and consideration by production companies and literary representatives. This competition is open to any writer, 18 or older without produced feature film credits. Scripts must be accompanied by a) completed official entry form, b) the appropriate entry fee, c) completed original feature screenplay. Multiple entries are OK, provided a signed entry form and entry fee is attached to each submission. Multiple authorship is acceptable. Screenplays must be the original work of the author. Registering scripts with the WGA or copyrighting your material with the Library of Congress is recommended.

N: SCRIPTREP.COM, PMB 360, 7095 Hollywood Blvd., Los Angeles CA 90028. E-mail: info@scriptrep.com. Website: www.scriptrep.com. **Contact:** Brian Hennessy. Submissions must be unoptioned. Scriptrep.com seeks to introduce aspiring screenwriters to the Hollywood film industry. **Deadline:** July 1. Charges $25 (check or money order only) fee. **Prize:** $1,000 cash and a pitch meeting with a working Hollywood professional. All submissions must be typewritten with a minimum of 50 pages and a maximum of 130 pages. Any script entered after 200 submissions are received will automatically be entered into the next contest. Sign entry form with terms and conditions attached and enclose screenplay along with entry fee.

N: SCRIPTWRITERS NETWORK/CARL SAUTTER MEMORIAL SCRIPTWRITING COMPETITION, 11684 Ventura Blvd., Suite 508, Studio City CA 91604. (323)848-9477. Website: http://scriptwritersnetwork.com. **Contact:** Billy Lundy. Submissions required to be unoptioned. Offered as part of a nonprofit, all volunteer run support and networking organization for people pursuing a screenwriting career. **Deadline:** February 8. Visit website for guidelines. Charges $35 for 1st script, $30 for any additional scripts. **Prize:** Guaranteed reads by major production companies/agencies/networks/show winners; books, gift certificates, movie passes, subscriptions, computer software, free writing seminars/conferences (including "Selling to Hollywood"). Cool trophy. You must be a current member of the Network or join at time of competition entry. Open to scripts for feature films, MOWs, 1-hour and ½hour TV. No limit on number of entries per person.

N: SLAMDANCE FILM FESTIVAL SCREENPLAY COMPETITION, 5634 Melrose Ave., Los Angeles CA 90038. (323)466-1786. Fax: (323)466-1784. E-mail: screenplay@slamdance.com. Website: www.slamdance.com/screencomp. **Contact:** Cianna Chuchere. Submissions required to be unproduced, unoptioned, unpurchased. The purpose of the competition is to recognize and support new filmmakers and screenwriters on an ongoing basis. **Deadline:** March (early); June (late). Visit website for guidelines. Charges $45 (early), $55 (final) fee. **Prizes:** Cash, software and free coverage. Competition open to writers who have never had a script produced. Screenplays must be in English. Screenplays must be feature length 70-130 pages or short length 1-60 pages typed in 12-point Courier font. Writers with a previous feature screenplay produced and distributed are ineligible.

N: STEP UP WOMEN'S NETWORK SCREENWRITING CONTEST, 8424-A Santa Monica Blvd., #857, West Hollywood CA 90069. (323)549-5347. E-mail: stepupsymposium@aol.com. Website: www.stepupwomensnetwork.org. Submissions required to be unproduced, unoptioned, unsold. Step Up's Screenwriting Contest is an event in which unknown and untapped screenwriters have an exceptional opportunity to gain knowledge of script development and make contact with agents, writers, producers and directors. Visit website for deadlines and guidelines. Charges $35 fee. **Prize:** $3,000 (first), a pitch meeting with a prominent management/production company, and the opportunity to be interviewed on Zide/Perry Entertainment's website, www.Inzide.com, a heavily trafficed website for writers; $500 (runner-up) and a pitch meeting. Both finalists and runner-up will be the focus of a one-day workshop, The Writers Lab. Screenplays must be the original work of the applicant's. If based on author's life, applicant(s) must include a grant of their rights to use the story. Any genre will be considered. It is the applicant's sole responsibility to register or copyright the material. You may submit more than one screenplay, but each must be accompanied by an entry form, release and entry fee. Screenplays will not be returned. Applicant's name, address or phone number should not appear on the cover, title page, or any other pages.

N THE SUNDANCE FEATURE FILM PROGRAM, The Sundance Institute, 8857 W. Olympic Blvd., Beverly Hills CA 90211. (310)394-4662. Website: www.sundance.org. **Contact:** Michelle Satter. The Sundance Institute is interested in supporting original, compelling, human stories that reflect the independent vision of the writer and/or writer/director. Visit website for spring deadlines and guidelines. Charges $30 fee. **Prize:** Participation in the prestigious residential lab and travel expenses. 10-15 winners. Non-US citizens living abroad cannot be considered. Do not send the screenplay. Submit an application, cover letter, résumé/bio, synopsis not to exceed two pages, first five pages of the script, and the entry fee.

N WINNER TAKE ALL SCREENWRITING & SHORT FILM COMPETITION, 10606 Camino Ruiz, #8-352, San Diego CA 92126. (619)991-1926. E-mail: info@winner-takeall.com. Website: www.winner-takeall.com. **Contact:** John Goodman. Submissions required to be unproduced. "Winner Take All is a screenwriting and filmmaking contest with rules that favor talent. Not arbitrary opinions." **Deadline:** May 15 ($40); June 30 ($45); August 15 ($50); December 2 ($55). Visit website for guidelines. Charges $40-55, depending on early or late submission. **Prize:** $5,000 and production company/agent consideration. Open to anyone without produced feature film credits.

N WRITEMOVIES.COM, 1041 N. Formosa Ave., Fomosa Bldg., Suite 214, West Hollywood CA 90046. E-mail: agr@writemovies.com. Website: www.writemovies.com. **Contact:** Alex Ross, founder. The purpose of this contest is to find the best screenplays, books, plays, short stories and articles with cinematic potential. Visit our website for deadlines and guidelines. Charges $29 (early); $39 (late); $49 (books) fee. **Prize:** $2,000, trip to LA to meet producers and agents, top three projects submitted to the studios and production companies; up to $70,000 in option moneys from Russ WW Media Productions; Final Draft software plus, the top three entries will be pitched to high-ranking executives at all the studios; a minimum of ten production companies (such as Castle Rock, Bruckheimer Films, and Scott Rudin Productions); and several literary agencies. Material is also submitted to non-US companies. Open to anyone (material written in English, French and German allowed). No material that has been shopped around the industry. Submissions will not be returned.

N WRITERS NETWORK SCREENPLAY COMPETITION, 289 S. Robertson Blvd., Beverly Hills CA 90211. (800)646-3896. Fax: (310)275-0298. E-mail: writersnet@aol.com. Website: www.fadeinonline.com. **Contact:** Audrey Kelly. Purpose of competition is to give new and talented writers the chance to pursue a career in film and television. **Deadline:** May. Visit website for guidelines. Charges $35 fee. **Prize:** $2,000 cash award and representation for up to 2 projects for 1 year. Judged by industry professionals including agents from ICM, William Morris, Endeavor and UTA. Open to screenwriters, playwrights, TV writers and novelists worldwide. "Competition is based solely on storytelling talent."

Independent Publicists

You spent years writing your book, then several more months sending queries to agents. You finally find an agent who loves your work, but then you have to wait even more time as she submits your manuscript to editors. After a few months, your agent closes a great deal for your work with a publishing house you really admire. Now you can sit back and wait for the money to start rolling in, right?

If you've learned anything about publishing so far, you've learned that getting a book published takes a lot of work. And once you find a publisher, your work doesn't stop. You have to focus now on selling your book to make money and to ensure that publishing companies will work with you again. Industry experts estimate that 50,000 books are published each year in the U.S. This number is only going to increase with the ease of Internet publishing. What can you do to ensure that your book succeeds with this amount of competition?

While most publishing houses do have in-house publicists, their time is often limited and priority is usually given to big-name authors who have already proved they will make money for the publisher. Often writers feel their books aren't getting the amount of publicity they had hoped for. Because of this, many authors have decided to work with an independent publicist.

To help you market your book after publication, we've included a section of independent publicists, or speakers' agents, in this book. Like agents, publicists view publishing as a business. And their business goal is to see that your book succeeds. And usually publicists are more than happy to work in conjunction with your editor, your publisher, and your agent. Together they can form a strong team that will help make you a publishing sensation.

What to look for in a publicist

When choosing an independent publicist, you'll want someone who has business savvy and experience in sales. And, of course, you'll want someone who is enthusiastic about you and your writing. When looking through the listings in this section, look at each person's experience both prior to and after becoming a publicist. The radio and television shows on which their clients have appeared can indicate the caliber of their contacts, and the recent promotions they have done for their clients' books can reveal their level of creativity.

You'll also want to look for a publicist who is interested in your subject area. Like agents and publishing houses, most independent publicists specialize. By focusing on specific areas, publicists can actually do more for their clients. For example, if a publicist is interested in cookbooks, she can send her clients to contacts she has on Cooking Network shows, editors at gourmet cooking magazines, bookstores which have cafés, and culinary conferences. The more knowledge a publicist has about your subject, the more opportunities she will find to publicize your work.

How to make the initial contact

Contacting independent publicists should be much less stressful than the query process you've gone through to find an agent. Most publicists are open to a phone call, though some still prefer to receive a letter or an e-mail as the initial contact. Often you can receive a referral to a publicist through an agent, an editor, or even another writer. Because publicists do cost more out-of-pocket money than an agent, there isn't the same competition for their time. Of course, not every publicist you call will be the best fit for you. Be prepared to hear that the publicist already has a full client load, or even that she doesn't have the level of interest in your work that you want a publicist to have.

How much money should I spend?

As you read over the listings of independent publicists, you'll quickly notice that many charge a substantial amount of money for their services. The cost of a publicist can be daunting, especially to a new writer. *You should only pay what you feel comfortable paying and what you can reasonably afford.* Keep in mind, however, that any money you spend on publicity will come back to you in the form of more sold books. A general rule of thumb is to budget one dollar for every copy of your book that is printed. For a print run of 10,000, you should expect to spend $10,000.

There are ways you can make working with a publicist less of a strain on your purse strings. If you received an advance for your book, you can use part of it to help with your marketing expenses. Some publishers will agree to match the amount of money an author pays on outside publicity. If your publicist's bill is $2,000, you would pay half and your publisher would pay the other half. Be sure to ask your publishing house if this option is available to you. Most publicists are very willing to work with their clients on a marketing budget.

"WE WANT TO PUBLISH YOUR WORK."

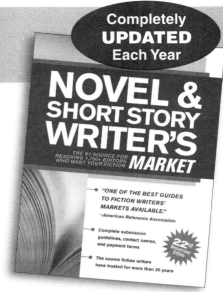

You would give anything to hear an editor speak those six magic words. So you work hard for weeks, months, even years to make that happen. You create a brilliant piece of work and a knock-out presentation, but there's still one vital step to ensure publication. You still need to submit your work to the right buyers. With rapid changes in the publishing industry it's not always easy to know who those buyers are. That's why each year thousands of writers, just like you, turn to the most current edition of this indispensable market guide.

Keep ahead of the changes by ordering *2004 Novel & Short Story Writer's Market* today! You'll save the frustration of getting manuscripts returned in the mail stamped MOVED: ADDRESS UNKNOWN, and of NOT submitting your work to new listings because you don't know they exist. All you have to do to order next year's edition — at this year's price — is complete the attached order card and return it with your payment. Lock in the 2003 price for 2004 — order today!

2004 Novel & Short Story Writer's Market will be published and ready for shipment in November 2003.

New Writer's Digest Books!

The Complete Handbook of Novel Writing
This compilation of the best interviews from *Writer's Digest* magazine, books and annuals will guide you through the craft, art and process of writing your novel. Includes interviews and articles from bestselling authors including Margaret Atwood, Tom Clancy, James Patterson, Nora Roberts, Kurt Vonnegut and more!
#10825-K/$17.99/400p/pb

Writing Mysteries
Second Edition
Sue Grafton weaves the expertise of America's top mystery writers into a comprehensive mystery "how-to." Contributors include Jonathan Kellerman, Sara Paretsky, Michael Connelly, and more!
#10782-K/$16.99/256p/pb

Urge to Kill
Don't undercut the effectiveness of your crime novel with procedural and technical inaccuracies — delve into this compelling mix of case studies, instruction and photographs to create believable crime scenes, plots and characters.
#10795-K/$24.99/192p/pb

The Criminal Mind
Correct common misconceptions about the criminal psyche to create credible characters. Plus, discover how forensic psychology is used to catch nefarious n'er-do-wells.
10763-K/$17.99/256p/pb

Fiction First Aid
Instantly heal those wounded spots in your manuscript — where it's just not working — with these clever remedies modeled after a first-aid manual. Novice and more experienced writers alike will learn to diagnose problems, review specific cures, and apply therapies to avoid problems in the future.
#10722-K/$16.99/256p/pb

2003 Guide to Literary Agents
Your search for powerful representation and the perfect writer's contract begins here. Find the right agent to get your fiction, nonfiction or screenplay into the hands of the publishers who can make your dreams come true! With 100% updated listings of 600+ agents who sell what you write.
#10811-K/$23.99/400p/pb

How to Find the Publicist You Need

BY JAY CONRAD LEVINSON, RICK FRISHMAN & MICHAEL LARSEN

When you look for a publicist, take the following factors into consideration:

1. Book publicity is a specialty. You need someone with experience promoting books on a national scale, someone who has contacts with trade and consumer print, broadcast and electronic book media around the country. When you hire a publicist, you are basically paying for four things: ability, contacts, experience and enthusiasm.

   It's not that a publicist who promotes clothing doesn't have the ability to help you. In fact, if you were writing a book about clothing, such a publicist might be your best bet even though he or she has no book experience.

   That concern aside, the ideal publicist for you is the one who
   - is the most successful
   - has the most experience
   - is the most passionate about your book
   - you have the most confidence in

2. The rapport you establish with the publicist is also a key factor in choosing one. As with your agent and editor, try to meet with the publicist before you make a commitment.

   If you can, meet prospective publicists, see their offices, the press materials they produce for their clients and what they have accomplished for clients. Be sure to meet any other publicists in the agency as well as anybody else in the office who will be involved with your book. Talk to present and former clients to learn what it's like to work with the agency. You want someone with whom you will enjoy working.

   Only your books are more important to your success than the personal relationships you create, and no relationship is more important than the one between you and your publicist.

3. Geography may be a factor in your decision. Does a publicist have to be in New York City to be effective? Not every publicist in New York is a genius, and there are many excellent publicists who reside elsewhere. Some of them were staff or freelance publicists in New York before they literally headed out to greener pastures.

   What you need is a publicist who can convince you that, based on the agency's experience and results, he can do the job you want done.

   Another factor to consider: If you will hire a publicist whom you will mention in the promotion plan you send to New York publishers, try to make it someone whose name at least the staff publicists will know. Better still, her name should be recognized by the editor and others whose enthusiasm will help convince the house to buy the book.

   If nobody recognizes the name, they won't have a clue how effective the publicist is. This diminishes the value of your commitment. This is more of a problem with out-of-town publicists, because publishers may feel that if publicists are in the Big Apple, they must know what they're doing.

   If you're going to hire a publicist whose name big publishers won't recognize, solve this problem in advance by including
   - how long the publicist has been in business
   - whether the publicist has worked in New York

This article is excerpted from Guerrilla Marketing for Writers © *2001 by* **JAY CONRAD LEVINSON, RICK FRISHMAN** *and* **MICHAEL LARSEN**. *Used with kind permission from Writer's Digest Books, a division of F&W Publications. For credit card orders phone toll free 1-800-448-0915.*

- the titles of successful books from New York houses for which the publicist ran national campaigns
- any other information that will raise the publisher's comfort level
- the publicist's brochure if it's impressive

4. The best time to contact prospective publicists is after you've prepared the first version of your promotion plan. Your plan will benefit from the practical advice of a pro. Publishers who receive your work will assume that the publicist you mention in your plan assisted you in preparing it. Having your publicist advise you on how to create your promotion plan will increase the likelihood your book will sell.

Ask prospective publicists to advise you on how to prepare a publicity campaign for your book using what's left of your budget after your other expenses are accounted for. Then together, you can integrate your plan with his and write the final version.

After you and your publicist agree on the most effective plan for promoting your book, ballpark the cost of every item so you can come up with a reasonably accurate "guesstimate" of the total that is best for your budget. It can't be exact, but it also can't be too far off base, or publishers will think that either the plan or the budget is not realistic.

5. How flexible a publicist is about structuring fees may affect your choice. If publicists are short on experience, they will be more eager to make a mark in the field and perhaps more open to trying new ideas. As in other fields, their fees will reflect their experience.

Among the questions for you to ask publicists about fees are:

- Would the publicist be willing to accept being written into the contract to receive a certain percentage of the royalties? This would certainly be an incentive for the publicist to go all-out to make sure your book is successful. Advertising agencies working with high-tech start-ups are taking stock instead of cash. Mint those guerrilla greenbacks any way you can.
- Would the publicist accept being used on an assignment basis, for example, to create a news release and then let you send it out?
- Would the publicist be willing to serve only as a consultant?
  She can
    —share the sample press kits with you
    —give you feedback on the publicity materials you create

The basic notion: the publicist shows you what to do, you do it, and the publicist looks over your shoulder to make sure you're doing it right.

Publicity organizations have monthly meetings with guest speakers and helpful monthly newsletters. Joining one or more of them is a worthwhile investment for building your network and keeping up to speed on new developments in the field.

Questions to Ask a Publicist Before Hiring One

You need answers to the following questions. But before you ask them, research the answers in directories and in agencies' brochures, media kits and websites. Publicists will be impressed with your professionalism if you know about them before you meet.

- How long have you been in business?
- Have you handled any books like mine?
- I have a budget of $X. What's the best way for you to help me within that budget?
- What is your payment schedule?
- Are you a member of any professional associations?
- How do you like to work with your clients?
- When should I expect to hear from you?
- How can I help you?

Independent Publicists

When reading through the listings of independent publicists, use the following key to help you fully understand the information provided:

SUBHEADS FOR QUICK ACCESS TO INFORMATION

Each listing is broken down into subheads to make locating specific information easier. In this first paragraph, you'll find contact information for each independent publicist. Further information is provided which indicates the company's size and experience in the publishing industry. **Members:** To help you find a publicist with a firm understanding of your book's subject and audience, we include the names of all publicists and their specialties. The year the member joined the company is also provided, indicating an individual's familiarity with book publicity. **Specializations:** Similar to the agents listed in this book, most publicists have specific areas

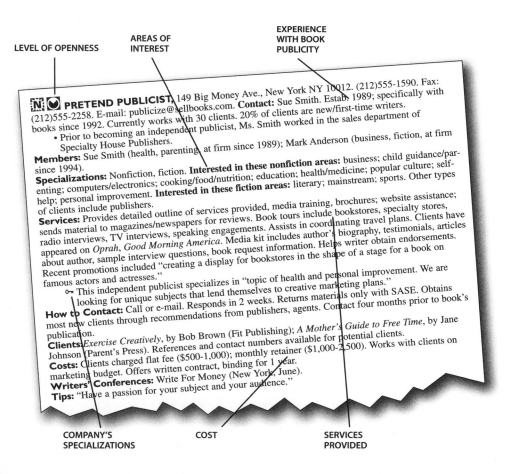

LEVEL OF OPENNESS

AREAS OF INTEREST

EXPERIENCE WITH BOOK PUBLICITY

PRETEND PUBLICIST, 149 Big Money Ave., New York NY 10012. (212)555-1590. Fax: (212)555-2258. E-mail: publicize@sellbooks.com. **Contact:** Sue Smith. Estab. 1989; specifically with books since 1992. Currently works with 30 clients. 20% of clients are new/first-time writers.
• Prior to becoming an independent publicist, Ms. Smith worked in the sales department of Specialty House Publishers.
Members: Sue Smith (health, parenting, at firm since 1989); Mark Anderson (business, fiction, at firm since 1994).
Specializations: Nonfiction, fiction. **Interested in these nonfiction areas:** business; child guidance/parenting; computers/electronics; cooking/food/nutrition; education; health/medicine; popular culture; self-help; personal improvement. **Interested in these fiction areas:** literary; mainstream; sports. Other types of clients include publishers.
Services: Provides detailed outline of services provided, media training, brochures; website assistance; sends material to magazines/newspapers for reviews. Book tours include bookstores, specialty stores, radio interviews, TV interviews, speaking engagements. Assists in coordinating travel plans. Clients have appeared on *Oprah*, *Good Morning America*. Media kit includes author's biography, testimonials, articles about author, sample interview questions, book request information. Helps writer obtain endorsements. Recent promotions included "creating a display for bookstores in the shape of a stage for a book on famous actors and actresses."
  ◑ This independent publicist specializes in "topic of health and personal improvement. We are looking for unique subjects that lend themselves to creative marketing plans."
How to Contact: Call or e-mail. Responds in 2 weeks. Returns materials only with SASE. Obtains most new clients through recommendations from publishers, agents. Contact four months prior to book's publication.
Clients: *Exercise Creatively*, by Bob Brown (Fit Publishing); *A Mother's Guide to Free Time*, by Jane Johnson (Parent's Press). References and contact numbers available for potential clients.
Costs: Clients charged flat fee ($500-1,000); monthly retainer ($1,000-2,500). Works with clients on marketing budget. Offers written contract, binding for 1 year.
Writers' Conferences: Write For Money (New York, June).
Tips: "Have a passion for your subject and your audience."

COMPANY'S SPECIALIZATIONS

COST

SERVICES PROVIDED

Quick Reference Icons

- **[N]** Independent publicist new to this edition.
- **○** New independent publicist actively seeking clients.
- **◐** Independent publicist interested in working with both new and established writers.
- **◑** Independent publicist open only to established writers.
- **◎** Independent publicist who specializes in specific types of work.
- **⊘** Independent publicist not currently open to new clients.

of interest. A publicist with a knowledge of your book's subject will have contacts in your field and a solid sense of your audience.

Services: This subhead provides important details about what the publicist can do for you, including a list of services available for clients, book tour information, television shows on which clients have appeared, contents of media kits, and examples of recent promotions done by the publicist.

☞ Look for the key icon to quickly learn the publicist's areas of specialization and specific marketing strengths.

How to Contact: Unlike literary agents, most independent publicists are open to phone calls, letters, and e-mail—check this subhead to see the individual publicist's preference. Also pay close attention to the time frame the publicist needs between your initial contact and your book's publication date.

Clients: To give a better sense of their areas of interest, independent publicists list authors they have helped to promote. Publicists also indicate here if they are willing to provide potential clients with references.

Costs: Specific details are provided on how publicists charge their clients. Although the costs seem high, the payback in terms of books sold is usually worth the additional expense. Publicists indicate if they work with clients on a marketing budget and if they offer a written contract.

Writers' Conferences: A great way to meet and learn more about publicists is at writers' conferences. Here publicists list the ones they attend. For more information about a specific conference, check the **Writers' Conferences** section starting on page 283.

Tips: Advice and additional instructions are given for writers interested in working with an independent publicist.

SPECIAL INDEXES

Independent Publicists Indexed by Openness to Submissions: This index lists publicists according to their receptivity to new clients.

Geographic Index: For writers looking for an agent close to home, this index lists independent publicists state-by-state.

Listing Index: This index lists all agencies, independent publicists, and writers' conferences listed in the book.

For More Information

For more information on working with independent publicists, read "How to Find the Publicist You Need" beginning on page 267.

◗ ACHESON-GREUB, INC., P.O. Box 735, Friday Harbor WA 98250-0735. (360)378-2815. Fax: (360)378-2841. **Contact:** Alice B. Acheson. Estab. 1981; specifically with books for 31 years. Currently works with 9 clients. 20% of clients are new/first-time writers.

• Prior to becoming a freelance publicist, Ms. Acheson was a high school Spanish teacher and worked as a trade book editor.

Specializations: Nonfiction, fiction, children's books. **Interested in these nonfiction areas:** art/architecture/design, biography/autobiography, juvenile nonfiction, language/literature/criticism, memoirs, multicultural, music/dance/theater/film, nature/environment, photography. **Interested in these fiction areas:** contemporary issues, historical, juvenile, literary, mainstream, multicultural, mystery/suspense, picture book.

Services: Provides detailed outline of services provided, media training, market research, sends material to magazines/newspapers for reviews, brochures. Book tours include bookstores, radio interviews, TV interviews, newspaper interviews, magazine interviews. Assists in coordinating travel plans. Clients have appeared on CBS-TV, *Early Show*, CNN, and innumerable radio, TV shows nationwide. Media kit includes author's biography, testimonials, articles about author, basic information on book, professional photos, sample interview questions. Clients responsible for assisting with promotional material. Helps writer obtain endorsements.

○➔ "We mentor so writers can do the work on their own for their next projects."

How to Contact: Call or e-mail. Send letter with SASE. Responds in 2 weeks unless on teaching trip. Returns materials only with SASE. Obtains most new clients through recommendations from others and conferences. Contact 8 months prior to book's publication.

Clients: *Africa*, by Art Wolfe (Wildlands Press); *Divorce Hangover*, by Anne Newton Walther, M.S. (Tapestries Publishing); *Great Lodges of the National Parks*, by Christine Barnes (W.W. West, Inc.). References and contact numbers available for potential clients.

Costs: Clients charged hourly fee. Works with clients on marketing budget. Offers written contract. Contract can be terminated upon written notification.

◖N◗ ◗ THE AMERICAN PROGRAM BUREAU, 36 Crafts St., Newton MA 02458. (800)225-4575, ext. 1614. Fax: (617)614-1705. E-mail: tray@apbspeakers.com. Website: www.apbspeakers.com. **Contact:** Trinity J. Ray. Estab. over 35 years; specifically with books for over 35 years. Currently works with over 200 clients. 10% of clients are new/first-time writers.

• Prior to becoming a publicist Ms. Ray was a programmer and event coordinator.

Members: Trinity J. Ray (art/literary).

Specializations: Nonfiction, fiction, children's books. Other types of clients include speakers on all areas and interests with a particular focus on speakers of diversity.

Services: Provides brochures, website publicity. Book tours include speaking engagements, conferences, libraries, schools, universities. Assists in coordinating travel plans. Clients have appeared on all programs . . . *Oprah*, *"Today"* Show, CSPAN, etc. Media kit includes author's biography, testimonials, articles about author, basic information on book, professional photos.

○➔ We're one of the oldest and largest speaker's bureaus in the country. We have an inhouse travel agency and 24-hour customer service.

How to Contact: Call, e-mail, fax. Send query letter with bio, photo, book copies, video, letters of recommendation with SASE. Responds in 6 weeks. Discards unwanted queries and mss. Obtains most new clients through recommendations from others, queries/solicitations. Contact 3 months prior to book's publication or after book's publication.

Clients: *Nader Reader*, by Ralph Nader; *Color of Water* and *Miracle at St. Anna*, by James McBride; *The Wind Done Gone*, by Alice Randall; *87th Precinct* series, by Evan Hunter (pen name Ed McBain). Other clients include Rick Bragg, John Updike, Dave Barry.

Costs: Clients charged commission. Offers written contract.

Tips: "A paid speaking career is a logical next step to publishing a successful book. We do not arrange the traditional "book tour" per say. We are speaker agents, we find paid speaking dates for qualified authors. This is a service separate from the traditional literary agent role."

◖◗ ◎ BRODY PUBLIC RELATIONS, 145 Route 519, Stockton NJ 08559-1711. (609)397-3737. Fax: (609)397-3666. E-mail: bebrody@aol.com. Website: http://members.aol.com/bethbrodyPR. **Contact:** Beth Brody. Estab. 1988; specifically with books for 14 years. Currently works with 8-10 clients. 10% of clients are new/first-time writers.

Members: Beth Brody (nonfiction, at firm for 14 years).

Specializations: Nonfiction. **Interested in these nonfiction areas:** business; child guidance/parenting; education; health/medicine; how-to; money/finance/economics; music/dance/theater/film; popular culture; psychology; self-help/personal improvement; travel. **Interested in these fiction areas:** cartoons/comic. Other types of clients include musicians, artists, dotcoms, healthcare.

Services: Provides detailed outline of services provided, fax news releases, electronic news releases, sends material to magazines/newspapers for reviews, brochures, website assistance, website publicity. Book tours include bookstores, specialty stores, radio interviews, TV interviews, newspaper interviews, magazine interviews, speaking engagements, conferences, libraries, schools, universities. Assists in coordinating travel plans. Clients have appeared on *Oprah Winfrey Show*, *Sally Jessy Raphael*, *Good Morning America*. Media kit includes author's biography, testimonials, articles about author, basic information on book, sample interview questions, book request information. Helps writer obtain endorsements.

How to Contact: Call or e-mail. Responds in 48 hours. Obtains most new clients through recommendations from others. Contact 6 months prior to book's publication.

Clients: Music Sales Corporation, Crown Business, Random House, Berkeley Publishing. Other clients include Dow Jones, Don & Bradstreet, Foundations Behaviorial Health, JVC Music, Magweb.com. References and contact numbers available for potential clients.

Costs: Clients charged hourly fee or monthly retainer. Offers written contract.

Tips: "Contact a publicist after you have secured a publisher and distributor."

◎ EVENT MANAGEMENT SERVICES, INC., 519 Cleveland St., Suite 205, Clearwater FL 33757. (727)443-7115, ext. 201. E-mail: mfriedman@event-management.com. Website: www.event-management.com. **Contact:** Marsha Friedman. Estab. 1990; specifically with books for 12 years. Currently works with 15 clients. 0% of clients are new/first-time writers.

● Prior to becoming a freelance publicist, Ms. Friedman worked in PR and event management.

Members: Martha Conway (senior campaign manager, partner); Amy Summers (account manager, at firm for 4 years); Rich Ghazzarian (account manager, at firm for 4 years); Ben Ice (business development, at firm for 3 years).

Specializations: Nonfiction. **Interested in these nonfiction areas:** cooking/food/nutrition; current affairs; government/politics/law; health/natural; how-to; interior design/decorating; money/finance/economics; nature/environment; science/technology; sports; travel. Other types of clients include corporations in natural health industry, entertainment industry and food industry.

Services: Provides detailed outline of services provided. Book tours include bookstores, radio interviews, TV interviews, newspaper interviews, magazine interviews. Clients have appeared on *GMA*, *Today*, *60 Minutes*, *CBS This Morning*, *Maury Povich*, *Montel*, talk radio shows around the country, many major newspapers and magazines. Media kit includes author's biography, press release that gives the actual show idea or story.

　　O╼ "We are paid on performance and our specialty is radio and TV. We book anywhere from 30 to 80 interviews per week!"

How to Contact: Call, e-mail or fax. Send letter with SASE. Responds in 2 weeks. Obtains most new clients through recommendations from others or an initial contact on our part. Contact 6 months prior to book's publication or after book's publication.

Clients: *Anti Aging Bible*, by Dr. Earl Mindell (Simon & Schuster); *Slimdown For Life*, by Larry North (Kensington); *Special Trust*, by Robert McFarlane (Multi Media); *Selling Online*, by Jim Carrol and Rick Broadhead (Dearborn). Other clients include Jimmy Hoffa, Jr., Harry Browne, The Temptations. References and contact numbers available for potential clients.

Costs: Clients charged on per placement basis $165 (radio)-$5,000 (national TV). Works with clients on marketing budget. Offers written contract.

Tips: "Check references to see how much media they book every week/month. Find out if they have knowledge of your area of expertise."

◗ FIRSTWORD AGENCY, P.O. Box 521534, Salt Lake City UT 84152-1534. (801)463-0976. Fax: (801)463-1650. E-mail: info@firstwordagency.com. Website: www.firstwordagency.com. **Contact:** Stephanie Kallbacka, president. Estab. 2000; specifically with books for 3 years. Currently works with 10 clients. 75% of clients are new/first-time writers.

● Prior to becoming a freelance publicist, Ms. Kallbacka worked in public relations.

Members: Stephanie Kallbacka (media relations, at firm for 3 years).

Specializations: Nonfiction, fiction, children's book, academic. **Interested in these nonfiction areas:** art/architecture/design; biography/autobiography; business; child guidance/parenting; computers/electronics; cooking/food/nutrition; history; how-to; humor; language/literature/criticism; memoirs; military/war; music/dance/theater/film; New Age/metaphysics; popular culture; self-help/personal improvement; sports; travel; women's issues/women's studies; young adult. **Interested in these fiction areas:** action/adventure; detective/police/crime; experimental; historical; horror; humor/satire; juvenile; literary; mainstream; mystery/suspense; New Age/metaphysical; thriller/espionage; westerns/frontier; young adult. Other types of clients include music labels, film directories.

Services: Provides detailed outline of services provided, media training, international publicity, if applicable, fax news releases, electronic news releases, sends material to magazines/newspapers for reviews, brochures, website assistance, website publicity. Book tours include bookstores, specialty stores, radio interviews, TV interviews, newspaper interviews, magazine interviews, speaking engagements, conferences, libraries, schools, universities. Assists in coordinating travel plans. Media kit includes résumé, author's biography, testimonials, articles about author, basic information on book, suggested story topics, professional photos, sample interview questions, book request information. Helps writer obtain endorsements.

　　O╼ FirstWord Agency offers personal interaction with the author. "We help first time authors gain media exposure through creative and unique publicity campaigns."

How to Contact: E-mail, fax, send letter with 3 sample chapters with SASE. Responds in 2 months. Returns materials only with SASE. Obtains most new clients through recommendations from others, queries/solicitations. Contact 1-6 months prior to book's publication.

Clients: *Hairdresser to the Stars*, by Ginger Blymyer (Xlibris); *The Sandscrapers*, by Griffin T. Garnett (Infinity Publishing); *Baseball's Greatest Players: The Saga Continues*, by David Shiner (Superior Books); *Hearing Footsteps*, by Edward Kallbacka (Infinity Publishing); *The Malco Polia Quartette*, by Gilbert Buchanan; *Novice of Souls*, by Kevin Holochwost; *Dawn of the New Man*, by Eduard Pugovecki. Other clients include Talking Cloud Records. References and contact numbers available for potential clients.

Costs: Clients charged flat fee $100-1,000/project; hourly retainer fee $20-60; monthly retainer $1,000-2,500. Works with clients on marketing budget. Offers written contract, usually binding for 3-12 months; negotiable. 1 month notice must be given to terminate contract.

Writers' Conferences: Book Expo America (Chicago IL, 2002); Infinity Publishing (Philadelphia PA).

Tips: "At FirstWord Agency, it is important for both us and the author to be dedicated to the subject of our authors' work. We value close relationships with each of our clients and work together to achieve success on their behalf."

THE FORD GROUP, 1250 Prospect St., Suite Ocean-5, La Jolla CA 92037. (858)454-3314. Fax: (858)454-3319. E-mail: kat@fordsisters.com. Website: www.fordsisters.com. **Contact:** Arielle Ford. Estab. 1987; specifically with books since 1990. Currently works with 10 clients. 50% of clients are new/first-time writers.

• Ms. Ford has been a publicist since 1976.

Members: Katherine Kellmeyer (self-help, health, spirituality, relationships, at firm since 1997).

Specializations: Nonfiction. **Interested in these nonfiction areas:** health/medicine; how-to; New Age/metaphysics; psychology; religious/inspirational; self-help/personal improvement.

Services: Provides detailed outline of services provided, audio/video tapes, media training, fax news releases, electronic news releases, sends material to magazines/newspapers for reviews. Book tours include bookstores, radio interviews, TV interviews, newspaper interviews, magazine interviews, speaking engagements (limited amount). Clients have appeared on *Oprah*, *Larry King Live*, *Good Morning America*, *AP Radio*, *The Today Show*, *CNN*, *Fox News*, *Art Bell Show*. Media kit includes author's biography, testimonials, articles about author, basic information on book, professional photos, sample interview questions. Helps writer obtain endorsements. "We created the 'World's Largest Pot of Chicken Soup' to serve 7,000 homeless on Thanksgiving 6 years ago to launch one of the *Chicken Soup for the Soul* books. We ended up on NBC-TV network news and had a photo in *USA Today*."

O—¬ "We live and breathe our niche: self-help, alternative medicine and spirituality—we completely understand the category and love promoting it."

How to Contact: Call, e-mail or fax. Responds within 3 days. Returns unwanted material. Obtains most new clients through recommendations from others. Contact 6 months prior to book's publication.

Clients: *Familiar Strangers*, by Gotham Chopra (Doubleday); *Secret of the Shadow*, by Debbie Ford; *Dr. Shapiro's Picture Perfect Weightloss 30-day Plan* (Rodale); *The Energy of Money*, by Maria Nemeth.

Costs: Charges clients flat fee ($6,000-26,000); monthly retainer ($4,000-7,000). Works with clients on marketing budget. Offers written contract, binding on a book-by-book basis. 30-day notice must be given to terminate contract.

Tips: "Make sure your publicist (the person who actually will be making the calls on your behalf) is passionate about your book and is experienced in pitching your subject matter."

GARIS AGENCY—NATIONAL PUBLICISTS, 6965 El Camino Real, #105-110, La Costa CA 92009-4195. (760)471-4807. Fax: (253)390-4262. E-mail: publicists@aol.com. Website: www.publicists.bizland.com. **Contact:** R.J. Garis. Estab. 1989; specifically with books since 1989. Currently works with 50 clients. 20% of clients are new/first-time writers.

• Prior to becoming a publicist, Mr Garis was a promoter and producer.

Members: Taryn Roberts (associate national publicist, at firm since 1997); R.J. Garis.

Specializations: Nonfiction, fiction, script. **Interested in these nonfiction areas:** animals; biography/autobiography; business; child guidance/parenting; current affairs; gay/lesbian issues; government/politics/law; health/medicine; how-to; humor; interior design/decorating; juvenile nonfiction; memoirs; military/war; money/finance/economics; multicultural; music/dance/theater/film; nature/environment; New Age/metaphysics; photography; popular culture; psychology; science/technology; self-help/personal improvement; sociology; sports; travel; true

FOR EXPLANATIONS OF THESE SYMBOLS,
SEE THE INSIDE FRONT AND BACK COVERS OF THIS BOOK

crime/investigative; women's issues/women's studies; young adult. **Interested in these fiction areas:** action/ adventure; cartoon/comic; contemporary issues; detective/police/crime; erotica; ethnic; family saga; fantasy; feminist; gay/lesbian; glitz; horror; humor/satire; juvenile; literary; mainstream; multicultural; mystery/suspense; New Age/metaphysical; picture book; psychic/supernatural; romance; science fiction; sports; thriller/espionage; westerns/frontier; young adult.

Services: Provides media training, nationwide publicity, if applicable, fax news releases, electronic news releases, material to magazines/newspapers for reviews, website assistance, website publicity. Book tours include bookstores, specialty stores, radio interviews, TV interviews, newspaper interviews, magazine interviews, speaking engagements, conferences. Assists in coordinating travel plans. Clients have appeared on *Oprah, Dateline, Larry King, Fox, Sally, Extra, 48 Hours, Good Morning America, Montel, Inside Edition, 20/20, Today.* Media kits include résumé, author's biography, testimonials, articles about author, basic infomation on book, professional photos, sample interview questions, book request information. Helps writer obtain endorsements. "We designed media information for author Missy Cummings (*Hornet's Nest*)—which resulted in TV interviews on *Extra, Inside Edition* and a print feature in *The Star.*"

   O→ This company specializes in "quality media that works! Morning radio, national TV, regional TV, major newspapers and national magazines. We currently book over 2,000 media interviews a year."

How to Contact: E-mail. Responds in 3 days. Discards unwanted materials. Obtains most new clients through recommendations from others. Contact 4-6 months prior to book's publication.

Clients: *Hornet's Nest*, by Missy Cummings (iUniverse); *Little Kids Big Questions*, by Dr. Judi Craig (Hearst Books); *There Are No Accidents*, by Robert Hopcke (Penguin Putnam); *Anger Work*, by Dr. Robert Puff (Vantage Press). References and contact numbers available for potential clients.

Costs: Charges clients contract fee based on the project; monthly retainer. Offers written contract, binding for a minimum of 3 months. 30-day notice must be given to terminate contract.

Tips: "Check references. Look for a publicist with a long history, it takes many years to establish powerful media contacts."

■ ○ **CAMERON GRAY COMMUNICATIONS**, 13109 Hearthside Lane, Fairfax VA 22033. (703)725-9300. Fax: (703)832-0711. E-mail: cameron@camerongray.com. **Contact:** Cameron Gray. Estab. 2000; specifically with books since 2000.

   • Prior to becoming a publicist, Mr. Gray was an assistant producer and guest coordinator with the *G. Gordon Liddy Show* for eight years.

Members: Cameron Gray (nonfiction, lifestyle, pop culture, political works).

Specializations: Nonfiction. **Interested in these nonfiction areas:** biography/autobiography; business; child guidance/parenting; computers/electronics; current affairs; education; government/politics/law; health/medicine; military/war; money/finance/economics; popular culture; psychology; science/technology; self-help/personal improvement; sociology; sports; true crime/investigative; women's issues/women's studies. Other types of clients include "anyone looking for affordable, broad radio exposure."

Services: Provides international publicity, if applicable, fax news releases, electronic news releases. Book tours include radio interviews, selected chat room events. Clients have appeared on *The G. Gordon Liddy Show, The Roger Hedgecock Show, Daybreak USA, Online Tonight,* and countless other radio shows. Media kit includes author's biography, testimonials, articles about author, basic information on book, sample interview questions.

   O→ Cameron Gray Communications is "one of the nation's only publicity firms that specifically targets radio outlets, and radio sells the most books of any media."

How to Contact: Call, e-mail, or fax, or send letter with entire ms, outline/proposal. Responds in 1 week. Discards unwanted material. Obtains most new clients through recommendations from others. Contact after book's publication.

Clients: *Avoiding Mr. Wrong*, by Stephen Arterburn (Thomas Nelson Publishers); *Get Anyone To Do Anything*, by David Lieberman (St. Martin's Press); *Beyond Valor*, by Patrick O'Donnell (Free Press); *Dr. Atkins Age Defying Diet*, by Dr. Robert Atkins (St. Martin's Press). References and contact numbers available for potential clients.

Costs: Client charged monthly retainer. Offers written contract.

◑ **GREATER TALENT NETWORK, INC.**, 437 Fifth Ave., New York NY 10016-2205. (212)645-4200. Fax: (212)627-1471. E-mail: gtn@greatertalent.com. Website: www.gtnspeakers.com. **Contact:** Don Epstein. Estab. 1980; specifically with books for 20 years. Currently works with 100 clients.

Members: Don Epstein (corporate/literary, at firm over 21 years); Debra Greene (corporate/literary, at firm 22 years); Kenny Rahtz (corporate/associations, at firm 22 years); Barbara Solomon (health/hospitals/public relations, at firm 17 years); David Evenchick (Fortune 1000, at firm for 9 years); Josh Yablon (technology/corporate management, at firm for 10 years); Lisa Bransdorf (college/university, at firm for 8 years).

Specializations: Nonfiction, fiction, academic. **Interested in these nonfiction areas:** business, computers/ electronics, current affairs, education, government/politics/law, humor, money/finance/economics, multicultural, popular culture, science/technology, sports, women's issues/women's studies. Other types of clients include government officials, athletes, CEO's, technology, media.

Services: Provides detailed outline of services provided, international publicity, if applicable, fax news releases, brochures, website publicity. Book tours include radio interviews, TV interviews, newspaper interviews, speaking engagements. Assists in coordinating travel plans. Clients have appeared on all major networks. Media kit includes author's biography, testimonials, articles about author, professional photos, book request information.

○─ "We understand authors' needs and publishers' wants."

How to Contact: Call, e-mail, fax. Discards unwanted queries and mss. Obtains most new clients through recommendations from others. Contact once a platform is started.

Clients: *The CEO of the Sofa*, by P.J. O'Rourke (Atlantic Monthly Press); *Stupid White Men*, by Michael Moore (HarperCollins); *Hidden Power*, by Kati Marton (Pantheon); *The Travel Detective*, by Peter Greenberg (Villard); *American Gods*, by Neil Gaiman (Wm. Morrow). Other clients include Homer Hickman, Tom Wolfe, John Douglas, Christopher Buckley, Michael Lewis. References and contact numbers available for potential clients.

Costs: Clients charged variable commission. Offers written contract.

◨ ◎ **KSB PROMOTIONS, (Specializes: general lifestyle books)**, 55 Honey Creek NE, Ada MI 49301-9768. (616)676-0758. Fax: (616)676-0759. E-mail: pr@ksbpromotions.com. Website: www.ksbpromotions.com. **Contact:** Kate Bandos. Estab. 1988; specifically with books since 1988. Currently works with 20-40 clients; 25% of clients are new/first-time writers.

• Prior to becoming a publicist, Ms. Bandos was a PR director for several publishers.

Members: Kate Bandos (travel, cookbooks, at firm since 1988); Doug Bandos (radio/TV, at firm since 1989).

Specializations: Nonfiction, children's books. **Interested in these nonfiction areas:** child guidance/parenting; cooking/food/nutrition; health/medicine; travel; gardening; home/how-to; general lifestyle.

Services: Provides detailed outline of services provided, sends material to magazines/newspapers for reviews. Book tours include radio interviews, TV interviews, newspaper interviews, magazine interviews. Clients have appeared on *Good Morning America, CNN, Business News Network, Parent's Journal, New Attitudes* and others. Media kit includes author's biography, testimonials, articles about author, basic information on book, sample interview questions, book request information, recipes for cookbooks, other excerpts as appropriate. Helps writers obtain endorsements.

○─ This company specializes in cookbooks, travel guides, parenting books, and other general lifestyle books. "Our specialty has allowed us to build relationships with key media in these areas. We limit ourselves to those clients we can personally help."

How to Contact: Call or e-mail. Responds in 2 weeks. Returns unwanted material only with SASE. Obtains most new clients through recommendations from others, conferences, listings in books on publishing. Contact 6-8 months prior to book's publication. Can do limited PR after book's publication.

Clients: *The Home Depot 1-2-3 Series*, (Meredith Books); *Along Interstate 75*, by Dave Hunter (Mile Oak Publishing). Other clients include AAA Publishing, PassPorter, World Leisure Corp. References and contact numbers available for potential clients.

Costs: Client charged per service fee ($500 minimum). "Total of contracted services is divided into monthly payments." Offers written contract. 30-day notice must be given to terminate contract.

Writers' Conferences: PMA University; BookExpo America.

Tips: "Find a publicist who has done a lot with books in the same area of interest since they will know the key media, etc."

◨ **KT PUBLIC RELATIONS**, 1905 Cricklewood Cove, Fogelsville PA 18051-1509. (610)395-6298. Fax: (610)395-6299. E-mail: KT4PR@aol.com. Website: www.webbookstars.com. **Contact:** Kae Tienstra. Estab. 1993; specifically with books for 23 years. Currently works with 6 clients. 60% of clients are new/first-time writers.

• Prior to becoming a freelance publicist, Ms. Tienstra was a freelance writer.

Members: Kae Tienstra (writing, client contact, media relations, at firm 9 years); Jon Tienstra (editing, administration, at firm 6 years); Jan Hooker-Haring (writing, booking, at firm 4 years).

Specializations: Nonfiction, fiction. **Interested in these nonfiction areas:** agriculture/horticulture, animals, child guidance/parenting, cooking/food/nutrition, crafts/hobbies, health/medicine, how-to, interior design/decorating, nature/environment, New Age/metaphysics, psychology, religious/inspirational, self-help/personal improvement, travel, relationships. **Interested in these fiction areas:** mainstream, women's fiction. Other types of clients include nonprofit institutions, publishers.

Services: Provides detailed outline of services provided, media training, sends material to magazines/newspapers for reviews, brochures. Book tours include bookstores, radio interviews, TV interviews, newspaper interviews, magazine interviews, speaking engagements, universities. Assists in coordinating travel plans. Clients have appeared on *Today*, CNN, CBS Radio, *Sally Jesse Raphael, Today Weekend Edition, Home Matters, Christopher Lowell*. Media kit includes author's biography, testimonials, articles about author, basic information on book, professional photos, sample interview questions, book request information, segment suggestions for TV, radio, pitch letter. Helps writer obtain endorsements.

○─ "Our personal, hands-on approach assures authors the one-on-one guidance they need. Our subsidiary service, WEBbookSTARS.com provides special, low-cost, self-paced author publicity service."

How to Contact: Call, e-mail or fax. Send letter with sample chapters and SASE. Responds in 1 week. Returns materials only with SASE. Obtains most new clients through recommendations from others and conferences. Contact 6 months prior to book's publication or after book's publication once a platform is started.

Clients: *Lasting Love*, by Paddy S. Welles, Ph.D. (Avalon Publisher); *Flea Market Decorating*, by Vickie Ingham (Meredith); *Weight Loss for African American Women*, by George Edmund Smith, M.D. (Hilton Publishing). Other clients include Visible Ink Press, Better Homes & Gardens Books, Etruscan Press, Stillwater Publishing. References and contact numbers available for potential clients.

Costs: Clients charged per service fee $1,500; monthly retainer $1,500. Works with clients on marketing budget. Offers written contract, binding for 6 months minimum. 1 month notice must be given to terminate contract.

Tips: "We are a small, focused organization, designed to provide personal service. Authors who sign on with us work with us, not with junior staffers."

GAIL LEONDAR PUBLIC RELATIONS, 21 Belknap St., Arlington MA 02474-6605. (781)648-1658. E-mail: glpr@aol.com. **Contact:** Gail Leondar-Wright. Estab. 1992; specifically with books for 10 years. Currently works with 16 clients. 50% of clients are new/first-time writers.
- Prior to becoming a freelance publicist, Ms. Leondar-Wright directed theater.

Specializations: Nonfiction, fiction, academic, any books on progressive social issues. **Interested in these nonfiction areas:** Biography/autobiography, current affairs, education, ethnic/cultural interests, gay/lesbian issues, government/politics/law, history, multicultural, music/dance/theater/film, sociology, women's issues/women's studies. **Interested in these fiction areas:** feminist, gay/lesbian.

Services: Provides detailed outline of services provided. Book tours include bookstores, radio interviews, TV interviews, newspaper interviews. Clients have appeared on *Fresh Air Morning Edition*, *Weekend Edition*, CNN, C-SPAN. Media kit includes author's biography, testimonials, articles about author, basic information on book, professional photos, sample interview questions. Clients responsible for writing promotional material.
- GLPR promotes only books on progressive social interviews. Our contacts give excellent interviews, primarily on noncommercial radio, including NPR.

How to Contact: Call or e-mail. Responds in less than 1 week. Returns materials only with SASE. Obtains most new clients through recommendations from others. Contact 6 months prior to book's publication.

Clients: *A Desperate Passion*, by Dr. Helen Caldicott (Norton); *The Good Heart*, by The Dalai Lama (Wisdom); *Love Canal*, by Lois Gibbs (New Society Publishers); *Gender Outlaw*, by Kate Bornstein (Routledge). Other clients include The Lambda Literary Awards. References and contact numbers available for potential clients.

Costs: Clients charged flat fee $2,000-15,000. Works with clients on marketing budget. Offers written contract, binding for typically 3 months.

MEDIA MASTERS PUBLICITY, 1957 Trafalger Dr., Romeoville IL 60446. (815)254-7383. Fax: (815)254-1948. E-mail: tracey@mmpublicity.com. Website: www.mmpublicity.com. **Contact:** Tracey Daniels. Estab. 1998. Currently works with 10 clients. 10% of clients are new/first-time writers.
- Prior to becoming an independent publicist, Ms. Daniels worked in English Education—middle school and high school.

Members: Karen Wadsworth (marketing, events, at firm since 2001); Marie Garcarz (marketing, at firm since 2001).

Specializations: Children's books, nonfiction. **Interested in these nonfiction areas:** biography/autobiography; child guidance/parenting; cooking/food/nutrition; education; how-to; juvenile nonfiction; young adult. **Interested in these fiction areas:** juvenile; picture book; young adult. Other types of clients include publishers.

Services: Provides detailed outline of services provided, fax news releases, electronic news releases, material to magazines/newspapers for reviews, brochures, website assistance, website publicity. Book tours include bookstores, specialty stores, radio interviews, TV interviews, newspaper interviews, magazine interviews, schools. Clients have appeared on *CNN*, *Talk America*, CBS, ABC, VOA, *USA Radio Network*, *AP Radio Network*, *20/20*. "Each media kit varies depending on focus, client needs and budget." Helps writer obtain endorsements.
- "I have over eight years of book publicity experience. My company delivers 'publicity with personality'—we go beyond just covering the basics."

How to Contact: E-mail or send letter with outline/proposal and sample chapters. Responds in 2 weeks. Returns materials only with SASE. Obtains most new clients through recommendations from others. Contact 3 months prior to book's publication.

Clients: Clients include Fitzhenry & Whiteside Children's Books, HarperCollins Children's Books, Reader's Digest Trade Books, NorthSouth Books, NorthWord Books for Young Readers, Boyds Mills Press, Insomniac Press, plus individual authors. Reference and contact numbers available for potential clients.

Costs: Charges for services depend on client's needs and budget. Offers written contract. 90-day notice must be given to terminate contract.

Writers' Conferences: BEA, ALA.

PHENIX & PHENIX LITERARY PUBLICISTS, INC., 2525 W. Anderson Lane, Suite 540, Austin TX 78257. (512)478-2028. Fax: (512)478-2117. E-mail: info@bookpros.com. Website: www.bookpros.com. **Contact:** Champ Covington. Estab. 1994; specifically with books since 1994. Currently works with 40 clients. 50% of clients are new/first-time writers.

Members: Marika Flatt (national media director); Andrew Berzanskis (publicist); Leann Phenix (CEO); Elaine Froelich (publicist); Andy Morales (publicist); Mike Odam (president); Steve Joiner (vice president).

Specializations: Nonfiction, fiction, children's books, academic, coffee table books, biographies. **Interested in these nonfiction areas:** animals; biography/autobiography; business; child guidance/parenting; computers/ electronics; current affairs; health/medicine; money/finance/economics; multicultural; religious/inspirational; self-help/personal improvement; sports; travel; true crime/investigative; women's issues/women's studies; young adult. **Interested in these fiction areas:** action/adventure; confessional; contemporary issues; detective/police/ crime; family saga; historical; humor/satire; multicultural; mystery/suspense; regional; religious/inspirational; sports; young adult. Other types of clients include publishers.

Services: Provides detailed outline of services provided, media training, fax news releases, electronic news releases, material to magazines/newspapers for reviews, brochures, website publicity. Book tours include bookstores, specialty stores, radio interviews, TV interviews, newspaper interviews, magazine interviews. Clients have appeared on *Oprah*, CNN, CNBC, *Fox News Network, Leeza, Montel, Good Morning America, Talk America Radio Network, Business News Network, Westwood One Radio Network, UPI Radio Network*. Media kit includes author's biography, testimonials, articles about author, basic information on book, professional photos, sample interview questions, book request information, press releases, excerpts. Recent promotions included video press releases, mystery contest, online publicity campaigns, creative angles for fiction positioning.

○┅ This company has a first 30-day strategy (develop strategy, positioning, press materials), and created 4 bestsellers in 1999.

How to Contact: Call, e-mail, fax or send letter with entire ms. Responds in 5 days. Discards unwanted material. Obtains most new clients through recommendations from others, conferences, website. Contact 2-4 months prior to book's publication or after book's publication.

Clients: *Kiss of God*, by Marshall Ball (Health Communications); *True Women/Hill Country*, by Janice Woods Windle (Longstreet Press); *Wizard of Ads*, by Roy Williams (Bard Press); *Faith on Trial*, by Pamela Ewen (Broadman & Holman). Other clients include Dr. Ivan Misner, Lisa Shaw-Brawley, Michele O'Donnell, Patrick Seaman (Timberwolf Press), Continuum Press. References and contact numbers available for potential clients.

Costs: Charges clients monthly retainer ($2,500-6,500). Works with clients on a marketing budget. Offers written contract binding for 4-6 months.

Writers' Conferences: Craft of Writing (Denton, TX), BEA (New York).

Tips: "Find a publicist that will offer a guarantee. Educate yourself on the book/publicity process."

◎ **RAAB ASSOCIATES**, 345 Millwood Rd., Chappaqua NY 10514. (914)241-2117. Fax: (914)241-0050. E-mail: info@raabassociates.com. Website: www.raabassociates.com. **Contact:** Susan Salzman Raab. Estab. 1986; specifically with books since 1986. Currently works with 10 clients. 10% of clients are new/first-time writers.

● Prior to becoming an independent publicist, Ms. Salzman Raab worked on staff at major publishing houses in the children's book industry.

Members: Susanna Reich (associate, at firm since 2000); Susan Salzman Raab (partner, at firm since 1986).

Specializations: Children's books, parenting books. **Interested in these nonfiction areas:** child guidance/ parenting, juvenile nonfiction, young adult. **Interested in these fiction areas:** juvenile, picture book, young adult, parenting. Other types of clients include publishers, toy companies, audio companies.

Services: Provides detailed outline of services provided, market research, sends material to magazines/newspapers for review, website assistance, website development, extensive online publicity. Book tours include bookstores, specialty stores, radio interviews, TV interviews, newspaper interviews, magazine interviews, schools and libraries. Can also assist in coordinating travel plans. Clients have appeared on NPR, CNN, C-Span, Radio-Disney, PRI. Media kit includes author's biography, testimonials, articles about author, basic information on book, sample interview questions, book request information. Helps writer obtain endorsements.

○┅ "We are the only PR agency to specialize in children's and parenting books."

How to Contact: Call or e-mail. Responds in 2 weeks. Returns materials only with SASE. Obtains most new clients through recommendations from others, conferences. Contact 4 months prior to book's publication.

Clients: Sometimes references and contact numbers available to potential clients (most often to publishers, rather than authors).

Costs: Clients charged per service fee. Offers written contract. 90-day notice must be given to terminate contract.

Writers' Conferences: Society of Children's Book Writers & Illustrators (New York National); Society of Children's Book Writers & Illustrators (Regional Meeting); Book Expo America (Chicago, May/June); American Library Association (Chicago, July); Bologna Bookfair (April).

◤ **ROCKS-DEHART PUBLIC RELATIONS (BOOK PUBLICITY)**, 811 Boyd Ave., Suite 101, Pittsburgh PA 15238. (412)820-3004. Fax: (412)820-3007. E-mail: celiarocks@aol.com. Website: www.celiarocks.com. **Contact:** Celia Rocks. Estab. 1993; specifically with books since 1993. Currently works with 10 clients; 20% of clients are new/first-time writers.

● Prior to becoming a publicist, Ms. Rocks was a publicity specialist at Burson Marsteller.

Members: Dottie DeHart (principal, at firm since 1993); 8 other staff members.

Specializations: Nonfiction, business, lifestyle. **Interested in these nonfiction areas:** biography/autobiography; business; cooking/food/nutrition; current affairs; health/medicine; how-to; humor; popular culture; psychology; religious/inspirational; self-help/personal improvement; sociology; travel; women's issues/women's studies. Other types of clients include major publishing houses.

Services: Provides detailed outline of services provided. Book tours include bookstores, specialty stores, radio interviews, TV interviews, newspaper interviews, magazine interviews, speaking engagements, conferences, libraries, schools, universities. Clients have appeared on *ABC World News, Oprah* and others, as well as in *Time* and *Newsweek.* Media kit includes author's biography, testimonials, articles about author, basic information on book, professional photos, sample interview questions, book request information, breakthrough plan materials, and "any other pieces that are helpful." Helps writers obtain endorsements. Recent promotions included "taking a book like *Fishing for Dummies* and sending gummy worms with packages."

⊶ This company specializes in IDG "Dummies" Books, business, management, and lifestyle titles. "We are a highly creative firm that understands the best way to obtain maximum publicity."

How to Contact: Call or e-mail. Responds in 1 day. Obtains most new clients through recommendations from others. Contact 2-4 months prior to book's publication.

Clients: Clients include John Wiley & Sons, AAA Publishing, Dearborn, Jossey-Bass.

Costs: Clients charged monthly retainer ($3,000-5,000). Works with clients on marketing budget. Offers written contract. 30-day notice must be given to terminate contract.

◖ **SHERRI ROSEN PUBLICITY**, 80 S. Main St., Suite 2A, Milltown NJ 08850. Phone/fax: (732)448-9441. E-mail: sherri@sherrirosen.com. Website: www.sherrirosen.com. **Contact:** Sherri Rosen. Estab. 1997, specifically with books for 12 years. Currently works with 4 clients. 50% of clients are new/first-time writers.

• Prior to becoming a freelance publicist, Ms. Rosen was an actress. She also assists writers in their search for a competent literary agent. Ms. Rosen's first client, Naura Hayden, was on the New York Times Best Seller List for 63 weeks.

Specializations: Nonfiction, fiction, children's book, events, healers. **Interested in these nonfiction areas:** child guidance/parenting, cooking/food/nutrition, current affairs, education, ethnic/cultural interests, gay/lesbian issues, health/medicine, how-to, humor, juvenile nonfiction, memoirs, music/dance/theater/film, New Age/metaphysics, popular culture, psychology, religious/inspirational, self-help/personal improvement, travel, women's issues/women's studies, young adult. **Interested in these fiction areas:** action/adventure, confessional, erotica, ethnic, experimental, family saga, fantasy, feminist, humor/satire, literary, mainstream, multicultural, New Age/metaphysical, psychic/supernatural, religious/inspirational, romance, young adult. Other types of clients include healers, business people, spiritual teachers.

Services: Provides detailed outline of services provided, audio/video tapes, international publicity, if applicable, sends material to magazines/newspapers for reviews, brochures. Book tours include bookstores, radio interviews, TV interviews, newspaper interviews, magazine interviews, speaking engagements, conferences, libraries, schools, universities. Assists in coordinating travel plans. Clients have appeared on *Oprah, Montel, Politically Incorrect, Leeza, Men are from Mars, The Sally Show, The Other Half.* Media kit includes author's biography, testimonials, articles about author, basic information on book, professional photos, sample interview questions, book request information. Will write all of the promotional material or collaborate with client. Helps writer obtain endorsements.

⊶ "I work with eclectic clientele—sex books, spiritual books, personal inspirational, self-help books. What is distinct is I will only work with people I like, and I have to like and respect what they are doing."

How to Contact: E-mail. Responds immediately. Discards unwanted queries or returns materials only with SASE. Obtains most new clients through recommendations from others, listings with other services in our industry. Contact 3 months prior to book's publication if possible; after book's publication once a platform is started.

Clients: *How to Satisfy a Woman*, by Naura Hayden (self-published); *Men Who Can't Love*, by Steven Carten (HarperCollins); *Rebirth of the Goddess*, by Carol Christ (Addison-Wesley); *Buddhism Without Belief*, by Stephen Batchelor (Riberhead). Other clients include Eli Jaxon-Bear, Sandra Rothenberger, Elizabeth Ayres. References and contact numbers available for potential clients.

Costs: Clients charged hourly retainer fee $125; monthly retainer $4,000. Offers written contract. One month notice must be given to terminate contract.

Tips: "Make sure you like who you will be working with, because you work so closely."

◗ **ROYCE CARLTON, INC.**, 866 United Nations Plaza, Suite 587, New York, NY 10017. (212)335-7700. Fax: (212)888-8659. E-mail: info@roycecarlton.com. Website: www.roycecarlton.com. **Contact:** Carlton Sedgeley. Estab. 1968. Currently works with 60 clients.

CONTACT THE EDITOR of *Guide to Literary Agents* by e-mail at literaryagents @fwpubs.com with your questions and comments.

• Royce Carlton, Inc. is a lecture agency and management firm for some 60 speakers who are available for lectures and special engagements.

Members: Carlton S. Sedgeley, president (at firm since 1968); Lucy Lepage, executive vice president (at firm since 1968); Helen Churko, vice president (at firm since 1984).

Specializations: Royce Carlton works with many different types of speakers. Other clients include celebrities, writers, journalists, scientists, etc.

Services: Provides "full service for all our clients to lecture."

○━ "We are the only lecture agency representing all our clients exclusively."

How to Contact: Call, e-mail, or fax. Discards unwanted material. Obtains most new clients through recommendations from others, or initiates contact directly.

Clients: *Tuesdays with Morrie*, by Mitch Albom; *House Made of Dawn*, by N. Scott Momaday. Other clients include Joan Rivers, Elaine Pagels, Walter Mosley, David Halberstam, Tom Friedman, Fareed Zakaria, Susan Sontag. References and contact numbers available for potential clients.

Costs: Client charged per placement; commission. Offers written contract. 30-day notice must be given to terminate contract.

✓ ◐ **SMITH PUBLICITY**, 57 S. Main St., Yardley PA 19067. (215)369-4858. Fax: (215)369-4849. E-mail: info@smithpublicity.com. Website: www.smithpublicity.com. **Contact:** Dan Smith. Estab. 1997; specifically with books for 4 years. Currently works with 10 clients. 70% of clients are new/first-time writers.

• Prior to starting Smith Publicity in 1997, Mr. Smith was a freelance public relations specialist and promotional writer.

Members: Dan Smith (president, marketing analysis, campaign management, at firm 6 years); Jeremy Trout (creative director); Fran Rubin (marketing, business development, at firm 5 years); Alexis Berger (research, at firm 3 years).

Specializations: Nonfiction, fiction. **Interested in these nonfiction areas:** government/politics/law, how-to, humor, multicultural, New Age/metaphysics, popular culture, self-help/personal improvement, true crime/investigative. **Interested in these fiction areas:** confessional, experimental, family saga, humor/satire, mainstream, New Age/metaphysical, psychic/supernatural. Other types of clients include entrepreneurs, business specialties.

Services: Provides detailed outline of services provided, media training, international publicity, if applicable, market research, fax news releases, electronic news releases, send material to magazines/newspapers for reviews, website assistance, website publicity. Book tours include bookstores, radio interviews, TV interviews, newspaper interviews, magazine interviews, speaking engagements. Assists in coordinating travel plans. Clients have appeared on CNN, *Montel, Sally Jessy Raphael, Extra, Good Morning America, Howard Stern, O'Reilly Factor, Ken Hamblin, Mike Gallagher, Daybreak USA*. Media kit includes author's biography, testimonials, articles about author, basic information on book, sample interview questions. Developed "Mob Lingo and Trivia Quiz" for fictional organized crime novel, which resulted in more than 40 interviews for the author.

○━ "We find angles which interest the media, while offering affordable rates with unparalled customer service."

How to Contact: Call, e-mail or fax. Responds in 1 week. Returns materials only with SASE. Obtains most new clients through recommendations from others, queries/solicitations, conferences. Contact 4 months prior to book's publication or after book's publication.

Clients: *Conversations with Tom*, by Walda Woods (White Rose Publishing); *The Old Boys: The American Elite and the Origins of the CIA*, by Burton Hersh; *Emotionally Intelligent Parenting*, by Dr. Steven Tobias (Random House). Other clients include John Paul Christ, Jack Nadel, Peter DeVico, Lester O'Shea, Suzanne Harrill, Dr. Arnold Nerenberg. References and contact numbers available for potential clients.

Costs: Clients charged flat fee $500-1,200; monthly retainer $500-1,800. Offers written contract. 3-month notice must be given to terminate contract.

Writers' Conferences: Book Expo America (New York City).

Tips: "Don't be afraid to ask questions. Speak with at least three different publicists before deciding. Have fun with your project and enjoy the ride!"

◐ **THE SPIZMAN AGENCY**, Atlanta GA 30327. E-mail: spizagency@aol.com. www.spizmanagency.com. **Contact:** Robyn or Willy Spizman. Estab. 1981; specifically with books for 21 years. 50% of clients are new/first-time writers.

• Prior to becoming a freelance publicist, co-owner Robyn Spizman was the author of more than 70 published books and a consumer reporter on TV.

Specializations: Nonfiction, fiction, children's book, academic. **Interested in these nonfiction areas:** business, child guidance/parenting, computers/electronics, cooking/food/nutrition, crafts/hobbies, current affairs, education, ethnic/cultural interests, health/medicine, history, how-to, humor, interior design/decorating, juvenile nonfiction, language/literature/criticism, memoirs, military/war, money/finance/economics, multicultural, music/dance/theater/film, nature/environment, New Age/metaphysics, photography, popular culture, psychology, religious/inspirational, science/technology, self-help/personal improvement, sociology, sports, travel, true crime/investigative, women's issues/women's studies, young adult. **Interested in these fiction areas:** contemporary issues, Internet, mainstream, inspirational, young adult.

Services: Provides detailed outline of services provided, media training, international publicity, if applicable, market research, fax news releases, electronic news releases, sends material to magazines/newspapers for reviews, brochures, website assistance, website publicity. Book tours include bookstores, specialty stores, radio interviews, TV interviews, newspaper interviews, magazine interviews, satellite media tours, speaking engagements, conferences, libraries, schools, universities. Assists in coordinating travel plans. Clients have appeared on *Oprah*, CNN, *NBC Today*, HGTV. Media kit includes, author's biography, testimonials, articles about author, basic information on book, professional photos, sample interview questions, book request information. Helps writer obtain endorsements. Recent promotions included a one hour show on a client's book on CNN.
How to Contact: E-mail. Responds in 1 week. Returns materials only with SASE. Obtains most new clients through recommendations from others. Contact 6 months prior to book's publication, once a platform is started.
Clients: *Immutable Laws of the Internet*, by Al and Laura Ries (HarperCollins); *Live, Learn & Pass It On*, by H. Jackson Brown, Jr. (Rutledge Hill). Other clients include Turner Broadcasting, GlaxoSmithKline, Reproductive Biology Associates. References and contact numbers available for potential clients.
Costs: Monthly retainer. Works with clients to help create a marketing budget. Offers written contract. 1-month notice must be given to terminate contract.
Writers' Conferences: Book Expo (Chicago).
Tips: "It gets down to one thing—who they know and what they know, plus years of successful clients. We score high on all counts."

WARWICK ASSOCIATES, 18340 Sonoma Hwy., Sonoma CA 95476. (707)939-9212. Fax: (707)938-3515. E-mail: sws@vom.com. Website: www.warwickassociates.net. **Contact:** Simon Warwick-Smith, president. Estab. 1983; specifically with books for 19 years. Currently works with 24 clients. 12% of clients are new/first-time writers.
  • Prior to becoming a freelance publicist, Mr. Warwick-Smith was Senior Vice President Marketing, Associated Publishers Group (books).
Members: Patty Vadinsky (celebrity, sports, at firm 7 years); Simon Warwick-Smith (metaphysics, business, at firm 19 years); Warren Misuraca (travel, writing, at firm 9 years).
Specializations: Nonfiction, children's books, spirituality. **Interested in these nonfiction areas:** biography/autobiography, business, child guidance/parenting, computers/electronics, cooking/food/nutrition, government/politics/law, health/medicine, how-to, New Age/metaphysics, psychology, religious/inspirational, self-help/personal improvement, sports, travel. Other types of clients include celebrity authors.
Services: Provides media training, market research, fax news releases, electronic news releases, sends material to magazines/newspapers for reviews, brochures, website assistance, website publicity. Book tours include bookstores, specialty stores, radio interviews, TV interviews, newspaper interviews, magazine interviews, speaking engagements, online interviews. Assists in coordinating travel plans. Clients have appeared on *Larry King*, *Donahue*, *Oprah*, *Good Morning America*. Media kit includes résumé, author's biography, testimonials, articles about author, basic information on book, professional photos, sample interview questions, book request information. Helps writer obtain endorsements.
How to Contact: See website. Responds in 2 weeks. Returns material only with SASE. Obtains most new clients through recommendations from others and on website. Contact 6 months prior to book's publication.
Clients: References and contact numbers available for potential clients.
Costs: Works with clients on marketing budget. Offers written contract binding for specific project.

WORLD CLASS SPEAKERS & ENTERTAINERS, 28025 Dorothy Dr., Suite 202, Aqoura Hills CA 91301. (818)991-5400. Fax: (818)991-2226. E-mail: info@speak.com. Website: www.speak.com. **Contact:** Joseph I. Kessler. Estab. 1965.
Specializations: Nonfiction, academic. **Interested in these nonfiction areas:** business; humor; money/finance/economics; psychology; science/technology; self-help/personal improvement; sociology; sports; women's issues; women's studies; high profile/famous writers. Other types of clients include experts in all fields.
Services: Provides market research, sends material to magazines/newspapers for reviews, brochures, website publicity. Book tours include radio interviews, TV interviews, newspaper interviews, magazine interviews, speaking engagements, conferences, universities. Assists in coordinating travel plans. Media kits include author's biography, testimonials, articles about author, professional photos. Helps writer obtain endorsements.
How to Contact: Call, e-mail or fax. Responds in 1 week. Discards unwanted materials. Obtains most new clients through recommendations from others. Contact prior to book's publication.
Costs: Charges clients per placement basis ($1,500 minimum); 30% commission. Works with clients on marketing budget. Offers written contract. 60- to 90-day notice must be given to terminate contract.

THE WRITE PUBLICIST & CO., 120 Adair Circle, Fayetteville GA 30215-8234. (770)716-3323. E-mail: thewritepublicist@earthlink.net. Website: www.thewritepublicist.com. **Contact:** Regina Lynch-Hudson. Estab. 1990; specifically with books for 11 years. Currently works with 5 clients. 50% of clients are new/first-time writers.
  • Prior to becoming a publicist Ms. Lynch-Hudson was Public Relations director for a 4-star resort.
Specializations: Nonfiction, fiction, children's books, multicultural, ethnic and minority market books. **Interested in these nonfiction areas:** biography/autobiography, business, education, ethnic/cultural interests, health/

medicine, how-to, juvenile nonfiction, multicultural, religious/inspirational, women's issues/women's studies. **Interested in these fiction areas:** confessional, contemporary issues, erotica, ethnic, family saga, humor/satire, mainstream, multicultural, religious/inspirational, romance, science fiction, sports. Other types of clients include physicians, lawyers, entertainers, artists.

Services: Provides international publicity, if applicable, electronic news releases, sends material to magazines/newspapers for reviews, website publicity. Book tours include bookstores, radio interviews, TV interviews, newspaper interviews, magazine interviews, schools, universities. Assists in coordinating travel plans. Clients have appeared on *Oprah*, all national TV networks. Media kit includes author's biography, basic information on book, professional photos, book request information, propriety innovative enclosures that insure and increase the opportunity for publication. Helps writer obtain endorsements. "We paired Dr. Marcus Wells, Bariatrics specialist, with obese readers in various cities. He flew in and became consultant to many readers."

　　O→ Twelve years experience publicizing people, places, products, performances. Owner of company was syndicated columnist to 215 newspapers, which solidified media contacts.

How to Contact: E-mail. Send book or ms. Responds in 1 week. Returns materials only with SASE. Obtains most new clients through recommendations from others. "90% of our clients are referred nationally." Contact 1 month prior to book's publication or after book's publication.

Clients: *Lifestyles for the 21st Century*, by Dr. Marcus Wells (Humanics Publishing); *Preconceived Notions*, by Robyn Williams (Noble Press); *Fed Up With the Fanny*, by Franklin White (Simon & Schuster). Other clients include Vernon Jones, CEO of DeKalb County; Atlanta Perinatal Associates; Tonda Smith, news anchor. "Our clients' contracts state that they will not be solicited by prospective clients. Our website shows photos of clients who give their recommendation by consenting to be placed on our website."

Costs: Clients charged flat fee $9,500-15,000. Works with clients on marketing budget. Offers written contract. Three-day notice before our company has invested time interviewing the client and writing their release must be given to terminate a contract.

Tips: "Does the publicist have a website that actually pictures clients? Our site ranks No. 1 with Yahoo!—as one of few PR sites that actually depicts clients."

◢ MERYL ZEGAREK PUBLIC RELATIONS, INC., 255 W. 108th St., Suite 9D1, New York NY 10025. (917)493-3601. Fax: (917)493-3598. E-mail: mz@mzpr.com. Website: www.mzpr.com. **Contact:** Meryl Zegarek. Worked specifically with books for 25 years.

　　● Prior to becoming a freelance publicist, Ms. Zegarek was a publicity director of two divisions of Knopf Books, Random House.

Specializations: Nonfiction, fiction. **Interested in these nonfiction areas:** animals, anthropology/archaeology, art/architecture/design, current affairs, ethnic/cultural interests, government/politics/law, health/medicine, history, how-to, humor, interior design/decorating, language/literature/criticism, multicultural, music/dance/theater/film, nature/environment, New Age/metaphysics, photography, popular culture, psychology, religious/inspirational, science/technology, self-help/personal improvement, sociology, travel, true crime/investigative, women's issues/women's studies. **Interested in these fiction areas:** action/adventure, contemporary issues, detective/police/crime, ethnic, historical, literary, multicultural, mystery/suspense, New Age/metaphysical, psychic/supernatural, religious/inspirational, science fiction, thriller/espionage. Other types of clients include organizations, nonprofits, business, human rights organizations, international publishers.

Services: Provides detailed outline of services provided, media training, sends material to magazines/newspapers for reviews, website publicity. Book tours include bookstores, radio interviews, TV interviews, newspaper interviews, magazine interviews, speaking engagements, universities. Assists in coordinating travel plans. Clients have appeared on *Oprah*, *Good Morning America*, *Fresh Air* (NPR), *Morning Edition* (NPR). Media kit includes résumé, author's biography, testimonials, articles about author, basic information on book, professional photos, sample interview questions, book request information. Plans nationwide print and radio campaigns with give-aways—with National Television and radio producing *New York Times* best-sellers.

　　O→ Specializes in Jewish and nonreligious spiritual books and authors. "I have been a publicity director for three major publishing houses during a twenty-five year career in book publicity. I have experience in every genre of book with established contacts in TV, radio and print—as well as bookstores and speaking venues."

How to Contact: Call, e-mail or fax. Send letter with entire ms or gallery, outline/proposal, sample chapters with SASE. Responds in 2 weeks. Returns material only with SASE. Obtains most new clients through recommendations from others. Contact 5-6 months prior to book's publication, if possible.

VISIT WWW.WRITERSMARKET.COM to obtain a searchable database of agents and publishers, and to receive updates on your specific interests on your computer.

Clients: *In My Brothers Image*, by Eugene Pogany (Viking/Penguin); *You Can't Do That on Broadway*, by Philip Rose (Limelight); *Hitler's Niece*, by Ron Hanson (HarperCollins); *Lit From Within*, by Victoria Moran (Harper SF). Other clients include Bright Sky Press, Hidden Spring Books, Jewish Publication Society, Serpent's Tail, Red Wheel/Weiser. References and contact numbers available for potential clients.

Costs: Clients charged flat fee, hourly retainer fee for consultations, monthly retainer (divide up flat fee payable by month). Offers written contract. One-month notice must be given to terminate contract.

Tips: "Call early."

Writers' Conferences

Attending a writers' conference that includes agents gives you the opportunity to listen and learn more about what agents do, as well as the chance to show an agent your work. Ideally, a conference should include a panel or two with a number of agents to give writers a sense of the variety of personalities and tastes of different agents.

Not all agents are alike: some are more personable and sometimes you simply click better with one agent over another. When only one agent attends a conference there is tendency for every writer at that conference to think, "Ah, this is the agent I've been looking for!" When the number of agents attending is larger, you have a wider group from which to choose and you may have less competition for the agent's time.

Besides including panels of agents discussing what representation means and how to go about securing it, many of these gatherings also include time, either scheduled or impromptu, to meet briefly with an agent to discuss your work.

If they're impressed with what they see and hear about your work, they will invite you to submit a query, a proposal, a few sample chapters, or possibly your entire manuscript. Some conferences even arrange for agents to review manuscripts in advance and schedule one-on-one sessions where you can receive specific feedback or advice on your work. Such meetings often cost a small fee, but the input you receive is usually worth the price. For helpful hints on how to make the most of meetings with agents, see "Three Agents Discuss the Dos and Dont's of Writers' Conferences" by Will Allison on page 284.

Ask writers who attend conferences and they'll tell you that at the very least you'll walk away with more knowledge than you came with. At the very best, you'll receive an invitation to send an agent your material!

Three Agents Discuss the Dos and Don'ts of Writers' Conferences

BY WILL ALLISON

For most writers, conferences represent their only opportunity to meet literary agents. It can be a nerve-wracking experience—for both the writer and the agent. In the following interview, three agents share their views on conferences and offer suggestions on how to establish successful relationships with agents while avoiding some common conference faux pas.

The agents

Prior to joining Sanford J. Greenburger Associates in 1999, Julie Barer worked for two years at Shakespeare & Co., an independent bookstore in New York City. She specializes in literary fiction and emerging authors, and her nonfiction interests include religion, cultural studies, memoir, biography, history, and narrative nonfiction. Among her book sales are *The Best of Animals: Stories* by Lauren Grodstein (Persea Books), *The Winter Zoo: A Novel* by John Beckman (Henry Holt), *An Everyday Savior* by Kathryn Larrabee (Four Walls Eight Windows), *Live from New York: The KGB Bar Fiction Anthology* (St. Martin's Press), and *A Company of Three* by Varley O'Connor (Algonquin).

Frances Kuffel has worked in publishing for thirteen years after doing graduate work in creative writing and English literature. She is executive vice president of Maria Carvainis Agency, Inc., in New York and has a client list of 30 writers—one-third children's books (she's signing no new writers of juvenile literature), one-third nonfiction (biography, science, history, memoirs), and one-third fiction (established mystery writers, high-end historicals, literary fiction). Her book sales include *White Star* by Marty Crisp (Holiday House), *The Devil's Hearth* by Phillip DePoy (St. Martin's Press), *Rebuilding the Indian* by Fred Haefele (Riverhead), *The Puppeteer's Apprentice* by D. Anne Love (Margaret McElderry Books), *Elizabeth: Grand Duchess of Russia* by Hugo Mager (Carroll & Graf), *The Place at the Edge of the Earth* by Bebe Rice (Clarion Books), *Last Breath* by Peter Stark (Ballantine), and *Princess Naughty and the Voodoo Cadillac* by Fred Willard (Longstreet Books).

Christina (Kit) Ward heads the Christina Ward Literary Agency in the Boston area. She represents a diverse list that includes writers of literary fiction and nonfiction, mystery and suspense novels, natural history, memoir, biography, and practical nonfiction on a variety of subjects. Her recent sales include *He Sleeps* by Reginald McKnight; *The New Covenant, a New Translation of The Four Gospels and Apocalypse* by Willis Barnstone; and *Program Your Baby's Health* by Barbara Luke and Tamara Eberlein.

In what ways are writers' conferences valuable to you as an agent?

Julie Barer: One thing I love about conferences is the experience of being surrounded by people—writers, editors, agents, teachers—who are passionate and excited about writing. The exchange of energy and ideas is often very inspiring. Obviously, conferences can be great places

WILL ALLISON *(willalliso@aol.com) is former editor at large of* Zoetrope: All-Story, *former executive editor of* Story, *and former editor of* Novel & Short Story Writer's Market.

to seek out potential clients and let aspiring writers know what kind of material you're looking for. But they also provide wonderful opportunities to talk one-on-one with someone whose work you're interested in, or who's interested in you.

Frances Kuffel: I attend conferences in hopes of finding new writers and have been successful in signing several writers I've met through these opportunities.

It has worked in two ways:

1. I discover the writer (as opposed to the writer discovering me). I have come across promising work through scheduled meetings, particularly those where I've heard or read an excerpt from a project. I've also met writers whom I've signed because s/he looks interesting. And sometimes it's been a casual conversation in which a writer reveals some knowledge that I've been able to explore further with that writer.

2. I've also signed conferees long after a conference. I will get a query letter from a writer who heard or met me and who listened carefully and thoughtfully to all of what they've heard at a conference (and part of what they'll hear from me, at least, is to join a writers' group, take classes, go to more conferences: by the time a writer who has followed my remarks approaches me, s/he has had a lot of exposure to the writing and revision process, and to the business). Having put that information into practice, the writer now has both much better work and the research and exposure to a number of agents: s/he has a real sense that it's me they want for their agent—that their needs and work now match my tastes and interests, expectations and abilities.

Kit Ward: When I first launched my agency ten years ago, I attended every writers' conference I was invited to, large or small, in part to prospect for new clients but also to get my presence "out there" in the larger world of writers and publishing professionals. (As a former editor from Little, Brown, I knew lots of agents but relatively few editors from other houses.) In the years since then, I've grown to love the whole experience of a good writers' conference—the readings, the camaraderie, the teaching and learning that go on in the workshops and lectures. I enjoy meeting writers at all levels, from the faculty to the relative beginners, and the experience reminds me afresh of the challenges writers face in their careers. This is, I find, valuable perspective for an author's representative. As for the prospecting—I've found several wonderful clients at conferences, but it's probably impossible to calculate the referrals that develop subsequently. Sometimes it's years before a writer I met at a conference has a book ready to send me. Though these developments are hard to measure, they're certainly facilitated by the conference connection.

Tell us some of your conference success stories.

Julie Barer: My biggest conference successes have been establishing wonderful business and personal relationships. The Squaw Valley Community of Writers, which I attended in August 2001, is a perfect example. I had the chance to meet and develop relationships with some remarkable people, including writers, editors, and other agents. At the Faulker Festival in New Orleans, I had the chance to spend time with a client I had been working with for a long time, but had never met. Often, forging these relationships can be even more valuable than discovering one particular project.

Frances Kuffel: Conference stories about writers would make me nervous to read, so I'll tell you about the conference where I felt most welcomed. My first conference was in Lafayette, Louisiana, which was also my first visit south of the Mason-Dixon Line and that conference's first agent from north of it. I didn't know that the aim of having me there was to hold me hostage: any time I wasn't obligated to the conference schedule, someone from the host group would take me sightseeing. I got insights into the area—which is, of course, enchanting in and of itself—but also into the writers who were showing me around. I still wish, ardently, that several of those hosts would turn to their distinct and wonderfully rich material and put it to literary use.

This has happened several times: in visiting an area with a writer/host who knows it well and is focused not on me as an agent but on me as a sightseer, I have been able to enthuse, "Write about that! No one knows about that—it deserves a book!"

Kit Ward: In recent years, I've restricted my conference attendance to one or two per summer, in an effort to balance agency business with the summer schedules of teenaged sons. The Bread Loaf Writers' Conference has been a top priority for me when I'm fortunate enough to be invited, and my recent visits there have brought me several clients whose books I've sold. Helen Husher's delightful travel-cum-history of Vermont, *Off the Leash*, was published by Countryman/Norton. Patrick Downes's first short story was sold to *Story* magazine and resulted in an offer from Dial Press for Patrick's first novel. Dana Cameron, a mystery writer in David Bradley's workshop at Bread Loaf, now has a three-book contract with Avon for her series of mysteries featuring archaeologist Emma Fielding. And I'm continuing to work with several writers on works in progress from the conference.

What's your preferred etiquette for writer-agent relations at conferences? (Is it okay if writers approach you? Should they schedule meetings with you? Should they bring complete manuscripts or proposals? What are your pet peeves and turnoffs?)

Julie Barer: I'm totally fine with writers approaching me at conferences—that's what I'm there for! In general, I like to make appointments to talk with potential clients, but I find it helpful to first have a look at a sample of their work before we meet. I never mind looking at the first chapter or a brief proposal, but an entire manuscript is a lot to manage when you're there for only a few days, or even a week. (Plus it's a pain to carry home on the plane!) I generally like to see a chapter or two, and then if I'm interested I'll ask for more. While I'm always happy to answer questions and welcome queries being sent to my office, I tend to get turned off at conferences when someone walks right up and starts pitching me his or her story without even asking if I'm interested in hearing it. I'm also turned off by writers who focus too much on trying to sell themselves, rather than letting their work stand on its own.

Frances Kuffel: Approach me like I'm a person—not prey, not a deity. If I look tired, in a hurry, on my way to eat or to the bathroom, consider how you would feel if someone came up and said, "I'd like to tell you about . . ." for possibly the sixtieth time that day.

The nicest impromptu meetings have been when groups of writers who obviously like each other have invited me to join them and have included me in their conversation with gentle questions as a natural tangent of that conversation. They learn more about me and my style, tastes, experience, more about the writing/publishing process, and I feel welcomed and therefore much more curious and receptive.

Meetings are fine if they're on the conference's agenda and scheduled through the structure of the conference. If such meetings are not a part of my responsibilities, and I want to meet with a writer, I'll do the suggesting.

Do not bring material unless it has been requested, by me or through the structure of the conference. Ask if, when, and how much material I would like to have sent to me at my office after my return to New York.

The conferee who is going to strike an immediate discord is pretty much the opposite of all the qualities I've mentioned above. This writer is desperate to bag an agent, any agent, as quickly as possible, and will hound, shadow, watch, and otherwise pester me and everyone else for the length of the conference. I will hear from editors in attendance that this writer or that is on the prowl; other attendees avoid this writer because s/he monopolizes the agents and editors, is competitive, and is determined to prove his/her expertise in workshop/social settings. Insisting that I take his/her manuscript—now—and read it—now—this is the writer who will be least willing to listen to criticism or caution, to consider my knowledge of the industry, and to be most likely to fire off a lot of questions about who I know, how many books I've sold, how I conduct my business, who my clients are. My privacy has now been assaulted both because I am so intensely wanted and so intensely judged.

Kit Ward: Most of the conferences I've attended set up scheduled meetings between writers and agents (and other publishing professionals). Sometimes I meet with small groups of writers, particularly when the topic is to be the basics of working with an agent. Unless I've been sent the writers' submissions in advance (which is sometimes the arrangement), there isn't time for me to read and respond to the writers' work at the conference. The meetings are opportunities for writers to tell me what they're working on, what experience if any they've had in submitting or publishing their work, and to ask any questions I might be able to answer. It's best not to tell me the plot, but to describe the project in more general terms—literary fiction, mystery, memoir about growing up on a commune (or whatever). The object in most cases is for me to read and respond to your work after the conference. Rather than give me the material on the spot, plan to send me the manuscript, or proposal if nonfiction, as soon after the conference as you can (with, alas, the usual SASE for submissions).

Also, I welcome the chance encounters that every conference produces, be they brief conversations, shared mealtimes, and so forth. I should stress, though, that the most fruitful contact does not involve the writer's attempt to "sell" me his or her work on the spot. Only my response to reading the manuscript or proposal can "sell" me on a project.

What's your best piece of insider advice for a writer who attends a conference in hopes of establishing a relationship with an agent?

Julie Barer: One of the most important things is to find out how the agent would like to hear about or read your work. Rather than walking up to agents at dinner and immediately launching into your pitch, approach them after a workshop or panel or discussion and ask them what they would prefer. Would they like to hear about your project now, or would they like to make an appointment for sometime during the conference? Would they like to look at a sample of your work during the conference, or would they prefer to receive something in the mail after the conference is over? Be honest about what stage your manuscript is in, and be honest about whether or not you've shared your work with other agents at the conference. Most importantly, find out ahead of time what each individual agent specializes in—handing a noir mystery to an agent who specializes in gardening books is a waste of everyone's time.

Frances Kuffel: Be sensitive to how much pressure is on an agent during and in the aftermath of the conference. I don't hang out much, but another agent may be in the bar until two in the morning, welcoming all comers. Realize there are as many different styles as there are agents: observe their modus operandi, listen to what s/he says, and form your approach from that information.

Kit Ward: My best piece of insider advice to writers attending a conference? Don't be in a hurry to sell your book before it's ready. There's no substitute for a wonderful manuscript or, for nonfiction, a persuasive book proposal. To paraphrase the Zen proverb, when the book is ready, the agent will come. I've had first-time writers ask me, at our meeting, whether they "had to finish the novel" before approaching publishers. (We all hear about contracts offered on the basis of a few pages, and while this does happen, it's almost always for a writer of a very high level of accomplishment.) What's the hurry? The manuscript will have to be finished at some point! A good conference is an opportunity for writers to focus on their craft in an environment of rich experience and inspiration. Give yourself over to it. The publishing connections will fall into place when the time is right.

Writers' Conference Calendar

To see which conferences are being held in the upcoming months, check the writers' conference calendar listing each conference alphabetically by the month it occurs. It's often to your advantage to register for the conference you want to attend a few months in advance. This ensures you get the best prices and priority meeting slots available for consultations with the agents or editors. For screenwriters, some of the most popular conferences are UCLA's Los Angeles Writers Conference (February), the American Screenwriting Association's Selling to Hollywood (August), and the Santa Fe Screenwriting Conference (October).

For writers interested in screenplays or books, the San Diego State University Writers' Conference (January), the Maui Writers Conference (August), and the Southwest Writers Conference (September) are popular choices for their beautiful locations as well as for the large number of high-quality industry professionals who lead workshops and meet one-on-one with attendees. Who says you can't mix business with pleasure? Many of the conferences have discount hotel rates and airline fares. Why not plan to attend a conference on your next vacation?

January

San Diego State University Writers' Conference (San Diego, CA)
Society of Southwestern Authors Writers' Conference—Wrangling with Writing (Tucson, AZ)

February

American Christian Writers (based in Nashville TN) (Little Rock, AR; Houston, Austin & Dallas, TX)
Florida Christian Writers Conference (Brandenton, FL)
Florida Suncoast Writers' Conference (Tampa, FL)
Los Angeles Writers Conference (see UCLA Extension Writers' Program) (Los Angeles, CA)
Sleepless in Silverdale (Silverdale, WA)
Southern California Writers' Conference (San Diego, CA)
Whidbey Island Writers' Conference (Langley, WA)

March

American Christian Writers (based in Nashville TN) (Oklahoma City, OK; Fort Wayne, IN)
IWWG Early Spring In California Conference (New York, NY)
Writing Today (Birmingham, AL)

April

American Christian Writers (based in Nashville TN) (Richmond, VA; Charlotte, NC)
The College of New Jersey Writers' Conference (Ewing, NJ)
IWWG Meet the Authors, Agents and Editors (New York, NY)
Mount Hermon Christian Writers Conference (Mount Hermon, CA)
Northeast Texas Community College (Mount Pleasant, TX)
Pikes Peak Writers Conference (Colorado Springs, CO)
The William Saroyan Writers' Conference (Fresno, CA)
Sinipee Writers' Workshop (Dubuque, IA)

Society of Children's Book Writers & Illustrators / Hofstra Children's Literature Conference
   (Hemstead, NY)
Waterside Publishing Conference (Berkley, CA)

May

American Christian Writers (based in Nashville TN) (Atlanta, GA; Columbus, OH)
ASJA Writer's Conference (New York, NY)
The Bay Area Writers League Annual Conference (Seabrook, TX)
Florida First Coast Writers' Festival (Jacksonville, FL)
Midland Writers Conference (Midland, MI)
Pima Writers' Workshop (Tucson, AZ)
Washington Independent Writers (Washington DC)
Washington Writers Conference (Seattle, WA)
Writers' Retreat Workshop (Erlanger, KY)

June

American Christian Writers (based in Nashville TN) (Grand Rapids, MI; Syracuse, NY)
Aspen Summer Words Writing Retreat (Aspen, CO)
Bloody Words (Nepean, Ontario, Canada)
Frontiers in Writing (Amarillo, TX)
Heartland Writers Conference (Kennett, MO)
Highland Summer Conference (Radford, VA)
Jackson Hole Writers Conference (Jackson Hole, WY)
Mendocino Coast Writers Conference (Fort Bragg, CA)
National Writers Association Foundation Conference (Aurora, CO)
The New Letters Weekend Writers Conference (Kansas City, MO)
Of Dark & Story Nights, Mystery Writers of America (Muncie, IN)
Police Writers Conference (Ashburn, TN)
Santa Barbara Writers' Conference (Montecito, CA)
Short Course on Professional Writing (Norman, OK)
Southeastern Writers Conference (Decatur, GA)
Taos Poetry Circus (Taos, NM)
Wesleyan Writers Conference (Middletown, CT)

July

Agents! Agents! Agents! & Editors Too! (see Writers' League of Texas) (Austin, TX)
American Christian Writers (based in Nashville TN) (Orlando, FL; Nashville, TN)
A Day for Writers (Steamboat Springs, CO)
Festival of Words (Moose Jaw, Saskatchewan, Canada)
Highlights Foundation Writers Workshop (Chautauqua, NY)
Hofstra University Summer Writers' Conference (Hempstead, NY)
New England Writers Conference (Windsor, VT)
Pacific Northwest Writers Association (Seattle, WA)
Romance Writers of America National Conference (various)
Sewanee Writers' Conference (Sewanee, TN)
Writers Workshop in Science Fiction (Lawrence, KS)

August

American Christian Writers (based in Nashville TN) (Quad Cities, IA/IL; Minneapolis, MN)
Bread Loaf Writers' Conference (Middlebury, VT)
The Festival of the Written Arts (Sechelt, British Columbia, Canada)

Illustrating for Children (Los Angeles, CA)
Maui Writers Conference (Kihei, HI)
Rocky Mountain Fiction Writers Colorado Gold (Denver, CO)
Sage Hill Writing Experience (Saskatoon, Saskatchewan, Canada)
Selling to Hollywood International Screenwriters Conference (Los Angeles, CA)
Society of Children's Book Writers and Illustrators/National Conference on Writing and
Squaw Valley Community of Writers Fiction Workshop (Squaw Valley, CA)
Willamette Writers Conference (Portland, OR)

September

American Christian Writers (based in Nashville TN) (Colorado Springs, CO; Boise, ID; Seattle, WA)
The Columbus Writers Conference (Columbus, OH)
Lost State Writers Conference 2004 (Greeneville, TN)
National Museum Publishing Seminar 2004 (Chicago, IL)
Southwest Writers Conference (Albuquerque, NM)
Winnipeg International Writers Festival (Winnipeg, Manitoba, Canada)

October

American Christian Writers (based in Nashville TN) (Sacramento, Anaheim, San Diego, CA; Phoenix, AZ)
Austin Film Festival & Heart of Film Screenwriters Conference (Austin, TX)
Central Ohio Fiction Writers (Westerville, OH)
Blue Ridge Writers Conference (Blacksburg, VA)
Flathead River Writers Conference (Whitefish, MT)
The Mid America Crime Fiction Festival (Muncie, IN)
Oakland University Writers' Conference (Rochester, MI)
Ozark Creative Writers Inc. (Little Rock, AR)
Santa Fe Screenwriting Conference (Santa Fe, NM)
The Vancouver International Writers Festival (Granville Island, Vancouver, Canada)
A Writer's W*O*R*L*D / Surrey Writers' Conference (Surrey, British Columbia, Canada)

November

American Christian Writers (based in Nashville TN) (Fort Lauderdale, FL; Caribbean cruise)
Baltimore Writers' Alliance Conference (Riderwood, MD)
North Carolina Writers' Network Fall Conference (Carrboro, NC)
Sage Hill Writing Experience (Saskatoon, Saskatchewan, Canada)

December

Words & Music: A Literary Feast (New Orleans, LA)

Writers' Conferences

Many writers try to make it to at least one conference a year, but cost and location can count as much as subject matter when determining which conference to attend. There are conferences in almost every state and province that can provide answers to your questions about writing and the publishing industry. Conferences also connect you with a community of other writers. Such connections help you learn about the pros and cons of different agents writers have worked with, and give you a renewed sense of purpose and direction in your own writing.

When reading through this section, keep in mind the following information to help you pick the best conference for your needs:

REGIONS

To make it easier for you to find a conference close to home—or to find one in an exotic locale to fit into your vacation plans—we've separated this section into geographical regions. The regions are as follows:

Northeast (pages 294-295): Connecticut, Maine, Massachusetts, New Hampshire, New York, Rhode Island, Vermont.
Midatlantic (pages 295-296): Washington DC, Delaware, Maryland, New Jersey, Pennsylvania.
Midsouth (pages 296-298): North Carolina, South Carolina, Tennessee, Virginia, West Virginia.
Southeast (pages 298-299): Alabama, Arkansas, Florida, Georgia, Louisiana, Mississippi, Puerto Rico.
Midwest (pages 299-302): Illinois, Indiana, Kentucky, Michigan, Ohio.
North Central (page 302): Iowa, Minnesota, Nebraska, North Dakota, South Dakota, Wisconsin.
South Central (pages 302-306): Colorado, Kansas, Missouri, New Mexico, Oklahoma, Texas.
West (pages 307-310): Arizona, California, Hawaii, Nevada, Utah.
Northwest (page 310-312): Alaska, Idaho, Montana, Oregon, Washington, Wyoming.
Canada (pages 312-313).

REGION   COST   SIZE   FOCUS

Midsouth (NC, SC, TN, VA, WV)

PRETEND WRITERS' CONFERENCE, Southern University, 123 Network Way, Memphis TN 36589. (615)555-3135. E-mail: conference@aol.com. Website: www.writing.com. **Contact:** Sue Jones, director. Estab. 1982. Annual. Conference held July 14-21. Average attendance: 150. Conference offers seminars on publishing, writing fiction and nonfiction, and finding an agent. **Agents/speakers attending include:** B.L. Smith, R.W. Lane. Agents will be speaking and available for meetings with attendees. **Costs:** $800 for the week (includes 2 meals/day). **Accommodations:** Dormitory rooms available for $350. There are also many hotels in the area. **Additional Information:** Submit a 10-page writing sample for critique. "There are always at least two agents available to meet with writers." Conference brochures are available for SASE. Inquires by e-mail OK.

AGENTS IN ATTENDANCE

SUBHEADS

Each listing is divided into subheads to make locating specific information easier. In the first section, you'll find contact information for each conference. Also given are conference dates, specific focus, and size. If a conference is small, you may receive more individual attention from speakers. If it is large, there may be a greater number and variety of agents in attendance. Finally, names of agents who will be speaking or have spoken in the past are listed along with details about their availability during the conference. Calling or e-mailing a conference director to verify the names of agents in attendance is always a good idea.

Costs: Looking at the price of seminars, plus room and board, may help writers on a tight budget narrow their choices.

Accommodations: Here conferences list overnight accommodation and travel information. Often conferences held in hotels will reserve rooms at a discount price and may provide a shuttle bus to and from the local airport.

Additional Information: A range of features are given here, including information on contests, individual meetings, and the availability of brochures.

Quick Reference Icons

At the beginning of some listings, you will find one or more of the following symbols for quick identification of features particular to that listing.

N Conference new to this edition.

✓ Change in address, contact information, phone number or e-mail address from last year's edition.

Canadian conference.

International conference.

Get the Most from a Conference

Squeeze the most out of a conference by getting organized and staying involved. Follow these steps to ensure a worthwhile event.

Before you go:
- **Become familiar with all the pre-conference literature,** particularly the agenda. Study the maps of the area, especially the locations of the rooms in which your meetings/events are scheduled.
- **Make a list of three to five objectives you'd like to obtain,** e.g., whom you want to meet, what you want to learn more about, what you want to improve on, how many new markets you want to find.

At the conference:
- **Budget your time.** Label a map so you know ahead of time where, when and how to get to each session. Note what you want to do most. Then, schedule time with agents and editors for critique sessions.
- **Don't be afraid to explore new areas.** You are there to learn. Pick one or two sessions you wouldn't typically attend. This is an education; keep your mind open to new ideas and advice.
- **Allow time for mingling.** Some of the best information is given after the session. Find out "frank truths" and inside scoops. Asking people what they've learned at the conference will trigger a conversation that may branch into areas you want to know more about but won't hear from the speakers.
- **Learn about agents, editors and new markets.** Which are more open to new writers? Find a new contact in your area for future support.
- **Collect everything:** guidelines, sample issues, promotional fliers, and especially business cards. Make notes about the personalities of the people you meet to remind you later who to contact and who to avoid.
- **Find inspiration for future projects.** While you're away from home, people-watch, take a walk, a bike ride, or drive. You may even want to take pictures to enhance your memory.

After the conference:
- **Evaluate.** Write down the answers to these questions: Would I attend again? What were the pluses and minuses, e.g., speakers, location, food, topics, cost, lodging? What do I want to remember for next year? What should I try to do next time? Who would I like to meet?
- **Write a thank-you letter** to an agent or editor who has been particularly helpful. They'll remember you when you later submit.

Northeast (CT, MA, ME, NH, NY, RI, VT)

☑ **ASJA WRITERS CONFERENCE**, (formerly Writers Conference 2002), Amercian Society of Journalists and Authors, 1501 Broadway, Suite 302, New York NY 10036. (212)997-0947. Fax: (212)768-7414. E-mail: staff@asja.org. Website: www.asja.org. **Contact:** Brett Harvey, executive director. Estab. 1971. Annual. Conference held May 3-4, 2003. Conference duration: 2 days. Average attendance: 500. Nonfiction, screenwriting. Held at Grand Hyatt in New York. For 2002, panels included "Packaging and Re-selling Your Work," "Writing for the Web," "Networking Secrets from Pro Writers." **Previous agents/speakers have included:** Dominick Dunne, James Brady, Dana Sobel. Agents will be speaking.
Costs: $195 (includes lunch).
Accommodations: "The hotel holding our conference always blocks out discounted rooms for attendees."
Additional Information: Brochures available in February. Registration form on website. Inquiries by e-mail and fax OK.

BREAD LOAF WRITERS' CONFERENCE, Middlebury College, Middlebury VT 05753. (802)443-5286. Fax: (802)443-2087. E-mail: blwc@middlebury.edu. Website: www.middlebury.edu/~blwc. **Contact:** Noreen Cargill, administrative manager. Estab. 1926. Annual. Conference held in late August. Conference duration: 11 days. Average attendance: 230. For fiction, nonfiction and poetry. Held at the summer campus in Ripton, Vermont (belongs to Middlebury College).
Costs: $1,850 (includes room/board) (2002).
Accommodations: Accommodations are on campus in Ripton.

☑ **HOFSTRA UNIVERSITY SUMMER WRITERS' CONFERENCE**, 250 Hofstra University, UCCE, Hempstead NY 11549-1090. (516)463-5016. Fax: (516)463-4833. E-mail: uccelibarts@hofstra.edu. Website: www.hofstra.edu-writers (includes details on dates, faculty, general description, tuition). **Contact:** Marion Flomenhaft, director, Liberal Arts Studies. Estab. 1972. Annual (every summer, starting week after July 4). Conference held July 7-18, 2003. Average attendance: 65. Conference offers workshops in short fiction, nonfiction, poetry, juvenile fiction, stage/screenwriting and, on occasion, one other genre such as detective fiction or science fiction. Workshops in prose and poetry for high school student writers are also offered. Site is the university campus, a suburban setting, 25 miles from NYC. **Previous agent/speakers have incuded:** Roberta Allen, Ronald Bazarini, Carole Crowe, Brian Heinz and Rebecca Wolff. Agents will be speaking and available for meetings with attendees.
Costs: Non-credit (2 meals, no room): approximately $425 per workshop or $650 for two workshops. Credit: Approximately $1,100/workshop (2 credits) and $2,100/workshop (4 credits), graduate and undergraduate. Continental breakfast and lunch are provided daily; tuition also includes cost of banquet.
Accommodations: Free bus operates between Hempstead Train Station and campus for those commuting from NYC. Dormitory rooms are available for approximately $350 for the 2 week conference.
Additional Information: "All workshops include critiquing. Each participant is given one-on-one time for a half hour with workshop leader. We submit work to the Shaw Guides Contest and other writers' conferences, retreats and contests when appropriate."

IWWG MEET THE AUTHORS, AGENTS AND EDITORS: THE BIG APPLE WORKSHOPS, % International Women's Writing Guild, P.O. Box 810, Gracie Station, New York NY 10028-0082. (212)737-7536. Fax: (212)737-9469. E-mail: iwwg@iwwg.com. Website: www.iwwg.com. **Contact:** Hannelore Hahn, executive director. Estab. 1980. Conferences held generally the third weekend in April and the second weekend in October. Average attendance: 200. Workshops to promote creative writing and professional success. Held at the City Athletic Club of New York, mid-town New York City. **Previous agents/speakers have included:** Meredith Bernstein and Rita Rosenkranz. Sunday afternoon openhouse with agents and editors. Agents will be speaking and available for meetings with attendees.
Costs: $110 for members for the weekend; $130 for nonmembers for the weekend.
Accommodations: Information on transportation arrangements and overnight accommodations made available.
Additional Information: Workshop brochures/guidelines are available for SASE. Inquires by fax and e-mail OK. "Many contacts have been made between agents and authors over the years."

NEW ENGLAND WRITERS CONFERENCE, Box 483, Windsor VT 05089-0483. (802)674-2315. E-mail: newvtpoet@aol.com. Website: www.hometown.aol.com/newvtpoet/myhomepage/profile/html. **Contact:** Dr. Frank and Susan Anthony, co-directors. Estab. 1986. Annually. Conference held third Saturday in July. Conference duration: 1 day. Average attendance: 150. Held at the Grace-Outreach building 1 mile from Dartmouth campus. Panel on agents, children's publishing, fiction, nonfiction, and poetry. **Previous agents/speakers have included:** John Talbot Agency, Dana Gioia, Wesley McNair, Michael C. White.
Costs: $20 (includes seminar sessions, open readings, light lunch, writers' panel and ticket drawings).
Accommodations: "Hotel list can be made available. There are many hotels in the area."

Additional Information: "This annual conference continues our attempt to have a truly affordable writers conference that has as much as most 3-4 day events." Brochures available for SASE or on website. Inquiries by e-mail OK.

☑ SOCIETY OF CHILDREN'S BOOK WRITERS & ILLUSTRATORS CONFERENCE/HOFSTRA CHILDREN'S LITERATURE CONFERENCE, University College for Continuing Education, 250 Hofstra University, Hempstead NY 11549-1090. (516)463-5016. Fax: (516)463-4833. E-mail: uccelibarts@hofstra.edu. **Contact:** Marion Flomenhaft. Estab. 1985. Annual. Conference to be held April 2003. Average attendance: 200. Conference to encourage good writing for children. "The conference brings together writers, illustrators, librarians, agents, publishers, teachers and other professionals who are interested in writing for children. Each year we organize the program around a theme. Last year it was 'Finding Your Voice.'" The conference takes place at the Student Center Building of Hofstra University, located in Hempstead, Long Island. "We have two general sessions, five break-out groups." **Previous agents/speakers have included:** Paula Danziger and Ann M. Martin, and a panel of children's book editors who critique randomly selected first-manuscript pages submitted by registrants. Agents will be speaking and available for meetings with attendees.
Costs: $70 (previous year) for SCBWI members; $78 for nonmembers. Continental breakfast and full luncheon included.
Additional Information: Special interest groups are offered in submission procedures, fiction, nonfiction, writing picture books, illustrating picture books, poetry and scriptwriting.

WESLEYAN WRITERS CONFERENCE, Wesleyan University, Middletown CT 06459. (860)685-3604. Fax: (860)685-2441. E-mail: agreene@wesleyan.edu. Website: www.wesleyan.edu/writing/conferen.html. **Contact:** Anne Greene, director. Estab. 1956. Annual. Conference held the third week in June. Average attendance: 100. Fiction techniques, novel, short story, poetry, screenwriting, nonfiction, literary journalism, memoir. The conference is held on the campus of Wesleyan University, in the hills overlooking the Connecticut River. Features readings of new fiction, guest lectures on a range of topics including publishing and daily seminars. "Both new and experienced writers are welcome." **Agents/speakers attending include:** Edmond Harmsworth (Zachary Schuster Agency); Daniel Mandel (Sanford J. Greenburger Associates); Dorian Karchmar. Agents will be speaking and available for meetings with attendees.
Costs: In 2001, day rate $725 (includes meals); boarding students' rate $845 (includes meals and room for 5 nights).
Accommodations: "Participants can fly to Hartford or take Amtrak to Meriden, CT. We are happy to help participants make travel arrangements." Meals and lodging are provided on campus. Overnight participants stay on campus.
Additional Information: Manuscript critiques are available as part of the program but are not required. Participants may attend seminars in several different genres. Scholarships and teaching fellowships are available, including the Jakobson awards for fiction writers and poets and the Jon Davidoff Scholarships for journalists. Inquiries by e-mail and fax OK.

☑ WRITERS RETREAT WORKSHOP, % Write It/Sell It, 2507 S. Boston Place, Tulsa OK 74114. (800)642-2494. Fax: (918)583-7625. E-mail: wrwisi@cox.net. Website: www.writerstreatworkshop.com. **Contact:** Gail Provost Stockwell, director. Executive Director: Lance Stockwell. Editor-in-Residence: Lorin Oberweger. Estab. 1987. Conference held May 24-June 2, 2002. Held at Marydale Retreat Center in northern KY. Workshop duration: 10 days. Average attendance: 30. Focus on novels in progress. All genres. "Teaches a proven step-by-step process for developing and completing a novel for publication, developed originally by the late Gary Provost. The practical application of lessons learned in classes, combined with continual private consultations with staff members, guarantees dramatic improvement in craft, writing technique and self-editing skills." **Previous speakers/agents have included:** Donald Maass, Marcy Posner, Jennifer Jackson.
Costs: $1,695 for new students; $1,575 for returning students (includes lodging, meals, consultations and course materials).
Accomodations: Costs (discount for past participants) $1,695 for 10 days which includes all food and lodging, tuition and private consultations. The Marydale Retreat Center is 5 miles from the Cincinnati airport and offers shuttle services.

Midatlantic (DC, DE, MD, NJ, PA)

BALTIMORE WRITERS' ALLIANCE CONFERENCE, P.O. Box 410, Riderwood MD 21139. (410)377-5265. E-mail: bdiehl@jhsph.edu. Website: www.baltimorewriters.org. **Contact:** Barbara Diehl, coordinator. Estab. 1994. Annual. Conference held in November. Conference duration: 1 day. Average attendance: 150-200. Writing and getting published—all areas. Held at Towson University. Topics have included: mystery, science fiction, poetry, children's writing, legal issues, grant funding, working with an agent, book and magazine panels. **Previous agents/speakers have included:** Nat Sobel (Sobel/Weber Associates); Nina Graybill (Graybill and English). Agents will be speaking.

Costs: $70-80 (includes all-day conference, lunch and snacks). Manuscript critiques for additional fee.
Accommodations: Hotels close by, if required.
Additional Information: Inquiries by e-mail OK. May register through BWA website.

THE COLLEGE OF NEW JERSEY WRITERS' CONFERENCE, English Dept., The College of New Jersey, P.O. Box 7718, Ewing NJ 08628-0718. (609)771-3254. Fax: (609)637-5112. E-mail: write@tcnj.edu. **Contact:** Jean Hollander, director. Estab. 1980. Annual. Conference held in April. Conference duration: 9 a.m. to 10 p.m. Average attendance: 600-1,000. "Conference concentrates on fiction (the largest number of participants), poetry, children's literature, play and screenwriting, magazine and newspaper journalism, overcoming writer's block, nonfiction and memoir writing. Conference is held at the student center at the college in two auditoriums and workshop rooms; also Kendall Theatre on campus. We focus on various genres: romance, detective, mystery, TV writing, etc." Topics have included "How to Get Happily Published," "How to Get an Agent" and "Earning a Living as a Writer." The conference usually presents 20 or so authors, editors and agents, plus two featured speakers. **Previous agents/speakers have included:** Arthur Miller, Saul Bellow, Toni Morrison, Joyce Carol Oates, Erica Jong, Alice Walker and John Updike. Last year's evening presentation featured keynote speaker Margaret Atwood. Agents will be speaking and available for meetings with attendees.
Costs: General registration $50 for entire day, plus $10 for evening presentation. Lower rates for students.
Additional Information: Brochures/guidelines available.

N: HIGHLIGHTS FOUNDATION WRITERS WORKSHOP AT CHAUTAUQUA, Dept. NM, 814 Court St., Honesdale PA 18431. (570)253-1192. Fax: (570)253-0179. E-mail: contact@highlightsfoundation.org. **Contact:** Kent Brown, Jr., executive director. Estab. 1985. Annual. Workshop held July 12-19, 2003. Average attendance: 100. "Writer workshops geared toward those who write for children of beginner, intermediate, advanced levels. Small group workshops, one-to-one interaction between faculty and participants plus panel sessions, lectures and large group meetings. Workshop site is the picturesque community of Chautauqua, New York." Classes offered include "Point of View," "Writing Dialogue," "Characterization and Developing Plot." **Previous faculty/speakers have included:** Eve Bunting, James Cross Giblin, Jane Yolen, Dayton O. Hyde, Patricia Gauch, Jerry Spinelli, Joy Cowley and Ed Young.
Accommodations: "We coordinate ground transportation to and from airports, trains and bus stations in the Erie, PA and Jamestown/Buffalo, NY area. We also coordinate accommodations for conference attendees."
Additional Information: "We offer the opportunity for attendees to submit a manuscript for review at the conference." Workshop brochures/guidelines are available after January. More information available at www.high lightsfoundation.org.

✓ WASHINGTON INDEPENDENT WRITERS (WIW) SPRING WRITERS CONFERENCE, 733 15th St. NW, Suite 220, Washington DC 20005. (202)347-4973. Fax: (202)628-0298. E-mail: info@washwriter.o rg. Website: www.washwriter.org. **Contact:** Aishling McGinty, membership coordinator. Estab. 1975. Annual. Conference held May 16-17. Conference duration: Friday and Saturday. Average attendance: 250. Fiction, nonfiction, screenwriting, poetry, children's, technical. "Gives participants a chance to hear from and talk with dozens of experts on book and magazine publishing as well as on the craft, tools and business of writing." **Previous agents/speakers have included:** Erica Jong, John Barth, Kitty Kelley, Vanessa Leggett and Diana McLellan. New York and local agents at every conference.
Costs: $125 members; $175 nonmembers; $210 membership and conference.
Additional Information: Brochures/guidelines available for SASE in mid-February.

Midsouth (NC, SC, TN, VA, WV)

AMERICAN CHRISTIAN WRITERS CONFERENCES, P.O. Box 110390, Nashville TN 37222-0390. (800)21-WRITE. Fax: (615)834-7736. E-mail: regaforder@aol.com. Website: www.ACWriters.com (includes schedule of cities). **Contact:** Reg Forder, director. Estab. 1981. Annual. Conference duration: 2 days. Average attendance: 60. Fiction, nonfiction, scriptwriting. To promote all forms of Christian writing. Conferences held throughout the year in 36 US cities.
Costs: Approximately $169 plus meals and accommodation.
Accommodations: Special rates available at host hotel. Usually located at a major hotel chain like Holiday Inn.
Additional Information: Conference brochures/guidelines are available for SASE.

BLUE RIDGE WRITERS CONFERENCE, 911 Allendale Court, Blacksburg VA 24060. (540)961-3115. Fax: (540)231-3306. E-mail: agoethe@usit.net. **Contact:** Ann Goethe, president. Estab. 1984. Annual. Conference held in October. Conference duration: 1 day. Average attendance: 70-90. Novels, children's literature, poetry, adult fiction, creative nonfiction, journalism and the memoir. Held on the Virginia Tech campus, Blacksburg. **Previous speakers/agents have included:** Fred Chappell, Pinkney Bennett, Lee Smith, Ellen Gilchrist, John Casey and Katharine Soniat.

Costs: $65 general, $30 students. "No other costs included."
Accommodations: Information is available in brochure.

HIGHLAND SUMMER CONFERENCE, Box 7014, Radford University, Radford VA 24142-7014. (540)831-5366. Fax: (540)831-5004. E-mail: jasbury@radford.edu. Website: www.radford.edu/~arsc. **Contact:** JoAnn Asbury, assistant to director. Chair, Appalachian Studies Program: Dr. Grace Toney Edwards. Estab. 1978. Annual. Conference held in June. Conference duration: 15 days. Average attendance: 25. Fiction, nonfiction, screenwriting. **Previous speakers/agents have included:** Bill Brown, Robert Morgan, Sharyn McCrumb, Nikki Giovanni, Wilma Dykeman, Jim Wayne Miller. Agents will be speaking and available for meetings with attendees.
Costs: "The cost is based on current Radford tuition for 3 credit hours plus an additional conference fee. On-campus meals and housing are available at additional cost. In 2002, conference tuition was $409 for in-state undergraduates, $1,177 for out-of-state undergraduates, $501 for in-state graduates, $994 for out-of-state graduates."
Accommodations: "We do not have special rate arrangements with local hotels. We do offer accommodations on the Radford University Campus in a recently refurbished residence hall. (In 2002 cost was $19-28 per night.)"
Additional Information: "Conference leaders typically critique work done during the two-week conference, but do not ask to have any writing submitted prior to the conference beginning." Conference brochures/guidelines are available after February for SASE. Inquiries by e-mail and fax OK.

LOST STATE WRITERS CONFERENCE, P.O. Box 1442, Greeneville TN 37744. (423)636-6738. E-mail: tamarac@xtn.net. Website: www.loststatewriters.com. **Contact:** Tamara Chapman, director. Estab. 1998. Annually. Conference held in September 2004. Conference duration: 3 days. Average attendance: 300. Fiction, nonfiction, screenwriting, writing for children, poetry. Held at The General Morgan Inn & Conference Center, an historic hotel in Greeneville TN. Panels include fiction, nonfiction, poetry, an editor and agent panel, and a Southern writers panel. **Agents/speakers attending include:** representatives from William Morris, Virginia Barber, Harper-Collins and Random House. Agents will be speaking and available for meetings with attendees.
Costs: $200 (includes all workshops and partial meals).
Accommodations: List of area hotels on website and brochure. Cost for on-site accommodations: $69.
Additional Information: Scholarships available. Brochures available for SASE. Inquiries by e-mail OK.

✓ **NORTH CAROLINA WRITERS' NETWORK FALL CONFERENCE**, P.O. Box 954, Carrboro NC 27510-0954. (919)967-9540. Fax: (919)929-0535. E-mail: mail@ncwriters.org. Website: www.ncwriters.org (includes "history and information about the NC Writers' Network and our programs. Also has a links page to other writing-related websites"). **Contact:** Jan Wheaton, program & services director. Estab. 1985. Annual. "2002 Conference will be held in Rese Arch Triangle Park, NC, November 15-17." Average attendance: 450. Fiction, nonfiction, screenwriting. "The conference is a weekend full of workshops, panels, readings and discussion groups. We try to have a variety of genres represented. In the past we have had fiction writers, poets, journalists, editors, children's writers, young adult writers, storytellers, playwrights, screenwriters, technical writing, web-based writing, etc. We take the conference to a different location in North Carolina each year in order to best serve our entire state. We hold the conference at a conference center with hotel rooms available." **Previous agents/speakers have included:** Christy Fletcher and Neal Bascomb (Carlisle & Co.); Delin Cormeny (PMA Literary & Film Agency); Joe Regal (Viking Press). Agents will be speaking and available for meetings with attendees.
Costs: "Conference cost is approximately $200-225 and includes two meals."
Accommodations: "Special conference hotel rates are available, but the individual makes his/her own reservations."
Additional Information: Conference brochures/guidelines are available by sending street address to mail@ncwriters.org or on website. Inquiries by fax and e-mail OK.

✓ **POLICE WRITERS CONFERENCE**, Police Writers Association, P.O. Box 738, Ashburn VA 20146. (703)723-4740. Fax: (703)723-4743. E-mail: leslye@policewriter.com. Website: www.policewriter.com. **Contact:** Leslyeann Rolik. Estab. 1996. Annually. Conference held June 2002. Conference duration: 2 days. Average attendance: 50. Related writing—both fiction and nonfiction. Focuses on police. Held in various hotels in various regions, determined annually. "Each year the conference focuses on helping club members get their work polished and published." **Previous agents/speakers have included:** Paul Bishop (novelist), Ed Dee (novelist), Roger Fulton (editor).
Costs: $175-300 in 2002 (includes all classes and seminars, fiction and nonfiction writing contest entries and awards luncheons).

CAN'T FIND A CONFERENCE? Conferences are listed by region. Check the introduction to this section for a list of regional categories.

Accommodations: Hotel arrangements, at special conference rates, are available.
Additional Information: "Unpublished police genre writers are welcomed at the conference and as Police Writers Association Members." Brochures available on website. Inquiries by fax OK.

☑ SEWANEE WRITERS' CONFERENCE, 310 St. Luke's Hall, Sewanee TN 37383-1000. (931)598-1141. E-mail: cpeters@sewanee.edu. Website: www.sewaneewriters.org (includes general conference information and schedule of events). **Contact:** Cheri B. Peters, creative writing programs manager. Estab. 1990. Annual. Conference held in July. Conference duration: 12 days. Average attendance: 110. "We offer genre-based workshops (in fiction, poetry and playwriting), not theme-based workshops. The Sewanee Writers' Conference uses the facilities of the University of the South. Physically, the University is a collection of ivy-covered Gothic-style buildings, located on the Cumberland Plateau in mid-Tennessee. Editors, publishers and agents structure their own presentations, but there is always opportunity for questions from the audience." **Previous agents/speakers have included:** Tony Earley, Barry Hannah, Romulus Linney, Alice McDermott, Erin McGraw, Padgett Powell, Daisy Foote, Debora Greger, Robert Hass, John Hollander, Margot Livesey, William Logan, Alison Lurie, Tim O'Brien.
Costs: Full conference fee is $1,325 (includes tuition, board, and basic room).
Accommodations: Participants are housed in University dormitory rooms. Motel or B&B housing is available but not abundantly so. Dormitory housing costs are included in the full conference fee.
Additional Information: Complimentary chartered bus service is available, on a limited basis, on the first and last days of the conference. "We offer each participant (excepting auditors) the opportunity for a private manuscript conference with a member of the faculty. These manuscripts are due one month before the conference begins." Conference brochures/guidelines are available, "but no SASE is necessary. The conference has available a limited number of fellowships and scholarships; these are awarded on a competitive basis."

Southeast (AL, AR, FL, GA, LA, MS, Puerto Rico)

FLORIDA CHRISTIAN WRITERS CONFERENCE, 2344 Armour Court, Titusville FL 32780. (321)269-5831. Website: www.flwriter.org. **Conference Director:** Billie Wilson. Estab. 1988. Annual. Conference is held in February. Conference duration: 5 days. Average attendance: 200. To promote "all areas of writing." Conference held at Christian Retreat Center in Brandenton FL. Editors will represent over 45 publications and publishing houses.
Costs: Tuition is $400 (includes tuition, food); $500 (double occupancy); $600 (single occupancy).
Accommodations: "We provide shuttle from the Tampa airport."
Additional Information: Critiques available. "Each writer may submit two works for critique. We have specialists in every area of writing." Conference brochures/guidelines are available for SASE and on website.

☑ FLORIDA FIRST COAST WRITERS' FESTIVAL, 9911 Old Baymeadows Rd., Room C1301, FCCJ, Jacksonville FL 32256. (904)997-2669. Fax: (904)997-2746. E-mail: kclower@fccj.org. Website: ww.fccj.org/wf (includes festival workshop speakers, contest information). **Contacts:** Kathy Clower and Howard Denson. Estab. 1985. Annual. Conference held May 15-17, 2003. Held at Sea Turtle Inn, Atlantic Beach, FL. Average attendance: 300. All areas: mainstream plus genre. Fiction, nonfiction, scriptwriting, poetry, mystery, humor, freelancing, etc. Offers seminars on narrative structure and plotting character development. **Invited agents/speakers include:** Kitty Oliver, John Dufresne, Robert Inman, Arthur Rosenfeld, Kathy Pories (editor), Shelley Mickle, Sandra Kitt, Sheree Bykofsky (agent), Elizabeth Lund, David Poyer, Lenoe Hart and more to be announced. Agents will be speaking and available for meetings with attendees.
Costs: Maximum of $150 for 2 days, with 2 meals.
Accommodations: Sea Turtle Inn, (904)249-7402 or 1(800)874-6000, has a special festival rate.
Additional Information: Conference brochures/guidelines are available for SASE. Sponsors a contest for short fiction, poetry and novels. Novel judges are David Poyer and Lenore Hart. Entry fees: $30, novels; $10, short fiction; $5, poetry. Deadline: December 1. "We offer one-on-one sessions at no additional costs for attendees to speak to selected writers, editors, agents on first-come, first-served basis."

FLORIDA SUNCOAST WRITERS' CONFERENCE, University of South Florida, Division of Professional & Workforce Development, 4202 E. Fowler Ave., MHH-116, Tampa FL 33620-6610. (813)974-2403. Fax: (813)974-5421. E-mail: mglakis@admin.usf.edu. Directors: Steve Rubin, Ed Hirshberg, Betty Moss and Lagretta Lenkar. Estab. 1970. Annual. Held February 6-8, 2003. Conference duration: 3 days. Average attendance: 400. Conference covers poetry, short story, novel and nonfiction, including science fiction, detective, travel writing, drama, TV scripts, photojournalism and juvenile. "We do not focus on any one particular aspect of the writing profession but instead offer a variety of writing related topics. The conference is held on the picturesque university campus fronting the bay in St. Petersburg, Florida." Features panels with agents and editors. **Previous speakers/agents have included:** Lady P.D. James, William Styron, John Updike, Joyce Carol Oates, Francine Prose, Frank McCourt, David Guterson and Jane Smiley.
Costs: Call for information.
Accommodations: Special rates available at area motels. "All information is contained in our brochure."

Get the 2004 EDITION
at this year's price!

You already know an agent can be the key to selling your work. But, how do you know when you're ready to sign on with one? And, how do you select an agent that's right for you? To make such crucial decisions you need the most up-to-date information on the agents out there and what they can offer you. That's exactly what you'll find in *Guide to Literary Agents*.

Through this special offer, you can get a jump on next year today! If you order now, you'll get the *2004 Guide to Literary Agents* at the 2003 price—just $23.99—no matter how much the regular price may increase!

2004 Guide to Literary Agents will be published and ready for shipment in November 2003.

Turn Over for More Great Books to Help You Write and Sell Your Work!

Write Better and Sell More
with Help from These Writer's Digest Books!

Agents, Editors and You
Dozens of industry professionals provide you with essential information on everything from preparing your manuscript and getting it into the hands of the right editor, to the finer points of e-publishing.
#10817-K/$17.99/256p/pb

The Complete Handbook of Novel Writing
This compilation of the best interviews from *Writer's Digest* magazine, books and annuals will guide you through the craft, art and process of writing your novel. Includes interviews and articles from bestselling authors including Margaret Atwood, Tom Clancy, James Patterson, Nora Roberts, Kurt Vonnegut and more!
#10825-K/$17.99/400p/pb

How to Get Your e-Book Published
This authoritative, step-by-step guide to conquering the e-book market will help you understand digital rights management, select the best delivery format, market your work and more!
#10776-K/$16.99/256p/pb

Writer's Market FAQs
You'll find fast answers on how to get published more easily, more often and for more money. With tips on how to succeed with traditional publishing houses as well as in the wired world of e-publishing. Plus, how to protect your work, handle agents and editors and more!
#10754-K/$18.99/240p/pb

Writer's Online Marketplace
Discover more than 250 paying Internet markets, and get advice on the unique marketing and writing techniques needed to succeed in the wired world. Includes interviews with online editors, and a list of agents who handle e-work.
#10697-K/$17.99/240p/pb

Guerrilla Marketing for Writers
Packed with more than 100 low-cost weapons to help you sell your books, before and after they're finished. You'll also get insider insight into how the publishing industry works to help you develop a complete, professional promotion plan.
#10667-K/$14.99/224p/pb

Additional Information: Participants may submit work for critiquing. Extra fee charged for this service. Conference brochures/guidelines are available November 2002. Inquiries by e-mail and fax OK.

OZARK CREATIVE WRITERS INC., 75 Robinwood Dr., Little Rock, AR 72227. (501)225-8619. **Contact:** Marcia Camp, conference business manager. Estab. 1975. Annual. Conference held second weekend in October. Conference duration: Thursday through Saturday. Average attendance: 150. Includes programs for all types of writing, about one half of attendees are already published. Conference held at conference center and inn in the Arkansas Ozark mountains. **Previous agents/speakers have included:** Dan Slater (editor, Penguin Putnam); Stephan Harrigan (novelist, screenwriter).
Costs: $60 before August 25, $70 after August 25 (includes cocktail party, continental breakfast for 2 days). Friday and Saturday night banquet are optional for an additional fee.
Accommodations: Special conference rates available at the Inn of the Ozarks.
Additional Information: "The conference has a friendly atmosphere and conference speakers are available. Many speakers return to the conference for the companionship of writers and speakers." Brochures available for SASE.

SOUTHEASTERN WRITERS CONFERENCE, 1399 Vista Leaf Dr., Decatur GA 30033-2028. (404)636-1316. E-mail: g&dworth@gsu.edu. **Contact:** Dorothy Williamson Worth, president. Estab. 1975. Annual. Conference held June 15-21, 2003. Conference duration: 1 week. Average attendence: 100 (limited to 100 participants). Concentration is on fiction, poetry, juvenile, nonfiction, playwriting, storytelling and genre. Site is St. Simons Island, GA. Conference held at Epworth-by-the-Sea Conference Center—tropical setting, beaches. "Each year we offer market advice, agent updates. All our instructors are professional writers presently selling in New York."
Agents/speakers attending included: Carolyn Grayson (Ashley-Grayson Literary Agency), Cricket Pechstein (The Christina Pechstein Agency), Jeff Gerecke (JCA Literary Agency). Agents will be speaking and available for meetings with attendees.
Costs: $250 for early bird registration before April 15, 2003. $290 regular tuition. Meals and lodging are separate.
Accommodations: Information on overnight accommodations is made available. "On-site facilities at a remarkably low cost. Facilities are motel style of excellent quality. Other hotels are available on the island."
Additional Information: "Three manuscript submissions of one chapter each are allowed in three different categories." Sponsors several contests, MANY cash prizes. Brochures are available in March for SASE.

WORDS & MUSIC: A LITERARY FEAST IN NEW ORLEANS, 632 Pirates Alley, New Orleans LA 70116. (504)586-1609. Fax: (504)522-9725. E-mail: faulkhouse@aol.com. Website: www.Wordsandmusic.org. Conference Director: Rosemary James DeSalvo. Estab. 1997. Annual. Conference held December 5-9, 2002. Conference duration: 5 days. Average attendance: 350-400. Presenters include authors, agents, editors and publishers. **Previous agents/speakers have included:** Deborah Grosvenor (Deborah Grosvenor Literary Agency); Jenny Bent (Harvey Klinger Agency); M.T. Caen. Agents will be speaking and available for meetings with attendees.
Costs: $350 tuition fee.
Accommodations: Hotel Monteleone in New Orleans.
Additional Information: Write for additional information.

✓ **WRITING TODAY—BIRMINGHAM-SOUTHERN COLLEGE**, Box 549003, Birmingham AL 35254. (205)226-4921. Fax: (205)226-3072. E-mail: dcwilson@bsc.edu. Website: www.bsc.edu. **Contact:** Dee Wilson. Estab. 1978. Annual. Conference scheduled March 7-8, 2003. Average attendance: 400-500. "This is a two-day conference with approximately 18 workshops, lectures and readings. We try to offer workshops in short fiction, novels, poetry, children's literature, magazine writing, and general information of concern to aspiring writers such as publishing, agents, markets and research. The conference is sponsored by Birmingham-Southern College and is held on the campus in classrooms and lecture halls." **Previous agents/speakers included:** Eudora Welty, Pat Conroy, Ernest Gaines, Ray Bradbury, Erskine Caldwell, John Barth, Galway Kinnell, Edward Albee. Agents will be speaking and available for meetings with attendees.
Costs: $120 for both days (includes lunches, reception, and morning coffee and rolls).
Accommodations: Attendees must arrange own transporation. Local hotels and motels offer special rates, but participants must make their own reservations.
Additional Information: "We usually offer a critique for interested writers. For those who request and send manuscripts by the deadline, we have had poetry and short story critiques. There is an additional charge for these critiques." Conference sponsors the Hackney Literary Competition Awards for poetry, short story and novels. Brochures available for SASE.

Midwest (IL, IN, KY, MI, OH)

N CAPON SPRINGS WRITERS' WORKSHOP, P.O. Box 11116, Cincinnati OH 45211-0116. (513)481-9884. Fax: (513)481-2646. E-mail: beckcomm@fuse.net. **Contact:** Wendy Beckman, director. Estab. 2000. Bian-

nual. Conference held mid-June or mid-September in even years. Conference duration: 3 days. Fiction, poetry, creative nonfiction. Conference held at Farm Resort, 5,000-acre secluded mountain resort in West Virginia. In 2000, theme was "A Sense of Place."
Costs: $375, in 2000 (includes seminars, meals, lodging, manuscript critique).
Accommodations: Facility has swimming, hiking, fishing, tennis, badminton, volleyball, basketball, ping pong, campfire sing along. Nine-hole golf course available for additional fee.
Additional Information: Brochures available for SASE. Inquiries by fax and e-mail OK.

CENTRAL OHIO FICTION WRITERS READERS & WRITERS HOLIDAY: A conference for book lovers, P.O. Box 1981, Westerville OH 43086-1981. E-mail: sargtaz@yahoo.com. Website: www.cofw.org. **Contact:** Patricia Sargeant-Matthews, 2002 conference chair. Estab. 1991. Annually. Conference held October 4-5, 2002. Conference duration: 1½ days. Average attendance: 100 attendees. Fiction, nonfiction, screenwriting, writing for children, poetry, etc. The conference is designed to address the needs of writers in all genres of fiction. The purpose of the conference is to explore fiction-writing trends, and discuss the business as well as the craft of writing. Central Ohio Fiction Writers's conference keynote speaker is usually a popular fiction author who can discuss writing trends. We also invite a publishing house editor and a literary agent to discuss the business side of writing. We offer a writing workshop. Attendees also are offered the opportunity to pitch their completed mss to the guest editor and/or agent. A continental breakfast and hearty lunch—complete with dessert—is part of the conference registration. The conference hosts a book fair with a number of popular fiction authors present to talk to readers and aspiring authors, as well as to autograph their books. Door prizes and raffles also are held. Held in a Columbus, Ohio-area hotel. The main events are held in a large ballroom. The workshop, book fair, editor and agent appointments are held in separate rooms. As part of the contractual agreement, the hotel offers Central Ohio Fiction Writers's conference guests a discounted rate for rooms. "During our upcoming conference, October 4-5, 2002, our workshop will help attendees polish their manuscript pitch to editors and agents." **Speakers in 2002 included:** Jennifer Crusie and Barbara Samuel/Ruth Wind, discussed the writing muse and how to get the most of her; Barbara Collins Rosenberg, the Rosenberg Group discussed publishing contracts; Cindy Hwang, Penguin Putnam discussed the trends for Penguin Putnam.
Costs: The agent appointment was $10 for non-Central Ohio Fiction Writers members; free for members. $60 for Central Ohio Fiction Writers members; $70 for non-Central Ohio Fiction Writers members. Fee includes conference registration, Friday night workshop, continental breakfast Saturday, writers' resource booklet and Saturday luncheon.
Accommodations: As part of our contractual agreement with the hotel, Central Ohio Fiction Writers's conference attendees are given discounted hotel accommodations. For the 2002 conference, the host hotel, The Wyndham Dublin Hotel, offers conference attendees double rooms for $79/night.

THE COLUMBUS WRITERS CONFERENCE, P.O. Box 20548, Columbus OH 43220. (614)451-3075. Fax: (614)451-0174. E-mail: AngelaPL28@aol.com. Website: creatiavevista.com. Director: Angela Palazzolo. Estab. 1993. Annual. Conference held in September. Average attendance: over 300. "The conference covers a wide variety of fiction and nonfiction topics presented by writers, editors and literary agents. Writing topics have included novel, short story, children's, young adult, science fiction, fantasy, humor, mystery, playwriting, screenwriting, personal essay, travel, humor, cookbook, technical, magazine writing, query letter, corporate, educational and greeting cards. Other topics for writers: finding and working with an agent, targeting markets, research, time management, obtaining grants and writers' colonies." **Previous agents/speakers have included:** Lee K. Abbott, Lore Segal, Jeff Herman, Andrea Brown, Simon Lipskar, Doris S. Michaels, Sheree Bykofsky, Mike Harden, Oscar Collier, Maureen F. McHugh, Ralph Keyes, Stephanie S. Tolan, Bonnie Pryor, Dennis L. McKiernan, Karen Harper, Rita Rosenkranz, Mark D. Ryan, Melvin Helitzer, Susan Porter, Les Roberts, Tracey E. Dils, J. Patrick Lewis and many other professionals in the writing field.
Costs: Early registration fee is $189 for full conference (includes Friday and Saturday sessions, Friday dinner program, Friday open mic sessions, and Saturday continental breakfast, lunch, and afternoon refreshments); otherwise, fee is $209. Early registration fee for Friday only is $70; otherwise, fee is $85. Friday dinner program is $38. Early registration fee for Saturday only is $154; otherwise, fee is $174. Friday dinner program is $38.
Additional Information: Call, write, e-mail or send fax to obtain a conference brochure, available mid-summer.

KENTUCKY WOMEN WRITERS CONFERENCE, P.O. Box 1042, Lexington KY 40588-1042. (859)254-4175. Fax: (859)281-1151. E-mail: kywwc@hotmail.com. Website: www.carnegieliteracy.org. **Contact:** Brenda Weber. Annual. Conference held in spring 2003. Fiction, nonfiction, poetry. "Gathering of women writers and scholars—novelists, poets, playwrights, essayists, biographers, journalists—and readers and students of literature. For the past twenty years, several days of reading, lectures, workshops, musical and theater performances and panel discussions about women writers and women's writing have been held both on campus and out in the community." Future sites will be in various venues in the community. Also traditional activities will involve creative writing of all kinds. **Previous agents/speakers have included:** Alice Walker, Barbara Kingsolver, Margaret Atwood, Sandra Maria-Esteves, Peggy Seeger, Lynn Pruett, Nalo Hopkinson.
Costs: To be announced for 2003.
Accommodations: A list of area hotels will be provided by the Lexington Convention & Tourist Bureau upon request. Call (859)233-1221.

Additional Information: "Manuscript critiques of pre-submitted fiction, poetry, playwriting and nonfiction by registered conference participants will be provided by regional writers." Scholarships are available for those who would otherwise be unable to attend. "For details, contact us at kywwc@hotmail.com."

THE MID AMERICA CRIME FICTION FESTIVAL, (formerly The Mid America Mystery Conference), Magna cum Murder, The E.B. Ball Center, Ball State University, Muncie IN 47306. (765)285-8975. Fax: (765)747-9566. E-mail: kennisonk@aol.com. Website: www.magnacummurder.com. **Contact:** Kathryn Kennison, director. Estab. 1994. Annual. Conference held from October 25-27, 2002. Average attendance: 400. Fiction, nonfiction. Held in the Horizon Convention Center and Historic Radisson Hotel Roberts. Conference for crime and detective fiction. **Previous agents/speakers have included:** Val McDermid and Donald Westlake. This year's guests of honor are Michael Connelly and Frances Fyfield.
Costs: $175 (includes continental breakfast, boxed lunches, a reception and a banquet).

MIDLAND WRITERS CONFERENCE, Grace A. Dow Memorial Library, 1710 W. St. Andrews, Midland MI 48640-2698. (989)837-3430. Fax: (989)837-3468. E-mail: ajarvis@midland-mi.org. Website: www.midland-mi.org/gracedowlibrary. Conference Chair: Katherine Redwine. **Contact:** Ann Jarvis, librarian. Estab. 1980. Annual. Conference held in June. Average attendance: 100. Fiction, nonfiction, children's and poetry. "The Conference is composed of a well-known keynote speaker and six workshops on a variety of subjects including poetry, children's writing, nonfiction, freelancing, agents, etc. The attendees are both published and unpublished authors. The Conference is held at the Grace A. Dow Memorial Library in the auditorium and conference rooms."
Previous speakers/agents have included: James W. Armstrong, Ruth Dukelow, Steve Griffin, Tom Powers, Brenda Shannon Yee, Sarah Zettle. Agents will be speaking.
Costs: Adult, $50; students, senior citizens and handicapped, $40. A box lunch is available. Costs are approximate until plans for upcoming conference are finalized.
Accommodations: A list of area hotels is available.
Additional Information: Conference brochures/guidelines are mailed mid-April. Call or write to be put on mailing list. Inquiries by e-mail and fax OK.

NATIONAL MUSEUM PUBLISHING SEMINAR, University of Chicago, Graham School of General Studies, 1427 E. 60th St., Chicago IL 60637. (773)702-1682. Fax: (773)702-6814. E-mail: s-medlock@uchicago.edu. **Contact:** Stephanie Medlock, director. Estab. 1988. Biennially. Conference September 2004. Themes include: the concept of branding, the conflict between popular and academic catalogs, how to conduct photo research, and much more. Conference duration: 2½ days. Average attendance: 250. Primarily nonfiction, writing and editing in museums. "Conference moves to a new city every time and is co-sponsored by the University and different museums." Agents will be attending.
Costs: $425, includes a dinner sponsored by the Shedd Aquarium, a lunch, and materials.
Accomodations: Accomodations at the Chicago Hilton will be $185/night.
Additional Information: Brochures available for SASE after June 1, 2002. Inquiries by fax and e-mail OK.

☑ **OAKLAND UNIVERSITY WRITERS' CONFERENCE**, 221 Varner Hall, Rochester MI 48309-4401. (248)370-3125. Fax: (248)370-4280. E-mail: gjboddy@oakland.edu. Website: www.oakland.edu/contin-ed/writer sconf/. **Contact:** Gloria J. Boddy, program director. Estab. 1961. Annual. Conference held in October 18-19, 2002. Average attendance: 400. Held at Oakland University: Oakland Center. Conference covers all aspects and types of writing in 36 concurrent workshops on Saturday. "It is a conference for beginning and established writers. It provides an opportunity to exchange ideas and perfect writing skills by meeting with agents, editors and successful writers." Major writers from various genres are speakers for the Saturday conference and luncheon program. Individual critiques, one-day writer retreats and hands-on writing workshops are conducted Friday. Areas: nonfiction, young adult fiction, poetry, short fiction, chapbooks, magazine fiction, essay, script writing.
Previous agents/speakers have included: Delen Cormeny, agent; Arthur Evans, university press editor; Karen Renaud, small presses. Agents will be speaking and available for meetings with attendees.
Costs: 2002: Conference registration: $95; lunch, $10; individual mss, $68; writing workshop, $58.
Accommodations: Hotel list is available.
Additional Information: Conference brochure/guidelines available after August 2002 for SASE. Inquiries by e-mail and fax OK.

OF DARK & STORMY NIGHTS, Mystery Writers of America—Midwest Chapter, P.O. Box 1944, Muncie IN 47308-1944. (765)288-7402. E-mail: spurgeonmwa@juno.com. Website: www.zoss.com/stormynig hts/. **Contact:** W.W. Spurgeon, workshop director. Estab. 1982. Annual. Workshop held June 8, 2002. Workshop

---

TO FIND A LIST OF CONFERENCES occurring in upcoming months, check the conference calendar in the introduction to this section beginning on page 288.

duration: 1 day. Average attendance: 200. Fiction, nonfiction, scriptwriting, children, young adult. Dedicated to "writing *mystery* fiction and crime-related nonfiction. Workshops and panels presented on plotting, dialogue, promotion, writers' groups, dealing with agents, synopsis and manuscript presentation, plus various technical aspects of crime and mystery." Held at the Holiday Inn, Rolling Meadows IL (suburban Chicago). **Previous agents/speakers have included:** Kimberley Cameron (Reese Halsey North), Javan Kienzle, Victoria Houston, William X. Kienzele, Jay Bonansinga, Brandon DuBois, S.J. Rozan, Barbara D'Amato, Joe Hensley, Hariette Gillem Robinet, Michael Raleigh, James Brewer, Jeremiah Healy. "Our agents speak, do critiques and schmooze with those attending." Agents will be speaking and available for meetings with attendees.
Costs: $130 for MWA members; $160 for nonmembers; $50 extra for ms critique.
Accommodations: Easily accessible by car or train (from Chicago) Holiday Inn, Rolling Meadows $96/night plus tax; free airport bus (Chicago O'Hare) and previously arranged rides from train.
Additional Information: "We accept manuscripts for critique (first 30 pages maximum); $50 cost. Writers meet with critics during workshop for one-on-one discussions." Brochures available for SASE after January 1.

WRITERS' RETREAT WORKSHOP, Write It/Sell It, 2507 S. Boston Place, Tulsa OK 74114. (800)642-2494. Fax: (918)583-7625. E-mail: wrwwisi@cox.net. Website: www.writersretreatworkshop.com. **Contact:** Gail Provost Stockwell, director. Estab. 1987. Annual. Conference held May 23-June 1, 2003. Conference duration: 10 days. Average attendance: 30. Novels-in-progress, all genres, narrative nonfiction. Held at Marydale Retreat Center in northern KY. "Teaches a proven step-by-step process for developing and completing a novel for publication, developed originally by the late Gary Provost. The practical application of lessons learned in classes, combined with continual private consultations with staff members, guarantees dramatic improvement in craft, writing technique and self-editing skills." **Agents/Speakers attending include:** Elizabeth Lyon, editor; Marcy Posner, agent; Jennifer Jackson, agent; T.J. MacGregor, author; Nancy Pickard, author.
Costs: $1,695, new students; $1,525 returning students (includes lodging, meals, consultations and course materials.)
Accommodations: Marydale Retreat Center provides complimentary shuttle services between Cincinnati airport and the center.

North Central (IA, MN, NE, ND, SD, WI)

☑ SINIPEE WRITERS' WORKSHOP, Loras College, 1450 Alta Vista, Dubuque IA 52004-0178. (563)588-7139. Fax: (563)588-4962. E-mail: cneuhaus@loras.edu. Website: www.loras.edu. **Contact:** Chris Neuhaus, secretary of continuing education. Director Emeritus: John Tigges. Estab. 1985. Annual. Conference scheduled for April 12, 2003. Average attendance: 50-75. The workshop is held on the campus of Loras College in Dubuque. "This campus holds a unique atmosphere and everyone seems to love the relaxed and restful mood it inspires. This in turn carries over to the workshop, and friendships are made that last in addition to learning and experiencing what other writers have gone through to attain success in their chosen field." **Previous agents/speakers include:** Shirley Damsgaard, Larry Goldberg, Pam Kress, Jim Shaffer, Kathryn Struck. Agents will be speaking and available for meetings with attendees.
Costs: $65 early registration; $75 at the door (includes all handouts, necessary materials for the workshop, coffee/snack break, lunch, drinks and snacks at autograph party following workshop). Discounts available for fulltime students and senior citizens.
Accommodations: Information is available for out-of-town participants, concerning motels, etc., even though the workshop is 1-day long.
Additional Information: Offers The John Tigges Writing Contest for Short Fiction, Nonfiction and Poetry. Limit 1,500 words (fiction or nonfiction), 40 lines (poetry). 1st prize in all 3 categories: $100 plus publication in an area newspaper or magazine; 2nd prize all categories: $50; 3rd prize in all categories: $25. Entry fee: $5/ entry in any category. Written critique service available for contest entries, $15 extra. Deadline: In-hand by March 24, 2003. Conference brochures/guidelines are available in February for SASE.

South Central (CO, KS, MO, NM, OK, TX)

A DAY FOR WRITERS, P.O. Box 774284, Steamboat Springs CO 80477. (970)879-8079. E-mail: mshfreiberge r@cs.com. **Contact:** Harriet Freiberger, director. Estab. 1981. Annual. Conference held in July. Conference duration: 1 day. Average attendance: 35. Featured areas of instruction change each year. Held at the restored train depot, home of the Steamboat Springs Arts Council. **Previous agents/speakers have included:** Jim Fergus, Avi, Robert Greer, Renate Wood.
Costs: $35 prior to June 1; $45 after June 1 (includes seminars, catered luncheon). Pre-conference dinner also available at $13/person. Limited enrollment.
Additional Information: Brochures available in April for SASE. Inquiries by e-mail OK.

■ **ASPEN SUMMER WORDS WRITING RETREAT AND LITERARY FESTIVAL**, (formerly Aspen Summer Words), Aspen Writers' Foundation, 110 E. Hallam St., #116, Aspen CO 81611. (800)925-2526. Fax (970)920-5700. E-mail: info@aspenwriters.org. Website: www.aspenwriters.org. **Contact:** Julie Comins, executive director. Estab. 1976. Annual. Conference held in late June. Conference duration: 1 week. Average attendance: 50 at writing retreat, 1,500 at literary festival. Retreat for fiction, poetry, creative nonfiction. Festival includes author readings, panel discussions with publishing industry insiders, professional consultations with editors and agents and social gatherings. **Previous agents/speakers have included:** Suzanne Gluck, Elizabeth Sheinkman and Jody Hotchkiss (agents); Jordan Pavlin and Hilary Black (editors); Pam Houston, Mark Salzman, Larry Watson and Chip Kidd (fiction); Harold Kushner, Ted Conover, Laura Fraser and Peter Stark (nonfiction); Mary Jo Salter and J.D. McClatchy (poetry); and many more.
Costs: $350/retreat; $135/festival; $460/both.
Accommodations Rates for 2002: $65/night double; $130/night single.
Additional Information: Manuscripts to be submitted for review by faculty prior to conference. Conference brochures are available for SASE or on website.

■ **AUSTIN FILM FESTIVAL & HEART OF FILM SCREENWRITERS CONFERENCE**, 1604 Nueces St., Austin TX 78701. (800)310-3378 or (512)478-4795. Fax:(512)478-6205. E-mail: austinfilm@aol.com. Website: www.austinfilmfestival.com. **Contact:** Sharon Henry, office manager. Estab. 1994. Annual. Conference held October 10-14, 2002. Conference duration: 4 days. Average attendance: 1,500. The Austin Film Festival & Heart of Film Screenwriters Conference is a nonprofit organization committed to furthering the art, craft and business of screenwriters, and recognizing their contribution to the filmmaking industry. The 4-day Screenwriters Conference presents over 60 panels, roundtables, and workshops that address various aspects of screenwriting and filmmaking. Held at the Omni and Driskill Hotels, located in downtown Austin. **Agents/Speakers attending include: Bill Broyles** (*Unfaithful*), Lam Dobbs (*The Score*), Larry Doyle (*Duplex*), Scott Frank (*Minority Report*), Robert Gordon (*MIB*), Brain Helgeland (*The Sin Eater*), Philip Levens (TV writer for *Smallville* and many others). Agents will be speaking and available for meetings with attendees.
Costs: $350 before May 15. Includes entrance to all panels, workshops and roundtables during the 4-day conference, as well as all films during the 8-night Film Exhibition, the Opening Night Party, and Closing Night Party.
Accommodations: Discounted rates on hotel accommodations are available to conference attendees if the reservations are made through the Austin Film Festival office. Contact Austin Film Festival for holds and rates. Continental Airlines offers discounted fares to conference attendees. Contact Austin Film Festival for more information.
Additional Information: "The Austin Film Festival is considered one of the most accessible festivals, and Austin is the premiere town for networking because when industry people are here, they are relaxed and friendly." Brochures available January 1 for SASE or on website. Inquiries by e-mail and fax OK.

■ **THE BAY AREA WRITERS LEAGUE ANNUAL CONFERENCE**, P.O. Box 580007, Seabrook TX 77586. (281)268-7500. Fax: (409)762-4787. E-mail: seamus@compuserve.com. Website: www.angelfire.com/tx2/bawl. **Contact:** Jim Casey, webmaster. Estab. 1988. Annual. Conference held May 9-10, 2003. Conference duration: 2 days. Average attendance: 100. "We present a comprehensive range of topics." Conference held at the University of Houston-Clear Lake. **Previous agents/speakers have included:** Michelle Brummer (Donald Maass Agency), Angela Adair-Hoy. Agents will be speaking and available for meetings with attendees.
Costs: $125, plus $25 for annual membership (includes all sessions, lunch on both days, Friday evening dinner and reception). One-day price is $75.
Accommodations: Information is available. "We attempt to assist out-of-town attendees individually."
Additional Information: "We have a contest for novice writers in conjunction with the conference." Brochures available in March for SASE or on website. Inquiries by e-mail OK.

FRONTIERS IN WRITING, P.O. Box 19303, Amarillo TX 79114. (806)354-2305. E-mail: pcs@arn.net. Website: www.users.arn.net/~ppw/. Estab. 1980. Annual. Conference held in June. Duration: 2 days. Average attendance: 200. Nonfiction, poetry, scriptwriting and fiction (including mystery, romance, mainstream, science fiction and fantasy). **Previous agents/speakers have included:** Don Maass (agent), Cherise Grant (Simon & Schuster editor), Melanie Rigney (*Writer's Digest* editor), bestseller Nancy Taylor Rosenberg and 1999 Pulitzer Prize winner Michael Cunningham.
Costs: 2001 conference: $125 Members; $145 Non-members ($30 for membership). (Includes Friday night dinner, Saturday breakfast, lunch and beverages—lodging and transportation separate.)
Accommodations: Special conference room rate.
Additional information: Sponsors a contest. Guidelines available for SASE or on website.

HEARTLAND WRITERS CONFERENCE, P.O. Box 652. Kennett MO 63857. (573)297-3325. Fax: (573)297-3352. E-mail: hwg@heartlandwriters.org. Website: www.heartlandwriters.org. **Contact:** Judy Stamms, attendee liaison. Estab. 1990. Biennial (even years). Conference to be held June 2004. Conference duration: 3 days. Average attendance: 160. Popular fiction (all genres), nonfiction, children's, screenwriting, poetry. Held at the Best Western Coach House Inn in Sikeston MO. Previous panels included "Christopher Vogler's Myth

Adventures: The Storytellers Journey" and "Finding the Time and Will to Write" and "Putting Reality into Your Genre Fiction." **Previous agents/speakers attending include:** Alice Orr, Jennifer Jackson, Ricia Mainhardt, Christy Fletcher, Sue Yuen. Agents will be speaking and available for meetings with attendees.
Costs: $215 for advance registration, $250 for general registration (includes lunch on Friday and Saturday, awards banquet Saturday, hospitality room and get-acquainted mixer Thursday night).
Accommodations: Blocks of rooms are available at special conference rate at conference venue and at two nearby motels. Cost: $55-85/night (2002 price).
Additional Information: Brochures available late January 2004. Inquiries by e-mail and fax OK.

NATIONAL WRITERS ASSOCIATION FOUNDATION CONFERENCE, 3140 S. Peoria, #295, Aurora CO 80014. (303)841-0246. Fax: (303)841-2607. E-mail: sandywriter@aol.com. Website: www.nationalwriters.c om. **Contact:** Sandy Whelchel, executive director. Estab. 1926. Annual. Conference held June 13-15, 2003. Conference held in Denver, CO. Conference duration: 3 days. Average attendance: 200-300. General writing and marketing.
Costs: $200 (approx.).
Additional Information: Awards for previous contests will be presented at the conference. Conference brochures/guidelines are available for SASE.

☑ **THE NEW LETTERS WEEKEND WRITERS CONFERENCE**, University of Missouri-Kansas City, College of Arts and Sciences Continuing Ed. Division, 215 4825 Troost Bldg., 5100 Rockhill Rd., Kansas City MO 64110-2499. (816)235-2736. Fax: (816)235-2611. E-mail: newletters@umkc.edu. Website: www.umkc.edu/ newletters. **Contact:** Betsy Beasley or Sharon Seaton, administrative associates. Estab. in the mid-70s as The Longboat Key Writers Conference. Annual. Conference held in late June. Conference duration is 3 weeks. Average attendance: 75. Fiction, nonfiction, scriptwriting, poetry, playwriting, journalism. "The New Letters Weekend Writers Conference brings together talented writers in many genres for lectures, seminars, readings, workshops and individual conferences. The emphasis is on craft and the creative process in poetry, fiction, screenwriting, playwriting and journalism; but the program also deals with matters of psychology, publications and marketing. The conference is appropriate for both advanced and beginning writers. The conference meets at the beautiful Diastole conference center of The University of Missouri-Kansas City."
Costs: Several options are available. Participants may choose to attend as a noncredit student or they may attend for 1 hour of college credit from the University of Missouri-Kansas City. Conference registration includes continental breakfasts, Saturday and Sunday lunch. For complete information, contact the University of Missouri-Kansas City.
Accommodations: Registrants are responsible for their own transportation, but information on area accommodations is made available.
Additional Information: Those registering for college credit are required to submit a ms in advance. Manuscript reading and critique is included in the credit fee. Those attending the conference for noncredit also have the option of having their ms critiqued for an additional fee. Conference brochures/guidelines are available for SASE after March. Inquiries by e-mail and fax OK.

NORTHEAST TEXAS COMMUNITY COLLEGE & NETWO ANNUAL CONFERENCE, Continuing Education, Northeast Texas Community College, P.O. Box 1307, Mount Pleasant TX 75456-9991. (903)572-1911, ext. 241. Fax: (903)572-6712. E-mail: aduke@ntcc.cc.tx.us. Website: www.ntcc.cc.tx.us/instruction/conted.html. **Contact:** Angie Duke, program developer. Estab. 1987. Annual. Conference held April. Conference duration: 1 day. Presenters include agents, writers, editors and publishers.
Additional Information: Write for additional information. Conference is co-sponsored by the Northeast Texas Writers Organization (NETWO).

PIKES PEAK WRITERS CONFERENCE, P.O. Box 6726, Colorado Springs CO 80934. E-mail: info@ppwc. net. Website: www.ppwc.net. Estab. 1994. Annual. Conference held April 25-27, 2003. Conference duration: Friday 11 a.m. to Sunday 2 p.m. Average attendance: 400. Commercial fiction. Held at the Wyndham Hotel. "Workshops, presentations and panels focus on writing and publishing genre fiction—romance, scifi and fantasy, suspense thrillers, action adventure, mysteries. Agents and editors are available for meetings with attendees."
Costs: $250 (includes all meals).
Accommodations: Wyndham Colorado Springs holds a block of rooms for conference attendees until March 30 at a special $75 rate (1-800-962-6982).
Additional Information: Readings with critique are available on Friday afternoon. One-on-one meetings with editors and agents available Saturday and Sunday. Brochures available in October. Inquiries by e-mail OK. Registration form available on website. Contest for unpublished writers; need not attend conference to enter contest.

ROCKY MOUNTAIN FICTION WRITERS COLORADO GOLD, P.O. Box 260244, Denver CO 80226-0244. (303)791-3941. Website: www.rmfw.org (includes contest, membership, conference, critique). Estab. 1983. Annual. Conference held weekend after Labor Day. Conference duration: 3 days. Average attendance: 250. For novel length fiction. The conference will be held in Denver. Themes included general novel length fiction, genre

fiction, contemporary romance, mystery, sf/f, mainstream, history. Guest speakers and panelists have included Terry Brooks, Dorothy Cannell, Patricia Gardner Evans, Diane Mott Davidson, Constance O'Day, Connie Willis, Clarissa Pinkola Estes and Michael Palmer; approximately 4 editors and 5 agents annually.
Costs: In 2002, cost was $169 early, $189 walk in (includes conference, reception, banquet). Editor workshop $20 additional.
Accommodations: Information on overnight accommodations made available of area hotels. The conference will be at the Renaissance Denver Hotel. Conference rates available.
Additional Information: Editor conducted workshops are limited to 10 participants for critique with auditing available. Workshops in science fiction, mainstream, mystery, historical, contemporary romance. Sponsors a contest. For 20-page mss and 8-page synopsis; categories mentioned above. First rounds are done by qualified members, published and nonpublished, with editors doing the final ranking; 2 copies need to be submitted without author's name. $20 entry only, $40 entry and (one) critique. Guidelines available for SASE. Deadline June 1.

ROMANCE WRITERS OF AMERICA NATIONAL CONFERENCE, 3707 FM 1960 West, Suite 555, Houston TX 77068. (281)440-6885, ext. 27. Fax: (281)440-7510. E-mail: info@rwanational.com. Website: www.rwanational.com. **Contact:** Chris McEachern, communications manager. Executive Director: Allison Kelley. Estab. 1981. Annual. Conference held in late July or early August. Average attendance: 1,500. Fiction writers, scriptwriters. Over 100 workshops on writing, researching and the business side of being a working writer. Publishing professionals attend and accept appointments. Keynote speaker is renowned romance writer. Conference has been held in Chicago, Washington, DC and Denver.
Costs: $300.
Additional Information: Annual RITA awards are presented for romance authors. Annual Golden Heart awards are presented for unpublished writers. Conference brochures/guidelines are available for SASE.

SANTA FE SCREENWRITING CONFERENCE, P.O. Box 28423. Sante Fe NM 87592-8423. (505)424-1501. Fax: (505)471-7126. E-mail: writeit@sfesc.com. Website: www.sfesc.com. **Contact:** Rick Reichman or Larry N. Stouffer, co-executive directors. Estab. 1999. Annual. Conference held October 4-7, 2002. Conference duration: 4 days. Average attendance: 200. The Santa Fe Screenwriting Conference is designed to teach the art and craft of screenwriting. Held at the scenic campus of St. John's College in Santa Fe, New Mexico. **Previous agents/speakers have included:** Jeff Aghassi (The Alpern Group); Nicole Graham (Writers & Artists Agency). Agents will be speaking and available for meetings with attendees.
Costs: $495 (early); $595 (regular). Includes 9 hours of in-depth classroom instruction, 24 one and one-half hour workshops, a panel discussion, live scene readings, Fade In breakfast, Fade Out Luncheon, door prizes, and the outrageous "J.W. Eaves Movie Ranch Barbeque Blowout and Wild West Fiesta" party on Sunday night.
Accommodations: Accommodations are available at both the dorms at St. John's College and through Santa Fe Accommodations which represent hotels, motels, B&B's and condos with a variety of price ranges. Santa Fe Accommodations room prices range from $115 (including breakfast) and up. St. John's dorm prices range from $75-98 (including breakfast and lunch). Shuttle services to and from Albuquerque Airport cost $21 each way (it is a 65 mile drive to Santa Fe). Shuttle service to downtown Santa Fe and to the J.W. Eaves Movie Ranch are provided by the Conference at no cost to the attendees. The Conference has an arrangement with Southwest Airlines to give conference attendees a 10% discount.
Additional Information: "Unique to any other screenwriting conference in the world, the Santa Fe Screenwriting Conference is devoted almost exclusively toward teaching the art and craft of writing screenplays. The Conference is suitable for beginning, intermediate and advanced screenwriters. What separates this from other conferences is the nine hours of in-depth instruction from one Mentor. Classrooms will have no more than 40 students which encourages interactive participation. There will be a minimum of eight classes. Each class will have no more than 40 students and be led by a recognized Mentor in the field of screenwriting. "Mentors include Jeff Arch (*Sleepless in Seattle*), Richard Krevolin (screenwriting professor, playwright, screenwriter and poet), Daniel Pyne (film writer and director), Christopher Vogler (screenwriting consultant), and Cynthia Whitcomb (*Buffalo Gals* plus 25 produced screenplays)."

SHORT COURSE ON PROFESSIONAL WRITING, University of Oklahoma, 860 Van Vleet Oval, Room 101, Norman OK 73071-0270. (405)325-2721. Fax: (405)325-7565. E-mail: jmadisondavis@ou.edu. Website: http://jmc.ou.edu/shortcourse. **Contact:** J. Madison Davis, professor of professional writing. Estab. 1938. Annual. Conference held June 2003. Conference duration: 3 days. Average attendance: 100-200. All areas of writing for publication, excluding poetry. Held in Norman, at the NCED Postal training center, a resort-like facility with recreational amenities. **Agents/speakers attending include:** Alison Bond, Sheree Bykofsky, Albert Zuckerman, Bob Mecoy, Donald Maass, Betsey Lerner, Peter Rubie. Agents will be speaking and available for meetings with attendees.
Costs: $230 (includes banquet, all sessions). In addition: Private ms consultations for $45. Graduate or undergrad credit available for additional cost.
Accommodations: Special rates available: with meals included.
Additional Information: "A warm, friendly and supportive conference." Brochures available in April and on website. Inquiries by e-mail and fax OK.

✔ **SOUTHWEST WRITERS CONFERENCE**, (formerly Southwest Writers Workshop Conference). 8200 Mountain Rd., NE, Suite 106, Albuquerque NM 87110. (505)265-9485. Fax: (505)265-9483. E-mail: swriters@aol.com. Website: www.southwestwriters.org. Estab. 1983. Annual. Conference held in September 2003. Average attendance: about 500. "Speakers include writers, editors, agents, publicists and producers. All areas of writing, including screenwriting and poetry, are represented. Pre-conference workshops and conference sessions are available for beginning or experienced writers."

Costs: Fee includes conference sessions, 2 luncheons, 2 banquets.

Accommodations: Usually have official airline and hotel discount rates.

Additional Information: Sponsors a contest judged by authors, editors and agents from New York, Los Angeles, etc., and from major publishing houses. Eighteen categories. Deadline: May 1. Entry fee is $29 (members) or $39 (nonmembers). Brochures/guidelines available for SASE. Inquiries by e-mail and fax OK. "An appointment (10 minutes, one-on-one) may be set up at the conference with editor or agent of your choice on a first-registered/first-served basis."

TAOS POETRY CIRCUS, 5275 NDCBU, Taos NM 87571. (505)758-1800. E-mail: wpba@laplaza.org. Website: www.poetrycircus.org. **Contact:** Anne, director. Estab. 1982. Annual. Festival held in June. Duration: 9 days. Average attendance: 2,000. Poetry. Held in Taos NM.

Costs: $3-75 per event.

Accommodations: Special room rates are available from $69-85/double. Special rental car rates available with Enterprise.

Additional Information: Festival includes readings, slams, seminars, a performance and poetics workshop, poetry video showing and free events. Main event is the World Heavyweight Championship Poetry Bout. Brochures available April for SASE. Inquiries by e-mail OK.

✔ **WRITERS' LEAGUE OF TEXAS**, 1501 W. Fifth St., Suite E-2, Austin TX 78703. (512)499-8914. Fax: (512)499-0441. E-mail: awl@writersleague.org. Website: www.writersleague.org. **Contact:** Stephanie Sheppard, executive director. Estab. 1982. Conference held in summer. Conference duration: varies according to program. Average attendance 200. Fiction, nonfiction. Programs held at Writers' League Resource Center/Library, other sites in Austin and Texas. Topics include: finding and working with agents and publishers; writing and marketing short fiction; dialogue; characterization; voice; research; basic and advanced fiction writing/focus on the novel; business of writing; also workshops for genres. **Agents/speakers attending include:** Ken Atchity, Sheree Bykofsky, Mary Evans, Felicia Eth, Michael Larsen, Elizabeth McHugh, Elizabeth Pomada, Nancy Stender, Andrew Whelchel, Tim Bent, Karen V. Haas, Kati Hesford, Ron Martirano. Agents will be speaking and available for meetings with attendees. Each summer the League holds its annual Agents! Agents! Agents! Conference which provides writers with the opportunity to meet top agents from New York and the West Coast.

Costs: Varies, depending on program. Most classes, $80-200; workshops $50; conferences: $125-185.

Accommodations: Special rates given at some hotels for program participants.

Additional Information: Critique sessions offered at some programs. Individual presenters determine critique requirements. Those requirements are then made available through Writers' League office and in workshop promotion. Contests and awards programs are offered separately. Brochures/guidelines are available on request.

✔ **WRITERS WORKSHOP IN SCIENCE FICTION**, English Department/University of Kansas, Lawrence KS 66045-2115. (785)864-3380. Fax: (785)864-1159. E-mail: jgunn@ku.edu. Website: www.ku.edu/~sfcenter/. **Contact:** James Gunn, professor. Estab. 1985. Annual. Conference held in July. Average attendance: 15. Conference for writing and marketing science fiction. "Classes meet in university housing on the University of Kansas campus. Workshop sessions operate informally in a lounge." **Previous agents/speakers have included:** Frederick Pohl, Kij Johnson, Chris McKitterick.

Costs: Tuition: $400. Housing and meals are additional.

Accommodations: Housing information available. Several airport shuttle services offer reasonable transportation from the Kansas City International Airport to Lawrence. During past conferences, students were housed in a student dormitory at $12.50/day double, $23.50/day single.

Additional Information: "Admission to the workshop is by submission of an acceptable story. Two additional stories should be submitted by the middle of June. These three stories are copied and distributed to other participants for critiquing and are the basis for the first week of the workshop; one story is rewritten for the second week." Brochures/guidelines are available for SASE. "The Writers Workshop in Science Fiction is intended for writers who have just started to sell their work or need that extra bit of understanding or skill to become a published writer."

CONTACT THE EDITOR of *Guide to Literary Agents* by e-mail at literaryagents @fwpubs.com with your questions and comments.

West (AZ, CA, HI, NV, UT)

IWWG EARLY SPRING IN CALIFORNIA CONFERENCE, International Women's Writing Guild, P.O. Box 810, Gracie Station, New York NY 10028-0082. (212)737-7536. Fax: (212)737-9469. E-mail: iwwg@iwwg.com. Website: www.IWWG.com. **Contact:** Hannelore Hahn, executive director. Estab. 1982. Annual. Conference gennerally held on the 2nd weekend in March. Conference duration: 3 days. Average attendance: 80. Conference to promote "creative writing, personal growth and empowerment." Site is a redwood forest mountain retreat in Santa Cruz, California.
Costs: $350 for weekend program with room and board, $150 for weekend program without room and board.
Accommodations: Accommodations are all at conference site.
Additional Information: Conference brochures/guidelines are available for SASE. Inquiries by e-mail and fax OK or view on web: www.IWWG.com.

MAUI WRITERS CONFERENCE, P.O. Box 1118, Kihei HI 96753. (808)879-0061. Fax: (808)879-6233. E-mail: writers@maui.net. Website: www.mauiwriters.com (includes information covering all programs offered, writing competitions, presenters past and present, writers forum bulletin board, published attendees books, dates, price, hotel and travel information). **Contact:** Shannon and John Tullius. Estab. 1993. Annual. Conference held the end of August (Labor Day weekend). Conference duration: 4 days. Conference held at Outrigger Wailea Resort. Average attendance: 800. For fiction, nonfiction, poetry, children's, young adult, horror, mystery, romance, science fiction, journalism, screenwriting. Manuscript Marketplace, held twice a year, is a mail in service where your book idea is reviewed by participating agents and editors. **Previous agents attending have included:** Andrea Brown (Andrea Brown Literary Agency); Kimberley Cameron (The Reece Halsey Agency); Susan Crawford (Crawford Literary Agency); Laurie Horwitz (Creative Artists Agency); Amy Kossow (Linda Allen Literary Agency); Owen Laster (William Morris); Jillian Manus (Manus & Associates Literary Agency); Craig Nelson (The Craig Nelson Co.); Elizabeth Pomada (Larsen/Pomada Literary Agency); Susan Travis (Susan Travis Literary Agency). Agents will be speaking and available for consultations with attendees.
Additional Information: "We offer a comprehensive view of the business of publishing, with over 2,000 consultation slots with industry agents, editors and screenwriting professionals as well as workshops and sessions covering writing instruction." Write or call for additional information.

MENDOCINO COAST WRITERS CONFERENCE, 1211 Del Mar. Fort Bragg CA 95437. (707)964-6810. Fax: (707)961-1255. E-mail: mcwc@jps.org. Website: www.mcwcwritewhale.com. **Contact:** Jan Boyd, registrar. Estab. 1988. Annually. Conference held June 5-7, 2003. Conference duration: 3 days. Average attendance: 90. All areas of writing covered. Provides workshops for fiction, nonfiction, scriptwriting, children's, mystery, writing for social change. Held at small community college campus on the northern Pacific Coast. **Previous agents/ speakers attending have included:** Jandy Nelson, Ted Weinstein, Ellen Meloy, Valerie Miner, Roy Parvin, John Lescroart, Maxine Schur, and others. Agents will be speaking and available for meetings with attendees.
Costs: $250-300 (includes one day intensive in one subject and two days of several short sessions; panels; meals; two socials with guest readers; one open to the public event. Kayakk trip extra on Sunday.)
Accommodations: Information on overnight accommodations is made available. Special conference attendee accommodations made in some cases. Shared rides from San Francisco Airport are available.
Additional Information: Emphasis on writers who are also good teachers. Brochures available for SASE in January or on website now. Inquiries by e-mail and fax OK.

MOUNT HERMON CHRISTIAN WRITERS CONFERENCE, P.O. Box 413, Mount Hermon CA 95041-0413. (831)335-4466 or (888)MH-CAMPS. Fax: (831)335-9413. E-mail: dtalbot@mhcamps.org. Website: www. mounthermon.org. **Contact:** David R. Talbott, director of adult ministries. Estab. 1970. Annual. Conference held Friday-Tuesday over Palm Sunday weekend, April 11-15, 2003. Average attendance: 450. "We are a broadranging conference for all areas of Christian writing, including fiction, children's, poetry, nonfiction, magazines, inspirational and devotional writing, books, educational curriculum and radio and TV scriptwriting. This is a working, how-to conference, with many workshops within the conference involving on-site writing assignments. The conference is sponsored by and held at the 440-acre Mount Hermon Christian Conference Center near San Jose, California, in the heart of the coastal redwoods. The faculty/student ratio is about 1:6 or 7. The bulk of our more than 60 faculty are editors and publisher representatives from major Christian publishing houses nationwide." **Agents/speakers attending include:** Janet Kobobel Grant, Elaine W. Colvin, Chip MacGregor, Karen Solem and others. Agents will be speaking and available for meetings with attendees.
Costs: Registration fees include tuition, conference sessions, resource notebook, refreshment breaks, room and board and vary from $620 (economy) to $915 (deluxe), double occupancy (2002 fees).
Accommodations: Registrants stay in hotel-style accommodations, and full board is provided as part of conference fees. Meals are taken family style, with faculty joining registrants. Airport shuttles are available from the San Jose International Airport. Housing is not required of registrants, but about 95% of our registrants use Mount Hermon's own housing facilities (hotel style double-occupancy rooms). Meals with the conference are required and are included in all fees.

Additional Information: "The residential nature of our conference makes this a unique setting for one-on-one interaction with faculty/staff. There is also a decided inspirational flavor to the conference, and general sessions with well-known speakers are a highlight." Registrants may submit 2 works for critique in advance of the conference, then have personal interviews with critiquers during the conference. No advance work is required however. Conference brochures/guidelines are available December 1. Inquiries by e-mail and fax OK. Tapes of past conference workshops also available.

PIMA WRITERS' WORKSHOP, Pima College, 2202 W. Anklam Rd., Tucson AZ 85709. (520)206-6974. Fax: (520)206-6020. E-mail: mfiles@pimacc.pima.edu. **Contact:** Meg Files, director. Estab. 1988. Annual. Conference held May 23-25, 2003. Conference duration 3 days. Average attendance 250. Fiction, nonfiction, poetry, scriptwriting. "For anyone interested in writing—beginning or experienced writer. The workshop offers sessions on writing short stories, novels, nonfiction articles and books, children's and juvenile stories, poetry and screenplays." Sessions are held in the Center for the Arts on Pima Community College's West Campus. **Previous agents/speakers have included:** Michael Blake, Ron Carlson, Gregg Levoy, Nancy Mairs, Linda McCarriston, Larry McMurty, Barbara Kingsolver, Jerome Stern, Connie Willis, Jack Heffron, Jeff Herman, Robert Morgan. Agents will be speaking and available for meetings with attendees.
Costs: $65 (can include ms critique). Participants may attend for college credit, in which case fees are $87 for Arizona residents and $215 for out-of-state residents. Meals and accommodations not included.
Accommodations: Information on local accommodations is made available, and special workshop rates are available at a specified motel close to the workshop site (about $60/night).
Additional Information: "The workshop atmosphere is casual, friendly, and supportive, and guest authors are very accessible. Readings and panel discussions are offered as well as talks and manuscript sessions." Participants may have up to 20 pages critiqued by the author of their choice. Mss must be submitted 3 weeks before the workshop. Conference brochure/guidelines available for SASE. Inquiries by e-mail OK.

SAN DIEGO STATE UNIVERSITY WRITERS' CONFERENCE, SDSU College of Extended Studies, San Diego CA 92182-1920. (619)594-2517. Fax: (619)594-8566. E-mail: xtension@mail.sdsu.edu. Website: www.ces.sdsu.edu/writersconference.html. **Contact:** Paula Pierce, coordinator, SDSU extension programs. Estab. 1984. Annual. Conference held the third weekend in January. Conference duration: 2 days. Average attendance: approximately 375. Fiction, nonfiction, scriptwriting, e-books. Held at the Doubletree Hotel, Mission Valley. "Each year the SDSU Writers Conference offers a variety of workshops for the beginner and the advanced writer. This conference allows the individual writer to choose which workshop best suits his/her needs. In addition to the workshops, editor/agent appointments and office hours are provided so attendees may meet with speakers, editors and agents in small, personal groups to discuss specific questions. A reception is offered Saturday immediately following the workshops where attendees may socialize with the faculty in a relaxed atmosphere. Last year 18 agents attended in addition to editors and screenwriting experts." **Agents/speakers attending include:** Betsy Amster, Loretta Barrett, Julie Castiglia, Laurie Horowitz, Angela Rinaldi. Agents will be speaking and available for meetings with attendees.
Costs: Approximately $280 (includes all conference workshops and office hours, coffee and pastries in the morning, lunch and reception Saturday evening).
Accommodations: Doubletree Hotel (800)222-TREE. Attendees must make their own travel arrangements.
Additional Information: Editor/agent appointments are private, one-on-one opportunities to meet with editors and agents to discuss your submission. To receive a brochure, e-mail, call or send a postcard with address to: SDSU Writers Conference, College of Extended Studies, 5250 Campanile Drive, San Diego State University, San Diego CA 92182-1920. No SASE required.

N SANTA BARBARA WRITERS' CONFERENCE, P.O. Box 304, Carpinteria CA 93014. (805)684-2250. Fax: (805)684-7003. Website: www.sbwc.online.com. **Contact:** Mary or Barnaby Conrad, conference directors. Estab. 1973. Annual. Conference held June 20-27 2003, at Westmont College in Montecito. Average attendance: 350. For poetry, fiction, nonfiction, journalism, playwriting, screenplays, travel writing, children's literature. **Previous agents/speakers have included:** Kenneth Atchity, Michael Larson, Elizabeth Pomada, Linda Mead, Stuart Miller, Gloria Stern. Agents will be speaking and available for meetings with attendees.
Accommodations: Onsite accommodations available. Additional accommodations available at area hotels.
Additional Information: Individual critiques are also available. Submit 1 ms of no more than 3,000 words in advance with SASE. Competitions with awards sponsored as part of the conference. Send SASE for brochure and registration forms.

THE WILLIAM SAROYAN WRITERS' CONFERENCE, P.O. Box 5331, Fresno CA 93755-5331. Phone/fax: (559)224-2516. E-mail: law@pacbell.net. Website: www.homestead.com/winwinorg. **Contact:** Linda West. Estab. 1992. Annual. Conference held in April. Conference duration: 3 days. Average attendance: 150. "This conference is designed to provide insights that could lift you out of the pack and into publication. You will learn from masters of the writing craft, you will discover current and future market trends, and you will meet and network with editors and agents who can sell, buy, or publish your manuscript." Fiction, nonfiction, scriptwriting. Held at the Piccadilly Inn Hotel across from the Fresno Airport. **Previous agents/speakers have included:**

Leonard Bishop, David Brin, John Dunning, Marcia Preston, Andrea Brown, Kathleen Brenzel, Linda Mead, Nancy Ellis-Bell, Liz Pentacoff, Rita Robinson, Stephen Mattee. Agents will be speaking and available for meetings with attendees.
Costs: $240 for 3 days (includes some meals). Single day fees: $95 for Friday, $175 for Saturday, $60 for Sunday.
Accommodations: Special lodging rate at the Piccadilly Inn Hotel: $68 single, $78 double plus room tax. "Be sure to mention the William Saroyan Writers' Conference to obtain this special rate. Reservations must be made two weeks in advance to assure availability of room at the conference site."
Additional Information: Offers "Persie" writing contest in connection with conference. Also offers a pre-conference ms critique service for fiction and nonfiction mss. Fees: $35/book chapter or short story, maximum length 20 pgs., double-spaced. Send SASE for brochure and guidelines. Fax and e-mail inquiries OK.

N: SELLING TO HOLLYWOOD INTERNATIONAL SCREENWRITERS CONFERENCE, 269 S. Beverly Dr., Suite 2600, Beverly Hills CA 90212-3807. Phone/fax: (866)265-9091. E-mail: asa@goasa.com. Website: www.goasa.com. **Contact:** John Johnson, director. Estab. 1988. Annual. Conference held in August in LA area. Conference duration: 3 days. Average attendance: 275. "Conference targets scriptwriters and fiction writers, whose short stories, books, or scripts have strong cinematic potential, and who want to make valuable contacts in the film industry. Full conference registrants receive a private consultation with the film industry producer or professional of his/her choice who make up the faculty. Panels, workshops, pitching discussion groups and networking sessions include over 50 agents, professional film and TV scriptwriters, and independent as well as studio and TV and feature film producers." **Agents/speakers attending include:** Michael Hauge, Lew Hunter, Linda Seger, Syd Field, Blain Richwood, Billy Mernit, Richard Walter, Heidi Wall.
Costs: In 2002: full conference by May 31, $560; after May 31: $600. Includes some meals.
Accommodations: $140/night (in LA) for private room; $70/shared room. Discount with designated conference airline.
Additional Information: "This is the premier screenwriting conference of its kind in the world, unique in its offering of an industry-wide perspective from pros working in all echelons of the film industry. Great for making contacts." Conference brochure/guidelines available March; phone, e-mail, fax or send written request.

SOCIETY OF CHILDREN'S BOOK WRITERS AND ILLUSTRATORS/NATIONAL CONFERENCE ON WRITING & ILLUSTRATING FOR CHILDREN, 8271 Beverly Blvd., Los Angeles CA 90048-4515. (323)782-1010. Fax: (323)782-1892. E-mail: scbwi@scbwi.org. Website: www.scbwi.org. **Contact:** Stephen Mooser, president. Estab. 1972. Annual. Conference held in August. Conference duration: 4 days. Average attendance: 500. Writing and illustrating for children. Held at the Century Plaza Hotel in Los Angeles. **Previous agents/speakers have included:** Andrea Brown, Steven Malk, Scott Treimel (agents), Ashley Bryan, Bruce Coville, Karen Hesse, Harry Mazer, Lucia Monfried and Russell Freedman. Agents will be speaking and available for meetings with attendees.
Costs: $370 (members); $395 (late registration, members); $415 (nonmembers). Cost does not include hotel room.
Accommodations: Information on overnight accommodations made available.
Additional Information: Ms and illustration critiques are available. Conference brochures/guidelines are available June with SASE.

SOCIETY OF SOUTHWESTERN AUTHORS WRITERS' CONFERENCE—WRANGLING WITH WRITING, P.O. Box 30355, Tucson AZ 85751-0355. (520)546-9382. Fax: (520)296-0409. E-mail: wporter202 @aol.com and apetrillo@earthlink.net. Website: www.azstarnet.com/nonprofit/ssa. **Contact:** Penny Porter or Al Petrillo, conference chairs. Estab. 1972. Annual. Two-day conference held 4th weekend in January. Maximum attendance: 400. Fiction, nonfiction, screenwriting, poetry. Conference offers 30 workshops covering all genres of writing; pre-scheduled one-on-one interviews with 22 agents, editors and publishers representing major book houses and magazines. **Keynote speakers for 2003 include:** J.A. Jance, Frances Weaver, Vince De Pierro and one more pending.
Costs: $250 (general; $200 (member). Scholarships available.
Additional Information: Conference brochures/guidelines are available for SASE.

▼ SOUTHERN CALIFORNIA WRITERS' CONFERENCE, 4406 Park Blvd., Suite E, San Diego CA 92116. Phone/fax: (619)233-4651. E-mail: wewrite@writersconference.com. Website: www.writersconference.c om. **Contact:** Michael Steven Gregory, executive director. Estab. 1986. Annually. Conference held Februrary 14-17, 2003. Conference duration: 3 days. Average attendance: 250. Fiction and nonfiction, with particular emphasis on reading and critiquing. Held at Holiday Inn Hotel and Suites located in Old Town, San Diego. "Extensive reading and critiquing workshops by working writers. Over 3 dozen 2-hour workshops and no time limit late-night sessions." Agents will be speaking and available for meetings with attendees.
Costs: $275 (includes all workshops and events, as well as Saturday evening banquet).
Accommodations: Discounted rates available at Holiday Inn. Complimentary shuttle service provided from airport and Amtrak.

Additional Information: Late-night read and critique workshops run until 3 or 4 a.m. Brochures available for SASE or on website. Inquiries by e-mail and fax OK.

☑ **SQUAW VALLEY COMMUNITY OF WRITERS FICTION WORKSHOP**, P.O. Box 1416. Nevada City CA 95959-1416. (530)274-8551. E-mail: svcw@oro.net. Website: www.squawvalleywriters.org. **Contact:** Ms. Brett Hall Jones, executive director. Estab. 1969. Annual. Conference held August. Conference duration: 1 week. Average attendance: 125. Fiction, nonfiction, memoir. Held in Squaw Valley, California—the site of the 1960 Winter Olympics. The workshops are held in a ski lodge at the foot of this spectacular ski area. **Previous agents/speakers have included:** Betsy Amster, Julie Barer, Michael Carlisle, Elyse Cheney, Mary Evans, Christy Fletcher, Theresa Park, B.J. Robbins. Agents will be speaking and available for meetings with attendees.
Costs: $650 (includes tuition, dinners). Housing is extra.
Accommodations: Rooms available. Single: $450/week. Double: $285/week per person. Multiple room: $185/week per person. Airport shuttle available for additional cost. Contact conference for more information.
Additional Information: Brochures available March for SASE or on website. Inquiries by e-mail OK.

☑ **UCLA EXTENSION WRITERS' PROGRAM**, 10995 Le Conte Ave., #440, Los Angeles CA 90024. (310)825-9415 or (800)388-UCLA. Fax: (310)206-7382. E-mail: writers@unex.ucla.edu. Website: www.uclaexte nsion.org/writers. **Contact:** Rick Noguchi, program manager. Estab. 1891. Courses held year-round with one-day or intensive weekend workshops to 12-week courses. Los Angeles Writers Conference held February 6-9, 2003. Fiction, nonfiction, scriptwriting. "The diverse offerings span introductory seminars to professional novel and script completion workshops. The annual Los Angeles Writers Conference and a number of 1-, 2- and 4-day intensive workshops are popular with out-of-town students due to their specific focus and the chance to work with industry professionals. The most comprehensive and diverse continuing education writing program in the country, offering over 500 courses a year including: screenwriting, fiction, writing for young people, poetry, nonfiction, playwriting, publishing and writing for interactive multimedia. Courses are offered in Los Angeles on the UCLA campus and Universal City as well as online over the Internet. Adult learners in the UCLA Extension Writers' Program study with professional screenwriters, fiction writers, playwrights, poets, nonfiction writers, and interactive multimedia writers, who bring practical experience, theoretical knowledge, and a wide variety of teaching styles and philosophies to their classes." Online courses are also available. Call for details.
Costs: Vary from $90 for a 1-day workshops to $450 for a 12-week course to $2,850 for the 9-month Master Class.
Accommodations: Students make own arrangements. The program can provide assistance in locating local accommodations.
Additional Information: "Some advanced-level classes have manuscript submittal requirements; instructions are always detailed in the quarterly UCLA Extension course catalog." Screenwriting prize, the Diane Thomas Award, is given annually. Contact program for details. Conference brochures/guidelines are available in the Fall. Inquiries by e-mail and fax OK.

WATERSIDE PUBLISHING CONFERENCE, 2191 San Elijo Ave., Cardiff CA 92007. (760)632-9190. Fax: (760)632-9295. E-mail: admin@waterside.com. Website: www.waterside.com. **Contact:** Kimberly Valentini, controller. Estab. 1990 Annually. Conference held April 10-12, 2003. Conference duration: 3 days. Average attendance: 200. Focused on computer and technology, books and their writers and publishers. Issues in the industry that affect the genre. Held at the Radisson Hotel in Berkley, CA. A bayside hotel with full amenities and beautiful view. Past themes: Digital Delivery; Ask the Buyer; Author Taxes, Branding, Contracts. **Previous agents/speakers have included:** Paul Hilts (*Publishers Weekly*); Carla Bayha (Borders Books); Bob Ipsen (John Wiley & Sons); Microsoft; Mighty Words.com. Agents will be speaking and available for meetings with attendees.
Costs: In 2002: $500 general; $250 for authors (includes all sessions and parties, meals, coffee breaks). Conference attendees get a discounted room rate at the Radisson.
Accommodations: Other hotels are in the area if conference hotel is booked or too expensive.
Additional Information: Brochures available via fax or e-mail, or call.

Northwest (AK, ID, MT, OR, WA, WY)

FLATHEAD RIVER WRITERS CONFERENCE, P.O. Box 7711, Whitefish MT 59904-7711. Fax: (406)862-4839. E-mail: hows@centurytel.net. **Contact:** Jake How, chairman. Estab. 1990. Annual. Conference held early October. Conference duration: 3 days. Average attendance: 110. "We provide several small, intense three-day workshops before the general weekend conference on a wide variety of subjects every year, including fiction, nonfiction, screenwriting, and working with editors and agents." Held at Grouse Mountain Lodge. Workshops, panel discussions and speakers focus on novels, nonfiction, screenwriting, short stories, magazine articles, and the writing industry. **Previous agents/speakers have included:** Rob Simbeck, Marcela Landres, Amy Rennert, Ben Mikaelsen, Esmond Harmsworth, Terry Borst, Ron Carlson. Agents will be speaking and available for meetings with attendees.
Costs: $135 (includes breakfast and lunch, but does not include lodging).

Accommodations: Rooms available at discounted rates: $90/night. Whitefish is a resort town, and less expensive lodging can be arranged.

Additional Information: "By limiting attendance to 100 people, we assure a quality experience and informal, easy access to the presentors and other attendees." Brochures available June. Inquiries by e-mail OK.

☑ **JACKSON HOLE WRITERS CONFERENCE**, University of Wyoming, Box 3972, Laramie WY 82071-3972. (877)733-3618, #2. Fax: (307)766-3914. E-mail: kguille@uwyo.edu. Website: www.jacksonholewriters.org. **Contact:** Keith Buille, conference coordinator. Estab. 1991. Annual. Conference held in June/July. Conference duration: 4 days. Average attendance: 70. For fiction, creative nonfiction, screenwriting. Offers critiques from authors, agents and editors. Write for additional information or visit website.

PACIFIC NORTHWEST WRITERS ASSOCIATION, 2608 Third Ave., Suite B, Seattle WA 98121-1214. (206)443-3807. E-mail: jmaread@aol.com. Website: www.pnwa.org. **Contact:** Scott McDonaldEstab. 1955. Annual. Conference held in July. Conference duration: 4 days. Information available May. Average attendance: 400. Conference focuses on "fiction, nonfiction, poetry, film, drama, self-publishing, the creative process, critiques, core groups, advice from pros and networking." Site is Hilton Seattle Airport and Conference Center. "Editors and agents come from both coasts. They bring lore from the world of publishing. The PNWA provides opportunities for writers to get to know editors and agents. The literary contest provides feedback from professionals and possible fame for the winners." **Previous agents have included:** Sheree Bykofsky, Kimberley Cameron, Jennie Dunham, Donald Maass and Jandy Nelson.

Costs: For 2002: $350 (members) and $400 (nonmembers). Meals and lodging are available at hotel.

Accommodations: Hilton, conference special rate $119 per night.

Additional Information: On-site critiques are available in small groups. Literary contest in these categories: Stella Cameron Romance, adult article/essay, adult genre novel, adult mainstream novel, adult short story, juvenile/young adult, screenwriting, nonfiction book, playwriting and poetry. Deadline: February 13. Over $9,000 awarded in prizes. Send SASE for guidelines.

🅽 **SLEEPLESS IN SILVERDALE**, Peninsula Chapter RWA, P.O. Box 4551, Rolling Bay WA 98061. Chapter E-mail: penrwa2002@hotmail.com. Conference E-mail: defee@peoplepc.com. Website: www.penrwa.com. **Contact:** Ann Defee, conference chair 2003 and chapter contact. Estab. 1984. Biannual. Conference held February 21-23, 2003. Conference duration: 3 days. Average attendance: 250. Women's fiction, romance writing, publishing industry information. Held at beautiful West Coast Silverdale on the Bay Hotel. Waterfront. Centrally located close to mall shopping and restaurants. 1 hour from Seattle via Bainbridge Island Ferry. **Keynote speakers attending include:** NYT best selling authors Teresa Medieros and Kristin Hannagh, plus Stef Ann Holm. **Workshop speakers include:** Multi-published authors, many *New York Times* best sellers. Top editors, top agents. Multiple tracks workshops something for all levels. Relaxed, fun, and the famous Pajama Party Saturday Night Dessert blow-out. **Agents/speakers attending include:** Editors from Avon HarperCollins, Harlequin, Silhouette, Ballentine, 14 authors, agent from Rotrosen Agency, many more. Agents will be speaking and available for meetings with attendees.

Costs: $189 (early, January 10th), $209 (late) (includes all workshops, Friday multi-author book signing, Saturday breakfast, lunch Pajama Party Dessert, Sunday breakfast.)

Accommodations: West Coast Silverdale Hotel offers converence discount rate of $89 per night single. 3073 NW Bucklin Hill Rd., Silverdale WA 98383. (360)698-1000. Fax: (360)692-0932. Seattle: (206)382-0717. Reservations: 1(800)426-0670. Shuttle service is available fro SeaTac Airport to hotel.

Additional Information: Sleepless in Silverdale is famous for fun, informative weekend to help aspiring and published romance writers further their career in the romantic fiction industry. Brochures or guidelines available for SASE in September. Check website for information. Inquiries by e-mail OK.

🅽 **WASHINGTON WRITER'S CONFERENCE, WIW**, 220 Woodward Bldg., 733 15th St. NW, Washington DC 20005. (202)347-4973. Fax: (202)628-0298. E-mail: info@washwriter.org. Website: www.washwriter.org/events/. Conference held in May. Conference duration: 2 days. For fiction, nonfiction, scripts and business writing. **Agents/speakers attending have included:** Mirium Altshuler, Jeff Kleinman, Peter Rubie, Carol Mann. Last year 18 agents attended. Agents will be speaking and available for meetings with attendees.

WHIDBEY ISLAND WRITERS' CONFERENCE, P.O. Box 1289, Langley WA 98260. (360)331-6714. E-mail: writers@whidbey.com. Website: www.whidbey.com/writers. **Contact:** Celeste Mergens, director. Annual. Conference held February 28-March 2, 2003. Conference duration: 3 days. Average attendance: 260. Fiction, nonfiction, screenwriting, writing for children, poetry, travel and naturalist. Conference held at conference hall, and break-out fireside chats in local homes near sea. Panels include: "Meeting the Challenges of Writing," "The Art of Revision." **Agents/speakers attending include:** Jandy Nelson, Laurie Liss, Esmond Harmsworth, Katharine Sands; updated list on website.

Costs: $275 before September 1. $325 after. Volunteer discounts available; early registration encouraged.

Accommodations: Information available for SASE.

Additional Information: Brochures available for SASE or on website. Inquiries by e-mail OK.

WILLAMETTE WRITERS CONFERENCE, 9045 SW Barbur, Suite 5-A, Portland OR 97219. (503)452-1592. Fax: (503)452-0372. E-mail: wilwrite@willamettewriters.com. Website: www.willamettewriters.com. **Contact:** Bill Johnson. Estab. 1968. Annual. Conference held second weekend in August 2003. Average attendance: 400. Fiction, nonfiction, scriptwriting. "Willamette Writers is open to all writers, and we plan our conference accordingly. We offer workshops on all aspects of fiction, nonfiction, marketing, scriptwriting, the creative process, etc. Also we invite top notch inspirational speakers for key note addresses. Recent theme was 'Writing Your Future.' We always include at least one agent or editor panel and offer a variety of topics of interest to both fiction, screenwriters and nonfiction writers." **Previous agents/speakers have included:** Donald Maass, Noah Lukeman, Bob Mecoy, Angela Rinaldi, Lisa Dicker, Richard Morris, Andrew Whelchel. Agents will be speaking and available for meetings with attendees.
Costs: Cost for full conference including meals is $250 members; $286 nonmembers.
Accommodations: If necessary, these can be made on an individual basis. Some years special rates are available.
Additional Information: Conference brochures/guidelines are available for catalog-size SASE.

Canada

■N■ ■■ BLOODY WORDS, 40 Glendenning Dr., Nepean, Ontario K2H 7Y9 Canada. E-mail: info@bloodywords.com. Website: www.bloodywords.com. **Contact:** Linda Wilken or Sue Pike, co-chairs. Estab. 1999. Annual. Conference held June 13-15, 2003. Conference duration: 3 days. Average attendance: 225. Focus on mystery fiction—to provide a showcase for Canadian mystery fiction writers and readers, and to provide writing information to aspiring writers. Held at the Lord Elgin Hotel in downtown Toronto. "We will present two tracks of programming: one on Just the Facts, where everyone from coroners to toxicologists to Tactical Police Units present how things are done in the real world; and The Book track, where authors and readers discuss their favorite themes. Then we have the Mystery Café, where thirteen authors read and discuss their work." **Agents/speakers attending will include:** Agents, forensic specialists and RCMP spokespeople. Agents will be speaking and available for meetings with attendees.
Costs: $125-140 (Canadian).
Accommodations: Special conference rate available at the Lord Elgin Hotel.
Additional Information: Brochures available on website. Inquiries by e-mail OK.

■■ THE FESTIVAL OF THE WRITTEN ARTS, Box 2299, Sechelt, British Columbia V0N 3A0 Canada. (800)565-9631 or (604)885-9631. Fax: (604)885-3967. E-mail: info@writersfestival.ca. Website: www.writersfestival.ca. **Contact:** Gail Bull, festival producer. Estab. 1983. Annual. Festival held August 7-10, 2003. Average attendance: 3,500. To promote "all writing genres." Festival held at the Rockwood Centre. "The Centre overlooks the town of Sechelt on the Sunshine Coast. The lodge around which the Centre was organized was built in 1937 as a destination for holidayers arriving on the old Union Steamship Line; it has been preserved very much as it was in its heyday. A new twelve-bedroom annex was added in 1982, and in 1989 the Festival of the Written Arts constructed a 500-seat Pavilion for outdoor performances next to the annex. The festival does not have a theme. Instead, it showcases 25 or more Canadian writers in a wide variety of genres each year." **Previous agents/speakers have included:** Jane Urquhart, Sholagh Rogers, David Watmough, Zsuzsi Gartner, Gail Bowen, Charlotte Gray, Bill Richardson, P.K. Page, Richard B. Wright, Madeleine Thien, Ronald Wright, Michael Kusugak, Bob McDonald. Agents will be speaking.
Costs: $12 per event or $175 for a four-day pass (Canadian).
Accommodations: Lists of hotels and bed/breakfast available.
Additional Information: The festival runs contests during the 3½ days of the event. Prizes are books donated by publishers. Brochures/guidelines are available.

■■ ■■ FESTIVAL OF WORDS, 250 Thatcher Dr. E., Moose Jaw, Saskatchewan S6J 1L7 Canada. (306)691-0557. Fax: (306)693-2994. E-mail: word.festival@sk.sympatico.ca. Website: www.3.sk.sympatico.ca/praifes. **Contact:** Gary Hyland, coordinator; or Lori Dean, operations manager. Estab. 1997. Annual. Festival held in July. Festival duration: 4 days. The festival celebrates the imaginative uses of language, and features fiction and nonfiction writers, screenwriters, poets, children's authors, songwriters, dramatists and film makers. Held at the Moose Jaw Public Library/Art Museum complex and in Crescent Park. **Previous agents/speakers have included:** Alistair McLeaod, Roch Carrier, Jane Urquhart, Susan Musgrave, M.T. Kelly, Terry Jordan, Sharon Butala, Maryann Kovalski, Allan Fotheringham, Pamela Wallin, Bonnie Burnard, Erika Ritter, Wayson Choy, Koozma Tarasoff, Lorna Crozier, Sheree Fitch, Nino Ricci.
Costs: $115 (includes 3 meals).
Accommodations: Motels, hotels, campgrounds, bed and breakfasts.
Additional Information: "Our festival is an ideal meeting ground for people who love words to meet and mingle, promote their books and meet their fans." Brochures available for SASE. Inquiries by e-mail and fax OK.

■■ SAGE HILL WRITING EXPERIENCE, Box 1731, Saskatoon, Saskatchewan S7K 2Z4 Canada. Phone/fax: (306)652-7395. E-mail: sage.hill@sasktel.net. Website: www.lights.com/sagehill (features complete program, including application and scholarship information). **Contact:** Steven Ross Smith, executive director. Annual. Workshops held in August and November. Workshop duration 10-21 days. Attendance: limited to 40-50. "Sage Hill Writing Experience offers a special working and learning opportunity to writers at different stages of development. Top quality instruction, low instructor-student ratio and the beautiful Sage Hill settings offer conditions ideal for the pursuit of excellence in the arts of fiction, nonfiction, poetry and playwriting." The Sage Hill location features "individual accommodation, in-room writing area, lounges, meeting rooms, healthy meals, walking woods and vistas in several directions." Seven classes are held: Introduction to Writing Fiction & Poetry; Fiction Workshop; Nonfiction Workshop; Writing Young Adult Fiction Workshop; Poetry Workshop; Poetry Colloquium; Fiction Colloquium; Novel ColloquiumPlaywriting Lab; Fall Poetry Colloquium. 2002 Application deadlines are: April 25, July 30. **Previous agents/authors speakers have included in 2002:** Warren Canou, Robert Kroetsch, Betsy Warland, David Carpenter, Marilyn Dumont, Floyd Favel Starr.

Costs: $775 (Canadian) includes instruction, accommodation, meals and all facilities. Fall Poetry Colloquium: $975.

Accommodations: On-site individual accommodations located at Lumsden 45 kilometers outside Regina. Fall Colloquium is at Muenster, Saskatchewan, 150 kilometers east of Saskatoon.

Additional Information: For Introduction to Creative Writing: A five-page sample of your writing or a statement of your interest in creative writing; list of courses taken required. For workshop and colloquium program: A résumé of your writing career and a 12-page sample of your work plus 5 pages of published work required. Guidelines are available for SASE. Inquiries by e-mail and fax OK. Scholarships and bursaries are available.

THE VANCOUVER INTERNATIONAL WRITERS FESTIVAL, 1398 Cartwright St., Vancouver, British Columbia V6H 3R8 Canada. (604)681-6330. Fax: (604)681-6400. E-mail: viwf@writersfest.bc.ca. Website: www.writersfest.bc.ca (includes information on festival). **Contact:** Jane Davidson, general manager. Estab. 1988. Annual. Held in October. Average attendance: 11,000. "This is a festival for readers and writers. The program of events is diverse and includes readings, panel discussions, seminars. Lots of opportunities to interact with the writers who attend." Held on Granville Island—in the heart of Vancouver. Two professional theaters are used as well as Performance Works (an open space). "We try to avoid specific themes. Programming takes place between February and June each year and is by invitation." **Previous agents/speakers have included:** Margaret Atwood, Maeve Binchy, J.K. Rowling.

Costs: Tickets are $6-20 (Canadian).

Accommodations: Local tourist info can be provided when necessary and requested.

Additional Information: Brochures/guidelines are available for SASE after August. Inquiries by e-mail and fax OK. "A reminder—this is a festival, a celebration, not a conference or workshop."

WINNIPEG INTERNATIONAL WRITERS FESTIVAL, 624-100 Arthur St., Winnipeg, Manitoba R3B 1H3 Canada. (204)927-7323. Fax: (204)927-7320. E-mail: info@winnipegwords.com. Website: www.winnipegwords.com. **Contact:** Kathleen Darby, executive director/producer. Estab. 1997. Annual. Conference held last week of September. Conference duration: 6 days. Average attendance: 10,000. Fiction, nonfiction, scriptwriting. All areas of written/spoken word. Previous themes: Words of Wisdom, Diverse Voices. **Previous speakers/agents have included:** Michael Ondaatje, George Elliot Clarke, Esta Spalding. Agents will be speaking.

Costs: $10-30.

Additional Information: Brochures available on website. Inquiries by e-mail and fax OK.

A WRITER'S W*O*R*L*D, Surrey Writers' Conference, 10707 146th St., Surrey, British Columbia V3R 1T5 Canada. (604)589-2221. Fax: (604)588-9286. E-mail: ikmason@bc.sympatico.ca. Website: www.surreywritersconference.BC.ca. Principal: Bonnie Deren. Estab. 1992. Annual. Conference held October 18-20, 2002. Conference duration: 3 days. Average attendance: 400. Conference for fiction (romance/science fiction/fantasy/mystery—changes focus depending upon speakers and publishers scheduled), nonfiction, scriptwriting and poetry. "For everyone from beginner to professional." Conference held at Sheraton Guildford. **Agent/speakers attending have included:** Meredith Bernstein (Meredith Bernstein Literary Agency), Charlotte Gusay (Charlotte Gusay Literary Agency), Donald Maass (Donald Maass Literary Agency), Denise Marcil (Denise Marcil Literary Agency), Anne Sheldon and Michael Vidor (The Hardy Agency). Agents will be speaking and available for meetings with attendees.

Costs: Approximately $399.

Accommodations: On request will provide information on hotels and B&Bs. Conference rate: $109 (1999). Attendee must make own arrangements for hotel and transportation. For accomodations, call (800)661-2818.

Additional Information: Writer's contest entries must be submitted about 1 month early. Length: 1,000 words fiction, nonfiction, poetry, young writers (19 or less). Cash prizes awarded. Contest is judged by a qualified panel of writers and educators. Write, call or e-mail for additional information.

TO FIND A LIST OF CONFERENCES occurring in upcoming months, check the conference calendar in the introduction to this section beginning on page 288.

Resources
Professional Organizations

ORGANIZATIONS FOR AGENTS
Association of Authors' Representatives (AAR), P.O. Box 237201, Ansonia Station, New York NY 10003. Website: www.aar-online.org. A list of member agents is available for $7 and SAE with 99¢ postage.
Association of Authors' Agents, 62 Grafton Way, London W1P 5LD, England. (011) 44 7387 2076.

ORGANIZATIONS FOR WRITERS
The following professional organizations publish newsletters and hold conferences and meetings at which they often share information on agents. Organizations with an asterisk (*) have members who are liaisons to the AAR

Academy of American Poets, 588 Broadway, Suite 1203, New York NY 10012-3210. (212)274-0343. Website: www.poets.org/index.cfm.

American Medical Writers Association, 40 W. Gude Dr., Suite 101, Rockville MD 20850-1192. (301)294-5303. Website: www.amwa.org.

*American Society of Journalists & Authors, 1501 Broadway, Suite 302, New York NY 10036. (212)997-0947. Website: www.asja.org.

American Translators Association, 225 Reinekers Lane, Suite 590, Alexandria VA 22314. (703)683-6100. Website: www.atanet.org.

Asian American Writers' Workshop, 16 W. 32nd St., Suite 10A, New York NY 10001. (212)494-0061. Website: www.aaww.org

*Associated Writing Programs, The Tallwood House, Mail stop 1E3, George Mason University, Fairfax VA 22030. (703)993-4301. Website: www.awpwriter.org.

*The Authors Guild Inc., 31 E. 28th St., 10th Floor, New York NY 10016. (212)563-5904. Website: www.authorsguild.org.

The Authors League of America, Inc., 31 E. 28th St., 10th Floor, New York NY 10016. (212)564-8350.

Council of Writers Organizations, 12724 Sagamore Rd., Leawood KS 66209. (913)451-9023. Website: www.councilofwriters.com.

*The Dramatists Guild, 1501 Broadway, Suite 701, New York NY 10036. (212)398-9366.

Education Writers Association, 2122 P St. NW, Suite 201, Washington DC 20037. (202)452-9830. Website: www.ewa.org.

*Horror Writers Association, S.P. Somtow, President, P.O. Box 50577, Palo Alto CA 94303. Website: www.horror.org.

International Association of Crime Writers Inc., North American Branch, P.O. Box 8674, New York NY 10016. (212)243-8966.

International Television Association, 9202 N. Meridian St., Suite 200, Indianapolis IN 46260. (317)816-6269. Website: www.itva.org.

The International Women's Writing Guild, P.O. Box 810, Gracie Station, New York NY 10028-0082. (212)737-7536. Website: www.iwwg.com. Provides a literary agent list to members and holds "Meet the Agents and Editors" in April and October.

*Mystery Writers of America (MWA), 17 E. 47th St., 6th Floor, New York NY 10017. (212)888-8171. Website: www.mysterywriters.org.

National Association of Science Writers, Box 890, Hedgesville WV 25427. (304)754-5077. Website: www.nasw.org.

National League of American Pen Women, 1300 17th St. NW, Washington DC 20036-1973. (202)785-1997. Website: http://members.aol.com/penwomen/pen.htm.

National Writers Association, 3140 S. Peoria, Suite 295, Aurora CO 80014. (303)841-0246. Website: www.nationalwriters.com. In addition to agent referrals, also operates an agency for members.

*National Writers Union, 113 University Place, 6th Floor, New York NY 10003. (212)254-0279. Website: www.nwu.org. A trade union, this organization has an agent database available to members.

*PEN American Center, 568 Broadway, New York NY 10012-3225. (212)334-1660. Website: www.pen.org.

*Poets & Writers, 72 Spring St., New York NY 10012. (212)226-3586. Website: www.pw.org. Operates an information line, taking calls from 11-3 EST Monday through Friday.

Poetry Society of America, 15 Gramercy Park, New York NY 10003. (212)254-9628. Website: www.poetrysociety.org.

*Romance Writers of America, 3707 F.M. 1960 West, Suite 555, Houston TX 77068. (281)440-6885. Website: www.rwanational.com. Publishes an annual agent list for members for $10.

*Science Fiction and Fantasy Writers of America, P.O. Box 171, Unity ME 04988-0171. Website: www.sfwa.org.

Society of American Business Editors & Writers, University of Missouri, School of Journalism, 76 Gannett Hall, Columbia MO 65211. (573)882-7862. Website: www.sabew.org.

Society of American Travel Writers, 1500 Sunday Dr., Suite 102, Raleigh NC 27607. (919)787-5181. Website: www.satw.org.

*Society of Children's Book Writers & Illustrators, 8271 Beverly Blvd., Los Angeles CA 90048. (323)782-1010. Website: www.scbwi.org.

Volunteer Lawyers for the Arts, One E. 53rd St., 6th Floor, New York NY 10022. (212)319-2787. Website: www.vlany.org.

Washington Independent Writers, 220 Woodward Bldg., 733 15th St. NW, Washington DC 20005. (202)347-4973. Website: www.washwriter.org/.

Western Writers of America, 1012 Fair St., Franklin TN 37064. (615)791-1444. Website: www.westernwriters.org.

Writers Guild of Alberta, Main Floor, Percy Page Centre, 11759 Groat Rd., Edmonton, Alberta T5M 3K6 Canada. (780)422-8174. Website: http://writersguild.ab.ca.

*Writers Guild of America-East, 555 W. 57th St., Suite 1230, New York NY 10019. (212)767-7800. Website: www.wgaeast.org/. Provides list of WGA signatory agents for $1.29.

Writers Guild of America-West, 7000 W. Third St., Los Angeles CA 90048. (323)951-4000. Website: www.wga.org. Provides a list of WGA signatory agents for $2.50 and SASE sent to Agency Department.

Websites of Interest

WRITING

Fiction Addiction (www.fictionaddiction.net)
This site features articles and listings of publishers, agents, workshops and contests for fiction writers.

Writer's Exchange (http://writerexchange.about.com)
This site, hosted by writer Susan Molthrop, is a constantly updated resource devoted to the business of writing. Molthrop's goal is to include "everything I can discover to make your writing better, easier, and more fun."

Writing-World.com (www.writing-world.com)
This site offers a free biweekly newsletter for writers as well as instructional articles.

AGENTS

WritersNet (www.writers.net)
This site includes a bulletin board where writers can discuss their experiences with agents.

Agent Research and Evaluation (www.agentresearch.com)
This is the website of AR&E, a company that specializes in keeping tabs on literary agents. For a fee you can order their varied services to learn more about a specific agent.

The Query Guild (www.queryguild.com)
A working tool where writers can post queries for samples or receive feedback from other authors.

Writer Beware (www.sfwa.org/beware)
The Science Fiction Writers of America's page of warnings about agents and subsidy publishers.

Writer's Market (www.writersmarket.com)
This giant, searchable database includes agents and publishers, and offers daily updates tailored to your individual needs.

SCREENWRITING

Hollywoodlitsales.com (www.hollywoodlitsales.com)
Find out what your fellow scribes are writing by reading their loglines on this website sponsored by two major hollywood production companies.

The Hollywood Reporter (www.hollywoodreporter.com)
Online version of print magazine for screenwriters. Get the buzz on the movie biz.

Hollywood Scriptwriter (www.hollywoodscriptwriter.com)
This online site for the print magazine features articles and interviews.

Hollywood Creative Directory (www.hcdonline.com)
By joining this website, you'll have access to listings of legitimate players in the film, television, and new media industry.

MovieBytes (www.moviebytes.com)
Subscribe to **MovieBytes'** Who's Buying What for listings of the latest screenplay sales. Free access to one of the most comprehensive lists of screenplay contests is also offered on this site.

Daily Variety (www.variety.com)
This site archives the top stories from *Daily Variety.* Check here for the latest scoop on the movie and TV biz.

Samuel French, Inc. (www.samuelfrench.com/index.html)
This is the website of play publisher Samuel French that includes an index of authors and titles.

Screenwriter Web (www.breakingin.net) Screenplay marketing advice about agents, format, marketing, contests and more is edited by screenwriter Lenore Wright.

Screenwriter's Heaven (www.impactpc.freeserve.co.uk)
This is a page of links to many resources for screenwriters from workshops and competitions to scripts and software.

Done Deal (www.scriptsales.com)
The most useful features of this screenwriting site include descriptions of recently sold scripts, a list of script agents, and a list of production companies.

Wordplay (www.wordplayer.com)
The columns on this site are written by Academy Award-nominated writers Terry Rossio and Ted Elliott (*Shrek, Aladdin, The Mark of Zorro,* etc.) Consider it a free college-level scriptwriting course.

MARKETING AND PUBLICISTS

BookTalk (www.booktalk.com)
This site "offers authors an opportunity to announce and market new releases to millions of viewers across the globe."

Book Marketing Update (http://bookmarket.com)
This website by John Kremer, author of *1001 Ways to Market Your Book*, offers helpful tips for marketing books and many useful links to publishing websites. Also offers an e-newsletter so writers may share their marketing success stories.

Guerrilla Marketing (www.gmarketing.com)
The writers of *Guerrilla Marketing for Writers* provide many helpful resources to help you successfully market your book.

About Publishing (http://publishing.about.com)
This website provides a wide range of information about publishing, including several articles on independent publicists.

Authorlink (www.authorlink.com)
"The news, information and marketing community for editors, literary agents and writers." Showcases manuscripts of experienced and beginning writers.

BookWire (www.bookwire.com)
BookWire bills itself as the book industry's most comprehensive online information source. The site includes industry news, features, reviews, fiction, events, interviews, and links to other book sites.

Publishers Lunch (www.publisherslunch.com)
This site allows you to sign up for the free newsletter, which offers daily updates on what's going on in the wonderful world of publishing. It's a good way to keep on top of the market.

Publishers Weekly (www.publishersweekly.com)
Read the latest book publishing news on this electronic version of the popular print magazine.

Writer's Digest (www.writersdigest.com)
This site includes information about writing books and magazines from *Writer's Digest*. It also has a huge, searchable database of writer's guidelines from thousands of publishers.

ORGANIZATIONS

The Association of Authors' Representatives (www.aar-online.org)
This association page includes a list of member agents, their newsletter and their canon of ethics.

National Writer's Union (www.nwu.org/)
Site of the National Writer's Union—the trade union for freelance writers of all genres publishing in the U.S.

PEN American Center (www.pen.org)
Site of the organization of writers and editors that seek to defend the freedom of expression and promote contemporary literature.

Writer's Guild of America (www.wga.org)
The WGA site includes advice and information on the art and craft of professional screenwriting for film, television, and interactive projects. This site offers script registration and a list of WGA signatory agencies.

TABLE OF ACRONYMS

The organizations and their acronyms listed below are frequently referred to in the listings and are widely used in the industries of agenting and writing.

AAA	Association of Authors' Agents	NLAPW	National League of American Pen Women
AAP	American Association of Publishers	NWA	National Writers Association
AAR	Association of Authors' Representatives	OWAA	Outdoor Writers Association of America, Inc.
ABA	American Booksellers Association	RWA	Romance Writers of America
ABWA	Associated Business Writers of America	SAG	Screen Actor's Guild
AEB	Association of Editorial Businesses	SATW	Society of American Travel Writers
AFTRA	American Federation of TV and Radio Artists	SCBWI	Society of Children's Book Writers & Illustrators
AGVA	American Guild of Variety Artists	SFRA	Science Fiction Research Association
AMWA	American Medical Writer's Association	SFWA	Science Fiction and Fantasy Writers of America
ASJA	American Society of Journalists and Authors	SPWA	South Plains Writing Association
ATA	Association of Talent Agents	WGA	Writers Guild of America
AWA	Aviation/Space Writers Association	WIA	Women in the Arts Foundation, Inc.
CAA	Canadian Authors Association	WIF	Women in Film
DGA	Director's Guild of America	WICI	Women in Communications, Inc.
GWAA	Garden Writers Association of America	WIW	Washington Independent Writers
HWA	Horror Writers of America	WMG	Women's Media Group
IACP	International Association of Culinary Professionals	WNBA	Women's National Book Association
MOW	Movie of the Week	WRW	Washington Romance Writers (chapter of RWA)
MWA	Mystery Writers of America, Inc.	WWA	Western Writers of America
NASW	National Association of Science Writers		

Glossary

Above the line. A budgetary term for movies and TV. The line refers to money budgeted for creative talent, such as actors, writers, directors, and producers.

Advance. Money a publisher pays a writer prior to book publication, usually paid in installments, such as one-half upon signing the contract; one-half upon delivery of the complete, satisfactory manuscript. An advance is paid against the royalty money to be earned by the book. Agents take their percentage off the top of the advance as well as from the royalties earned.

Auction. Publishers sometimes bid for the acquisition of a book manuscript with excellent sales prospects. The bids are for the amount of the author's advance, guaranteed dollar amounts, advertising and promotional expenses, royalty percentage, etc.

Backlist. Those books still in print from previous years' publication.

Backstory. The history of what has happened before the action in your script takes place, affecting a character's current behavior.

Beat. Major plot points of a story.

Below the line. A budgetary term for movies and TV, referring to production costs, including production manager, cinematographer, editor and crew members such as gaffers, grips, set designers, make-up, etc.

Bible. The collected background information on all characters and storylines of all existing episodes, as well as projections of future plots.

Bio. Brief (usually one page) background information about an artist, writer, or photographer. Includes work and educational experience.

Boilerplate. A standardized publishing contract. Most authors and agents make many changes on the boilerplate before accepting the contract.

Book club rights. Rights to sell a book through a book club.

Book packager. Draws elements of a book together, from the initial concept to writing and marketing strategies, then sells the book package to a book publisher and/or movie producer. Also known as book producer or book developer.

Business-size envelope. Also known as a #10 envelope.

Castable. A script with attractive roles for known actors.

Category fiction. A term used to include all various types of fiction. See *genre*.

Client. When referring to a literary or script agent, "client" is used to mean the writer whose work the agent is handling.

Clips. Writing samples, usually from newspapers or magazines, of your published work.

Commercial novels. Novels designed to appeal to a broad audience. These are often broken down into categories such as western, mystery, and romance. See also *genre*.

Concept. A statement that summarizes a screenplay or teleplay—before the outline or treatment is written.

Contributor's copies. Copies of the author's book sent to the author. The number of contributor's copies is often negotiated in the publishing contract.

Co-agent. See *subagent*.

Co-publishing. Arrangement where author and publisher share publication costs and profits of a book. Also known as cooperative publishing.

Copyediting. Editing of a manuscript for writing style, grammar, punctuation, and factual accuracy.

Copyright. A means to protect an author's work.

Cover letter. A brief descriptive letter sent with a manuscript submitted to an agent or publisher.

Coverage. A brief synopsis and analysis of a script, provided by a reader to a buyer considering purchasing the work.

Critiquing service. A service offered by some agents in which writers pay a fee for comments on the saleability or other qualities of their manuscript. Sometimes the critique includes suggestions on how to improve the work. Fees vary, as do the quality of the critiques. See also *editing service*.

Curriculum vitae. Short account of one's career or qualifications (i.e., résumé).

D person. Development person. Includes readers and story editors through creative executives who work in development and acquisition of properties for TV and movies.

Deal memo. The memorandum of agreement between a publisher and author that precedes the actual contract and includes important issues such as royalty, advance, rights, distribution, and option clauses.

Development. The process where writers present ideas to producers overseeing the developing script through various stages to finished product.

Division. An unincorporated branch of a company.

Docudrama. A fictional film rendition of recent newsmaking events or people.

Editing service. A service offered by some agents in which writers pay a fee—either lump sum or per-page—to have their manuscript edited. The quality and extent of the editing varies from agency to agency. See also *critiquing service*.

Electronic rights. Secondary or subsidiary rights dealing with electronic/multimedia formats (e.g., the Internet, CD-ROMs, electronic magazines).

Elements. Actors, directors, and producers attached to a project to make an attractive package.

El-hi. Elementary to high school. A term used to indicate reading or interest level.

Episodic drama. Hour-long continuing TV show, often shown at 10 p.m.

Evaluation fees. Fees an agent may charge to evaluate material. The extent and quality of this evaluation varies, but comments usually concern the saleability of the manuscript.

Exclusive. Offering a manuscript, usually for a set period of time, to just one agent and guaranteeing that agent is the only one looking at the manuscript.

Film rights. May be sold or optioned by author to a person in the film industry, enabling the book to be made into a movie.

Flap copy. The text which appears on the inside covers of a published book which briefly tell the book's premise. Also called jacket copy.

Floor bid. If a publisher is very interested in a manuscript he may offer to enter a floor bid when the book goes to auction. The publisher sits out of the auction, but agrees to take the book by topping the highest bid by an agreed-upon percentage (usually 10 percent).

Foreign rights. Translation or reprint rights to be sold abroad.

Foreign rights agent. An agent who handles selling the rights to a country other than that of the first book agent. Usually an additional percentage (about 5 percent) will be added on to the first book agent's commission to cover the foreign rights agent.

Genre. Refers to either a general classification of writing such as a novel, poem, or short story or to the categories within those classifications, such as problem novels or sonnets. Genre fiction is a term that covers various types of commercial novels such as mystery, romance, western, science fiction, or horror.

Ghosting/ghostwriting. A writer puts into literary form the words, ideas, or knowledge of another person under that person's name. Some agents offer this service; others pair ghostwriters with celebrities or experts.

Green light. To give the go-ahead to a movie or TV project.

Half-hour. A 30-minute TV show, also known as a *sitcom.*

High concept. A story idea easily expressed in a quick, one-line description.

Hook. Aspect of the work that sets it apart from others.

Imprint. The name applied to a publisher's specific line of books.

IRC. International Reply Coupon. Buy at a post office to enclose with material sent outside your country to cover the cost of return postage. The recipient turns them in for stamps in their own country.

Log line. A one-line description of a plot as it might appear in *TV Guide.*

Long-form TV. Movies of the week (MOW) or *miniseries.*

Mainstream fiction. Fiction on subjects or trends that transcend popular novel categories such as mystery or romance. Using conventional methods, this kind of fiction tells stories about people and their conflicts.

Marketing fee. Fee charged by some agents to cover marketing expenses. It may be used to cover postage, telephone calls, faxes, photocopying or any other expense incurred in marketing a manuscript.

Mass market paperbacks. Softcover book, usually around 4×7, on a popular subject directed at a general audience and sold in groceries and drugstores as well as bookstores.

MFTS. Made for TV series. A series developed for television. See also episodics.

Middle reader. The general classification of books written for readers 9-11 years old.

Midlist. Those titles on a publisher's list expected to have limited sales. Midlist books are mainstream, not literary, scholarly, or genre, and are usually written by new or relatively unknown writers.

Miniseries. A limited dramatic series written for television, often based on a popular novel.

MOW. Movie of the week. A movie script written especially for television, usually seven acts with time for commercial breaks. Topics are often contemporary, sometimes controversial, fictional accounts. Also known as a made-for-TV-movie.

Multiple contract. Book contract with an agreement for a future book(s).

Net receipts. One method of royalty payment based on the amount of money a book publisher receives on the sale of the book after the booksellers' discounts, special sales discounts and returned copies.

Novelization. A novel created from the script of a popular movie, usually called a movie "tie-in" and published in paperback.

Novella. A short novel or long short story, usually 7,000 to 15,000 words. Also called a novelette.

One-time rights. This right allows a short story or portions of a fiction or nonfiction book to be published. The work can be printed again without violating the contract.

Option. Also known as a script option. Instead of buying a movie script outright, a producer buys the right to a script for a short period of time (usually six months to one year) for a small down payment. At the end of the agreed time period, if the movie has not begun production and the producer does not wish to purchase the script, the rights revert back to the scriptwriter.

Option clause. A contract clause giving a publisher the right to publish an author's next book.

Outline. A summary of a book's contents in 5 to 15 double-spaced pages; often in the form of chapter headings with a descriptive sentence or two under each one to show the scope of the book. A script's outline is a scene-by-scene narrative description of the story (10-15 pages for a ½-hour teleplay; 15-25 pages for 1-hour; 25-40 pages for 90 minutes; and 40-60 pages for a 2-hour feature film or teleplay).

Over-the-transom. Slang for the path of an unsolicited manuscript into the slush pile.

Packaging. The process of putting elements together, increasing the chances of a project being made. See also *book packager.*

Platform. A writer's speaking experience, interview skills, website, and other abilities which helps form a following of potential buyers for that author's book.

Picture book. A type of book aimed at the preschool to 8-year-old that tells the story primarily or entirely with artwork. Agents and reps interested in selling to publishers of these books often handle both artists and writers.

Pitch. The process where a writer meets with a producer and briefly outlines ideas that could be developed if the writer is hired to write a script for the project.

Proofreading. Close reading and correction of a manuscript's typographical errors.

Property. Books or scripts forming the basis for a movie or TV project.

Proposal. An offer to an editor or publisher to write a specific work, usually a package consisting of an outline and sample chapters.

Prospectus. A preliminary, written description of a book, usually one page in length.

Query. A letter written to an agent or a potential market, to elicit interest in a writer's work.

Reader. A person employed by an agent or buyer to go through the slush pile of manuscripts and scripts and select those worth considering.

Release. A statement that your idea is original, has never been sold to anyone else, and that you are selling negotiated rights to the idea upon payment.

Remainders. Leftover copies of an out-of-print or slow-selling book purchased from the publisher at a reduced rate. Depending on the contract, a reduced royalty or no royalty is paid on remaindered books.

Reporting time. The time it takes the agent to get back to you on your query or submission.

Reprint rights. The rights to republish your book after its initial printing.

Royalties. A percentage of the retail price paid to the author for each copy of the book that is sold. Agents take their percentage from the royalties earned as well as from the advance.

SASE. Self-addressed, stamped envelope; should be included with all correspondence.

Scholarly books. Books written for an academic or research audience. These are usually heavily researched, technical, and often contain terms used only within a specific field.

Screenplay. Script for a film intended to be shown in theaters.

Script. Broad term covering teleplay, screenplay, or stage play. Sometimes used as a shortened version of the word "manuscript" when referring to books.

Serial rights. The right for a newspaper or magazine to publish sections of a manuscript.

Simultaneous submission. Sending a manuscript to several agents or publishers at the same time. Simultaneous queries are common; simultaneous submissions are unacceptable to many agents or publishers.

Sitcom. Situation comedy. Episodic comedy script for a television series. Term comes from the characters dealing with various situations with humorous results.

Slush pile. A stack of unsolicited submissions in the office of an editor, agent or publisher.

Spec script. A script written on speculation without confirmation of a sale.

Standard commission. The commission an agent earns on the sales of a manuscript or script. For literary agents, this commission percentage (usually between 10 and 20 percent) is taken from the advance and royalties paid to the writer. For script agents, the commission is taken from script sales; if handling plays, agents take a percentage from the box office proceeds.

Story analyst. See *reader*.

Storyboards. Series of panels which illustrates a progressive sequence or graphics and story copy for a TV commercial, film, or filmstrip.

Subagent. An agent handling certain subsidiary rights, usually working in conjunction with the agent who handled the book rights. The percentage paid the book agent is increased to pay the subagent.

Subsidiary. An incorporated branch of a company or conglomerate (e.g., Alfred Knopf, Inc. is a subsidiary of Random House, Inc.).

Subsidiary rights. All rights other than book publishing rights included in a book publishing contract, such as paperback rights, bookclub rights, movie rights. Part of an agent's job is to negotiate those rights and advise you on which to sell and which to keep.

Syndication rights. The right which allows a television station to rerun a sit-com or drama, even if the show appeared originally on a different network.

Synopsis. A brief summary of a story, novel. or play. As a part of a book proposal, it is a comprehensive summary condensed in a page or page and a half, single-spaced. See also *outline*.

Tearsheet. Published samples of your work, usually pages torn from a magazine.

Teleplay. Script for television.

Terms. Financial provisions agreed upon in a contract.

Textbook. Book used in a classroom on the elementary, high school, or college level.

Trade book. Either a hard cover or soft cover book; subject matter frequently concerns a special interest for a general audience; sold mainly in bookstores.

Trade paperback. A softbound volume, usually around 5×8, published and designed for the general public, available mainly in bookstores.

Translation rights. Sold to a foreign agent or foreign publisher.

Treatment. Synopsis of a television or film script (40-60 pages for a 2-hour feature film or teleplay).

Turnaround. When a script has been in development but not made in the time allotted, it can be put back on the market.

Unsolicited manuscript. An unrequested manuscript sent to an editor, agent, or publisher.

Young adult. The general classification of books written for readers age 12-18.

Young reader. Books written for readers 5-8 years old, where artwork only supports the text.

Contributors to the Insider Reports

JEFFREY HILLARD
Jeff Hillard is a poet, journalist, novelist, and screenwriter who has written three books of poetry. Additionally, he is an associate professor of English at the College of Mount St. Joseph in Cincinnati, Ohio.

TERRI SEE
Terri See is a freelance writer and editor living near Philadelphia. She is a former staff editor for Writer's Digest Books.

W.E. REINKA
W.E. Reinka is a fulltime freelance writer of fiction and nonfiction. Now living in Eugene, Oregon, he is former books editor of the *Berkeley Insider* and the *Berkeley Voice*. He has published reviews, personal essays, profiles, business articles and travel pieces in publications nationwide.

RODNEY A. WILSON
Rodney A. Wilson (www.geocities.com/rodney_a_wilson) is a professional freelance writer and editor living in the wilds of suburban Kentucky. When not slaving over pages of text, Rodney can be found enjoying domestic life with his beautiful wife Carla.

Literary Agents Specialties Index

The subject index is divided into fiction and nonfiction subject categories for Literary Agents. To find an agent interested in the type of manuscript you've written, see the appropriate sections under subject headings that best describe your work.

FICTION

Action/Adventure: ABS Literary Agency, Inc. **76**; Acacia House Publishing Services Ltd. **76**; Ahearn Agency, Inc., The **78**; Alive Communications, Inc. **78**; Allred and Allred Literary Agents **79**; Amsterdam Agency, Marcia **81**; Authentic Creations Literary Agency **82**; Baldi Literary Agency, Malaga **82**; Barrett Books Inc., Loretta **83**; Bial Agency, Daniel **84**; Brandt & Hochman Literary Agents Inc. **91**; Brown Ltd., Curtis **92**; Browne Ltd., Pema **93**; Buck Agency, Howard **93**; Congdon Associates Inc., Don **97**; Crawford Literary Agency **99**; Donovan Literary, Jim **104**; Ducas, Robert **105**; Dupree/Miller and Associates Inc. Literary **106**; Dystel Literary Management, Inc., Jane **106**; Farber Literary Agency Inc. **110**; Fort Ross Inc. Russian-American Publishing Projects **113**; Goldfarb & Associates **116**; Goodman Associates **117**; Grace Literary Agency, Carroll **117**; Greenburger Associates, Inc., Sanford J. **118**; Gregory and Company Authors' Agents **118**; Halsey Agency, Reece **120**; Halsey North, Reece **120**; Hamilburg Agency, Mitchell J., The **120**; Harris Literary Agency, Inc., The Joy **121**; Hartline Literary Agency **121**; Hawkins & Associates, Inc., John **121**; Henshaw Group, Richard **122**; Jabberwocky Literary Agency **125**; JCA Literary Agency **126**; Kleinman, Esq., Jeffrey M. **128**; Klinger, Inc., Harvey **129**; Koster Literary Agency, LLC, Elaine **130**; Kraas Agency, Irene **130**; Kritzer Productions, Eddie **131**; Lampack Agency, Inc., Peter **132**; Larsen/Elizabeth Pomada Literary Agents, Michael **132**; Lasher Agency, The Maureen **133**; Lazear Agency Incorporated **133**; Levine Literary Agency, Paul S. **135**; Lincoln Literary Agency, Ray **136**; Literary Group, The **137**; Marshall Agency, The Evan **148**; McBride Literary Agency, Margret **148**; Morrison, Inc., Henry **151**; Mura Literary, Dee **152**; Naggar Literary Agency, Jean V. **153**; National Writers Literary Agency **153**; Norma-Lewis Agency, The **155**; Paraview, Inc. **156**; Picard, Literary Agent, Alison J. **158**; Quicksilver Books Literary Agents **161**; RLR Associates, Ltd. **169**; Rotrosen Agency, LLC, Jane **172**; Rubie Literary Agency, The Peter **173**; Russell and Volkening **173**; Sanders & Associates, Victoria **174**; Scherf, Inc., Literary Properties **174**; Sedgeband Literary Associates **177**; Simmons Literary Agency, Jeffrey **179**; Treimel NY, Scott **187**; Venture Literary **191**; Vines Agency, Inc., The **192**; Wald Associates, Inc., Mary Jack **192**; Weiner Literary Agency, Cherry **195**; Wonderland Press, Inc., The **197**; Writers House **198**; Wylie-Merrick Literary Agency **199**

Cartoon/Comic: Bial Agency, Daniel **84**; Brown Ltd., Curtis **92**; Halsey North, Reece **120**; Hamilburg Agency, Mitchell J., The **120**; Harris Literary Agency, Inc., The Joy **121**; Hawkins & Associates, Inc., John **121**; Jabberwocky Literary Agency **125**; Lazear Agency Incorporated **133**; Levine Literary Agency, Paul S. **135**; Nazor Literary Agency **154**; Pevner, Inc., Stephen **157**; Preskill Literary Agency, Robert **159**; RLR Associates, Ltd. **169**; Treimel NY, Scott **187**; Van Der Leun & Associates **191**; Writers House **198**

Confessional: Allred and Allred Literary Agents **79**; Barrett Books Inc., Loretta **83**; Bial Agency, Daniel **84**; Brown Ltd., Curtis **92**; Buck Agency, Howard **93**; Hamilburg Agency, Mitchell J., The **120**; Harris Literary Agency, Inc., The Joy **121**; Kritzer Productions, Eddie **131**; Lazear Agency Incorporated **133**; Levine Literary Agency, Paul S. **135**; March Tenth, Inc. **147**; Simmons Literary Agency, Jeffrey **179**; Writers House **198**

Contemporary Issues: Ahearn Agency, Inc., The **78**; Alive Communications, Inc. **78**; Authentic Creations Literary Agency **82**; Baldi Literary Agency, Malaga **82**; Barrett Books Inc., Loretta **83**; Bernstein & Associates, Inc., Pam **84**; Bial Agency, Daniel **84**; BookEnds, LLC **86**; Books & Such **87**; Brandt & Hochman Literary Agents Inc. **91**; Brandt Agency, The Joan **91**; Brown Associates Inc., Marie **91**; Brown Ltd., Curtis **92**; Browne Ltd., Pema **93**; Buck Agency, Howard **93**; Castiglia Literary Agency **95**; Clark Associates, William **96**; Doyen Literary Services, Inc. **104**; Ducas, Robert

105; Dupree/Miller and Associates Inc. Literary **106**; Dystel Literary Management, Inc., Jane **106**; Elmo Agency Inc., Ann **109**; Farber Literary Agency Inc. **110**; Freymann Literary Agency, Sarah Jane **114**; Goldfarb & Associates **116**; Goodman Associates **117**; Greenburger Associates, Inc., Sanford J. **118**; Grosjean Literary Agency, Jill **119**; Grosvenor Literary Agency, The **119**; Halsey Agency, Reece **120**; Hamilburg Agency, Mitchell J., The **120**; Harris Literary Agency, Inc., The Joy **121**; Hartline Literary Agency **121**; Hawkins & Associates, Inc., John **121**; Jabberwocky Literary Agency **125**; JCA Literary Agency **126**; Jenks Agency, The **126**; Kleinman, Esq., Jeffrey M. **128**; Koster Literary Agency, LLC, Elaine **130**; Kouts, Literary Agent, Barbara S. **130**; Kritzer Productions, Eddie **131**; Larsen/Elizabeth Pomada Literary Agents, Michael **132**; Lazear Agency Incorporated **133**; Levine Communications, Inc., James **134**; Levine Literary Agency, Paul S. **135**; Lincoln Literary Agency, Ray **136**; Literary Group, The **137**; LitWest Group, LLC **140**; Lowenstein Associates **141**; Markowitz Literary Agency, Barbara **147**; McGrath, Helen **149**; Multimedia Product Development, Inc. **152**; Mura Literary, Dee **152**; Naggar Literary Agency, Jean V. **153**; Paraview, Inc. **156**; Pevner, Inc., Stephen **157**; Picard, Literary Agent, Alison J. **158**; Pinder Lane & Garon-Brooke Associates, Ltd. **158**; Rees Literary Agency, Helen **162**; Rhodes Literary Agency, Jodie **162**; RLR Associates, Ltd. **169**; Robbins Literary Agency, B.J. **170**; Sanders & Associates, Victoria **174**; Schiavone Literary Agency, Inc. **175**; Schulman, A Literary Agency, Susan **175**; Singer Literary Agency Inc., Evelyn **179**; Skolnick Literary Agency, Irene **180**; Spectrum Literary Agency **181**; Spitzer Literary Agency, Philip G. **182**; Stauffer Associates, Nancy **182**; Straus Agency, Inc., Robin **183**; Tabian/Literary Agent, Robert E. **185**; Treimel NY, Scott **187**; Van Der Leun & Associates **191**; Vines Agency, Inc., The **192**; Wald Associates, Inc., Mary Jack **192**; Wales, Literary Agency, Inc. **193**; Watt & Associates, Sandra **194**; Wecksler-Incomco **195**; Weiner Literary Agency, Cherry **195**; Wieser & Wieser, Inc. **197**; Witherspoon Associates, Inc. **197**; Writers House **198**; Zachary Shuster Harmsworth **199**

Detective/Police/Crime: ABS Literary Agency, Inc. **76**; Abel Literary Agency, Inc., Dominick **76**; Acacia House Publishing Services Ltd. **76**; Ahearn Agency, Inc., The **78**; Alive Communications, Inc. **78**; Allred and Allred Literary Agents **79**; Amsterdam Agency, Marcia **81**; Anubis Literary Agency **81**; Appleseeds Management **82**; Authentic Creations Literary Agency **82**; Baldi Literary Agency, Malaga **82**; Barrett Books Inc., Loretta **83**; Bial Agency, Daniel **84**; BookEnds, LLC **86**; Brandt Agency, The Joan **91**; Brown Ltd., Curtis **92**; Browne Ltd., Pema **93**; Buck Agency, Howard **93**; Collin Literary Agency, Frances **97**; Congdon Associates Inc., Don **97**; Core Creations **98**; Cornerstone Literary, Inc. **99**; DHS Literary, Inc. **102**; Donovan Literary, Jim **104**; Dorian Literary Agency **104**; Ducas, Robert **105**; Dupree/Miller and Associates Inc. Literary **106**; Dystel Literary Management, Inc., Jane **106**; Elmo Agency Inc., Ann **109**; Fort Ross Inc. Russian-American Publishing Projects **113**; Goldfarb & Associates **116**; Goodman Associates **117**; Grace Literary Agency, Carroll **117**; Greenburger Associates, Inc., Sanford J. **118**; Gregory and Company Authors' Agents **118**; Grosvenor Literary Agency, The **119**; Halsey Agency, Reece **120**; Halsey North, Reece **120**; Hamilburg Agency, Mitchell J., The **120**; Harris Literary Agency, Inc., The Joy **121**; Hawkins & Associates, Inc., John **121**; Henshaw Group, Richard **122**; J de S Associates Inc. **125**; Jabberwocky Literary Agency **125**; JCA Literary Agency **126**; Klinger, Inc., Harvey **129**; Koster Literary Agency, LLC, Elaine **130**; Kraas Agency, Irene **130**; Kritzer Productions, Eddie **131**; Lampack Agency, Inc., Peter **132**; Larsen/Elizabeth Pomada Literary Agents, Michael **132**; Lasher Agency, The Maureen **133**; Lazear Agency Incorporated **133**; Levine Literary Agency, Paul S. **135**; Lincoln Literary Agency, Ray **136**; Literary Group, The **137**; LitWest Group, LLC **140**; Lowenstein Associates **141**; Maass Literary Agency **142**; Markowitz Literary Agency, Barbara **147**; Marmur Associates, Ltd., Mildred **148**; McBride Literary Agency, Margret **148**; McGrath, Helen **149**; Morrison, Inc., Henry **151**; Multimedia Product Development, Inc. **152**; Mura Literary, Dee **152**; Naggar Literary Agency, Jean V. **153**; Norma-Lewis Agency, The **155**; Picard, Literary Agent, Alison J. **158**; Pinder Lane & Garon-Brooke Associates, Ltd. **158**; Pine Associates, Inc., Arthur **159**; Preskill Literary Agency, Robert **159**; Protter Literary Agent, Susan Ann **160**; RLR Associates, Ltd. **169**; Robbins Literary Agency, B.J. **170**; Rotrosen Agency, LLC, Jane **172**; Rubie Literary Agency, The Peter **173**; Russell and Volkening **173**; Schulman, A Literary Agency, Susan **175**; Seligman, Literary Agent, Lynn **177**; Simmons Literary Agency, Jeffrey **179**; Spitzer Literary Agency, Philip G. **182**; Treimel NY, Scott **187**; Venture Literary **191**; Vines Agency, Inc., The **192**; Wald Associates, Inc., Mary Jack **192**; Ware Literary Agency, John A. **193**; Watt & Associates, Sandra **194**; Weiner Literary Agency, Cherry **195**; Whittaker, Literary Agent, Lynn **196**; Wieser & Wieser, Inc. **197**; Witherspoon Associates, Inc. **197**; Writers House **198**; Zachary Shuster Harmsworth **199**; Zeckendorf Assoc. Inc., Susan **200**

Erotica: Baldi Literary Agency, Malaga **82**; Bial Agency, Daniel **84**; Brown Ltd., Curtis **92**; Browne Ltd., Pema **93**; Cornerstone Literary, Inc. **99**; DHS Literary, Inc. **102**; Goodman Associates **117**; Hamilburg Agency, Mitchell J., The **120**; Lazear Agency Incorporated **133**; Levine Literary Agency, Paul S. **135**; Lowenstein Associates **141**; Marshall Agency, The Evan **148**; New Brand Agency Group,

LLC **154**; Pevner, Inc., Stephen **157**; Picard, Literary Agent, Alison J. **158**; Writers House **198**

Ethnic: Ahearn Agency, Inc., The **78**; Allred and Allred Literary Agents **79**; Amster Literary Enterprises, Betsy **80**; Baldi Literary Agency, Malaga **82**; Barrett Books Inc., Loretta **83**; Bent, Harvey Klinger, Inc., Jenny **84**; Bernstein & Associates, Inc., Pam **84**; Bial Agency, Daniel **84**; Bleeker Street Associates, Inc. **85**; Book Deals, Inc. **86**; BookEnds, LLC **86**; Brandt & Hochman Literary Agents Inc. **91**; Brown Associates Inc., Marie **91**; Brown Ltd., Curtis **92**; Browne Ltd., Pema **93**; Buck Agency, Howard **93**; Castiglia Literary Agency **95**; Clark Associates, William **96**; Cohen, Inc. Literary Agency, Ruth **97**; Collin Literary Agency, Frances **97**; Cornerstone Literary, Inc. **99**; Daves Agency, Joan **101**; Dawson Associates, Liza **101**; DeFiore and Company **101**; DHS Literary, Inc. **102**; Dijkstra Literary Agency, Sandra **102**; Dunham Literary **105**; Dupree/Miller and Associates Inc. Literary **106**; Dystel Literary Management, Inc., Jane **106**; Elmo Agency Inc., Ann **109**; Eth Literary Representation, Felicia **109**; Freymann Literary Agency, Sarah Jane **114**; Goldfarb & Associates **116**; Goodman Associates **117**; Greenburger Associates, Inc., Sanford J. **118**; Halsey Agency, Reece **120**; Halsey North, Reece **120**; Hamilburg Agency, Mitchell J., The **120**; Harris Literary Agency, Inc., The Joy **121**; Hawkins & Associates, Inc., John **121**; Henshaw Group, Richard **122**; Hill & Barlow Agency **123**; Jabberwocky Literary Agency **125**; Jenks Agency, The **126**; Kern Literary Agency, Natasha **127**; Kleinman, Esq., Jeffrey M. **128**; Koster Literary Agency, LLC, Elaine **130**; Larsen/Elizabeth Pomada Literary Agents, Michael **132**; Lazear Agency Incorporated **133**; Levine Literary Agency, Paul S. **135**; Lincoln Literary Agency, Ray **136**; Literary Group, The **137**; LitWest Group, LLC **140**; Lowenstein Associates **141**; March Tenth, Inc. **147**; Markowitz Literary Agency, Barbara **147**; Marshall Agency, The Evan **148**; McBride Literary Agency, Margret **148**; Multimedia Product Development, Inc. **152**; Mura Literary, Dee **152**; Naggar Literary Agency, Jean V. **153**; Nazor Literary Agency **154**; Nine Muses and Apollo Inc. **155**; Paraview, Inc. **156**; Pevner, Inc., Stephen **157**; Picard, Literary Agent, Alison J. **158**; Rhodes Literary Agency, Jodie **162**; RLR Associates, Ltd. **169**; Robbins Literary Agency, B.J. **170**; Rubie Literary Agency, The Peter **173**; Russell and Volkening **173**; Sanders & Associates, Victoria **174**; Schiavone Literary Agency, Inc. **175**; Seligman, Literary Agent, Lynn **177**; Singer Literary Agency Inc., Evelyn **179**; Treimel NY, Scott **187**; Vines Agency, Inc., The **192**; Wald Associates, Inc., Mary Jack **192**; Wales, Literary Agency, Inc. **193**; Whittaker, Literary Agent, Lynn **196**; Witherspoon Associates, Inc. **197**; Writers House **198**; Zachary Shuster Harmsworth **199**; Zeckendorf Assoc. Inc., Susan **200**

Experimental: Baldi Literary Agency, Malaga **82**; Brown Ltd., Curtis **92**; Buck Agency, Howard **93**; Dupree/Miller and Associates Inc. Literary **106**; Hamilburg Agency, Mitchell J., The **120**; Harris Literary Agency, Inc., The Joy **121**; Hawkins & Associates, Inc., John **121**; Larsen/Elizabeth Pomada Literary Agents, Michael **132**; Lazear Agency Incorporated **133**; Levine Literary Agency, Paul S. **135**; Mura Literary, Dee **152**; Pevner, Inc., Stephen **157**; Picard, Literary Agent, Alison J. **158**; RLR Associates, Ltd. **169**; Sedgeband Literary Associates **177**; Treimel NY, Scott **187**; Vines Agency, Inc., The **192**; Wald Associates, Inc., Mary Jack **192**; Whittaker, Literary Agent, Lynn **196**; Writers House **198**

Family Saga: Ahearn Agency, Inc., The **78**; Alive Communications, Inc. **78**; Allred and Allred Literary Agents **79**; Authentic Creations Literary Agency **82**; Barrett Books Inc., Loretta **83**; BookEnds, LLC **86**; Books & Such **87**; Brandt & Hochman Literary Agents Inc. **91**; Brandt Agency, The Joan **91**; Brown Ltd., Curtis **92**; Buck Agency, Howard **93**; Collin Literary Agency, Frances **97**; Cornerstone Literary, Inc. **99**; Daves Agency, Joan **101**; Dawson Associates, Liza **101**; Dorian Literary Agency **104**; Doyen Literary Services, Inc. **104**; Ducas, Robert **105**; Dupree/Miller and Associates Inc. Literary **106**; Dystel Literary Management, Inc., Jane **106**; Elmo Agency Inc., Ann **109**; Feigen/Parrent Literary Management **110**; Goodman Associates **117**; Grace Literary Agency, Carroll **117**; Greenburger Associates, Inc., Sanford J. **118**; Grosvenor Literary Agency, The **119**; Halsey Agency, Reece **120**; Halsey North, Reece **120**; Hamilburg Agency, Mitchell J., The **120**; Harris Literary Agency, Inc., The Joy **121**; Hartline Literary Agency **121**; Hawkins & Associates, Inc., John **121**; Henshaw Group, Richard **122**; Jabberwocky Literary Agency **125**; JCA Literary Agency **126**; Kleinman, Esq., Jeffrey M. **128**; Klinger, Inc., Harvey **129**; Koster Literary Agency, LLC, Elaine **130**; Kouts, Literary Agent, Barbara S. **130**; Lampack Agency, Inc., Peter **132**; Larsen/Elizabeth Pomada Literary Agents, Michael **132**; Lasher Agency, The Maureen **133**; Lazear Agency Incorporated **133**; Levine Literary Agency, Paul S. **135**; Lincoln Literary Agency, Ray **136**; Literary Group, The **137**; LitWest Group, LLC **140**; March Tenth, Inc. **147**; Marmur Associates, Ltd., Mildred **148**; Morrison, Inc., Henry **151**; Multimedia Product Development, Inc. **152**; Mura Literary, Dee **152**; Naggar Literary Agency, Jean V. **153**; Norma-Lewis Agency, The **155**; Picard, Literary Agent, Alison J. **158**; Pinder Lane & Garon-Brooke Associates, Ltd. **158**; Pine Associates, Inc., Arthur **159**; Rhodes Literary Agency, Jodie **162**; RLR Associates, Ltd. **169**; Rotrosen Agency, LLC, Jane **172**; Sanders & Associates, Victoria **174**; Schiavone Literary Agency, Inc. **175**; Simmons Literary Agency, Jeffrey **179**; Spieler Agency, The **182**; Straus Agency, Inc., Robin **183**; Treimel NY, Scott **187**; Vines Agency, Inc., The **192**; Wald Associates, Inc., Mary Jack **192**; Watt & Associates, Sandra **194**; Weiner Literary Agency, Cherry **195**; Witherspoon Associates, Inc. **197**; Writers House **198**

Fantasy: Allred and Allred Literary Agents **79**; Anubis Literary Agency **81**; Brown Ltd., Curtis **92**; Collin Literary Agency, Frances **97**; Dorian Literary Agency **104**; Ellenberg Literary Agency, Ethan **108**; Fleury Agency, B.R. **112**; Fort Ross Inc. Russian-American Publishing Projects **113**; Gislason Agency, The **115**; Grace Literary Agency, Carroll **117**; Hamilburg Agency, Mitchell J., The **120**; Hawkins & Associates, Inc., John **121**; Henshaw Group, Richard **122**; Jabberwocky Literary Agency **125**; Kidd Agency, Inc. Virginia **128**; Kleinman, Esq., Jeffrey M. **128**; Larsen/Elizabeth Pomada Literary Agents, Michael **132**; Lazear Agency Incorporated **133**; Lincoln Literary Agency, Ray **136**; Literary Group, The **137**; Maass Literary Agency **142**; Mura Literary, Dee **152**; New Brand Agency Group, LLC **154**; Perkins Associates, L. **157**; Pinder Lane & Garon-Brooke Associates, Ltd. **158**; Rubie Literary Agency, The Peter **173**; Seligman, Literary Agent, Lynn **177**; Spectrum Literary Agency **181**; Sternig & Byrne Literary Agency **183**; Treimel NY, Scott **187**; Viciananza, Ltd., Ralph **192**; Weiner Literary Agency, Cherry **195**; Writers House **198**; Wylie-Merrick Literary Agency **199**

Feminist: Ahearn Agency, Inc., The **78**; Allred and Allred Literary Agents **79**; Baldi Literary Agency, Malaga **82**; Barrett Books Inc., Loretta **83**; Bial Agency, Daniel **84**; BookEnds, LLC **86**; Brown Ltd., Curtis **92**; Browne Ltd., Pema **93**; Buck Agency, Howard **93**; Dupree/Miller and Associates Inc. Literary **106**; Eth Literary Representation, Felicia **109**; Feigen/Parrent Literary Management **110**; Greenburger Associates, Inc., Sanford J. **118**; Hamilburg Agency, Mitchell J., The **120**; Harris Literary Agency, Inc., The Joy **121**; Hawkins & Associates, Inc., John **121**; Hill & Barlow Agency **123**; Kern Literary Agency, Natasha **127**; Kleinman, Esq., Jeffrey M. **128**; Koster Literary Agency, LLC, Elaine **130**; Kouts, Literary Agent, Barbara S. **130**; Larsen/Elizabeth Pomada Literary Agents, Michael **132**; Lasher Agency, The Maureen **133**; Lazear Agency Incorporated **133**; Levine Literary Agency, Paul S. **135**; Lincoln Literary Agency, Ray **136**; Literary Group, The **137**; LitWest Group, LLC **140**; Lowenstein Associates **141**; Marmur Associates, Ltd., Mildred **148**; Mura Literary, Dee **152**; Naggar Literary Agency, Jean V. **153**; Nazor Literary Agency **154**; Paraview, Inc. **156**; Picard, Literary Agent, Alison J. **158**; RLR Associates, Ltd. **169**; Sanders & Associates, Victoria **174**; Seligman, Literary Agent, Lynn **177**; Singer Literary Agency Inc., Evelyn **179**; Spieler Agency, The **182**; Treimel NY, Scott **187**; Vines Agency, Inc., The **192**; Wald Associates, Inc., Mary Jack **192**; Wales, Literary Agency, Inc. **193**; Whittaker, Literary Agent, Lynn **196**; Witherspoon Associates, Inc. **197**; Writers House **198**; Zachary Shuster Harmsworth **199**

Gay/Lesbian: Ahearn Agency, Inc., The **78**; Allred and Allred Literary Agents **79**; Barrett Books Inc., Loretta **83**; Brown Ltd., Curtis **92**; Browne Ltd., Pema **93**; Buck Agency, Howard **93**; Dupree/Miller and Associates Inc. Literary **106**; Greenburger Associates, Inc., Sanford J. **118**; Hamilburg Agency, Mitchell J., The **120**; Harris Literary Agency, Inc., The Joy **121**; Hawkins & Associates, Inc., John **121**; Jabberwocky Literary Agency **125**; Kleinman, Esq., Jeffrey M. **128**; Larsen/Elizabeth Pomada Literary Agents, Michael **132**; Lazear Agency Incorporated **133**; Levine Literary Agency, Paul S. **135**; Mura Literary, Dee 152Pevner, Inc., Stephen **157**; Pevner, Inc., Stephen **157**; Picard, Literary Agent, Alison J. **158**; Wald Associates, Inc., Mary Jack **192**; Writers House **198**

Glitz: Ahearn Agency, Inc., The **78**; Allred and Allred Literary Agents **79**; Baldi Literary Agency, Malaga **82**; Barrett Books Inc., Loretta **83**; Bial Agency, Daniel **84**; BookEnds, LLC **86**; Brown Ltd., Curtis **92**; Browne Ltd., Pema **93**; Buck Agency, Howard **93**; Cornerstone Literary, Inc. **99**; Daves Agency, Joan **101**; DeFiore and Company **101**; DHS Literary, Inc. **102**; Dupree/Miller and Associates Inc. Literary **106**; Dystel Literary Management, Inc., Jane **106**; Eth Literary Representation, Felicia **109**; Feigen/Parrent Literary Management **110**; Greenburger Associates, Inc., Sanford J. **118**; Hamilburg Agency, Mitchell J., The **120**; Harris Literary Agency, Inc., The Joy **121**; Hawkins & Associates, Inc., John **121**; Henshaw Group, Richard **122**; Hill & Barlow Agency **123**; Jabberwocky Literary Agency **125**; Kidd Agency, Inc. Virginia **128**; Kleinman, Esq., Jeffrey M. **128**; Klinger, Inc., Harvey **129**; Larsen/Elizabeth Pomada Literary Agents, Michael **132**; Lazear Agency Incorporated **133**; Levine Literary Agency, Paul S. **135**; Lincoln Literary Agency, Ray **136**; Lowenstein Associates **141**; Multimedia Product Development, Inc. **152**; Mura Literary, Dee **152**; Pevner, Inc., Stephen **157**; Picard, Literary Agent, Alison J. **158**; Pinder Lane & Garon-Brooke Associates, Ltd. **158**; Quicksilver Books Literary Agents **161**; RLR Associates, Ltd. **169**; Rubie Literary Agency, The Peter **173**; Sanders & Associates, Victoria **174**; Schulman, A Literary Agency, Susan **175**; Seligman, Literary Agent, Lynn **177**; Spieler Agency, The **182**; Teal Literary Agency, Patricia **185**; Treimel NY, Scott **187**; Vines Agency, Inc., The **192**; Wald Associates, Inc., Mary Jack **192**; Wales, Literary Agency, Inc.

193; Weiner Literary Agency, Cherry **195**; Witherspoon Associates, Inc. **197**; Writers House **198**; Zachary Shuster Harmsworth **199**

Gothic: Brown Ltd., Curtis **92**; Hamilburg Agency, Mitchell J., The **120**; Hawkins & Associates, Inc., John **121**; Lazear Agency Incorporated **133**; Writers House **198**

Hi-Lo: Brown Ltd., Curtis **92**; Hamilburg Agency, Mitchell J., The **120**; Harris Literary Agency, Inc., The Joy **121**; Hawkins & Associates, Inc., John **121**; Lazear Agency Incorporated **133**; Writers House **198**

Historical: ABS Literary Agency, Inc. **76**; Ahearn Agency, Inc., The **78**; Alive Communications, Inc. **78**; Allen Literary Agency, Linda **79**; Allred and Allred Literary Agents **79**; Altair Literary Agency **80**; Anubis Literary Agency **81**; Baldi Literary Agency, Malaga **82**; Barrett Books Inc., Loretta **83**; Bernstein & Associates, Inc., Pam **84**; Bleeker Street Associates, Inc. **85**; BookEnds, LLC **86**; Books & Such **87**; Brandt & Hochman Literary Agents Inc. **91**; Brown Ltd., Curtis **92**; Browne Ltd., Pema **93**; Buck Agency, Howard **93**; Carvainis Agency, Inc., Maria **94**; Clark Associates, William **96**; Cohen, Inc. Literary Agency, Ruth **97**; Collin Literary Agency, Frances **97**; Connor Literary Agency **98**; Cornerstone Literary, Inc. **99**; Dawson Associates, Liza **101**; Donovan Literary, Jim **104**; Dorian Literary Agency **104**; Doyen Literary Services, Inc. **104**; Dupree/Miller and Associates Inc. Literary **106**; Elmo Agency Inc., Ann **109**; English, Elaine P. **109**; Fogelman Literary Agency **112**; Goodman Associates **117**; Grace Literary Agency, Carroll **117**; Greenburger Associates, Inc., Sanford J. **118**; Gregory and Company Authors' Agents **118**; Grosjean Literary Agency, Jill **119**; Grosvenor Literary Agency, The **119**; Halsey Agency, Reece **120**; Halsey North, Reece **120**; Hamilburg Agency, Mitchell J., The **120**; Harris Literary Agency, Inc., The Joy **121**; Hartline Literary Agency **121**; Hawkins & Associates, Inc., John **121**; Henshaw Group, Richard **122**; Hopkins Literary Associates **124**; J de S Associates Inc. **125**; Jabberwocky Literary Agency **125**; JCA Literary Agency **126**; Jenks Agency, The **126**; Kern Literary Agency, Natasha **127**; Kidd Agency, Inc. Virginia **128**; Kleinman, Esq., Jeffrey M. **128**; Koster Literary Agency, LLC, Elaine **130**; Kouts, Literary Agent, Barbara S. **130**; Lampack Agency, Inc., Peter **132**; Larsen/Elizabeth Pomada Literary Agents, Michael **132**; Lasher Agency, The Maureen **133**; Lazear Agency Incorporated **133**; Levine Literary Agency, Paul S. **135**; Lincoln Literary Agency, Ray **136**; LitWest Group, LLC **140**; Lowenstein Associates **141**; Maass Literary Agency **142**; March Tenth, Inc. **147**; Markowitz Literary Agency, Barbara **147**; Marshall Agency, The Evan **148**; McBride Literary Agency, Margret **148**; McHugh Literary Agency **149**; Morrison, Inc., Henry **151**; Multimedia Product Development, Inc. **152**; Mura Literary, Dee **152**; Naggar Literary Agency, Jean V. **153**; New Brand Agency Group, LLC **154**; Norma-Lewis Agency, The **155**; Picard, Literary Agent, Alison J. **158**; Rees Literary Agency, Helen **162**; Rhodes Literary Agency, Jodie **162**; RLR Associates, Ltd. **169**; Rotrosen Agency, LLC, Jane **172**; Rowland Agency, The Damaris **172**; Rubie Literary Agency, The Peter **173**; Schiavone Literary Agency, Inc. **175**; Schulman, A Literary Agency, Susan **175**; Seligman, Literary Agent, Lynn **177**; Singer Literary Agency Inc., Evelyn **179**; Spectrum Literary Agency **181**; Straus Agency, Inc., Robin **183**; Treimel NY, Scott **187**; Vines Agency, Inc., The **192**; Wald Associates, Inc., Mary Jack **192**; Wecksler-Incomco **195**; Weiner Literary Agency, Cherry **195**; Whittaker, Literary Agent, Lynn **196**; Wieser & Wieser, Inc. **197**; Witherspoon Associates, Inc. **197**; Writers House **198**; Wylie-Merrick Literary Agency **199**; Zachary Shuster Harmsworth **199**; Zeckendorf Assoc. Inc., Susan **200**

Horror: Allred and Allred Literary Agents **79**; Amsterdam Agency, Marcia **81**; Anubis Literary Agency **81**; Brown Ltd., Curtis **92**; Congdon Associates Inc., Don **97**; Connor Literary Agency **98**; Core Creations **98**; Donovan Literary, Jim **104**; Dorian Literary Agency **104**; Fleury Agency, B.R. **112**; Fort Ross Inc. Russian-American Publishing Projects **113**; Grace Literary Agency, Carroll **117**; Halsey North, Reece **120**; Hamilburg Agency, Mitchell J., The **120**; Hawkins & Associates, Inc., John **121**; Henshaw Group, Richard **122**; Jabberwocky Literary Agency **125**; Kleinman, Esq., Jeffrey M. **128**; Lazear Agency Incorporated **133**; Literary Group, The **137**; Maass Literary Agency **142**; Marshall Agency, The Evan **148**; New Brand Agency Group, LLC **154**; Norma-Lewis Agency, The **155**; Perkins Associates, L. **157**; Pevner, Inc., Stephen **157**; Picard, Literary Agent, Alison J. **158**; RLR Associates, Ltd. **169**; Rotrosen Agency, LLC, Jane **172**; Schiavone Literary Agency, Inc. **175**; Sedgeband Literary Associates **177**; Seligman, Literary Agent, Lynn **177**; Sternig & Byrne Literary Agency **183**; Treimel NY, Scott **187**; Vines Agency, Inc., The **192**; Writers House **198**

Humor/Satire: Ahearn Agency, Inc., The **78**; Alive Communications, Inc. **78**; Allred and Allred Literary Agents **79**; Barrett Books Inc., Loretta **83**; Bial Agency, Daniel **84**; Brown Ltd., Curtis **92**; Browne Ltd., Pema **93**; Buck Agency, Howard **93**; Congdon Associates Inc., Don **97**; Cornerstone Literary, Inc. **99**; Dupree/Miller and Associates Inc. Literary **106**; Farber Literary Agency Inc. **110**; Fleury Agency, B.R. **112**; Greenburger Associates, Inc., Sanford J. **118**; Gregory and Company Authors' Agents **118**; Grosjean Literary Agency, Jill **119**; Hamilburg Agency, Mitchell J., T Harris Literary Agency, Inc., The Joy **121**; Hawkins & Associates, Inc., John **121**; Henshaw Richard **122**; Jabberwocky Literary Agency **125**; Kleinman, Esq., Jeffrey M. **128**; Kroll Agency Inc., Edite **131**; Larsen/Elizabeth Pomada Literary Agents, Michael **132**; Lazear Incorporated **133**; Levine Literary Agency, Paul S. **135**; Lincoln Literary Agency, Ray **136** Group, The **137**; LitWest Group, LLC **140**; March Tenth, Inc. **147**; Markowitz Literary Barbara **147**; Marshall Agency, The Evan **148**; McBride Literary Agency, Margret **148**; Mur Dee **152**; Norma-Lewis Agency, The **155**; Pevner, Inc., Stephen **157**; Picard, Literary Agent, Alison J. **158**; RLR Associates, Ltd. **169**; Schiavone Literary Agency, Inc. **175**; Seligman, Literary Agent, Lynn **177**; Spieler Agency, The **182**; Treimel NY, Scott **187**; Van Der Leun & Associates **191**; Vines Agency, Inc., The **192**; Writers House **198**

Juvenile: Alive Communications, Inc. **78**; Allred and Allred Literary Agents **79**; Books & Such **87**; Briggs, M. Courtney **91**; Brown Associates Inc., Marie **91**; Brown Literary Agency, Inc., Andrea **92**; Brown Ltd., Curtis **92**; Browne Ltd., Pema **93**; Cohen, Inc. Literary Agency, Ruth **97**; Dunham Literary **105**; Dwyer & O'Grady, Inc. **106**; Farber Literary Agency Inc. **110**; Flannery Literary **111**; Fort Ross Inc. Russian-American Publishing Projects **113**; Hamilburg Agency, Mitchell J., The **120**; Hawkins & Associates, Inc., John **121**; J de S Associates Inc. **125**; Kouts, Literary Agent, Barbara S. **130**; Kroll Literary Agency Inc., Edite **131**; Lazear Agency Incorporated **133**; Lincoln Literary Agency, Ray **136**; Livingston Cooke **140**; Maccoby Agency, Gina **143**; Markowitz Literary Agency, Barbara **147**; Marmur Associates, Ltd., Mildred **148**; Multimedia Product Development, Inc. **152**; Mura Literary, Dee **152**; National Writers Literary Agency **153**; New Brand Agency Group, LLC **154**; Norma-Lewis Agency, The **155**; Picard, Literary Agent, Alison J. **158**; Rhodes Literary Agency, Jodie **162**; Schiavone Literary Agency, Inc. **175**; Treimel NY, Scott **187**; Wald Associates, Inc., Mary Jack **192**; Wecksler-Incomco **195**; Writers House **198**

Literary: ABS Literary Agency, Inc. **76**; Acacia House Publishing Services Ltd. **76**; Ahearn Agency, Inc., The **78**; Alive Communications, Inc. **78**; Allred and Allred Literary Agents **79**; Altshuler Literary Agency, Miriam **80**; Amster Literary Enterprises, Betsy **80**; Authentic Creations Literary Agency **82**; Baldi Literary Agency, Malaga **82**; Barrett Books Inc., Loretta **83**; Bent, Harvey Klinger, Inc., Jenny **84**; Bernstein Literary Agency, Meredith **84**; Bial Agency, Daniel **84**; Black Literary Agency, David **85**; Bleeker Street Associates, Inc. **85**; Book Deals, Inc. **86**; BookEnds, LLC **86**; Borchardt Inc., Georges **87**; Brady Literary Management **90**; Brandt & Hochman Literary Agents Inc. **91**; Brandt Agency, The Joan **91**; Brown Associates Inc., Marie **91**; Brown Ltd., Curtis **92**; Browne Ltd., Pema **93**; Buck Agency, Howard **93**; Bykofsky Associates, Inc. Sheree **94**; Carlisle & Company **94**; Carvainis Agency, Inc., Maria **94**; Castiglia Literary Agency **95**; Clark Associates, William **96**; Cohen, Inc. Literary Agency, Ruth **97**; Collin Literary Agency, Frances **97**; Congdon Associates Inc., Don **97**; Connor Literary Agency **98**; Coover Agency, The Doe **98**; Cornerstone Literary, Inc. **99**; Darhansoff & Verrill Literary Agency **100**; Daves Agency, Joan **101**; Dawson Associates, Liza **101**; DeFiore and Company **101**; DHS Literary, Inc. **102**; Dijkstra Literary Agency, Sandra **102**; Donovan Literary, Jim **104**; Dorian Literary Agency **104**; Doyen Literary Services, Inc. **104**; Ducas, Robert **105**; Dunham Literary **105**; Dupree/Miller and Associates Inc. Literary **106**; Dystel Literary Management, Inc., Jane **106**; Ellison, Inc., Nicholas **108**; Elmo Agency Inc., Ann **109**; Eth Literary Representation, Felicia **109**; Farber Literary Agency Inc. **110**; Feigen/Parrent Literary Management **110**; Fleury Agency, B.R. **112**; Fogelman Literary Agency **112**; Franklin Associates, Ltd., Lynn C. **114**; Freymann Literary Agency, Sarah Jane **114**; Gelfman Schneider Literary Agents, Inc. **115**; Goldfarb & Associates **116**; Goodman Associates **117**; Grace Literary Agency, Carroll **117**; Greenburger Associates, Inc., Sanford J. **118**; Gregory and Company Authors' Agents **118**; Grosjean Literary Agency, Jill **119**; Grosvenor Literary Agency, The **119**; Halsey Agency, Reece **120**; Halsey North, Reece **120**; Hamilburg Agency, Mitchell J., The **120**; Harris Literary Agency, Inc., The Joy **121**; Hartline Literary Agency **121**; Hawkins & Associates, Inc., John **121**; Henshaw Group, Richard **122**; Hill & Barlow Agency **123**; Hill Bonnie Nadell, Inc., Frederick **123**; Hornfischer Literary Management, Inc. **124**; J de S Associates Inc. **125**; Jabberwocky Literary Agency **125**; JCA Literary Agency **126**; Jenks Agency, The **126**; Kidd Agency, Inc. Virginia **128**; Kleinman, Esq., Jeffrey M. **128**; Klinger, Inc., Harvey **129**; Knight Agency, The **129**; Koster Literary Agency, LLC, Elaine **130**; Kouts, Literary Agent, Barbara S. **130**; Lampack Agency, Inc., Peter **132**; Larsen/Elizabeth Pomada Literary Agents, Michael **132**; Lasher Agency, The Maureen **133**; Lazear Agency Incorporated **133**; Levine Communications, Inc., James **134**; Levine Literary Agency, Inc., Ellen **135**; Levine Literary Agency, Paul S. **135**; Lincoln Literary Agency, Ray **136**; LitWest Group, LLC **140**; Livingston Cooke **140**; Lowenstein Associates **141**; Maass Literary Agency **142**; Maccoby Agency, Gina **143**; Mann Agency, Carol **143**; Manus & Associates Literary Agency, Inc. **143**; March Tenth, Inc. **147**; Marmur Associates, Ltd., Mildred **148**; Marshall Agency, The Evan **148**; McBride Literary Agency, Margret

148; McGrath, Helen 149; Michaels Literary Agency, Inc., Doris S. 150; Multimedia Product Development, Inc. 152; Mura Literary, Dee 152; Naggar Literary Agency, Jean V. 153; Nazor Literary Agency 154; New Brand Agency Group, LLC 154; Nine Muses and Apollo Inc. 155; Paraview, Inc. 156; Paton Literary Agency, Kathi J. 157; Perkins Associates, L. 157; Pevner, Inc., Stephen 157; Picard, Literary Agent, Alison J. 158; Pinder Lane & Garon-Brooke Associates, Ltd. 158; Pine Associates, Inc., Arthur 159; Popkin, Julie 159; Preskill Literary Agency, Robert 159; Rees Literary Agency, Helen 162; Rein Books, Inc., Jody 162; Rhodes Literary Agency, Jodie 162; Rinaldi Literary Agency, Angela 166; Rittenberg Literary Agency, Inc., Ann 166; RLR Associates, Ltd. 169; Robbins Literary Agency, B.J. 170; Robbins Office, Inc., The 170; Rosenberg Group, The 170; Ross Literary Agency, The Gail 171; Rowland Agency, The Damaris 172; Rubie Literary Agency, The Peter 173; Russell and Volkening 173; Sanders & Associates, Victoria 174; Sandum and Associates 174; Scherf, Inc., Literary Properties 174; Schiavone Literary Agency, Inc. 175; Schulman, A Literary Agency, Susan 175; Sedgeband Literary Associates 177; Seligman, Literary Agent, Lynn 177; Sherman Associates, Inc., Wendy 178; Simmons Literary Agency, Jeffrey 179; Singer Literary Agency Inc., Evelyn 179; Skolnick Literary Agency, Irene 180; Slopen Literary Agency, Beverley 180; Spieler Agency, The 182; Spitzer Literary Agency, Philip G. 182; Stauffer Associates, Nancy 182; Straus Agency, Inc., Robin 183; Susijn Agency, The 184; Tabian/Literary Agent, Robert E. 185; Talbot Agency, The John 185; Trace Inc., The Tracy Sherrod Literary Agency 186; Travis Literary Agency, Susan 186; Treimel NY, Scott 187; Van Der Leun & Associates 191; Venture Literary 191; Viciananza, Ltd., Ralph 192; Vines Agency, Inc., The 192; Wald Associates, Inc., Mary Jack 192; Wales, Literary Agency, Inc. 193; Watkins Loomis Agency, Inc. 194; Waxman Literary Agency 195; Wecksler-Incomco 195; Weingel-Fidel Agency, The 196; Whittaker, Literary Agent, Lynn 196; Wieser & Wieser, Inc. 197; Witherspoon Associates, Inc. 197; Wonderland Press, Inc., The 197; Writers House 198; Writers' Representatives, Inc. 199; Zachary Shuster Harmsworth 199; Zeckendorf Assoc. Inc., Susan 200

Mainstream/Contemporary: ABS Literary Agency, Inc. 76; Acacia House Publishing Services Ltd. 76; Ahearn Agency, Inc., The 78; Alive Communications, Inc. 78; Allred and Allred Literary Agents 79; Altshuler Literary Agency, Miriam 80; Amsterdam Agency, Marcia 81; Authentic Creations Literary Agency 82; Baldi Literary Agency, Malaga 82; Barrett Books Inc., Loretta 83; Bent, Harvey Klinger, Inc., Jenny 84; Bernstein & Associates, Inc., Pam 84; Black Literary Agency, David 85; Book Deals, Inc. 86; BookEnds, LLC 86; Books & Such 87; Brady Literary Management 90; Brandt & Hochman Literary Agents Inc. 91; Brandt Agency, The Joan 91; Briggs, M. Courtney 91; Brown Associates Inc., Marie 91; Brown Ltd., Curtis 92; Browne Ltd., Pema 93; Buck Agency, Howard 93; Bykofsky Associates, Inc. Sheree 94; Carlisle & Company 94; Carvainis Agency, Inc., Maria 94; Castiglia Literary Agency 95; Clark Associates, William 96; Cohen, Inc. Literary Agency, Ruth 97; Collin Literary Agency, Frances 97; Congdon Associates Inc., Don 97; Connor Literary Agency 98; Coover Agency, The Doe 98; Cornerstone Literary, Inc. 99; Daves Agency, Joan 101; DeFiore and Company 101; DHS Literary, Inc. 102; Dijkstra Literary Agency, Sandra 102; Donovan Literary, Jim 104; Dorian Literary Agency 104; Doyen Literary Services, Inc. 104; Ducas, Robert 105; Dunham Literary 105; Dupree/Miller and Associates Inc. Literary 106; Dystel Literary Management, Inc., Jane 106; Ellison, Inc., Nicholas 108; Elmo Agency Inc., Ann 109; English, Elaine P. 109; Eth Literary Representation, Felicia 109; Farber Literary Agency Inc. 110; Fogelman Literary Agency 112; Franklin Associates, Ltd., Lynn C. 114; Freymann Literary Agency, Sarah Jane 114; Gelfman Schneider Literary Agents, Inc. 115; Gislason Agency, The 115; Goldfarb & Associates 116; Goodman Associates 117; Grace Literary Agency, Carroll 117; Greenburger Associates, Inc., Sanford J. 118; Gregory and Company Authors' Agents 118; Grosjean Literary Agency, Jill 119; Grosvenor Literary Agency, The 119; Halsey Agency, Reece 120; Halsey North, Reece 120; Hamilburg Agency, Mitchell J., The 120; Harris Literary Agency, Inc., The Joy 121; Hawkins & Associates, Inc., John 121; Henshaw Group, Richard 122; Hill & Barlow Agency 123; Hill Bonnie Nadell, Inc., Frederick 123; Hopkins Literary Associates 124; Hornfischer Literary Management, Inc. 124; J de S Associates Inc. 125; Jabberwocky Literary Agency 125; JCA Literary Agency 126; Jenks Agency, The 126; Kern Literary Agency, Natasha 127; Kidd Agency, Inc. Virginia 128; Kleinman, Esq., Jeffrey M. 128; Klinger, Inc., Harvey 129; Knight Agency, The 129; Koster Literary Agency, LLC, Elaine 130; Kouts, Literary Agent, Barbara S. 130; Kritzer Productions, Eddie 131; Lampack Agency, Inc., Peter 132; Larsen/Elizabeth Pomada Literary Agents, Michael 132; Lasher Agency, The Maureen 133; Lazear Agency Incorporated 133; Levine Communications, Inc., James 134; Levine Literary Agency, Paul S. 135; Lincoln Literary Agency, Ray 136; Lipkind Agency, Wendy 137; LitWest Group, LLC 140; Lowenstein Associates 141; Maass Literary Agency 142; Maccoby Agency, Gina 143; Manus & Associates Literary Agency, Inc. 143; March Tenth, Inc. 147; Markowitz Literary Agency, Barbara 147; Marmur Associates, Ltd., Mildred 148; Marshall Agency, The Evan 148; McBride Literary Agency, Margret 148; McGrath, Helen 149; McHugh Literary Agency 149; Multi-

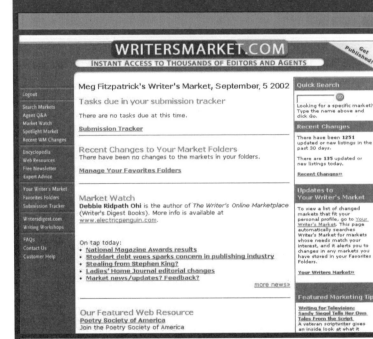

WRITERSMARKET.COM

INSTANT ACCESS TO THOUSANDS OF EDITORS AND AGENTS

Sure, you already know *Writer's Market* is the essential tool for selling your writing — after all, a new edition has come out every year for almost a century! And now, to complement your trusty "freelance writer's bible," you can subscribe to WritersMarket.com! It's cool… it's quick…and it's $10 off the regular price!

Here's what you'll find at WritersMarket.com:

→ **EASY-TO-USE SEARCHABLE DATABASE** — Simply enter your search parameters, and voila! Zero in on potential markets in seconds.

→ **SUBMISSION TRACKER** — Have trouble remembering what you've sent to whom, or if you've heard back? The Submission Tracker does the work for you!

→ **PERSONALIZED MARKET LISTS** — Set up a personal profile and get news, new listings and market changes that match your interests…the second you sign on!

→ **MORE MARKETS** — Yes, there are 1,000+ pages in the book, but believe it or not, there are several hundred listings that just couldn't fit! You'll find even more markets and agents at WritersMarket.com, and we keep adding to the database whenever new listings become available!

→ **LISTINGS UPDATED DAILY** — It doesn't look good to address your query letter to the wrong editor or agent…and with WritersMarket.com, that will never happen again. You'll be on top of all the industry developments…as soon as they happen!

→ **LINKS TO WRITING RESOURCES** including a comprehensive library of writing tips, myriad fact books and dictionaries, media research, writing magazines, online workshops, and more!

WRITERSMARKET.COM

SUBSCRIBE TODAY AND SAVE $10!

03GLA

media Product Development, Inc. **152**; Mura Literary, Dee **152**; Naggar Literary Agency, Jean V. **153**; National Writers Literary Agency **153**; New Brand Agency Group, LLC **154**; Nine Muses and Apollo Inc. **155**; Norma-Lewis Agency, The **155**; Paraview, Inc. **156**; Paton Literary Agency, Kathi J. **157**; Pevner, Inc., Stephen **157**; Picard, Literary Agent, Alison J. **158**; Pinder Lane & Garon-Brooke Associates, Ltd. **158**; Pine Associates, Inc., Arthur **159**; Popkin, Julie **159**; Rees Literary Agency, Helen **162**; Rein Books, Inc., Jody **162**; Rhodes Literary Agency, Jodie **162**; Rinaldi Literary Agency, Angela **166**; RLR Associates, Ltd. **169**; Robbins Literary Agency, B.J. **170**; Robbins Office, Inc., The **170**; Rotrosen Agency, LLC, Jane **172**; Rowland Agency, The Damaris **172**; Russell and Volkening **173**; Scherf, Inc., Literary Properties **174**; Schiavone Literary Agency, Inc. **175**; Schulman, A Literary Agency, Susan **175**; Sedgeband Literary Associates **177**; Seligman, Literary Agent, Lynn **177**; Simmons Literary Agency, Jeffrey **179**; Singer Literary Agency Inc., Evelyn **179**; Skolnick Literary Agency, Irene **180**; Spectrum Literary Agency **181**; Spitzer Literary Agency, Philip G. **182**; Stauffer Associates, Nancy **182**; Steele-Perkins Literary Agency **183**; Straus Agency, Inc., Robin **183**; Tabian/Literary Agent, Robert E. **185**; Teal Literary Agency, Patricia **185**; Travis Literary Agency, Susan **186**; Treimel NY, Scott **187**; Van Der Leun & Associates **191**; Venture Literary **191**; Viciananza, Ltd., Ralph **192**; Vines Agency, Inc., The **192**; Wald Associates, Inc., Mary Jack **192**; Wales, Literary Agency, Inc. **193**; Watt & Associates, Sandra **194**; Wecksler-Incomco **195**; Weiner Literary Agency, Cherry **195**; Weingel-Fidel Agency, The **196**; Wieser & Wieser, Inc. **197**; Witherspoon Associates, Inc. **197**; Writers House **198**; Zachary Shuster Harmsworth **199**; Zeckendorf Assoc. Inc., Susan **200**

Military/War: Brown Ltd., Curtis **92**; Buck Agency, Howard **93**; Goodman Associates **117**; Hamilburg Agency, Mitchell J., The **120**; Harris Literary Agency, Inc., The Joy **121**; Hawkins & Associates, Inc., John **121**; Lazear Agency Incorporated **133**; Treimel NY, Scott **187**; Writers House **198**

Multicultural: Brown Ltd., Curtis **92**; Buck Agency, Howard **93**; Goodman Associates **117**; Hamilburg Agency, Mitchell J., The **120**; Harris Literary Agency, Inc., The Joy **121**; Hawkins & Associates, Inc., John **121**; Kleinman, Esq., Jeffrey M. **128**; Lazear Agency Incorporated **133**; Treimel NY, Scott **187**; Van Der Leun & Associates **191**; Writers House **198**

Mystery/Suspense: ABS Literary Agency, Inc. **76**; Abel Literary Agency, Inc., Dominick **76**; Acacia House Publishing Services Ltd. **76**; Ahearn Agency, Inc., The **78**; Alive Communications, Inc. **78**; Allred and Allred Literary Agents **79**; Amsterdam Agency, Marcia **81**; Appleseeds Management **82**; Authentic Creations Literary Agency **82**; Axelrod Agency, The **82**; Baldi Literary Agency, Malaga **82**; Barrett Books Inc., Loretta **83**; Bernstein & Associates, Inc., Pam **84**; Bernstein Literary Agency, Meredith **84**; Bleeker Street Associates, Inc. **85**; BookEnds, LLC **86**; Brandt & Hochman Literary Agents Inc. **91**; Brandt Agency, The Joan **91**; Brown Ltd., Curtis **92**; Browne Ltd., Pema **93**; Buck Agency, Howard **93**; Carvainis Agency, Inc., Maria **94**; Castiglia Literary Agency **95**; Cohen, Inc. Literary Agency, Ruth **97**; Collin Literary Agency, Frances **97**; Congdon Associates Inc., Don **97**; Cornerstone Literary, Inc. **99**; Crawford Literary Agency **99**; Dawson Associates, Liza **101**; DeFiore and Company **101**; DHS Literary, Inc. **102**; Dijkstra Literary Agency, Sandra **102**; Donovan Literary, Jim **104**; Dorian Literary Agency **104**; Ducas, Robert **105**; Dunham Literary **105**; Dupree/Miller and Associates Inc. Literary **106**; Dystel Literary Management, Inc., Jane **106**; Elmo Agency Inc., Ann **109**; Farber Literary Agency Inc. **110**; Fort Ross Inc. Russian-American Publishing Projects **113**; Freymann Literary Agency, Sarah Jane **114**; Gelfman Schneider Literary Agents, Inc. **115**; Gislason Agency, The **115**; Goldfarb & Associates **116**; Goodman Associates **117**; Grace Literary Agency, Carroll **117**; Greenburger Associates, Inc., Sanford J. **118**; Grosjean Literary Agency, Jill **119**; Grosvenor Literary Agency, The **119**; Halsey Agency, Reece **120**; Halsey North, Reece **120**; Hamilburg Agency, Mitchell J., The **120**; Harris Literary Agency, Inc., The Joy **121**; Hartline Literary Agency **121**; Hawkins & Associates, Inc., John **121**; Henshaw Group, Richard **122**; J de S Associates Inc. **125**; JCA Literary Agency **126**; Jenks Agency, The **126**; Kern Literary Agency, Natasha **127**; Kidd Agency, Inc. Virginia **128**; Klinger, Inc., Harvey **129**; Koster Literary Agency, LLC, Elaine **130**; Kouts, Literary Agent, Barbara S. **130**; Kraas Agency, Irene **130**; Lampack Agency, Inc., Peter **132**; Larsen/Elizabeth Pomada Literary Agents, Michael **132**; Lazear Agency Incorporated **133**; Lescher & Lescher Ltd. **134**; Levine Communications, Inc., James **134**; Levine Literary Agency, Inc., Ellen **135**; Levine Literary Agency, Paul S. **135**; Lincoln Literary Agency, Ray **136**; Lipkind Agency, Wendy **137**; Literary Group, The **137**; LitWest Group, LLC **140**; Love Literary Agency, Nancy **141**; Lowenstein Associates **141**; Maass Literary Agency **142**; Maccoby Agency, Gina **143**; Manus & Associates Literary Agency, Inc. **143**; Markowitz Literary Agency, Barbara **147**; Marmur Associates, Ltd., Mildred **148**; Marshall Agency, The Evan **148**; McBride Literary Agency, Margret **148**; McGrath, Helen **149**; McHugh Literary Agency **149**; Multimedia Product Development, Inc. **152**; Mura Literary, Dee **152**; Naggar Literary Agency, Jean V. **153**; National Writers Literary Agency **153**; New

Brand Agency Group, LLC **154**; Norma-Lewis Agency, The **155**; Picard, Literary Agent, Alison J. **158**; Pinder Lane & Garon-Brooke Associates, Ltd. **158**; Popkin, Julie **159**; Protter Literary Agent, Susan Ann **160**; Quicksilver Books Literary Agents **161**; Rees Literary Agency, Helen **162**; Rein Books, Inc., Jody **162**; Rhodes Literary Agency, Jodie **162**; RLR Associates, Ltd. **169**; Robbins Literary Agency, B.J. **170**; Roghaar Literary Agency, Inc., Linda **170**; Rotrosen Agency, LLC, Jane **172**; Russell and Volkening **173**; Scherf, Inc., Literary Properties **174**; Schulman, A Literary Agency, Susan **175**; Sedgeband Literary Associates **177**; Seligman, Literary Agent, Lynn **177**; Simmons Literary Agency, Jeffrey **179**; Singer Literary Agency Inc., Evelyn **179**; Slopen Literary Agency, Beverley **180**; Spectrum Literary Agency **181**; Spitzer Literary Agency, Philip G. **182**; Sternig & Byrne Literary Agency **183**; Tabian/Literary Agent, Robert E. **185**; Talbot Agency, The John **185**; Teal Literary Agency, Patricia **185**; Treimel NY, Scott **187**; Venture Literary **191**; Vines Agency, Inc., The **192**; Wald Associates, Inc., Mary Jack **192**; Ware Literary Agency, John A. **193**; Watt & Associates, Sandra **194**; Weiner Literary Agency, Cherry **195**; Whittaker, Literary Agent, Lynn **196**; Wieser & Wieser, Inc. **197**; Witherspoon Associates, Inc. **197**; Writers House **198**; Wylie-Merrick Literary Agency **199**; Zachary Shuster Harmsworth **199**; Zeckendorf Assoc. Inc., Susan **200**

Occult: Brown Ltd., Curtis **92**; Doyen Literary Services, Inc. **104**; Goodman Associates **117**; Hamilburg Agency, Mitchell J., The **120**; Hawkins & Associates, Inc., John **121**; Lazear Agency Incorporated **133**; Vines Agency, Inc., The **192**; Writers House **198**

Picture Book: Books & Such **87**; Briggs, M. Courtney **91**; Brown Ltd., Curtis **92**; Browne Ltd., Pema **93**; Cohen, Inc. Literary Agency, Ruth **97**; Dunham Literary **105**; Dupree/Miller and Associates Inc. Literary **106**; Dwyer & O'Grady, Inc. **106**; Flannery Literary **111**; Hamilburg Agency, Mitchell J., The **120**; Harris Literary Agency, Inc., The Joy **121**; Hawkins & Associates, Inc., John **121**; Kouts, Literary Agent, Barbara S. **130**; Kroll Literary Agency Inc., Edite **131**; Lazear Agency Incorporated **133**; Multimedia Product Development, Inc. **152**; Norma-Lewis Agency, The **155**; Picard, Literary Agent, Alison J. **158**; Russell and Volkening **173**; Tobias, A Literary Agency for Chilren's Books, Ann **186**; Treimel NY, Scott **187**; Van Der Leun & Associates **191**; Wald Associates, Inc., Mary Jack **192**; Wecksler-Incomco **195**; Writers House **198**; Wylie-Merrick Literary Agency **199**

Plays: Brown Ltd., Curtis **92**; Hamilburg Agency, Mitchell J., The **120**; Hawkins & Associates, Inc., John **121**; Lazear Agency Incorporated **133**; Treimel NY, Scott **187**; Writers House **198**

Poetry: Brown Ltd., Curtis **92**; Hamilburg Agency, Mitchell J., The **120**; Harris Literary Agency, Inc., The Joy **121**; Hawkins & Associates, Inc., John **121**; Lazear Agency Incorporated **133**; Robbins Office, Inc., The **170**; Tobias, A Literary Agency for Chilren's Books, Ann **186**; Treimel NY, Scott **187**; Van Der Leun & Associates **191**; Writers House **198**

Poetry in Translation: Brown Ltd., Curtis **92**; Hamilburg Agency, Mitchell J., The **120**; Harris Literary Agency, Inc., The Joy **121**; Hawkins & Associates, Inc., John **121**; Lazear Agency Incorporated **133**; Treimel NY, Scott **187**; Van Der Leun & Associates **191**; Writers House **198**

Psychic/Supernatural: Ahearn Agency, Inc., The **78**; Allred and Allred Literary Agents **79**; Barrett Books Inc., Loretta **83**; Brown Ltd., Curtis **92**; Browne Ltd., Pema **93**; Buck Agency, Howard **93**; Collin Literary Agency, Frances **97**; Doyen Literary Services, Inc. **104**; Dupree/Miller and Associates Inc. Literary **106**; Fleury Agency, B.R. **112**; Grace Literary Agency, Carroll **117**; Greenburger Associates, Inc., Sanford J. **118**; Hamilburg Agency, Mitchell J., The **120**; Hawkins & Associates, Inc., John **121**; Henshaw Group, Richard **122**; Hornfischer Literary Management, Inc. **124**; Jabberwocky Literary Agency **125**; Kleinman, Esq., Jeffrey M. **128**; Lazear Agency Incorporated **133**; Levine Literary Agency, Paul S. **135**; Lincoln Literary Agency, Ray **136**; Literary Group, The **137**; Maass Literary Agency **142**; McGrath, Helen **149**; Mura Literary, Dee **152**; Naggar Literary Agency, Jean V. **153**; Pevner, Inc., Stephen **157**; Picard, Literary Agent, Alison J. **158**; Treimel NY, Scott **187**; Vines Agency, Inc., The **192**; Weiner Literary Agency, Cherry **195**; Writers House **198**

Regional: Ahearn Agency, Inc., The **78**; Allred and Allred Literary Agents **79**; Baldi Literary Agency, Malaga **82**; Brown Ltd., Curtis **92**; Buck Agency, Howard **93**; Collin Literary Agency, Frances **97**; Dawson Associates, Liza **101**; Elmo Agency Inc., Ann **109**; Goodman Associates **117**; Greenburger Associates, Inc., Sanford J. **118**; Grosjean Literary Agency, Jill **119**; Hamilburg Agency, Mitchell J., The **120**; Harris Literary Agency, Inc., The Joy **121**; Hartline Literary Agency **121**; Hawkins & Associates, Inc., John **121**; Jabberwocky Literary Agency **125**; Kleinman, Esq., Jeffrey M. **128**; Koster Literary Agency, LLC, Elaine **130**; Lazear Agency Incorporated **133**; Levine Literary Agency, Paul S. **135**; Lincoln Literary Agency, Ray **136**; Mura Literary, Dee **152**; Nazor Literary Agency **154**; Paraview, Inc. **156**; Picard, Literary Agent, Alison J. **158**; Singer Literary Agency Inc.,

Evelyn **179**; Stauffer Associates, Nancy **182**; Treimel NY, Scott **187**; Vines Agency, Inc., The **192**; Wales, Literary Agency, Inc. **193**; Watt & Associates, Sandra **194**; Writers House **198**

Religious/Inspirational: Alive Communications, Inc. **78**; Allred and Allred Literary Agents **79**; Barrett Books Inc., Loretta **83**; Books & Such **87**; Brown Ltd., Curtis **92**; Browne Ltd., Pema **93**; Dupree/Miller and Associates Inc. Literary **106**; Hamilburg Agency, Mitchell J., The **120**; Harris Literary Agency, Inc., The Joy **121**; Hartline Literary Agency **121**; Hawkins & Associates, Inc., John **121**; Hornfischer Literary Management, Inc. **124**; Kern Literary Agency, Natasha **127**; Larsen/Elizabeth Pomada Literary Agents, Michael **132**; Lazear Agency Incorporated **133**; Levine Literary Agency, Paul S. **135**; LitWest Group, LLC **140**; Marshall Agency, The Evan **148**; Multimedia Product Development, Inc. **152**; Picard, Literary Agent, Alison J. **158**; Seymour Agency, The **177**; Watt & Associates, Sandra **194**; Writers House **198**; Wylie-Merrick Literary Agency **199**

Romance: Ahearn Agency, Inc., The **78**; Allred and Allred Literary Agents **79**; Amsterdam Agency, Marcia **81**; Authentic Creations Literary Agency **82**; Axelrod Agency, The **82**; Barrett Books Inc., Loretta **83**; Bent, Harvey Klinger, Inc., Jenny **84**; Bernstein & Associates, Inc., Pam **84**; Bernstein Literary Agency, Meredith **84**; Bleeker Street Associates, Inc. **85**; BookEnds, LLC **86**; Books & Such **87**; Brandt & Hochman Literary Agents Inc. **91**; Brown Ltd., Curtis **92**; Browne Ltd., Pema **93**; Buck Agency, Howard **93**; Carvainis Agency, Inc., Maria **94**; Collin Literary Agency, Frances **97**; Cornerstone Literary, Inc. **99**; Dorian Literary Agency **104**; Ellenberg Literary Agency, Ethan **108**; Elmo Agency Inc., Ann **109**; English, Elaine P. **109**; Feigenbaum Publishing Consultants, Inc. **110**; Fogelman Literary Agency **112**; Fort Ross Inc. Russian-American Publishing Projects **113**; Gislason Agency, The **115**; Goodman Associates **117**; Grace Literary Agency, Carroll **117**; Gregory and Company Authors' Agents **118**; Grosjean Literary Agency, Jill **119**; Grosvenor Literary Agency, The **119**; Hartline Literary Agency **121**; Henshaw Group, Richard **122**; Hopkins Literary Associates **124**; Jenks Agency, The **126**; Kern Literary Agency, Natasha **127**; Knight Agency, The **129**; Larsen/Elizabeth Pomada Literary Agents, Michael **132**; Lazear Agency Incorporated **133**; Levine Literary Agency, Paul S. **135**; Lincoln Literary Agency, Ray **136**; Literary Group, The **137**; Lowenstein Associates **141**; Maass Literary Agency **142**; Manus & Associates Literary Agency, Inc. **143**; Marshall Agency, The Evan **148**; McGrath, Helen **149**; McHugh Literary Agency **149**; Multimedia Product Development, Inc. **152**; Mura Literary, Dee **152**; New Brand Agency Group, LLC **154**; Norma-Lewis Agency, The **155**; Paraview, Inc. **156**; Picard, Literary Agent, Alison J. **158**; Pinder Lane & Garon-Brooke Associates, Ltd. **158**; Pine Associates, Inc., Arthur **159**; Rosenberg Group, The **170**; Rotrosen Agency, LLC, Jane **172**; Rowland Agency, The Damaris **172**; Sedgeband Literary Associates **177**; Seligman, Literary Agent, Lynn **177**; Seymour Agency, The **177**; Spectrum Literary Agency **181**; Steele-Perkins Literary Agency **183**; Teal Literary Agency, Patricia **185**; Travis Literary Agency, Susan **186**; Vines Agency, Inc., The **192**; Weiner Literary Agency, Cherry **195**; Wieser & Wieser, Inc. **197**; Writers House **198**; Wylie-Merrick Literary Agency **199**

Science Fiction: ABS Literary Agency, Inc. **76**; Allred and Allred Literary Agents **79**; Amsterdam Agency, Marcia **81**; Anubis Literary Agency **81**; Brown Ltd., Curtis **92**; Collin Literary Agency, Frances **97**; Core Creations **98**; Dorian Literary Agency **104**; Ellenberg Literary Agency, Ethan **108**; Fort Ross Inc. Russian-American Publishing Projects **113**; Gislason Agency, The **115**; Halsey Agency, Reece **120**; Halsey North, Reece **120**; Hamilburg Agency, Mitchell J., The **120**; Hawkins & Associates, Inc., John **121**; Henshaw Group, Richard **122**; Jabberwocky Literary Agency **125**; Kidd Agency, Inc. Virginia **128**; Kleinman, Esq., Jeffrey M. **128**; Kraas Agency, Irene **130**; Lazear Agency Incorporated **133**; Maass Literary Agency **142**; Marshall Agency, The Evan **148**; McGrath, Helen **149**; Mura Literary, Dee **152**; National Writers Literary Agency **153**; New Brand Agency Group, LLC **154**; Perkins Associates, L. **157**; Pinder Lane & Garon-Brooke Associates, Ltd. **158**; Protter Literary Agent, Susan Ann **160**; Rubie Literary Agency, The Peter **173**; Schiavone Literary Agency, Inc. **175**; Seligman, Literary Agent, Lynn **177**; Spectrum Literary Agency **181**; Sternig & Byrne Literary Agency **183**; Treimel NY, Scott **187**; Vicananza, Ltd., Ralph **192**; Vines Agency, Inc., The **192**; Weiner Literary Agency, Cherry **195**; Writers House **198**; Wylie-Merrick Literary Agency **199**

Short Story Collections: Brown Ltd., Curtis **92**; Buck Agency, Howard **93**; Congdon Associates Inc., Don **97**; Hamilburg Agency, Mitchell J., The **120**; Harris Literary Agency, Inc., The Joy **121**; Hawkins & Associates, Inc., John **121**; Lazear Agency Incorporated **133**; Paton Literary Agency, Kathi J. **157**; Van Der Leun & Associates **191**; Writers House **198**

Spiritual: Barrett Books Inc., Loretta **83**; Brown Ltd., Curtis **92**; Hamilburg Agency, Mitchell J., The **120**; Harris Literary Agency, Inc., The Joy **121**; Hawkins & Associates, Inc., John **121**; Lazear Agency Incorporated **133**; Writers House **198**

Sports: Allred and Allred Literary Agents **79**; Authentic Creations Literary Agency **82**; Barrett Books Inc., Loretta **83**; Brown Ltd., Curtis **92**; Donovan Literary, Jim **104**; Ducas, Robert **105**; Dupree/Miller and Associates Inc. Literary **106**; Goodman Associates **117**; Greenburger Associates, Inc., Sanford J. **118**; Hamilburg Agency, Mitchell J., The **120**; Harris Literary Agency, Inc., The Joy **121**; Hawkins & Associates, Inc., John **121**; Henshaw Group, Richard **122**; Jabberwocky Literary Agency **125**; JCA Literary Agency **126**; Lasher Agency, The Maureen **133**; Lazear Agency Incorporated **133**; Levine Literary Agency, Paul S. **135**; Lincoln Literary Agency, Ray **136**; Literary Group, The **137**; LitWest Group, LLC **140**; Markowitz Literary Agency, Barbara **147**; Multimedia Product Development, Inc. **152**; Mura Literary, Dee **152**; National Writers Literary Agency **153**; Picard, Literary Agent, Alison J. **158**; RLR Associates, Ltd. **169**; Robbins Literary Agency, B.J. **170**; Russell and Volkening **173**; Spitzer Literary Agency, Philip G. **182**; Treimel NY, Scott **187**; Venture Literary **191**; Vines Agency, Inc., The **192**; Whittaker, Literary Agent, Lynn **196**; Writers House **198**

Thriller/Espionage: ABS Literary Agency, Inc. **76**; Acacia House Publishing Services Ltd. **76**; Ahearn Agency, Inc., The **78**; Alive Communications, Inc. **78**; Allred and Allred Literary Agents **79**; Altshuler Literary Agency, Miriam **80**; Amsterdam Agency, Marcia **81**; Authentic Creations Literary Agency **82**; Baldi Literary Agency, Malaga **82**; Barrett Books Inc., Loretta **83**; Bernstein & Associates, Inc., Pam **84**; Bleeker Street Associates, Inc. **85**; BookEnds, LLC **86**; Brandt & Hochman Literary Agents Inc. **91**; Brandt Agency, The Joan **91**; Brown Ltd., Curtis **92**; Buck Agency, Howard **93**; Carvainis Agency, Inc., Maria **94**; Congdon Associates Inc., Don **97**; Connor Literary Agency **98**; Cornerstone Literary, Inc. **99**; Crawford Literary Agency **99**; Dawson Associates, Liza **101**; DeFiore and Company **101**; DHS Literary, Inc. **102**; Dijkstra Literary Agency, Sandra **102**; Donovan Literary, Jim **104**; Dorian Literary Agency **104**; Ducas, Robert **105**; Dunham Literary **105**; Dupree/Miller and Associates Inc. Literary **106**; Dystel Literary Management, Inc., Jane **106**; Ellenberg Literary Agency, Ethan **108**; Elmo Agency Inc., Ann **109**; Eth Literary Representation, Felicia **109**; Farber Literary Agency Inc. **110**; Fleury, B.R. **112**; Fort Ross Inc. Russian-American Publishing Projects **113**; Freymann Literary Agency, Sarah Jane **114**; Gislason Agency, The **115**; Goldfarb & Associates **116**; Goodman Associates **117**; Grace Literary Agency, Carroll **117**; Greenburger Associates, Inc., Sanford J. **118**; Gregory and Company Authors' Agents **118**; Grosjean Literary Agency, Jill **119**; Grosvenor Literary Agency, The **119**; Halsey Agency, Reece **120**; Halsey North, Reece **120**; Hamilburg Agency, Mitchell J., The **120**; Harris Literary Agency, Inc., The Joy **121**; Hartline Literary Agency **121**; Hawkins & Associates, Inc., John **121**; Henshaw Group, Richard **122**; Hornfischer Literary Management, Inc. **124**; Jabberwocky Literary Agency **125**; JCA Literary Agency **126**; Jenks Agency, The **126**; Kern Literary Agency, Natasha **127**; Kleinman, Esq., Jeffrey M. **128**; Klinger, Inc., Harvey **129**; Koster Literary Agency, LLC, Elaine **130**; Kraas Agency, Irene **130**; Lampack Agency, Inc., Peter **132**; Lasher Agency, The Maureen **133**; Lawyer's Literary Agency, Inc. **133**; Lazear Agency Incorporated **133**; Levine Communications, Inc., James **134**; Levine Literary Agency, Inc., Ellen **135**; Levine Literary Agency, Paul S. **135**; Lincoln Literary Agency, Ray **136**; Literary Group, The **137**; LitWest Group, LLC **140**; Love Literary Agency, Nancy **141**; Lowenstein Associates **141**; Maass Literary Agency **142**; Maccoby Agency, Gina **143**; Manus & Associates Literary Agency, Inc. **143**; Markowitz Literary Agency, Barbara **147**; Marmur Associates, Ltd., Mildred **148**; McBride Literary Agency, Margret **148**; McGrath, Helen **149**; McHugh Literary Agency **149**; Multimedia Product Development, Inc. **152**; Mura Literary, Dee **152**; Naggar Literary Agency, Jean V. **153**; New Brand Agency Group, LLC **154**; Norma-Lewis Agency, The **155**; Pevner, Inc., Stephen **157**; Picard, Literary Agent, Alison J. **158**; Pine Associates, Inc., Arthur **159**; Preskill Literary Agency, Robert **159**; Protter Literary Agent, Susan Ann **160**; Quicksilver Books Literary Agents **161**; Rees Literary Agency, Helen **162**; Rhodes Literary Agency, Jodie **162**; RLR Associates, Ltd. **169**; Robbins Literary Agency, B.J. **170**; Rotrosen Agency, LLC, Jane **172**; Rubie Literary Agency, The Peter **173**; Russell and Volkening **173**; Sanders & Associates, Victoria **174**; Scherf, Inc., Literary Properties **174**; Simmons Literary Agency, Jeffrey **179**; Singer Literary Agency Inc., Evelyn **179**; Spitzer Literary Agency, Philip G. **182**; Tabian/Literary Agent, Robert E. **185**; Treimel NY, Scott **187**; Venture Literary **191**; Vicananza, Ltd., Ralph **192**; Vines Agency, Inc., The **192**; Wald Associates, Inc., Mary Jack **192**; Ware Literary Agency, John A. **193**; Watt & Associates, Sandra **194**; Weiner Literary Agency, Cherry **195**; Wieser & Wieser, Inc. **197**; Witherspoon Associates, Inc. **197**; Wonderland Press, Inc., The **197**; Writers House **198**; Wylie-Merrick Literary Agency **199**; Zachary Shuster Harmsworth **199**; Zeckendorf Assoc. Inc., Susan **200**

Translation: Brown Ltd., Curtis **92**; Buck Agency, Howard **93**; Goodman Associates **117**; Hamilburg Agency, Mitchell J., The **120**; Harris Literary Agency, Inc., The Joy **121**; Hawkins & Associates, Inc., John **121**; Lazear Agency Incorporated **133**; Treimel NY, Scott **187**; Van Der Leun & Associates **191**; Writers House **198**

Western/Frontier: Alive Communications, Inc. **78**; Allred and Allred Literary Agents **79**; Amsterdam Agency, Marcia **81**; Brown Ltd., Curtis **92**; DHS Literary, Inc. **102**; Donovan Literary, Jim **104**; Grace Literary Agency, Carroll **117**; Hamilburg Agency, Mitchell J., The **120**; Hawkins & Associates, Inc., John **121**; J de S Associates Inc. **125**; Lazear Agency Incorporated **133**; Levine Literary Agency, Paul S. **135**; Literary Group, The **137**; Marshall Agency, The Evan **148**; McBride Literary Agency, Margret **148**; McHugh Literary Agency **149**; Mura Literary, Dee **152**; New Brand Agency Group, LLC **154**; Norma-Lewis Agency, The **155**; Seymour Agency, The **177**; Treimel NY, Scott **187**; Vines Agency, Inc., The **192**; Weiner Literary Agency, Cherry **195**; Writers House **198**

Women's: Axelrod Agency, The **82**; Bleeker Street Associates, Inc. **85**; Book Deals, Inc. **86**; Brown Ltd., Curtis **92**; Buck Agency, Howard **93**; Castiglia Literary Agency **95**; Congdon Associates Inc., Don **97**; Connor Literary Agency **98**; Ellenberg Literary Agency, Ethan **108**; English, Elaine P. **109**; Halsey Agency, Reece **120**; Halsey North, Reece **120**; Harris Literary Agency, Inc., The Joy **121**; Hawkins & Associates, Inc., John **121**; Hopkins Literary Associates **124**; Knight Agency, The **129**; Lazear Agency Incorporated **133**; Levine Communications, Inc., James **134**; Levine Literary Agency, Inc., Ellen **135**; Maass Literary Agency **142**; Manus & Associates Literary Agency, Inc. **143**; Michaels Literary Agency, Inc., Doris S. **150**; Moran Agency, Maureen **151**; Nazor Literary Agency **154**; Paraview, Inc. **156**; Rhodes Literary Agency, Jodie **162**; Rosenberg Group, The **170**; Rotrosen Agency, LLC, Jane **172**; Sherman Associates, Inc., Wendy **178**; Steele-Perkins Literary Agency **183**; Van Der Leun & Associates **191**; Vines Agency, Inc., The **192**; Writers House **198**

Young Adult: Alive Communications, Inc. **78**; Allred and Allred Literary Agents **79**; Amsterdam Agency, Marcia **81**; Books & Such **87**; Brandt & Hochman Literary Agents Inc. **91**; Briggs, M. Courtney **91**; Brown Literary Agency, Inc., Andrea **92**; Brown Ltd., Curtis **92**; Browne Ltd., Pema **93**; Carvainis Agency, Inc., Maria **94**; Cohen, Inc. Literary Agency, Ruth **97**; Dorian Literary Agency **104**; Dunham Literary **105**; Dwyer & O'Grady, Inc. **106**; Farber Literary Agency Inc. **110**; Flannery Literary **111**; Fort Ross Inc. Russian-American Publishing Projects **113**; Hamilburg Agency, Mitchell J., The **120**; Hawkins & Associates, Inc., John **121**; J de S Associates Inc. **125**; Kidd Agency, Inc. Virginia **128**; Kouts, Literary Agent, Barbara S. **130**; Lazear Agency Incorporated **133**; Lincoln Literary Agency, Ray **136**; Maccoby Agency, Gina **143**; Markowitz Literary Agency, Barbara **147**; Marmur Associates, Ltd., Mildred **148**; Mura Literary, Dee **152**; National Writers Literary Agency **153**; Norma-Lewis Agency, The **155**; Picard, Literary Agent, Alison J. **158**; Rhodes Literary Agency, Jodie **162**; Schiavone Literary Agency, Inc. **175**; Schulman, A Literary Agency, Susan **175**; Tobias, A Literary Agency for Chilren's Books, Ann **186**; Treimel NY, Scott **187**; Wald Associates, Inc., Mary Jack **192**; Watt & Associates, Sandra **194**; Writers House **198**; Wylie-Merrick Literary Agency **199**

NONFICTION

Agriculture/Horticulture: Baldi Literary Agency, Malaga **82**; Brown Ltd., Curtis **92**; Casselman Literary Agency, Martha **95**; Curtis Associates, Inc., Richard **99**; Doyen Literary Services, Inc. **104**; Dupree/Miller and Associates Inc. Literary **106**; Fernandez, Justin E. **111**; Gartenberg, Literary Agent, Max **115**; Greenburger Associates, Inc., Sanford J. **118**; Hamilburg Agency, Mitchell J., The **120**; Hawkins & Associates, Inc., John **121**; Kleinman, Esq., Jeffrey M. **128**; Krages, Attorney at Law, Bert P. **131**; Lazear Agency Incorporated **133**; Lieberman Associates, Robert **136**; Limelight Management **136**; Multimedia Product Development, Inc. **152**; Mura Literary, Dee **152**; Paraview, Inc. **156**; Seymour Agency, The **177**; Snell Literary Agency, Michael **181**; Treimel NY, Scott **187**; Watt & Associates, Sandra **194**

Americana: Barrett Books Inc., Loretta **83**; Brown Ltd., Curtis **92**; Buck Agency, Howard **93**; Bykofsky Associates, Inc. Sheree **94**; Curtis Associates, Inc., Richard **99**; Doyen Literary Services, Inc. **104**; Dupree/Miller and Associates Inc. Literary **106**; Fernandez, Justin E. **111**; Goodman Associates **117**; Greenburger Associates, Inc., Sanford J. **118**; Hamilburg Agency, Mitchell J., The **120**; Hawkins & Associates, Inc., John **121**; Lazear Agency Incorporated **133**; Paraview, Inc. **156**; Seymour Agency, The **177**; Snell Literary Agency, Michael **181**; Treimel NY, Scott **187**

Animals: Acacia House Publishing Services Ltd. **76**; Ahearn Agency, Inc., The **78**; Baldi Literary Agency, Malaga **82**; Balkin Agency, Inc. **83**; Barrett Books Inc., Loretta **83**; Bent, Harvey Klinger, Inc., Jenny **84**; Bernstein Literary Agency, Meredith **84**; Bial Agency, Daniel **84**; Bleeker Street Associates, Inc. **85**; BookEnds, LLC **86**; Boston Literary Group, The **90**; Briggs, M. Courtney **91**; Brown Literary Agency, Inc., Andrea **92**; Brown Ltd., Curtis **92**; Bykofsky Associates, Inc. Sheree **94**; Castiglia Literary Agency **95**; Curtis Associates, Inc., Richard **99**; Doyen Literary Services, Inc.

104; Ducas, Robert **105**; Dupree/Miller and Associates Inc. Literary **106**; Dystel Literary Management, Inc., Jane **106**; Eth Literary Representation, Felicia **109**; Fernandez, Justin E. **111**; Fredericks Literary Agency, Jeanne **114**; Freymann Literary Agency, Sarah Jane **114**; Gartenberg, Literary Agent, Max **115**; Gislason Agency, The **115**; Goodman Associates **117**; Greenburger Associates, Inc., Sanford J. **118**; Grosvenor Literary Agency, The **119**; Hamilburg Agency, Mitchell J., The **120**; Hawkins & Associates, Inc., John **121**; Henshaw Group, Richard **122**; Jenks Agency, The **126**; Kern Literary Agency, Natasha **127**; Kleinman, Esq., Jeffrey M. **128**; Krages, Attorney at Law, Bert P. **131**; Kritzer Productions, Eddie **131**; Lasher Agency, The Maureen **133**; Lazear Agency Incorporated **133**; Levine Communications, Inc., James **134**; Lincoln Literary Agency, Ray **136**; Literary Group, The **137**; Lowenstein Associates **141**; McHugh Literary Agency **149**; Multimedia Product Development, Inc. **152**; Mura Literary, Dee **152**; National Writers Literary Agency **153**; Nine Muses and Apollo Inc. **155**; Paraview, Inc. **156**; Parks Agency, The Richard **156**; Picard, Literary Agent, Alison J. **158**; RLR Associates, Ltd. **169**; Roghaar Literary Agency, Inc., Linda **170**; Rosenkranz Literary Agency, Rita **171**; Schiavone Literary Agency, Inc. **175**; Seymour Agency, The **177**; Snell Literary Agency, Michael **181**; Straus Agency, Inc., Robin **183**; Teal Literary Agency, Patricia **185**; Treimel NY, Scott **187**; Venture Literary **191**; Wales, Literary Agency, Inc. **193**; Ware Literary Agency, John A. **193**; Watt & Associates, Sandra **194**; Whittaker, Literary Agent, Lynn **196**; Writers House **198**; Zachary Shuster Harmsworth **199**

Anthropology/Archaeology: Allred and Allred Literary Agents **79**; Authentic Creations Literary Agency **82**; Baldi Literary Agency, Malaga **82**; Balkin Agency, Inc. **83**; Barrett Books Inc., Loretta **83**; Bial Agency, Daniel **84**; Borchardt Inc., Georges **87**; Boston Literary Group, The **90**; Brown Literary Agency, Inc., Andrea **92**; Brown Ltd., Curtis **92**; Buck Agency, Howard **93**; Bykofsky Associates, Inc. Sheree **94**; Casselman Literary Agency, Martha **95**; Castiglia Literary Agency **95**; Collin Literary Agency, Frances **97**; Congdon Associates Inc., Don **97**; Coover Agency, The Doe **98**; Curtis Associates, Inc., Richard **99**; Dijkstra Literary Agency, Sandra **102**; Doyen Literary Services, Inc. **104**; Dunham Literary **105**; Dupree/Miller and Associates Inc. Literary **106**; Dystel Literary Management, Inc., Jane **106**; Educational Design Services, Inc. **107**; Elek Associates, Peter **107**; Eth Literary Representation, Felicia **109**; Fernandez, Justin E. **111**; Freymann Literary Agency, Sarah Jane **114**; Goodman Associates **117**; Greenburger Associates, Inc., Sanford J. **118**; Grosvenor Literary Agency, The **119**; Hamilburg Agency, Mitchell J., The **120**; Hawkins & Associates, Inc., John **121**; Hill & Barlow Agency **123**; Hochmann Books, John L. **123**; Hornfischer Literary Management, Inc. **124**; James Peter Associates, Inc. **125**; JCA Literary Agency **126**; Kern Literary Agency, Natasha **127**; Kleinman, Esq., Jeffrey M. **128**; Krages, Attorney at Law, Bert P. **131**; Larsen/Elizabeth Pomada Literary Agents, Michael **132**; Lasher Agency, The Maureen **133**; Lazear Agency Incorporated **133**; Levine Literary Agency, Inc., Ellen **135**; Lieberman Associates, Robert **136**; Lincoln Literary Agency, Ray **136**; Literary Group, The **137**; Lowenstein Associates **141**; Lownie Literary Agency Ltd., Andrew **142**; Mann Agency, Carol **143**; McHugh Literary Agency **149**; Miller Agency, The **150**; Morrison, Inc., Henry **151**; Multimedia Product Development, Inc. **152**; Mura Literary, Dee **152**; Paraview, Inc. **156**; Parks Agency, The Richard **156**; Picard, Literary Agent, Alison J. **158**; Quicksilver Books Literary Agents **161**; RLR Associates, Ltd. **169**; Roghaar Literary Agency, Inc., Linda **170**; Rosenkranz Literary Agency, Rita **171**; Ross Literary Agency, The Gail **171**; Russell and Volkening **173**; Schiavone Literary Agency, Inc. **175**; Schulman, A Literary Agency, Susan **175**; Seligman, Literary Agent, Lynn **177**; Seymour Agency, The **177**; Singer Literary Agency Inc., Evelyn **179**; Slopen Literary Agency, Beverley **180**; Snell Literary Agency, Michael **181**; Straus Agency, Inc., Robin **183**; Treimel NY, Scott **187**; United Tribes **190**; Venture Literary **191**; Ware Literary Agency, John A. **193**; Watt & Associates, Sandra **194**; Witherspoon Associates, Inc. **197**

Art/Architecture/Design: Allred and Allred Literary Agents **79**; Baldi Literary Agency, Malaga **82**; Barrett Books Inc., Loretta **83**; Boston Literary Group, The **90**; Brown Associates Inc., Marie **91**; Brown Literary Agency, Inc., Andrea **92**; Brown Ltd., Curtis **92**; Buck Agency, Howard **93**; Bykofsky Associates, Inc. Sheree **94**; Clark Associates, William **96**; Curtis Associates, Inc., Richard **99**; Donnaud & Associates, Inc., Janis A. **103**; Doyen Literary Services, Inc. **104**; Dunham Literary **105**; Dupree/Miller and Associates Inc. Literary **106**; Fernandez, Justin E. **111**; Forthwrite Literary Agency **113**; Freymann Literary Agency, Sarah Jane **114**; Gartenberg, Literary Agent, Max **115**; Goldfarb & Associates **116**; Greenburger Associates, Inc., Sanford J. **118**; Grosjean Literary Agency, Jill **119**; Grosvenor Literary Agency, The **119**; Hamilburg Agency, Mitchell J., The **120**; Hawkins & Associates, Inc., John **121**; Hochmann Books, John L. **123**; James Peter Associates, Inc. **125**; Kleinman, Esq., Jeffrey M. **128**; Krages, Attorney at Law, Bert P. **131**; Larsen/Elizabeth Pomada Literary Agents, Michael **132**; Lasher Agency, The Maureen **133**; Lazear Agency Incorporated **133**; Levine Communications, Inc., James **134**; Levine Literary Agency, Paul S. **135**; Lieberman Associates, Robert **136**; Limelight Management **136**; Lincoln Literary Agency, Ray **136**; Mann Agency, Carol

Agency, Susan **175**; Sedgeband Literary Associates **177**; Seligman, Literary Agent, Lynn **177**; Seymour Agency, The **177**; Simmons Literary Agency, Jeffrey **179**; Singer Literary Agency Inc., Evelyn **179**; Skolnick Literary Agency, Irene **180**; Slopen Literary Agency, Beverley **180**; Smith Literary Agency Ltd., Robert **180**; Snell Literary Agency, Michael **181**; Spieler Agency, The **182**; Spitzer Literary Agency, Philip G. **182**; Stauffer Associates, Nancy **182**; Straus Agency, Inc., Robin **183**; Susijn Agency, The **184**; Teal Literary Agency, Patricia **185**; Treimel NY, Scott **187**; 2M Communications Ltd. **187**; United Tribes **190**; Van Der Leun & Associates **191**; Venture Literary **191**; Viciananza, Ltd., Ralph **192**; Vines Agency, Inc., The **192**; Wald Associates, Inc., Mary Jack **192**; Wales, Literary Agency, Inc. **193**; Ware Literary Agency, John A. **193**; Waterside Productions, Inc. **194**; Watkins Loomis Agency, Inc. **194**; Wecksler-Incomco **195**; Weingel-Fidel Agency, The **196**; Weinstein Literary Management, Ted **196**; Whittaker, Literary Agent, Lynn **196**; Witherspoon Associates, Inc. **197**; Wonderland Press, Inc., The **197**; Writers House **198**; Zachary Shuster Harmsworth **199**; Zeckendorf Assoc. Inc., Susan **200**

Business/Ecomomics: Alive Communications, Inc. **78**; Amster Literary Enterprises, Betsy **80**; Baldi Literary Agency, Malaga **82**; Barrett Books Inc., Loretta **83**; Bernstein Literary Agency, Meredith **84**; Bial Agency, Daniel **84**; Black Literary Agency, David **85**; Bleeker Street Associates, Inc. **85**; Book Deals, Inc. **86**; BookEnds, LLC **86**; Boston Literary Group, The **90**; Brown Associates Inc., Marie **91**; Brown Ltd., Curtis **92**; Browne Ltd., Pema **93**; Buck Agency, Howard **93**; Bykofsky Associates, Inc. Sheree **94**; Carlisle & Company **94**; Carvainis Agency, Inc., Maria **94**; Castiglia Literary Agency **95**; Coover Agency, The Doe **98**; Curtis Associates, Inc., Richard **99**; Dawson Associates, Liza **101**; DeFiore and Company **101**; DHS Literary, Inc. **102**; Dijkstra Literary Agency, Sandra **102**; Donovan Literary, Jim **104**; Doyen Literary Services, Inc. **104**; Ducas, Robert **105**; Dunham Literary **105**; Dupree/Miller and Associates Inc. Literary **106**; Dystel Literary Management, Inc., Jane **106**; Educational Design Services, Inc. **107**; Elmo Agency Inc., Ann **109**; Eth Literary Representation, Felicia **109**; Feigen/Parrent Literary Management **110**; Fernandez, Justin E. **111**; Fogelman Literary Agency **112**; Forthwrite Literary Agency **113**; Freymann Literary Agency, Sarah Jane **114**; Goldfarb & Associates **116**; Goodman Associates **117**; Greenburger Associates, Inc., Sanford J. **118**; Grosvenor Literary Agency, The **119**; Hamilburg Agency, Mitchell J., The **120**; Hartline Literary Agency **121**; Hawkins & Associates, Inc., John **121**; Henshaw Group, Richard **122**; Herman Agency LLC, The Jeff **122**; Hill & Barlow Agency **123**; Hornfischer Literary Management, Inc. **124**; J de S Associates Inc. **125**; Jabberwocky Literary Agency **125**; James Peter Associates, Inc. **125**; JCA Literary Agency **126**; Jordan Literary Agency, Lawrence **127**; Kern Literary Agency, Natasha **127**; Ketz Agency, Louise B. **127**; Kleinman, Esq., Jeffrey M. **128**; Knight Agency, The **129**; Konner Literary Agency, Linda **130**; Koster Literary Agency, LLC, Elaine **130**; Krages, Attorney at Law, Bert P. **131**; Kritzer Productions, Eddie **131**; Larsen/Elizabeth Pomada Literary Agents, Michael **132**; Lasher Agency, The Maureen **133**; Lazear Agency Incorporated **133**; Levine Communications, Inc., James **134**; Levine Literary Agency, Paul S. **135**; Lieberman Associates, Robert **136**; Lincoln Literary Agency, Ray **136**; Literary and Creative Artists, Inc. **137**; Literary Group, The **137**; LitWest Group, LLC **140**; Livingston Cooke **140**; Lowenstein Associates **141**; Mann Agency, Carol **143**; Manus & Associates Literary Agency, Inc. **143**; Marmur Associates, Ltd., Mildred **148**; McBride Literary Agency, Margret **148**; McGrath, Helen **149**; Michaels Literary Agency, Inc., Doris S. **150**; Millard Literary Agency, Martha **150**; Miller Agency, The **150**; Moore Literary Agency **151**; Multimedia Product Development, Inc. **152**; Mura Literary, Dee **152**; Nazor Literary Agency **154**; New Brand Agency Group, LLC **154**; New England Publishing Associates Inc. **154**; Nine Muses and Apollo Inc. **155**; Paraview, Inc. **156**; Parks Agency, The Richard **156**; Paton Literary Agency, Kathi J. **157**; Picard, Literary Agent, Alison J. **158**; Pine Associates, Inc., Arthur **159**; Preskill Literary Agency, Robert **159**; Quicksilver Books Literary Agents **161**; Rabiner, Literary Agent, Inc., Susan **161**; Rees Literary Agency, Helen **162**; Rein Books, Inc., Jody **162**; Rinaldi Literary Agency, Angela **166**; RLR Associates, Ltd. **169**; Rosenkranz Literary Agency, Rita **171**; Ross Literary Agency, The Gail **171**; Roth, Literary Representation, Carol Susan **172**; Rotrosen Agency, LLC, Jane **172**; Russell and Volkening **173**; Scherf, Inc., Literary Properties **174**; Sebastian Literary Agency **176**; Seligman, Literary Agent, Lynn **177**; Seymour Agency, The **177**; Shepard Agency, The Robert **178**; Singer Literary Agency Inc., Evelyn **179**; Slopen Literary Agency, Beverley **180**; Snell Literary Agency, Michael **181**; Spieler Agency, The **182**; Spitzer Literary Agency, Philip G. **182**; Swayne Agency Literary Management & Consulting, Inc., The **184**; Tabian/Literary Agent, Robert E. **185**; Trace Inc., The Tracy Sherrod Literary Agency **186**; United Tribes **190**; Venture Literary **191**; Viciananza, Ltd., Ralph **192**; Vines Agency, Inc., The **192**; Waterside Productions, Inc. **194**; Waxman Literary Agency **195**; Wecksler-Incomco **195**; Weinstein Literary Management, Ted **196**; Wieser & Wieser, Inc. **197**; Witherspoon Associates, Inc. **197**; Writers House **198**; Zachary Shuster Harmsworth **199**

Child Guidance/Parenting: ABS Literary Agency, Inc. **76**; Ahearn Agency, Inc., The **78**;

Alive Communications, Inc. **78**; Amster Literary Enterprises, Betsy **80**; Amsterdam Agency, Marcia **81**; Authentic Creations Literary Agency **82**; Barrett Books Inc., Loretta **83**; Bernstein Literary Agency, Meredith **84**; Bial Agency, Daniel **84**; Bleeker Street Associates, Inc. **85**; Book Deals, Inc. **86**; BookEnds, LLC **86**; Books & Such **87**; Boston Literary Group, The **90**; Brown Ltd., Curtis **92**; Browne Ltd., Pema **93**; Bykofsky Associates, Inc. Sheree **94**; Castiglia Literary Agency **95**; Charlton Associates, James **95**; Congdon Associates Inc., Don **97**; Connor Literary Agency **98**; Coover Agency, The Doe **98**; Curtis Associates, Inc., Richard **99**; Dawson Associates, Liza **101**; DeFiore and Company **101**; DHS Literary, Inc. **102**; Dijkstra Literary Agency, Sandra **102**; Donnaud & Associates, Inc., Janis A. **103**; Donovan Literary, Jim **104**; Doyen Literary Services, Inc. **104**; Dupree/Miller and Associates Inc. Literary **106**; Dystel Literary Management, Inc., Jane **106**; Educational Design Services, Inc. **107**; Elek Associates, Peter **107**; Eth Literary Representation, Felicia **109**; Farber Literary Agency Inc. **110**; Fernandez, Justin E. **111**; Fogelman Literary Agency **112**; Forthwrite Literary Agency **113**; Fredericks Literary Agency, Jeanne **114**; Freymann Literary Agency, Sarah Jane **114**; Gartenberg, Literary Agent, Max **115**; Goodman Associates **117**; Greenburger Associates, Inc., Sanford J. **118**; Grosvenor Literary Agency, The **119**; Hamilburg Agency, Mitchell J., The **120**; Hartline Literary Agency **121**; Hawkins & Associates, Inc., John **121**; Henshaw Group, Richard **122**; Hill & Barlow Agency **123**; Hornfischer Literary Management, Inc. **124**; James Peter Associates, Inc. **125**; Kern Literary Agency, Natasha **127**; Kleinman, Esq., Jeffrey M. **128**; Knight Agency, The **129**; Konner Literary Agency, Linda **130**; Koster Literary Agency, LLC, Elaine **130**; Kouts, Literary Agent, Barbara S. **130**; Krages, Attorney at Law, Bert P. **131**; Lasher Agency, The Maureen **133**; Lazear Agency Incorporated **133**; Levine Communications, Inc., James **134**; Levine Literary Agency, Paul S. **135**; Lincoln Literary Agency, Ray **136**; Literary Group, The **137**; LitWest Group, LLC **140**; Livingston Cooke **140**; Love Literary Agency, Nancy **141**; Lowenstein Associates **141**; Mann Agency, Carol **143**; Manus & Associates Literary Agency, Inc. **143**; McHugh Literary Agency **149**; Millard Literary Agency, Martha **150**; Miller Agency, The **150**; Multimedia Product Development, Inc. **152**; Mura Literary, Dee **152**; Naggar Literary Agency, Jean V. **153**; National Writers Literary Agency **153**; Nazor Literary Agency **154**; New England Publishing Associates Inc. **154**; Norma-Lewis Agency, The **155**; Paraview, Inc. **156**; Parks Agency, The Richard **156**; Paton Literary Agency, Kathi J. **157**; Picard, Literary Agent, Alison J. **158**; Quicksilver Books Literary Agents **161**; Rein Books, Inc., Jody **162**; Rhodes Literary Agency, Jodie **162**; Rinaldi Literary Agency, Angela **166**; RLR Associates, Ltd. **169**; Robbins Literary Agency, B.J. **170**; Rosenkranz Literary Agency, Rita **171**; Rotrosen Agency, LLC, Jane **172**; Schiavone Literary Agency, Inc. **175**; Schulman, A Literary Agency, Susan **175**; Seligman, Literary Agent, Lynn **177**; Seymour Agency, The **177**; Singer Literary Agency Inc., Evelyn **179**; Snell Literary Agency, Michael **181**; Spieler Agency, The **182**; Straus Agency, Inc., Robin **183**; Teal Literary Agency, Patricia **185**; Travis Literary Agency, Susan **186**; 2M Communications Ltd. **187**; United Tribes **190**; Waterside Productions, Inc. **194**; Writers House **198**; Zeckendorf Assoc. Inc., Susan **200**

Computers/Electronics: Barrett Books Inc., Loretta **83**; Bleeker Street Associates, Inc. **85**; Brown Ltd., Curtis **92**; Buck Agency, Howard **93**; Bykofsky Associates, Inc. Sheree **94**; Curtis Associates, Inc., Richard **99**; Doyen Literary Services, Inc. **104**; Dupree/Miller and Associates Inc. Literary **106**; Fernandez, Justin E. **111**; Greenburger Associates, Inc., Sanford J. **118**; Hamilburg Agency, Mitchell J., The **120**; Henshaw Group, Richard **122**; Herman Agency LLC, The Jeff **122**; Kleinman, Esq., Jeffrey M. **128**; Krages, Attorney at Law, Bert P. **131**; Kritzer Productions, Eddie **131**; Lazear Agency Incorporated **133**; Levine Communications, Inc., James **134**; Levine Literary Agency, Paul S. **135**; Lieberman Associates, Robert **136**; Michaels Literary Agency, Inc., Doris S. **150**; Moore Literary Agency **151**; Mura Literary, Dee **152**; Nazor Literary Agency **154**; Paraview, Inc. **156**; Rosenkranz Literary Agency, Rita **171**; Seymour Agency, The **177**; Snell Literary Agency, Michael **181**; Swayne Agency Literary Management & Consulting, Inc., The **184**; Waterside Productions, Inc. **194**

Cooking/Foods/Nutrition: ABS Literary Agency, Inc. **76**; Agents Incorporated for Medical and Mental Health Professionals **77**; Allred and Allred Literary Agents **79**; Barrett Books Inc., Loretta **83**; Bial Agency, Daniel **84**; Bleeker Street Associates, Inc. **85**; BookEnds, LLC **86**; Brown Ltd., Curtis **92**; Browne Ltd., Pema **93**; Buck Agency, Howard **93**; Bykofsky Associates, Inc. Sheree **94**; Carlisle & Company **94**; Casselman Literary Agency, Martha **95**; Castiglia Literary Agency **95**; Charlton Associates, James **95**; Clausen, Mays & Tahan, LLC **96**; Congdon Associates Inc., Don **97**; Connor Literary Agency **98**; Coover Agency, The Doe **98**; Curtis Associates, Inc., Richard **99**; DeFiore and Company **101**; DHS Literary, Inc. **102**; Dijkstra Literary Agency, Sandra **102**; Donnaud & Associates, Inc., Janis A. **103**; Doyen Literary Services, Inc. **104**; Dupree/Miller and Associates Inc. Literary **106**; Dystel Literary Management, Inc., Jane **106**; Elmo Agency Inc., Ann **109**; Farber Literary Agency Inc. **110**; Fernandez, Justin E. **111**; Forthwrite Literary Agency **113**; Fredericks

Literary Agency, Jeanne **114**; Freymann Literary Agency, Sarah Jane **114**; Goldfarb & Associates **116**; Goodman Associates **117**; Greenburger Associates, Inc., Sanford J. **118**; Hamilburg Agency, Mitchell J., The **120**; Hartline Literary Agency **121**; Hawkins & Associates, Inc., John **121**; Henshaw Group, Richard **122**; Hill Bonnie Nadell, Inc., Frederick **123**; Hochmann Books, John L. **123**; Jabberwocky Literary Agency **125**; Jordan Literary Agency, Lawrence **127**; Kleinman, Esq., Jeffrey M. **128**; Klinger, Inc., Harvey **129**; Koster Literary Agency, LLC, Elaine **130**; Krages, Attorney at Law, Bert P. **131**; Kritzer Productions, Eddie **131**; Larsen/Elizabeth Pomada Literary Agents, Michael **132**; Lasher Agency, The Maureen **133**; Lazear Agency Incorporated **133**; Lescher & Lescher Ltd. **134**; Levine Communications, Inc., James **134**; Levine Literary Agency, Paul S. **135**; Limelight Management **136**; Lincoln Literary Agency, Ray **136**; Literary and Creative Artists, Inc. **137**; Literary Group, The **137**; Love Literary Agency, Nancy **141**; Marmur Associates, Ltd., Mildred **148**; McBride Literary Agency, Margret **148**; McHugh Literary Agency **149**; Millard Literary Agency, Martha **150**; Miller Agency, The **150**; Multimedia Product Development, Inc. **152**; Nolan Literary Agency, Betsy **155**; Norma-Lewis Agency, The **155**; Paraview, Inc. **156**; Parks Agency, The Richard **156**; Picard, Literary Agent, Alison J. **158**; Quicksilver Books Literary Agents **161**; RLR Associates, Ltd. **169**; Rosenkranz Literary Agency, Rita **171**; Rotrosen Agency, LLC, Jane **172**; Rubie Literary Agency, The Peter **173**; Russell and Volkening **173**; Seligman, Literary Agent, Lynn **177**; Seymour Agency, The **177**; Smith Literary Agency Ltd., Robert **180**; Snell Literary Agency, Michael **181**; Spieler Agency, The **182**; Straus Agency, Inc., Robin **183**; Travis Literary Agency, Susan **186**; United Tribes **190**; Van Der Leun & Associates **191**; Wieser & Wieser, Inc. **197**; Writers House **198**

Crafts/Hobbies: Allred and Allred Literary Agents **79**; Authentic Creations Literary Agency **82**; Barrett Books Inc., Loretta **83**; BookEnds, LLC **86**; Brown Ltd., Curtis **92**; Bykofsky Associates, Inc. Sheree **94**; Connor Literary Agency **98**; Curtis Associates, Inc., Richard **99**; Doyen Literary Services, Inc. **104**; Dupree/Miller and Associates Inc. Literary **106**; Fernandez, Justin E. **111**; Forthwrite Literary Agency **113**; Greenburger Associates, Inc., Sanford J. **118**; Hamilburg Agency, Mitchell J., The **120**; Hawkins & Associates, Inc., John **121**; Kleinman, Esq., Jeffrey M. **128**; Krages, Attorney at Law, Bert P. **131**; Lazear Agency Incorporated **133**; Levine Literary Agency, Paul S. **135**; Limelight Management **136**; Lincoln Literary Agency, Ray **136**; Literary Group, The **137**; Lowenstein Associates **141**; Multimedia Product Development, Inc. **152**; Norma-Lewis Agency, The **155**; Paraview, Inc. **156**; Parks Agency, The Richard **156**; Rosenkranz Literary Agency, Rita **171**; Seymour Agency, The **177**; Snell Literary Agency, Michael **181**; Watt & Associates, Sandra **194**

Creative Nonfiction: Barrett Books Inc., Loretta **83**; Bernstein Literary Agency, Meredith **84**; Brown Ltd., Curtis **92**; Buck Agency, Howard **93**; Bykofsky Associates, Inc. Sheree **94**; Congdon Associates Inc., Don **97**; Curtis Associates, Inc., Richard **99**; Donnaud & Associates, Inc., Janis A. **103**; Doyen Literary Services, Inc. **104**; Dupree/Miller and Associates Inc. Literary **106**; Fernandez, Justin E. **111**; Goldfarb & Associates **116**; Goodman Associates **117**; Greenburger Associates, Inc., Sanford J. **118**; Hamilburg Agency, Mitchell J., The **120**; Hawkins & Associates, Inc., John **121**; Kleinman, Esq., Jeffrey M. **128**; Lazear Agency Incorporated **133**; Levine Literary Agency, Inc., Ellen **135**; Levine Literary Agency, Paul S. **135**; Lincoln Literary Agency, Ray **136**; Literary Group, The **137**; Lowenstein Associates **141**; Manus & Associates Literary Agency, Inc. **143**; Multimedia Product Development, Inc. **152**; Paraview, Inc. **156**; Rein Books, Inc., Jody **162**; Rubie Literary Agency, The Peter **173**; Russell and Volkening **173**; Sebastian Literary Agency **176**; Seymour Agency, The **177**; Snell Literary Agency, Michael **181**; Stauffer Associates, Nancy **182**; Treimel NY, Scott **187**; Van Der Leun & Associates **191**; Wecksler-Incomco **195**

Current Affairs: Ahearn Agency, Inc., The **78**; Allen Literary Agency, Linda **79**; Allred and Allred Literary Agents **79**; Authentic Creations Literary Agency **82**; Baldi Literary Agency, Malaga **82**; Balkin Agency, Inc. **83**; Barrett Books Inc., Loretta **83**; Bial Agency, Daniel **84**; Bleeker Street Associates, Inc. **85**; BookEnds, LLC **86**; Borchardt Inc., Georges **87**; Boston Literary Group, The **90**; Brandt & Hochman Literary Agents Inc. **91**; Brown Literary Agency, Inc., Andrea **92**; Brown Ltd., Curtis **92**; Buck Agency, Howard **93**; Bykofsky Associates, Inc. Sheree **94**; Castiglia Literary Agency **95**; Clark Associates, William **96**; Congdon Associates Inc., Don **97**; Connor Literary Agency **98**; Curtis Associates, Inc., Richard **99**; Cypher, The Cypher Agency, James R. **100**; DHS Literary, Inc. **102**; Donnaud & Associates, Inc., Janis A. **103**; Donovan Literary, Jim **104**; Doyen Literary Services, Inc. **104**; Ducas, Robert **105**; Dunham Literary **105**; Dupree/Miller and Associates Inc. Literary **106**; Dystel Literary Management, Inc., Jane **106**; Educational Design Services, Inc. **107**; Elmo Agency Inc., Ann **109**; Eth Literary Representation, Felicia **109**; Feigen/Parrent Literary Management **110**; Fernandez, Justin E. **111**; Flaming Star Literary Enterprises **111**; Fogelman Literary Agency **112**; Forthwrite Literary Agency **113**; Franklin Associates, Ltd., Lynn C. **114**; Freymann Literary Agency, Sarah Jane **114**; Gartenberg, Literary Agent, Max **115**; Goldfarb & Associates **116**; Goodman Associates **117**; Greenburger Associates, Inc., Sanford J. **118**; Grosvenor Literary Agency, The **119**; Halsey Agency, Reece **120**; Hamilburg Agency, Mitchell J., The **120**; Hawkins & Associates, Inc., John **121**; Henshaw Group, Richard **122**; Hill & Barlow Agency **123**; Hill Bonnie Nadell, Inc., Frederick **123**; Hochmann Books, John L. **123**; Hornfischer Literary Management, Inc. **124**; J de S Associates Inc. **125**; Jabberwocky Literary Agency **125**; James Peter Associates, Inc. **125**; JCA Literary Agency **126**; Kern Literary Agency, Natasha **127**; Ketz Agency, Louise B. **127**; Kleinman, Esq., Jeffrey M. **128**; Knight Agency, The **129**; Koster Literary Agency, LLC, Elaine **130**; Kouts, Literary Agent, Barbara S. **130**; Krages, Attorney at Law, Bert P. **131**; Kritzer Productions, Eddie **131**; Larsen/Elizabeth Pomada Literary Agents, Michael **132**; Lasher Agency, The Maureen **133**; Lazear Agency Incorporated **133**; Levine Literary Agency, Inc., Ellen **135**; Levine Literary Agency, Paul S. **135**; Lincoln Literary Agency, Ray **136**; Lipkind Agency, Wendy **137**; Literary Group, The **137**; LitWest Group, LLC **140**; Livingston Cooke **140**; Love Literary Agency, Nancy **141**; Lowenstein Associates **141**; Lownie Literary Agency Ltd., Andrew **142**; Maccoby Agency, Gina **143**; Mann Agency, Carol **143**; Manus & Associates Literary Agency, Inc. **143**; March Tenth, Inc. **147**; Markowitz Literary Agency, Barbara **147**; Marmur Associates, Ltd., Mildred **148**; McBride Literary Agency, Margret **148**; McGrath, Helen **149**; McHugh Literary Agency **149**; Menza Literary Agency, Claudia **149**; Michaels Literary Agency, Inc., Doris S. **150**; Millard Literary Agency, Martha **150**; Miller Agency, The **150**; Multimedia Product Development, Inc. **152**; Mura Literary, Dee **152**; Naggar Literary Agency, Jean V. **153**; Nazor Literary Agency **154**; Nine Muses and Apollo Inc. **155**; Norma-Lewis Agency, The **155**; Paraview, Inc. **156**; Parks Agency, The Richard **156**; Picard, Literary Agent, Alison J. **158**; Pine Associates, Inc., Arthur **159**; Preskill Literary Agency, Robert **159**; Protter Literary Agent, Susan Ann **160**; Quicksilver Books Literary Agents **161**; Raymond, Literary Agent, Charlotte Cecil **161**; Rees Literary Agency, Helen **162**; Rein Books, Inc., Jody **162**; Rinaldi Literary Agency, Angela **166**; RLR Associates, Ltd. **169**; Robbins Literary Agency, B.J. **170**; Rosenberg Group, The **170**; Rosenkranz Literary Agency, Rita **171**; Rotrosen Agency, LLC, Jane **172**; Rubie Literary Agency, The Peter **173**; Russell and Volkening **173**; Sanders & Associates, Victoria **174**; Schiavone Literary Agency, Inc. **175**; Schulman, A Literary Agency, Susan **175**; Sebastian Literary Agency **176**; Seligman, Literary Agent, Lynn **177**; Seymour Agency, The **177**; Shepard Agency, The Robert **178**; Simmons Literary Agency, Jeffrey **179**; Singer Literary Agency Inc., Evelyn **179**; Skolnick Literary Agency, Irene **180**; Slopen Literary Agency, Beverley **180**; Snell Literary Agency, Michael **181**; Spieler Agency, The **182**; Spitzer Literary Agency, Philip G. **182**; Stauffer Associates, Nancy **182**; Straus Agency, Inc., Robin **183**; Swayne Agency Literary Management & Consulting, Inc., The **184**; Treimel NY, Scott **187**; United Tribes **190**; Van Der Leun & Associates **191**; Venture Literary **191**; Vines Agency, Inc., The **192**; Wald Associates, Inc., Mary Jack **192**; Wales, Literary Agency, Inc. **193**; Ware Literary Agency, John A. **193**; Watkins Loomis Agency, Inc. **194**; Watt & Associates, Sandra **194**; Wecksler-Incomco **195**; Weinstein Literary Management, Ted **196**; Whittaker, Literary Agent, Lynn **196**; Wieser & Wieser, Inc. **197**; Witherspoon Associates, Inc. **197**; Zachary Shuster Harmsworth **199**

Education: Allred and Allred Literary Agents **79**; Barrett Books Inc., Loretta **83**; Brown Ltd., Curtis **92**; Buck Agency, Howard **93**; Bykofsky Associates, Inc. Sheree **94**; Curtis Associates, Inc., Richard **99**; Doyen Literary Services, Inc. **104**; Dunham Literary **105**; Dupree/Miller and Associates Inc. Literary **106**; Dystel Literary Management, Inc., Jane **106**; Educational Design Services, Inc. **107**; Fernandez, Justin E. **111**; Fogelman Literary Agency **112**; Goldfarb & Associates **116**; Goodman Associates **117**; Greenburger Associates, Inc., Sanford J. **118**; Hamilburg Agency, Mitchell J., The **120**; Hawkins & Associates, Inc., John **121**; Hill & Barlow Agency **123**; Kleinman, Esq., Jeffrey M. **128**; Krages, Attorney at Law, Bert P. **131**; Lazear Agency Incorporated **133**; Levine Literary Agency, Paul S. **135**; Lieberman Associates, Robert **136**; Literary Group, The **137**; Lowenstein Associates **141**; McHugh Literary Agency **149**; Menza Literary Agency, Claudia **149**; Millard Literary Agency, Martha **150**; Mura Literary, Dee **152**; National Writers Literary Agency **153**; Paraview, Inc. **156**; Picard, Literary Agent, Alison J. **158**; Rabiner, Literary Agent, Inc., Susan **161**; RLR Associates, Ltd. **169**; Roghaar Literary Agency, Inc., Linda **170**; Ross Literary Agency, The Gail **171**; Russell and Volkening **173**; Schiavone Literary Agency, Inc. **175**; Schulman, A Literary Agency, Susan **175**; Seligman, Literary Agent, Lynn **177**; Seymour Agency, The **177**; Snell Literary Agency, Michael **181**; Treimel NY, Scott **187**; United Tribes **190**

Ethnic/Cultural Interests: Ahearn Agency, Inc., The **78**; Allred and Allred Literary Agents **79**; Altshuler Literary Agency, Miriam **80**; Amster Literary Enterprises, Betsy **80**; Baldi Literary Agency, Malaga **82**; Barrett Books Inc., Loretta **83**; Bent, Harvey Klinger, Inc., Jenny **84**; Bial Agency, Daniel **84**; Bleeker Street Associates, Inc. **85**; Book Deals, Inc. **86**; BookEnds, LLC **86**; Boston Literary Group, The **90**; Brandt & Hochman Literary Agents Inc. **91**; Brown Associates Inc., Marie **91**; Brown Literary Agency, Inc., Andrea **92**; Brown Ltd., Curtis **92**; Browne Ltd., Pema **93**; Buck Agency, Howard **93**; Bykofsky Associates, Inc. Sheree **94**; Castiglia Literary Agency **95**; Clark

Associates, William **96**; Congdon Associates Inc., Don **97**; Connor Literary Agency **98**; Coover Agency, The Doe **98**; Curtis Associates, Inc., Richard **99**; Cypher, The Cypher Agency, James R. **100**; DHS Literary, Inc. **102**; Dijkstra Literary Agency, Sandra **102**; Doyen Literary Services, Inc. **104**; Dunham Literary **105**; Dupree/Miller and Associates Inc. Literary **106**; Dystel Literary Management, Inc., Jane **106**; Educational Design Services, Inc. **107**; Eth Literary Representation, Felicia **109**; Fernandez, Justin E. **111**; Fogelman Literary Agency **112**; Freymann Literary Agency, Sarah Jane **114**; Goldfarb & Associates **116**; Goodman Associates **117**; Greenburger Associates, Inc., Sanford J. **118**; Hamilburg Agency, Mitchell J., The **120**; Hawkins & Associates, Inc., John **121**; Hill & Barlow Agency **123**; J de S Associates Inc. **125**; James Peter Associates, Inc. **125**; Jenks Agency, The **126**; Kern Literary Agency, Natasha **127**; Kleinman, Esq., Jeffrey M. **128**; Knight Agency, The **129**; Koster Literary Agency, LLC, Elaine **130**; Kouts, Literary Agent, Barbara S. **130**; Larsen/Elizabeth Pomada Literary Agents, Michael **132**; Lasher Agency, The Maureen **133**; Lazear Agency Incorporated **133**; Levine Literary Agency, Paul S. **135**; Lincoln Literary Agency, Ray **136**; Literary Group, The **137**; LitWest Group, LLC **140**; Love Literary Agency, Nancy **141**; Lowenstein Associates **141**; Maccoby Agency, Gina **143**; Mann Agency, Carol **143**; Manus & Associates Literary Agency, Inc. **143**; Marmur Associates, Ltd., Mildred **148**; McBride Literary Agency, Margret **148**; Menza Literary Agency, Claudia **149**; Millard Literary Agency, Martha **150**; Miller Agency, The **150**; Multimedia Product Development, Inc. **152**; Mura Literary, Dee **152**; Nazor Literary Agency **154**; Nine Muses and Apollo Inc. **155**; Norma-Lewis Agency, The **155**; Paraview, Inc. **156**; Parks Agency, The Richard **156**; Pevner, Inc., Stephen **157**; Picard, Literary Agent, Alison J. **158**; Popkin, Julie **159**; Quicksilver Books Literary Agents **161**; Raymond, Literary Agent, Charlotte Cecil **161**; Rein Books, Inc., Jody **162**; Rhodes Literary Agency, Jodie **162**; RLR Associates, Ltd. **169**; Robbins Literary Agency, B.J. **170**; Rosenkranz Literary Agency, Rita **171**; Ross Literary Agency, The Gail **171**; Rubie Literary Agency, The Peter **173**; Russell and Volkening **173**; Sanders & Associates, Victoria **174**; Schiavone Literary Agency, Inc. **175**; Schulman, A Literary Agency, Susan **175**; Sedgeband Literary Associates **177**; Seligman, Literary Agent, Lynn **177**; Seymour Agency, The **177**; Shepard Agency, The Robert **178**; Singer Literary Agency Inc., Evelyn **179**; Snell Literary Agency, Michael **181**; Spitzer Literary Agency, Philip G. **182**; Stauffer Associates, Nancy **182**; Straus Agency, Inc., Robin **183**; Swayne Agency Literary Management & Consulting, Inc., The **184**; Travis Literary Agency, Susan **186**; Treimel NY, Scott **187**; 2M Communications Ltd. **187**; United Tribes **190**; Van Der Leun & Associates **191**; Venture Literary **191**; Vines Agency, Inc., The **192**; Wald Associates, Inc., Mary Jack **192**; Wales, Literary Agency, Inc. **193**; Waterside Productions, Inc. **194**; Watkins Loomis Agency, Inc. **194**; Waxman Literary Agency **195**; Whittaker, Literary Agent, Lynn **196**; Witherspoon Associates, Inc. **197**; Wonderland Press, Inc., The **197**

Gardening: Amster Literary Enterprises, Betsy **80**; Brown Ltd., Curtis **92**; Bykofsky Associates, Inc. Sheree **94**; Curtis Associates, Inc., Richard **99**; Doyen Literary Services, Inc. **104**; Dupree/Miller and Associates Inc. Literary **106**; Fernandez, Justin E. **111**; Fredericks Literary Agency, Jeanne **114**; Greenburger Associates, Inc., Sanford J. **118**; Grosjean Literary Agency, Jill **119**; Hamilburg Agency, Mitchell J., The **120**; Hawkins & Associates, Inc., John **121**; Kern Literary Agency, Natasha **127**; Lazear Agency Incorporated **133**; Levine Communications, Inc., James **134**; Limelight Management **136**; Lincoln Literary Agency, Ray **136**; McHugh Literary Agency **149**; Paraview, Inc. **156**; Parks Agency, The Richard **156**; Rittenberg Literary Agency, Inc., Ann **166**; Seymour Agency, The **177**; Snell Literary Agency, Michael **181**; Treimel NY, Scott **187**; Van Der Leun & Associates **191**

Gay/Lesbian Issues: Ahearn Agency, Inc., The **78**; Baldi Literary Agency, Malaga **82**; Barrett Books Inc., Loretta **83**; Bial Agency, Daniel **84**; BookEnds, LLC **86**; Brown Ltd., Curtis **92**; Browne Ltd., Pema **93**; Buck Agency, Howard **93**; Bykofsky Associates, Inc. Sheree **94**; Core Creations **98**; Curtis Associates, Inc., Richard **99**; Cypher, The Cypher Agency, James R. **100**; Daves Agency, Joan **101**; DeFiore and Company **101**; Doyen Literary Services, Inc. **104**; Ducas, Robert **105**; Dunham Literary **105**; Dupree/Miller and Associates Inc. Literary **106**; Dystel Literary Management, Inc., Jane **106**; Eth Literary Representation, Felicia **109**; Feigen/Parrent Literary Management **110**; Fernandez, Justin E. **111**; Greenburger Associates, Inc., Sanford J. **118**; Hamilburg Agency, Mitchell J., The **120**; Hawkins & Associates, Inc., John **121**; Henshaw Group, Richard **122**; Hill & Barlow Agency **123**; Hochmann Books, John L. **123**; Jabberwocky Literary Agency **125**; James Peter Associates, Inc. **125**; Kleinman, Esq., Jeffrey M. **128**; Konner Literary Agency, Linda **130**; Larsen/Elizabeth Pomada Literary Agents, Michael **132**; Lazear Agency Incorporated **133**; Levine Communications, Inc., James **134**; Levine Literary Agency, Paul S. **135**; Lincoln Literary Agency, Ray **136**; Livingston Cooke **140**; Lowenstein Associates **141**; Miller Agency, The **150**; Mura Literary, Dee **152**; Paraview, Inc. **156**; Parks Agency, The Richard **156**; Pevner, Inc., Stephen **157**; Picard, Literary Agent, Alison J. **158**; RLR Associates, Ltd. **169**; Rosenkranz Literary Agency, Rita **171**; Ross Literary Agency, The Gail **171**; Russell and Volkening **173**; Sanders & Associates, Victoria **174**; Schiavone Literary Agency,

Inc. **175**; Schulman, A Literary Agency, Susan **175**; Shepard Agency, The Robert **178**; Snell Literary Agency, Michael **181**; Spieler Agency, The **182**; Treimel NY, Scott **187**; 2M Communications Ltd. **187**; United Tribes **190**; Wales, Literary Agency, Inc. **193**; Whittaker, Literary Agent, Lynn **196**; Witherspoon Associates, Inc. **197**; Zachary Shuster Harmsworth **199**

Government/Politics/Law: Baldi Literary Agency, Malaga **82**; Barrett Books Inc., Loretta **83**; Bernstein Literary Agency, Meredith **84**; Bial Agency, Daniel **84**; Black Literary Agency, David **85**; Bleeker Street Associates, Inc. **85**; Boston Literary Group, The **90**; Brandt & Hochman Literary Agents Inc. **91**; Brown Ltd., Curtis **92**; Buck Agency, Howard **93**; Bykofsky Associates, Inc. Sheree **94**; Congdon Associates Inc., Don **97**; Connor Literary Agency **98**; Curtis Associates, Inc., Richard **99**; Cypher, The Cypher Agency, James R. **100**; Dijkstra Literary Agency, Sandra **102**; Doyen Literary Services, Inc. **104**; Ducas, Robert **105**; Dunham Literary **105**; Dupree/Miller and Associates Inc. Literary **106**; Dystel Literary Management, Inc., Jane **106**; Educational Design Services, Inc. **107**; Eth Literary Representation, Felicia **109**; Feigen/Parrent Literary Management **110**; Fernandez, Justin E. **111**; Flaming Star Literary Enterprises **111**; Fogelman Literary Agency **112**; Goldfarb & Associates **116**; Goodman Associates **117**; Greenburger Associates, Inc., Sanford J. **118**; Grosvenor Literary Agency, The **119**; Hamilburg Agency, Mitchell J., The **120**; Hawkins & Associates, Inc., John **121**; Henshaw Group, Richard **122**; Herman Agency LLC, The Jeff **122**; Hill & Barlow Agency **123**; Hill Bonnie Nadell, Inc., Frederick **123**; Hochmann Books, John L. **123**; Hornfischer Literary Management, Inc. **124**; J de S Associates Inc. **125**; Jabberwocky Literary Agency **125**; James Peter Associates, Inc. **125**; JCA Literary Agency **126**; Kleinman, Esq., Jeffrey M. **128**; Krages, Attorney at Law, Bert P. **131**; Kroll Literary Agency Inc., Edite **131**; Larsen/Elizabeth Pomada Literary Agents, Michael **132**; Lasher Agency, The Maureen **133**; Lawyer's Literary Agency, Inc. **133**; Lazear Agency Incorporated **133**; Levine Literary Agency, Paul S. **135**; Lincoln Literary Agency, Ray **136**; Literary and Creative Artists, Inc. **137**; Literary Group, The **137**; Love Literary Agency, Nancy **141**; Lowenstein Associates **141**; Lownie Literary Agency Ltd., Andrew **142**; Mann Agency, Carol **143**; Marmur Associates, Ltd., Mildred **148**; McBride Literary Agency, Margret **148**; Morrison, Inc., Henry **151**; Mura Literary, Dee **152**; Naggar Literary Agency, Jean V. **153**; National Writers Literary Agency **153**; Nazor Literary Agency **154**; New England Publishing Associates Inc. **154**; Norma-Lewis Agency, The **155**; Paraview, Inc. **156**; Parks Agency, The Richard **156**; Picard, Literary Agent, Alison J. **158**; Popkin, Julie **159**; Preskill Literary Agency, Robert **159**; Rees Literary Agency, Helen **162**; Rein Books, Inc., Jody **162**; Rhodes Literary Agency, Jodie **162**; RLR Associates, Ltd. **169**; Robbins Office, Inc., The **170**; Rosenkranz Literary Agency, Rita **171**; Ross Literary Agency, The Gail **171**; Russell and Volkening **173**; Sanders & Associates, Victoria **174**; Schiavone Literary Agency, Inc. **175**; Schulman, A Literary Agency, Susan **175**; Seligman, Literary Agent, Lynn **177**; Seymour Agency, The **177**; Shepard Agency, The Robert **178**; Simmons Literary Agency, Jeffrey **179**; Singer Literary Agency Inc., Evelyn **179**; Snell Literary Agency, Michael **181**; Spieler Agency, The **182**; Spitzer Literary Agency, Philip G. **182**; Straus Agency, Inc., Robin **183**; Treimel NY, Scott **187**; United Tribes **190**; Venture Literary **191**; Weinstein Literary Management, Ted **196**; Witherspoon Associates, Inc. **197**; Zachary Shuster Harmsworth **199**

Health/Medicine: Agents Incorporated for Medical and Mental Health Professionals **77**; Ahearn Agency, Inc., The **78**; Allen Literary Agency, Linda **79**; Allred and Allred Literary Agents **79**; Amster Literary Enterprises, Betsy **80**; Baldi Literary Agency, Malaga **82**; Balkin Agency, Inc. **83**; Barrett Books Inc., Loretta **83**; Bent, Harvey Klinger, Inc., Jenny **84**; Bernstein & Associates, Inc., Pam **84**; Bernstein Literary Agency, Meredith **84**; Bleeker Street Associates, Inc. **85**; Book Deals, Inc. **86**; BookEnds, LLC **86**; Boston Literary Group, The **90**; Brandt & Hochman Literary Agents Inc. **91**; Briggs, M. Courtney **91**; Brown Ltd., Curtis **92**; Browne Ltd., Pema **93**; Buck Agency, Howard **93**; Bykofsky Associates, Inc. Sheree **94**; Carlisle & Company **94**; Carvainis Agency, Inc., Maria **94**; Casselman Literary Agency, Martha **95**; Castiglia Literary Agency **95**; Charlton Associates, James **95**; Clausen, Mays & Tahan, LLC **96**; Collin Literary Agency, Frances **97**; Congdon Associates Inc., Don **97**; Connor Literary Agency **98**; Coover Agency, The Doe **98**; Curtis Associates, Inc., Richard **99**; Cypher, The Cypher Agency, James R. **100**; Dawson Associates, Liza **101**; DeFiore and Company **101**; Dijkstra Literary Agency, Sandra **102**; Donnaud & Associates, Inc., Janis A. **103**; Donovan Literary, Jim **104**; Doyen Literary Services, Inc. **104**; Ducas, Robert **105**; Dunham Literary **105**; Dupree/Miller and Associates Inc. Literary **106**; Dystel Literary Management, Inc., Jane **106**; Ellenberg Literary Agency, Ethan **108**; Elmo Agency Inc., Ann **109**; Eth Literary Representation, Felicia **109**; Feigen/Parrent Literary Management **110**; Fernandez, Justin E. **111**; Flaming Star Literary Enterprises **111**; Fleury Agency, B.R. **112**; Fogelman Literary Agency **112**; Forthwrite Literary Agency **113**; Franklin Associates, Ltd., Lynn C. **114**; Fredericks Literary Agency, Jeanne **114**; Freymann Literary Agency, Sarah Jane **114**; Gartenberg, Literary Agent, Max **115**; Gislason Agency, The **115**; Goldfarb & Associates **116**; Goodman Associates **117**; Greenburger Associates, Inc., Sanford J. **118**;

Grosvenor Literary Agency, The **119**; Halsey North, Reece **120**; Hamilburg Agency, Mitchell J., The **120**; Hawkins & Associates, Inc., John **121**; Henshaw Group, Richard **122**; Herman Agency LLC, The Jeff **122**; Hill & Barlow Agency **123**; Hochmann Books, John L. **123**; Hornfischer Literary Management, Inc. **124**; J de S Associates Inc. **125**; Jabberwocky Literary Agency **125**; James Peter Associates, Inc. **125**; JCA Literary Agency **126**; Jordan Literary Agency, Lawrence **127**; Kern Literary Agency, Natasha **127**; Kleinman, Esq., Jeffrey M. **128**; Klinger, Inc., Harvey **129**; Knight Agency, The **129**; Konner Literary Agency, Linda **130**; Koster Literary Agency, LLC, Elaine **130**; Kouts, Literary Agent, Barbara S. **130**; Krages, Attorney at Law, Bert P. **131**; Kritzer Productions, Eddie **131**; Larsen/Elizabeth Pomada Literary Agents, Michael **132**; Lasher Agency, The Maureen **133**; Lazear Agency Incorporated **133**; Levine Communications, Inc., James **134**; Levine Literary Agency, Inc., Ellen **135**; Levine Literary Agency, Paul S. **135**; Lieberman Associates, Robert **136**; Limelight Management **136**; Lincoln Literary Agency, Ray **136**; Lipkind Agency, Wendy **137**; Literary and Creative Artists, Inc. **137**; Literary Group, The **137**; LitWest Group, LLC **140**; Livingston Cooke **140**; Love Literary Agency, Nancy **141**; Lowenstein Associates **141**; Mann Agency, Carol **143**; Manus & Associates Literary Agency, Inc. **143**; March Tenth, Inc. **147**; Marmur Associates, Ltd., Mildred **148**; McBride Literary Agency, Margret **148**; McGrath, Helen **149**; McHugh Literary Agency **149**; Menza Literary Agency, Claudia **149**; Michaels Literary Agency, Inc., Doris S. **150**; Millard Literary Agency, Martha **150**; Miller Agency, The **150**; Multimedia Product Development, Inc. **152**; Mura Literary, Dee **152**; Naggar Literary Agency, Jean V. **153**; New Brand Agency Group, LLC **154**; New England Publishing Associates Inc. **154**; Nine Muses and Apollo Inc. **155**; Norma-Lewis Agency, The **155**; Paraview, Inc. **156**; Parks Agency, The Richard **156**; Picard, Literary Agent, Alison J. **158**; Pine Associates, Inc., Arthur **159**; Protter Literary Agent, Susan Ann **160**; Quicksilver Books Literary Agents **161**; Rees Literary Agency, Helen **162**; Rein Books, Inc., Jody **162**; Rhodes Literary Agency, Jodie **162**; Rinaldi Literary Agency, Angela **166**; RLR Associates, Ltd. **169**; Robbins Literary Agency, B.J. **170**; Rosenkranz Literary Agency, Rita **171**; Ross Literary Agency, The Gail **171**; Roth, Literary Representation, Carol Susan **172**; Rotrosen Agency, LLC, Jane **172**; Russell and Volkening **173**; Schiavone Literary Agency, Inc. **175**; Schulman, A Literary Agency, Susan **175**; Sebastian Literary Agency **176**; Seligman, Literary Agent, Lynn **177**; Seymour Agency, The **177**; Singer Literary Agency Inc., Evelyn **179**; Smith Literary Agency Ltd., Robert **180**; Snell Literary Agency, Michael **181**; Spitzer Literary Agency, Philip G. **182**; Straus Agency, Inc., Robin **183**; Tabian/Literary Agent, Robert E. **185**; Teal Literary Agency, Patricia **185**; Trace Inc., The Tracy Sherrod Literary Agency **186**; Travis Literary Agency, Susan **186**; 2M Communications Ltd. **187**; United Tribes **190**; Ware Literary Agency, John A. **193**; Waterside Productions, Inc. **194**; Waxman Literary Agency **195**; Weinstein Literary Management, Ted **196**; Wieser & Wieser, Inc. **197**; Witherspoon Associates, Inc. **197**; Wonderland Press, Inc., The **197**; Writers House **198**; Zachary Shuster Harmsworth **199**; Zeckendorf Assoc. Inc., Susan **200**

History: Ahearn Agency, Inc., The **78**; Allen Literary Agency, Linda **79**; Allred and Allred Literary Agents **79**; Altair Literary Agency **80**; Altshuler Literary Agency, Miriam **80**; Amster Literary Enterprises, Betsy **80**; Authentic Creations Literary Agency **82**; Baldi Literary Agency, Malaga **82**; Balkin Agency, Inc. **83**; Barrett Books Inc., Loretta **83**; Bent, Harvey Klinger, Inc., Jenny **84**; Bial Agency, Daniel **84**; Black Literary Agency, David **85**; Bleeker Street Associates, Inc. **85**; Book Deals, Inc. **86**; Borchardt Inc., Georges **87**; Boston Literary Group, The **90**; Brandt & Hochman Literary Agents Inc. **91**; Brown Associates Inc., Marie **91**; Brown Literary Agency, Inc., Andrea **92**; Brown Ltd., Curtis **92**; Buck Agency, Howard **93**; Bykofsky Associates, Inc. Sheree **94**; Carlisle & Company **94**; Carvainis Agency, Inc., Maria **94**; Castiglia Literary Agency **95**; Clark Associates, William **96**; Clausen, Mays & Tahan, LLC **96**; Collin Literary Agency, Frances **97**; Congdon Associates Inc., Don **97**; Coover Agency, The Doe **98**; Curtis Associates, Inc., Richard **99**; Cypher, The Cypher Agency, James R. **100**; Dawson Associates, Liza **101**; Dijkstra Literary Agency, Sandra **102**; Donovan Literary, Jim **104**; Doyen Literary Services, Inc. **104**; Ducas, Robert **105**; Dunham Literary **105**; Dupree/Miller and Associates Inc. Literary **106**; Dystel Literary Management, Inc., Jane **106**; Educational Design Services, Inc. **107**; Ellenberg Literary Agency, Ethan **108**; Elmo Agency Inc., Ann **109**; Eth Literary Representation, Felicia **109**; Fernandez, Justin E. **111**; Fort Ross Inc. Russian-American Publishing Projects **113**; Forthwrite Literary Agency **113**; Franklin Associates, Ltd., Lynn C. **114**; Fredericks Literary Agency, Jeanne **114**; Freymann Literary Agency, Sarah Jane **114**; Gartenberg, Literary Agent, Max **115**; Goldfarb & Associates **116**; Goodman Associates **117**; Grace Literary Agency, Carroll **117**; Greenburger Associates, Inc., Sanford J. **118**; Gregory and Company Authors' Agents **118**; Grosvenor Literary Agency, The **119**; Halsey Agency, Reece **120**; Halsey North, Reece **120**; Hamilburg Agency, Mitchell J., The **120**; Hawkins & Associates, Inc., John **121**; Herman Agency LLC, The Jeff **122**; Hill & Barlow Agency **123**; Hochmann Books, John L. **123**; Hornfischer Literary Management, Inc. **124**; J de S Associates Inc. **125**; Jabberwocky Literary Agency **125**; James Peter Associates, Inc. **125**; JCA Literary Agency **126**; Jenks Agency, The **126**; Ketz Agency, Louise B. **127**; Kleinman,

Esq., Jeffrey M. **128**; Knight Agency, The **129**; Koster Literary Agency, LLC, Elaine **130**; Kouts, Literary Agent, Barbara S. **130**; Krages, Attorney at Law, Bert P. **131**; Larsen/Elizabeth Pomada Literary Agents, Michael **132**; Lasher Agency, The Maureen **133**; Lazear Agency Incorporated **133**; Levine Literary Agency, Inc., Ellen **135**; Levine Literary Agency, Paul S. **135**; Lincoln Literary Agency, Ray **136**; Lipkind Agency, Wendy **137**; Literary Group, The **137**; LitWest Group, LLC **140**; Love Literary Agency, Nancy **141**; Lowenstein Associates **141**; Lownie Literary Agency Ltd., Andrew **142**; Maccoby Agency, Gina **143**; Mann Agency, Carol **143**; March Tenth, Inc. **147**; Marmur Associates, Ltd., Mildred **148**; McBride Literary Agency, Margret **148**; McGrath, Helen **149**; McHugh Literary Agency **149**; Menza Literary Agency, Claudia **149**; Michaels Literary Agency, Inc., Doris S. **150**; Millard Literary Agency, Martha **150**; Morrison, Inc., Henry **151**; Mura Literary, Dee **152**; Naggar Literary Agency, Jean V. **153**; Nazor Literary Agency **154**; New England Publishing Associates Inc. **154**; Norma-Lewis Agency, The **155**; Paraview, Inc. **156**; Parks Agency, The Richard **156**; Pevner, Inc., Stephen **157**; Picard, Literary Agent, Alison J. **158**; Popkin, Julie **159**; Preskill Literary Agency, Robert **159**; Quicksilver Books Literary Agents **161**; Rabiner, Literary Agent, Inc., Susan **161**; Raymond, Literary Agent, Charlotte Cecil **161**; Rees Literary Agency, Helen **162**; Rein Books, Inc., Jody **162**; Rhodes Literary Agency, Jodie **162**; Rittenberg Literary Agency, Inc., Ann **166**; RLR Associates, Ltd. **169**; Roghaar Literary Agency, Inc., Linda **170**; Rosenkranz Literary Agency, Rita **171**; Russell and Volkening **173**; Sanders & Associates, Victoria **174**; Schiavone Literary Agency, Inc. **175**; Schulman, A Literary Agency, Susan **175**; Sebastian Literary Agency **176**; Sedgeband Literary Associates **177**; Seligman, Literary Agent, Lynn **177**; Seymour Agency, The **177**; Shepard Agency, The Robert **178**; Simmons Literary Agency, Jeffrey **179**; Snell Literary Agency, Michael **181**; Spieler Agency, The **182**; Spitzer Literary Agency, Philip G. **182**; Straus Agency, Inc., Robin **183**; Tabian/Literary Agent, Robert E. **185**; Treimel NY, Scott **187**; United Tribes **190**; Van Der Leun & Associates **191**; Venture Literary **191**; Viciananza, Ltd., Ralph **192**; Vines Agency, Inc., The **192**; Wald Associates, Inc., Mary Jack **192**; Wales, Literary Agency, Inc. **193**; Ware Literary Agency, John A. **193**; Watkins Loomis Agency, Inc. **194**; Waxman Literary Agency **195**; Wecksler-Incomco **195**; Weinstein Literary Management, Ted **196**; Whittaker, Literary Agent, Lynn **196**; Wieser & Wieser, Inc. **197**; Witherspoon Associates, Inc. **197**; Wonderland Press, Inc., The **197**; Writers House **198**; Zachary Shuster Harmsworth **199**; Zeckendorf Assoc. Inc., Susan **200**

How-to: ABS Literary Agency, Inc. **76**; Alive Communications, Inc. **78**; Allred and Allred Literary Agents **79**; Authentic Creations Literary Agency **82**; Balkin Agency, Inc. **83**; Barrett Books Inc., Loretta **83**; Bernstein & Associates, Inc., Pam **84**; Bial Agency, Daniel **84**; Bleeker Street Associates, Inc. **85**; Book Deals, Inc. **86**; BookEnds, LLC **86**; Brown Literary Agency, Inc., Andrea **92**; Brown Ltd., Curtis **92**; Browne Ltd., Pema **93**; Bykofsky Associates, Inc. Sheree **94**; Charlton Associates, James **95**; Clausen, Mays & Tahan, LLC **96**; Connor Literary Agency **98**; Core Creations **98**; Curtis Associates, Inc., Richard **99**; Cypher, The Cypher Agency, James R. **100**; Doyen Literary Services, Inc. **104**; Dupree/Miller and Associates Inc. Literary **106**; Elmo Agency Inc., Ann **109**; Feigen/Parrent Literary Management **110**; Fernandez, Justin E. **111**; Fleury Agency, B.R. **112**; Forthwrite Literary Agency **113**; Fredericks Literary Agency, Jeanne **114**; Greenburger Associates, Inc., Sanford J. **118**; Grosvenor Literary Agency, The **119**; Hamilburg Agency, Mitchell J., The **120**; Hawkins & Associates, Inc., John **121**; Henshaw Group, Richard **122**; Herman Agency LLC, The Jeff **122**; Hornfischer Literary Management, Inc. **124**; Kleinman, Esq., Jeffrey M. **128**; Knight Agency, The **129**; Konner Literary Agency, Linda **130**; Koster Literary Agency, LLC, Elaine **130**; Krages, Attorney at Law, Bert P. **131**; Kritzer Productions, Eddie **131**; Larsen/Elizabeth Pomada Literary Agents, Michael **132**; Lasher Agency, The Maureen **133**; Lazear Agency Incorporated **133**; Levine Literary Agency, Paul S. **135**; Literary and Creative Artists, Inc. **137**; Literary Group, The **137**; LitWest Group, LLC **140**; Love Literary Agency, Nancy **141**; Lowenstein Associates **141**; Manus & Associates Literary Agency, Inc. **143**; McBride Literary Agency, Margret **148**; McGrath, Helen **149**; McHugh Literary Agency **149**; Millard Literary Agency, Martha **150**; Multimedia Product Development, Inc. **152**; Mura Literary, Dee **152**; National Writers Literary Agency **153**; Nazor Literary Agency **154**; Paraview, Inc. **156**; Parks Agency, The Richard **156**; Picard, Literary Agent, Alison J. **158**; Preskill Literary Agency, Robert **159**; Quicksilver Books Literary Agents **161**; Rein Books, Inc., Jody **162**; Robbins Literary Agency, B.J. **170**; Rosenkranz Literary Agency, Rita **171**; Rotrosen Agency, LLC, Jane **172**; Scherf, Inc., Literary Properties **174**; Schiavone Literary Agency, Inc. **175**; Schulman, A Literary Agency, Susan **175**; Seligman, Literary Agent, Lynn **177**; Seymour Agency, The **177**; Singer Literary Agency Inc., Evelyn **179**; Snell Literary Agency, Michael **181**; Swayne Agency Literary Management & Consulting, Inc., The **184**; Tabian/Literary Agent, Robert E. **185**; Teal Literary Agency, Patricia **185**; Travis Literary Agency, Susan **186**; United Tribes **190**; Vines Agency, Inc., The **192**; Watt & Associates, Sandra **194**; Wonderland Press, Inc., The **197**; Wylie-Merrick Literary Agency **199**; Zachary Shuster Harmsworth **199**

Humor: Allred and Allred Literary Agents **79**; Barrett Books Inc., Loretta **83**; Bial Agency, Daniel **84**; BookEnds, LLC **86**; Books & Such **87**; Brown Ltd., Curtis **92**; Buck Agency, Howard **93**; Bykofsky Associates, Inc. Sheree **94**; Charlton Associates, James **95**; Clausen, Mays & Tahan, LLC **96**; Congdon Associates Inc., Don **97**; Connor Literary Agency **98**; Core Creations **98**; Curtis Associates, Inc., Richard **99**; Donnaud & Associates, Inc., Janis A. **103**; Doyen Literary Services, Inc. **104**; Dupree/Miller and Associates Inc. Literary **106**; Dystel Literary Management, Inc., Jane **106**; Fernandez, Justin E. **111**; Fleury Agency, B.R. **112**; Goldfarb & Associates **116**; Greenburger Associates, Inc., Sanford J. **118**; Grosjean Literary Agency, Jill **119**; Hamilburg Agency, Mitchell J., The **120**; Hawkins & Associates, Inc., John **121**; Henshaw Group, Richard **122**; Hornfischer Literary Management, Inc. **124**; Jabberwocky Literary Agency **125**; Kleinman, Esq., Jeffrey M. **128**; Kritzer Productions, Eddie **131**; Larsen/Elizabeth Pomada Literary Agents, Michael **132**; Lazear Agency Incorporated **133**; Levine Literary Agency, Paul S. **135**; Literary Group, The **137**; LitWest Group, LLC **140**; Lowenstein Associates **141**; March Tenth, Inc. **147**; Multimedia Product Development, Inc. **152**; Mura Literary, Dee **152**; New Brand Agency Group, LLC **154**; Paraview, Inc. **156**; Parks Agency, The Richard **156**; Pevner, Inc., Stephen **157**; Picard, Literary Agent, Alison J. **158**; Preskill Literary Agency, Robert **159**; Rein Books, Inc., Jody **162**; RLR Associates, Ltd. **169**; Robbins Literary Agency, B.J. **170**; Rosenkranz Literary Agency, Rita **171**; Rotrosen Agency, LLC, Jane **172**; Sanders & Associates, Victoria **174**; Schiavone Literary Agency, Inc. **175**; Seligman, Literary Agent, Lynn **177**; Snell Literary Agency, Michael **181**; Treimel NY, Scott **187**; Vines Agency, Inc., The **192**; Waterside Productions, Inc. **194**; Watt & Associates, Sandra **194**

Interior Design/Decorating: Allred and Allred Literary Agents **79**; Baldi Literary Agency, Malaga **82**; Barrett Books Inc., Loretta **83**; Brown Ltd., Curtis **92**; Bykofsky Associates, Inc. Sheree **94**; Connor Literary Agency **98**; Curtis Associates, Inc., Richard **99**; Doyen Literary Services, Inc. **104**; Dupree/Miller and Associates Inc. Literary **106**; Fernandez, Justin E. **111**; Forthwrite Literary Agency **113**; Fredericks Literary Agency, Jeanne **114**; Freymann Literary Agency, Sarah Jane **114**; Greenburger Associates, Inc., Sanford J. **118**; Grosjean Literary Agency, Jill **119**; Hamilburg Agency, Mitchell J., The **120**; Hawkins & Associates, Inc., John **121**; Kleinman, Esq., Jeffrey M. **128**; Larsen/Elizabeth Pomada Literary Agents, Michael **132**; Lazear Agency Incorporated **133**; Levine Literary Agency, Paul S. **135**; Limelight Management **136**; Lincoln Literary Agency, Ray **136**; Paraview, Inc. **156**; Preskill Literary Agency, Robert **159**; RLR Associates, Ltd. **169**; Rosenkranz Literary Agency, Rita **171**; Seligman, Literary Agent, Lynn **177**; Seymour Agency, The **177**; Snell Literary Agency, Michael **181**; Wonderland Press, Inc., The **197**; Writers House **198**

Juvenile Nonfiction: Allred and Allred Literary Agents **79**; Books & Such **87**; Briggs, M. Courtney **91**; Brown Associates Inc., Marie **91**; Brown Literary Agency, Inc., Andrea **92**; Brown Ltd., Curtis **92**; Browne Ltd., Pema **93**; Curtis Associates, Inc., Richard **99**; Doyen Literary Services, Inc. **104**; Dunham Literary **105**; Dupree/Miller and Associates Inc. Literary **106**; Dwyer & O'Grady, Inc. **106**; Elek Associates, Peter **107**; Fernandez, Justin E. **111**; Flannery Literary **111**; Greenburger Associates, Inc., Sanford J. **118**; Hamilburg Agency, Mitchell J., The **120**; Hawkins & Associates, Inc., John **121**; Kouts, Literary Agent, Barbara S. **130**; Lazear Agency Incorporated **133**; Lincoln Literary Agency, Ray **136**; Literary Group, The **137**; Maccoby Agency, Gina **143**; Markowitz Literary Agency, Barbara **147**; Millard Literary Agency, Martha **150**; Morrison, Inc., Henry **151**; Multimedia Product Development, Inc. **152**; Mura Literary, Dee **152**; Naggar Literary Agency, Jean V. **153**; New Brand Agency Group, LLC **154**; Norma-Lewis Agency, The **155**; Paraview, Inc. **156**; Picard, Literary Agent, Alison J. **158**; Schiavone Literary Agency, Inc. **175**; Schulman, A Literary Agency, Susan **175**; Seymour Agency, The **177**; Singer Literary Agency Inc., Evelyn **179**; Snell Literary Agency, Michael **181**; Tobias, A Literary Agency for Chilren's Books, Ann **186**; Treimel NY, Scott **187**; Wald Associates, Inc., Mary Jack **192**; Wecksler-Incomco **195**; Writers House **198**; Wylie-Merrick Literary Agency **199**

Language/Literature/Criticism: Acacia House Publishing Services Ltd. **76**; Allred and Allred Literary Agents **79**; Altshuler Literary Agency, Miriam **80**; Baldi Literary Agency, Malaga **82**; Balkin Agency, Inc. **83**; Barrett Books Inc., Loretta **83**; Bial Agency, Daniel **84**; Brown Ltd., Curtis **92**; Buck Agency, Howard **93**; Bykofsky Associates, Inc. Sheree **94**; Castiglia Literary Agency **95**; Congdon Associates Inc., Don **97**; Connor Literary Agency **98**; Coover Agency, The Doe **98**; Curtis Associates, Inc., Richard **99**; Cypher, The Cypher Agency, James R. **100**; Dijkstra Literary Agency, Sandra **102**; Doyen Literary Services, Inc. **104**; Dunham Literary **105**; Dupree/Miller and Associates Inc. Literary **106**; Educational Design Services, Inc. **107**; Fernandez, Justin E. **111**; Goldfarb & Associates **116**; Goodman Associates **117**; Greenburger Associates, Inc., Sanford J. **118**; Grosvenor Literary Agency, The **119**; Halsey Agency, Reece **120**; Hamilburg Agency, Mitchell J., The **120**; Hawkins & Associates, Inc., John **121**; Hill & Barlow Agency **123**; Hill Bonnie Nadell, Inc., Frederick

123; Jabberwocky Literary Agency **125**; James Peter Associates, Inc. **125**; JCA Literary Agency **126**; Jenks Agency, The **126**; Kleinman, Esq., Jeffrey M. **128**; Lazear Agency Incorporated **133**; Levine Literary Agency, Paul S. **135**; Lincoln Literary Agency, Ray **136**; Literary Group, The **137**; Lowenstein Associates **141**; March Tenth, Inc. **147**; Miller Agency, The **150**; New England Publishing Associates Inc. **154**; Nine Muses and Apollo Inc. **155**; Paraview, Inc. **156**; Parks Agency, The Richard **156**; Pevner, Inc., Stephen **157**; Preskill Literary Agency, Robert **159**; Quicksilver Books Literary Agents **161**; RLR Associates, Ltd. **169**; Robbins Office, Inc., The **170**; Rosenkranz Literary Agency, Rita **171**; Russell and Volkening **173**; Sanders & Associates, Victoria **174**; Schiavone Literary Agency, Inc. **175**; Seligman, Literary Agent, Lynn **177**; Seymour Agency, The **177**; Simmons Literary Agency, Jeffrey **179**; Snell Literary Agency, Michael **181**; Spitzer Literary Agency, Philip G. **182**; Straus Agency, Inc., Robin **183**; Treimel NY, Scott **187**; United Tribes **190**; Wald Associates, Inc., Mary Jack **192**; Ware Literary Agency, John A. **193**; Watt & Associates, Sandra **194**; Whittaker, Literary Agent, Lynn **196**; Wonderland Press, Inc., The **197**; Zachary Shuster Harmsworth **199**

Memoirs: Acacia House Publishing Services Ltd. **76**; Altshuler Literary Agency, Miriam **80**; Baldi Literary Agency, Malaga **82**; Barrett Books Inc., Loretta **83**; Bial Agency, Daniel **84**; Black Literary Agency, David **85**; Bleeker Street Associates, Inc. **85**; BookEnds, LLC **86**; Borchardt Inc., Georges **87**; Brown Ltd., Curtis **92**; Buck Agency, Howard **93**; Bykofsky Associates, Inc. Sheree **94**; Carlisle & Company **94**; Carvainis Agency, Inc., Maria **94**; Clark Associates, William **96**; Clausen, Mays & Tahan, LLC **96**; Congdon Associates Inc., Don **97**; Coover Agency, The Doe **98**; Curtis Associates, Inc., Richard **99**; Cypher, The Cypher Agency, James R. **100**; Dawson Associates, Liza **101**; Doyen Literary Services, Inc. **104**; Ducas, Robert **105**; Dupree/Miller and Associates Inc. Literary **106**; Feigen/Parrent Literary Management **110**; Fernandez, Justin E. **111**; Fort Ross Inc. Russian-American Publishing Projects **113**; Franklin Associates, Ltd., Lynn C. **114**; Freymann Literary Agency, Sarah Jane **114**; Goldfarb & Associates **116**; Goodman Associates **117**; Greenburger Associates, Inc., Sanford J. **118**; Hamilburg Agency, Mitchell J., The **120**; Hawkins & Associates, Inc., John **121**; Hornfischer Literary Management, Inc. **124**; James Peter Associates, Inc. **125**; JCA Literary Agency **126**; Jordan Literary Agency, Lawrence **127**; Larsen/Elizabeth Pomada Literary Agents, Michael **132**; Lazear Agency Incorporated **133**; Levine Literary Agency, Inc., Ellen **135**; Levine Literary Agency, Paul S. **135**; Lieberman Associates, Robert **136**; Literary and Creative Artists, Inc. **137**; Literary Group, The **137**; LitWest Group, LLC **140**; Love Literary Agency, Nancy **141**; Lowenstein Associates **141**; Lownie Literary Agency Ltd., Andrew **142**; Manus & Associates Literary Agency, Inc. **143**; McHugh Literary Agency **149**; Michaels Literary Agency, Inc., Doris S. **150**; Millard Literary Agency, Martha **150**; Multimedia Product Development, Inc. **152**; Mura Literary, Dee **152**; Naggar Literary Agency, Jean V. **153**; New Brand Agency Group, LLC **154**; Paraview, Inc. **156**; Parks Agency, The Richard **156**; Pevner, Inc., Stephen **157**; Picard, Literary Agent, Alison J. **158**; Preskill Literary Agency, Robert **159**; Protter Literary Agent, Susan Ann **160**; Quicksilver Books Literary Agents **161**; Rhodes Literary Agency, Jodie **162**; Rittenberg Literary Agency, Inc., Ann **166**; RLR Associates, Ltd. **169**; Robbins Literary Agency, B.J. **170**; Robbins Office, Inc., The **170**; Rosenberg Group, The **170**; Seymour Agency, The **177**; Simmons Literary Agency, Jeffrey **179**; Smith Literary Agency Ltd., Robert **180**; Snell Literary Agency, Michael **181**; Spieler Agency, The **182**; Susijn Agency, The **184**; Treimel NY, Scott **187**; 2M Communications Ltd. **187**; United Tribes **190**; Van Der Leun & Associates **191**; Venture Literary **191**; Vines Agency, Inc., The **192**; Wales, Literary Agency, Inc. **193**; Watt & Associates, Sandra **194**; Weingel-Fidel Agency, The **196**; Whittaker, Literary Agent, Lynn **196**; Witherspoon Associates, Inc. **197**; Zachary Shuster Harmsworth **199**

Military/War: Acacia House Publishing Services Ltd. **76**; Allred and Allred Literary Agents **79**; Barrett Books Inc., Loretta **83**; Bial Agency, Daniel **84**; Black Literary Agency, David **85**; Bleeker Street Associates, Inc. **85**; Boston Literary Group, The **90**; Brown Ltd., Curtis **92**; Browne Ltd., Pema **93**; Buck Agency, Howard **93**; Bykofsky Associates, Inc. Sheree **94**; Charlton Associates, James **95**; Circle of Confusion Ltd.; Congdon Associates Inc., Don **97**; Curtis Associates, Inc., Richard **99**; Dijkstra Literary Agency, Sandra **102**; Donovan Literary, Jim **104**; Doyen Literary Services, Inc. **104**; Ducas, Robert **105**; Dupree/Miller and Associates Inc. Literary **106**; Dystel Literary Management, Inc., Jane **106**; Educational Design Services, Inc. **107**; Ellenberg Literary Agency, Ethan **108**; Fernandez, Justin E. **111**; Flaherty, Literary Agent, Joyce A.; Gartenberg, Literary Agent, Max **115**; Goldfarb & Associates **116**; Goodman Associates **117**; Greenburger Associates, Inc., Sanford J. **118**; Grosvenor Literary Agency, The **119**; Gusay Literary Agency, The Charlotte; Hamilburg Agency, Mitchell J., The **120**; Harris Literary Agency, Inc., The Joy; Hawkins & Associates, Inc., John **121**; Henshaw Group, Richard **122**; Hochmann Books, John L. **123**; Hoffman Literary Agency, Berenice; Hornfischer Literary Management, Inc. **124**; J de S Associates Inc. **125**; Jabberwocky Literary Agency **125**; James Peter Associates, Inc. **125**; JCA Literary Agency **126**; Ketz Agency, Louise B. **127**; Krages, Attorney at Law, Bert P. **131**; Lake Agency, The Candace; Lazear Agency Incorporated **133**;

Levine Literary Agency, Paul S. **135**; Literary Group, The **137**; LitWest Group, LLC **140**; Lownie Literary Agency Ltd., Andrew **142**; McGrath, Helen **149**; McHugh Literary Agency **149**; Madsen Agency, Robert; Mura Literary, Dee **152**; New England Publishing Associates Inc. **154**; Paraview, Inc. **156**; Parks Agency, The Richard **156**; Pelter, Rodney; Picard, Literary Agent, Alison J. **158**; Preskill Literary Agency, Robert **159**; Rhodes Literary Agency, Jodie **162**; Rosenkranz Literary Agency, Rita **171**; Russell and Volkening **173**; Schiavone Literary Agency, Inc. **175**; Seymour Agency, The **177**; Shapiro-Lichtman; Sherman & Associates, Ken; Snell Literary Agency, Michael **181**; Spitzer Literary Agency, Philip G. **182**; Treimel NY, Scott **187**; Venture Literary **191**; Vines Agency, Inc., The **192**; Visionary Entertainment; Writers House **198**

Money/Finance/Economics:
Altair Literary Agency **80**; Amster Literary Enterprises, Betsy **80**; Baldi Literary Agency, Malaga **82**; Barrett Books Inc., Loretta **83**; Bial Agency, Daniel **84**; Black Literary Agency, David **85**; Bleeker Street Associates, Inc. **85**; Book Deals, Inc. **86**; BookEnds, LLC **86**; Boston Literary Group, The **90**; Brown Ltd., Curtis **92**; Browne Ltd., Pema **93**; Buck Agency, Howard **93**; Bykofsky Associates, Inc. Sheree **94**; Castiglia Literary Agency **95**; Clausen, Mays & Tahan, LLC **96**; Connor Literary Agency **98**; Coover Agency, The Doe **98**; Curtis Associates, Inc., Richard **99**; Cypher, The Cypher Agency, James R. **100**; DeFiore and Company **101**; Dijkstra Literary Agency, Sandra **102**; Donovan Literary, Jim **104**; Doyen Literary Services, Inc. **104**; Ducas, Robert **105**; Dupree/Miller and Associates Inc. Literary **106**; Dystel Literary Management, Inc., Jane **106**; Educational Design Services, Inc. **107**; Elmo Agency Inc., Ann **109**; Feigen/Parrent Literary Management **110**; Fernandez, Justin E. **111**; Fleury Agency, B.R. **112**; Fredericks Literary Agency, Jeanne **114**; Gartenberg, Literary Agent, Max **115**; Goldfarb & Associates **116**; Goodman Associates **117**; Greenburger Associates, Inc., Sanford J. **118**; Grosvenor Literary Agency, The **119**; Hamilburg Agency, Mitchell J., The **120**; Hartline Literary Agency **121**; Hawkins & Associates, Inc., John **121**; Henshaw Group, Richard **122**; Hill & Barlow Agency **123**; Hornfischer Literary Management, Inc. **124**; Jabberwocky Literary Agency **125**; James Peter Associates, Inc. **125**; JCA Literary Agency **126**; Kern Literary Agency, Natasha **127**; Kleinman, Esq., Jeffrey M. **128**; Knight Agency, The **129**; Konner Literary Agency, Linda **130**; Koster Literary Agency, LLC, Elaine **130**; Krages, Attorney at Law, Bert P. **131**; Larsen/Elizabeth Pomada Literary Agents, Michael **132**; Lazear Agency Incorporated **133**; Levine Communications, Inc., James **134**; Levine Literary Agency, Paul S. **135**; Lieberman Associates, Robert **136**; Lincoln Literary Agency, Ray **136**; Literary Group, The **137**; LitWest Group, LLC **140**; Lowenstein Associates **141**; Mann Agency, Carol **143**; Manus & Associates Literary Agency, Inc. **143**; Marmur Associates, Ltd., Mildred **148**; McBride Literary Agency, Margret **148**; McHugh Literary Agency **149**; Millard Literary Agency, Martha **150**; Multimedia Product Development, Inc. **152**; Mura Literary, Dee **152**; New England Publishing Associates Inc. **154**; Paraview, Inc. **156**; Parks Agency, The Richard **156**; Paton Literary Agency, Kathi J. **157**; Picard, Literary Agent, Alison J. **158**; Pine Associates, Inc., Arthur **159**; Preskill Literary Agency, Robert **159**; Rees Literary Agency, Helen **162**; Rinaldi Literary Agency, Angela **166**; RLR Associates, Ltd. **169**; Rosenkranz Literary Agency, Rita **171**; Ross Literary Agency, The Gail **171**; Roth, Literary Representation, Carol Susan **172**; Rotrosen Agency, LLC, Jane **172**; Russell and Volkening **173**; Scherf, Inc., Literary Properties **174**; Schulman, A Literary Agency, Susan **175**; Sebastian Literary Agency **176**; Seligman, Literary Agent, Lynn **177**; Seymour Agency, The **177**; Shepard Agency, The Robert **178**; Singer Literary Agency Inc., Evelyn **179**; Snell Literary Agency, Michael **181**; Spieler Agency, The **182**; United Tribes **190**; Venture Literary **191**; Vines Agency, Inc., The **192**; Waterside Productions, Inc. **194**; Waxman Literary Agency **195**; Whittaker, Literary Agent, Lynn **196**; Wieser & Wieser, Inc. **197**; Witherspoon Associates, Inc. **197**; Writers House **198**; Zachary Shuster Harmsworth **199**

Music/Dance:
Acacia House Publishing Services Ltd. **76**; Ahearn Agency, Inc., The **78**; Allred and Allred Literary Agents **79**; Altshuler Literary Agency, Miriam **80**; Andrews & Associates, Bart **81**; Baldi Literary Agency, Malaga **82**; Balkin Agency, Inc. **83**; Barrett Books Inc., Loretta **83**; Bial Agency, Daniel **84**; Brown Associates Inc., Marie **91**; Brown Ltd., Curtis **92**; Buck Agency, Howard **93**; Bykofsky Associates, Inc. Sheree **94**; Clark Associates, William **96**; Congdon Associates Inc., Don **97**; Curtis Associates, Inc., Richard **99**; Cypher, The Cypher Agency, James R. **100**; Donovan Literary, Jim **104**; Doyen Literary Services, Inc. **104**; Dunham Literary **105**; Dupree/Miller and Associates Inc. Literary **106**; Elmo Agency Inc., Ann **109**; Farber Literary Agency Inc. **110**; Fernandez, Justin E. **111**; Gartenberg, Literary Agent, Max **115**; Goodman Associates **117**; Greenburger Associates, Inc., Sanford J. **118**; Grosvenor Literary Agency, The **119**; Hamilburg Agency, Mitchell J., The **120**; Hawkins & Associates, Inc., John **121**; Henshaw Group, Richard **122**; Hill & Barlow Agency **123**; Hochmann Books, John L. **123**; Jabberwocky Literary Agency **125**; James Peter Associates, Inc. **125**; JCA Literary Agency **126**; Kleinman, Esq., Jeffrey M. **128**; Knight Agency, The **129**; Kouts, Literary Agent, Barbara S. **130**; Larsen/Elizabeth Pomada Literary Agents, Michael **132**; Lazear Agency Incorporated **133**; Levine Literary Agency, Paul S. **135**; Lieberman Associates, Robert **136**;

Lincoln Literary Agency, Ray **136**; Literary Group, The **137**; Lowenstein Associates **141**; Lownie Literary Agency Ltd., Andrew **142**; March Tenth, Inc. **147**; Markowitz Literary Agency, Barbara **147**; Marmur Associates, Ltd., Mildred **148**; McBride Literary Agency, Margret **148**; Menza Literary Agency, Claudia **149**; Michaels Literary Agency, Inc., Doris S. **150**; Millard Literary Agency, Martha **150**; Nazor Literary Agency **154**; Norma-Lewis Agency, The **155**; Paraview, Inc. **156**; Parks Agency, The Richard **156**; Pevner, Inc., Stephen **157**; Picard, Literary Agent, Alison J. **158**; Preskill Literary Agency, Robert **159**; Rein Books, Inc., Jody **162**; RLR Associates, Ltd. **169**; Robbins Literary Agency, B.J. **170**; Rosenkranz Literary Agency, Rita **171**; Rubie Literary Agency, The Peter **173**; Russell and Volkening **173**; Sanders & Associates, Victoria **174**; Schulman, A Literary Agency, Susan **175**; Seligman, Literary Agent, Lynn **177**; Seymour Agency, The **177**; Simmons Literary Agency, Jeffrey **179**; Smith Literary Agency Ltd., Robert **180**; Snell Literary Agency, Michael **181**; Spieler Agency, The **182**; Spitzer Literary Agency, Philip G. **182**; Straus Agency, Inc., Robin **183**; Treimel NY, Scott **187**; 2M Communications Ltd. **187**; United Tribes **190**; Venture Literary **191**; Wald Associates, Inc., Mary Jack **192**; Ware Literary Agency, John A. **193**; Wecksler-Incomco **195**; Weingel-Fidel Agency, The **196**; Witherspoon Associates, Inc. **197**; Writers House **198**; Zachary Shuster Harmsworth **199**; Zeckendorf Assoc. Inc., Susan **200**

Nature/Environment: Acacia House Publishing Services Ltd. **76**; Altshuler Literary Agency, Miriam **80**; Baldi Literary Agency, Malaga **82**; Balkin Agency, Inc. **83**; Barrett Books Inc., Loretta **83**; Bial Agency, Daniel **84**; Bleeker Street Associates, Inc. **85**; Boston Literary Group, The **90**; Brandt & Hochman Literary Agents Inc. **91**; Brown Literary Agency, Inc., Andrea **92**; Brown Ltd., Curtis **92**; Browne Ltd., Pema **93**; Buck Agency, Howard **93**; Bykofsky Associates, Inc. Sheree **94**; Castiglia Literary Agency **95**; Collin Literary Agency, Frances **97**; Congdon Associates Inc., Don **97**; Coover Agency, The Doe **98**; Curtis Associates, Inc., Richard **99**; Cypher, The Cypher Agency, James R. **100**; Dijkstra Literary Agency, Sandra **102**; Donovan Literary, Jim **104**; Doyen Literary Services, Inc. **104**; Ducas, Robert **105**; Dunham Literary **105**; Dupree/Miller and Associates Inc. Literary **106**; Elek Associates, Peter **107**; Eth Literary Representation, Felicia **109**; Fernandez, Justin E. **111**; Flaming Star Literary Enterprises **111**; Forthwrite Literary Agency **113**; Fredericks Literary Agency, Jeanne **114**; Freymann Literary Agency, Sarah Jane **114**; Gartenberg, Literary Agent, Max **115**; Goldfarb & Associates **116**; Goodman Associates **117**; Greenburger Associates, Inc., Sanford J. **118**; Grosjean Literary Agency, Jill **119**; Grosvenor Literary Agency, The **119**; Hamilburg Agency, Mitchell J., The **120**; Hawkins & Associates, Inc., John **121**; Henshaw Group, Richard **122**; Hill & Barlow Agency **123**; Hornfischer Literary Management, Inc. **124**; Jabberwocky Literary Agency **125**; JCA Literary Agency **126**; Jenks Agency, The **126**; Kern Literary Agency, Natasha **127**; Kleinman, Esq., Jeffrey M. **128**; Koster Literary Agency, LLC, Elaine **130**; Kouts, Literary Agent, Barbara S. **130**; Krages, Attorney at Law, Bert P. **131**; Larsen/Elizabeth Pomada Literary Agents, Michael **132**; Lasher Agency, The Maureen **133**; Lazear Agency Incorporated **133**; Levine Communications, Inc., James **134**; Levine Literary Agency, Paul S. **135**; Lieberman Associates, Robert **136**; Limelight Management **136**; Lincoln Literary Agency, Ray **136**; Literary Group, The **137**; Love Literary Agency, Nancy **141**; Lowenstein Associates **141**; Manus & Associates Literary Agency, Inc. **143**; Markowitz Literary Agency, Barbara **147**; Marmur Associates, Ltd., Mildred **148**; McHugh Literary Agency **149**; Multimedia Product Development, Inc. **152**; Mura Literary, Dee **152**; Nazor Literary Agency **154**; New England Publishing Associates Inc. **154**; Norma-Lewis Agency, The **155**; Paraview, Inc. **156**; Parks Agency, The Richard **156**; Paton Literary Agency, Kathi J. **157**; Picard, Literary Agent, Alison J. **158**; Preskill Literary Agency, Robert **159**; Quicksilver Books Literary Agents **161**; Raymond, Literary Agent, Charlotte Cecil **161**; Rein Books, Inc., Jody **162**; RLR Associates, Ltd. **169**; Roghaar Literary Agency, Inc., Linda **170**; Rosenkranz Literary Agency, Rita **171**; Ross Literary Agency, The Gail **171**; Rotrosen Agency, LLC, Jane **172**; Russell and Volkening **173**; Schiavone Literary Agency, Inc. **175**; Schulman, A Literary Agency, Susan **175**; Seligman, Literary Agent, Lynn **177**; Seymour Agency, The **177**; Singer Literary Agency Inc., Evelyn **179**; Snell Literary Agency, Michael **181**; Spieler Agency, The **182**; Spitzer Literary Agency, Philip G. **182**; Straus Agency, Inc., Robin **183**; United Tribes **190**; Venture Literary **191**; Vines Agency, Inc., The **192**; Wald Associates, Inc., Mary Jack **192**; Wales, Literary Agency, Inc. **193**; Ware Literary Agency, John A. **193**; Waterside Productions, Inc. **194**; Watkins Loomis Agency, Inc. **194**; Watt & Associates, Sandra **194**; Wecksler-Incomco **195**; Whittaker, Literary Agent, Lynn **196**; Wieser & Wieser, Inc. **197**; Writers House **198**

New Age/Metaphysics: Allred and Allred Literary Agents **79**; Barrett Books Inc., Loretta **83**; Bial Agency, Daniel **84**; Bleeker Street Associates, Inc. **85**; BookEnds, LLC **86**; Brown Ltd., Curtis **92**; Browne Ltd., Pema **93**; Bykofsky Associates, Inc. Sheree **94**; Castiglia Literary Agency **95**; Curtis Associates, Inc., Richard **99**; Doyen Literary Services, Inc. **104**; Dupree/Miller and Associates Inc. Literary **106**; Dystel Literary Management, Inc., Jane **106**; Ellenberg Literary Agency, Ethan **108**; Fernandez, Justin E. **111**; Flaming Star Literary Enterprises **111**; Fleury Agency, B.R. **112**; Franklin

Associates, Ltd., Lynn C. **114**; Gislason Agency, The **115**; Greenburger Associates, Inc., Sanford J. **118**; Grosvenor Literary Agency, The **119**; Hamilburg Agency, Mitchell J., The **120**; Hawkins & Associates, Inc., John **121**; Henshaw Group, Richard **122**; Hill & Barlow Agency **123**; J de S Associates Inc. **125**; Kern Literary Agency, Natasha **127**; Koster Literary Agency, LLC, Elaine **130**; Larsen/Elizabeth Pomada Literary Agents, Michael **132**; Lazear Agency Incorporated **133**; Levine Communications, Inc., James **134**; Levine Literary Agency, Paul S. **135**; Limelight Management **136**; Love Literary Agency, Nancy **141**; Lowenstein Associates **141**; Millard Literary Agency, Martha **150**; Miller Agency, The **150**; Naggar Literary Agency, Jean V. **153**; New Brand Agency Group, LLC **154**; Paraview, Inc. **156**; Pevner, Inc., Stephen **157**; Picard, Literary Agent, Alison J. **158**; Quicksilver Books Literary Agents **161**; Rosenkranz Literary Agency, Rita **171**; Roth, Literary Representation, Carol Susan **172**; Schulman, A Literary Agency, Susan **175**; Smith Literary Agency Ltd., Robert **180**; Snell Literary Agency, Michael **181**; Vines Agency, Inc., The **192**; Watt & Associates, Sandra **194**

Philosophy: Barrett Books Inc., Loretta **83**; Brown Ltd., Curtis **92**; Buck Agency, Howard **93**; Bykofsky Associates, Inc. Sheree **94**; Curtis Associates, Inc., Richard **99**; Doyen Literary Services, Inc. **104**; Dupree/Miller and Associates Inc. Literary **106**; Fernandez, Justin E. **111**; Goodman Associates **117**; Greenburger Associates, Inc., Sanford J. **118**; Hamilburg Agency, Mitchell J., The **120**; Hawkins & Associates, Inc., John **121**; Lazear Agency Incorporated **133**; Literary and Creative Artists, Inc. **137**; Paraview, Inc. **156**; Popkin, Julie **159**; Seymour Agency, The **177**; Snell Literary Agency, Michael **181**; Treimel NY, Scott **187**

Photography: Allred and Allred Literary Agents **79**; Baldi Literary Agency, Malaga **82**; Barrett Books Inc., Loretta **83**; Boston Literary Group, The **90**; Brown Literary Agency, Inc., Andrea **92**; Brown Ltd., Curtis **92**; Buck Agency, Howard **93**; Bykofsky Associates, Inc. Sheree **94**; Connor Literary Agency **98**; Curtis Associates, Inc., Richard **99**; Doyen Literary Services, Inc. **104**; Dunham Literary **105**; Dupree/Miller and Associates Inc. Literary **106**; Fernandez, Justin E. **111**; Fredericks Literary Agency, Jeanne **114**; Greenburger Associates, Inc., Sanford J. **118**; Grosvenor Literary Agency, The **119**; Hamilburg Agency, Mitchell J., The **120**; Hawkins & Associates, Inc., John **121**; Kleinman, Esq., Jeffrey M. **128**; Krages, Attorney at Law, Bert P. **131**; Larsen/Elizabeth Pomada Literary Agents, Michael **132**; Lazear Agency Incorporated **133**; Levine Literary Agency, Paul S. **135**; Limelight Management **136**; Menza Literary Agency, Claudia **149**; Millard Literary Agency, Martha **150**; Nazor Literary Agency **154**; Norma-Lewis Agency, The **155**; Paraview, Inc. **156**; Pevner, Inc., Stephen **157**; RLR Associates, Ltd. **169**; Rosenkranz Literary Agency, Rita **171**; Russell and Volkening **173**; Seligman, Literary Agent, Lynn **177**; Seymour Agency, The **177**; Snell Literary Agency, Michael **181**; Treimel NY, Scott **187**; Vines Agency, Inc., The **192**; Wald Associates, Inc., Mary Jack **192**; Wecksler-Incomco **195**; Wonderland Press, Inc., The **197**

Popular Culture: Ahearn Agency, Inc., The **78**; Allred and Allred Literary Agents **79**; Altair Literary Agency **80**; Altshuler Literary Agency, Miriam **80**; Amsterdam Agency, Marcia **81**; Balkin Agency, Inc. **83**; Barrett Books Inc., Loretta **83**; Bent, Harvey Klinger, Inc., Jenny **84**; Bernstein & Associates, Inc., Pam **84**; Bial Agency, Daniel **84**; Bleeker Street Associates, Inc. **85**; Book Deals, Inc. **86**; Brown Literary Agency, Inc., Andrea **92**; Brown Ltd., Curtis **92**; Browne Ltd., Pema **93**; Buck Agency, Howard **93**; Bykofsky Associates, Inc. Sheree **94**; Carlisle & Company **94**; Charlton Associates, James **95**; Clark Associates, William **96**; Congdon Associates Inc., Don **97**; Connor Literary Agency **98**; Curtis Associates, Inc., Richard **99**; Cypher, The Cypher Agency, James R. **100**; Daves Agency, Joan **101**; DeFiore and Company **101**; DHS Literary, Inc. **102**; Donovan Literary, Jim **104**; Doyen Literary Services, Inc. **104**; Dunham Literary **105**; Dupree/Miller and Associates Inc. Literary **106**; Dystel Literary Management, Inc., Jane **106**; Elek Associates, Peter **107**; Elmo Agency Inc., Ann **109**; Eth Literary Representation, Felicia **109**; Fernandez, Justin E. **111**; Fogelman Literary Agency **112**; Goldfarb & Associates **116**; Goodman Associates **117**; Greenburger Associates, Inc., Sanford J. **118**; Grosvenor Literary Agency, The **119**; Halsey Agency, Reece **120**; Hamilburg Agency, Mitchell J., The **120**; Hawkins & Associates, Inc., John **121**; Henshaw Group, Richard **122**; Hill & Barlow Agency **123**; Hornfischer Literary Management, Inc. **124**; Jabberwocky Literary Agency **125**; James Peter Associates, Inc. **125**; JCA Literary Agency **126**; Kern Literary Agency, Natasha **127**; Kleinman, Esq., Jeffrey M. **128**; Knight Agency, The **129**; Konner Literary Agency, Linda **130**; Koster Literary Agency, LLC, Elaine **130**; Larsen/Elizabeth Pomada Literary Agents, Michael **132**; Lasher Agency, The Maureen **133**; Lazear Agency Incorporated **133**; Levine Literary Agency, Inc., Ellen **135**; Levine Literary Agency, Paul S. **135**; Literary Group, The **137**; LitWest Group, LLC **140**; Livingston Cooke **140**; Love Literary Agency, Nancy **141**; Lowenstein Associates **141**; Lownie Literary Agency Ltd., Andrew **142**; Maccoby Agency, Gina **143**; Manus & Associates Literary Agency, Inc. **143**; March Tenth, Inc. **147**; Markowitz Literary Agency, Barbara **147**; McBride Literary Agency, Margret **148**; McHugh Literary Agency **149**; Michaels Literary Agency, Inc., Doris S. **150**; Millard

Literary Agency, Martha **150**; Multimedia Product Development, Inc. **152**; National Writers Literary Agency **153**; Nazor Literary Agency **154**; New Brand Agency Group, LLC **154**; Norma-Lewis Agency, The **155**; Paraview, Inc. **156**; Parks Agency, The Richard **156**; Perkins Associates, L. **157**; Pevner, Inc., Stephen **157**; Picard, Literary Agent, Alison J. **158**; Preskill Literary Agency, Robert **159**; Quicksilver Books Literary Agents **161**; Rein Books, Inc., Jody **162**; Rinaldi Literary Agency, Angela **166**; RLR Associates, Ltd. **169**; Robbins Literary Agency, B.J. **170**; Roghaar Literary Agency, Inc., Linda **170**; Rosenberg Group, The **170**; Rosenkranz Literary Agency, Rita **171**; Rotrosen Agency, LLC, Jane **172**; Rubie Literary Agency, The Peter **173**; Russell and Volkening **173**; Sanders & Associates, Victoria **174**; Scherf, Inc., Literary Properties **174**; Schiavone Literary Agency, Inc. **175**; Schulman, A Literary Agency, Susan **175**; Seligman, Literary Agent, Lynn **177**; Seymour Agency, The **177**; Shepard Agency, The Robert **178**; Simmons Literary Agency, Jeffrey **179**; Smith Literary Agency Ltd., Robert **180**; Snell Literary Agency, Michael **181**; Spitzer Literary Agency, Philip G. **182**; Straus Agency, Inc., Robin **183**; Susijn Agency, The **184**; Swayne Agency Literary Management & Consulting, Inc., The **184**; Tabian/Literary Agent, Robert E. **185**; Travis Literary Agency, Susan **186**; Treimel NY, Scott **187**; United Tribes **190**; Venture Literary **191**; Viciananza, Ltd., Ralph **192**; Vines Agency, Inc., The **192**; Wales, Literary Agency, Inc. **193**; Ware Literary Agency, John A. **193**; Waterside Productions, Inc. **194**; Watkins Loomis Agency, Inc. **194**; Watt & Associates, Sandra **194**; Weinstein Literary Management, Ted **196**; Whittaker, Literary Agent, Lynn **196**; Wonderland Press, Inc., The **197**

Psychology: Agents Incorporated for Medical and Mental Health Professionals **77**; Allred and Allred Literary Agents **79**; Altshuler Literary Agency, Miriam **80**; Amster Literary Enterprises, Betsy **80**; Baldi Literary Agency, Malaga **82**; Barrett Books Inc., Loretta **83**; Bent, Harvey Klinger, Inc., Jenny **84**; Bernstein & Associates, Inc., Pam **84**; Bernstein Literary Agency, Meredith **84**; Bial Agency, Daniel **84**; Bleeker Street Associates, Inc. **85**; Book Deals, Inc. **86**; BookEnds, LLC **86**; Boston Literary Group, The **90**; Brandt & Hochman Literary Agents Inc. **91**; Brown Ltd., Curtis **92**; Browne Ltd., Pema **93**; Buck Agency, Howard **93**; Bykofsky Associates, Inc. Sheree **94**; Carlisle & Company **94**; Castiglia Literary Agency **95**; Clausen, Mays & Tahan, LLC **96**; Congdon Associates Inc., Don **97**; Coover Agency, The Doe **98**; Core Creations **98**; Curtis Associates, Inc., Richard **99**; Cypher, The Cypher Agency, James R. **100**; Dawson Associates, Liza **101**; DeFiore and Company **101**; Dijkstra Literary Agency, Sandra **102**; Donnaud & Associates, Inc., Janis A. **103**; Doyen Literary Services, Inc. **104**; Dunham Literary **105**; Dupree/Miller and Associates Inc. Literary **106**; Dystel Literary Management, Inc., Jane **106**; Elmo Agency Inc., Ann **109**; Eth Literary Representation, Felicia **109**; Farber Literary Agency Inc. **110**; Feigen/Parrent Literary Management **110**; Fernandez, Justin E. **111**; Fogelman Literary Agency **112**; Fort Ross Inc. Russian-American Publishing Projects **113**; Forthwrite Literary Agency **113**; Franklin Associates, Ltd., Lynn C. **114**; Fredericks Literary Agency, Jeanne **114**; Freymann Literary Agency, Sarah Jane **114**; Gartenberg, Literary Agent, Max **115**; Gislason Agency, The **115**; Goodman Associates **117**; Greenburger Associates, Inc., Sanford J. **118**; Grosvenor Literary Agency, The **119**; Hamilburg Agency, Mitchell J., The **120**; Hawkins & Associates, Inc., John **121**; Henshaw Group, Richard **122**; Herman Agency LLC, The Jeff **122**; Hill & Barlow Agency **123**; Hornfischer Literary Management, Inc. **124**; James Peter Associates, Inc. **125**; Kern Literary Agency, Natasha **127**; Kleinman, Esq., Jeffrey M. **128**; Klinger, Inc., Harvey **129**; Knight Agency, The **129**; Konner Literary Agency, Linda **130**; Koster Literary Agency, LLC, Elaine **130**; Kouts, Literary Agent, Barbara S. **130**; Krages, Attorney at Law, Bert P. **131**; Larsen/Elizabeth Pomada Literary Agents, Michael **132**; Lasher Agency, The Maureen **133**; Lazear Agency Incorporated **133**; Levine Communications, Inc., James **134**; Levine Literary Agency, Inc., Ellen **135**; Levine Literary Agency, Paul S. **135**; Lieberman Associates, Robert **136**; Lincoln Literary Agency, Ray **136**; Literary Group, The **137**; LitWest Group, LLC **140**; Love Literary Agency, Nancy **141**; Lowenstein Associates **141**; Mann Agency, Carol **143**; Manus & Associates Literary Agency, Inc. **143**; McBride Literary Agency, Margret **148**; McGrath, Helen **149**; Menza Literary Agency, Claudia **149**; Millard Literary Agency, Martha **150**; Miller Agency, The **150**; Multimedia Product Development, Inc. **152**; Naggar Literary Agency, Jean V. **153**; New Brand Agency Group, LLC **154**; New England Publishing Associates Inc. **154**; Nine Muses and Apollo Inc. **155**; Paraview, Inc. **156**; Parks Agency, The Richard **156**; Paton Literary Agency, Kathi J. **157**; Picard, Literary Agent, Alison J. **158**; Pine Associates, Inc., Arthur **159**; Preskill Literary Agency, Robert **159**; Protter Literary Agent, Susan Ann **160**; Quicksilver Books Literary Agents **161**; Rabiner, Literary Agent, Inc., Susan **161**; Raymond, Literary Agent, Charlotte Cecil **161**; Rein Books, Inc., Jody **162**; Rinaldi Literary Agency, Angela **166**; RLR Associates, Ltd. **169**; Robbins Literary Agency, B.J. **170**; Rosenberg Group, The **170**; Rosenkranz Literary Agency, Rita **171**; Ross Literary Agency, The Gail **171**; Rotrosen Agency, LLC, Jane **172**; Russell and Volkening **173**; Sanders & Associates, Victoria **174**; Scherf, Inc., Literary Properties **174**; Schiavone Literary Agency, Inc. **175**; Schulman, A Literary Agency, Susan **175**; Sebastian Literary Agency **176**; Seligman, Literary Agent, Lynn **177**; Seymour Agency, The **177**; Sherman Associates,

Inc., Wendy **178**; Singer Literary Agency Inc., Evelyn **179**; Slopen Literary Agency, Beverley **180**; Snell Literary Agency, Michael **181**; Spitzer Literary Agency, Philip G. **182**; Straus Agency, Inc., Robin **183**; Tabian/Literary Agent, Robert E. **185**; Teal Literary Agency, Patricia **185**; Travis Literary Agency, Susan **186**; United Tribes **190**; Venture Literary **191**; Vines Agency, Inc., The **192**; Ware Literary Agency, John A. **193**; Waterside Productions, Inc. **194**; Watt & Associates, Sandra **194**; Weingel-Fidel Agency, The **196**; Wieser & Wieser, Inc. **197**; Wonderland Press, Inc., The **197**; Writers House **198**; Zachary Shuster Harmsworth **199**; Zeckendorf Assoc. Inc., Susan **200**

Recreation: Barrett Books Inc., Loretta **83**; Brown Ltd., Curtis **92**; Buck Agency, Howard **93**; Bykofsky Associates, Inc. Sheree **94**; Curtis Associates, Inc., Richard **99**; Doyen Literary Services, Inc. **104**; Dupree/Miller and Associates Inc. Literary **106**; Fernandez, Justin E. **111**; Goodman Associates **117**; Greenburger Associates, Inc., Sanford J. **118**; Hamilburg Agency, Mitchell J., The **120**; Hawkins & Associates, Inc., John **121**; Lazear Agency Incorporated **133**; McHugh Literary Agency **149**; Paraview, Inc. **156**; Seymour Agency, The **177**; Snell Literary Agency, Michael **181**; Treimel NY, Scott **187**

Religious/Inspirational: Alive Communications, Inc. **78**; Allred and Allred Literary Agents **79**; Barrett Books Inc., Loretta **83**; Bernstein & Associates, Inc., Pam **84**; Bial Agency, Daniel **84**; Bleeker Street Associates, Inc. **85**; Book Deals, Inc. **86**; BookEnds, LLC **86**; Books & Such **87**; Brown Associates Inc., Marie **91**; Brown Ltd., Curtis **92**; Browne Ltd., Pema **93**; Buck Agency, Howard **93**; Bykofsky Associates, Inc. Sheree **94**; Castiglia Literary Agency **95**; Clark Associates, William **96**; Clausen, Mays & Tahan, LLC **96**; Crawford Literary Agency **99**; Curtis Associates, Inc., Richard **99**; DeFiore and Company **101**; Doyen Literary Services, Inc. **104**; Dupree/Miller and Associates Inc. Literary **106**; Dystel Literary Management, Inc., Jane **106**; Ellenberg Literary Agency, Ethan **108**; Fernandez, Justin E. **111**; Forthwrite Literary Agency **113**; Franklin Associates, Ltd., Lynn C. **114**; Freymann Literary Agency, Sarah Jane **114**; Greenburger Associates, Inc., Sanford J. **118**; Grosvenor Literary Agency, The **119**; Hamilburg Agency, Mitchell J., The **120**; Hartline Literary Agency **121**; Hill & Barlow Agency **123**; Hornfischer Literary Management, Inc. **124**; Jordan Literary Agency, Lawrence **127**; Kern Literary Agency, Natasha **127**; Knight Agency, The **129**; Krages, Attorney at Law, Bert P. **131**; Larsen/Elizabeth Pomada Literary Agents, Michael **132**; Lazear Agency Incorporated **133**; Levine Communications, Inc., James **134**; Levine Literary Agency, Inc., Ellen **135**; Levine Literary Agency, Paul S. **135**; Literary Group, The **137**; LitWest Group, LLC **140**; Love Literary Agency, Nancy **141**; Lowenstein Associates, Ltd., Mildred **148**; Marmur Associates, Ltd., Mildred **148**; McBride Literary Agency, Margret **148**; McHugh Literary Agency **149**; Multimedia Product Development, Inc. **152**; Naggar Literary Agency, Jean V. **153**; New Brand Agency Group, LLC **154**; Paraview, Inc. **156**; Paton Literary Agency, Kathi J. **157**; Pevner, Inc., Stephen **157**; Picard, Literary Agent, Alison J. **158**; Quicksilver Books Literary Agents **161**; Rein Books, Inc., Jody **162**; RLR Associates, Ltd. **169**; Roghaar Literary Agency, Inc., Linda **170**; Rosenkranz Literary Agency, Rita **171**; Ross Literary Agency, The Gail **171**; Roth, Literary Representation, Carol Susan **172**; Scherf, Inc., Literary Properties **174**; Schulman, A Literary Agency, Susan **175**; Seymour Agency, The **177**; Singer Literary Agency Inc., Evelyn **179**; Snell Literary Agency, Michael **181**; United Tribes **190**; Van Der Leun & Associates **191**; Viciananza, Ltd., Ralph **192**; Vines Agency, Inc., The **192**; Watt & Associates, Sandra **194**; Waxman Literary Agency **195**

Science/Technology: Agents Incorporated for Medical and Mental Health Professionals **77**; Allred and Allred Literary Agents **79**; Altair Literary Agency **80**; Authentic Creations Literary Agency **82**; Baldi Literary Agency, Malaga **82**; Balkin Agency, Inc. **83**; Barrett Books Inc., Loretta **83**; Bernstein Literary Agency, Meredith **84**; Bial Agency, Daniel **84**; Bleeker Street Associates, Inc. **85**; Book Deals, Inc. **86**; Boston Literary Group, The **90**; Brandt & Hochman Literary Agents Inc. **91**; Brown Literary Agency, Inc., Andrea **92**; Brown Ltd., Curtis **92**; Buck Agency, Howard **93**; Bykofsky Associates, Inc. Sheree **94**; Carlisle & Company **94**; Carvainis Agency, Inc., Maria **94**; Castiglia Literary Agency **95**; Clark Associates, William **96**; Congdon Associates Inc., Don **97**; Curtis Associates, Inc., Richard **99**; Cypher, The Cypher Agency, James R. **100**; Dijkstra Literary Agency, Sandra **102**; Doyen Literary Services, Inc. **104**; Ducas, Robert **105**; Dunham Literary **105**; Dupree/Miller and Associates Inc. Literary **106**; Dystel Literary Management, Inc., Jane **106**; Educational Design Services, Inc. **107**; Elek Associates, Peter **107**; Ellenberg Literary Agency, Ethan **108**; Elmo Agency Inc., Ann **109**; Eth Literary Representation, Felicia **109**; Fernandez, Justin E. **111**; Flaming Star Literary Enterprises **111**; Gartenberg, Literary Agent, Max **115**; Gislason Agency, The **115**; Goodman Associates **117**; Greenburger Associates, Inc., Sanford J. **118**; Grosvenor Literary Agency, The **119**; Halsey North, Reece **120**; Hamilburg Agency, Mitchell J., The **120**; Hawkins & Associates, Inc., John **121**; Henshaw Group, Richard **122**; Hill & Barlow Agency **123**; Hornfischer Literary Management, Inc. **124**; Jabberwocky Literary Agency **125**; JCA Literary Agency **126**; Jordan Literary

Agency, Lawrence **127**; Kern Literary Agency, Natasha **127**; Ketz Agency, Louise B. **127**; Kleinman, Esq., Jeffrey M. **128**; Klinger, Inc., Harvey **129**; Krages, Attorney at Law, Bert P. **131**; Larsen/ Elizabeth Pomada Literary Agents, Michael **132**; Lasher Agency, The Maureen **133**; Lazear Agency Incorporated **133**; Levine Communications, Inc., James **134**; Levine Literary Agency, Inc., Ellen **135**; Levine Literary Agency, Paul S. **135**; Lieberman Associates, Robert **136**; Lincoln Literary Agency, Ray **136**; Lipkind Agency, Wendy **137**; Literary Group, The **137**; Livingston Cooke **140**; Love Literary Agency, Nancy **141**; Lowenstein Associates **141**; Manus & Associates Literary Agency, Inc. **143**; Marmur Associates, Ltd., Mildred **148**; McBride Literary Agency, Margret **148**; McHugh Literary Agency **149**; Multimedia Product Development, Inc. **152**; Mura Literary, Dee **152**; National Writers Literary Agency **153**; Nazor Literary Agency **154**; New England Publishing Associates Inc. **154**; Paraview, Inc. **156**; Parks Agency, The Richard **156**; Picard, Literary Agent, Alison J. **158**; Protter Literary Agent, Susan Ann **160**; Quicksilver Books Literary Agents **161**; Rabiner, Literary Agent, Inc., Susan **161**; Rein Books, Inc., Jody **162**; Rhodes Literary Agency, Jodie **162**; RLR Associates, Ltd. **169**; Rosenkranz Literary Agency, Rita **171**; Ross Literary Agency, The Gail **171**; Rubie Literary Agency, The Peter **173**; Russell and Volkening **173**; Schiavone Literary Agency, Inc. **175**; Sebastian Literary Agency **176**; Seligman, Literary Agent, Lynn **177**; Seymour Agency, The **177**; Shepard Agency, The Robert **178**; Singer Literary Agency Inc., Evelyn **179**; Snell Literary Agency, Michael **181**; Susijn Agency, The **184**; Tabian/Literary Agent, Robert E. **185**; Treimel NY, Scott **187**; United Tribes **190**; Venture Literary **191**; Viciananza, Ltd., Ralph **192**; Vines Agency, Inc., The **192**; Wales, Literary Agency, Inc. **193**; Ware Literary Agency, John A. **193**; Watkins Loomis Agency, Inc. **194**; Weingel-Fidel Agency, The **196**; Weinstein Literary Management, Ted **196**; Whittaker, Literary Agent, Lynn **196**; Witherspoon Associates, Inc. **197**; Writers House **198**; Zachary Shuster Harmsworth **199**; Zeckendorf Assoc. Inc., Susan **200**

Self-Help/Personal Improvement: ABS Literary Agency, Inc. **76**; Agents Incorporated for Medical and Mental Health Professionals **77**; Ahearn Agency, Inc., The **78**; Alive Communications, Inc. **78**; Allred and Allred Literary Agents **79**; Amsterdam Agency, Marcia **81**; Authentic Creations Literary Agency **82**; Barrett Books Inc., Loretta **83**; Bent, Harvey Klinger, Inc., Jenny **84**; Bernstein & Associates, Inc., Pam **84**; Bial Agency, Daniel **84**; Bleeker Street Associates, Inc. **85**; Book Deals, Inc. **86**; BookEnds, LLC **86**; Books & Such **87**; Briggs, M. Courtney **91**; Brown Associates Inc., Marie **91**; Brown Ltd., Curtis **92**; Browne Ltd., Pema **93**; Bykofsky Associates, Inc. Sheree **94**; Castiglia Literary Agency **95**; Connor Literary Agency **98**; Crawford Literary Agency **99**; Curtis Associates, Inc., Richard **99**; Cypher, The Cypher Agency, James R. **100**; DeFiore and Company **101**; Doyen Literary Services, Inc. **104**; Dupree/Miller and Associates Inc. Literary **106**; Elmo Agency Inc., Ann **109**; Feigen/Parrent Literary Management **110**; Fernandez, Justin E. **111**; Flaming Star Literary Enterprises **111**; Fleury Agency, B.R. **112**; Fort Ross Inc. Russian-American Publishing Projects **113**; Forthwrite Literary Agency **113**; Franklin Associates, Ltd., Lynn C. **114**; Fredericks Literary Agency, Jeanne **114**; Freymann Literary Agency, Sarah Jane **114**; Gartenberg, Literary Agent, Max **115**; Gislason Agency, The **115**; Greenburger Associates, Inc., Sanford J. **118**; Grosvenor Literary Agency, The **119**; Hamilburg Agency, Mitchell J., The **120**; Hartline Literary Agency **121**; Hawkins & Associates, Inc., John **121**; Henshaw Group, Richard **122**; Herman Agency LLC, The Jeff **122**; Hill & Barlow Agency **123**; Hornfischer Literary Management, Inc. **124**; J de S Associates Inc. **125**; James Peter Associates, Inc. **125**; Jordan Literary Agency, Lawrence **127**; Kern Literary Agency, Natasha **127**; Kleinman, Esq., Jeffrey M. **128**; Klinger, Inc., Harvey **129**; Knight Agency, The **129**; Konner Literary Agency, Linda **130**; Koster Literary Agency, LLC, Elaine **130**; Kouts, Literary Agent, Barbara S. **130**; Krages, Attorney at Law, Bert P. **131**; Kritzer Productions, Eddie **131**; Larsen/ Elizabeth Pomada Literary Agents, Michael **132**; Lasher Agency, The Maureen **133**; Lazear Agency Incorporated **133**; Levine Communications, Inc., James **134**; Levine Literary Agency, Paul S. **135**; Limelight Management **136**; Lincoln Literary Agency, Ray **136**; Literary Group, The **137**; LitWest Group, LLC **140**; Love Literary Agency, Nancy **141**; Lowenstein Associates **141**; Mann Agency, Carol **143**; Manus & Associates Literary Agency, Inc. **143**; McBride Literary Agency, Margret **148**; McGrath, Helen **149**; McHugh Literary Agency **149**; Menza Literary Agency, Claudia **149**; Michaels Literary Agency, Inc., Doris S. **150**; Millard Literary Agency, Martha **150**; Miller Agency, The **150**; Multimedia Product Development, Inc. **152**; Mura Literary, Dee **152**; Naggar Literary Agency, Jean V. **153**; New Brand Agency Group, LLC **154**; New England Publishing Associates Inc. **154**; Norma-Lewis Agency, The **155**; Paraview, Inc. **156**; Parks Agency, The Richard **156**; Picard, Literary Agent, Alison J. **158**; Pine Associates, Inc., Arthur **159**; Preskill Literary Agency, Robert **159**; Quicksilver Books Literary Agents **161**; Rein Books, Inc., Jody **162**; Rinaldi Literary Agency, Angela **166**; RLR Associates, Ltd. **169**; Robbins Literary Agency, B.J. **170**; Roghaar Literary Agency, Inc., Linda **170**; Rosenkranz Literary Agency, Rita **171**; Ross Literary Agency, The Gail **171**; Roth, Literary Representation, Carol Susan **172**; Rotrosen Agency, LLC, Jane **172**; Scherf, Inc., Literary Properties **174**; Schiavone Literary Agency, Inc. **175**; Schulman, A Literary Agency, Susan **175**; Sebastian

Literary Agency 176; Seligman, Literary Agent, Lynn 177; Seymour Agency, The 177; Singer Literary Agency Inc., Evelyn 179; Smith Literary Agency Ltd., Robert 180; Snell Literary Agency, Michael 181; Teal Literary Agency, Patricia 185; Trace Inc., The Tracy Sherrod Literary Agency 186; Travis Literary Agency, Susan 186; 2M Communications Ltd. 187; United Tribes 190; Vines Agency, Inc., The 192; Watt & Associates, Sandra 194; Weiner Literary Agency, Cherry 195; Weinstein Literary Management, Ted 196; Witherspoon Associates, Inc. 197; Wonderland Press, Inc., The 197; Writers House 198; Wylie-Merrick Literary Agency 199; Zachary Shuster Harmsworth 199

Sociology: Agents Incorporated for Medical and Mental Health Professionals 77; Allred and Allred Literary Agents 79; Altshuler Literary Agency, Miriam 80; Amster Literary Enterprises, Betsy 80; Baldi Literary Agency, Malaga 82; Balkin Agency, Inc. 83; Barrett Books Inc., Loretta 83; Bernstein & Associates, Inc., Pam 84; Bial Agency, Daniel 84; Bleeker Street Associates, Inc. 85; Boston Literary Group, The 90; Brown Literary Agency, Inc., Andrea 92; Brown Ltd., Curtis 92; Buck Agency, Howard 93; Bykofsky Associates, Inc. Sheree 94; Castiglia Literary Agency 95; Clark Associates, William 96; Congdon Associates Inc., Don 97; Coover Agency, The Doe 98; Curtis Associates, Inc., Richard 99; Cypher, The Cypher Agency, James R. 100; Dawson Associates, Liza 101; Dijkstra Literary Agency, Sandra 102; Doyen Literary Services, Inc. 104; Dunham Literary 105; Dupree/Miller and Associates Inc. Literary 106; Educational Design Services, Inc. 107; Eth Literary Representation, Felicia 109; Fernandez, Justin E. 111; Gislason Agency, The 115; Goldfarb & Associates 116; Goodman Associates 117; Greenburger Associates, Inc., Sanford J. 118; Grosvenor Literary Agency, The 119; Hamilburg Agency, Mitchell J., The 120; Hawkins & Associates, Inc., John 121; Henshaw Group, Richard 122; Hill & Barlow Agency 123; Hochmann Books, John L. 123; Hornfischer Literary Management, Inc. 124; J de S Associates Inc. 125; Jabberwocky Literary Agency 125; JCA Literary Agency 126; Kleinman, Esq., Jeffrey M. 128; Krages, Attorney at Law, Bert P. 131; Kroll Literary Agency Inc., Edite 131; Larsen/Elizabeth Pomada Literary Agents, Michael 132; Lasher Agency, The Maureen 133; Lazear Agency Incorporated 133; Levine Communications, Inc., James 134; Levine Literary Agency, Paul S. 135; Lieberman Associates, Robert 136; Lincoln Literary Agency, Ray 136; Literary Group, The 137; LitWest Group, LLC 140; Love Literary Agency, Nancy 141; Lowenstein Associates 141; Mann Agency, Carol 143; McBride Literary Agency, Margret 148; Multimedia Product Development, Inc. 152; Mura Literary, Dee 152; Naggar Literary Agency, Jean V. 153; Nazor Literary Agency 154; New England Publishing Associates Inc. 154; Paraview, Inc. 156; Parks Agency, The Richard 156; Pevner, Inc., Stephen 157; Quicksilver Books Literary Agents 161; Raymond, Literary Agent, Charlotte Cecil 161; Rein Books, Inc., Jody 162; Rinaldi Literary Agency, Angela 166; RLR Associates, Ltd. 169; Robbins Literary Agency, B.J. 170; Ross Literary Agency, The Gail 171; Russell and Volkening 173; Schiavone Literary Agency, Inc. 175; Schulman, A Literary Agency, Susan 175; Sebastian Literary Agency 176; Seligman, Literary Agent, Lynn 177; Seymour Agency, The 177; Shepard Agency, The Robert 178; Simmons Literary Agency, Jeffrey 179; Slopen Literary Agency, Beverley 180; Snell Literary Agency, Michael 181; Spieler Agency, The 182; Spitzer Literary Agency, Philip G. 182; Straus Agency, Inc., Robin 183; Treimel NY, Scott 187; United Tribes 190; Vines Agency, Inc., The 192; Wald Associates, Inc., Mary Jack 192; Waterside Productions, Inc. 194; Weiner Literary Agency, Cherry 195; Weingel-Fidel Agency, The 196; Zeckendorf Assoc. Inc., Susan 200

Sports: Agents Incorporated for Medical and Mental Health Professionals 77; Alive Communications, Inc. 78; Allred and Allred Literary Agents 79; Authentic Creations Literary Agency 82; Barrett Books Inc., Loretta 83; Bial Agency, Daniel 84; Black Literary Agency, David 85; Bleeker Street Associates, Inc. 85; Brown Literary Agency, Inc., Andrea 92; Brown Ltd., Curtis 92; Browne Ltd., Pema 93; Buck Agency, Howard 93; Bykofsky Associates, Inc. Sheree 94; Charlton Associates, James 95; Connor Literary Agency 98; Curtis Associates, Inc., Richard 99; Cypher, The Cypher Agency, James R. 100; DeFiore and Company 101; DHS Literary, Inc. 102; Donovan Literary, Jim 104; Doyen Literary Services, Inc. 104; Ducas, Robert 105; Dunham Literary 105; Dupree/Miller and Associates Inc. Literary 106; Fernandez, Justin E. 111; Flaming Star Literary Enterprises 111; Fogelman Literary Agency 112; Fredericks Literary Agency, Jeanne 114; Gartenberg, Literary Agent, Max 115; Goldfarb & Associates 116; Goodman Associates 117; Greenburger Associates, Inc., Sanford J. 118; Hamilburg Agency, Mitchell J., The 120; Hawkins & Associates, Inc., John 121; Henshaw Group, Richard 122; Hornfischer Literary Management, Inc. 124; J de S Associates Inc. 125; Jabberwocky Literary Agency 125; JCA Literary Agency 126; Jordan Literary Agency, Lawrence 127; Ketz Agency, Louise B. 127; Klinger, Inc., Harvey 129; Larsen/Elizabeth Pomada Literary Agents, Michael 132; Lasher Agency, The Maureen 133; Lazear Agency Incorporated 133; Levine Communications, Inc., James 134; Levine Literary Agency, Paul S. 135; Limelight Management 136; Lincoln Literary Agency, Ray 136; Literary Group, The 137; LitWest Group, LLC 140; Lowenstein Associates 141; Markowitz Literary Agency, Barbara 147; Marmur Associates, Ltd., Mildred 148; McGrath, Helen

Justin E. **111**; Fleury Agency, B.R. **112**; Fogelman Literary Agency **112**; Fort Ross Inc. Russian-American Publishing Projects **113**; Gartenberg, Literary Agent, Max **115**; Goldfarb & Associates **116**; Goodman Associates **117**; Grace Literary Agency, Carroll **117**; Greenburger Associates, Inc., Sanford J. **118**; Grosvenor Literary Agency, The **119**; Halsey Agency, Reece **120**; Hamilburg Agency, Mitchell J., The **120**; Hawkins & Associates, Inc., John **121**; Henshaw Group, Richard **122**; Hornfischer Literary Management, Inc. **124**; Jabberwocky Literary Agency **125**; JCA Literary Agency **126**; Kleinman, Esq., Jeffrey M. **128**; Klinger, Inc., Harvey **129**; Kritzer Productions, Eddie **131**; Larsen/Elizabeth Pomada Literary Agents, Michael **132**; Lasher Agency, The Maureen **133**; Lawyer's Literary Agency, Inc. **133**; Lazear Agency Incorporated **133**; Levine Literary Agency, Paul S. **135**; Literary Group, The **137**; LitWest Group, LLC **140**; Love Literary Agency, Nancy **141**; Lownie Literary Agency Ltd., Andrew **142**; Marmur Associates, Ltd., Mildred **148**; McHugh Literary Agency **149**; Millard Literary Agency, Martha **150**; Multimedia Product Development, Inc. **152**; Mura Literary, Dee **152**; New England Publishing Associates Inc. **154**; Norma-Lewis Agency, The **155**; Paraview, Inc. **156**; Picard, Literary Agent, Alison J. **158**; Preskill Literary Agency, Robert **159**; Quicksilver Books Literary Agents **161**; Rinaldi Literary Agency, Angela **166**; RLR Associates, Ltd. **169**; Robbins Literary Agency, B.J. **170**; Ross Literary Agency, The Gail **171**; Rotrosen Agency, LLC, Jane **172**; Russell and Volkening **173**; Scherf, Inc., Literary Properties **174**; Schiavone Literary Agency, Inc. **175**; Schulman, A Literary Agency, Susan **175**; Sedgeband Literary Associates **177**; Seligman, Literary Agent, Lynn **177**; Seymour Agency, The **177**; Simmons Literary Agency, Jeffrey **179**; Slopen Literary Agency, Beverley **180**; Smith Literary Agency Ltd., Robert **180**; Snell Literary Agency, Michael **181**; Spitzer Literary Agency, Philip G. **182**; Teal Literary Agency, Patricia **185**; Treimel NY, Scott **187**; Venture Literary **191**; Vines Agency, Inc., The **192**; Wald Associates, Inc., Mary Jack **192**; Ware Literary Agency, John A. **193**; Watkins Loomis Agency, Inc. **194**; Watt & Associates, Sandra **194**; Wieser & Wieser, Inc. **197**; Witherspoon Associates, Inc. **197**; Writers House **198**; Zachary Shuster Harmsworth **199**

Women's Issues/Women's Studies: Ahearn Agency, Inc., The **78**; Alive Communications, Inc. **78**; Allred and Allred Literary Agents **79**; Altshuler Literary Agency, Miriam **80**; Amster Literary Enterprises, Betsy **80**; Authentic Creations Literary Agency **82**; Baldi Literary Agency, Malaga **82**; Barrett Books Inc., Loretta **83**; Bent, Harvey Klinger, Inc., Jenny **84**; Bernstein & Associates, Inc., Pam **84**; Bial Agency, Daniel **84**; Bleeker Street Associates, Inc. **85**; BookEnds, LLC **86**; Books & Such **87**; Borchardt Inc., Georges **87**; Boston Literary Group, The **90**; Brandt & Hochman Literary Agents Inc. **91**; Brown Associates Inc., Marie **91**; Brown Ltd., Curtis **92**; Browne Ltd., Pema **93**; Buck Agency, Howard **93**; Bykofsky Associates, Inc. Sheree **94**; Carvainis Agency, Inc., Maria **94**; Casselman Literary Agency, Martha **95**; Castiglia Literary Agency **95**; Clausen, Mays & Tahan, LLC **96**; Congdon Associates Inc., Don **97**; Connor Literary Agency **98**; Coover Agency, The Doe **98**; Cornerstone Literary, Inc. **99**; Crawford Literary Agency **99**; Curtis Associates, Inc., Richard **99**; Cypher, The Cypher Agency, James R. **100**; Daves Agency, Joan **101**; Dawson Associates, Liza **101**; Dijkstra Literary Agency, Sandra **102**; Doyen Literary Services, Inc. **104**; Dunham Literary **105**; Dupree/Miller and Associates Inc. Literary **106**; Dystel Literary Management, Inc., Jane **106**; Educational Design Services, Inc. **107**; Eth Literary Representation, Felicia **109**; Feigen/Parrent Literary Management **110**; Fernandez, Justin E. **111**; Fogelman Literary Agency **112**; Forthwrite Literary Agency **113**; Fredericks Literary Agency, Jeanne **114**; Freymann Literary Agency, Sarah Jane **114**; Gartenberg, Literary Agent, Max **115**; Goldfarb & Associates **116**; Goodman Associates **117**; Grace Literary Agency, Carroll **117**; Greenburger Associates, Inc., Sanford J. **118**; Grosjean Literary Agency, Jill **119**; Grosvenor Literary Agency, The **119**; Halsey Agency, Reece **120**; Hamilburg Agency, Mitchell J., The **120**; Hartline Literary Agency **121**; Hawkins & Associates, Inc., John **121**; Henshaw Group, Richard **122**; Hill & Barlow Agency **123**; Hill Bonnie Nadell, Inc., Frederick **123**; Jabberwocky Literary Agency **125**; James Peter Associates, Inc. **125**; JCA Literary Agency **126**; Jenks Agency, The **126**; Kern Literary Agency, Natasha **127**; Kleinman, Esq., Jeffrey M. **128**; Klinger, Inc., Harvey **129**; Konner Literary Agency, Linda **130**; Koster Literary Agency, LLC, Elaine **130**; Kouts, Literary Agent, Barbara S. **130**; Kroll Literary Agency Inc., Edite **131**; Larsen/Elizabeth Pomada Literary Agents, Michael **132**; Lasher Agency, The Maureen **133**; Lazear Agency Incorporated **133**; Levine Communications, Inc., James **134**; Levine Literary Agency, Inc., Ellen **135**; Levine Literary Agency, Paul S. **135**; Lincoln Literary Agency, Ray **136**; Lipkind Agency, Wendy **137**; Literary Group, The **137**; LitWest Group, LLC **140**; Love Literary Agency, Nancy **141**; Lowenstein Associates **141**; Maccoby Agency, Gina **143**; Mann Agency, Carol **143**; Manus & Associates Literary Agency, Inc. **143**; Markowitz Literary Agency, Barbara **147**; Marmur Associates, Ltd., Mildred **148**; McBride Literary Agency, Margret **148**; McGrath, Helen **149**; McHugh Literary Agency **149**; Michaels Literary Agency, Inc., Doris S. **150**; Millard Literary Agency, Martha **150**; Miller Agency, The **150**; Multimedia Product Development, Inc. **152**; Mura Literary, Dee **152**; Naggar Literary Agency, Jean V. **153**; Nazor Literary Agency **154**; New Brand Agency Group, LLC **154**; New England Publishing Associ-

Script Agents Specialties Index

This subject index is divided into script subject categories. To find an agent interested in the type of screenplay you've written, see the appropriate sections under subject headings that best describe your work.

DISCOVER A WORLD OF WRITING SUCCESS

Get 2 FREE ISSUES of Writer's Digest!

Are you ready to be praised, published, and paid for your writing? It's time to invest in your future with *Writer's Digest*! Beginners and experienced writers alike have been enjoying *Writer's Digest*, the world's leading magazine for writers, for more than 80 years — and it keeps getting better! Each issue is brimming with:

- Inspiration from writers who have been in your shoes
- Detailed info on the latest contests, conferences, markets, and opportunities in every genre
- Tools of the trade, including reviews of the latest writing software and hardware
- Writing prompts and exercises to overcome writer's block and rekindle your creative spark
- Expert tips, techniques, and advice to help you get published
- And so much more!

That's a lot to look forward to every month. Let *Writer's Digest* put you on the road to writing success!

NO RISK!
Send No Money Now!

☐ **Yes!** Please rush me my 2 FREE issues of *Writer's Digest* — the world's leading magazine for writers. If I like what I read, I'll get a full year's subscription (12 issues, including the 2 free issues) for only $19.96. That's 67% off the newsstand rate! If I'm not completely happy, I'll write "cancel" on your invoice, return it and owe nothing. The 2 FREE issues are mine to keep, no matter what!

Name_____

Address_____

City_____

State_____ZIP_____

Annual newsstand rate is $59.88. Orders outside the U.S. will be billed an additional $10 (includes GST/HST in Canada.) Please allow 4-6 weeks for first-issue delivery.

Writer's ® Digest

www.writersdigest.com

T6LM3

Get 2 FREE TRIAL ISSUES

of Writer's® Digest

Packed with creative inspiration, advice, and tips to guide you on the road to success, *Writer's Digest* will offer you everything you need to take your writing to the next level! You'll discover how to:

- Create dynamic characters and page-turning plots
- Submit query letters that publishers won't be able to refuse
- Find the right agent or editor for you
- Make it out of the slush-pile and into the hands of the right publisher
- Write award-winning contest entries
- And more!

See for yourself by ordering your 2 FREE trial issues today!

Westerns/Frontier

Script Agents Format Index:

This subject index will help you determine agencies interested in handling scripts for particular types of movies or TV programs. These formats are delineated into ten categories: animation, documentary; episodic drama; feature film; miniseries; movie of the week (MOW); sitcom; soap opera; stage play; variety show.

Agencies Indexed by Openness to Submissions

We've ranked the agencies and independent publicists according to their openness to submissions. Check this index to find an agent or independent publicist who is appropriate for your level of experience. Some companies are listed under more than one category.

☐ NEW AGENCY ACTIVELY SEEKING CLIENTS

Literary agents
Collins McCormick Literary Agency
English, Elaine P.
Grosjean Literary Agency, Jill
Rights Unlimited, Inc.
Venture Literary

Publicists
Gray Communications, Cameron

☑ AGENCIES SEEKING BOTH NEW AND ESTABLISHED WRITERS

Literary agents
ABS Literary Agency, Inc.
Acacia House Publishing Services Ltd.
Agents Incorporated for Medical and Mental Health Professionals
Ahearn Agency, Inc., The
Allen Literary Agency, Linda
Allred and Allred Litarary Agents
Altair Literary Agency
Altshuler Literary Agency, Miriam
Amster Literary Enterprises, Betsy
Amsterdam Agency, Marcia
Andrews & Associates, Bart
Anubis Literary Agency
Appleseeds Management
Balkin Agency, Inc.
Barrett Books Inc., Loretta
Bent, Harvey Klinger, Inc., Jenny
Bernstein Literary Agency, Meredith
Bial Agency, Daniel
Bigscore Productions Inc.
Book Deals, Inc.

Brandt & Hochman Literary Agents Inc.
Brandt Agency, The Joan
Brown Literary Agency, Inc., Andrea
Brown Ltd., Curtis
Browne Ltd., Pema
Bykofsky Associates, Inc. Sheree
Carvainis Agency, Inc., Maria
Castiglia Literary Agency
Charlton Associates, James
Clausen, Mays & Tahan, LLC
Client First—a/k/a Leo P. Haffey Agency
Cohen, Inc. Literary Agency, Ruth
Connor Literary Agency
Coover Agency, The Doe
Cornerstone Literary, Inc.
Crawford Literary Agency
Cypher, The Cypher Agency, James R.
Darhansoff & Verrill Literary Agency
Daves Agency, Joan
Dawson Associates, Liza
DeFiore and Company
Donovan Literary, Jim
Dorian Literary Agency
Ducas, Robert
Dunham Literary
Dupree/Miller and Associates Inc. Literary
Dystel Literary Management, Inc., Jane
Educational Design Services, Inc.
Elek Associates, Peter
Ellenberg Literary Agency, Ethan
Ellison, Inc., Nicholas
ES Agency, The
Eth Literary Agency, Felicia
Farber Literary Agency Inc.
Feigen/Parrent Literary Management

Fernandez, Justin E.
Flaming Star Literary Enterprises
Flannery Literary
Fleming Agency, Peter
Fleury Agency, B.R.
Forthwrite Literary Agency
Franklin Associates, Ltd., Lynn C.
Gelfman Schneider Literary Agents, Inc.
Gislason Agency, The
Greenburger Associates, Inc., Sanford J.
Gregory and Company Authors' Agents
Grosvenor Literary Agency, The
H.W.A. Talent Representatives
Halsey North, Reece
Hamilburg Agency, Mitchell J., The
Harris Literary Agency, Inc., The Joy
Herman Agency LLC, The Jeff
Hill Bonnie Nadell, Inc., Frederick
Hornfischer Literary Management, Inc.
Jabberwocky Literary Agency
James Peter Associates, Inc.
JCA Literary Agency
Jordan Literary Agency, Lawrence
Kern Literary Agency, Natasha
Ketz Agency, Louise B.
Kidd Agency, Virginia
Kirchoff/Wohlberg, Inc., Authors' Representation Division
Kleinman, Esq., Jeffrey M.
Konner Literary Agency, Linda
Kouts, Literary Agent, Barbara S.
Kraas Agency, Irene
Kritzer Productions, Eddie
Lake Agency, The Candace
Lazear Agency Incorporated

Lescher & Lescher LTD
Levine Literary Agency, Paul S.
Literary Group, The
Litwest Group, LLC
Livingston Cooke
Love Literary Agency, Nancy
Lownie Literary Agency Ltd.,
  Andrew
Maass Literary Agency, Donald
Mann Agency, Carol
March Tenth, Inc.
Markowitz Literary Agency,
  Barbara
McHugh Literary Agency
Menza Literary Agency, Claudia
Morris Agency, Inc., William
Mura Literary, Dee
National Writers Literary Agency
Nazor Literary Agency
New Brand Agency Group, LLC
New England Publishing
  Associates Inc.
Nine Muses and Apollo Inc.
Norma-Lewis Agency, The
Paton Literary Agency, Kathi J.
Perkins Associates, L.
Pevner, Inc., Stephen
Picard, Literary Agent, Alison J.
Pinder Lane & Garon-Brooke
  Associates, Ltd.
Popkin, Julie
Quicksilver Books Literary
  Agents
Rabiner, Literary Agent, Inc.,
  Susan
Rees Literary Agency, Helen
Rhodes Literary Agency, Jodie
RLR Associates, Ltd.
Robbins Literary Agency, B.J.
Roghaar Literary Agency, Inc.,
  Linda
Rosenberg Group, The
Rosenkranz Literary Agency,
  Rita
Roth, Literary Representation,
  Carol Susan
Rubie Literary Agency, The
  Peter
Russell and Volkening
Sagalyn Agency
Sanders and Associates, Victoria
Sandum and Associates
Schwartz Agency, Laurens R.
Sedgeband Literary Associates
Seligman, Literary Agent, Lynn
Seymour Agency, The
Shepard Agency, The Robert
Sherman Associates, Inc.,
  Wendy
Simmons Literary Agency,
  Jeffrey

Smith Literary Agency Ltd.,
  Robert
Snell Literary Agency, Michael
Sobel Weber Associates
Spectrum Literary Agency
Spieler Agency, The
Steele-Perkins Literary Agency
Susijn Agency, The
Talesmyth Entertainment, Inc.
Tobias, A Literary Agency for
  Chilren's Books, Ann
Trace Inc., The Tracy Sherrod
  Literary Agency
Travis Literary Agency, Susan
2M Communications Ltd.
United Tribes
Van Der Leun & Associates ,
Vines Agency, Inc., The
Wales, Literary Agency, Inc.
Ware Literary Agency, John A.
Waterside Productions, Inc.
Watkins Loomis Agency, Inc.
Waxman Literary Agency, Inc.
Wecksler-Incomco
Weinstein Literary Management,
  Ted
Whittaker, Literary Agent, Lynn
Witherspoon Associates, Inc.
Wonderland Press, Inc., The
Writers House
Zachary Shuster Harmsworth
Zack Company, Inc., The
Zeckendorf Assoc. Inc., Susan

Script agents

Abrams Artists Agency
Allred and Allred, Literary
  Agents
Alpern Group, The
Amsterdam Agency, Marcia
Brown Ltd., Curtis
Bulger and Associates, Kelvin C.
Client First-a/k/a/ Leo P. Haffey
  Agency
Communications Management
  Associates
ES Agency, The
Feigen/Parrent Literary
  Management
Fleury Agency, B.R.
Freedman Dramatic Agency,
  Inc., Robert A. Gage Group,
  The
Graham Agency
H.W.A. Talent Representatives
Hart Literary Management
Hudson Agency
Jaret Entertainment
Kerin-Goldberg Associates
Ketay Agency, The Joyce
Kritzer Productions, Eddie
Lake Agency, The Candace

Larchmont Literary Agency
Legacies
Levine Literary Agency, Paul S.
Livingston Cooke
Luedtke Agency, The
Management Company, The
Manus & Associates Literary
  Agency, Inc.
Miller Co., The Stuart M.
Mura Enterprises, Inc., Dee
Nelson Literary Agency &
  Lecture Bureau, BK
Oscard Agency, Inc., Fifi
Perelman Agency, Barry
Pevner, Inc., Stephen
Picture of You, A
Scagnetti Talent & Literary
  Agency, Jack
Silver Screen Placements
Sorice Agency, Camille
Stanton & Associates Literary
  Agency
Talent Source
Talesmyth Entertainment, Inc.
Wardlow and Associates
Wauhob Agency, Donna
Whittlesey Agency, Peregrine
Wright Representatives, Ann
Writer Store

Publicists

Acheson-Greub, Inc.
Brody Public Relations
Ford Group, The
Garis Agency—National
  Publicists
KSB Promotions
KT Public Relations
Media Masters Publicity
Phenix & Phenix Literary
  Publicists, Inc.
Rocks-Dehart Public Relations
  (Book Publicity)
Rosen Publicity, Sherri
Spizman Agency, The
World Class Speakers &
  Entertainers
Zegarek Public Relations, Inc.,
  Meryl

☑ AGENCIES PREFERRING TO WORK WITH ESTABLISHED WRITERS, MOSTLY OBTAIN NEW CLIENTS THROUGH REFERRALS

Literary agents

Alive Communications, Inc.
Authentic Creations Literary
  Agency
Axelrod Agency, The

Black Literary Agency, David
Bleeker Street Associates, Inc.
Books & Such
Borchardt Inc., Georges
Boston Literary Group, The
Brady Literary Management
Buck Agency, Howard
Casselman Literary Agency,
    Martha
Clark Associates, William
Collin Literary Agency, Frances
Communications and
    Entertainment, Inc.
Congdon Associates Inc., Don
Curtis Associates, Inc., Richard
DH Literary, Inc.
DHS Literary, Inc.
Donnaud & Associates, Inc.,
    Janis A.
Doyen Literary Services, Inc.
Elmo Agency Inc., Ann
Fogelman Literary Agency
Fort Ross Inc. Russian-American
    Publishing Projects
Freymann Literary Agency,
    Sarah Jane
Gartenberg, Literary Agent, Max
Goldfarb & Associates
Goodman Associates
Grady Agency, The Thomas
Grayson Literary Agency, Ashley
Gregory, Inc., Blanche
Halsey Agency, Reece
Hartline Literary Agency
Hawkins & Associates, Inc., John
Hill & Barlow Agency
Hochmann Books, John L.
Hogenson Agency, Barbara
J de S Associates Inc.
Jenks Agency, The
Koster Literary Agency, LLC,
    Elaine
Lampack Agency, Inc., Peter
Lasher Agency, The Maureen
Lawyer's Literary Agency, Inc.
Levine Communications, Inc.,
    James
Levine Literary Agency, Inc.,
    Ellen
Lieberman Associates, Robert
Limelight Management
Lincoln Literary Agency, Ray
Lipkind Agency, Wendy
Literary and Creative Artists, Inc.
Maccoby Agency, Gina
March Tenth, Inc.
Markson Literary Agency, Elaine
Marmur Associates, Ltd.,
    Mildred
McGrath, Helen

Michaels Literary Agency, Inc.,
    Doris S.
Miller Agency, The
Moore Literary Agency
Moran Agency, Maureen
Morrison, Inc., Henry
Multimedia Product
    Development, Inc.
Naggar Literary Agency, Jean V.
Ober Associates, Harold
Oscard Agency Inc., Fifi
Paraview, Inc.
Parks Agency, The Richard
Pine Associates, Inc., Arthur
Preskill Literary Agency, Robert
Protter Literary Agent, Susan
    Ann
Raymond, Literary Agent,
    Charlotte Cecil
Rein Books, Inc., Jody
Rittenberg Literary Agency, Inc.,
    Ann
Riverside Literary Agency
Robbins Office, Inc., The
Robinson Talent and Literary
    Management
Ross Literary Agency, The Gail
Rotrosen Agency LLC, Jane
Rowland Agency, The Damaris
Ryan Publishing Enterprises,
    Inc., Regina
Schulman, A Literary Agency,
    Susan
Scovil Chichak Galen Literary
    Agency
Sebastian Literary Agency
Shukat Company Ltd., The
Siegel, International Literary
    Agency, Inc., Rosalie
Singer Literary Agency Inc.,
    Evelyn
Skolnick Literary Agency, Irene
Slopen Literary Agency,
    Beverley
Spitzer Literary Agency, Philip
    G. Stauffer Associates, Nancy
Sternig & Byrne Literary Agency
Straus Agency, Inc., Robin
Swayne Agency Literary
    Management & Consulting,
    Inc., The
Talbot Agency, The John
Targ Literary Agency, Inc.,
    Roslyn
Teal Literary Agency, Patricia
Treimel NY, Scott
Weingel-Fidel Agency, The
Wieser & Wieser, Inc.
Williams Literary Agency
Wright Representatives, Ann
Writers' Representatives, Inc.

Wylie-Merrick Literary Agency

Script agents

Above the Line Agency
Acme Talent & Literary
    Agency, The
Amato Agency, Michael
Baskow Agency
Berman Boals and Flynn, Inc.
Bohrman Agency, The
Brodie Representation, Alan
Buchwald & Associates, Inc.,
    Don
Cedar Grove Agency
    Entertainment
Communications and
    Entertainment, Inc.
Coppage Company, The
Douroux & Co.
Epstein-Wyckoff-Corsa-Ross and
    Associates
Fitzgerald Literary Management
Freed Co., The Barry
French, Inc., Samuel
Gelff Literary and Talent Agency,
    The Laya
Grant, Savic, Kopaloff &
    Associates
Gurman Agency, The Susan
Hodges Agency, Carolyn
Hogenson Agency, Barbara
Kallen Agency, Leslie
Monteiro Rose Agency
Niad Management
Omniquest Entertainment
Palmer, Dorothy
Preminger Agency , Jim
Redler Entertainment, Dan
Robins & Associates, Michael D.
Schulman, A Literary Agency,
    Susan
Shapiro-Lichtman
Sherman & Associates, Ken
Stein Agency
Suite A Management Talent &
    Literary Agency
Visionary Entertainment
Windfall Management
Writers & Artists Agency

Publicists

Royce Carlton, Inc.
Warwick Associates
Write Publicist & Co., The

◎ AGENCIES HANDLING ONLY CERTAIN TYPES OF WORK OR WORK BY WRITERS UNDER CERTAIN CIRCUMSTANCES

Literary agents

ABS Literary Agency, Inc.
Andrews & Associates, Bart

Books & Such
Brown Literary Agency, Inc.,
   Andrea
Casselman Literary Agency,
   Martha
Dwyer & O'Grady, Inc.
Educational Design Services,
   Inc.
Feigenbaum Publishing
   Consultants, Inc.
Flannery Literary
Ghosts & Collaborators
   International
Kidd Agency, Inc. Virginia
Kirchoff/Wohlberg, Inc.,
   Authors' Representation
   Division
Paraview, Inc.
Roth, Literary Representation,
   Carol Susan
Schulman, A Literary Agency,
   Susan
Tobias, A Literary Agency for
   Chilren's Books, Ann
Treimel NY, Scott
Valcourt Agency, Inc., Richard R.

Script agents
Dramatic Publishing
Kohner, Inc., Paul
Schulman, A Literary Agency,
   Susan
Not Seeking New Clients
   (Literary)
Abel Literary Agency, Inc.,
   Dominick
Abel Literary Agent, Carole
Arcadia
Bach Literary Agency, Julian
Bijur, Vicky
Boates Literary Agency, Reid
Brann Agency, Inc., The Helen
Braun Associates, Inc., Barbara
Brown Associates Inc., Marie
Burger Associates, Ltd., Knox

Chelius Literary Agency, Jane
Cine Lit Representation
Core Creations
Creative Culture, Inc., The
Dail Literary Agency, Inc., Laura
Dijkstra Literary Agency, Sandra
Dolger Agency, The Jonathan
Dorian Literary Agency
Dunow Literary Agency, Henry
Dwyer & O'Grady, Inc.
Edelstein Literary Agency, Anne
Fallon Literary Agency
Foley Literary Agency, The
Fox Chase Agency, Inc.
Goldin, Frances
Grace Literary Agency, Carroll
Groffsky Literary Agency,
   Maxine
Hanson Literary Agency, Jeanne
   K.
Harden Curtis Associates
International Creative
   Management
Krichevsky Literary Agency, Inc.
Lazin, Sarah
Leavitt Agency, The Ned
Marshall Agency, The Evan
Matson Co. Inc., Harold
Mattes, Inc., Jed
McCauley, Gerard
McClellan Associates, Anita D.
Merrill, Ltd., Helen
Morhaim Literary Agency,
   Howard
Roberts, Flora
Rosentstone/Wender
Scherf, Inc., Literary
   Management
Selman Agency, Edythia Ginis
   Selman
Sheedy Agency, Charlotte
Smith-Skolnik Literary
Sommer, Elyse
Stuhlmann, Author's
   Representative, Gunther
Valcourt Agency, Inc., Richard R.
   Van Duren Agency, Annette

Viciananza, Ltd., Ralph
Vigliano Literary Agency, David
Wald Associates, Inc., Mary Jack
Wasserman Literary Agency,
   Harriet
Watt & Associates, Sandra
Weil Agency, Inc., The Wendy
Weiner Literary Agency, Cherry
Wolf Literary Agency, Audrey A.
Writers' Productions
Yost Associates, Inc., Mary

Publicists
Brody Public Relations
KSB Promotions
Leondar Public Relations, Gail
Raab Associates

AGENCIES NOT CURRENTLY SEEKING NEW CLIENTS
Literary agents
Bernstein and Associates, Inc.,
   Pam
Chester, Linda
Millard Literary Agency, Martha
Wallace, LTD, T.C.

Script agents
Chadwick & Gros Literary
   Agency
Filmwriters Literary Agency
International Creative
   Management
International Leonards Corp.
Lantz Office, The
Marton Agency Inc., The
   Elisabeth
Merrill, Ltd., Helen
Morris, William
Panda Talent
Quillco Agency, The
Stone Manners Agency
United Talent Agency
Van Duren Agency, Annette

Geographic Index

Some writers prefer to work with an agent or independent publicist in their vicinity. If you're such a writer, this index offers you the opportunity to easily select agents closest to home. Agencies and independent publicists are separated by state. We've also arranged them according to the sections in which they appear in the book (Literary agents, Script agents or Publicists). Once you find the agency you're interested in, refer to the Listing Index for the page number.

CALIFORNIA

Literary agents

Agents Incorporated for Medical and Mental Health Professionals
Allen Literary Agency, Linda
Allred and Allred Literary Agents
Amster Literary Enterprises, Betsy
Andrews & Associates, Bart
Appleseeds Management
Books & Such
Brown Literary Agency, Inc., Andrea
Browne Ltd., Pema
Casselman Literary Agency, Martha
Castiglia Literary Agency
Cine Lit Representation
Cohen, Inc. Literary Agency, Ruth
Cornerstone Literary, Inc.
Dijkstra Literary Agency, Sandra
ES Agency, The
Eth Literary Agency, Felicia
Feigen/Parrent Literary Management
Fleming Agency, Peter
Forthwrite Literary Agency
Grayson Literary Agency, Ashley
H.W.A. Talent Representatives
Halsey Agency, Reece
Halsey North, Reece
Hamilburg Agency, Mitchell J., The
Hill Bonnie Nadell, Inc., Frederick
Kritzer Productions, Eddie
Lake Agency, The Candace
Larsen/Elizabeth Pomada Literary Agents, Michael
Lasher Agency, The Maureen
Lawyer's Literary Agency, Inc.
Levine Literary Agency, Paul S.
Litwest Group, LLC

Manus & Associates Literary Agency, Inc.
Markowitz Literary Agency, Barbara
McBride Literary Agency, Margret
McGrath, Helen
Popkin, Julie
Preskill Literary Agency, Robert
Rhodes Literary Agency, Jodie
Rinaldi Literary Agency, Angela
Robbins Literary Agency, B.J.
Robinson Talent and Literary Management
Roth, Literary Representation, Carol Susan
Shepard Agency, The Robert
Teal Literary Agency, Patricia
Travis Literary Agency, Susan
Van Duren Agency, Annette
Venture Literary
Waterside Productions, Inc.
Watt & Associates, Sandra
Weinstein Literary Management, Ted

Script agents

Above the Line Agency
Acme Talent & Literary Agency, The
Allred and Allred, Literary Agents
Alpern Group, The
Bohrman Agency, The
Buchwald & Associates, Inc., Don
Coppage Company, The
Douroux & Co.
Epstein-Wyckoff-Corsa-Ross and Associates
ES Agency, The
Feigen/Parrent Literary Management
Freed Co., The Barry
Gage Group, The
Gelff Literary and Talent Agency, The Laya

Grant, Savic, Kopaloff & Associates
H.W.A. Talent Representatives
Hart Literary Management
Jaret Entertainment
Kallen Agency, Leslie
Kohner, Inc., Paul
Kritzer Productions, Eddie
Lake Agency, The Candace
Larchmont Literary Agency
Levine Literary Agency, Paul S.
Management Company, The
Miller Co., The Stuart M.
Monteiro Rose Agency
Niad Management
Omniquest Entertainment
Panda Talent
Perelman Agency, Barry
Preminger Agency, Jim
Quillco Agency, The
Redler Entertainment, Dan
Robins & Associates, Michael D.
Scagnetti Talent & Literary Agency, Jack
Shapiro-Lichtman
Sherman & Associates, Ken
Sorice Agency, Camille
Stein Agency
Stone Manners Agency
Suite A Management Talent & Literary Agency
Van Duren Agency, Annette
Visionary Entertainment
Wardlow and Associates
Windfall Management
Wright Concept, The

Publicists

Ford Group, The
Garis Agency—National Publicists
Warwick Associates
World Class Speakers & Entertainers

COLORADO
Literary agents
Alive Communications, Inc.
Core Creations
National Writers Literary Agency
Rein Books, Inc., Jody
Script agents

Hodges Agency, Carolyn

CONNECTICUT
Literary agents
Arcadia
Brann Agency, Inc., The Helen
Ducas, Robert
Fredericks Literary Agency,
    Jeanne
Ghosts & Collaborators
    International
J de S Associates Inc.
James Peter Associates, Inc.
New England Publishing
    Associates Inc.
Stauffer Associates, Nancy
Writers' Productions

DISTRICT OF COLUMBIA
Literary agents
English, Elaine P.
Goldfarb & Associates
Kleinman, Esq., Jeffrey M.
Literary and Creative Artists, Inc.
Ross Literary Agency, The Gail
Whittaker, Literary Agent, Lynn
Wolf Literary Agency, Audrey A.

FLORIDA
Literary agents
Communications and
    Entertainment, Inc.
Fleury Agency, B.R.
Grace Literary Agency, Carroll
New Brand Agency Group, LLC
Schiavone Literary Agency, Inc.

Script agents
Communications and
    Entertainment, Inc.
Fleury Agency, B.R.
Legacies

Publicists
Event Management Services,
    Inc.

GEORGIA
Literary agents
Authentic Creations Literary
    Agency
Brandt Agency, The Joan
Knight Agency, The

Script agents
Talent Source
Writer Store

Publicists
Spizman Agency, The
Write Publicist & Co., The

IOWA
Literary agents
Doyen Literary Services, Inc.

IDAHO
Literary agents
McHugh Literary Agency

ILLINOIS
Literary agents
Flannery Literary
Multimedia Product
    Development, Inc.

Script agents
Bulger and Associates, Kelvin C.
Dramatic Publishing
Silver Screen Placements

Publicists
Media Masters Publicity

INDIANA
Literary agents
Wylie-Merrick Literary Agency

Scripts
International Leonards Corp.

LOUISIANA
Literary agents
Ahearn Agency, Inc., The

Scripts
Chadwick & Gros Literary
    Agency

MAINE
Literary agents
Kroll Literary Agency Inc., Edite

Script agents
Talesmyth Entertainment, Inc.

MASSACHUSETTS
Literary agents
Balkin Agency, Inc.
Boston Literary Group, The
Coover Agency, The Doe
Hill & Barlow Agency
Jenks Agency, The
McClellan Associates, Anita D.
Moore Literary Agency
Nazor Literary Agency
Picard, Literary Agent, Alison J.

Raymond, Literary Agent,
    Charlotte Cecil
Rees Literary Agency, Helen
Roghaar Literary Agency, Inc.,
    Linda
Rosenberg Group, The
Snell Literary Agency, Michael
Stuhlmann, Author's
    Representative, Gunther

Publicists
American Program Bureau, The
Leondar Public Relations, Gail

MARYLAND
Literary agents
Grosvenor Literary Agency, The
Sagalyn Agency

MICHIGAN
Publicists
KSB Promotions

MINNESOTA
Literary agents
Connor Literary Agency
Gislason Agency, The
Hanson Literary Agency, Jeanne
    K.
Lazear Agency Incorporated
Sebastian Literary Agency

MISSISSIPPI
Literary agents
Williams Literary Agency

NEW HAMPSHIRE
Literary agents
Crawford Literary Agency
Dwyer & O'Grady, Inc.

NEW JERSEY
Literary agents
Boates Literary Agency, Reid
BookEnds, LLC
Elek Associates, Peter
March Tenth, Inc.
Marshall Agency, The Evan
McCarthy Agency, LLC, The
Millard Literary Agency, Martha
Seligman, Literary Agent, Lynn
Siegel, International Literary
    Agency, Inc., Rosalie
Smith-Skolnik Literary
Stimola Literary Studio
Weiner Literary Agency, Cherry

Publicists
Brody Public Relations
Rosen Publicity, Sherri

NEW MEXICO
Literary agents
Kraas Agency, Irene

Script agents
Fitzgerald Literary Management

NEVADA
Literary agents
Scherf, Inc., Literary Management

Script agents
Baskow Agency
Wauhob Agency, Donna

NEW YORK
Literary agents
Abel Literary Agency, Inc., Dominick
Abel Literary Agent, Carole
Altair Literary Agency
Altshuler Literary Agency, Miriam
Amsterdam Agency, Marcia
Axelrod Agency, The
Bach Literary Agency, Julian
Barrett Books Inc., Loretta
Bent, Harvey Klinger, Inc., Jenny
Bernstein & Associates, Inc., Pam
Bernstein Literary Agency, Meredith
Bial Agency, Daniel
Bijur, Vicky
Black Literary Agency, David
Bleeker Street Associates, Inc.
Book Deals, Inc.
Borchardt Inc., Georges
Brandt & Hochman Literary Agents Inc.
Braun Associates, Inc., Barbara
Brown Associates Inc., Marie
Brown Ltd., Curtis
Buck Agency, Howard
Burger Associates, Ltd., Knox
Bykofsky Associates, Inc. Sheree
Carlisle & Company
Carvainis Agency, Inc., Maria
Charlton Associates, James
Chelius Literary Agency, Jane
Chester and Associates, Linda
Clark Associates, William
Clausen, Mays & Tahan, LLC
Collins McCormick Literary Agency
Congdon Associates Inc., Don
Creative Culture, Inc., The
Curtis Associates, Inc., Richard
Cypher, The Cypher Agency, James R.
Dail Literary Agency, Inc., Laura

Darhansoff & Verrill Literary Agency
Daves Agency, Joan
Dawson Associates, Liza
DeFiore and Company
DH Literary, Inc.
Dolger Agency, The Jonathan
Donnaud & Associates, Inc., Janis A.
Dunham Literary
Dunow Literary Agency, Henry
Dystel Literary Management, Inc., Jane
Edelstein Literary Agency, Anne
Educational Design Services, Inc.
Ellenberg Literary Agency, Ethan
Ellison, Inc., Nicholas
Elmo Agency Inc., Ann
Fallon Literary Agency
Farber Literary Agency Inc.
Flaming Star Literary Enterprises
Foley Literary Agency, The
Fort Ross Inc. Russian-American Publishing Projects
Franklin Associates, Ltd., Lynn C.
Freymann Literary Agency, Sarah Jane
Gartenberg, Literary Agent, Max
Gelfman Schneider Literary Agents, Inc.
Goldin, Frances
Goodman Associates
Greenburger Associates, Inc., Sanford J.
Gregory, Inc., Blanche
Groffsky Literary Agency, Maxine
Grosjean Literary Agency, Jill
Harden Curtis Associates
Harris Literary Agency, Inc., The Joy
Hawkins & Associates, Inc., John
Herman Agency LLC, The Jeff
Hochmann Books, John L.
Hogenson Agency, Barbara
International Creative Management
Jabberwocky Literary Agency
JCA Literary Agency
Jordan Literary Agency, Lawrence
Ketz Agency, Louise B.
Kirchoff/Wohlberg, Inc., Authors' Representation Division
Klinger, Inc., Harvey
Konner Literary Agency, Linda

Koster Literary Agency, LLC, Elaine
Kouts, Literary Agent, Barbara S.
Krichevsky Literary Agency, Inc.
Lampack Agency, Inc., Peter
Lazin, Sarah
Leavitt Agency, The Ned
Lescher & Lescher Ltd.
Levine Communications, Inc., James
Levine Literary Agency, Inc., Ellen
Lieberman Associates, Robert
Lipkind Agency, Wendy
Literary Group, The
Love Literary Agency, Nancy
Lowenstein Associates
Maass Literary Agency, Donald
Maccoby Agency, Gina
Mann Agency, Carol
Markson Literary Agency, Elaine
Marmur Associates, Ltd., Mildred
Matson Co. Inc., Harold
Mattes, Inc., Jed
McCauley, Gerard
McIntosh and Otis
Menza Literary Agency, Claudia
Merrill, Ltd., Helen
Michaels Literary Agency, Inc., Doris S.
Miller Agency, The
Moran Agency, Maureen
Morhaim Literary Agency, Howard
Morris Agency, Inc., William
Morrison, Inc., Henry
Mura Literary, Dee
Naggar Literary Agency, Jean V.
Nine Muses and Apollo Inc.
Nolan Literary Agency, Betsy
Norma-Lewis Agency, The
Ober Associates, Harold
Oscard Agency Inc., Fifi
Parks Agency, The Richard
Paton Literary Agency, Kathi J.
Perkins Associates, L.
Pevner, Inc., Stephen
Pinder Lane & Garon-Brooke Associates, Ltd.
Pine Associates, Inc., Arthur
Pratt, Inc., Helen F.
Priest Literary Agency, Aaron M.
Protter Literary Agent, Susan Ann
Quicksilver Books Literary Agents
Rabiner, Literary Agent, Inc., Susan
Rights Unlimited, Inc.

VIRGINIA
Script agents
Filmwriters Literary Agency

Publicists
Gray Communications, Cameron

WASHINGTON
Literary agents
Wales, Literary Agency, Inc.

Script agents
Cedar Grove Agency
    Entertainment

Publicists
Acheson-Greub, Inc

WISCONSIN
Literary agents
Sternig & Byrne Literary Agency

INTERNATIONAL
Literary agents
Acacia House Publishing
    Services Ltd.
Anubis Literary Agency
Dorian Literary Agency
Gregory and Company Authors'
    Agents
Limelight Management
Livingston Cooke
Lownie Literary Agency Ltd.,
    Andrew

Paraview, Inc.
Simmons Literary Agency,
    Jeffrey
Slopen Literary Agency,
    Beverley
Smith Literary Agency Ltd.,
    Robert
Susijn Agency, The

Script agents
Brodie Representation, Alan
Cooke

Agents Index

This index of agent names can help you locate agents you may have read or heard about even when you do not know the name of their agency. Agent names are listed with their agencies' names.

A

Abate, Richard (International Creative Management)

Abecassis, A.L. (Ann Elmo Agency Inc.)

Adams, Tracey (McIntosh & Otis)

Aghassi, Jeff (The Alpern Group)

Agyeman, Janell Walden (Marie Brown Associates Inc.)

Ahearn, Pamela G. (The Ahearn Agency, Inc.)

Ahuile, Leylha (Carol Mann Agency)

Ajlouny, Joseph (Joseph Ajlouny Literary Agency)

Allred, Kim (Allred and Allred Literary Agents)

Allred, Robert (Allred and Allred Literary Agents)

Alpern, Jeff (The Alpern Group)

Altshuler, Miriam (Miriam Altshuler Literary Agency)

Amato, Marcy Ann (Legacies)

Amato, Michael (Michael Amato Agency)

Amparan, Joann (Wecksler-Incomco)

Amster, Betsy (Betsy Amster Literary Enterprises)

Amsterdam, Marcia (Marcia Amsterdam Agency)

Andiman, Lori (Arthur Pine Associates, Inc.)

Andrews, Bart (Bart Andrews & Associates)

Ashley, Kris (Karen Nazor Literary Agency)

Auclair, Kristin (Goldfarb & Associates)

Axelrod, Steven (The Axelrod Agency; The Damaris Rowland Agency)

B

Baldi, Malaga (Malaga Baldi Literary Agency)

Balkin, Rick (Balkin Agency, Inc.)

Bankoff, Lisa (International Creative Management)

Banks, Toni (Lawrence Jordan Literary Agency)

Barber, Dave (Curtis Brown Ltd.)

Barber, Virginia (William Morris Agency, Inc.)

Barer, Julie (Sanford J. Greenburger Associates, Inc.)

Barlow, Jane (Gregory and Company Authors' Agents)

Barnes-Zeleke, Melanie (Kevin C. Bulger and Associates)

Barrett, Loretta A. (Loretta Barrett Books Inc.)

Barron, Manie (William Morris Agency, Inc.)

Barry, Susan (The Swayne Agency Literary Management & Consulting, Inc.)

Bartlett, Bruce (Above the Line Agency)

Baskow, Jaki (Baskow Agency)

Bearden, James (Communications and Entertainment, Inc.)

Belushi, Traci (Omniquest Entertainment)

Bender, Faye (Doris S. Michaels Literary Agency, Inc.)

Benrey, Janet (Hartline Literary Agency)

Bent, Jenny (Harvey Kilinger, Inc.)

Berger, Mel (William Morris Agency, Inc.)

Berkey, Jane R. (Jane Rotrosen Agency LLC)

Berkower, Amy (Writers House)

Bernstein, Meredith (Meredith Bernstein Literary Agency)

Bernstein, Pam (Pam Bernstein & Associates, Inc.)

Bernstein, Robert (Carlisle & Company)

Bial, Daniel (Daniel Bial Agency)

Bilmes, Joshua (Jabberwocky Literary Agency)

Birnbaum, Agnes (Bleeker Street Associates, Inc.)

Black, David (David Black Literary Agency)

Blackstone, Anne (Lazear Agency Incorporated)

Blanton, Sandra (Peter Lampack Agency, Inc.)

Blasdell, Caitlin (Liza Dawson Associates)

Blickers, Beth (Helen Merrill, Ltd.)

Boals, Judy (Berman Boals and Flynn Inc.)

Boates, Reid (Reid Boates Literary Agency)

Boeshaar, Andrea Kuhn (Hartline Literary Agency)

Bohrman, Caren (The Bohrman Agency)

Bontemps, Sandy (The Robbins Office, Inc.)

Bookman, Leo (Acme Talent & Literary)

Borchardt, Anne (Georges Borchardt Inc.)

Borchardt, Georges (Georges Borchardt Inc.)

Borchardt, Valerie (Georges Borchardt Inc.)

Borodyanskaya, Olga (Fort Ross Inc. Russian-American Publishing Projects)

Bourret, Michael (Jane Dystel Literary Management, Inc.)

Boyle, Katie (LitWest Group, LLC)

Brady, Upton (Brady Literary Management)

Brandt, Carl (Brandt & Hochman Literary Agents Inc.)

Brandt, Joan (The Joan Brandt Agency)

Braun, Barbara (Barbara Braun Associates, Inc.)

Bregman, Gertrude (Blanche C. Gregory, Inc.)

Breitwieser, Helen (Cornerstone Literary, Inc.)

Bresnick, Paul (Carlisle & Company)

Briggs, M. Courtney (M. Courtney Briggs)

Brissie, Gene (Ghosts & Collaborators International)

Brissie, Gene (James Peter Associates, Inc.)

Brockish, Milissa (Moneiro Rose Agency)

Brodie, Alan (Alan Brodie Representation)

Brophy, Philppa (Sterling Lord Literistic, Inc.)

Broussard, Michael (Dupree/Miller and Associates Inc. Literary)

Brown, Andrea (Andrea Brown Literary Agency, Inc.)

Brown, Marie (Marie Brown Associates Inc.)

Brown, Robert (Wylie-Merrick Literary Agency)

Browne, Jane Jordan (Multimedia Product Development, Inc.)

Browne, Pema (Pema Browne Ltd.)

Browne, Perry (Pema Browne Ltd.)

Brummer, Michelle (Donald Maass Literary Agency)

Buchjsbaum, Steven (Jack Scagnetti Talent & Literary Agency)

Buchwald, Don (Don Buchwald & Associates, Inc.)

Buck, Howard (Howard Buck Agency)

Buckley, Megan (Sheree Bykofsky Associates, Inc.)

Bulger, Kevin C. (Kevin C. Bulger and Associates)

Burger, Knox (Harold Ober Associates)

Burgess, Thomas (Talesmyth Entertainment, Inc.)

Bykofsky, Sheree (Sheree Bykofsky Associates, Inc.)

Byrne, Jack (Sternig & Byrne Literary Agency)

C

Calcutt, Steve (Anubis Literary Agency)

Calhoun, Chris (Sterling Lord Literistic, Inc.)

Camardi, Ben (Harold Matson Co. Inc.)

Cameron, Kimberley (Reece Halsey North)

Campbell, John (The Wonderland Press, Inc.)

Cangialosi, Jason S. (National Writers Literary Agency)

Cardenas, Christi (Lazear Agency Incorporated)

Cardona, Moses (John Hawkins & Associates, Inc.)

Carducci, Brett (Epstein-Wyckoff-Corsa-Ross and Associates)

Carlisle, Michael (Carlisle & Company)

Carlson, Jennifer (Henry Dunow Literary Agency)

Carney, Caroline Francis (Book Deals, Inc.)

Carubba, David J. (Chadwick & Gros Literary Agency)

Carvainis, Maria (Maria Carvainis Agency, Inc.)

Cashman, Ann (The Maureen Lasher Agency)

Casselman, Martha (Martha Casselman Literary Agency)

Castiglia, Julie (Castiglia Literary Agency)

Cavanaugh, Elizabeth (Meredith Bernstein Literary Agency)

Cesare, Kara (Jane Rotrosen Agency LLC)

Cheney, Elyse (Sanford J. Greenburger Associates, Inc.)

Chester, Linda (Linda Chester and Associates)

Cho, Kyung (Henry Dunow Literary Agency)

Choate, Michael (Lescher & Lescher Ltd.)

Choron, Harry (March Tenth, Inc.)

Christian, Rick (Alive Communications, Inc.)

Chu, Lynn (Writers' Representatives, Inc.)

Cirillo, Andrea (Jane Rotrosen Agency LLC)

Clark, June (The Peter Rubie Literary Agency)

Clark, Steven Day (The Candace Lake Agency)

Clark, William (WM Clark Associates)

Cleary, Kevin (Acme Talent & Literary)

Coccia, Miek (James Levine Communications, Inc.)

Coffey, Nancy (Pinder Lane &

Garon-Brooke Associates, Ltd.)

Cohen, Christine (Virginia Kidd Agency, Inc.)

Cohen, Ruth (Ruth Cohen, Inc. Literary Agency)

Cohen, Susan (Writers House)

Cohen, Susan Lee (Riverside Literary Agency)

Cohen, Susan Perlman (Rosenstone/Wender)

Cohn, Sam (International Creative Management)

Coker, Deborah (Connor Literary Agency)

Collette, Ann (Helen Rees Literary Agency)

Collin, Frances (Frances Collin Literary Agent)

Concepcion, Cristina (Don Congdon Associates Inc.)

Congdon, Don (Don Congdon Associates Inc.)

Congdon, Michael (Don Congdon Associates Inc.)

Cooke, Dean (Livingston Cooke)

Coover, Doe (The Doe Coover Agency)

Cope, Eileen (Lowenstein Associates)

Coppage, Judy (The Coppage Company)

Cottle, Anna (Cine/Lit Representation)

Craver, William (Writers & Artists Agency)

Crawford, Lorne (Crawford Literary Agency)

Crawford, Susan (Crawford Literary Agency)

Cronin, Mari (Ann Elmo Agency Inc.)

Cross, Claudia (Sterling Lord Literistic, Inc.)

Crumlish, Christian (Waterside Productions, Inc.)

Curtis, Richard (Richard Curtis Associates, Inc.)

Cypher, James R. (James R. Cypher, The Cypher Agency)

D

Dahl, Kristine (International Creative Management)

Dail, Laura (Laura Dail Literary Agency, Inc.)

Damen, Kimberlee (Goldfarb & Associates)

Darhansoff, Liz (Darhansoff & Verrill Literary Agents)

Publishing Associates, Inc.)

Frost-Knappman, Elizabeth (New England Publishing Associates, Inc.)

Fugate, David (Waterside Productions, Inc.)

Fuhrman, Candice (Candice Fuhrman Literary Agency)

G

Galen, Russell (Scovil Chichak Galen Literary Agency)

Gamber, Steve (The Management Company)

Gartenberg, Max (Max Gartenberg, Literary Agent)

Gates, Jennifer (Zachary Shuster Harmsworth)

Geiger, Ellen (Curtis Brown Ltd.)

Gelff, Laya (The Laya Gelff Literary and Talent Agency)

Gelfman, Jane (Gelfman Schneider Literary Agents, Inc.)

Gentilie, Juliet (Peter Elek Associates)

Gerecke, Jeff (JCA Literary Agency)

Ghosh, Anna (Scovil Chichak Galen Literary Agency)

Giles, Meg (Brandt & Hochman Literary Agents Inc.)

Ginsberg, Peter L. (Curtis Brown Ltd.)

Ginsburg, Susan (Writers House)

Giordano, Sue (Hudson Agency)

Gladstone, Bill (Waterside Productions, Inc.)

Glasford, Linda (Alive Communications, Inc.)

Glasser, Carla (The Betsy Nolan Literary Agency)

Glick, Stacey (Jane Dystel Literary Management, Inc.)

Glislason, Barbara J. (The Glislason Agency)

Gluck, Suzanne (William Morris Agency, Inc.)

Goderich, Miriam (Jane Dystel Literary Management, Inc.)

Goldfard, Ronald (Goldfarb & Associates)

Goldman, David (Jack Scagnetti Talent & Literary Agency)

Goldstein, Debra (The Creative Culture, Inc.)

Goldstein, Kim (Carol Mann Agency)

Goodman, Arnold P. (Goodman Associates)

Goodman, Elise Simon (Goodman Associates)

Gordijn, Perry (Jane Rotrosen Agency LLC)

Grady, Thomas (The Thomas Grady Agency)

Grant, Janet Kobobel (Books & Such)

Grant, Susan (Grant, Savic, Kopaloff & Associates)

Graybill, Nina (Graybill & English)

Grayson, Ashley (Ashley Grayson Literary Agency)

Grayson, Carolyn (Ashley Grayson Literary Agency)

Greco, Gerardo (Peter Elek Associates)

Greenberg, Daniel (James Levine Communications, Inc.)

Greer, Rima Bauer (Above the Line Agency)

Gregory, Jane (Gregory and Company Authors' Agents)

Gregory, Lynda (Blanche C. Gregory, Inc.)

Griffen, Elizabeth (Livingston Cooke)

Grosjean, Jill (Jill Grosjean Literary Agency)

Grosvenor, Deborah C. (The Grosvenor Literary Agency)

Gudovitz, Neil (Waterside Productions, Inc.)

Guerth, Jan-Erik (United Tribes)

Guma, Matthew (Arthur Pine Associates, Inc.)

Gurman, Susan (The Susan Gurman Agency)

Gwiazda, Ronald (Rosenstone/Wender)

H

Habjan, Linda (Dramatic Publishing)

Hackworth, Jennifer (Richard Curtis Associates, Inc.)

Haffey, Leo (Client First-A/K/A Leo P. Haffey Agency)

Hagan, Lisa (Paraview, Inc.)

Hales, Kristen (Crawford Literary Agency)

Halpern, David (The Robbins Office, Inc.)

Halsey, Dorris (Reece Halsey Agency)

Hamilburg, Michael (The Mitchell J. Hamilburg Agency)

Hamlin, Faith (Sanford J. Greenburger Associates, Inc.)

Harding, Elizabeth (Curtis Brown Ltd.)

Hare, Robbie Anne (Goldfarb & Associates)

Harlow, Victoria (New England Publishing Associates, Inc.)

Harmsworth, Esmond (Zachary Shuster Harmsworth)

Harper, Laurie (Sebastian Literary Agency)

Harriet, Sydney H. (Agents Inc. for Medical and Mental Health Professionals)

Harris, Joy (The Joy Harris Literary Agency, Inc.)

Harris, Sloan (International Creative Management)

Harrison, Renuka (Robert Smith Literary Agency Ltd.)

Hart, A.L. (Fox Chase Agency, Inc.)

Hart, Jo C. (Fox Chase Agency, Inc.)

Hart, Joyce A. (Hartline Literary Agency)

Hart, Susan (Hart Literary Management)

Hartley, Glen (Writers' Representatives, Inc.)

Harty, Pamela (The Knight Agency)

Hawkins, Anne (John Hawkins & Associates, Inc.)

Hawkins, John (John Hawkins & Associates, Inc.)

Heavey, Maggie (Anubis Literary Agency)

Heifetz, Merrilee (Writers House)

Heindel, DeAnna (Georges Borchardt Inc.)

Helmers, Kathryn (Alive Communications, Inc.)

Hendin, David (DH Literary, Inc.)

Henshaw, Rich (Richard Henshaw Group)

Herman, Jeffrey (The Jeff Herman Agency LLC)

Herold, Patrick (Helen Merrill, Ltd.)

Higgs, Lisa (The Glislason Agency)

Hill, Fred (Frederick Hill Bonnie Nadell, Inc.)

Hochman, Gail (Brandt & Hochman Literary Agents Inc.)

Hochmann, John L. (John L. Hochmann Books)

Hodges, Carolyn (Carolyn Hodges Agency)

Hogenson, Barbara (Barbara Hogenson Agency)

Levine, Ellen (Ellen Levine Literary Agency, Inc.)

Levine, James (James Levine Communications, Inc.)

Levine, Paul S. (Paul S. Levine Literary Agency)

Lewis, Greg (Larchmont Literary Agency)

Lichtenstein, Jessica (Wendy Sherman Associates, Inc.)

Lieberman, Robert (Robert Lieberman Associates)

Liebert, Norma (The Norma-Lewis Agency)

Lincoln, Jerome A. (Ray Lincoln Liteary Agency)

Lincoln, Ray (Ray Lincoln Liteary Agency)

Linder, Bertram L. (Educational Design Services, Inc.)

Lindo, Lisa (Acme Talent & Literary)

Lindsay, Fiona (Limelight Management)

Lindsey, Kathryn (Jim Donovan Literary)

Lipkind, Wendy (Wendy Lipkind Agency)

Lipskar, Simon (Writers House)

Liss, Laurie (Sterling Lord Literistic, Inc.)

Loomis, Gloria (Watkins Loomis Agency, Inc.)

Lord, Sterling (Sterling Lord Literistic, Inc.)

Lorenz, Brad (Samuel French, Inc.)

Lotts, Chris (Ralph Vicinanza, Ltd.)

Love, Nancy (Nancy Love Literary Agency)

Lowenstein, Barbara (Lowenstein Associates)

Lownie, Andrew (Andrew Lownie Literary Agency Ltd.)

Lucas, Ling (Nine Muses and Apollo Inc.)

Luedtke, Penny (The Luedtke Agency)

Lumley, Dorothy (Dorian Literary Agency)

Luttinger, Selma (Robert A. Freedman Dramatic Agency, Inc.)

Lynch, Marlene Connor (Connor Literary Agency)

Lyons, Jennifer (Joan Daves Agency; Writers House)

M

Maass, Donald (Donald Maass Literary Agency)

Maccoby, Gina (Gina Maccoby Agency)

MacGregor, Jerry "Chip" (Alive Communications, Inc.)

Mack, Elizabeth (The Boston Literary Group)

MacKenzie, Renee (Cedar Grove Agency Entertainment)

Mackey, Sandy (The Quillco Agency)

Madan, Neeti (Sterling Lord Literistic, Inc.)

Malk, Steven (Writers House)

Malpas, Pamela (Harold Ober Associates)

Manchur, W. Gail (ABS Literary Agency, Inc.)

Mandel, Dan (Sanford J. Greenburger Associates, Inc.)

Mandel, Jay (William Morris Agency, Inc.)

Manges, Kristen (Curtis Brown Ltd.)

Manguera, Jennifer (The Gail Ross Literary Agency)

Mann, Carol (Carol Mann Agency)

Manus, Janet (Manus & Associates Literary Agency, Inc.)

Manus, Jillian (Manus & Associates Literary Agency, Inc.)

Markowitz, Barbara (Barbara Markowitz Literary Agency)

Markson, Elaine (Elaine Markson Literary Agency)

Marlow, Marilyn (Curtis Brown Ltd.)

Marmur, Mildred (Mildred Marmur Associates, Ltd.)

Marshall, Evan (The Evan Marshall Agency)

Martin, Paul (Silver Screen Placements)

Martin, S. A. (Wylie-Merrick Literary Agency)

Marton, Elisabeth (Elisabeth Marton Agency Inc.)

Marton, Tonda (Elisabeth Marton Agency Inc.)

Massie, Maria (Witherspoon Associates, Inc.)

Matson, Jonathan (Harold Matson Co. Inc.)

Matson, Peter (Sterling Lord Literistic, Inc.)

Mattis, Lawrence (Circle of Confusion Ltd.)

Mayo, Julie (Lazear Agency Incorporated)

Mays, Stedman (Clausen, Mays & Tahan, LLC)

Mays, Sunny (Carroll Grace Literary Agency)

Mazmanian, Joan (Helen Rees Literary Agency)

McAndrews, Rob (B.J. Robbins Literary Agency)

McBride, Margret (Margret McBride Literary Agency)

McCarter, Bob (Jodie Rhodes Literary Agency)

McCarthy, Shawna (The McCarthy Agency, LLC)

McCauley, Gerard (Gerard McCauley)

McClendon, Carole (Waterside Productions, Inc.)

McCloskey, Nanci (Virginia Kidd Agency, Inc.)

McCord, Margaret (Julie Popkin)

McCutcheon, Clark (Jodie Rhodes Literary Agency)

McGrath, Helen (Helen McGrath)

McHugh, Elisabet (McHugh Literary Agency)

McKenna, Deborah (Moore Literary Agency)

McNair, Sarah (Alan Brodie Representation)

McQuilkin, Rob (Hill & Barlow Agency)

McShane, Kevin (Fifi Oscard Agency Inc.)

Mead, Linda (LitWest Group, LLC)

Meehan, Mike (Moore Literary Agency)

Mendel, Scott (Multimedia Product Development, Inc.)

Menza, Claudia (Claudia Menza Literary Agency)

Meo, Amy Victoria (Richard Curtis Associates, Inc.)

Merola, Marianne (Brandt & Hochman Literary Agents Inc.)

Meth, David L. (Writers' Productions)

Michaels, Doris S. (Doris S. Michaels Literary Agency, Inc.)

Millard, Martha (Martha Millard Literary Agency)

Miller, Angela (The Miller Agency)

Miller, Jan (Dupree/Miller and Associates Inc. Literary)

Miller, Stuart (The Stuart M. Miller Co.)

Millner, Joel (Larchmont Literary Agency)

Raihofer, Susan (David Black Literary Agency)

Ramer, Susan (Don Congdon Associates Inc.)

Randall, Kevin Lee (Lawyer's Literary Agency, Inc.)

Ratneshwar, Priya (The Literary Group)

Ray, Roslyn (Communications and Entertainment, Inc.)

Raymond, Charlotte Cecil (Charlotte Cecil Raymond, Literary Agent)

Read, Melissa (Jim Preminger Agency)

Reamer, Jodie (Writers House)

Redler, Dan (Dan Redler Entertainment)

Rein, Jody (Jody Rein Books, Inc.)

Reiss, William (John Hawkins & Associates, Inc.)

Rengold, Anne (Elisabeth Marton Agency Inc.)

Rennert, Laura (Andrea Brown Literary Agency, Inc.)

Rex, Calvin (Core Creations, LLC)

Rhodes, Jodie (Jodie Rhodes Literary Agency)

Rifkind, Barbara (Helen Rees Literary Agency)

Rinaldi, Angela (Angela Rinaldi Literary Agency)

Rittenberg, Ann (Ann Rittenberg Literary Agency, Inc.)

Rivas, Maribel (The Shukat Company Ltd.)

Robbins, B.J. (B.J. Robbins Literary Agency)

Robbins, Kathy P. (The Robbins Office, Inc.)

Roberts, Jane (Literary and Creative Artists, Inc.)

Roberts, Karen (Dee Mura Literary)

Robey, Annelise (Jane Rotrosen Agency LLC)

Robie, David A. (Bigscore Productions Inc.)

Robins, Michael D. (Michael D. Robins & Associates)

Robinson, Lloyd (Suite A Management & Literary Agency)

Rodman, Andy (Jack Scagnetti Talent & Literary Agency)

Rogers, Elaine (Hill & Barlow Agency)

Roghaar, Linda L. (Linda Roghaar Literary Agency, Inc.)

Rose, Fredda (Moneiro Rose Agency)

Rosen, Janet (Sheree Bykofsky Associates, Inc.)

Rosenberg, Barbara Collins (The Rosenberg Group)

Rosenkranz, Rita (Rita Rosenkranz Literary Agency)

Rosenstone, Howard (Rosenstone/Wender)

Rosenthal, Judith (Barbara Markowitz Literary Agency)

Ross, Gail (The Gail Ross Literary Agency)

Ross, Lisa M. (The Spieler Agency)

Roston, Stephanie Kip (James Levine Communications, Inc.)

Roth, Carol Susan (Carol Susan Roth, Literary Representation)

Rowland, Damaris (The Damaris Rowland Agency)

Rowland, Laureen (David Black Literary Agency)

Roy, Mark S. (DeFiore and Company)

Rubie, Peter (The Peter Rubie Literary Agency)

Rubin, Michele (Writers House)

Rudes, Jerry (Fifi Oscard Agency Inc.)

Rue, Robin (Writers House)

Ruley, Margaret (Jane Rotrosen Agency LLC)

Rutman, Jim (Sterling Lord Literistic, Inc.)

Ruwe, Stephen (Literary and Creative Artists, Inc.)

Ryan, Ali (The Vines Agency, Inc.)

Ryan, Mark (New Brand Agency Group, LLC)

Ryan, Regina (Regina Ryan)

Ryba, Richard (The Candace Lake Agency)

S

Sach, Jacky (Bookends, LLC)

Sagalyn, Raphael (The Sagalyn Agency)

Saidullah, Jawahara K. (Waterside Productions, Inc.)

Sanders, Victoria (Victoria Sanders & Associates)

Sandum, Howard E. (Sandum & Associates)

Sansevieri, Penny C. (Waterside Productions, Inc.)

Santell, Nathan (Jaret Entertainment)

Santone, Cheri (Hudson Agency)

Sarulus, Crivolus (Baskow Agency)

Saul, Ryan L. (Jim Preminger Agency)

Sawyer, Peter (Fifi Oscard Agency Inc.)

Scagnetti, Jack (Jack Scagnetti Talent & Literary Agency)

Scatoni, Frank R. (Venture Literary)

Schelling, Chris (Ralph Vicinanza, Ltd.)

Scherf, Dietmar (Scherf, Inc. Literary Properties)

Schiavi, Kristine (New England Publishing Associates, Inc.)

Schiavone, James (Schiavone Literary Agency, Inc.)

Schlessiger, Charles (Brandt & Hochman Literary Agents Inc.)

Schneider, Deborah (Gelfman Schneider Literary Agents, Inc.)

Schramm, Dean (Jim Preminger Agency)

Schroeder, Heather (International Creative Management)

Schubert, Linda (Julie Popkin)

Schulman, Susan (Susan Schulman, A Literary Agency)

Schwartz, Laurens R. (Laurens R. Schwartz Agency)

Scovil, Jack (Scovil Chichak Galen Literary Agency)

Scriven-Marzani, Lysna (The Shukat Company Ltd.)

Seigan, Tony (Chadwick & Gros Literary Agency)

Seldes, Timothy (Russell & Volkening)

Seligman, Lynn (Lynn Seligman, Literary Agent)

Selman, Edythia Ginis (Edythia Ginis Selman Agency)

Selman, Richard (Edythia Ginis Selman Agency)

Seymour, Mary Sue (The Seymour Agency)

Shannon, Denise (International Creative Management)

Sharpe, Shayne (National Writers Literary Agency)

Sheedy, Charlotte (Sterling Lord Literistic, Inc.)

Sheinkman, Elizabeth (Elaine Markson Literary Agency)

Listing Index

Agencies that appeared in the 2002 *Guide to Literary Agents* but are not included this year are identified by a two-letter code explaining why the agency is not listed: (**ED**)—Editorial Decision, (**NS**)—Not Accepting Submissions/Too Many Queries, (**NR**)—No (or Late) Response to Listing Request, (**OB**)—Out of Business, (**RR**)—Removed by Agency's Request, (**UF**)—Uncertain Future, (**UC**)—Unable to Contact, (**RP**)—Business Restructured or Sold.